T0351838

Conceptualizing Capitalism

Conceptualizing Capitalism

Institutions, Evolution, Future

GEOFFREY M. HODGSON

THE UNIVERSITY OF CHICAGO PRESS   CHICAGO AND LONDON

GEOFFREY M. HODGSON is research professor at Hertfordshire Business School, University of Hertfordshire, England, and the author or coauthor of over a dozen books, including *Darwin's Conjecture* and *From Pleasure Machines to Moral Communities*, both also published by the University of Chicago Press.

The University of Chicago Press, Chicago 60637
The University of Chicago Press, Ltd., London
© 2015 by The University of Chicago
All rights reserved. Published 2015.
Printed in the United States of America
24 23 22 21 20 19 18 17 16 15   2 3 4 5

ISBN-13: 978-0-226-16800-5 (cloth)
ISBN-13: 978-0-226-16814-2 (e-book)
DOI: 10.7208/chicago/9780226168142.001.0001

Library of Congress Cataloging-in-Publication Data

Hodgson, Geoffrey Martin, 1946– author.
  Conceptualizing capitalism : institutions, evolution, future / Geoffrey M. Hodgson.
    pages cm
  Includes bibliographical references and index.
  ISBN 978-0-226-16800-5 (cloth : alk. paper)—ISBN 978-0-226-16814-2 (e-book)
  1. Capitalism—Philosophy.   I. Title.
  HB501.H528 2015
  330.12′2—dc23

                                                           2014044825

TO THE UNNAMED, UNCOUNTED, AND UNSUNG PAST HEROES OF MANY
NATIONS WHO HAVE INCREMENTALLY TINKERED AND EXPERIMENTED:
THEIR INNUMERABLE INSTITUTIONAL INNOVATIONS HAVE LED TO
MASSIVE WEALTH.

AND TO THE MANY UNKNOWN CHAMPIONS TO COME WHO WILL HELP
ENSURE THAT THE PROCEEDS OF THE SYSTEM SHALL BE MORE FAIRLY
DISTRIBUTED, THAT ECONOMIC GROWTH SHALL LEAD NEITHER TO
ARMAGEDDON NOR TO THE RUINATION OF OUR NATURAL ENVIRONMENT
AND THAT HUMANITY MAY MOVE TOWARD AN EVEN BETTER FUTURE—
MAYBE EVEN BEYOND THE BOUNDARIES OF CAPITALISM ITSELF.

Contents

Preface   ix

Introduction   1

PART I.   Discovering Capitalism

CHAPTER 1. Distilling the Essence   25

CHAPTER 2. Social Structure and Individual Motivation   53

CHAPTER 3. Law and the State   76

CHAPTER 4. Property, Possession, and Contract   101

CHAPTER 5. Commodity Exchange and Markets   129

CHAPTER 6. Money and Finance   147

CHAPTER 7. Meanings of Capital   173

CHAPTER 8. Firms and Corporations   204

CHAPTER 9. Labor and Employment   235

CHAPTER 10. A Definition of Capitalism   251

PART II.   Capitalism and Beyond

CHAPTER 11. Conceptualizing Production   265

CHAPTER 12. Socialism, Capitalism, and the State   282

CHAPTER 13. How Does Capitalism Evolve?   315

CHAPTER 14. The Future of Global Capitalism   332

CHAPTER 15. Addressing Inequality   352

CHAPTER 16. After Capitalism?   366

Glossary   385

References   393

Index   473

Preface

Whether capitalism be retained, reformed, or replaced, we must understand what it is and how it works. This requires sharp categories as well as factual knowledge. Capitalism is a complex constellation of different institutions. To comprehend it we need clear understandings of property, exchange, markets, money, capital, and other elements. Once I had the idea of writing a modern version of Thomas Robert Malthus's *Definitions in Political Economy* (1827) where the meanings of such concepts would have been tackled. But the economic crash of 2008 gave me the idea of focusing instead on capitalism and its essence.

This book is about the nature of capitalism. I argue that our understanding of that system has been impaired by the deep corruption within the social sciences of key terms such as *property*, *exchange*, and *capital* as well as by the ongoing preoccupation by economists with mathematical technique over real-world substance. Conceptual precision is as vital as mathematical precision, yet economists pay relatively little attention to the former.

I have been inspired by great writers on capitalism—including Karl Marx, Max Weber, Joseph A. Schumpeter, John Maynard Keynes, and Friedrich A. Hayek—but their accounts have limitations, as I explain below. While the present book is eclectic, I adopt a distinctive theoretical approach; it puts the role of law at the center without reducing everything to law alone. It is described as *legal institutionalism*. This emphasis on legal realities helps establish sharper and superior concepts of property, exchange, market, firm, and capital.

Much of the core narrative and basic structure of the book was tested on a group of economics students with a series of lectures in 2011 at Shandong University in China. It was received with some enthusiasm, and the book project was born. Its title emerged from a 2012 seminar at the Center for the History of Political Economy at Duke University, where Bruce Caldwell kindly invited me to outline my book venture for critical discussion. During a rerun of the course in 2012 at Shandong University, the students remained enthusiastic and even corrected some flaws in my argument. I also received helpful feedback from students who attended a fuller series of lectures based on the book given at the Université Paris I Panthéon-Sorbonne in early 2014. Among the many who have helped me with discussions and comments are Richie Adelstein, Amitai Aviram, Christian Barrère, Jens Beckert, Peter Boettke, Marcel Boumans, Robert Butler, Bruce Caldwell, Ana Castro, Rutger Claassen, Michael D. Cohen, Jean-Philippe Colin, Frank Currie, Hulya Dagdeviren, John B. Davis, Simon Deakin, Frank Decker, Christine Desan, Ronald Dore, Gary Dymski, Christoph Engel, Chukwunonye Emenalo, Steve Fleetwood, Nicolai Foss, David Friedman, Francesca Gagliardi, Pierre Gervais, David Gindis, Charles Goodhart, Avner Greif, Jerry Hough, Anne-Claire Hoyng, Kainan Huang, Geoffrey Ingham, Thorbjørn Knudsen, Richard Langlois, John Linarelli, Richard Lipsey, Vinny Logan, Tariq Malik, Renate Mayntz, Deirdre McCloskey, Perry Mehrling, Claude Ménard, Philippe Minard, Zhihong Mo, Paolo Moreira Franco, Grimot Nane, Guinevere Nell, Richard Nelson, Klaus Nielsen, Bart Nooteboom, Ugo Pagano, Katharina Pistor, Bharat Punjabi, Ernesto Screpanti, Itai Sened, J.-C. Spender, Robert Steinfeld, Rolf Steppacher, Virgil Storr, Arthur Stinchcombe, Wolfgang Streeck, Andrew Tylecote, Richard Van Den Berg, Derek Wall, Randy Wray, Xueqi Zhang, and anonymous referees.

I am grateful to the Association for Evolutionary Economics, Edward Elgar Publishing, and the Cambridge Political Economy Society Trust for permission to use material from published articles in chapters 3, 5, and 7.

Throughout the text, all emphases in quotes are in the original, unless otherwise noted.

Introduction

The Great Financial Crash of 2008 and the subsequent global crisis have led many people to question the viability of capitalism or
to consider major reforms to its financial and corporate institutions.
Alongside this, spectacular economic growth rates in China, India, and
elsewhere since 1980 have revealed the potential dynamism of private
enterprise and markets as well as the role of strategic guidance by governments. We need to understand the nature of capitalism, the sources
of its dynamism, and its frailties.

The word *capitalism* was once unfashionable, except among opponents to that system. That has changed. In 2012 the words *capitalism* and
socialism were the two most consulted entries in the Merriam-Webster
online dictionary (Merriam-Webster 2012).[1] This book addresses capitalism, with a much shorter critical discussion (in chapter 12) of socialism.

Readers looking here for an ideological tract, either for or against
capitalism, will be disappointed. Although I consider the future of capitalism near the end of this volume, my main purpose is to understand
the nature of the beast and to establish some conceptual tools to dissect
its inner structure. I shall also argue that some mix of market competition and state regulation is unavoidable in any complex modern economy, thus disappointing advocates of unfettered market competition and
of socialism (at least as originally defined). Some further policy questions are raised in chapters 15 and 16—particularly the thorny problem of inequality. But generally the book is more about understanding
capitalism than policy. Consequently, for example, analysis of the post-

---

1. They were followed, incidentally, by touché, bigot, marriage, democracy, profession-
alism, and globalization.

1970s rise of neoliberal ideology is consigned elsewhere (Crouch 2011; Mirowski 2013).

Although recent events and developments are mentioned, the book does not focus on them. Instead, it addresses the nature of capitalism and its possible future in the twenty-first century. The supreme purpose is to understand what capitalism is and to establish it as a historically specific and relatively recent phenomenon. It is neither a historical analysis nor an exposition of models. There is no new theory of its origins here, and I do not develop a new analysis of capitalist growth or development.

Instead, I point to the explosion of growth that started in Europe in the eighteenth century and try to identify institutional developments that preceded or coincided with this expansion. Thereby some possible causes are suggested: future empirical work by economic historians will have to test their relative significance. But no empirical inquiry can start without some initial identification of key institutional developments that make up the modern order. This is not a trivial task.

The Contribution of This Volume in Brief

There are many books on capitalism: so what is added here? My position is different from both Marxism and much promarket libertarianism. This is apparent from my overall analytic approach, including my assessment of the constitutive role of law and the state within capitalism, my conceptual treatments of property and capital, and my appraisal of postcapitalist possibilities. From diametrically opposite policy positions, both Marxism and promarket libertarianism focus on markets. But just as important within modern capitalism is the role of property as collateral, to secure loans for enterprise. Specific legal and financial institutions are needed to make this possible, yet in many accounts of capitalism they are omitted.

Many define capitalism as private ownership plus markets. This loose definition fails to focus on the key features of the modern dynamic epoch. By most definitions, markets and private property are much older than capitalism, as it is defined here. If capitalism is a particular historical formation, then we must identify its essence more precisely. I argue that private ownership and markets are necessary but insufficient to define capitalism.

Some advocates of capitalism downgrade its distinctive features. By treating capitalism as (nearly) universal, they blur the boundaries of this historically specific system. Many see contractual exchange as a "natural" phenomenon. For one famous writer, *all human action* is "exchange." He and others see production as an "exchange with nature." Some treat politics as a matter of individual contract and exchange, thus viewing all power and authority as commerce. Every activity becomes an exchange, and delimited notions of commerce lose their meaning. Simultaneously, the concept of contract is itself devalued by notions of "psychological contract" or "implicit contract" that may involve neither individual consent nor legal enforceability. Capitalism is equated with markets, which in turn are regarded as synonymous with exchange. Some leading authors favor a "market for ideas" (treated as synonymous with freedom of expression), overlooking whether ideas are actually owned, bought, or sold (and maybe suggesting markets as the solution to almost every problem). Firms too become markets. Everything is a market. Markets and contracts become omnipresent. As terms, *market* and *contract* too lose their meaning. Against these degradations of our conceptual armory, an appraisal of the virtues and vices of capitalism requires a superior conceptual framework that is more sensitive to great institutional innovations in history.

In short, the language required to understand capitalism has been deeply corrupted by economists and other social scientists. Vital concepts—including law, property, exchange, markets, and capital—have become so degraded that mainstream, Marxist, and other approaches have difficulty identifying the core unique features of capitalism. A new understanding is required that builds on redefined concepts. Relatedly, the physicalist metaphors that underlie much of economic analysis have to be discarded for more adequate and illuminating alternatives.

Mainstream economics has further analytic problems in dealing with capitalism. Central to some prominent definitions of capitalism are institutions such as money and firms. But both are treated poorly. As Frank Hahn (1965, 1980, 1987, 1988) explained, general equilibrium theory cannot explain why agents hold on to money. If we follow Keynes (1936, 1937) and regard money as a means of dealing with uncertainty about the future, where *uncertainty* by definition refers to future events concerning which "there is no scientific basis on which to form any calculable probability whatever" (Keynes 1937, 215), then mainstream economics again proves inadequate because it has banished this concept of uncertainty from its discourse (Hodgson 2011a). I argue later that the concepts of capital in mainstream economics and in Marxism are also deficient. Turning to the firm, Frank H. Knight (1921, 271) argued that its existence is also "the direct result of the fact of uncertainty." A similar explanatory emphasis on uncertainty is endorsed by others, including accounts that rely on transaction costs (Loasby 1976; Dahlman 1979; Kay 1984; Langlois 1984). By downplaying uncertainty, mainstream economics also lacks an adequate explanation of the existence of the firm. Mainstream thinking has severe limitations in coping with core capitalist institutions such as money, markets, capital, and firms.[2]

I argue that, while markets are central to capitalism, capitalism is not simply a market system: unavoidably it contains different subsystems of governance, production, distribution, and exchange. Furthermore, capitalism cannot in principle have markets for everything or bring everything within the orbit of commodity exchange.

In particular, under capitalism there can never be a complete set of markets for future labor power. For there to be full futures markets for labor, all workers must enter into contracts for their expected working life. This would be tantamount to voluntary bondage, limiting the freedom of workers to quit their employment. Paradoxically, pushing markets to their limits would mean the return of slavery for the workforce.[3] Unlike owned capital, free labor power cannot be used as collateral to obtain loans for investment. At least in this respect, capital and labor do not meet on a level playing field, and this asymmetry is a major driver of inequality.

A further consequence of missing markets for future labor power was identified by the great economist Alfred Marshall (1920, 565). Marshall pointed out that, if the employer spends money on employee training and skill development, this investment cannot be secured by futures contracts and will be lost to the employer if the worker quits. As a re-

2. This exposes the limitations of MacKenzie's (2006) "performativity" thesis—that economics creates the phenomena it describes. Of course, many ideas from economics have changed the real world. But mainstream economics comprehends some features of capitalism so poorly that it cannot be primarily responsible for their creation. For further criticisms of the performativity thesis, see n. 5, chapter 2 below, and Hodgson (2010c).

3. Some libertarians—such as Nozick (1974)—have argued that voluntary slavery should be permitted. This goes with the assumption that the individual is always the best judge of his or her interests and that these judgments where possible should be honored. See Hodgson (2013b) for a critique of this assumption.

sult, without compensatory arrangements or incentives, employers will underinvest in human learning and education.

These missing markets and factor asymmetries are central to capitalism, but they are rarely discussed by modern economists. We need to look more closely at the system that dominates our world.

Despite the 2008 crash, most economists still seem more interested in mathematical technique than the big questions about modern capitalism.[4] Mathematics is an indispensable tool. But the dominance of mathematical technique in contemporary economics has crowded out valuable discourses seeking conceptual understanding of and precision concerning capitalism and other economic formations. Mathematics is said to bring rigor. But conceptual precision is also needed. Unfortunately, economists are not trained to be meticulous about concepts. Many do not even try. Mathematics involves symbolic constructions of beauty and finality. The task of conceptual precision is no less tough but much messier. It is always unfinished.

Theorists of Capitalism

Inspirational thinkers that have helped us understand capitalism include Karl Marx, Max Weber, Joseph A. Schumpeter, John Maynard Keynes, and Friedrich A. Hayek.[5] Over 150 years ago, Marx rightly predicted the global spread of capitalism. There has been a revival of Marxist thinking since the Great Crash of 2008, and much discourse on capitalism is unavoidably influenced by Marx. His contribution is magisterial. But, for reasons that I discuss in this book, I find Marxist and other approaches inadequate and invalid in key respects.

Marx put less emphasis than Schumpeter and others on finance, and, where he did so, he was burdened by a flawed substance theory of money,

4. The preoccupation of economists with mathematical technique over real-world substance has been criticized by Krueger (1991), McCloskey (1991), Blaug (1997, 1998), Friedman (1999), Krugman (2009), and many others. But I do not concur with Lawson's (1997) argument that mathematics is ruled out by the open and complex nature of economic phenomena (Hodgson 2006a, 2012).

5. Hayek (1973, 61–62) disapproved of the word capitalism because before the 1970s it was largely used by critics of the system. He wrote instead of the "free system" and the "Great Society." Clearly he was referring to a system dominated by market exchanges and individual private property.

where money was treated more as a substance such as gold and less as a system of shared rules, representations, and understandings. He was also impaired by the labor theory of value, which he inherited from Adam Smith and David Ricardo. Centering his account on the class struggle between workers and employers and on the role of labor as the circulating blood of the capitalist body, he gave relatively less attention to the dynamic combinations of finance, knowledge, and innovation.

Both Marx and Schumpeter were mistaken in regarding the evolution of the system as one of unfolding primarily or exclusively "from within"—from its own economic core.[6] The development of individual capitalist systems is important, but capitalism must also be understood as a global, interacting population of different national formations, each with different types of subsystems. Furthermore, capitalism is always conjoined with state power. Marx and Schumpeter paid insufficient attention to the constitutive and economic roles of the state and to capitalism's political and legal nature.[7]

While Schumpeter rightly emphasized the driving forces of money capital and finance, he saw the rhythms and crises of the system as resulting from inner, multiple-frequency cycles rather than from the interactions between different capitalisms or between different subsystems. Both Marx and Schumpeter failed to underline the role of collateralizable property in the creation of finance for enterprise.

Hayek and other Austrian school economists provided an invaluable understanding of the nature and role of knowledge and markets in eco-

6. Marx (1976, 619) focused on class antagonisms and "the development of the contradictions" that impelled the system down its preordained historical path. Schumpeter (1954, 391) favorably described Marx's theory of capitalism as "evolutionary" because "it tries to uncover the mechanism that, by its mere working and without the aid of external factors, turns any given state of society into another." Schumpeter (1934, 63) elaborated: "By 'development,' therefore, we shall understand only such changes in economic life as are not forced upon it from without but arise by its own initiative, from within." Schumpeter (1942, 83) also wrote of "industrial mutation . . . that increasingly revolutionizes the economic structure from within." Of course if we define the object of analysis sufficiently broadly—say global capitalism—then almost everything is from within, and nothing is external. But Marx and Schumpeter both referred to the development of national economic systems.

7. Marx (1976, 916) of course emphasized that capitalists "employ the power of the state," and he wrote: "Force is the midwife of every old society which is pregnant with a new one." But, while he highlighted the role of force in the historical development of capitalism, including in the subjection of the working class, he did not see the state and its legal system as constitutive of social relations or social classes.

nomic systems, despite their insufficient appreciation of capitalist institutions and the role of the state and their challengeable theory of money. From a very different policy perspective, John Maynard Keynes remains extremely important, particularly for his understanding of money, the fragility of markets, and the consequences of uncertainty.

Weber understood the role of the state and a "rational legal system" in capitalism. I also acknowledge the influence of others from the German historical school, including Albert Schäffle, Gustav Schmoller, and Werner Sombart. Members of this school understood long ago that neither laissez-faire nor wholesale planning would work and that the way ahead was a reformed and regulated capitalism that protected property and stimulated innovation.

No less important are the original American institutionalists, particularly Thorstein Veblen and John R. Commons. Although they lacked a comprehensive theory, they enhanced our understanding of the institutional and legal foundations of capitalism and also emphasized the role of technology in revolutionizing social life. I also draw on the work of other mainstream and heterodox economists as well as that of historians, sociologists, anthropologists, psychologists, philosophers, political scientists, and legal theorists.

Key Aims of This Work

Given the primary aim of understanding the essence of capitalism, matters of extensive historical exegesis and detailed empirical description are omitted. But of course we must rely on crucial facts of history, and of different capitalisms in time and space, to achieve this primary mission. This is not a book of economic history but one that relies on economic history and comparative analysis to reach a clarificatory and analytic goal.

This foremost objective gives rise to a number of other aims. While private property and markets are among the key defining institutions of capitalism and vital sources of its historically unprecedented dynamism, I argue that capitalism, property, money, markets, and corporations typically depend on, and are partly constituted by, the state. This does not simply mean that the state is necessary to correct "market failures" or that empirically the role of the state has been important. The state was vital to bring capitalism into being and is needed to sustain its existence. As Dani Rodrik (2011, xviii) argued: "Markets work best not when states are weakest, but when they are strong."

This again puts me at loggerheads with many libertarians and Marxists.[8] Despite their different political standpoints, they share the view that markets and private property can be understood with minimal reference to the state. For libertarians, the system is essentially a "spontaneous order," and state planners or designers play a secondary or even inessential role. For most Marxists, the system consists of economic relations between antagonistic social classes; the state is there mostly to represent the bourgeoisie and to keep the working class under control. The state and law are seen as part of the superstructure, but not of the "economic" base. There are nuggets of truth in both standpoints, but together they downplay the vital and constitutive role of law and the state.

It is not that any state will do. Crucial is the role of law. For capitalism to prosper, the state has to sustain and operate within an effective legal framework. Here again I counter leading libertarians who argue that law is essentially custom and does not necessarily require something like a state. Others argue that what matters is control or possession: not legal rights established by statutory courts and state legislatures. For example, Armen Alchian (1977, 238) defined a "property right" as the probability that a decision over use will be effective. Oliver Williamson (1985a, 184) argued explicitly that "transaction cost economics" should address "private ordering" rather than legal institutions such as courts.

Marx argued that law is part of the "superstructure" and focused instead on the underlying "relations of production" that make up "the economic structure of society, the real foundation." But how these vaguely defined "relations of production" (presumably involving property, rights, and rules) can be understood without immediate reference to law has always been a mystery to me. If social classes are defined in terms of ownership of the means of production or as employees of owners, then legal concepts such as the employment contract and property ownership are essential to these definitions. Reference to law is primary and essential.

---

8. Some Marxists and post-Marxists attempt to rescue Marx from his cruder and unacceptable formulations. I respect these efforts but ask why they wish to retain their "Marxist" affiliation? The answer, I speculate, may lie in a desire to maintain the political project to replace capitalism with socialism. If so, it would have more to do with ideology than science.

Law is a central mechanism of social power, and Marxists unconvincingly regard it as secondary.

In economics and sociology, law is often vaguely described as *formal* and then pushed aside, as if it were no part of the rules and relations of vital social organizations such as the firm and the family. An amazing consensus—treating law as epiphenomenal rather than constitutive—pervades the social sciences. But it has remarkably little supporting argument. In contrast, I argue that rules and relations constitute social reality and that some of the most important and powerful social rules are legal and statutory in nature.

Of course, an unenforced law or right is not an operative social rule in fact. But, when the rule of law prevails and laws are enforced, these become powerful social rules. They are backed by authority and have the perceived legitimacy of sovereign power. Transgressors face possible punishment. Much of the de jure then becomes de facto.

Taking law seriously does not mean ignoring rules and practices that are undefined in law. The "informal" norms of culture and convention also matter greatly. When law is nonexistent or ineffective, they are everything. And, even when law is strong, there are zones of discretion where much else is important. The fact that legal rules determine far from everything does not mean that law can be ignored.

Law is not treated here as set of statements or statutes in dusty books. Laws are made meaningful and have effect within legal institutions, including those of legislation, judgment, and enforcement. The legal focus here is on institutional facts, not proclamations alone.

Downgrading law does not simply mean that a crucial function of the modern state is neglected. The accounts of Marx, Alchian, Williamson, and others are inadequate in terms of human motivation as well. There is no recognition of legally sanctioned rights, and everything becomes a matter of mere possession. The individual is treated simply as a "pleasure machine," simply seeking the use of things to maximize his or her utility. Missing here—as highlighted by Adam Smith—are impulses to behave morally, respect authority, and seek justice alongside greed and the quest for pleasure (Hodgson 2013b).

The demotion of law and the conflation of property with mere possession cannot be defended on the grounds that they are sufficient to understand or predict behavior. To some degree, people take account of rules concerning justice and morality, even if their supreme motive is greed.

To understand capitalism we need a fuller account of multifaceted human nature. But this does not mean that capitalism is simply a reflection of the latter. Instead, it is a specific system with the capacity to harness human dispositions in a particular manner.

My third aim is to counter the still-widespread view that capitalism is an eternal or natural order. Along with Marx, the historical school, the original institutionalists, and others, I argue that capitalism is a relatively recent phenomenon. Capitalism is much younger than the state: it requires special forms of state that cannot confiscate property arbitrarily at will, that are effectively restrained by laws, that have internal checks and balances, and that are faced with countervailing (democratic or other) powers that help protect a relatively autonomous legal system. Such states are necessary to legitimate and protect property rights and to enforce contracts. They required peculiar circumstances and a long time to evolve. Foreshadowed in the Italian city-states, they did not appear on a national scale until the seventeenth century, in Britain and the Netherlands.

My fourth aim is to develop workable definitions of capitalism and of its constituent institutions. To do this, I must counter academic habits of neglect concerning definitional tasks. Lamentably few social scientists these days have a solid grounding in philosophy, including the philosophy of their own discipline. Many in my experience cannot distinguish acts of definition from those of abstraction or description. Many seem to believe that adequate definitions will emerge with little reflection, during or after some process of empirical investigation: stew the facts, and definitions will congeal. But all inquiry is theory driven: it requires conceptual guideposts, all of which depend on *prior* definitions.

As an example, consider Thomas Piketty's (2014) breakthrough work in *Capital in the Twenty-First Century*. The book is driven by forceful data and a little precise mathematics, so why do we need to care about concepts and definitions? The truth is that Piketty had to reverse more than two centuries of abuse of the notion of capital by economists and sociologists to make his case. After an age of terminological obscurantism, his data would have us return to the commercial meaning of the concept.[9]

I have had arguments with eminent social scientists who, in post-

---

9. While Piketty (2014, 46) commendably removed inalienable assets such as "human capital" and "social capital" from his definition of capital, it still requires sharpening, as noted in chapter 7 below.

modernist or poststructuralist fashion, have taken their "antiessential-ism" so far as to oppose all definitions. If they are right, then scientific conversation must stop because scientific progress requires researchers with shared understandings achieved through articulated definitions. Definitions are vital because science is a social process, requiring communication of meaning. Definitions are often fuzzy, and their meanings can shift. But they are still necessary.

The modern literature on varieties of capitalism counters the traditional Marxist and market-fundamentalist notions that only one type of capitalism (or one developmental track for capitalism) is feasible, normal, or desirable. Those counterarguments are important. But variety does not imply that it is impossible to define capitalism; this would be a misunderstanding of what *definition* means. As in biology, variation across a population does not preclude a common essence for a genus or a species. In fact, the understanding of that common essence helps us appreciate the nature and scope of the variation or change.

A particularly important definitional task is to help clear up a mess caused by the promiscuous application of the term *capital* by economists and sociologists. Today we find *human capital, social capital, cultural capital, natural capital, erotic capital,* and a great deal else. Of course, if this word *capital* were clearly defined (and typically it is not), then we could understand each other. But we would then need another term to describe *capital* in its original and pecuniary meaning. The phrases *human capital* and *social capital* end up as aids to misunderstanding what *capital*-ism is really about. Some may adopt a distinction between (say) *finance capital* and (say) *social capital*. But a problem here is that what is described as *social capital* has been around for millions of years. Given these confusions, one can misunderstand the whole meaning of *capitalism* and neglect the real *capital* at its core. Attention to definitions is not simply a means to improve clarity in communication. Inadequate definitions can obstruct understanding of the object of analysis. This has happened with capitalism.

The central role of the state within capitalism means that we must address politics as well as economics. John Kenneth Galbraith (1987, 299) wrote: "The separation of economics from politics and political motivation is a sterile thing. It is also a cover for the reality of economic power and motivation. And it is a prime source of misjudgment and error in economic policy." Similarly, Douglass C. North, John J. Wallis, and Barry R. Weingast (2009, 269) argued: "The seeming independence of the economic and political systems on the surface is apparent, not real. In fact, these systems are deeply intertwined." I also concur with Bruce R. Scott (2009, 4) in his claim that capitalism is both "a political phenomenon" and "an economic one" and that "specifically it requires the visible hands of political actors exercising power through political institutions." Capitalism always involves legal and political institutions: pure "anarchocapitalism" is an unrealizable fantasy.

Elements of Legal Institutionalism

The approach here differs from much of mainstream "law and economics," which is often about utility-maximizing individuals acting under legal constraints. Relatively little is learned from law itself. The approach of *legal institutionalism* is different.[10] It makes claims concerning the nature of social reality and (more complex) individual motivation, at least in modern, developed socioeconomic systems. It does not yet provide a full theoretical approach, but it does provide some tentative and limited indications concerning theory and policy.

In legal institutionalism there are three primary ontological claims. When addressing property rights many economists highlight agent-object relations, where objects are conceived in physical terms. Often neglected are agent-to-agent interactions that engender and sustain shared interpretations, meanings, understandings, rules, and institutional facts (Searle 1995). Among these many rules, and their matters of meaning and interpretation, are legal obligations and rights. Much economic activity consists of exchange, allocation, interpretation, or adjudication involving legal rights or obligations. An economy is much more than the physical creation, transformation, or transfer of material things.

The second ontological claim concerns the nature of law. It is argued that law (at least in the fullest and most developed sense) necessarily involves both the state (broadly construed to involve a realm of public ordering) and private or customary arrangements. Reduction of law to just

---

10. See Deakin, Gindis, Hodgson, Huang, and Pistor (in press). The term legal institutionalism has been used by some legal scholars to refer to institution-orientated theories of law (La Torre 1993; MacCormick 2007). I use it to denote legally grounded approaches to the institutional and economic analysis of capitalism, as envisioned by Commons (1924), Samuels (1989), and others.

one of these two aspects is mistaken. Law involves an institutionalized judiciary and a legislative apparatus.

The third ontological claim is that law—understood as an outcome of both state intervention and private ordering—accounts for many of the rules and structures of modern capitalist society. Consequently, law is not simply an expression of power relations but also a constitutive part of the institutionalized power structure and a major means through which power is exercised. This claim applies primarily to modern developed economies. In underdeveloped societies the rule of law may be compromised by greater arbitrary power. But, even in these cases, at least in the modern world, law still plays an important role.

Models of the spontaneous development of law typically rest on relatively small numbers of agents and underestimate the complexities and uncertainties in developed societies (Knight 1992; North 1994; Sened 1997; Mantzavinos 2001). Law is developed by organs of the state, including judges and legislatures. While it may often itself reflect customary experiences, it is a means of overcoming some of the complexity and uncertainty of multiple, complex, devolved interactions in large societies.

Legal institutionalism upholds that an understanding of crucial legal rules is necessary for economists and other social scientists. This is not to say that law is everything. Many social rules are not laws. The law is necessarily incomplete and sometimes self-contradictory. There are important areas of social life that rely on frequent interpersonal action rather than the anonymous generalities of law. Nevertheless, in analyzing modern capitalism an understanding of the role of law is vital.

Legal institutionalism shares with other institutional approaches a common emphasis on the importance of social rules. Indeed, constitutive and procedural rules are the stuff of social life, and institutions are essentially systems of shared social rules. Legal institutionalism adds to this the further claim that many of the more important and powerful rules are legal in character and that they are backed by the power and authority of the state.

One immediate consequence of this vision is the literal impossibility of complete deregulation or of an unregulated economy or market. Rules are everywhere: they are vital for social and economic life. All that can be attained is to change some rules or to remove some to allow others to do more work. Rather than universal deregulation, legal institutionalism addresses the difficult research question of what kind of rules are appropriate for each particular circumstance. Given the complexities involved, such an approach must be cautious and experimental and cannot proceed on the basis of complete prior design.

Legal institutionalism embraces a view of individual motivation that is much closer to Adam Smith with his "moral sentiments" than the unidimensional, utility-maximizing individual of modern mainstream economics. Individuals are often greedy and selfish, but there are also motives of morality or justice. To understand human behavior in society and business, this appreciation of morality and justice is just as necessary as one of greed and vested interests. All these factors help bind modern, complex, socioeconomic systems together (Hodgson 2013b; Smith 2013).

The role of authority is crucial, as dramatized in the famous experiments on obedience conducted by Stanley Milgram (1974). Some basic dispositions to obey authority are probably hardwired—a result of millions of years of evolution in social groups (Haidt and Joseph 2004, 2007). Law draws on these dispositions, along with feelings of morality and justice, to institutionalize authority within a system of law. We may follow customs out of habit or conformism, but in modern society law is too vast and complex to be obeyed simply by these means. Instead, we generally accept the authority of the law.

With this multidimensional view of human motivation it is impossible to separate the "economic" from the "legal." Many people want to adhere to the law and also pursue their self-interest. Consequently, the attempt to make a distinction between "economic property rights" and "legal (property) rights" fails. Yoram Barzel (1997, 3) saw "economic rights" as related to "what people ultimately seek" and law as simply "the means to achieve" those ends. But many people want more than simply "the ability to enjoy a piece of property"—they wish to own it, as a recognized and legitimate right, with assurances that it has not been acquired illegally or immorally. As Smith (1759/1976a, 159) put it in his *Moral Sentiments*, alongside our greed and "self-love" we also consider "what is fit and proper to be done or to be avoided": "It is thus that the general rules of morality are formed."

Legal institutionalism also highlights the problem of corruption. Corruption has its apologists, such as those who claim that it oils the wheels of commerce or that, if it is done by mutual consent, it must be Pareto efficient (Huntington 1968). Especially in the context of bureaucracy and underdevelopment, corruption may seem to be the only way to get things done. Once again, this view assumes that markets and business naturally operate outside law and state institutions; law and regulation are seen to give rise to corruption because they increase the costs of commerce. But, from the perspective of legal institutionalism, corruption is the negation of legal ordering.

As noted in chapter 14, empirical studies indicate that corruption has deleterious effects on economic performance (see Shleifer and Vishny 1993; Mauro 1995; Jain 2001; Mo 2001; Aidt 2003; and Pellegrini and Gerlagh 2004). The social costs of corruption may be huge (Hodgson and Jiang 2007). They include the corrosion of the legal system in favor of elite interests and nepotism. Evidence shows that corruption stultifies effective economic competition, undermines investment, inhibits the rule of law, undermines effective state administration, and promotes political instability.

What has legal institutionalism in common with the original American institutionalism in economics (including Thorstein Veblen and John Commons) and with the new institutional economics (including Ronald Coase, Douglass North, Mancur Olson, Elinor Ostrom, and Oliver Williamson)? How does it differ from them?

The answers are complex because both institutionalisms have contained a diverse range of thinkers, with some important overlap between the two traditions (Dequech 2002; Groenewegen, Kerstholt, and Nagelkerke 1995). In recognizing the historical specificity of property, contract, exchange, and firms, legal institutionalism shares an important insight from the original institutionalism. Furthermore, the original institutionalist Commons placed particular emphasis on the role of law, which he regarded as a historically specific combination of both legal decree and custom. Other leading original institutionalists recognized the economic role of law, to differing degrees. The contribution of Veblen, for example, had more to do with the general nature and evolution of institutions, although he underlined intangible assets plus vital legal concepts such as property and incorporation (Camic and Hodgson 2011).

New institutional economists have made major contributions to the development of the interface between law and economics, but sometimes they have treated law as a matter of custom or private ordering alone. But, on the other hand, North, Wallis, and Weingast (2009) have stressed the general role of statutory law and of legal incorporation of business firms in particular.[11]

---

11. Underlying the overlap between parts of the original and the new institutionalism, the Nobel laureate Ostrom (2004) chose Commons (1924) as one of the ten most important

Legal institutionalism draws from all these traditions, but it gives particular emphasis to the role of the state in the legal system and to the constitutive role of law in modern socioeconomic life.

Historical Explanations of Origins— a Brief and Derivative Summary

It is not the purpose of this work to examine the historical reasons for the emergence of capitalism. It is more concerned with the essence of capitalism. It uses history principally to identify when crucial institutional components of capitalism were established. But this clearly involves some preconception of what these components were. In identifying these particular institutions, I take capitalism as a relatively recent phenomenon and consider the rapid development of leading economies in the last few hundred years. By locating that takeoff, history helps us identify the key institutions that emerged and empowered the system.

The complex question of the origins of capitalism has long been debated by economic historians and others. I do not add anything new on that topic. A brief, eclectic account follows. As Jean Baechler (1975) argued, it is methodologically illegitimate to explain the origins of capitalism in terms of defining properties of capitalism itself. To do so would be to assume what has to be explained. The origins have to be understood in terms of factors outside the system's defining core, in terms of novel combinations of elements, or in terms of new institutions. Baechler (1975, 42) argued specifically that "the solution to the problem of the origins of capitalism must be sought within the political system."[12]

The importance of the state in the emergence of capitalism is already

---

books affecting her intellectual growth, alongside the influence of Simon (1981) and other volumes. The Nobel laureates Simon (1979, 499), Myrdal (1978, 771), and Williamson (Williamson 1975, 3, 254; Williamson 1985b, 3–5; Williamson 2002, 438–39) have all stressed the influence of Commons on their work.

12. Berman (1983) showed that religion played an important role in the development of medieval legal systems. Since Weber (1904–5/1930), the idea that Protestantism played a positive role in capitalist development has become the subject of endless controversy. Andrew Tylecote has suggested to me in conversation that Weber may have been partly right for the wrong reasons. Protestantism did more than Catholicism to promote literacy and an ethic of equal access to scriptural knowledge and other entitlements, thus aiding technical and legislative progress. But this issue is beyond the scope of the present work.

well established in numerous studies of law, property rights, markets, banking, manufacturing, and so on. A key factor was the development of a new and sophisticated state machine that was strong enough to protect property and trade, but adequately restrained by checks, balances, and countervailing power, to minimize confiscation or overtaxation, to protect a relatively autonomous legal system, and to allow the development of self-governing organizational forms that could engage in productive activity and reap the rewards of innovation.[13]

The plurality and rivalry of states in late medieval Europe helped create the conditions for the emergence of capitalism (Tilly 1975; Scott 2011). Water and mountains divided multiple lowland populations, making the continent difficult to unify politically (a feat now on the agenda but hitherto signaled by the Romans alone). This medieval political division had a number of important effects, particularly when merchant trade became well established from the eleventh century. The mobility of merchants and intellectuals within Europe, facilitated by some sharing of Latin, gave some the option to migrate to less-oppressive states (Weber 1968; Jones 1981; Pipes 1999). This created some pressure on relatively enlightened states to develop policies to encourage merchants and trade.

Once a merchant class became well established in a nation, it became a political lobby to defend its interests, reinforce countervailing power, and enable the development of a relatively autonomous system of law. In countries where merchants had greater power and autonomy (contrast England with Spain), the rewards of global trade made this class even more powerful and led to institutional changes that further checked the arbitrary power of the state. Access to emerging Atlantic trade routes enhanced this process of positive feedback between commerce and countervailing power (Cipolla 1965; Braudel 1984; Acemoglu, Johnson, and Robinson 2005a, 2005b; Acemoglu and Robinson 2012). To be effective, these changed institutions also had to bestow a degree of political stability within a complex system with divergent interests (Moore 1966).

---

13. Galbraith (1952, 1969) promoted the concept of "countervailing power" but referred specifically to the role of trade unions as a counterbalance to large corporations. North, Wallis, and Weingast (2009) referred more broadly to any organized power to check state tyranny. The earliest use of the term I have found is in a pamphlet by a stockholder that criticizes the lack of "countervailing power" within the governance structures of the East India College in Hertfordshire in England, where Malthus was a professor (Address to the Proprietors 1823).

Where they emerged, countervailing power within pluralist constellations of institutions created spaces for the intelligentsia, the Enlightenment, and the advancement of science (Mokyr 2003, 2010). They also encouraged financial investment on a larger scale.

War between rival states periodically devastated Europe and often checked its development. But in some cases—particularly in the island of Britain—production of material for military and naval use itself gave a huge boost to industry (Tilly 1975; O'Brien 1989, 1993, 1994; Scott 2011). Wars in the eighteenth century and the early nineteenth prompted the development of more efficient state administrations and reductions in public corruption (Neild 2001). The further development in the nineteenth century of the legal form of the corporation, the banking system, and other institutions provided additional incentives and possibilities for investment, innovation, and technical change.

Two important points emerge from this very brief summary of the emergence of capitalism. First, the roles of the state and trade have been vital. Second—and against both Marx and Schumpeter—the evolution of national capitalist systems cannot be understood as a process that is exclusively "from within." As in the biological world, evolution depends on the environment and rivalry with others as well as on the development of the organism itself.

The Structure and Outline of This Book

Much of this book addresses the definitions of key terms such as *law, property, exchange, markets, money, capital,* and *capitalism.* If it is at least partly successful in this respect alone, then this is no meager achievement. It means that the reader can delve selectively and unsequentially into chapters 3–10 in search of arguments for particular definitions.

But in addition there are some guiding threads that connect the chapters together, and the less casual reader may be interested in these. One of these is the general role of the state and law in constituting and sustaining capitalism. Another is the inevitability of missing markets in a system that is nevertheless dominated by commodity exchange. A third is the way that physicalist metaphors and a focus on associated agent-object relations together corrode our definitions and understandings of the system and its key components.

The first part of the book is entitled "Discovering Capitalism." The guiding narrative is toward the goal of a definition of capitalism in chapter 10. Preceding chapters have a connected, logical sequence. Hence, to understand capitalism we need to understand capital, to understand capital we need to understand money, to understand money we need to understand exchange, to understand exchange we need to understand property, and to understand property we need to understand law. There is also a chapter on firms and another on employment because these too may plausibly enter the definition of capitalism.

The opening two chapters are important preliminaries to this logical sequence. Chapter 1 considers the definitional problem of identifying key essential features of a class of phenomena of the same type. Pinpointing the essence of multiple capitalist social formations means identifying fundamental properties that make capitalism what it is, notwithstanding important variations between different national capitalisms. This chapter is the most philosophical, and some readers may be inclined to skip it. But I suggest that they read section 1.3 and definitely look at figure 1.1 on page 36. They are vital for what follows.

The next nine chapters are in descending levels of abstraction and rising degrees of historical specificity. Chapter 2 addresses issues of social structure and individual motivation that have been relevant for human societies at least since the development of a sophisticated language, very roughly 100,000 years ago (Oppenheimer 2004). It stresses dispositions such as conformism and obedience to authority that evolved in human societies long before the dawn of civilization.

Chapter 3 considers the constitutive role of law in modern society. Law is distinguished from custom. Law emerged in states with institutionalized judiciaries, as first found in antiquity. Chapter 4 continues on legal themes and insists on a difference between possession and property, where the latter involves legal rights and obligations. It also emphasizes a definition of exchange entailing property rights rather than social interaction alone.

Chapter 5 addresses the nature and definition of the market. Following common parlance, it defines a market as an organized forum of exchange rather than trade in general. Markets in this sense are relatively recent. A hitherto uncited Chinese text suggests that they may have existed ca. 3000 BC in China, but there is no other known record of them until the sixth century BC.

Chapter 6 considers money and compares spontaneous and state-

centered (or chartalist) views. It argues that money is essentially neither spontaneous nor entirely a creation of the state but that legal en-
forcements are vital for its existence. The chapter goes on to consider the
evolution of more complex financial systems that first emerged in Italy,
the Netherlands, and Great Britain. Chapter 7 considers the problematic word *capital* and how economists since Adam Smith progressively
changed its meaning and ended up losing sight of core characteristics
that are vital to understand *capital*-ism.

Chapter 8 considers firms and corporations, arguing that legal insights must be reintroduced in order to understand these institutions.
Chapter 9 addresses the labor process and the employment relationship
and weighs up their importance for the capitalist system. Chapter 10 finally reaches the point where the definition of capitalism is addressed.
Capitalism is defined therein as a socioeconomic system with the following six characteristics:

1. A legal system supporting widespread individual rights and liberties to own,
   buy, and sell private property
2. Widespread commodity exchange and markets involving money
3. Widespread private ownership of the means of production by firms producing
   goods or services for sale in the pursuit of profit
4. Much of production organized separately and apart from the home and
   family
5. Widespread wage labor and employment contracts
6. A developed financial system with banking institutions, the widespread use
   of credit with property as collateral, and the selling of debt

There are two optional, five-point variant definitions, namely, *S-
capitalism* (in honor of Schumpeter), which omits point (5) concerning
employment, and *M-capitalism* (in honor of Marx), which omits point
(6) concerning finance, credit, collateral, and the selling of debt. The
case is made in the book for adopting all six points, but, as with all definitions, there is no supreme court that can offer a final verdict on the six-
point definition's alleged superiority. The merits and demerits of different definitions have to be debated.

The second part of this book contains six further chapters and is entitled "Capitalism and Beyond." This addresses some key questions that
are now subjects of popular interest, particularly after the Great Crash
of 2008. These include the generic limitations of capitalism, its possible

development in the twenty-first century, the effects of ongoing globalization, the possibility of a new global economic leader to overtake the United States, the problem of inequality and its causes, and the possibility of postcapitalist developments such as socialism.

To understand possibilities beyond capitalism we must appreciate how any system organizes and interacts with the processes of production. Chapter 11 considers the general nature, or ontology, of the production process. While this question is not specific to capitalism, it is vital to understand its nature and any postcapitalist possibilities. This is an important preliminary to the following chapter, which is on the viability of socialism.

Chapter 12 argues that the abolition of private property and its replacement by comprehensive planning—which until about 1950 was the meaning of socialism held by almost all its adherents—is incompatible with efficient, large-scale production in a modern, complex economy under a democratic polity. In this respect I give qualified support to the Austrian school in the great "socialist calculation debate" of the 1930s and 1940s. But, on the other hand, the state has a greater role to play in a viable and dynamic capitalist system than many critics of socialism envisage. Furthermore, the Austrian school defense of capitalism was gravely weakened by its poor definitions of property, exchange, and markets.

The final four chapters consider how capitalism evolves, its prospects, and other possible postcapitalist directions. Chapter 13 considers the mechanisms of capitalist evolution using insights from recent work on evolutionary theory. Chapter 14 further considers tendencies of capitalist development and argues that, despite globalization, capitalism will not converge on a single type. This opens up a choice between different varieties of capitalism, including between different levels of economic inequality. Capitalism engenders equal commercial rights under the law but has generated greater inequalities in the distribution of income and wealth. Chapter 15 addresses the sources of this inequality and briefly considers some possible policy remedies. Chapter 16 considers further reforms of capitalist institutions and offers glimpses of possible routes beyond capitalism.

PART I

Discovering Capitalism

CHAPTER ONE

Distilling the Essence

If names are not right, words are misused. When words are misused, affairs go wrong. When affairs go wrong, courtesy and music droop, law and justice fail. And when law and justice fail them, a people can move neither hand nor foot. — Confucius, *Analects* (ca. 400 BC)

A definition is an account that signifies the essence. — Aristotle, *Topica* (ca. 350 BC)

By this it appears how necessary it is for any man that aspires to true Knowledge, to examine the Definitions of former Authors; and either to correct them, where they are negligently set down; or to make them himself. For the errors of Definitions multiply themselves, according as the reckoning proceeds; and lead men into absurdities, which at last they see, but cannot avoid, without reckoning anew from the beginning; in which lies the foundation of their errors. — Thomas Hobbes, *Leviathan* (1651)

This book is about capitalism and understanding the type of real-world entity to which the word *capitalism* most usefully should refer. Given this project, definitions are unavoidable. Like it or not, we must seek some precision with words, to help us dissect reality with sharp concepts of the mind. A definition must identify key essential features of the type it defines.[1] It cannot simply be a description of the entity or group of entities. Definitions demarcate different types: they are not mere lists of attributes. Identifying what is and what is not essential is tricky. We never reach fixed and final statements that are devoid of ambiguity or the need for further refinement. But we must first understand what an act of definition means: definition must be defined.

---

1. The word *essential* is ambiguous. It can refer to something that is part of the essence of a kind or to something that is vital to its existence. Unless otherwise indicated, *essential* here shall refer to part of the essence of a type.

Definitions are not mere wordplay. Questions of the form, "What is the meaning of X?" are not confined to philosophers. Comprehending the meaning of a word is often tied up with the understanding of real phenomena; the search for understanding drives scientific inquiry. For example, questions concerning the nature and meaning of gravity drove both the Newtonian and the Einsteinian Scientific Revolutions in physics. Scientists must first establish an agreed rough understanding of the phenomenon they are investigating. Then they try to focus on the problem, using a definition as a means of demarcation. They sometimes change this definition. Definitions matter at every stage. Science is driven in part by a search for meaning.

Some readers may wonder whether a philosophical discussion of definitions is any use. Others will accuse me of the cardinal sin of "essentialism," mock my naivety, and go their own way. I urge them to stay. I argue that much "antiessentialism" is mistaken and that it has created damaging confusion for the social sciences. I am not alone in this view. I further argue that—despite their neglect in the social sciences—definitions are vital for all science.

To identify capitalism we need to make explicit the features that distinguish it from other social formations. If this is agreed and the reader is not interested in the philosophical arguments, then he or she might skip sections 1.1 and 1.2 of this chapter and proceed to section 1.3, with its crucial facts about the explosion of productive activity around 1800. But, if the reader is interested in my defense of at least one version of essentialism, then read on.

Antiessentialism has been used as an excuse for avoiding precise definitions. But shared meanings are necessary for communication and mutual understanding. The more abstract and complex the discourse, the more serious this problem becomes. Even "antiessentialists" or "antirealists" must use words carefully and attempt to communicate intended meanings. Absolute precision, like absolute cleanliness, is impossible; but that does not imply that we should abandon our duties of linguistic housekeeping or personal hygiene.

1.1. Anti-Antiessentialism

The term *essentialism* was allegedly invented by the leading philosophers Karl Popper and Willem van Orman Quine (Wilkins 2012), but they used it in contrasting and challengeable ways. Quine (1960, 1966) faulted *essentialism* on the grounds that, if we considered a single entity, it was generally difficult and often impossible to disentangle essential from accidental attributes. A person is characterized by features that others do not possess—such as blue eyes—so they are accidental for humans as a whole but not for the individual concerned. Among other problems in his account, Douglas B. Rasmussen (1984) pointed out that Quine had shifted the discussion of essences from Aristotle's species or kinds to a single individual. This was a key error; it is only when we address species or kinds that the distinction between essential and accidental features becomes sufficiently meaningful.[2]

Popper (1945, 1963, 1972) criticized *essentialism*, but he gave it a different meaning. For him, essentialism was not about identification but about explanation. Hence, Popper (1945, 25ff.) critiqued *methodological essentialism*. Later Popper (1963, 103–4) wrote: "The essentialist doctrine I am contesting is solely *the doctrine that science aims at ultimate explanation;* that is to say, an explanation which (essentially, or by its very nature) cannot be further explained, and which is in no need of further explanation." But this is not the version of essentialism defended here, which involves the assertion of the existence and meaningfulness of essences. Popper (1963, 104) himself went on to say that his criticism "does not aim at establishing the non-existence of essences." So in this vital respect his view does not conflict with that proposed here. Popper was attacking a view of science rather than the notion of essence.

Another apparent challenge to essentialism derives from the American pragmatist tradition, stretching from Charles Sanders Peirce (1878, 1923), through John Dewey (1929), to Richard Rorty (1979). Peirce and Dewey criticized claims that essences are always knowable. But sophisticated essentialists would not uphold that they are. Furthermore, both Peirce and Dewey embrace forms of realism or naturalism, which would typically imply some commitment to types or kinds of entities.[3]

The version of essentialism adopted here involves the claim that es-

2. Robinson (1950, 154–56) made a similar criticism of the concept of essence. Relatedly, he too downplayed the role of definition in classifying groups of varied or varying entities, beyond single or unchanging things. White (1972) argued persuasively that Quine's account of Aristotle is inaccurate in several respects and has led to a widespread misspecification of the Greek philosopher's position (Wilkins 2009, 2012).

3. Note that I avoid the term *natural kind* here because it may connote things that are indifferent to our classifications or descriptions of them. "Kinds" or "types" in the social

sences are meaningful and real. For any kind of entity there is a set of characteristics that all entities of that kind must possess for it to be that kind of thing; if it does not possess them, it will be another kind of thing. This should not be confused with *foundationalism*, which is the view that all knowledge can be grounded on some foundation such as reason, sensation, or experience. Essentialism here is an ontological doctrine; foundationalism concerns epistemology. Likewise, essentialism here has nothing to do with correspondence or spectator theories of truth, which are also epistemological doctrines.

Dewey and Rorty rejected correspondence theories of truth as well as foundationalism. When Rorty rejected *essentialism*, it too was given a peculiar meaning, related to the linguistic and political themes of his work. Consequently, the authors and arguments cited above do not undermine the kind of essentialism adopted here. The notion of essences, in the Aristotelian sense of referring to kinds, is preserved. Influential philosophers such as Saul Kripke (1972) and Hilary Putnam (1975) have restored the reputation of essentialism, claiming that it is the task of a science to investigate the essential properties of the types of entity that it may address.

We should not ignore the role of the French in all this.[4] Writing in 1957, the philosopher Roland Barthes explored in his *Mythologies* how words can be used to assert particular values and become instruments of power for the media and the bourgeoisie. Fair enough. But then Barthes (1972, 75) went too far and condemned "this disease of thinking in essences." The fact that words can be instruments of power does not mean that we can or should abandon words. Social scientists have a duty to use words as precisely as possible. Inquiry is a social process. To carry out an investigation we have to communicate and refer to objects of analysis. This is not a disease. It is a vital part of science, without which it dies.

In his *For Marx*, Louis Althusser (1969) developed the concept of *overdetermination*, which roughly means that a single observed effect is simultaneously determined by multiple different causes, where fewer of

---

world can be themselves affected by our categorizations, as in Hacking's (1999) notion of "interactive kinds."

4. Or perhaps, more particularly, the Parisians. The philosopher Thomas Nagel (2002, 165) wrote: "There does seem to be something about the Parisian scene that is particularly hospitable to reckless verbosity." But France often leads in fashion, and Gallic garrulity has spread elsewhere.

them might be enough to account for the phenomenon. Althusser linked this to the Marxist idea of contradiction. Overdetermination signified internal, conflicting forces within a complex whole. Several Althusserians then argued that to focus on relatively few essential features was mistaken. Some went further, claiming that any account of an essence is a mistake. As far as I am aware, Althusser himself did not take that step, but he inspired others such as James Tomlinson (1982), Ernesto Laclau and Chantal Mouffe (1985), Barry Hindess (1987), and Stephen A. Resnick and Richard D. Wolff (1987) to move in this direction.

It is indeed necessary to understand a complex entity such as capitalism in terms of structurally dissimilar—or "contradictory"—elements. Because multiple varied elements are part of the system, it is necessary to understand it in terms of these dissimilar parts. But that begs a number of further questions, which I shall address later. Crucially, despite claims to the contrary, Althusser's concept of overdetermination does not counter the need or possibility of describing essences.

Considering the essence and meaning of a market, Hindess (1987, 149) wrote: "To write of essentialism in this context is to say that the market is analyzed in terms of an essence or inner principle which produces necessary effects by the mere fact of its presence." In a forensic response, John O'Neill (1998, 10) regarded this as "a caricature of what it is to say that an entity has an essence." Instead of "necessary effects," an essence involves dispositions: "It does not follow that these dispositions are always exhibited. . . . The criticisms are aimed at a position that nobody holds." O'Neill (1998, 2001) emphasized that essence precedes discovery, that many essential properties are dispositional properties that are actualized only in certain circumstances, and that some essential properties depend on others. O'Neill (1998, 9) explained: "The essential properties of an entity of a particular kind are those properties of the object that it must have if it is to be an object of that kind. Accidental properties of an entity of a particular kind are those properties it has, but could lack and still be an entity of that kind." O'Neill also countered claims that Ludwig Wittgenstein (1960) criticized essential properties. After a detailed examination of Wittgenstein's text, O'Neill (1998, 14) concluded: "The legitimate conclusion to be drawn from Wittgenstein's discussion is that one cannot assume in advance that there must be a set of essential properties shared by all entities that fall under some concept, not that there are no essential properties of objects."

But that was not the end of the story. By the 1980s *essentialism* had become a global term of abuse among anthropologists, feminists, and many others. It became a catchall word for many varied sins, including biological reductionism, economic reductionism, the notion of knowledge as representation, the imposition of Western values on other cultures, and overgeneralizations concerning gender differences (Fuss 1989; Nussbaum 1992; Assiter 1996; Sayer 1997). But essentialism does not itself imply that the (human) essence is biological, cultural, or economic. The essence of a kind can be social, biological, physical, chemical, ideational, or whatever, including often a combination of these: it all depends on the nature of that kind. Finally, claiming that essences exist does not imply that knowledge is representation: ontological and epistemological claims are different in character.

The rise of social constructivism led to further antiessentialist rhetoric. After declaring her own antiessentialism in *An Introduction to Social Constructivism*, Vivien Burr (1995, 4) explained: "Since the social world, including ourselves as people, is the product of social processes, it follows that there cannot be any given, determined nature to the world or people." But this does not follow. The social world—like anything else—is clearly the product of processes, but we cannot infer from this that it lacks any "given" or "determined" nature. The fact that a thing is created, or in movement, does not mean that it lacks an essence. Burr continued: "There are no 'essences' inside things or people that make them what they are." First, an essence is a property, and it is not strictly "inside" the entity. Second, if things lack factors "that make them what they are," then how can we account for their existence? Third, the defining properties of a type are generally insufficient to constitute that type or "make them what they are." Mass and structure help make things "what they are." But these are not necessarily defining properties. Burr also depicts essentialism as involving the view that persons have "some definable and discoverable nature, whether given by biology or by the environment." Essentialists believe that there is such a thing as human nature that helps define the essence of being human. But, contrary to Burr, essentialism does not imply that essences are always discoverable.

In the 1980s, antiessentialist rhetoric swept through several areas of inquiry, impairing social theory and its reputation. As Martha Nussbaum (1992) noted with concrete examples, antiessentialism joined forces with normative cultural relativism (where one culture is deemed to be as good or as bad as any other) even to defend traditional but harmful practices in the developing world. As Diana Fuss (1989) jested, an obsession with antiessentialism has become the "essence" of social theory. Fuss (1989, xi) further wrote: "Few [other] words in the vocabulary of contemporary critical theory are so persistently maligned, so little interrogated, and so predictably summoned as a term of infallible critique." But she too was obliged to describe herself as an antiessentialist. It had become a necessary shibboleth.

1.2. Essentialism without the Natural State Model

Another perceived attack on essentialism derived from interpretations of "population thinking" in evolutionary theory. The leading philosopher of biology, Ernst Mayr (1963, 1976, 1982, 1988), argued that one of Charles Darwin's (1859) greatest achievements was population thinking. This surpassed the alleged "typological essentialism" or "typologism" of Plato or others, where variety in a population is ignored to concentrate instead on an average, typical, or representative individual that served as a surrogate for the whole species. By contrast, in population thinking, variation is all important. Variation is a key feature of any species; it is the evolutionary fuel for natural selection. Consequently, the essence of any species cannot be understood without encompassing that variation.

Population thinking is relevant for economics as well as biology. When addressing an industry or economy, economists sometimes use simplifying notions such as the representative firm or the representative individual. But this simplification suppresses the variety in the population, which can account for distinct dynamics and serve as the fuel of evolutionary change (Metcalfe 1988; Nelson 1991; Kirman 1992; Hodgson 1993).

Does population thinking amount to a rejection of essentialism? David Hull (1965)—who studied under Popper—thought so. Mayr (1982, 38) himself cited Popper on essentialism and rejected any conception of "a limited number of fixed and unchanging forms . . . or essences." But a commitment to essences does not itself imply that forms are fixed or unchanging. Mayr's population thinking does not imply a general rejection of the notion of essence. We should not in this regard be misled by his critique of what he described as "typological essentialism."

In a neglected article, the philosopher of biology Elliott Sober (1980) made a major breakthrough. Instead of seeing population thinking as a negation of essentialism, he argued that the problems lay elsewhere. He showed that the classical essentialism of Aristotle involved additional questionable assumptions that had been given insufficient attention. For Sober (1980, 350) the key problematic addition in the Aristotelian account was the "natural state model" and its use to explain variation. It is this—and not essentialism as such—that "clashes with evolutionary theory." Sober explained the natural state model as follows: "Aristotle's hypothesis was that there is a distinction between the natural state of a kind of object and those states which are not natural. These latter are produced by subjecting the object to an interfering force. . . . Variability within nature is . . . to be accounted for as a deviation from what is natural" (360).

With the natural state model, "variation is deviation caused by interfering forces" (Sober 1980, 364), and hence "the search for invariances takes the form of a search for natural tendencies" (370). By contrast, Darwin brought about a great transformation in our thinking, involving "the realization that this diversity itself constituted an invariance, obeying its own laws" (365). Consequently: "Individual differences are not the effects of interfering forces confounding the expression of a prototype; rather they are the causes of events that are absolutely central to the history of evolution" (371).

Multiple coexisting capitalisms, or competing firms in an industry, have to be understood in population terms. Crucially, variation within a population (of capitalisms or of firms) is part of its species essence rather than a disturbance from one natural state. The essence itself embraces variation. We cannot identify an essence by seeking an illusory natural state for the species.

Sober further addressed the nature of the essential properties that group entities together in a population. He argued: "The membership condition must be *explanatory*. . . . A species essence will be a causal mechanism which works on each member of the species, making it the kind of thing it is" (1980, 354). Consequently, a species essence cannot simply be a set of descriptive characteristics.

Of course, there will always be problems drawing the line between what is a member of the species and what is not. For Sober: "Essentialism is in principle consistent with *vague essences*" (1980, 358). Sober construed "essentialism as a fairly flexible doctrine which, in at least some circumstances, can be seen to be quite consistent with the existence of insoluble line-drawing problems" (359). Consider entities that are constantly undergoing change. Given the variation in a population, some things may alter without changing the species essence. But there may come a point at which alterations lead to a change of essence and, thus, the entity becomes another kind of thing. But this does not mean the thing in question never had an essence.

Why is this relevant for our quest to understand capitalism? Versions of the natural state model are widespread in popular and academic discourse on capitalism, among both advocates and critics of the system. Marx was not simply an essentialist (Meikle 1985). He also adopted a version of Aristotle's natural state model. Marx (1976, 90) declared in the preface to the first edition of *Capital* (1867) that he was following physicists by studying the capitalist mode of production in its "most typical form . . . least affected by disturbing influences" and hence closest to its "pure state." He declared that England was then the "*locus classicus*" for capitalism and that Germany, among others, would follow the same road.

Marx promoted a modified natural state model, one in which the natural state of the entity is not a single outcome but a single path of development. Variation from this path would be short-lived and due to a "disturbing influence" rather than the opening of a new road ahead. Apart from these disturbances, every country is more or less obliged to follow the same path.

Francis Fukuyama (1992) famously declared that Western liberal-democratic capitalism was the end state of historical evolution for all politicoeconomic systems. He has since modified his position, but it is easy to find other examples of the idea that capitalism has a natural state toward which it gravitates. Often this natural state is deemed to be a Western-style capitalist economy.

The post-1990 literature on varieties of capitalism challenged both traditional Marxist and procapitalist natural state doctrines.[5] Instead of the idea that all capitalisms would eventually find approximately the same track and destination, this literature gave explanations for enduring differences between them. These included the influences of different cultures, path dependence, and institutional complementarities. I

---

5. On varieties of capitalism, see Albert (1993), Hodgson (1995, 1996), Berger and Dore (1996), Boyer (1999, 2005a, 2005b), Whitley (1999), Dore (2000), Amable (2000, 2003), Aoki (2001, 2010), Hall and Soskice (2001), Streeck and Yamamura (2001), Coates (2005), Crouch (2005), Elsner and Hanappi (2008), Amable and Palombarini (2009), Hall and Thelen (2009), and many others.

return to these issues later in this book. Here I note that the varieties-of-capitalism literature was partly an implicit revolt against the natural state model.

Economists rarely refer to the natural state model or seem to be aware of the underlying philosophical issues. A rare exception is Thorstein Veblen, who had an acute grasp of philosophy. In his critique of the economics of John Bates Clark, Veblen (1908d, 154–55) noted that the Clark's treatment of dynamics assumes a "'natural' state in which the phenomena of economic life are assumed to arrange themselves in a stable, normal scheme." Furthermore, "Mr. Clark's use of the word 'dynamic'" involves "a speculative inquiry as to how the equilibrium re-established itself when one or more of the quantities involved increases or decreases." Clark's dynamics were about disturbing forces acting on equilibrium and being corrected by negative feedback; lacking were qualitative changes and ongoing evolution. Later Veblen (1925, 51) extolled "evolutionary" principles that "hold attention to the changes that are going forward" rather than focusing it on that "natural state of man . . . to which the movement of history was believed inevitably to lead": "The question now before the body of economists is not how things stabilize themselves in a 'static state,' but how they endlessly grow and change."

Veblen thus rejected the idea of a natural socioeconomic order. His rejection of the natural state model was a first step in making economics a Darwinian and evolutionary science. But this did not imply a rejection of essentialism, as the notion is defined here.

1.3. Carving Reality at the Joints:
Degrees of Generality or Specificity

The role of a definition is to identify the essential distinguishing characteristics or to "carve" reality "where the joint is," as Plato reported of Socrates in the *Phaedrus*. We need to distinguish the essential from the accidental features of natural or social kinds. In practice we do this all the time, such as when we identify a group of people as familiar friends even though they have changed their clothes and are doing different things.

But what is deemed accidental or essential depends on the degree of generality we are seeking in locating the type of entity to be defined. Defining birds is different from defining finches. Among the class of birds is the genus of finches. In defining finches we need a fuller description of essence than we do in defining birds, where some characteristics that are accidental for birds as a whole become essential for finches. Going further, to define a specific species of finch—such as a common (European) chaffinch—we need to make the description of its essence even more detailed.

The problem of choosing the level of generality or specificity arises with definitions of capitalism. Many simply define it as a market system with private property. This broad definition concentrates on the (private) form of ownership and the (market) mechanism of distribution. In this approach, other features such as finance, corporate power, and the employment relationship are secondary. Whether they are added to the definition makes a big difference. It is not simply a matter of differentiating birds from finches; it affects our identification and hence our conception of the longevity and generality of the system.

Consider some historical facts. In the first seventeen hundred years after the birth of Christ, world GDP per capita increased by an overall factor of about 3.5 (Maddison 2007). But sometime after 1700 GDP per capita began to take off in Europe and accelerated further upward around 1800, sending developmental (and militaristic) shockwaves around the world.[6]

In terms of GDP per capita, four countries successively led the way. Figure 1.1 shows that Italy had the highest GDP per capita in Europe in the fifteenth century. It was overtaken by the Netherlands in the late sixteenth century, which in turn was overtaken by the United Kingdom in the early nineteenth century. Then the United States became the global leader around 1900. Some new form of social organization emerged in this period. It was refined as each new pioneer built on and developed the dynamic institutions of its predecessors.

Western European GDP per capita was about twenty times larger in 2003 than it was in 1700. World GDP per capita in 2003 was about eleven times larger than it was in 1700. In less than half the time, US GDP per capita in 2003 was about twelve times greater than it was in 1870. At the

---

6. Gross domestic product (GDP) measures have been criticized for several reasons, including their neglect of unpaid work and environmental damage (Costanza et al. 2014). Prominent alternative measures of economic activity show less rapid progress since the 1970s.

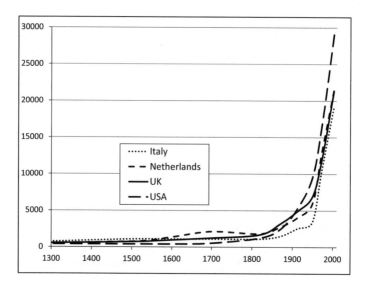

FIGURE 1.1. The birth of capitalism: GDP per capita in pioneering capitalist countries. *Data source*: Maddison (2007, 382). GDP (PPP) per capita in 1990 international dollars.

same time, global growth since 1700 has seen a widening gap between rich and poor nations (Milanovic 2011).

Nevertheless, as a result of technological developments in medicine and the improved average standard of living, between 1800 and 2000 life expectancy at birth rose from a global average of about thirty years to sixty-seven years and to more than seventy-five years in several developed countries (Riley 2001; Fogel 2004; Deaton 2013).

Something happened to cause this unprecedented explosion in production, innovation, and human longevity. Figure 1.1 prompts us to consider changes in the leading countries before 1800 that caused the subsequent takeoff. What were those changes?

A widespread view is that technology explains the takeoff in output. To be sure, technology was a necessary condition of much progress, and many explosions in productivity have resulted from new technologies— from steam engines to modern electronics. But what were the necessary conditions for the development and diffusion of new technology? Property rights were necessary to provide incentives, and finance was required to purchase materials and labor power. There had to be networked communities of scientists and engineers to scrutinize, share, and develop ideas. These communities required political conditions allowing relatively free and open inquiry and the uncensored publication of much scientific information. Addressing these necessary conditions, we are back to institutions again. Both technology and institutions must be part of the explanation.

In contrast, according to Deirdre McCloskey (2010, 26), ideas explain the takeoff: "Ideas, not mere trade or investment, did the creating and the releasing. The leading ideas were two: that the liberty to hope was a good idea and that a faithful economic life should give dignity and even honor to ordinary people." Of course, ideas were central, but were they everything? Something must account for the rise of these ideas and for the developments in the social system and culture that allowed them to spread and take hold. Ideas and rhetoric are vital, but their origins and spread among a population must also be explained.[7]

How do the facts and possible explanations outlined above relate to the definition of capitalism? McCloskey ruled out the possibility that the rise of capitalist institutions can have any explanatory role post-1700 because, for her, capitalism was defined in terms of "markets" (by which she meant any kind of trade) and the "market economy has existed since the caves" (2010, 16). For her: "Market participants are capitalists" (260). From this it seems that markets are sufficient to imply capitalism (this widespread view is criticized in later chapters). McCloskey was not alone in posing a very broad definition of capitalism. For example, the historian Alan Macfarlane (1978, 178) declared: "England was as 'capitalist' in 1250 as it was in 1550 or 1750." Definitions framed simply in terms of markets or private property are commonplace. The *Compact Oxford*

---

7. McCloskey (in press) further develops her argument that spectacular growth after 1800 was caused by "rhetorical and ethical" change. Yet her detailed argument is all about institutions: the growth of equality under the law, the removal of tariffs and other restrictions on trade, the failing grip of conservative institutions, and so on. Clearly, every innovation, every change, whether technological or institutional, was or is at some stage an idea. Humans are driven by ideas. So ideas propelled spectacular growth. Q.E.D. But social reality is not simply the sum of ideas in our heads. Society also consists of relations between individuals (albeit interpreted and understood through ideas) that typically are inadequately understood by social actors. Also, we do not simply think with the brain: our mind works through interactions with its material and social contexts. "Situated cognition" means that knowing is inseparable from doing and from its material setting (Lave and Wenger 1991; Hutchins 1995; Lane, Malerba, Maxfield, and Orsenigo 1996; Clark 1997a, 1997b). Ideas develop and play out in the world of material things. Human cognitive capacities are irreducible to individuals alone: they also depend on social structures and material cues. Ideas matter. But so do institutions. Each helps constitute the other.

English Dictionary, for example, defines capitalism as "an economic and political system in which a country's trade and industry are controlled by private owners for profit, rather than by the state." If we insert *most of* before *a country's* and treat *profit* loosely as pecuniary gain, then by this definition capitalism has been around for thousands of years. Its appearance long ago would have little connection with the post-1700 explosions in productivity.

It would make more sense to define capitalism more narrowly and apply it to something that became prominent in leading countries in the seventeenth and eighteenth centuries. This means adding some further stipulations to the definition, other than mere "markets" or "private ownership." We have to identify the kind of system that emerged in the eighteenth century and led to explosive growth.

But that does not mean that the additional stipulations are arbitrary or merely descriptive. Our focus is a massive growth of productive activity, so we must concentrate on the economic core of the system—the engine of growing production of goods and services. What defines this core?

Could it be wage labor? In the third volume of *Capital*, Marx (1981, 1019) saw wage labor as a "characteristic trait" of the capitalist mode of production. But using this as a criterion is not straightforward. As noted in chapter 9, extensive wage labor dates from medieval times. But widespread *industrial* wage labor emerged much later. As late as about 1803, when the Industrial Revolution was under way, industrial laborers (excluding agriculture and the armed forces) made up about 21 percent of heads of households (Lindert and Williamson 1982, 400). Marx's vision of a large industrial proletariat was realized in England no earlier than the nineteenth century. But why should the demarcation criterion focus solely on *industrial* wage labor?

As shown in later chapters, Marx put insufficient emphasis on the empowering role of the financial system and its use of debt to capitalize production. Instead, he concentrated on the emergence of wage labor and the organization of labor as the primary driving force. But that does not necessarily mean that his definition of capitalism should be rejected. The definition of an entity cannot include everything that is vital for the existence of that entity. Such an impractical definition would consist of an unending list of everything required for everything within the system to function.

But adding the financial system to Marx's definition of capitalism would help us date the emergence of the system in Western Europe. After the establishment of the Bank of England in 1694, other major developments in British financial institutions emerged in the eighteenth century (see Powell 1915; Bagehot 1873/1919; Dickson 1967; Kindleberger 1984; Roseveare 1991; and Wennerlind 2011). It is reasonable to consider an alternative finance-oriented definition of capitalism alongside the Marx-style definition highlighting the employment relationship. This is done in chapter 11.

1.4. Impurities and Internal Variety

Consider some subsystems such as child rearing. Every socioeconomic system depends for its reproduction on the rearing of children. But this could be done in a wide variety of ways, such as in the modern nuclear family, the extended family, or collectives such as the Israeli kibbutzim. So, although most developed capitalist countries have reared their children in nuclear families involving monogamy and heterosexual relations, this particular kind of child-rearing subsystem is clearly not the only possibility. The traditional Western nuclear family is optional in the sense that it results from the twists and turns of history. Family structures are evolving before our eyes. Some system of child rearing is necessary. But capitalism could operate with different child-rearing arrangements.

The mode of rearing children under capitalism, whatever it is, is an *unavoidable* impurity. Capitalism would no longer be capitalism if children were owned, farmed, and produced for profit like slaves. Although capitalism promotes markets and profit-seeking activity, it cannot in principle allow the family to be run along capitalist lines and remain capitalist.[8]

Another important subsystem is the state, which has played a vital role in economic development by protecting property and contract, underwriting the financial system, and helping promote investment.

---

8. Marx (1975, 365) recognized this in an 1844 manuscript: "When political economy maintains that supply and demand always balance each other, it immediately forgets its own assertion that the supply of *people* (the theory of population) always exceeds the demand and therefore the disproportion between supply and demand finds its most striking expression in what is the essential goal of production—the existence of man." But this never became a centerpiece of his analysis of capitalism. In *Capital*, it is negated by his strategy of trying to isolate a "pure" system.

Previously I have described vital subsystems—where they differ in their structure from the dominant mode of organization of the whole system—as "impurities" (Hodgson 1984, 1988, 1999). The *impurity principle* is the proposition that *every socioeconomic system must rely on at least one structurally dissimilar subsystem to function.* There must always be a plurality of production subsystems so that the social formation as a whole has requisite variety to promote and cope with change. And, if one type of structure is to dominate, other structures are necessary to enable the system as a whole to operate. Complexity and variety within the system are necessary so that the system can survive and deal with complexity, variety, and unforeseeable shocks in the real world.[9]

The impurity principle is not functionalist. Functionalism upholds that the existence of a component is explained by its function. But the impurity principle does not involve particular explanations of existence. Different sustaining subsystems are possible. Because the impurity principle does not purport to explain the existence of any one specific subsystem, it is not functionalism. Note also that the impurity principle is falsifiable: it would be falsified if a pure system were discovered.

Capitalism today depends on the *impurities* of the household and the state. Other systems exhibit impurities. The slave mode of production of classical times depended on the military organization of the state as well as on trade, markets, and money. European feudalism evidently relied on limited markets and a powerful church. Markets allowed adjustment for local surpluses or demands, while the church was an overarching institution providing limited welfare and ideological control. Finally, without extensive legal or illegal commodity exchanges, the Soviet-type systems of central planning would have ceased to function long before 1989. These massive planning systems had difficulty dealing with complexities and localized knowledge.

In each of these socioeconomic systems, at least one *impurity* has been necessary for the preservation and reproduction of the system as a whole. Markets are basic to the vitality of capitalism, but capitalism in

---

9. Inspiration for the impurity principle came partly from systems theory, including Ashby's (1952, 1956) "law of requisite variety." Beer (1972) and Espejo and Harnden (1989) applied Ashby's idea to management systems. Note also Schumpeter's (1942, 139) remarks concerning capitalism depending on noncapitalist "flying buttresses" that acted as "partners of the capitalist stratum, symbiosis with whom was an essential element of the capitalist schema."

principle—for reasons discussed later—cannot use markets everywhere. All economies, including capitalism, are mixed economies.

What is involved here is more than an empirical observation that different structures and systems have coexisted through history. It is claimed that some of these economic structures were *necessary* for the socioeconomic system to function over time. The impurity principle is a theoretical guideline, one based on ontological considerations. Like *population thinking*, it is not itself a theory.

The impurity principle indicates that to understand the workings of a relevant system we cannot confine our account to its principal essence alone. We have to include the other subsystems that are necessary for the system as a whole to function. There is a vital difference between defining the essence of a system and establishing the key components that are necessary to understand how the system works. The latter task must always include more components than those required to establish a definition.

In this respect Marx's theoretical strategy of isolating a pure capitalism is flawed and misleading. It is at best provisional and partial. Marx recognized the *empirical* existence of impurities, but not their functional role for the system as a whole. Hence, he concentrated on a single, pure form. He wrongly believed that the dynamic of the system could be understood simply by focusing in its essence. For him, the system unfolded in a Hegelian manner from its inner core, while other subsystems and external forces exerted no more than disturbing influences. In contrast, the study of the *impurities* is necessary to understand the evolution of the system, even if they are not part of its defining essence.[10]

Crucially, given that the impurities can typically take different forms, there is huge scope for variation in conceivable forms of capitalism. Capitalist systems are complex entities with a number of different internal subsystems. Major sources of variety in the population of different capitalisms include variation in the qualities of one or more particular subsystems common to all or variation in the way in which one or more subsystems connect with the others.

---

10. The concept of "pure capitalism" was central to the work of the Japanese Marxist Kozo Uno (1980). He argued that "actual capitalism in its liberal stage of development demonstrated a tendency toward self-perfection, divesting itself more and more of precapitalist economic relations" (Sekine 1975, 857). But, as Schumpeter (1942) and others have rightly argued, in reality such a complete divestment is impossible.

For this reason, a huge variety of forms of capitalism are conceivable. And, even if one optimal combination of subsystems was superior to all the others (by some efficiency or other criterion), then no system could readily overcome its history and modify its subsystems to move toward an optimal system. The impurity principle lends support to the varieties-of-capitalism research program.

As Darwin recognized in his population thinking, the essence of a population involves variation *between* entities of a given type. The impurity principle means that there is variation in the character of the subsystems *within* entities. The impurity principle reinforces population thinking and adds an additional dimension of variation.

1.5. Definition Is Different from Abstraction

Having refined the meaning of an essence, we can further tackle the matter of definition. To address some of the possible problems and misunderstandings in the way, I choose some examples from economics. Further examples of definitional confusions are given later in this book.

It is widely believed that Douglass North's definition of institutions excludes organizations and hence that for him organizations are not institutions (Khalil 1995; Ménard 1995; Pelikan 2003). In an often-quoted passage, North (1990a, 3–5) wrote:

> Institutions are the rules of the game in society or, more formally, are the humanly devised constraints that shape human interaction. In consequence they structure incentives in human exchange, whether political, social, or economic. . . . Conceptually, what must be clearly differentiated are the rules from the players. The purpose of the rules is to define the way the game is played. But the objective of the team within that set of rules is to win the game. . . . Modeling the strategies and skills of the team as it develops is a separate process from modeling the creation, evolution, and consequences of the rules.

North rightly insisted that rules must be "clearly differentiated . . . from the players." The distinction between players and rules is similar in some ways to the distinction between agents and structures, as discussed elsewhere (Archer 1995; Lawson 1997; Hodgson 2004). Structures depend on agents, but the two are different and distinct. North (1994, 361) also wrote: "It is the interaction between institutions and organizations that shapes the institutional evolution of an economy. If institutions are the rules of the game, organizations and their entrepreneurs are the players. Organizations are made up of groups of individuals bound together by some common purpose to achieve certain objectives."

As organizations North reasonably included political parties, firms, trade unions, schools, universities, and so on. People have interpreted North as saying that organizations are not institutions. But he did not actually write this. He simply established his own primary interest in macrolevel economic systems rather than the internal functioning of specific organizations. He was not so concerned with the social rules that are internal to organizations because he wanted to treat them as unitary players and focus on interactions at higher levels.

There is nothing in principle wrong with the idea that under some conditions organizations can be treated as single actors, such as when there are procedures for members of an organization to express a common or majority decision (Coleman 1982; Hindess 1989). But a problem arises if we *define* organizations as actors. This would amount to an unwarranted conflation of individual agency and organization. Organizations—such as firms and trade unions—are structures made up of individual actors, often with conflicting objectives. Even if mechanisms for reaching and acting on decisions are prevalent, the treatment of an organization as a social actor should not ignore the potential conflict within the organization. Any treatment of the organization as a social actor abstracts from such internal conflicts. Such an abstraction may be useful, but it should not become a principle or definition that would block all considerations of internal conflict or structure.

Abstraction and definition are entirely different analytic procedures. When mathematicians calculate the trajectory of a space vehicle or satellite, they often treat it as a singular particle. In other words, they ignore the spatial extension, internal structure, and rotation of the entity. But this abstraction does not mean that the vehicle or satellite is *defined* as a particle.

North did not make it sufficiently clear whether he was *defining* organizations as players or treating organizations as players as an *analytic abstraction*. This has created much confusion, with some of his readers insisting that organizations should be *defined* as players. But in correspondence North (2002a, 2002b) remarked that he treats organizations as players simply for the purpose of analysis of the socioeconomic system as a whole and that he does not regard organizations as essentially the same thing as players in all circumstances. In saying that "organizations are players," North was making an *abstraction* rather than *defining* organizations in this way.[11]

When North assumed that organizations "are made up of groups of individuals bound together by some common purpose," he was less interested in the internal mechanisms by which organizations coerce or persuade members to act together. Crucially, these mechanisms always involve systems of embedded rules. Organizations involve structures, and these cannot function without rules of communication, membership, or sovereignty. The unavoidable existence of rules within organizations means that, by North's own definition, organizations must be regarded as a type of *institution*. Indeed, North (2002b) accepted that organizations themselves have internal players and systems of rules and hence by implication that organizations are a special type of institution.

As North acknowledged, it is possible for organizations to be treated as actors in some circumstances *and* generally to be regarded as institutions. Individual agents act within the organizational rule system. In turn, under some conditions, organizations may be treated as actors within other, encompassing institutional rule systems. There are multiple levels at which organizations provide institutional rules for individuals. Possibly these organizations can also be treated as actors within broader institutional frameworks. For example, the individual acts within the na-

---

11. While North (2002b) clearly agreed that organizations may be treated as a special type of institution, North, Wallis, and Weingast (2009, 15) contradicted this: "In contrast to institutions, *organizations* consist of specific groups of individuals pursuing a mix of common and individual goals through partially coordinated behavior." If they had put, "In contrast to *other* institutions, organizations . . . ," then the contradiction would have disappeared. But it is misleading to define organizations as "specific groups of individuals" because "specific" individuals may leave or enter the organization without the organization changing its identity. Organizations are made up of social structures and positions occupied by individuals. But North, Wallis, and Weingast (2009, 16) went on to say that "most organizations have their own internal institutional structure," which suggests that most organizations contain institutions. For them the point of differentiation between organizations and institutions seems to be that individuals in organizations always have common purposes. But this is untrue. Workers in a firm often have goals different from those of their managers. Furthermore, individuals facing institutions can have shared purposes. This criterion is unsuccessful as a means of differentiation between organizations and institutions. Organizations are special institutions with rules of membership, sovereignty, command and responsibility.

tion, but in turn the nation can sometimes be treated as a singular actor within an international framework of rules and institutions.

Institutions are *systems of rules* (see North 1990a; Ostrom 1990; Knight 1992; Crawford and Ostrom 1995; Mantzavinos 2001; and Hodgson 2006c).[12] Some have expressed uneasiness with this definition of institution, which includes so many different things, from languages to political structures. Are such capacious definitions unwarranted?[13] Many definitions of kinds include very different things: the definition of a mammal includes elephants, whales, bats, and mice; the definition of an organism is even greater in its scope and variety; culture is normally defined in some way that includes a huge variety of types; the notion of social structure includes every possible set of social relations; the definition of an idea would include uncountable different instances; and so on. Those who reject a definition because it is too broad would have to reject all such definitions. Objecting to a definition simply on the grounds that it includes lots of very different items is deeply misguided. If required, definitions that delimit subsets can always be contrived to increase the specificity of a type of entity.

The fact that political structures, organizations, and languages are all institutions is entirely consistent with the fact that they are very different

---

12. There are alternative claims that institutions are game equilibria (Aoki 2001) or behavioral regularities (Schotter 1981). These can be treated as different sides of the same object (Hindriks and Guala, in press). In game theory, rules make up the *game form*, and an equilibrium is a possible *game outcome*.

13. Some writers wish to confine the term *institution* to overarching, "environmental," legal or customary rules and exclude organizations. But this is always tricky because legal systems and states also involve organizations. What is overarching or environmental depends on the analytic point of reference. The environment for an individual is different from the environment for a political state. Institutions are not all at one level: they are nested systems. Consider, e.g., Ménard's (1995) attempt to separate organizations from institutions, defining institutions as *"stable, abstract and impersonal rules, crystallized in traditions, customs or laws"* (167). Ménard also regarded markets as institutions. He continued: "Organizations, and especially firms, are specific institutional arrangements, different from those of markets" (172). This created a tangled terminology where an organization is an "institutional arrangement" but not an institution. He also wrote: "I see both markets and organizations as firmly *embedded* in institutions" (174). But this added further imprecision with the undefined term *embedded*. If a market is embedded in institutions and also itself an institution, then why cannot organizations be institutions too? Organizations also have specific customs. It would be far better to define institutions simply in terms of shared *"stable, abstract and impersonal rules"* without any attempt to confine them to overarching or environmental phenomena.

things. Definitions do not imply similarity within the class of defined entities. Instead, they imply some communality of minimal essential characteristics. Definition is different from abstraction.

1.6. Definition Is Different from Analysis and Description

There are different types of definition (Robinson 1950). When a triangle is defined as a polygon with three sides, this is a clear-cut designation. But in both the social and the biological worlds we have difficult problems of identifying species, often with no pure types. Here the role of a definition is to demarcate and assign a term to a type of entity: to distinguish one species from another, with possible fuzziness and boundary cases. Nevertheless, clear-cut and fuzzy-boundary definitions both have the principal purpose of demarcating a type; their role is not to analyze its functioning or development. A definition "should be empty of assertional content beyond its ability to explain meaning" (Belnap 1993, 122). After defining a type, analysts then have the big job of understanding the origin, nature, structure, composition, survival, operations, and functions of this type of entity. The definition is a necessary preliminary step—to ensure that the analysts are talking about the same thing. Definition and analysis are different tasks.

Definition is also different from description. Consider an example where the two were muddled. In their classic text on evolutionary economics, Richard Nelson and Sidney Winter sometimes treated routines as dispositions but otherwise described them as behaviors. For example, Nelson and Winter (1982, 14–15) saw routines as "regular and predictable behavioral patterns" as well as "dispositions . . . that shape the approach of the firm" to business problems. Another passage introduced the useful analogy between a routine and a computer program but repeated the same confusion. Nelson and Winter (1982, 97) saw a "routine" as being like a computer "program," referring to "a repetitive pattern of activity in an entire organization" as well as to skills or capacities. But this conflated a computer program with a computer's output or behavior. The computer program is an (often-fixed) rule-based system with a coding that, along with other inputs, determines the computer's (conditional and variable) output or behavior. Nelson and Winter confused generative and dispositional factors with outputs such a "repetitive pattern of activity" or "performance."

At root here there is a philosophical problem. The essence of what an entity *is* cannot be adequately defined in terms of what it *does* or by any patterns that it generates. If we make this confusion, then we wrongly imply that, when the entity interrupts its characteristic activity, it ceases to be such an entity. Sometimes birds fly. But what defines a bird is the (existing or ancestral) *capacity* to fly, not flying itself. If a bird were defined as a flying animal, then any bird sitting on a branch or pecking on the ground would cease to be a bird. If a firm were defined as an organization producing goods or services, then, when the workers were on holiday, the firm would cease to exist. It would be better to define a firm as an organization with the capacity to produce goods or services. This may seem a small point, but the substitution of behaviors for dispositions or capacities is one of the major methodological errors in the social sciences.

Accordingly, routines cannot be behavior; they are stored behavioral potentialities. Consider a firm in which all employees and managers work between 9 a.m. and 5 p.m. only. During this working day a number of organizational routines can be energized. At other times the firm is inactive. But the routines do not all disappear at 5 p.m., to reappear mysteriously the next day. The routines as capacities remain, as long as the individuals have the ability and disposition to work again together in the same context. Subject to this condition, the routines can be triggered the next day by appropriate stimuli.

The importance of potentialities over behavior was emphasized by Aristotle in the *Metaphysics*. Aristotle (1956, 227–28) identified the "paradoxes" engendered by the confusion of behavior with the capacity to act, as in the view of Eucleides of Megara and his school:

> Now if a man cannot have an art without having at some time learned it, and cannot later be without it unless he has lost it, are we to suppose that the moment he stops building he has lost his art? If so, how will he have recovered it if he immediately resumes building? The same is true of inanimate objects. . . . The Megaric view, in fact, does away with all change. On their theory that which stands will *always* stand, that which sits will *always* sit . . . Since we cannot admit this view . . . we must obviously draw a distinction between potentiality and actuality.

An enduringly relevant point here is that definitions or ontologies that are based principally on behavior cannot cope with instances where the behavior radically changes or ceases. But the capacity to produce the original characteristic behavior remains, and this potentiality, not the outcome, defines the essence of the entity. Although ancient, this point is not arcane; it is widely utilized in modern realist philosophy of science. Central to most strands of modern realist philosophy is the distinction between the *potential* and the *actual*, between dispositions and outcomes, where in each case the former are more fundamental than the latter.

In the early twentieth century the understanding of the social world in terms of capacities or potentialities was eclipsed by the rise of positivism and behaviorism (O'Donnell 1985; Lewin 1996; Hodgson 2004). Discussion of unobservables—including unperformed dispositions—was deemed unscientific.[14] The realization that all science had unavoidably to adopt some metaphysical assumptions took some time to be widely reestablished. A key essay by Quine (1951) helped turn the tables.[15] But positivist and behaviorist stances can still be found in the social sciences today.

Science is about the discovery of causal laws or principles. Causes are not events; they are generative mechanisms that under specific conditions can give rise to specific events. For example, a force impinging on an object does not always make that object move. The outcome also depends on friction, countervailing forces, and other factors. Causes relate to potentialities; they are not necessarily realized in outcomes. As Veblen (1899b, 128) put it: "The laws of nature are . . . of the nature of a propensity." Hence, there must be a distinction between an observed empirical regularity and any causal law that lies behind it. Similarly, there must be a distinction between the capacities and the behaviors of an entity.[16]

Habits and routines are thus understood as conditional, rule-like po-

14. For example, in psychology the term *instinct* shifted its meaning from an inherited disposition (as with James 1890) to a behavior. Given this mistaken move, it became easy to demonstrate that the list of hypothetical instincts could be expanded indefinitely—to relate to all behaviors and outcomes—and thus to cast doubt on the value and reliability of the concept (Ayres 1921, 1958). See Hodgson (2004) for the impact of these intellectual shifts on the original American institutional economics.

15. Veblen (1900, 241) astutely remarked that the "ultimate term or ground of knowledge is always of a metaphysical character." For Veblen (1900, 253), "a point of view must be chosen," and consequently the "endeavor to avoid all metaphysical premises fails here as everywhere." For him, unlike the positivists, *metaphysical* was not a term of abuse.

16. For realist accounts upholding a distinction between causal powers and outcomes or events, see Bhaskar (1975), Harré and Madden (1975), and Popper (1990).

tentialities or dispositions rather than behavior as such. The key distinction in the socioeconomic sphere is between habits and routines as dispositions, on the one hand, and manifest behavior, on the other.

In this light, any emphasis on the allegedly *predictable* character of routines is misplaced. Predictions relate to outcomes or events, not to causal laws, rules, or generative structures. The dependable feature of a routine, rule, or computer program is not one of predictability but one of existential durability. Routines (or rules or computer programs) are usually conditional on other inputs or events. As a result, any predictability stems not from the routine alone but from the predictability of these other inputs. For example, a firm may have a fixed markup pricing routine of adding 20 percent to the unit cost of its products. If costs were capricious and highly variable, as they might be under some circumstances, then the resulting price would be equally volatile. The relatively enduring and persistent quality of a routine is not its outcome but its persistent rule-like structure.

While a consensus has been established that a routine is an organizational rather than an individual phenomenon, some confusion remains on the above points, and this has led to some conceptual and empirical difficulties.[17] Some of these can be overcome by consistently treating a routine as an organizational capacity and generative structure, loosely analogous in some respects to biological genes or computer programs but having distinctive features of its own.

To their credit, both Nelson and Winter were later inclined to describe the routine in terms of a capacity. Nelson and Winter (2002, 30) wrote: "We treat *organizational routine* as the organizational analogue of individual skill." Much earlier, Barbara Levitt and James March (1988, 320) wrote: "The generic term 'routines' includes the forms, rules, procedures, conventions, strategies, and technologies around which organizations are constructed and through which they operate." Another useful definition of a routine as a potentiality or capability, rather than a behavior, is found in the discussion in Michael D. Cohen et al. (1996, 683): "A routine is an executable *capability* for repeated performance in some *context* that [has] been *learned* by an organization in response to *selective pressures*."[18]

---

17. For discussions of some of these difficulties, see Cohen et al. (1996), Becker (2001), and Lazaric (2000).

18. My own definition is as follows: *routines* are organizational dispositions to energize

Another example of inadequate definition is the claim by Jonathan Nitzan and Shimshon Bichler (2009) that "capital is power." Power may be a general attribute of capital (in some usages of that term), but that capacity alone is insufficient to define capital, unless the concepts of power and capital are conflated. Nitzan and Bichler also wrote: "All capital is finance and only finance" (262). The reader is left wondering which of their statements, if any, is an attempt at a definition.

1.7. Defending Definition: Summary and Conclusion

Adequately clear definitions are vital for all science. As Aristotle noted, definitions signal the essence of a type of entity.[19] In that sense, all acts of definition are essentialist. Tirades against vaguely defined essentialism in the social sciences since the 1980s have caused enormous damage.

But a problem in Aristotle's approach is his natural state model. This is his additional assumption that a kind has a natural state and that variations from that state are caused by interfering events or forces. In Darwinian population thinking, variation is regarded as a key feature of a group of entities of a specific type. Population thinking can be reconciled with essentialism once the natural state model is rejected. Contrary to much Marxist and some promarket discourse, we cannot focus on a single (existing or imagined) type of capitalism and simply assume that it represents capitalism's pure or natural state.

As with the classification of animal species, it is possible to have nested definitions with different degrees of generality. This book focuses on the type of socioeconomic system that was consolidated in the eighteenth century in parts of Western Europe and led eventually to an enormous explosion in productivity and innovation. It is reasonable to describe that system as *capitalist*. Hence the definition of capitalism should in part entail properties of the system that emerged

---

conditional patterns of behavior within organizations, involving repeated sequential responses to cues that are partly dependent on social positions in the organization.

19. The familiar definition of a mammal as an animal that suckles its young is a remarkably short signification of an essence. It works because this simple descriptive demarcation serves to divide the mammalian evolutionary lineage from other classes of animal. This case reinforces the point that a definition does not contain everything that is vital. In other cases, as so often in the social sciences, the elucidation of essences is more complex and difficult.

around the eighteenth century and led to a huge acceleration of economic growth.

Marx's definition of the capitalist mode of production—involving private property and wage labor—fits the system that emerged in Britain in the late eighteenth century. But his analysis of capitalism was in other respects flawed. Although the definition of an entity cannot list everything that is vital for the existence of that entity, it does not mean that other important subsystems can be pushed aside to concentrate the entire theoretical analysis of the system's dynamics on its definitional core. Marx made the mistake of concentrating largely on the core, without vital reference to interactions with other subsystems and external factors.

The *impurity principle* underlines the importance of the other subsystems, such as the household, the financial system, and the state. Because a large number of different types of subsystem could be combined in principle with the definitional core, a large variety of different capitalisms are possible.

Definitions are partly a matter of analytic usefulness, for the purposes of clarity and effective scientific communication. Definitions focus on the minimum number of common and essential features of a meaningful kind of entity. There is no fixed toolkit for making definitions, but they should ideally be based on underlying structures and relations rather than on secondary attributes or functional outcomes. Definitions are ill based on behaviors. A problem is that, if the behavior is interrupted, the definition suggests that the entity is no longer of that type. Some exceptions occur when those functions are permanent and act as reliable correlates of essential and shared structural characteristics, but generally definitions focus on dispositional properties.

Some features may be vital or important but unnecessary to define the phenomenon. What is vital to an entity is often not part of its essence. Such features have to be included at the theoretical rather than the definitional stage. Definitions of a kind do not imply that members of that kind are similar, but it does imply that there is some minimal communality in terms of their essence. Further chapters raise additional problems with definitions of relevant socioeconomic phenomena.

But, while stressing the importance of definitions, we should not be naive enough to believe that absolute precision or universal agreement is possible or even desirable. When it comes to the social sciences, the issue is even more difficult because the phenomena that we are trying to define in terms of words and ideas themselves involve words and ideas. The anthropologist Paul Bohannan (1965, 33) went so far as to argue that "in relation to a noetic unity like law, which is not represented by anything except man's ideas about it, definition can be no more than a set of mnemonics to remind the reader what has been talked about." Nevertheless, it is still necessary to explain, both in concise and in elaborated forms, what we are talking about.

Classification, as well as explanation, is basic to science. All sciences have to deal with both sameness and difference. As the biologists Richard Levins and Richard Lewontin (1985, 141) put it: "Things are similar: this makes science possible. Things are different: this makes science necessary." Definitions are vital as a means of classification, without ignoring differences within types. Definitions build on sufficient similarity and hence make science possible.

CHAPTER TWO

Social Structure and Individual Motivation

Social institutions form an element in a more general concept, known as social structure. The basic idea intended by the term is that societies show comprehensible and relatively enduring sets of relationships. . . . The function of social structure is . . . to canalize the varied potentialities of human nature. — Alan F. Wells (1970)

[In game theory] the *rules of the game* are *social*. . . . More generally, individual behavior is always mediated by social relations. These are as much part of the description of reality as is individual behavior. — Kenneth J. Arrow (1994)

Before we home in on the specific features of capitalism, there are reasons to consider the more general concept of social structure. Chapters 2–10 involve successively diminishing degrees of generality and increasing historical specificity. To help identify the system that generated post-1700 explosive growth, we successively add more features to the account, to highlight specificities of the modern era. We start with the most basic and general concepts and then move toward the particular.

This chapter addresses all human societies since the acquisition of sophisticated language, which was very roughly 100,000 years ago (Oppenheimer 2004; Tomasello 2008). Instead of a deep trawl through modern social ontology, the aim is simply to deal with some general issues that are necessary to move forward to the next stage and toward the main goal of understanding the nature of capitalism.

As well as considering social structures, I also establish a rudimentary account of basic individual motivation, which always is modified by culture in particular circumstances. This provides some building blocks for succeeding chapters. Basic universal characteristics of human nature have to be taken into account in understanding all social formations. But this is emphatically not an attempt to justify capitalism or any other systems on the grounds of an alleged correspondence to human nature. If this were true, it would be difficult to explain why this system has existed for only about three hundred years. It is inconceivable that something that is a fundamental expression of human nature would be so recent. Instead of claiming equivalence between capitalism and human nature, the aim here is to establish basic and long-lasting human characteristics, including conformism and the recognition of authority, that have evolved over millions of years and are needed to make all institutions work. While rejecting the notion that capitalism mirrors our longstanding nature, we still need to bring human nature into the picture.[1]

2.1. Social Structures

Understanding the nature of any economic system requires an appreciation of the concept of social structure. In his *Oxford Dictionary of Sociology*, Gordon Marshall (1998, 648–49) offered two definitions of social structure as either "any recurring pattern of social behaviour" or "the ordered inter-relationships between the different elements of a social system or society." As he noted: "The major divergence in sociological uses of structure is between those who see the term as referring to the observable patterned social practices . . . that make up social systems or societies, and those for whom structure comprises the underlying principles . . . that pattern these overt practices."

This rightly pinpointed the difference between outcomes and dispositions, which was raised in the preceding chapter. Definitions in terms of "observable patterned social practices" are generally flawed because they cannot account for the persistence of the entity during periods when the behavior is interrupted. This is Aristotle's objection to the "Megaric view." Accordingly, in *The Penguin Dictionary of Sociology*, Nicholas Abercrombie, Stephen Hill, and Bryan S. Turner (2000, 326–27) noted the two approaches and then favored definitions of social structure in terms of social relations rather than behavior: "Social struc-

---

1. Geras (1983) showed that Marx did not reject the notion of a universal human nature.

ture has been defined simply as any recurring pattern of social behaviour. . . . A more generally preferred approach is to say that social structure refers to the enduring, orderly and patterned relationships between elements of society."

A number of other definitions are broadly in line with this preference. Douglas Porpora (1989, 195ff.) posited a definition in terms of "systems of human relationships among social positions," a formulation that he regarded as close to Marx's. In *The Harper Collins Dictionary of Sociology*, David and Julia Jary (1991, 465) defined social structure as "any relative pattern of social elements." Finally, William Outhwaite and Tom Bottomore (1994, 613) wrote in their *Blackwell Dictionary of Twentieth Century Thought:* "Structure may be defined as an organized body of mutually connected parts." The common theme is that social structure involves relationships between individuals or social elements involving individuals. Porpora's (1989) definition was narrower because he required that social structure involves social positions, which encompass social roles. We may understand a social structure more broadly as a set of social relations between interacting individuals, where social positions are a specific form of social relation.

Social theorists get into complex debates at this point, particularly concerning whether social structures have "causal powers" and what that might mean (Harré and Varela 1996; Elder-Vass 2010). But the most important point is that interactive social relations exist in any society (Weissman 2000) and that the natures of those relations affect how actors think and behave. These interactive social relations typically include communications between and perceptions of others, but they are not confined to them. We do not necessarily have to claim that structures somehow impinge directly and causally on individuals; it is simply that our interactions with others depend on the type of relations involved.

It also must be stressed that a social structure is inseparable from the group of individuals in society and would not exist without them. But social structures do exist, and we are each born individually into a world where these structures have been already formed, prior to our own existence (Archer 1995; Hodgson 2004). Consequently, while social structures do not exist independently of humans as a whole, they do exist independently of each individual considered separately.[2]

2. Fleetwood (2008, 249) wrote: "Institutions (and social structures) are always and everywhere *external* to human agents." This cannot be true because, if humans ceased to ex-

While the concept of social structure is central to sociology, it is given much less prominence in economics. Mainstream economists give pride of place to the utility-maximizing individual—the famous "pleasure machine" (Hodgson 2013b). But, try as they will, economists never get rid of social relations and structures, even in their most simplified models. In the social sciences, there are no successful explanations of social phenomena in terms of individuals alone, without also taking into account relations between them. Kenneth Arrow (1994) pointed out that price mechanisms involve social interactions and structures that cannot be reduced entirely to individuals, without also including social relations. He rightly remarked: "Economic theories require social elements . . . even under the strictest acceptance of standard economic assumptions" (4).

In economics, all versions of contract theory and general equilibrium theory invoke individuals communicating with others or presuming the intentions of others. Exchange involves the transfer of property rights, with established rules. Property rights and contracts rely on other institutions for protection and enforcement. Apart from the fictional world of Robinson Crusoe, economic theories presume institutions and structured relations between individuals rather than mere individuals in isolation. These things are required for any meaningful application of economic theory to real business phenomena.

But, while the assumption of some social relations between individuals is unavoidable, economists have often concentrated on the features of the individual in isolation, plus relations of control between individuals and things. As explained in later chapters, physicalist and agent-object ontologies pervade economics, downplaying (but never successfully excluding) relations between individuals.

Individual choosers require conceptual frameworks to make sense of their world. The reception of information by an individual requires a paradigm or a cognitive frame to process and interpret that information. The acquisition of this cognitive apparatus involves processes of socialization and education, which in turn involve extensive interaction with others (Douglas 1986; Hodgson 1988; Bogdan 2000). Such means of understanding the world are necessarily acquired through social rela-

---

ist, so would all institutions. A distinction has to be made between (1) external to each human agent taken severally and (2) external to all human agents taken as whole. Institutions (and social structures) can be external in sense (1) but not sense (2). See Hodgson (2004, 34–36) for a fuller discussion and references to relevant literature on this point.

tionships and interactions. Cognition is a social as well as an individual process. Individual choice is impossible without these institutions and interactions.

Alexander Field (1979, 1981, 1984, 1991, 2001) showed that key attempts by economists to explain the origin of social institutions presume individuals acting in a particular context, with rules of behavior governing their interaction. In the presumed "state of nature," from which institutions are seen to have emerged in many accounts, a number of rules, structures, and cultural and social norms have already been (implicitly or explicitly) assumed. Field pointed out that, with explanations of the origin of institutions through game theory, several constraints, norms, and rules must inevitably be presumed at the start. There can be no games without constraints or rules, and thus game theory can never explain the original constraints or rules themselves.

Consequently, social structures are unavoidably presumed at the outset in any economic theory involving human interaction, including attempts to explain the evolution of institutions. Economists may wish to emphasize the role and importance of individuals, but social structures are also unavoidably part of the explanation. To understand the nature of an economic system it is insufficient to concentrate on the attributes of individuals: we also need to appreciate the specific structures of their interaction.

2.2. Social Positions, Institutions, Rules, and Organizations

What is the difference between a social structure and an institution? A social structure is defined as a set of social relations between interacting individuals. There is now a wide consensus that institutions are *integrated systems of rules that structure social interactions*.[3] Hence, an institution is a modular substructure involving an integrated system of rules.

These rules include norms of behavior and social conventions as well as legal rules.[4] Accordingly, systems of language, money, law, weights

---

3. See n. 12, chapter 1, on the claimed complementarity between rule-based and equilibria-oriented accounts.

4. The wildly ambiguous terminology of *formal* vs. *informal* institutions is often deployed but much less often defined. Sometimes *formal* is intended to mean "codified."

and measures, traffic conventions, table manners, and all organizations are institutions. But not all institutions are organizations. For example, language is an institution but not an organization.

Given that institutions are systems of rules, we need to clarify the nature of a rule. As a first approximation, we can understand a rule as a learned and mutually understood injunction or disposition, that in circumstances X do Y. In turn, "do Y" must be interpreted broadly, to include prohibitions as well as obligations (Crawford and Ostrom 1995). The "if X do Y" formulation applies to constitutive as well as procedural rules: the "do" can apply to understandings or assignments of status functions as well as to other actions.

The rules that make up institutions must be more than mere declarations by some authority. As Elinor Ostrom (1990, 2000, 2005) insisted, they must be rules in actual or potential use in a community and not merely rules in form. Even if the rule is never violated, it must act as a real constraint. There must also be some commitment in the community to follow the rule (Gilbert 1989, 2001). Rules include norms of behavior and social conventions as well as legal or formal rules.

Rules and institutions are the stuff of social life. Human life without them would be chaotic, brutish, and short. The rules of language are required in order to communicate. Other shared rules help make the behavior of others understandable or predictable. Rules and institutions enable, facilitate, and incentivize as well as constrain activity. Any notion of individual interaction without rules or institutions is untenable.

Examples of organizations are tribes, families, states, business firms, universities, and trade unions. In line with widespread usage, I define an organization as a special type of institution involving

a) criteria to establish its boundaries and to distinguish its members from its nonmembers,
b) principles of sovereignty concerning who is in charge, and
c) a structure delineating responsibilities within the organization.

These conditions imply the existence of social roles or positions that have properties irreducible to those of their incumbents. Social positions carry significant powers and obligations that do not emanate from

Others use it to mean "designed." Still others refer to "laws." The usage should always be clarified.

the characteristics of the individuals in those positions (Runciman 2001, 2002).

A social position is a specified social relationship with other individuals or social positions (such as priest, prime minister, production manager, or sales representative) that might in principle be occupied by alternative individuals. The occupant of a social position brings his or her own qualities and powers and acquires additional qualities, powers, and obligations associated with that position as well as enduring its constraints.

Organizations contain social positions that might in principle be occupied by alternative individuals. A congressman, manager, foreman, or bus driver occupying such a social position acquires powers associated with that role. Sophisticated institutions with such social positions involve "information encoded in rules governing the reciprocal behavior of interacting pairs of institutional role incumbents independently of their personal beliefs or values" (Runciman 2005, 138).

Social positions bring us to a still higher ontological level. Although the maintenance and replication of an organization and its social positions depend critically on habits of thought or behavior that sustain and buttress this social structure, they involve more than these individual thoughts and habits. The organizational relations between individuals, including the relevant social positions, have to be sustained as well. These organizational relations are often only partially understood by the people involved, and no one person may have a full understanding of the organization.

Despite having considered some special types and contingent features of social structures, we are still at a high level of abstraction. The concepts discussed above apply to all societies from tribalism to modern civilization. But we are now in a position to deploy some of these concepts and help our understanding of the nature of capitalism.

2.3. Ideology or Ideas as Essence?

Some "isms"—such as socialism—refer to both ideologies and actual or proposed types of social systems. But ideologies and systems are different, and a system is not simply a prevailing ideology. Among those untrained in social theory, it is a popular misconception that social systems simply amount to particular ideologies rooted in people's heads. This error is found among both supporters and opponents of capitalism. For example, the American Tea Party movement claimed on a Web site that "capitalism is an ideology" that is allegedly responsible for national success and individual freedom (Oregon Tea Party 2011). From a very different political viewpoint, a postcrisis blog asked: "Why occupy Wall Street?" Among its reasons for occupation, it declared: "Capitalism is an ideology that has gotten out of hand" (C-EM 2011). Both supporters and opponents of the capitalist system have treated it as an ideology.

The important element of truth here is that all social systems rely on ideologies and other ideas for reinforcement and acquiescence. Systems and structures depend on motivated individuals, and motivations partly depend on interpretations and ideas. In particular, as Max Weber (1927, 1968) pointed out, capitalism itself depends on forms of rational calculation that become operative in its bureaucracies and systems of monetary accounting. Ideas and ideologies matter.

But that does not mean that those ideas or ideologies are accurate or adequate pictures of the system itself. The Mayans practiced frequent ritual human sacrifice and built large monuments for that purpose, believing that the universe was sustained by the spilling of human blood. That does not mean that their theory was correct. Many people believe in a religious ideology and a divine being. But that does not itself mean that a divine being exists. The ideas that motivate people within a system or an institution do not have to be true. And generally these motivating ideas are incomplete and involve partially inaccurate representations of the actual system. Modern economies are extremely complex. So, if capitalism were simply a set if ideas, it would probably involve false claims and certainly be an inadequate depiction of the complex socioeconomic system to which it was related.

To participate in capitalism, people must be aware of some basic ideas. For example, they must have some notion that goods and services are exchangeable for money and that contracts involve agreements between parties. But that does not mean that they have anything approaching an adequate understanding of money or contract. Economists, philosophers, and social theorists know that money is a highly mysterious institution with contested interpretations. And, if ordinary people adequately understood the nature of contract, they would have achieved without tuition what it takes highly intelligent students of law more than a year to accomplish. Simple participation in capitalism does not require more than a tiny, fractional understanding of what capitalism is and how it works.

No one has a full understanding of the workings of capitalism. Consider the massive growth of markets in financial derivatives prior to the Great Crash of 2008. Gillian Tett (2009) in *Fool's Gold* showed that the precrash banks created complex financial instruments, designed and calibrated by highly intelligent mathematicians, that were inadequately understood by the bank directors and major shareholders. Highly paid quants promoted the myth that all bank risks in all circumstances could be effectively hedged. Their complex ideas were adopted but inadequately understood. Then their models were falsified in the subsequent crash.

Of course, ideas and ideologies about the system can have a major effect on the system itself. Legislation to deal with perceived problems within the system is guided by ideas or ideologies that can in principle be mistaken. For example, several times in the last hundred years, attitudes toward speculative activity within capitalist markets have switched back and forth from positive to negative and the reverse. These attitudes have affected legislation and the operation of real markets, for good or ill. Ideas and ideologies can have real institutional effects. But that does not mean that an institution or a social structure is simply a set of ideas.[5]

Instead of full awareness of the system, people make do with learned habits and tacit knowledge. We follow others without a complete understanding of what is involved. Few of us could specify fully the grammatical rules of the language that we use regularly or completely specify in detail some of our practical skills. We rely on learned habits. As Weber (1978, 105) pointed out in 1907, some rules are followed "without any subjective formulation in thought of the 'rule.'" Nevertheless, institutional rules are in principle codifiable, with the result that breaches of these rules can become subjects of discourse.

Institutions are not simply ideas in people's heads, although the internalization of particular values and concepts is a crucial feature of any in-

---

5. With his theory of "performativity," MacKenzie (2006) argued that economics creates the phenomena it describes. While economics clearly affects the real world—and it is not a simple reflection of it—this went too far. For example, influential models assume that agents are rational and have (nearly) perfect information, but that does not make these models true (Hodgson 2010c). Because it dispenses with such matters of truth, MacKenzie's argument has scientifically conservative implications: it ends up supporting mainstream models and ignoring heterodox criticisms (Mirowski and Nik-Khah 2007). Against MacKenzie, Felin and Foss (2009a, 2009b) argued persuasively that the capacity of economics to alter reality in its image is manifestly constrained by real factors, including some features of human nature.

stitutional reality (Searle 1995). Accordingly, the institutional structures of capitalism amount to more than ideology. Both the ideas and the social relations have to be understood. Albeit in different ways, Karl Marx, Werner Sombart, Max Weber, Joseph A. Schumpeter, and Friedrich A. Hayek appreciated this irreducible duality of structures and ideas. Capitalism is a set of historically specific relations among actors, and the workings of this complex array of relations are only partially understood by the actors themselves.[6] Even among economists they remain subjects of enduring debate.

2.4. Base, Superstructure, and Social Classes

If the prevailing ideology does not adequately characterize a socioeconomic system, then where do we find its essence? For Marx, the solution was located in his "base" and "superstructure" metaphor. In his 1859 preface to the *Contribution to the Critique of Political Economy*, Marx (1971, 20) argued that this base consisted of underlying "relations of production": "The totality of these relations of production constitutes the economic structure of society, the real foundation, on which arises a legal and political superstructure and to which correspond definite forms of social consciousness."

Marx (1971, 21) saw "property relations" as "merely" an expression "in legal terms" of these "relations of production" in society. He continued: "It is always necessary to distinguish between the material transformation of the economic conditions of production, which can be determined with the precision of natural science, and the legal, political, religious, artistic or philosophic—in short, ideological forms in which men become conscious of this conflict and fight it out."

A distinction between "ideological forms" and "relations of production" is consistent with the argument in the preceding section. But Marx's demotion of law is questionable. He saw law as just another ideological form. It was regarded as relatively superficial and of lower ontological status than the "material" and "economic conditions of production." A similar relegation of legal relations is found in the first volume

6. Note that this is not a *definition* of capitalism because other systems involve "historically specific relations among actors." It is more a statement of what such a definition must in part entail.

of *Capital* (first published in 1867). There Marx (1976, 178) wrote: "The juridical relation, whose form is the contract, whether as part of a developed legal system or not, is a relation between two wills which mirrors the economic relation. The content of this juridical relation (or relation of two wills) is itself determined by the economic relation."

This again suggests that such changes in the legal form of the contract are surface phenomena and not the real essence. A grain of truth in this argument is that legal formalities are never adequate or accurate summaries of economic or social relationships. But economic content is affected by legal relations as well as vice versa. Both directions of causality require us to recognize the reality and importance of the legal form. Accordingly, the legal form of the contract gives use clues about the underlying economic relation, even if the mirror to which Marx alludes is a distorting one.

Crucially, Marx failed to define adequately key terms such as *economic structure, relations of production, economic conditions of production*, or *economic relations*. The meanings of these concepts are not self-evident, and they have to be sufficiently clear to make sense of Marx's strict dichotomy between economic and legal relations. His failure to define the economic deprives his argument of analytic force.[7]

For Marx the essence of the economy does not include legal relations. The law is seen as an expression or reflection of these undefined economic relations or relations of production. Marx rules out the possibility that laws may be part of this essence. The danger here is that the importance and primary role of law is downgraded, in both analytic and policy terms.

Marx and Engels (1976, 59) wrote in the *German Ideology* in about 1845–47: "Ruling ideas are nothing more than the ideal expressions of the dominant material relations." Again, the meaning of *material relations* is undefined, but it is clear that Marx and Engels regard them as fundamental, while law is epiphenomenal and resides in the secondary realm of ideas and ideologies. In emphasizing matter over ideas, Marx

---

7. In the social sciences the term *economic* is used in several different ways. Meanings range from connotations of "material production" to being concerned with "economy" in a sense of cost reduction or efficiency. Marx hinted at the first meaning, but few economists today would confine the economy to material production. Economics is regarded by many mainstream economists as the study of choice under conditions of scarcity. Hence, a consensus is still lacking regarding the meaning of terms such as *economy, economic*, or *economic relation*.

and Engels were reacting against German idealism. Within their social ontology, legal relations were secondary to an imprecise "material" essence. Marx and Engels (1976, 41–42) attempted a justification of their "materialist" position with the statement: "Men must be in a position to live in order to be able to 'make history.' But life involves before everything else eating and drinking, housing, clothing and various other things. The first historical act is thus the production of the means to satisfy these needs, the production of material life itself."

There is an important element of truth here. Basic human needs, such as food and shelter, must be satisfied to make human life possible. But, as Marx and Engels emphasized, production and consumption are social processes, involving social structures and relations between individuals. Social relations and institutions are just as necessary for human existence as material production, which itself depends on social institutions such as language and on structured teams of hunters, gatherers, or producers.

The most primitive human societies involved social rules and customs. These governed the production of the means to sustain life. Hence, it does not follow from an emphasis on the production of material life that social rules and legal relations necessarily have a secondary status. The satisfaction of human needs involves social relations, social rules, and ideas as well as material objects. On this basis there is no convincing argument to give the latter priority or ontological primacy.

Marx and Engels depicted social classes as fundamental components of modern society. Their *Communist Manifesto* of 1848 (Marx 1973b, 67) famously began: "The history of all hitherto existing society is the history of class struggles." Classes were defined in terms of their relationship to the means of production. Hence, forty years later, Engels (Marx 1973b, 67n) added a note to the same work and defined the two main classes of modern capitalism, the bourgeoisie and the proletariat: "By bourgeoisie is meant the class of modern capitalists, owners of the means of social production and employers of wage labour. By proletariat, the class of modern wage labourers who, having no means of production of their own, are reduced to selling their labour power in order to live."

Clearly, when he defined these crucial classes, Engels was obliged to refer to *ownership*, the *employment* of waged laborers, and the *selling* of labor power. None of these terms can be defined adequately without reference to law and legal ideas. Ownership—in the fullest sense—implies legal rights, enforced by recognized contract and the legal powers of the state.[8] The employment contract is a specific legal form, differing from a contract for sales or services. Selling or hiring implies the legal transfer of some property rights. The hiring of labor power involves the legal transfer of limited rights of authority over the laborer and the use of his or her capacities for contracted purposes.

Attempts to reduce explanations to social class alone always face the problem of identifying the essence of class itself. Consequently, social formations such as capitalism and socialism cannot be categorized simply by determining which class is in power because social classes themselves are constituted in terms of legal and other rules. These rules themselves determine the nature of social formations; the configuration of class power is in part an expression of such legal rules.

Marx frequently used terms such as *owner* and *property* to describe social classes. In the third volume of *Capital*, in its unfinished chapter "Classes," Marx (1981, 1025; emphasis added) wrote: "The *owners* of mere labour-power, the *owners* of capital and the land*owners* . . . in other words wage-labourers, capitalists and landowners . . . form the three great classes of modern society based on the capitalist mode of production."

These are not mere formalities. The legal aspects of class relations are essential to define their character. In particular, if we ignore the legal nature and details of the employment relationship and concentrate solely on employee controls of the employer, then we have less ground to distinguish between capitalist employment and slavery. At their most polemical, Marx and Engels claimed that the proletariat was "enslaved" under capitalism or that wage labor was "slavery" (Marx and Engels 1989, 91), but in numerous other contexts they were keen to differentiate the capitalist mode of production from earlier forms where true slavery was predominant. Accordingly, Marx (1976, 271) wrote in *Capital* that in the employment contract "the proprietor of labour-power must always sell it for a limited period only, for if he were to sell it in a lump, once and for all, he would be selling himself, converting himself from a free man into a slave, from an owner of a commodity into a commodity." The wage laborer, in contrast to a slave, "manages both to alienate his labour-power and to avoid renouncing his rights of ownership over

---

8. In chapter 4 it is shown that both Marxist and mainstream conceptions of property or ownership are defective in terms of their understandings of rights.

it." Marx then added in a note: "Hence legislation in various countries fixes a maximum length for labour contracts." When he was analytically careful, Marx was obliged to make use of legal concepts—such as sale, contract, ownership, and legislation—to define the working class under capitalism.

Consequently, Marx and Engels were unconvincing in their rejection of law from the economic base. Law is constitutive of many important social relations and is necessary for the definition of modern social classes. It is not an epiphenomenon. In modern societies it is a central mechanism of social power.[9]

The mode of production does not have causal primacy over institutions (including law). Marx repeatedly made it clear that a mode of production involved social relations as well as technology. All human cooperation and interaction unavoidably involve decisions, rules, organization, and institutions. Without these, production cannot get off the ground.

But, in his enthralling study of the role of the state in economic development, Erik Reinert (2007, 65, 222) wrote: "Human institutions were determined by their mode of production rather than the other way round." He then criticized the new institutional economics of Douglass North and others for "blaming poverty on the lack of institutions rather than on a backward mode of production." Reinert opined: "Institutional changes . . . are surely important, but they are ancillary. . . . [T]he mode of production moulds and determines institutions—more than the other way round." But there must be rules and relations concerning how production is organized, who is in charge, who does what, who gets what, how the workforce is pressured to work, and so on. These systems of social rules and relations are institutions. Hence, institutions are part and parcel of any mode of production. So the argument whether institutions come before or after the mode of production is fundamentally misconceived.

Some of the institutions that help make up the mode of production in modern society are legal in character. In a large and complex society, legal enforcement is necessary to make important rules concern-

9. Some libertarian-individualist writers have adopted formulations uncannily similar to those of Marxism. For example, a book edited by Pejovich (1997) is titled *The Economic Foundations of Property Rights*. But the meaning of these "economic foundations," and how they are constituted before property rights are built on them, is unexplained.

ing property and other rights function effectively. The "new institutional economists" to whom Reinert (2007, 65) refers are right to emphasize institutions and incentives. A problem is that they sometimes have a narrow and unsophisticated view of human motivation, stressing "opportunism" and "self-interest seeking with guile" (Williamson 1975, 255).[10] Another problem is that much of this literature has taken technology as given, neglecting the role of technological change in prompting institutional change (Ruttan 1997, 2003, 2006). This can misinform the analysis of incentives, organizations, and enforcement. But incentives are still important. It is to the question of motivation that we now turn.

2.5. Individual Motivation

Economists have long assumed that individuals were self-interested and ignored the possible psychological or cultural determinations of self-interest. By contrast, in sociology and cultural anthropology, there has been much discussion of the cultural and structural determinants of human character. But these disciplines neglected the biological and instinctive foundations of human nature.[11] Yet an understanding of our evolved propensities and capacities as humans is also vital to understand social formations. In this point we may learn from Thorstein Veblen 1899c, 1914, 1919) and others inspired by evolutionary ideas.[12] Humans and their social structures have coevolved for millions of years.

Mainstream economic thinking is centered on the utility-maximizing individual. It defines the individual in terms of a preference function. Marxists similarly assume that individuals are optimizers: they seek ma-

---

10. Notably, Coase (1984, 231) thought otherwise, advising that we should "start with man as he is," thereby alluding to Marshall (1920, 26), who had a much fuller and more rounded understanding of human motivation.

11. By *instincts* I mean biologically inherited genetic propensities (Veblen 1914; Hodgson 2004). By contrast, habits, customs, and routines are culturally transmitted. Dual-inheritance theories acknowledge both types of process (Boyd and Richerson 1985).

12. *Evolution* is a vague term with several different meanings. The usage by Veblen and others was more specific. Veblen understood that the Darwinian principles of selection, variation, and inheritance applied to social institutions as well as biological entities (Hodgson and Knudsen 2010; Camic and Hodgson 2011). In this work, the terms *evolution* and *evolutionary* often connote this more specific Veblenian sense, although no attempt is made to limit their meaning to the usage.

terial wealth and minimize the labor required to obtain it. Although many accounts concentrate on self-regarding preferences, in principle the preference function can be modified to involve other-regarding or altruistic preferences as well (Bowles and Gintis 2011). Hence, the notions of ordered preferences and utility maximization can be stretched to cover every eventuality or behavior. They cover everything, thereby signifying next to nothing (Hodgson 2013b, chap. 3).

The notion of utility maximization is unfalsifiable. And it applies to everything down to bees and bacteria: it portrays nothing that is specifically human. The understanding of socioeconomic systems needs to proceed from a richer and more human account of individual motivation. For much of the twentieth century, the social sciences presented a choice between the absolutism of utility maximization in economics and some version of cultural determination taken from sociology or anthropology. Critics observed the dilemma between the under- and the oversocialized individual (Granovetter 1985). The solution to this problem lies not simply in some golden mean between the two extremes: evolution has to be brought into the picture.

Assumptions about human nature have to be consistent with our understanding of human (genetic and cultural) evolution. Guided by this principle, the modern investigation of human attributes and dispositions is rich and complex, with many unresolved questions. But we are in a position to sketch some central features of human motivation that are relevant for the analysis of all socioeconomic systems.

What can our understanding of evolution tell us about human selfishness? Instincts for self-preservation and cultural norms that emphasized individual survival would have a selection advantage in many circumstances, even in families or groups, where they were sometimes overridden by altruistic or cooperative dispositions. But that does not make individual selfishness the whole story.

As Darwin (1871) explained, cooperation within human groups is also important for survival (Sober and Wilson 1998; Bowles and Gintis 2011; Hodgson 2013b). There are good reasons to presume that the evolution of human cooperation involves both genetic and cultural elements.

Social species can evolve genetic dispositions for altruism. Genetic evolution involves changes in genotypes that lead to changes in individual characteristics. From this perspective, what matters is the survival of the gene. Given that we share many genes with close relatives, genetic selection can favor dispositions that increase the survival of offspring and close kin (Hamilton 1964). Genes disposing birds to give warning cries when they sense predators can have a selection advantage, even if the bird giving the warning cry is at greater risk, as long as the survival chances of a sufficient number of related birds are enhanced. For similar reasons, genes are selected that dispose us to care for our children. Hence, evolution does not bring about unalloyed individual selfishness, and there is some evolutionary grounding (at least among close kin) for altruism and what Veblen (1914) described as the "parental bent." These evolved dispositions can be greatly enhanced in cultural contexts that engender group cooperation (Darwin 1871; Bowles and Gintis 2011; Hodgson 2013b).

Culture has evolved because it encapsulates adaptable group knowledge that enhances the chances of our survival.[13] Culture itself requires strong dispositions to imitate or emulate others. There are at least two types of imitation among humans and primates. The first is *conformist transmission* (Boyd and Richerson 1985). Genes or instincts disposing individuals to conform would be selected in some contexts. Culture adds even greater pressure to conform to social groups (see also Veblen 1899c; Henrich and Boyd 1998, 2001; and Richerson and Boyd 2004). A second imitative mechanism is *prestige-based imitation* (Henrich and Gil-White 2001; Henrich 2004), where individuals learn advantageously from the more successful. Clearly this second mechanism must involve capabilities to recognize social hierarchy and prestige. In any social species such instinctive and cultural propensities are likely to be selected over time; they would bestow survival advantages for the individual and the group.

There are also learned or inherited dispositions, which are triggered in specific contexts, to punish those who break the rules or fail to enforce them.[14] Such inherited dispositions have evolved in our social species

---

13. Richerson, Boyd, and Bettinger (2001) addressed the reasons why sophisticated cultures evolved in humans.

14. For research on punishment and the development of cooperation through both genetic and cultural inheritance, see Boyd and Richerson (1992); Andreoni (1995); De Waal (1996); Ben-Ner and Putterman (2000); Fehr and Gächter (2000a, 2000b, 2002); Gintis (2000); Field (2001); Price, Cosmides, and Tooby (2002); Boyd, Gintis, Bowles, and Richerson (2003); Carpenter, Matthews, and Ong'Ong'a (2004); Gintis, Bowles, Boyd, and Fehr (2005); Wiessner (2005); Henrich et al. (2006); Fehr and Gintis (2007); Guzmán, Rodriguez-Sicken, and Rowthorn (2007); Carpenter and Matthews (2009); Henrich et al. (2010); and Bowles and Gintis (2011).

over millions of years. Some such punishment involves "strong reciprocity" (Gintis 2000), where, in addition to propensities to punish cheats,
free riders, rule breakers, and self-aggrandizers, there are also proclivities to punish others who fail to punish the offenders. Often these propensities are driven by emotions of anger.

For millions of years, humans and their ape-like ancestors have been
living in social groups. Typically, these groups have leaders and followers, although degrees of stratification have varied significantly.[15] The
long-standing existence of social hierarchy has conditioned the evolution
of genetic and cultural dispositions to cope with these structures. Peter
Richerson and Robert Boyd (1999, 2001) argue that modern social hierarchies (including armies) often involve tribal-sized groups at each level
that deploy instincts and capacities more suited to our earlier, tribal existence. Social cohesion within each level is thus maintained by deploying
inherited tribal mechanisms of group leadership and conformism. But
in large societies, people at the very bottom of the social hierarchy also
pay homage to those at its highest pinnacle, with whom they have had no
close or sustained contact. Some additional reasons must be found why
people acquiesce with authority at all levels.

Stanley Milgram (1974) conducted some amazing experiments on
obedience. Members of the public were recruited to help in a laboratory
study ostensibly about learning. A "scientist" asked these recruits to administer electric shocks to a subject, to punish wrong answers to questions. Milgram found that a majority of adults would administer shocks
that were apparently painful, dangerous, or even fatal if ordered to do
so by the person in authority. In fact, there were no shocks, and the subject was an actor, feigning agony or even death. This experiment showed
that people can willingly accept the orders of perceived authority figures
even when their own moral feelings are violated. Particular institutional
contexts, procedures, and surroundings can engender an "agentic state"
where people obey the commands of what they perceive to be legitimate
authority.[16]

15. On hierarchy in human hunter-gatherer societies, see Boehm (1999, 2000), Johnson
and Earle (2000), and Ludwig (2002). Primate societies exhibit hierarchies of power and
privilege (De Waal 1982). Hierarchies in hunter-gatherer societies typically accord status
and authority to tribal elders.

16. Perhaps because of the challenge posed to conventional notions of individual autonomy by Milgram's work, these striking experiments have had less impact on the social sciences than one might expect. Exceptions include Akerlof (1991), which emphasizes their

Milgram (1974, 124–25, 131) argued that our capacities to behave in this way emanate from the evolutionary survival advantages of cohesive social groups. He proposed that the human species has evolved an inherited, instinctive propensity for obedience that is triggered by specific cues and social circumstances. Conditional dispositions to accept authority, notwithstanding challenges and rebellions to the contrary, have evolved in order to enhance the chances of survival of both the individual and the group.[17] To become instinctive, conditional mechanisms to obey authority must have evolved in a hierarchal social context for a long period of time. In specific cultural settings, often cued by symbols and ceremonies, we learn to recognize individuals in social positions with authority over others.

Jonathan Haidt and Craig Joseph (2004, 2007) proposed that we have an innate value intuition to respect authority. Such inherited propensities are overlaid by culturally acquired proclivities. In particular, from the moment of our birth we learn to accept the authority of our parents. Instinctive triggers are likely to be relatively primitive, and deference to authority will rely heavily on nuanced habits of recognition and obeisance, largely acquired during childhood.[18]

From our culture we acquire habitual capacities to interpret aspects of clothing, decoration, bodily deportment, ceremony, and symbolism as possible markers of social authority and power. Habits to recognize and respect social positions evolve. Once authority is accepted as appropriate, additional habits trigger obeisance. Habits of obeisance are general, rule-like dispositions to accept and follow (present and future) rules imposed by those in authority. They have a second-order character; they are rules to follow other (possibly unknown) rules.

Effective systems of authority do not require that habits of obeisance are uniform or universal. All that is necessary is their prevalence among a critical mass of individuals of intermediate or higher social status. Habits of conformism and emulation can then ensure more wide-

challenge to mainstream assumptions in economics. Although scrutiny of the Milgram experiments revealed a complex interaction of context and personality (Blass 1991), their replication showed similar outcomes across several different cultures (Smith and Bond 1993).

17. The theory of group selection has been rehabilitated: it is now widely accepted that under specific conditions group selection is possible (Sober and Wilson 1998; Henrich 2004; Wilson and Wilson 2007; Hodgson and Knudsen 2010; Hodgson 2013b).

18. Habits are by definition acquired in a cultural and institutional context. But for their development they all depend on biologically inherited dispositions or instincts.

spread deference and consent to authority. But conformist habits are different from habits of obeisance: the latter means the acceptance of authority rather than the imitation of others. Conformist instincts and habits emerge in the early stages of cultural transmission, long before the evolution of states and other complex organizations. Habits of obeisance played an enhanced role after the emergence of more complex and stratified systems of power and authority. But their instinctive foundations must have been present earlier.

Habits of obeisance may come into conflict with other norms and dispositions, such as moral sentiments for fairness or equity. As the Milgram experiments illustrate, the powers of authority and obeisance may lead us to do things that we would otherwise regard as immoral.

The power of authority is not absolute. Systems of power rely on an ensemble of different habits and instincts, tangled among many varied individuals. Variation among individuals is vital to the Darwinian evolutionary approach on which this argument depends. Furthermore, habits of obeisance and conformism can work against the ruling order and among resolute dissident groups or organizations, potentially undermining popular support for an existing regime.

Dispositions to punish those who break social rules as well as dispositions to obey authority have both evolved over millions of years. But, while dispositions to punish had to be restrained for modern political and legal systems to function, this is not the case for habits of obeisance. Modern legal and political power is built partly on an ancient foundation of deferential traits.

There are strong arguments that morality has a genetic as well as a cultural foundation. In a complex culture, emotionally empowered rules can help enhance notions of justice and morality (Darwin 1871; De Waal 2006; Robinson, Kurzban, and Jones 2007; Krebs 2011; Hodgson 2013b). This means not that genes are sufficient to generate a moral system but that the cultural phenomenon of morality is fueled by biologically grounded emotions and value impulses. Through our genes we inherit the capacity to quickly respond to social dilemmas by developing emotions. These dispose us to make choices and help us form rapid judgments concerning what is morally right or wrong. In social settings the moral judgments help us justify our actions toward others and to exhort others to approve or imitate. Genetic dispositions to deal with social dilemmas by developing emotionally charged value intuitions can thus have strong survival value. These emotional capacities evolved by natural selection.

But our genes do not tell us what is moral or immoral. We have to learn that through engagement and communication in a social culture. The foundations of our moral capacity have evolved in the millions of years that we have been a social species. But the evolution of a sophisticated language roughly 100,000 years ago was vital to develop a system of morality with communicable, conditional, abstract rules. The subsequent development of human moral capacities has been dependent on particular cultural settings, allowing for multiple and contrasting moral systems on the basis of an instinctive bedrock (Hodgson 2013b).

Given that we also inherit genetically a long-evolved capacity to imitate others and a capacity for empathy, we are likely to conform to strong moral claims, especially when made by high-status or numerous individuals. Cultural mechanisms lead to conformity within the group. Although rebellion against the prevailing rules is possible, clashes are more likely between groups with different cultures. Cooperation emerges as a distinctively human combination of innate and learned behavior.

The discussion of human motivation in this section has revealed a complex ensemble of human dispositions. Individual human nature bears the stamp of our existence as social creatures for millions of years. Understanding individual incentives is vital for an appreciation of the workings of any socioeconomic system. Individual motivation is not entirely self-regarding: we take others into account (Bowles and Gintis 2011). Our social existence has also given rise to altruistic and moral propensities. Furthermore, we have dispositions to recognize, respect, and obey those in positions of authority. These features of human nature are particularly important for the functioning of law and the state.

2.6. Concluding Remarks on Structure and Individual Motivation

As argued above, although ideas play a vital role in determining the nature of an economic system, capitalism is not simply an ideology. Some of the basic elements of capitalism, such as money and contract, are so complex that people have a partial and incomplete understanding of them. People also have wrong ideas regarding how capitalism works.

The system is not simply ideas in people's heads—it consists of social relations and structures as well.

This chapter has also provided conceptual tools to help analyze the fundamental institutions of capitalism. It is argued that law is among the fundamental institutions of capitalist and some precapitalist societies. The Marxist attempt to place law in the superstructure is unconvincing; even Marxist definitions of social classes depend on legal terms.

In contrast to much mainstream economics, Marxism rightly emphasizes the importance of social structure. But it goes too far in subsuming individuals under social structures in its explanations of socioeconomic phenomena (Hodgson 2004). Hence, in *Capital* Marx (1976, 989) described how the actions of the capitalist are "no more" than the manifestation of capitalist relations: "The *functions* fulfilled by the capitalist are no more than the functions of capital . . . executed *consciously* and *willingly*. The capitalist functions only as *personified* capital, capital as a person, just as the worker is no more than *labour* personified." Similarly, in the third volume of *Capital*, Marx (1981, 1019–20; emphasis added) wrote: "The principal agents of this mode of production itself, the capitalist and the wage-labourer, are as such *simply* embodiments and personifications of capital and wage-labour–specific social characters that the social production process stamps on individuals, products of these specific social relations of production."

Explanations of individual agency were derived from "social relations" without recognition of individual diversity, cultural variation, or individual discretionary possibilities. Marx recognized both individuals and structured social relations between them. But what mattered ultimately was structure alone. Capitalists and workers were seen as simply expressions of social structure. People struggle as best they can, but within overriding structural limits. The individual was subsumed within a structural explanation. Through competition, the capitalist is forced to be greedy and seek profits or go under. The worker is impelled to struggle for higher wages. Veblen (1897, 137) criticized this view: "The materialistic [or Marxist] theory conceives of man as exclusively a social being, who counts in the process solely as a medium for the transmission and expression of social laws and changes; whereas he is, in fact, also an individual, acting out his own life as such."

For Veblen, in contrast to Marx, both the individual and the social relations and structures interact, interpenetrate, and mutually constitute one another. Veblen understood the importance of variation in an evolutionary process and wanted economics to be a "post-Darwinian" science. Inspired by Veblen and others, the post-Darwinian, evolutionary perspective adopted here provides a much richer account of human nature than is adopted in either Marxism or mainstream economics. Furthermore, it establishes characteristics—such as the capacity for moral judgment—that are specifically human.

Mainstream economics has a theory of human motivation that is based simply on pleasure seeking or the maximization of utility. It treats the individual as a "globule of desire," to use Veblen's (1898c, 389) sarcastic phrase. This approach fails to encapsulate vital economic factors such as rights, justice, and moral legitimacy. By contrast, Adam Smith (1759/1976a, 86) fully understood their importance, seeing justice as the "the main pillar that upholds the whole edifice" of society. Accordingly, individuals have a capacity to distinguish between matters of *want* and matters of *right*. This implies not that such judgments are always valid but that most of us know that claims to do the right thing are not the same as simply following a convention or acting out of preference or desire.

Capitalism is unique to our species and to the modern era. Accordingly, we require conceptual tools that to some extent reflect those specificities. But we are also products of a long process of human evolution. As well as other inclinations, we have evolved dispositions to make moral judgments and to respect authority: these have served the apparatuses of social power. In modern societies, moral legitimacy and respect for authority are major reasons why people are often disposed to obey the law.

It is suggested in the following chapters that a richer view of human motivation, with adequate notions of rights and justice, is crucial to understand basic concepts such as law, property, and contract.

CHAPTER THREE

Law and the State

As the grown man has long since forgotten the pains it cost him to learn to speak, so have the peoples, in the days of their mature growth of the state, forgotten what was required in order to free them from their primitive brutal savagery. — Johann Gottfried Hoffmann (1840)

It matters not how it came to be the law, whether it was prescribed by an autocrat or a legislative body, or arose from mere custom and usage, or the decrees of the courts—if the physical power of society, that is the State, is put forth for its vindication, it is law; if not, it is not law. — Joseph P. Bradley (1884/1902)

This book upholds that law is one of the core institutions of capitalism.[1] But we must clarify the nature of law and deal with rival conceptions. This chapter criticizes the idea that law can emerge spontaneously and simply through the interactions of individuals. Often such views dovetail with a notion of law as essentially custom. Arguments are provided here for a different understanding of law.

Law relates to hierarchical and complex societies with large numbers of individuals. Once we consider the problems of enforcement in complex legal systems with many agents and the motivational reasons why individuals might obey the law, then something like the state is required ultimately to ensure enforcement. The state is never monolithic and is broadly construed to refer to a realm of public ordering based on authority. Such a state must establish a monopoly of force within a territory, restrain vigilantism, and minimize extralegal violence. A state's commitment to operate within legal constraints can help enhance its own le-

---

1. This chapter extends and amends some material from Hodgson (2009).

gitimacy as a wielder of power. In practice, in large and complex societies, law has mostly required a state; conversely, the state is typically a necessary condition of law's existence.

Although custom is a source of law, this does not mean that "customary law" is always law proper.[2] Furthermore, contrary to the impression given by Hayek (1973) and others, common law (necessarily involving an institutionalized judiciary) is much more than much so-called customary law (Hasnas 2005). Generally, customary mechanisms are insufficient to explain adherence to large-scale, complex systems of law.

Where customary law is prevalent, it is generally associated with politicoeconomic underdevelopment. Separate customary law dominates only in parts where the state cannot reach, such as remote regions. The widening and development of capitalism has aided this encompassing process. In medieval England there was a variety of types of courts, relating to the church, feudal manors, guilds, and trade associations. Gradually, these were drawn into the clutches of the state (Pollock and Maitland 1898; Hasnas 2005), partly because of problems of plural, contested authority in circumstances of growing social complexity. Contracting parties found it easier to submit to a single, powerful legal apparatus. Historically, capitalism has reduced the multiplicity of legal authorities, in favor of the state.[3]

Of course, there is no law to prevent us defining law in a very broad sense so that it includes plain custom. But then we would have to subcategorize the law and label the important kind of law that depends on an institutionalized judiciary or the state. This subcategory is what many legal scholars and ordinary people mean by *law*. Although there is no fixed formula for definitional demarcations, the two questions of conven-

---

2. Gluckman (1967, 383) found resemblances between Western law and the judicial proceedings of the Barotse tribe in Africa, and concluded: "The most crucial concepts of law are elastic or of multiple meaning." But the elastic must not be stretched to the breaking point, when all meaning is lost. It is a question of where to draw the definitional line.

3. Private *lex mercatoria* or "law merchant" courts blossomed in Europe from the eleventh to the fourteenth centuries and were important in both internal and international trade. But they declined and were eventually absorbed or replaced by state enforcement (Baker 1979; Berman 1983, 333–56; Milgrom, North, and Weingast 1990; Rogers 1995; Masten, and Prüfer 2011). A major reason for their demise seems to be that they could not cope with the increasing scale and complexity of contracting. Greif and Tabellini (2010, 2012) argue persuasively that the formation of a single state legal system with associated moral norms was crucial in Europe's economic development.

tional usage and "carving reality at the joints" should be given appropriate weights. So we adopt a narrower conception, where law proper arose
when some customs were violated rather than followed and then some
permanent and institutionalized higher adjudication was required.

Conceptual dilemmas concerning law are redolent of Carl Menger's
(1871, 1981) famous critique of the German historical school on the question of money. As discussed in chapter 6 below, Menger argued that the
historical involvement of the state in the genesis of money showed that
the state was neither necessary for its creation nor essential to its nature.
He claimed that institutions such as money could emerge spontaneously
through the interaction of individuals, without the state. This contrasts
with alternative accounts of the nature and essence of money, including
"state" and "chartalist" theories (see Mitchell Innes 1914; Knapp 1924;
Keynes 1930; Ingham 1996, 2004; Wray 1998, 2004, 2012; Smithin 2000;
and Bell 2001). Hence, the dispute concerning the nature of law and the
roles of private ordering and the state has a parallel in the controversy
between spontaneous and state-based theories of money. A further parallel, discussed in chapter 8 below, exists in disputes over the role of the
state and law in constituting the business corporation (see Masten 1991;
Ellerman 1992; Phillips 1994; Blair 1999, 2003; Iwai 1999; Hodgson 2002;
Hansmann, Kraakman, and Squire 2006; Gindis 2007, 2009; Iacobucci
and Triantis 2007; Spulber 2009; Robé 2011; Deakin 2012; and Orts
2013). In each case there is one approach that focuses primarily on individual motivations and private ordering and another that also relies in
part on the existence of a state.

Addressing law, we require an explanation of how a system of complex and plentiful legal rules can be enforced. It is argued here that the
enforcement of law cannot rely simply on the self-interested calculations
of individuals. Law depends on varied complex motivations. Evidence
cited in the preceding chapter suggests that we have innate value intuitions to punish those who break the rules and also to respect authority. Law involves the cultural channeling of instincts to obey superiors
and constraints on dispositions to punish rule breakers. Generally, obedience to the law must be explained in terms of the penalties of violation
and also in terms of morally and emotionally infused dispositions to respect and follow those in power. The evolution of law must thus be understood in the context of biological, cultural, and institutional legacies,
and it cannot be understood adequately in terms of preferences alone.

Theorists who identify custom with law sometimes characterize their

opponents as "legal positivists" or "constructivists" who regard laws simply as decrees of the state.[4] In contrast, the position advanced here is
that the state is typically a necessary but *never a sufficient* condition for
a system of law. This does not amount to the mistaken "identity theory"
where the state and law are the same thing (Somek 2006). But while custom underpins much law, law cannot be reduced to custom.

Emphasizing the state does not mean that custom is unimportant.
John R. Commons (1924) correctly argued that to be enforceable (at
least in nontotalitarian societies) laws must be widely perceived as reasonable, appropriate, and fair. Consequently, law must conform to many
established customs, despite its being more than custom alone. Commons also emphasized that the collective power of the state also lay behind all property rights and transactions within capitalism.[5]

The following section addresses the intellectual tradition that equates
custom with law. A subsequent section addresses theories of the spontaneous emergence of law without the state. The third section raises the
question as to why customary or spontaneous law would be obeyed, including in large and complex societies. The fourth section relates evidence by legal historians and others that links the emergence of law with
the development of the state. The fifth section draws the threads together and concludes the chapter.

4. Hayek (1973, 73) wrote of "legal positivism which derives all law from the will of a
legislator." But actual doctrines of legal positivism are less simplistic. Primarily, they claim
a lack of correspondence between law and morality (Kramer 1999), and, secondarily, they
treat laws as identifiable institutional facts (Cotterrell 1999, 216). In his classic and influential work, Hart (1961) advanced a "soft" legal positivism upholding no necessary connection between law and morality. This contrasts with the legal positivist Kelsen (1967), who
wished also to sever the connection between law and the social sciences. Hayek's (1960,
238) association of Kelsen with the "definite eclipse of all traditions of limited government" is also inaccurate: Kelsen was a democrat who opposed fascism and communism.
Legal positivists generally oppose natural law theories and instead see law as a distinctive
human creation (but not necessarily an exclusive creation of the state). Hayek's caricature
of legal positivism omits such nuances.

5. Custom is also important in international law, where a developed international state
machine is absent. International legislation proceeds through treaties and other international institutions. Fuller (1969a, 2) wrote: "Much of international law, and perhaps the
most vital part of it, is essentially customary law." But international trade also rests on national law: parties choose one legal system for the default rules (backed by agreements
among states that choice of law in contracts shall be respected), and they choose a forum
(the place where disputes shall be resolved).

3.1. From Hume to Hayek: Custom as the Essence of Law

Several scholars suggest that custom is the key to understanding law, where custom is seen as evolving without overall guidance or design. Writers in this tradition include David Hume, Edmund Burke, Friedrich C. von Savigny, Henry S. Maine, James C. Carter, and Friedrich A. Hayek. Among these, Carter (1907, 173)—a resolute defender of common law and a president of the American Bar Association—wrote: "Law . . . *is* custom, and like custom, self-existing and irrepealable."

Within this tradition there are variants. Henry Maine (1861) and Numa Denis Fustel De Coulanges (1864/1980) argued additionally that religion was the basis of most laws, particularly concerning property rights. They argued that religion provided laws with moral salience, perceived enforcement incentives, and customary durability.[6]

Hayek's writings in this genre are among the most sophisticated and shall be highlighted here. Hayek (1973) opposed the constructivist idea of law as emanating from the state. Instead, he provided an evolutionary account of the development and selection of legal rules. He apparently removed the need for any explanatory deus ex machina by framing the account in (essentially Darwinian) evolutionary terms where the emergence of complex orders (as in nature) can occur without the need for overall guidance or design. But, while Hayek helped resolve the problem of explaining his initial assumptions by expressing his theory in such evolutionary terms, his account has remaining defects that are common to the entire tradition that sees law as essentially reducible to custom.[7]

Hayek (1973, 72) upheld that law "is older than legislation" and that law in some sense is "coeval with society." For him, laws are simply the "rules which govern men's conduct" (73). But, in contrast to the extreme libertarians, Hayek (1960) stressed the need in modern society for an

6. Durkheim's (1984) conception of law was influenced by both Maine and Fustel De Coulanges, but it is different in key respects (Sheleff 1997; Cotterrell 1999).

7. The so-called Freiburg school was founded by the economist Walter Eucken and the jurist Franz Böhm. Böhm (1980) developed the concept of the "private law society," in which the role of the state is to administer the "private law" system. Redolent of Hayek, this approach fails to draw a distinction between custom and law. For both definitional and operational reasons discussed below, in complex societies "private law" cannot become law proper without the state, notwithstanding the partial dependence of all functioning legal systems on private and customary rules.

overarching system of state and constitutional law within which contracts and markets can function.

The central concept in Hayek's mature theory of social and legal evolution is that of a *rule*. Hayek (1973, 11) wrote: "Man is as much a rule-following animal as a purpose-seeking one." For him, custom is a set of acquired rules that can be learned or innate: "*Rule* in this context means simply a propensity or disposition to act in a certain manner, which will manifest itself in what we call a *practice* or custom" (74–75). Hayek (1967, 66–67) earlier made it clear that the term *rule* is used for statements "by which a regularity of the conduct of individuals can be described, irrespective of whether such a rule is 'known' to the individuals in any other sense than they normally act in accordance with it."

Hayek (1979, 159–60) also explored the varied origins and "layers of rules" in human society. The lowest layer consisted of rules derived from the "little changing foundation of genetically inherited, 'instinctive' drives." Higher layers involve rules that were not deliberately chosen or designed but had evolved in society and rules that were consciously designed and inaugurated. Hayek (1967, 1973, 1979, 1988) developed an evolutionary explanation of the selection of social rules through the selection of the fitter social groups. For Hayek (1973, 9), institutions and practices, which had first "been adopted for other reasons, or even purely accidentally, were preserved because they enable the group in which they had arisen to prevail over others."[8]

But, as Roland Kley (1994, 44) pointed out, Hayek's notion of rule following is too broad. It includes behavior emanating from instinct as well as customary rules. Hayek's definition of a social rule as involving all behavioral dispositions should reasonably be modified to exclude instinctive or genetically transmitted dispositions (Hodgson 2006b).

What sustains the rule and gives it some durability through time? Hayek did not supply a sufficiently detailed answer, other than empha-

---

8. Hayek's analysis conflated the self-organization of a single order or entity with Darwinian (selectionist) accounts that focus on populations of entities (Hodgson 1993; Hodgson and Knudsen 2010). It juxtaposed selection mechanisms with the self-organizing and self-regulating processes found in "autopoiesis, cybernetics, homeostasis, spontaneous order, self-organization, synergetics, [and] systems theory" (Hayek 1988, 9). While both kinds of process are possible, Hayek did not carefully distinguish between them. On autopoietic accounts of law, see Teubner (1988, 1993) and Luhmann (1993) and the critique in Beck (1994). Stein (1980) and Hutchinson (2005) discuss evolutionary theories of law more broadly.

sizing the role of imitation in cultural transmission (Hayek 1967, 46–48; Hayek 1979, 155–57; Hayek 1988, 21, 24). This might help explain how behavioral regularities are reproduced, but we still lack a causal explanation of imitation and rule following itself. There are unfilled gaps in the theory.

Dispositions to imitate others or follow rules are either acquired culturally as habits or inherited biologically as instincts. Instinctive triggers are required to energize neural and behavioral responses that create the conditions for the cognition of appropriate information and the formation of habits. A habit is a disposition to engage in previously adopted or acquired behavior (including patterns of thought) that is triggered by an appropriate stimulus or context. In turn, habits are the preconditions for all reason and deliberation.[9]

The concept of habit appears infrequently in Hayek's work and is sometimes used to refer to settled behaviors (Hayek 1973, 11). Overall, Hayek subsumed both habit and instinct within his overly broad concept of a social rule, thus neglecting the cognitive and psychological foundations of rules themselves. He also lacked an adequate explanation of how customs are interpreted and why they are followed.

To understand why people follow rules we have to delve into psychology (Tyler 1990; Engel 2008; Tomasello et al. 2009). Once we attempt to identify the mechanisms involved, then problems appear in the standard account of a close relation or equivalence between custom and law. When these problems are addressed, important questions emerge about the nature and evolution of legal rules.

If customary rules were law, then all sorts of relatively minor rules, including grammatical rules of language and codes of politeness, would be laws. But there is a qualitative difference between custom and law, and a line must be drawn between societies dominated principally by customary rules and those where law proper has also emerged. This difference is illuminated by considering the psychological mechanisms involved when individuals adhere to customs and showing that law requires more complex social institutions. In addition, work by prominent anthropolo-

---

9. Our capacity for reason and deliberation must have itself evolved, and the evidence confirms that underlying drivers such as habit and emotion came first (James 1890; Bechara and Damasio 2005; Hodgson 2010b; see also Veblen 1919; Dewey 1922; Murphy 1994; Plotkin 1994; Ouellette and Wood 1998; Hodgson 2004, 2006b; Hodgson and Knudsen 2004; Wood and Neal 2007; Graybiel 2008; and Ravaisson 2008).

gists and legal historians shows that the evolution of law involves conflict resolution, powerful institutions, and the transcendence of mere customary arrangements. Hence, law is irreducible to custom.

The distinction between law and custom undermines theories that propose that all laws emerge entirely by allegedly "natural" processes, as in some accounts of the evolution of common law. On the other hand, it is not proposed here that all law emanates from legislative will or design. While spontaneous processes are significant, they can account for neither the totality nor the essential nature of legal systems. While law depends on the spontaneous evolution of custom, it also typically requires the powers and institutions of the state. Law in the modern sense did not exist in simpler and smaller societies. It generally requires a specialist judiciary within a stratified system of power.[10] Furthermore, in modern complex societies, law is not simply a matter of dispute resolution; there is a legislature that often acts proactively or in response to socioeconomic changes. Law typically requires major institutional interventions and arrangements promoted by the state.

3.2. Law as Spontaneous Order

Spontaneity itself has different meanings.[11] Many authors use it to refer to any institution that emerges without the intervention of the state (Friedman 1979; Benson 1989). Even when the state is acknowledged, theorists of spontaneous law regard statutory legislation as a ratification of prior customary arrangements—but not the essence of law. There is an emphasis on a bottom-up process of legal development, where statutory legislation typically ratifies customary precedents.[12]

---

10. Rare exceptions include the absence of a specialist judiciary for periods in ancient Athens and medieval Iceland.

11. For various accounts of spontaneous emergence, cf. Hayek (1973, 1979), Sugden (1986), Ellickson (1991), Parisi (1995), Dixit (2004), and Greif (2006). Amitai Aviram in personal correspondence has suggested that the term *spontaneous* is misleading because even private or customary arrangements are partly planned, albeit not by the state. But I have stuck with it here while giving it a health warning.

12. This explains their preference for Anglo-American systems of common law rather than Napoleonic or civil law. But the point here is not to debate the alleged advantages of common over civil law (Glaeser and Shleifer 2002; La Porta, Lopez-de-Silanes, and Shleifer 2008; Milhaupt and Pistor 2008; Armour, Deakin, Sarkar, Siems, and Singh 2009; Dea-

It is possible to stretch the meaning of *spontaneity* further to include outcomes that purportedly emerge from individuals alone, without any preexisting institutions. But, because emergence without any preexisting institutional foundation is unfeasible (Field 1979, 1981; Hodgson 1988; Aviram 2004), I confine myself to a narrower meaning, which refers to possible emergence in principle without the state. This narrower category includes cases where law is enforced by a nonstate authority as well as models where legal rules simply emerge from individual interactions.

The following claims are made in support of the idea that law is essentially a matter of self-organization rather than state enforcement:

i)   Some early legal systems emerged spontaneously (Friedman 1979; Jahnsen 1986; Benson 1989).

ii) Contract enforcement in medieval times evolved through the efforts of (often ethnic or religious) trading coalitions or town guilds (Greif 1989, 1993, 1994, 2006; North 1991; Greif, Milgrom, and Weingast 1994).[13]

iii) More recently, in some areas, trade among some ethnic or other groups has been sustained in the absence of adequate legal authorities (Landa 1994; Clay 1997; McMillan and Woodruff 1999, 2000; Leeson 2009).

iv) Trading networks or other "private orders" can enforce their own rules with minimal or zero recourse to state legal systems, even when they exist (Macaulay 1963; Ellickson 1991; Bernstein 1992, 2001; Williamson 1985a, 1985b, 2002).

The fact that many legal systems have relied heavily on the state is undisputed. Spontaneous-order theorists claim that, where the state is

---

kin 2009). Instead, we are primarily concerned with the nature of law per se. Hence, the argument here applies to both common and civil law. Note that the claim that English common law is largely a development of Anglo-Saxon customary law is questionable. The legal systems in England, France, Germany, Sweden, Poland, and the Netherlands were formed in the twelfth and thirteenth centuries under the influence of the new canon law of the church and the rediscovery of Justinian Roman law (Berman 1983, 2003; Hasnas 2005). Strangely, Hayek and other advocates of common law, alongside fulsome praise for Adam Smith, David Hume, and others of the Scottish Enlightenment, overlooked the fact that Scottish law is a fusion of common with civil law, where the latter is more pronounced than in the English system.

13. Greif's empirical account of the Maghribi traders was challenged by Edwards and Ogilvie (2008), who argued that there is no clear historical evidence for Maghribi coalitions. Edwards and Ogilvie maintained that these traders made use of a statutory legal system and took disputes before courts of law. Greif (2008) responded to these criticisms.

prominent, it serves principally to sanction or modify preexisting laws, as a statutory codification of existing customary arrangements. They propose that the essence of legal enforcement lies in interpersonal relations and incentives rather than state power. As Robert Sugden (1986, 5) argued, legal codes "merely formalize . . . conventions of behavior" that have evolved spontaneously out of individual interactions. The analytic focus on the spontaneous evolution of law does not necessarily derive from a claim that spontaneity was the historical norm. Instead, it arises from the notion that such spontaneous arrangements represent the essence of all legal systems, notwithstanding the widespread de facto involvement of the state.

Despite the manifest role of the state in legal systems, spontaneous-order theorists argue that the state or other strong third-party enforcers cannot play an ultimate role in the explanation because this would leave unanswered the question why "those who are supposed to enforce the rules do so" (Greif 2006, 8). The state is staffed by persons with their own interests, so why should it be assumed that they enforce legal rules? Instead, it is proposed that explanations must ultimately devolve on individuals and their interactions rather than state enforcement. As Avner Greif (2006, 8) put it: "Because institutions reflect human actions, we ultimately must study them as private order even when a state exists." To bring in the state as a deus ex machina to account for laws and their enforcement is to assume what has to be explained. Instead, many theorists have used game theory to show how interacting individuals give rise to legal and other "self-enforcing" institutions through the establishment of (Nash) equilibria in the game (Schotter 1981; Sugden 1986; Aoki 2001; Dixit 2004; Greif 2006).[14]

This argument must be taken seriously. But game theory does not provide an adequate answer because it too assumes things that must be explained. At least in classical game theory, individuals and their preferences, as well as the possible strategies and payoffs of the game, are assumed at the outset (Field 1979, 1981, 1984, 1991). More generally, there can be no games without rules, and game theory can never explain the primary rules themselves. At least one game with its structure and payoffs must be adopted at the beginning. Missing is some kind of cultural

14. Dixit (2004) made the important additional point that reliance on the courts or the state to enforce contracts is cumbersome and costly; hence, any adequate theory of law must consider interpersonal enforcement mechanisms.

or psychological account of the evolution of the original rules and preferences. Game-theoretic arguments may help explain the persistence of rules once they get established, but they cannot explain the origins of the elemental frameworks of human interaction and cooperation.

Some spontaneous models of the evolution of law attempt to explain it as a convention emerging through individual interactions. In an innovative essay, Gillian K. Hadfield and Barry R. Weingast (2012) treated law as an emergent convention. Unlike many accounts in the spontaneous-order tradition, theirs saw law as a "normative classification" involving possible punishment that "is the product of deliberate choice by an identifiable entity." Hence, law for them involves some institutional or personal agency, but not necessarily the state. Hadfield and Weingast dropped the common knowledge of rationality assumption, which dominates much game theory, and assumed that agents have their own "idiosyncratic logic." In place of rational calculation of the judgment of others, agents iterate toward a shifting framework of rules installed by a third party. Hadfield and Weingast assumed a trading arrangement with only two buyers and a single seller. They showed that an equilibrium order can emerge in their model, which settles on one set of behavioral rules, "delivered exclusively by decentralized collective punishment." They then argued that this system of rules is a "legal order" because it conforms to a picture of the law involving third-party deliberation and a system of punishment.

But their claim that they demonstrated the emergence of a legal order was based on a highly selective reading of a few philosophers of law. They cited the leading legal philosopher Herbert Hart (1961), to whom they attributed the "claim that the validity of law is ultimately a matter of social convention: a rule counts as a legal rule if the participants in a given legal community believe and behave as if it were a legal rule." But for Hart it was the *moral validity* of law that is a matter of convention, not the nature of law itself. As a legal positivist, Hart doubted that law can be validated by moral reasoning; instead, he saw *the moral content of law* as a matter of social convention. In pushing their notion that *law itself is formed as a convention*, Hadfield and Weingast overlooked the fact that Hart argued *against* that view. Hart (1961) made a distinction between being obliged, as a result merely of threats or constraints, and being obligated, as an outcome of law. He opposed the natural law tradition, arguing that law cannot be reduced merely to the imperatives of a social situation involving individual preferences. Acceptance of legal authority is more than the rational calculation of net benefits or of adherence to convention.

Hadfield and Weingast also referred to the prominent "legal realist" Lon Fuller. Again they missed a key point. Although Hart and Fuller differed on other issues, Fuller (1969b) saw law as typically involving the "morality of duty" beyond the exigencies of aspiration or circumstance.[15] This vital deontic dimension is diminished in many naturalistic accounts, including that of Hadfield and Weingast. But the relationship between morality and law is tricky. Some laws have much weaker moral imperatives than others—contrast traffic laws with laws against rape or murder. But the rule of law in general can carry a moral force. Evolved moral feelings and beliefs can enhance respect for the law.

Legal power relies on our evolved dispositions to respect authority, as discussed in the preceding chapter. Humans existing in social groups for millions of years have evolved dispositions to obey those in apparent authority. We also acquire general habits of obeisance that dispose us to obey the law even when we are unaware of its details. Not all authority is legal authority, but law relies on these dispositions. In turn, others imitate and conform to the rule followers (Milgram 1974; Haidt and Joseph 2004, 2007).

Some models of the emergence of law are based on reputation effects. Avner Greif (Greif 1989, 1993, 1994, 2006; Greif, Milgrom, and Weingast 1994) and Janet Landa (1994) have argued that a private system of legal enforcement can emerge by establishing the importance of the reputation of an ethnic, religious, or other group.[16] Once this happens, the group has an interest in enforcing rule compliance to maintain its reputation. These arguments apply to ethnically fractionalized societies where there is ineffective enforcement of general rules. They are less useful in explaining societies where there is general recognition of a singular system of legal authority that does not depend on the reputation of a group.

Many models of the spontaneous evolution of property and contract rely on reputation and other effects with small numbers of relatively well-informed traders. But these models typically break down or prove

15. Himma (2009) argued that in key respects "legal realism is not only consistent with [legal] positivism, but also presupposes the truth of all three of [legal] positivism's core theses."

16. Greif (2009) outlined the differences between his and Landa's approach.

intractable with larger numbers of players in more complex and uncertain circumstances. Consequently, private ordering models based on individual coordination equilibria or group reputational effects are inadequate to explain the enforcement of property rights in the real world (Knight 1992; Sened 1997; Mantzavinos 2001). As Douglass North (1994, 365) put it: "Cooperation is difficult to sustain . . . when information about the other players is lacking, and when there are large numbers of players." This suggests a vital role for the state (or another strong political authority) in the enforcement of property rights and contracts.

Amitai Aviram (2004) argued convincingly that private ordering is generally insufficient to create an enforceable legal authority. A newly formed spontaneous order cannot alone enforce compliance because mechanisms to secure this cooperation (such as the threat of exclusion) depend on its ability to confer benefits on its members, and a newborn order cannot yet confer such advantages because it lacks the critical mass to do so. Hence, what are described as "private legal systems" typically do not form spontaneously but build on preexisting institutional arrangements to secure initial compliance. Consequently, private ordering requires something such as the state or another strong prior institution.

Aviram's argument underlines the importance of the distinction between *explanations of origin* and *explanations of persistence.*[17] Crucially, it is difficult for spontaneously emerging systems of law to gain the critical mass to become pervasive, notwithstanding the possibility that, once established, they may be sustainable. Significantly, many of the historical examples of allegedly spontaneous legal systems had adjacent state systems of law or involved numerous people who previously had been enculturated in a state system. These could account for the diffusion of state-derived legal ideas and routines into a new environment where the hand of the state was more remote.

Although privately ordered legal systems are possible and have existed historically, there are significant difficulties concerning their establishment, endurance, and perceived moral legitimacy, especially in large and complex societies. Ronald Coase (1988, 10) wrote: "When the phys-

---

17. Hirst (1975) warned of the dangers of their conflation. Good explanations of persistence (such as the role of culture in sustaining norms) are entirely inadequate as explanations of origin (culture cannot adequately explain the emergence of morality or cooperation because the emergence of culture has to be demonstrated). See Field (2001) and Hodgson (2013b, chap. 3).

ical facilities are scattered and owned by a vast number of people with very different interests . . . the establishment and administration of a private legal system would be very difficult. Those operating in these markets have to depend, therefore, on the legal system of the State."

Jack Knight (1992) argued that distributional differences and power asymmetries, rather than spontaneous outcomes of individual interactions, explain how laws are established. Especially when large numbers of people are involved, a state machine based on a legal monopoly of force within a territory is typically required to sustain these rights.

3.3. Learning the Law: Problems of Complexity and Restraint of Punishment

How do we explain the origin of the specific motivations and dispositions to follow rules or obey laws? In some cases we have strong incentives to follow reigning conventions, whatever our marginal preferences. We willingly drive on the same side of the road as others and follow shared rules of linguistic communication. But these "coordination games" or "self-enforcing" institutions do not represent all cases (Vanberg 1994; Schultz 2001; Hodgson 2003, 2013b). We must explain enforcement in the many other instances where incentives for conformism are less obvious.

Clearly, the mere codification or proclamation of a rule is insufficient. It might simply be ignored, just as drivers everywhere break speed limits on roads. What matters in the construction of institutions are systems of established and prevalent social rules that structure social interactions rather than rules as such.

In searching for dispositions to follow rules, we may consider biologically inherited or culturally acquired propensities to imitate others. But a problem arises. *Once legal systems emerge with a minimal degree of complexity, then neither imitation, habit, nor instinct can be relied on to explain fully the enforcement of particular laws within intricate and extensive systems of law.* It would be absurd to suggest that most people follow a particular law in a complex legal system because they acquire a habit to do so. The number of laws becomes far too great for a population to adhere to them out of habit. Many laws are unknown, obscure, or difficult to understand. Imitating others can help explain conformity to some laws, but it cannot explain adherence to a law where the relevant behavior of others is unobserved. Habit and imitation are insufficient to carry the burdens of legislation and enforcement. Some other reason has to be found to explain how laws are enforced.

The answer involves institutionalized authority. Darwin (1871, 1:162–63) understood that propensities to obey leaders could enhance social cohesion and further the evolutionary selection of those social groups within which this property was prevalent. Similarly, Milgram (1974) argued that propensities to obey authority enhance group cohesion and bestow group survival advantages. Jonathan Haidt and Craig Joseph (2004, 2007) also proposed an innate disposition to respect authority. Accordingly, we have inherited propensities for obedience that can be enhanced by specific cultural cues. These propensities help explain why we obey the law even when the law itself is unfamiliar or complex. Evolved propensities to obey authority help explain obedience and respect for the law.

A second problem concerns punishment. As noted previously, there is anthropological and experimental evidence of learned or inherited dispositions to punish those who break social rules, or fail to enforce them, in specific contexts. The relevant inherited dispositions have evolved in our social species over millions of years and go back further to our apelike ancestors (De Waal 1982, 1996). Some such punishment involves "strong reciprocity" (Gintis 2000), where there is an additional propensity to punish those who fail to punish cheats, free riders, rule breakers, and self-aggrandizers. Often these propensities are driven by emotional feelings, including anger.

Given this long-standing instinct to punish transgressions of social norms, culture then moves in to enhance, refine, or divert these emotionally charged instincts, through the learning and imitation of habits of censoriousness or disapproval (Boyd and Richerson 1992; Runciman 2005; Bowles and Gintis 2011; Mesoudi 2011). Inherited instincts for the punishment of social transgressors are highly modified or diverted by culture.

A system of law removes the right to punish from unauthorized individuals; it becomes a legitimized monopoly of the judiciary. This implies the establishment of judicial institutions and mechanisms to suppress freelance dispositions to punish among the ordinary population. Law is not a system of reciprocal individual punishment. The qualitative change from custom to law entails a more complex and stratified society with developed judicial institutions. Institutions emerged to suppress and divert all rudimentary punitive emotions into legal channels.

Complexity and stratification came with the transition from groups and tribes to larger-scale societies, with greater divisions of labor. In societies where interaction is on a small and personal level, customs and norms may suffice to maintain order and cooperation. Larger, more complex and stratified societies make interaction more impersonal: other institutions are required to deal with internal conflict. Disputes had to be judged and punishments administered with procedures involving codifiable, abstract rules. Written legal records became necessary.

3.4. The State as an Institutional Foundation of Law

The first evidence of a state dates from about fourteen thousand years ago in the Levant (Bar-Yosef 1998, 2001). The detailed analysis of the origins of states in antiquity need not concern us here (see Carneiro 1970; Runciman 1982, 2001, 2005; Smith 2004; Yoffee 2005; and Blanton and Fargher 2008). Sedentism is a precondition for the emergence of states and social hierarchies. The finer division of labor in one location helped the further accumulation of wealth and enhanced the stratification of society. Eventually, trained armies became possible, and emergent states could resist or subdue weaker tribal adversaries (Diamond 1997). The evidence suggests that states did not appear until agglomerated populations rose into the hundreds of thousands.

Consider the emergence of legal institutions within states. Commons (1925, 687) argued that, while relying on it, even common law is more than custom and that it developed through dispute:

> It is out of these customs that the common law arises. But we do not reach the need of a common law until disputes arise which must be decided promptly in order to keep the association, or community, or nation, in a peaceable frame of coöperation. In this sense, there is a common law that arises in all private associations without any intervention of the State. . . . The peculiar common law of the State comes in only when a decision is made by a court which directs the use or the collective physical violence of the community.

The anthropologist Arthur Radcliffe-Brown (1933, 205) made a distinction between the existence of an "organized system of justice"—as found in many tribal societies—and a system of law. The former may lack a "juridical authority," which is a necessary condition for the latter: "An important step is taken toward the formation of a legal system where there are recognized arbitrators or judges who hear evidence, decide upon responsibility and assess damages; only the existence of some authority with power to enforce the judgments delivered by the judges is then lacking."

Accordingly, some legal historians stressed that the essence of law resides in its *transcendence of custom*, particularly at a stage when breaches of customary conventions arise (Diamond 1935; Seagle 1941; Redfield 1950, 1957). They claimed that law did not derive from religion.[18] Instead, disputes over *violations of custom* in large part gave rise to proto-legal actions and institutions. William Seagle's historical account is the most detailed. Far from custom alone, the emergence of law involved a state and a legal apparatus. Seagle (1941, 35) wrote: "It is in the process of retaliation that custom is shaped into law. Breach is the mother of law as necessity is the mother of invention. . . . [L]aw deals with the abnormal rather than the normal. . . . Only confusion can result from treating law and custom as interchangeable phenomena. If custom is in the truest sense of the terms spontaneous and automatic, law is the product of organized force." For Seagle (1941, 62): "The origin of the state was bound up with some form of social stratification. . . . The chief point of dispute is really whether social stratification resulted from external causes such as conquest . . . or from internal causes [such as] the division of labour, the accumulation of agricultural surpluses, or the exploitation of superior ability as well as superstition."

The state arose when society became complex, divided, and hierarchical. In emphasizing the state, the role of custom was not denied: customary social rules were often transformed into laws by the state apparatus. As Seagle (1941, 69) explained: "The custom had to be declared to be law by a judgement in order to receive the necessary étatistic stamp. . . . It is in this sense that there is no law until there are courts."

Robert Redfield (1950, 581) also argued that custom differed from law: "Custom is understood to exist whenever the members of a primitive group expect one another to follow one line of conduct rather than

---

18. Hoebel (1964, 258) argued that Diamond (1935) and others were wrong to say that Maine saw religion as the basis of law. Instead, Maine argued that law and religion were intertwined in early society. But this does not undermine the claims of Commons, Diamond, Seagle, and others that fully developed law depends on a strong organization such as the state.

another in circumstances that more or less repeat themselves, and when on the whole they do follow that line." For Redfield, law is associated with the potential use of force purportedly "on behalf of the whole group." The "beginning of law and the beginnings of the state are thus closely associated." Similarly, the jurisprudential theorist Dennis Lloyd (1964, 235) declared: "The vital contrast between primitive custom and developed law . . . is an absence of centralized government."

E. Allan Farnsworth (1969) examined the emergence of a system of contract where an agreement between two parties becomes enforceable in law. Today we take this for granted, but on reflection the automatic investment of pledges with legal enforceability is an extraordinary outcome, unlikely to evolve readily from custom. Farnsworth argued that the legal basis of contract emerged in ancient Rome: "The notion that a promise itself gives rise to a duty was an achievement of Roman law. It came, however, through the development of a series of exceptions rather than through the establishment of a general principle of the enforceability of promises" (588). Again, this undermines the view that law is a simple extension of custom and points to the role of disputes in the evolution of rules of contract and to the judicial functions of the state.

Statutory legal systems developed general laws concerning criminal offences, to replace tort and dispute resolution. Previously, many systems of penal law treated wrongs such as theft, injury, or murder principally as offences against the individual and his or her kin. Hence, the victim or the bereaved family or clan would bring a claim for restitution against the alleged perpetrator, under the procedures of civil law or tort. But in both ancient Greek and ancient Roman legal history there is a transformation of penal treatment from viewing offences as against individuals and their kin to treating them as injustices against the state or community as a whole. Penal law became state law while retaining a major role for tort outside the penal sphere. A major consequence of this transformation was to enhance the moral dimension of criminal law.[19]

The distinction between common law and civil law is important in the modern context but does not undermine the argument here. Common law evolves by the accumulation and modification of the decisions of judges. In the civil or Napoleonic system it is said that judges do not

---

19. See Sheleff (1997, chap. 6) for references. Sheleff uses this well-documented fact concerning the development of criminal law to undermine Durkheim's characterization of early law as largely "repressive" in character.

have the capacity to make law. But in both cases the very existence of a judiciary implies the existence of discernible and robust legal institutions that transcend arrangements based on popular custom. Indeed, both systems of law rely heavily on elements—including contract law—derived from the legal system of ancient Rome.[20]

As Seagle (1941, 153–60) argued, the distinction between the two systems is not as great as some scholars claim. Common law also depends on the machinery of the state. Obversely, as Curtis J. Milhaupt and Katharina Pistor (2008, 29–30) pointed out, statutory codes in civil law systems require interpretation, and "the interpretative function of courts in civil law systems is often indistinguishable from lawmaking." Furthermore, in their interpretations, "lower courts are highly conscious of prior rulings." So civil law systems also use precedents and adapt to circumstances. The differences between common law and civil law are important but should not be exaggerated.

Marxists stress that systems of law and the state emerged with the stratification of society into social classes and that law and the state are outcomes of class struggle (Engels 1902). But in other key respects the Marxist account is deficient. On the one hand, it underestimates the role of custom (Commons 1925), and, on the other, it treats law as a mere epiphenomenon of underlying but undefined "economic relations" (Hodgson 2003). Marxists presume that the state and law can both "wither away" under communism, without a clear account of what is to replace them.

Some scholars have pointed to historical examples of law without the state. One mistake in some cases was to overlook the crucial distinctions between law and custom (and between property and possession, as addressed in the next chapter). A second mistake in some cases was to claim that state authority was effectively absent where in fact it—or

20. Rather than being a spontaneous creation independent of the state, English common law owes a great deal to the reforms of the legal system by King Henry II in the twelfth century. There is evidence that Henry's reforms were inspired by Muslim ideas, imported via Sicily or the Crusader states in the Middle East (Cattan 1955, 213–18; Badr 1978; Boisard 1980; Gaudiosi 1988; Makdisi 1999). Among possible twelfth-century legal imports from the Islamic world is the jury system (which replaced trial by ordeal). And the Islamic *waqf* may have been an inspiration for English charity and corporate law. Later chapters of this book give other examples of institutional diffusion from one country to another, building a case that the evolution of social formations is often from without rather than exclusively from within.

a close substitute, authority—did bear on the situation. Finally, catastrophic examples of the breakdown of state authority are too frequently overlooked.

Consider David Friedman's (1979) study of the "private creation and enforcement of law" in Iceland in Viking times. Most Viking societies (which gave the word *law* to the English language) had limited state machines, with kings, chieftains, parliaments, and law courts. But in Iceland there was neither a king nor a central executive power. Instead, there was a supreme assembly that dealt with law and justice. Friedman underlines the heavy reliance of this legal system on local dispute mechanisms. But Viking Iceland still had a social hierarchy and coercive authority (Byock 1988). Local chieftains sometimes appointed judges and prosecuted criminals. Furthermore, many laws were imported from Norway or Denmark. The legal system was not simply a private, independent, spontaneous creation of free individuals. Perhaps significantly, in the thirteenth century the political and legal system began to disintegrate owing to internal strife.

Some writers claim that the Internet provides a contemporary case of rule enforcement without a central authority. These accounts downplay the presence of substantial legal rules and regulatory authorities (Radin and Wagner 1999). These include ICANN (Internet Corporation for Assigned Names and Numbers), which controls Internet name and site registrations.

The degree of self-regulation and spontaneous ordering in some cases is very impressive. But we must put these cases alongside those where state authority has broken down with catastrophic and deadly results. Examples include phases of the Chinese Cultural Revolution from 1966, Somalia from the 1990s, the Democratic Republic of Congo from 1998, and Iraq during the insurgency following the 2003 invasion. In these and other historical examples, the outcome of state breakdown has been not a well-regulated system of spontaneous law but the brutal ravages of armed gangs, indiscriminate mass killings, and widespread human misery.

It is a myth that before the rise of states societies were more peaceful. Although there is controversy over its extent, experts are agreed that violence in nonstate societies was ubiquitous (LeBlanc 2003; Nivette 2011). Despite the lethal and large-scale capabilities of modern military technology, the evidence suggests that group and tribal conflict in primitive societies was many times more deadly than twentieth-century warfare, where fatalities of conflict were calculated as a percentage of total deaths or as a percentage of the population (Keeley 1996; Bowles 2009). Douglass C. North, John J. Wallis, and Barry R. Weingast (2009) argued that the containment of violence is the primary precondition for the development of social order. The emergence of the state is a key institution in this process, notwithstanding the enduringly violent role of the state in punishment and war (Gat 2006).

Consider the claim of "legal pluralism"—that societies contain groups with rival rule systems and normative orders (Galanter 1981; Griffiths 1986; Merry 1988). Scholars pointed to the imperialist imposition of European legal systems on substrata of indigenous legal traditions in the colonial era. But these claims were not confined to less-developed countries. Sally Merry (1988, 871) argued: "Virtually every society is legally plural."

However, as Brian Tamanaha (1993) pointed out, theorists of legal pluralism regarded any normative order or system of social control as legal in character. With this vague and highly generous conception of law, claims of legal pluralism and the notion that much law does not emanate from the state all follow readily. Once again, the problem here is the conflation of law with custom and the failure to identify the distinctive features of legal systems.

All societies contain plural systems of normative rules, but this does not necessarily amount to plural systems of law. The more dramatic cases of conflicting systems of normative rules, in Africa and elsewhere, are marks not of a minimal-state utopia but of tribal or clan-based societies with high degrees of religious, cultural, and ethnic fragmentation that are arguably impediments to institutional, legal, and economic development (Easterly and Levine 1997; Alesina, Baquir, and Easterly 1999).[21]

---

21. Medieval Islamic legal systems were possible exceptions to this rule. In some cities, there coexisted separate courts and schools of law for Sunni, Shia, Christians, and Jews. In part these were possible because Islamic law derives its power more from grassroots religious commitment than from the state: in Islam, religion and law are fused. Nevertheless, within Islamic legal systems there were overarching laws that established the rights, obligations, and limits of minority legal orders. A plurality of legal subsystems, with significant variations in laws, existed within a single legal framework. As noted above, multiple courts and legal authorities existed in several countries in medieval Europe, but these became largely absorbed into the state at the time when the legal foundations of capitalism were being developed.

3.5. Law and the State: Summary and Conclusion

Those who view law as essentially custom and private ordering claim that the existence of the state cannot itself explain why people follow laws; we still require an explanation why state officials are themselves motivated to enforce them. Hence, real legal systems must be understood in terms of custom and spontaneous evolution, even when states are involved.

But theories of the spontaneous or custom-based evolution of law also rely on unexplained assumptions, often including the rationality and preferences of individuals. To place the explanation of the emergence of law in an evolutionary framework would require that one address theories in psychology that explain the evolution and transmission of relevant motivations and deliberations.

Once this is attempted, major problems arise. For example, imitation or habit cannot explain the widespread acceptance or observance of the enormous number of obscure and complex laws. This reveals a significant difference between the observance of custom and enforcement in a complex legal system. Another relevant psychological mechanism is a (partly instinctive) predisposition to punish those who break rules, as evident in primate communities and relatively simple human societies. But, once we move to complex systems of law, culture and institutions must suppress the emotions and behaviors triggered by these instincts so that the punishment of rule breakers is regulated more by the institutionalized enforcement of abstract legal principles than by emotionally charged actions by freelance individuals.

Historical evidence suggests that general systems of law emerged through disputes involving breaches of custom rather than through custom itself. Violations of rules were addressed by an institutionalized judiciary that emerged with organized state power in a sedentary and stratified society. Law relies to a large degree on custom, but it also depends on the existence of legal institutions and typically a state. Paul Bohannan (1965, 35–36) argued that "a fairly simple distinction" can be made between law and custom:

> Customs are norms or rules (more or less strict, and with greater or less support of moral, ethical, or even physical coercion) about the ways in which people must behave if social institutions are to perform their tasks and society

is to endure. All institutions (including legal institutions) develop customs. Some customs, in some societies, are reinstitutionalized at another level: they are restated for the more precise purposes of legal institutions. When this happens, therefore, law may be regarded as a custom that has been restated in order to make it amenable to the activities of the legal institutions.

It is argued in this chapter that legal institutions are generally tied up with the state and depend on the state monopoly of legitimate force. The legal philosopher D. Neil MacCormick (1998, 330) elaborated on the role of judicial and constitutional authorities in modern legal systems:

> How then shall we summarize the character of legal order? Where this is taken to be the legal order of a constitutional state . . . it requires a systematic interrelation of norms that empower the necessary public agencies. One agency must have judicial power under "rules of adjudication" stated in or made under the constitution, and with that must go the obligation to recognize and uphold the constitution itself and all the rules of public law, private law, and commercial law that are validly established and binding under the constitution, in accordance with a ranking of "sources of law" that the constitution recognizes.

It would be a grave mistake to regard all law as emanating from the will of legislators. But the state transforms custom into law, particularly by dealing with breaches or disputes. If customs were consistent and faithfully observed, then there would be no need for the involvement of the state or the courts. But such a utopia of customary consistency and fidelity has never existed.

Although many states have ruled by violence and terror, many also rely on some considerable degree of conscious support and consent. It is vital to understand how states manipulate public sentiment and gain the acquiescence or even the devotion of the masses. We need an explanation why many individuals accept authority and rules from above. The motivating forces behind individual conformity and obedience must be specified.

The role of authority is crucial. The Milgram (1974) experiments provide us with some striking empirical evidence. As both Darwin (1871) and Milgram suggested, we have long-evolved human propensities to obey authority, resulting from the survival advantages that effective authority bestows on social groups. In specific cultural settings, these trigger the development of habits of obeisance.

The very existence and functioning of complex state machines depends on the creation of habits of obeisance. In specific institutional and cultural circumstances, often involving the symbols and uniforms of state or legal power, we are disposed to accept and obey legal authority. Acting with specific contexts, a psychological basis for obedience to law is established. Previously, religious beliefs and institutions played a major part in the legitimation of law (Maine 1861; Fustel De Coulanges 1864/1980). Mixtures of nationalism and democratic involvement also help legitimate modern legal systems.[22]

Generally, habits are of the form: with sensory input X we are disposed to give a response Y. Habits of obeisance are more complex, involving the recognition of an authoritative individual or institution W. We follow a codified legal rule not necessarily because of any ingrained disposition to do so but often because of a disposition to obey authority. Obedience to authority leads us to follow rules that lie in some written record rather than our habits. These rules require habits of thought for their implementation, but they are not necessarily habits of thought themselves. Rather than simply "if X, then we are disposed to Y," the pattern becomes "if recognition of W, then (if X then Y)," where "if X then Y" is on the written record. This is the elemental structure of the power of legal authority.[23]

These insights are neglected in other accounts of the evolution of legal systems, largely because of the prevalence of approaches that take individual preferences or dispositions as given rather than also inquiring into their evolutionary origins. There is also a desire by some social scientists to attempt to establish principles that are true for all human existence rather than a historically specific period (Hodgson 2001).

While the state is a highly fallible and sometimes destructive institution, it is indispensable for legal systems. Rights and freedoms are not the antithesis of state power; they can be sustained only through the latter within an appropriate legal framework that protects individual liberties and rights.[24]

22. Tyler's (1990) evidence suggests that, the more people regard themselves as part of the process of law formation, the more likely they are to accept legal rulings, even if they disagree in particular cases.

23. Note the discussion of "rules of recognition" in legal theory, as in Hart (1961) and Kelsen (1967).

24. This is redolent of the legal realist Hale (1952), who had links with the Veblen-Commons tradition of institutional economics (Fried 1998; Vatiero 2013).

An aim of this chapter is to show that law has an essential hybridity, necessarily involving both custom and the state. In this way, purely spontaneous accounts of law are undermined, and it is shown that the evolution of law must necessarily involve biological instincts, culturally transmitted rules, and key institutions such as the state. As well as custom, legal enforcement requires the state or another strong third-party institution (see Commons 1924; Samuels 1989; Knight 1992; Sened 1997; Mantzavinos 2001; and Hodgson 2003).[25]

The following chapters consider key legal institutions at the core of capitalism.

25. There is not the space here to elaborate on the possibility of a third-party institution other than the state and the conditions under which it can arise and become an effective enforcer. But a key feature seems to be a monopoly or near monopoly of powers relevant to rule enforcement. In addition, given the importance of perceived justice for popular compliance, the perceived legitimacy of any authority is vital for widespread obedience.

CHAPTER FOUR

Property, Possession, and Contract

Commerce and manufactures can seldom flourish long in any state which does not enjoy a regular administration of justice, in which the people do not feel themselves secure in the possession of their property, in which the faith of contracts is not supported by law, and in which the authority of the state is not supposed to be regularly employed in enforcing the payment of debts from all those who are able to pay. Commerce and manufactures, in short, can seldom flourish in any state in which there is not a certain degree of confidence in the justice of government. — Adam Smith, *The Wealth of Nations* (1776)

And when we understand the meaning of the word Property, we shall find that it will throw a flood of light over the whole of Economic Science. . . . Most persons in modern times, when they speak or hear of Property, think of some material things, such as money, houses, lands, corn, timber, cattle, etc. But that is not the true meaning of the word Property. Property in its true and original sense is not a material thing, but the Right to something. — Henry Dunning MacLeod (1878)

A people to whom ownership was unknown, or who accorded it a minor place in their arrangements, who meant by *meum* and *tuum* no more than "what I (or you) presently hold" would live in a world that is not our world. — Antony M. Honoré (1961)

Property and contract are the principal pillars of commercial law. Codified as they were in ancient Rome and elsewhere, their history is much longer than that of modern industrial and financial capitalism. Yet they are a vital foundation of the modern economy: an understanding of their nature is crucial.

There is abundant evidence that infants have notions of possession (see, e.g., Hook 1993; Friedman 2008; Blake and Harris 2009; and Kanngiesser, Gjersoe, and Hoo 2010). Perhaps there is an instinctive basis for these cognitions and emotions: "Feelings of private property are hardwired into humans, or so anyone who has raised a two-year-old will attest" (McCloskey 2010, 332). Property, it is alleged, is part of our natural condition. Hence, socialist and statist threats to private property are counter to human nature. Private property, the very foundation of the capitalist system, is natural. So too is capitalism. Q.E.D.

I do not deny the deep-rooted nature and significance of feelings of possession (and I have helped raise two-year-olds). But the conclusions in the preceding paragraph are mistaken. McCloskey conflated two basically distinct categories: property and possession. The failure to distinguish between them is widespread, and this mistake is committed by both Marxists and free market libertarians.

Herbert Gintis (2007, 1) established a mechanism to explain the evolution of the "endowment effect," where "people value a good more highly than the same good when they do not possess it." He also cited evidence for a similar effect in other species, in the form of recognition of territorial incumbency. Theory and evidence point to the likely evolution under some conditions of possessive instincts. But the claim that possession has an instinctive and evolutionary basis (Stake 2004) should not lead us to the false conclusion that property and possession are the same (or to their terminological conflation, as found in Gintis's article and elsewhere). The term *property* should be reserved for cases of institutionalized possession with third-party mechanisms of adjudication and enforcement.[1]

For many theorists, the conflation of property and possession stems in part from the equivalent conflation of law and custom, as discussed in the preceding chapter. For Marxists, the distinction between property and possession is of little operational consequence because matters of law are superstructural and the notion of property refers to (vague and undefined) "economic relations" rather than legal superficialities.

This chapter has five sections. The first discusses the distinction between possession and property and its implications. The second addresses the concepts of contract and exchange. The third establishes a

---

1. There are interesting laboratory experiments in the emergence of property rights (Crockett, Smith, and Wilson 2009; Wilson, Jaworski, Schurter, and Smyth 2012). Kimbrough, Smith, and Wilson (2010) and Jaworski and Wilson (2013) show how pilfering may decrease if theft-averse individuals form more secure and productive coalitions. These experiments rely on reputation effects and engendered trust in relatively small groups. But Sened (1997) shows that such mechanisms are much less effective in large-scale and more complex communities. See Hodgson and Knudsen (2008) for a historically grounded model of the emergence of property rights that does not depend on reputation effects.

vital zone of interaction that cannot strictly be covered by enforceable legal contract. The fourth raises the question of "well-defined property rights" and argues that these rights are always and necessarily circumscribed. The fifth summarizes the key points. The chapter closes with an appendix that addresses the ambiguous usage of the term *commodity*.

4.1. The Distinction between Possession and Property

Possession refers to the control of a good or resource. As defined here, it is about the ability to make effective use: it is not about any implicit *right*. Possession is principally a relation between a person and a thing. It does not amount to legal ownership. As the historian Richard Pipes (1999, xv) put it: "Possession refers to the physical control of assets, material or incorporeal, without formal title to them." Property often implies but does not necessitate possession, and some laws recognize possession as separate right *in rem* (regarding things). But the two are not the same: "*Property* refers to the right of the owner or owners, formally acknowledged by public authority, both to exploit assets . . . and to dispose of them by sale or otherwise" (Pipes 1999, xv). The crucial difference concerns the declaration and granting of formal rights by public authority. Hence, property in its truest sense has another prerequisite— the political authority of the state. "Before the state there is only possession" (Pipes 1999, 117).[2]

Property is not simply a relationship between owner and object. It is a relationship between people involving rights with regard to tangible or intangible assets. The exchange of property involves a minimum of not two parties but three, where the third is the state or a "superior authority" (Commons 1924, 87). These social relations involve rights, benefits, and duties (Hallowell 1943). The basis of a right of ownership of a resource is an acknowledgment of that right by others, through mechanisms of institutional accreditation and legitimation. Property is "a creature of . . . the legal system" (Penner 1997, 3).

Property involves legitimate and enforceable rights. As Antony M. Honoré (1961, 115) wrote: "To have worked out the notion of 'having

---

2. Hegel ([1821] 1942), Proudhon ([1840] 1890), MacLeod (1878), and Commons (1924, 1934) all insisted on the distinction between possession and property. See Heinsohn and Steiger (2000, 2013) and Steiger (2008) for incisive discussions.

a right to' as distinct from merely 'having' . . . was a major intellectual achievement. Without it society would have been impossible." As Honoré (1961, 134) argued: "It is not enough for a legal system to recognize the possibility of people owning things. There must be rules laying down how ownership is acquired and lost and how claims to a thing are to rank *inter se*." The legal title to an object of property refers to the conditions that must be fulfilled in order that a person may acquire a claim to an asset.

The term *property* signifies multiple different types of possible right.[3] With their codified origin in Roman law, different types of property right include the right to use a tangible or intangible asset (*usus*), the right to appropriate the returns from the asset (*usus fructus*), the right to change a good in substance or location (*abusus*), the right to the capital derived from the use of the good as collateral, the right to sell a good (*alienation*), and several other rights or limitations (Hohfeld 1919; Honoré 1961; Pejovich 1990). The distinction between different types of property right is crucial for any modern economic system. For example, hiring or leasing something may confer a restricted right of use but not necessarily other rights, such as the right to sell it to others.

Crucially for the functioning of capitalism—evident in its daily processes—and unlike objects of mere possession, durable and alienable property can be used by its owner as collateral and can involve legal encumbrances (Heinsohn and Steiger 2000, 2013; Stadermann 2002; Arner, Booth, Lejot, and Hsu 2007; Steiger 2008). Consequently, the registration of much property—particularly land and buildings—and recorded means to identify both property and owners are crucial institutional mechanisms for economic development: they enable the use of such property as collateral for loans (see Simpson 1976; De Soto 2000; Banerjee and Iyer 2005; Arruñada 2012; and Bellemare 2013).[4] But these are not simple matters: precisely because property is much more than a relationship between individuals and objects, it requires an effective legal system and state administration. The vital role of property as collat-

---

3. Honoré (1961) uses the term *ownership* alone to refer to these multiple possible rights. Here *property* and *ownership* are treated as synonyms.

4. While, as Gilbert (2002) and others have pointed out, some experiments with legal registration in developing countries have failed, this does not necessarily mean that De Soto (2000) and others are wrong. It is more that political, legal, and financial institutions have to be sufficiently well developed before registration of legal title and individual identity can be effective.

eral for loans and raising capital is discussed further in later chapters of this book.

It would be a mistake to suggest that the distinction between property and possession amounts to one between de jure and de facto property. According to widespread usage, when something is in effect in reality without a law mandating it, then it is de facto rather than de jure. But legal rights cannot exist without law, so the notion of de facto property is problematic. "De facto property" is no longer property: property by definition entails legal rights. Key distinguishing attributes of property, including legal rights, potential legal enforceability, and collateralizability, cannot exist without legal mandation.

Many social scientists treat property principally as a relation between an individual and a good, thus downplaying the institution of property, social relations between individuals, and the relation between individuals and the state. Their primary focus is on individuals, goods, and self-regarding incentives. The institutions that sustain and legitimate property are given inadequate attention. This is true even among the most ardent defenders of the institution of private property.

Consider the Austrian school economist Ludwig von Mises. He argued that legal concepts could be largely relegated from economics and sociology. Hence, when von Mises (1981, 27) discussed the nature of ownership, he considered the legal aspect as merely a normative ("ought to have") justification of de facto "having" something: "From the sociological and economic point of view, ownership is the *having* of the goods. . . . This *having* may be called the natural or original ownership, as it is purely a physical relationship of man to the goods, independent of social relations between men or of a legal order. . . . Economically . . . the natural *having* alone is relevant, and the economic significance of the legal *should have* lies only in the support it lends to the acquisition, the maintenance, and the regaining of the natural *having*."

Hence, for von Mises, ownership was natural and ahistorical rather than legal or institutional. A physical rather than a social relationship, it was deemed independent of law or any other social institution. Von Mises downgraded the institutions required for the protection and enforcement of the capacity to have and neglected the social aspects of ownership and consumption, which may signal identity, power, or status. Contrary to von Mises, the law does not simply add a normative justification for having something: it also reinforces the de facto ability to use and hold on to the asset.

The resemblance to Marx's dismissal of law is uncanny: both Marx and von Mises concentrated on raw physical power over objects rather than legal rights. Marx's numerous discussions of "property" had little to say about legal rights, and he conflated property with possession. Hence Marx (1975, 351) in 1844 addressed "private property" and argued that "an object is only *ours* when we have it— . . . when we directly possess, eat, drink, wear, inhabit it, etc.,—in short, when we *use* it." With both Marx and von Mises, effective power over something is conflated with a de facto right. Legal and moral aspects of property are overshadowed.

Classic accounts by the economists Harold Demsetz (1967) and Richard Posner (1980) discussed the origin of "laws" of "property" in primitive societies. These are not so much wrong as mislabeled. Both writers conflated law with custom. Demsetz's discussion of property rights was about the motivations for customary rather than legal rights. He concentrated not so much on the origin of such rights as on how they become valuable. Posner addressed primitive arrangements concerning property, contract, and marriage. His main claim was that various forms of these institutions were rational in the context of prevailing information costs and other factors. But his arguments concerned custom rather than law. And instead of property he described possession.[5]

Armen Alchian (1965) defined private property rights in terms of the assignment of the ability to choose the use of goods (without affecting the property of other persons). While he referred to this as "exclusive authority" and mentioned the possible role of law alongside a greater stress on custom and convention, his definition was largely in terms of (constrained and assigned) de facto powers of control rather than legal or moral rights. Later, Alchian (1977, 238) defined the property rights of a person in universal, ahistorical, and institution-free terms, including "the probability that his decision about demarcated uses of the resource will determine the use." Alchian's definitions of property neglect the essential concept of legitimated, rightful ownership. They denote possession rather than property.[6] Grossman and Hart (1986, 694n)

5. To secure possession, Posner assumed elaborate "insurance" arrangements between parties that Knight (1992, 114) persuasively argued are unfeasible. Furthermore, Posner (1980, 5, 53) ducked the whole question of motivation to focus on "consequences rather than intentions." Yet criminal and contract law rely crucially on questions of intent.

6. Alchian's attempted definition is a probabilistic statement concerning behavioral outcomes. Generally, such formulations do not make good definitions: it is better to focus on essential features than behavioral outcomes.

claimed that ownership is "substantially the same" as possession. Following Alchian and others, the property rights economist Yoram Barzel (1994, 394) defined property as "an individual's net valuation, in expected terms, of the ability to directly consume the services of the asset, or to consume it indirectly through exchange. A key word is *ability:* the definition is concerned not with what people are legally entitled to do but with what they believe they can do."

This explicitly removed the question of legal title from the definition of property. The upshot of this is that, if a thief manages to keep stolen goods, he acquires a substantial property right in them, even if, on the contrary, legal or moral considerations would suggest that they remain the rightful property of their original owner. Elsewhere, Barzel (1997, 3) argued: "The term 'property rights' carries two distinct meanings in the economic literature. One . . . is essentially the ability to enjoy a piece of property. The other, much more prevalent and much older, is essentially what the state assigns to a person. I designate the first 'economic property rights' and the second 'legal (property) rights.' Economic rights are the end (that is, what people ultimately seek), whereas legal rights are the means to achieve the end. Legal rights play a primarily supporting role."

Barzel made it clear that his version of the economics of property rights is not about legalities. But it is misleading to describe "the ability to enjoy" something as a "right." Enjoyment can exist without rights and rights without enjoyment. Rights result from institutionalized rules involving assignments of benefit. They always involve relations between people as well as relations with things. The ability to enjoy may not involve more than an individual's relationship with an object.

Douglas Allen (2014, 4) put it even more simply: "Following others, economic property rights are defined as *the ability to freely exercise a choice.*" His formulation removes the matter of enjoyment and simply takes the reason for choice as given. This again does not necessarily imply any relation with others, let alone any matter of rights. Allen ignores specifically human concerns with rights, duties, and morality. His definition entails no more than possession. It would apply to robots or any living species, including animals that are nonsocial.[7] It fails to acknowl-

7. This universality is recognized by some property rights economists and touted as a strength of their approach (Tullock 1994; Landa 1999). On the contrary, I concur with Weber (1949, 72–80), who wrote in 1904 that highly general concepts can be less valuable be-

edge specifically human motivations that have evolved over millions of years and the much more recent human institutions that, in specific ways, exploit and mold our sense of justice and respect for authority. Such definitions of property rights by institutional economists are strangely free of institutions.

The insistence that property is a legal right does not imply that people never break the law or that law alone somehow predicts behavior. But the establishment of legal rights, through perceptions of moral legitimacy and the use of state power, can affect intentions or behavior. An economy involving mere possession is very different in nature and outcomes from one that has institutionalized rights of property.

The mistaken removal of legal rights from the definition of property cannot be justified on the ground that they are unnecessary to predict behavior. Any explanation of dispositions, choices, or preferences must take such factors on board. If economists are interested in predicting behavior, then they must take legal matters of motivation, possibility, and constraint into account. The focus on de facto control is descriptive rather than explanatory. It takes as given what has to be explained. Any predictive power is based on extrapolations of superficial observations, with inadequate explanation of what is observed. More reliable predictions require fuller theoretical explanations.

Furthermore, the focus on de facto control overlooks the use of property as collateral for loans. Such behavior—which relies on legal and financial institutions—cannot be predicted from possession alone. It involves institutions: relations between individuals as well as relations between individuals and things. While emphasizing the importance of property rights, much of this discourse sidelines the vital institutions that are required to sustain them and make them fully operational in a developed economy.

Ironically, much of the narrative in "the economics of property rights" (Furubotn and Pejovich 1972, 1974; Bush and Mayer 1974; Umbeck 1981; Barzel 1997) is about neither property nor rights. To the property rights economists, *the structure of property rights* refers primarily to a set of constraints on and incentives and disincentives for specific individual behaviors. The widespread misconception in economics that a property right is about the probability of control or the ability to enjoy

cause, "the more comprehensive their scope," the more they "lead away" from the task of explaining the historically specific phenomenon in question (Hodgson 2001).

would be strangely indifferent to whether property was publicly or privately owned or owned by an individual, a cooperative, or a corporation, as long as the denoted probabilities or abilities were unaltered.

It might be claimed that "the economics of property rights" abstracts from other considerations to focus simply on the "economic aspect" of property. Barzel's (1997, 3) claim that the "economic" is just about the *end* of enjoyment and not the *means* might be raised here. But, if we uphold economics as solely focusing on the enjoyment of things or experiences to the neglect of legally instituted rights, we must concede that economics cannot adequately appreciate the modern world order. To use the words of Antony Honoré (1961, 107), such economists seem to "live in a world that is not our world."

As Dean Lueck and Thomas J. Miceli (2007, 187) conclude, much of the literature in economics on property rights "remains ignorant of property law." As Benito Arruñada (2012, 24) pointed out, much economic analysis treats property as a relatively unproblematic distribution of entitlements and quickly moves analytic attention toward contracting difficulties and transaction costs. Property rights are too important to be left to economists.[8]

Like mainstream economists, Marxists also overlook the distinction between property and possession. By contrast, the distinction was central to Pierre-Joseph Proudhon's 1840 *What Is Property?* Proudhon ([1840] 1890) quoted the prominent French lawyers Charles Toullier and Alexandre Duranton. They both had insisted that property is a right and a legal power, whereas possession is a matter of fact, not of right. Marx stridently criticized Proudhon's work. But he paid little heed to its central distinction between possession and property. Marx and Engels also claimed that tribal and hunter-gatherer societies owned property in common. This was "primitive communism." In response, Veblen (1898a, 358) argued convincingly that ownership and property were later institutional developments: "No concept of ownership, either communal or individual, applies in the primitive community. The idea of communal ownership is of a relatively later growth."

While the distinction between possession and property is ignored by Marxists and most modern economists, it is of supreme analytic and

8. We cannot blame all economists. For example, Adam Smith (1759/1976a, 1776/1976b) repeatedly emphasized moral as well as selfish motivations and the importance of justice in dealings with trade and property rights.

practical significance. It is impossible to understand capitalism in terms of mere possession without an adequate conception of property.

Against this it may be objected that the growth success of, say, modern China (Stiglitz 1994, 12) has not depended on well-defined property rights: consequently, legal issues are of lesser importance. But, on the contrary, there are strong indications that legal systems and legal property rights matter even when they are imperfectly established (Ho 2005). China's explosive growth started when land use (*usus fructus*) rights were widely conceded to the peasants after 1978 (Zhou 1996; Oi 1999; Coase and Wang 2012). In this case, relevant legislation concerning land leasing followed rather than preceded this concession. But this does not mean that legal land use rights were unimportant. Local action from below tentatively established a de facto power that spread widely and became de jure when it was legally ratified by the state. This endorsement, along with the institutional arrangements established from below, was vital to safeguard these rights.[9]

Legalities matter, and the evidence suggests that they matter still more as capitalism develops. Further economic development in East Asia may depend in part on the installation of superior state legal and political systems governing and protecting property and contracts. Private ordering is important but insufficient. The cross-country evidence of Johan Torstensson (1994), Robert J. Barro (1997), and others suggests that economic growth is correlated with the rule of law, among other factors (Acemoglu and Johnson 2005).[10]

The failure of most economists to embrace an adequate concept of property is rooted in its conception in terms of agent-object relations. Often neglected are agent-to-agent interactions that engender and sustain shared interpretations, meanings, understandings, rules, and insti-

---

9. Nee and Opper (2013) showed that for decades from the beginning of reform in China in 1978 there were inadequate legal institutions protecting the property rights and enforcing the contracts of private firms. But the private sector still expanded rapidly. We cannot conclude from this that the law was unimportant. Nee and Opper themselves pointed out that, with inadequate legal protection, these private firms risked prosecution and arbitrary closure. The private sector lobbied successfully for the 2004 changes to the Chinese constitution to "protect the lawful rights and interests of the private sector" (Nee and Opper 2013, 7) on a legal basis equal to that of state-owned enterprises. Private sector lobbying also led to a new law on property rights in 2007. As the lobbyists themselves understood, the fact that legislation follows practice does not make legislation unimportant.

10. See also the evidence presented in chapter 14.

tutional facts (Searle 1995). Agent-object ontologies in economics have taken a number of different forms, but concerning property and possession there is a commonplace conflation. Property relations, which involve agent-to-agent relations and shared understandings concerning rules and rights, are mistakenly transformed into relations of possession between agents and physical objects or processes. A mapping (in the mathematical sense) is created between the set of physical entities and forces, on the one hand, and their possessors, on the other. Rather than from agent-to-agent interactions, economic value is seen as deriving from some measurable physical activity, substance, or sensation, such as embodied labor time or utility (Orléan 2011). In much of economics, relations between people appear loosely in depictions of acts of exchange, but not in the constitution of the property rights that are exchanged. The focus is on the individual making choices over the allocation of objects or activities.[11]

Marx turned social classes into agents, underlining social relations between them. But, while he repeatedly stressed the importance of social relations, generally they were conceived in terms of possession or otherwise of material means of production. Hence, for Marx (1976, 152) "the dominant social relation is the relation between men as possessors of commodities." In dealing with individual-to-individual relations that also involve associations between individuals and material things, Marx highlighted the agent-object relations "between men as possessors of commodities." Generally, he gave little attention to the social interactions and institutions that foster shared meanings and interpretations.[12]

Generally, an agent-object ontology cannot accommodate a concept of property that is anything more than possession; it lacks the key element of institutionally legitimated legal rights. Of course, agent-to-agent interactions are played out on the registers of material objects, and *property* may connote things as well as rights (Smith 2012), but we cannot understand property simple in terms of an agent-object relationship.

---

11. Hédoin (2013) proposed an interesting development of game theory that would incorporate agent-to-agent relations and institutional facts.

12. Marx (1976, 165) criticized "commodity fetishism," where a "definite social relation between men" assumed "the fantastic form of a relation between things." But his "social relations between men" were typically formulated in terms of comparative relations of possession between class agents and things. Hence, under capitalism, the predominant relation between capitalists and workers was regarded as one of possession and nonpossession, respectively, of the physical means of production. At least in this case, social relations were seen less as shared interpretations, institutionalized rights, or intersubjective meanings.

4.2. Contract and Exchange

Terms such as *exchange* or *contract* have suffered conceptual degradation in sociology as well as economics. Capitalism involves private property and widespread exchange. But, as with *property*, the meaning of *exchange* has been eroded of substance and historical specificity. Consider
the following cases.

In sociology, the "exchange theory" of George Homans (1961) and
Peter Blau (1964) proposed that a wide range of activities—including
gift giving and interpersonal communications—are "exchanges."[13] Similarly, the sociologist James Coleman (1990, 37) saw exchange as simply a
"pairwise exchange of resources" without the necessity of legal contracts
or property rights. In modern social science, even concepts such as *exchange, contract*, and *transaction* cannot be taken for granted. Yet the
terms are used habitually and without explanatory ado, as if their meaning is always crystal clear.

Von Mises (1949, 97) saw all action, even by an isolated individual, as
"exchange"—as an attempt to swap inferior for superior circumstances.
But, when he struggled alone to survive on his island, with whom did
Robinson Crusoe "exchange" rights to property? Who ensured that he
did not cheat in the deal? In 1907 the sociologist Georg Simmel (2004,
81) described production as an "exchange with nature," and in the same
year the economist Irving Fisher (1907, 37) wrote of producers "continually hunting . . . for bargains with Nature." One wonders who negotiates
on nature's behalf and whether she gets a fair price.

Allen (2014, 4) defined transaction costs as "*the costs of establishing
and maintaining economic property rights*," where property rights were
defined simply as "*the ability to freely exercise a choice*." These formulations imply that a transaction can simply be a matter of the choice of and
control over an object by one individual, as in von Mises's definition of

---

13. Blau (1964, 93) made a distinction between "social" and "economic" exchange,
where the latter is based on a "formal contract that stipulates the exact quantities to be
exchanged." But many business transactions do not involve such an exact specification.
This is especially the case with the employment contract, which is imperfectly and incompletely specified. Blau thus placed such business and employment issues outside the economy. This is an example of the recurring failure to define adequately the boundary between economics and sociology. It is now questionable whether this boundary is useful or
even meaningful (Hodgson 2008c).

exchange (Allen 1991). Such a "transaction" need not involve more than one person. This Crusoe world of "transaction costs" could be without institutions.

Such ahistorical or asocial concepts of exchange obscure its specific, contractual form in a market economy. In common business parlance, exchange involves multiple persons and means something more than the reciprocation of a polite greeting, a wave, or a smile. But it is more than a reciprocal transfer of resources. As Karl H. Rau (1835), Henry Dunning MacLeod (1878), and John R. Commons (1924) insisted, commodity exchange is a contractual interchange of *legal rights*, along with any transferred goods or money. Unless a transfer of rights is involved, it is not an exchange or a contract. Such rights are backed by legal sanctions. Exchange has to be understood in terms of the key social institutions that are required to sustain it.

A legal contract is a voluntary agreement by two or more parties *with the shared intention of creating legal obligations*. It may be made in writing, verbally, or by other signaled assent. It could involve the delivery of services or the exchange of goods. Voluntary contracts are not necessarily equal or fair. Consider employment contracts: they involve asymmetric authority. Marriage too involves a contract even if it involves asymmetric power.

But not all agreements between adults are legal contracts. Many are acts of reciprocity or interaction between friends and family without having recourse to law if they are breached. But, in the wider world of commerce, potential legal recourse to law to enforce contracts is vital to extend agreements beyond families and friends. An effective legal system involving contract law is needed to extend the sphere of exchange throughout society and reap the benefits of a wider and more complex division of labor.

Contracting rights are different from property rights. As Arruñada (2012) explained, these two types of right can come into conflict when legal ownership is unclear. Consider a person who claims ownership of a house and enters into a contract with a bank for a mortgage. A third party also claims ownership of the building, in conflict with the statement of the mortgagee. A judge might rule in favor of the third party, on the grounds that the mortgagee had no proven legal title to the property. This would be the enforcement of property rights (*in rem*), and it would imply the cancellation of the mortgage. Alternatively, the judge can rule that the contract between the mortgagee and the bank remains intact.

This would be the enforcement of contractually agreed rights between persons (*in personam*), and it would mean that the property rights of the third person were disregarded.

A contract is between contracting parties, typically relying on an enforcement authority only if matters come to grief. But the enforcement of a property right (in a thing) additionally requires that the legal owner is widely recognized as such. Institutional systems of land or other property registration can sometimes help. But continuous registration and re-registration of all property would be far too costly in practice.

In business, as Stewart Macaulay (1963) famously observed, most deals are enforced without any appeal to the courts and many even without written contracts. But this does not mean that legal institutions have no place in everyday commerce. As Avner Greif, Paul Milgrom, and Barry R. Weingast (1994, 746) put it: "The effectiveness of institutions for punishing contract violations is sometimes best judged like that of peacetime armies: by how little they must be used." Where the rule of law prevails, the mere possibility of access to the courts is sufficient for the legal system to bear down on contractual agreements. Hence, many apparently self-enforcing agreements are actually contracts made "in the shadow of the law" (Mnookin and Kornhauser 1979).

Contracts establish legally enforceable obligations. The success of capitalism depends on national systems of law enforcement. But these took a long time to establish. Even today, in much of the world, systems of law enforcement are weak, expensive, corrupt, or inaccessible. In their absence, people fall back on other means of establishing obligations and ensuring compliance. Commerce then works through clan or family ties, shared religion or ethnicity, bureaucratic co-option and corruption, or threats of violence to person or property. Systems of spontaneous enforcement show how commercial agreements can be maintained in the absence of adequate state systems of law. Such systems existed in history and persist today in some contexts, but this should not mislead us into believing that a fully developed modern capitalist system rests on purely spontaneous or customary foundations.

Nevertheless, there are limits to the reach of law, even within countries where there is a well-functioning legal system. We live in a world of complexity, information overload, enormous variety, uncertain events, and unforeseen outcomes. Hence, contracts are always imperfectly specified and incomplete. Somehow the world of commerce has to deal with these limitations.

Émile Durkheim argued in 1893 that every contract itself depends on elements beyond full deliberation or appraisal: "For in a contract not everything is contractual" (Durkheim 1984, 158). He explained that whenever a contract exists there are factors, not reducible to the intentions or agreements of individuals, that have regulatory and binding functions for the contract itself. These consist of rules and norms that are not necessarily codified in law. In a complex and ever-changing world, no complete and fully specified contract can be written. The parties to the agreement must rely on institutional rules and standard patterns of behavior that cannot for practical reasons be established or confirmed by detailed negotiation. Each person takes for granted a set of rules and norms and assumes that the other party does likewise.

The relevant information pertaining to the typical contract is too extensive, too complex, or too inaccessible for anything more than a small part of it to be subject to rational deliberation and contractual stipulation. The more complex the decision situation, the greater amount of information involved, or, the more tacit and dispersed the information itself, the more relevant Durkheim's argument becomes.

Even the simplest commercial activities rely on taken-for-granted institutional supports. The presentation of goods at a supermarket checkout invokes established legal meanings and precedents and depends on the prior existence of many institutions, routines, and conventions—banks, credit, and law—that are the antecedents and frameworks of socioeconomic action. Without such institutions, human activity would be paralyzed. Similar remarks apply to other everyday activities, such as mailing a letter or waiting for a bus. In every case, we habitually and unthinkingly depend on a dense network of established institutions and routines.

In such circumstances we often rely to some degree on trust. By definition, if we trust another party, that means we engage voluntarily in a course of action the outcome of which is contingent on choices made by that other party. Such an outcome is typically beyond our own control. Studies have shown that trust is vital, even in a cutthroat, competitive capitalist world (Nooteboom 2002; Nooteboom and Six 2003). Capitalist firms rely on values such as "common honesty and decency" (Macaulay 1963) when making deals. Even when high risks are involved, businesspeople do not necessarily respond by insisting on a formal contract that covers every possibility.

Legal rules and contracts always and necessarily rely on factors such as trust, custom, duty, and obligation. Accordingly, a contract takes on the hue of the particular social culture in which it is embedded. But this does not mean that legal enforcement mechanisms can be ignored. In any well-functioning legal system, law and culture sustain each other. Law depends on a measure of trust, and trust is itself sustained through well-functioning legal rules. Just as law needs trust, trust needs law (Lascaux 2008).

While capitalism is a system with contract at its center, there are vital activities that cannot be reduced to contract alone. Things like love, trust, and honor cannot be contracted without becoming severely degraded in the process (Fox 1974). Some contracts—like the buying and selling of slaves—are inconsistent with a developed capitalism resting on human equality under the law (despite capitalism being typically associated with inequalities of income and wealth). Other contracts—such as the buying and selling of votes—may be deemed morally undesirable or even corrosive of capitalist political or social institutions (Satz 2010; Sandel 2012). In any society there are limits to contract and the contractarian calculus. Capitalism is no exception.

Capitalism unleashes property and contract, creating incentives for trade and innovation. At the same time—like any society—it has to sustain vital activities that cannot be reduced to contract alone. Even if the pecuniary motivation is uppermost, moral and other motivations also play a vital role (Hodgson 2013b).

4.3. Legal Transaction Costs and the Zone of Legal Impermeability

Theories of the spontaneous emergence of law have difficulty explaining the initial emergence of rules concerning property and contract. To assume that the rules of property and contract could emerge through contract alone would leave contract itself unexplained. Not all the rules of contracting can themselves be contractible. Any assertion to the contrary must defy logic by assuming some rules of contracting at the outset. Durkheim's (1984, 158) argument that "in a contract not everything is contractual" reinforces the same conclusion of inevitably incomplete contractibility. All contracts are about rights and obligations, but some of these cannot be transacted: their transaction costs are infinite. Hence, there are limits to the penetration of both law and contract into key areas of social and economic life.

Law functions through an ongoing process of interpretation, decision, and codification by legal and judicial authorities. Custom does not. But, while law and custom are different, one shades into the other, creating a fuzzy and variable boundary between the two. This is vital to understand property, contract, and exchange.

The rule of law trivially implies its dominance. But, like kings, armies, and bureaucracies, its rule can be neither absolute nor complete. It can neither penetrate every nook and cranny of social interaction nor deal with all the changing complexities of evolving social order. As D. Neil MacCormick (1998, 330–31) argued, law entails "a schema of norms" arranged in a "pyramidal structure from the relatively concise set in the constitution itself, through the various tiers validated below that." He went on: "The conception of law as 'legal system' implies the always ongoing use of powers of interpretation and decision to resolve conflict and incoherence by interpretation and by declaring null, or quashing, or overruling norms that cannot by any reasonable interpretation be reconciled with governing higher or weightier norms of the system."

Yet, while law moves down from generalities to the rich specificities of social and economic life, it faces increasing problems in dealing with the quandaries and required flexibilities of interpersonal interaction. As Niklas Luhmann (1985) argued, every attempt to reduce complexity and vagueness by articulating explicit rules tends to generate a new complexity as dilemmas appear in relation to the new provision, calling for some new refined rule, and so on. There are many areas of social and economic life where we have to rely on lenience and give and take, albeit within a framework of legal rules. The legal theorist Lon Fuller (1969a, 29) quoted a US court judgment that, if a husband and wife were able to enter into binding contracts regulating their interpersonal relations, this would "open an endless field for controversy and bickering and would destroy the element of flexibility needed in making adjustments to new conditions."

Although law is dominant and irreducible to custom, it operates without constant recourse to judges and courts. These function "in reserve," coming into play when serious disputes arise. In addition, systems of law are always incomplete. Frequently, circumstances and cases arise that are addressed inadequately in the legal code.

Often people are dissatisfied in their dealings, but they lack the time or means to take things to court. The outcome of legal adjudication is often uncertain. Anticipated costs may outweigh expected remedies. These perceived costs are a variety of transaction cost because they relate to contract definition or enforcement (Dahlman 1979; Williamson 2000).[14] These costs mean that legal institutions cannot completely penetrate socioeconomic life even if the rule of law is well developed. There is always a variable zone of legal impermeability, involving tolerance, minor transgression, trust, custom, threat, or unresolvability. This is partially recognized in law with the concept of forbearance—the intentional holding back from the implementation of a legal right. Social interaction and commerce always involve degrees of lenience and give and take.

Recourse to law is avoided when the expected costs of using the legal system exceed the expected benefits. Even when there is cheap and widespread access to the law, the cost of using lawyers or courts can exceed expected remuneration.[15] There is a sizable zone of daily interaction that is difficult to pin down in enforceable contractual terms. Instead, there may be a reliance on relational development between the parties, to avoid contracting mishaps.

Other things held constant, the size of the zone of legal impermeability is monotonically related to the costliness of legal transactions involving lawyers, contracts, or courts. Although it is always important, the scale of the zone of legal impermeability is larger in societies where legal institutions are weak, unreliable, or corrupt. Developmental progress in modern economies partly consists in establishing more adequate legal institutions and compressing this zone, partly by reducing legal transaction costs. But it can never be entirely removed.

The magnitude of the zone of legal impermeability differs from individual to individual. It depends on multiple factors, from personal resources to moral resolve. It is generally larger for the poor than for the rich. While the rich can afford lawyers and the costs of legal enforcement, the poor often cannot, unless there is a generous system of legal

---

14. But note that here the term *transaction cost* refers to legal transactions between multiple agents. This is different from Allen's (1991, 2014) definition cited above.

15. Because moral motivations can come into play, these costs and benefits are complex summations of reasons and feelings and need not be confined to pecuniary calculation or self-interest (Hodgson 2013b).

aid. The security of property and the enforcement of contracts are more effective for some than for others.

Appreciation of a zone of legal impermeability is vital to understand the nature of firms, employment contracts, families, and civil society more generally; all these issues are discussed further in later chapters. For example, employment contracts are used as a framework with a degree of discretion to provide flexibility in a sphere of complexity and unpredictability (Simon 1951).

Regarding firms, Ronald Coase (1937, 390) pointed to the problem of transaction costs as the major reason for their existence. He referred primarily to "the cost of using the price mechanism."[16] We must also include the cost of using the institutional apparatus of legal codification and enforcement, especially in the context of the firm and the production process, with all its internal complexity and variability. Firms rely on psychological and social mechanisms of trust, cooperation, morality, and authority to establish the necessary degrees of commitment and flexibility that are beyond the capacities of even the most detailed employment contract (Minkler 2008). Social relations within firms are different from those in markets and to some degree "beyond contract" as well (Fox 1974).

It is important to investigate nonlegal enforcement mechanisms that apply to zones of legal impermeability. We can learn from the studies of Avner Greif (1989, 1993) of the Maghribi traders, Janet Landa (1994) of Chinese merchants, and Elinor Ostrom (1990) of the governance of common-pool resources in the underdeveloped world. These inquiries show how agreements or rules can be enforced in contexts where legal systems are weak or beyond reach. Greif and Landa underlined the importance of reputation effects. An ethnic or religious group may have an interest in enforcing contract compliance among its members because the reputation of the group may be at stake. Enforcement mechanisms include rebuke, disapproval, or more severe punishment. They are often more available and less costly than the use of lawyers or courts. Within relatively small and cohesive groups, Ostrom emphasized reputation, trust, and targeted sanctions as mechanisms for encouraging cooperation and compliance with customary rules.

Understanding the role of extralegal enforcement processes in the zone of legal impermeability is vital. But some researchers have errone-

---

16. Coase (1937) did not then use the term *transaction cost*, adopting it only later.

ously regarded extralegal devices as exemplars of all enforcement mechanisms in the system. Inflating the role of these mechanisms to represent the system as a whole is a serious error, especially in regard to societies where there are broadly effective legal systems. Extralegal mechanisms typically apply in small-scale contexts and are implausible for general enforcement in large, complex societies (Knight 1992; Sened 1997; Mantzavinos 2001). Their enduring role is confined to zones of legal impermeability.

4.4. Capitalism and Secure Property Rights

It is frequently claimed that capitalism depends on secure property rights and took off historically when they were established (North and Weingast 1989; Olson 2000; Acemoglu, Johnson, and Robinson 2005a; Acemoglu and Robinson 2012). Without doubt, secure property rights helped create incentives for investment and entrepreneurship. But there are complications, distortions, and missing elements in some accounts of their emergence.

Generally, property rights are neither complete nor absolute. They are always hedged and qualified. Rights over land, for example, often exclude rights to destroy or degrade (*abusus* rights), thus limiting ruination of the natural environment. These nuances are downplayed in definitions of property rights that concentrate on physical possession.

Crucially, the establishment of a property right often means the legal removal or denial of particular rights for others. Consider patent systems. To be effective, they must be widely accessible to inventors and capable of being enforced.[17] But, to avoid enduring monopoly, few patent systems make such property secure forever. The aim is to protect and encourage innovations in their initial stages, so patents will often lapse in about twenty years. Such intellectual property is not enduringly secure.

The enlargement of contract and trade under capitalism required the extension of legal rights to most of the population, with typical excep-

17. Limited patent systems existed in ancient Greece and in Italy and England in the fifteenth century. The British patent system was systematized and became more accessible during the reign of Queen Anne (1702–14), and its foundational rules spread to the American colonies and elsewhere (MacLeod 2002).

tions such as children, criminals, and the insane. But it also meant the removal of some rights. There can be a conflict between the security of property for the rich and the extension of property and other legal rights to the broader population. For example, tenants may obtain *usus* property rights that restrict the rights of landlords to evict them. For economic development, evidence suggests that the allocation of property rights is as important as their clarity and strength (Kennedy 2011).

This is most obvious with slavery. Before the early nineteenth century, slavery pervaded much of the British Empire. It survived longer in other countries, including Portugal, Spain, and the United States. The eventual abolition of slavery meant the removal of the possibility of any property right in other persons, thus diminishing the wealth of the slave owners. Giving slaves full legal rights—and thereby liberating them from slavery—meant taking away the rights of others to own slaves as property.[18]

Even after the abolition of slavery, forms of bonded labor, child labor, and other servitude persisted in Britain well into the nineteenth century (Steinfeld 2001; Naidu and Yuchtman 2011). Workers often entered into one-year contracts, giving their employers yearlong rights of control without the intermediate possibility of employee exit. Apprentices had no chance of leaving until their agreed term was completed. Employers could call for criminal prosecution of employees or apprentices who attempted to leave beforehand. Child laborers had little chance of release from their penury. These bonded and child workers were not strictly slaves, but their employers had extensive legal rights to use them as if they were chattels for a year or more. Ending child labor meant stopping the right of children to work and removing the rights of employers or parents to benefit. Enhancing the rights of adult employees in various ways meant removing still more rights from employers.

For much of the nineteenth century, women and children were treated as the property of the male head of the household (Hirschon 1984; Montgomery 1988). In Britain before 1870 a husband had the legal right over his wife's income. If the wife came to the marriage with property, then that became his. The Married Women's Property Act of 1870 allowed married women to retain such assets. Another act of 1882 made married women legal persons, with the right to own property as individuals.

---

18. I am suggesting not that advocates of secure property rights support slavery but that their account of property rights is often inadequate.

Both these extensions of rights to women meant the removal of significant property rights from men.

The development of capitalism requires the strengthening of some property rights and also the curtailment of some rights of rich and powerful actors, particularly as a result of extending rights to formerly deprived groups, including servants, women, children, and slaves. Despite divesting some rich people of some rights, overall this general extension helped spread incentives and extend trade more widely. Further rights were restricted as capitalism developed. For example, in an effective democracy there is no legal right to sell votes.

Furthermore, it is a pervasive myth that property rights were insecure in England before the seventeenth century.[19] For example, Daron Acemoglu, Simon Johnson, and James Robinson (2005a, 393) wrongly suggested that in the English Middle Ages there was a "lack of property rights for landowners, merchants and proto-industrialists" and that their "development" first occurred in the late seventeenth century, when "strengthening the property rights of both land and capital owners . . . spurred a process of financial and commercial expansion." They cited John M. Veitch (1986) to claim that there were "numerous financial defaults by medieval kings" (394). But at least in regard to England this is a severe exaggeration. While English kings sometimes seized property or defaulted on contracts, these were relatively isolated events.[20]

In England, with its long-established system of property, contract, and criminal law, property rights for the rich were quite well entrenched, at least since the thirteenth century. Of course, the poorer majority had few, if any, means to exercise their legal rights. Political changes in the seventeenth century improved the legal rights of some businessmen, but Britain remained a hierarchical and undemocratic society, and the vast

19. Clark (2007), Everest-Phillips (2008), and Bogart and Richardson (2011) challenged this myth.

20. In England, Edward I expelled the Jews and confiscated their property, Edward I, Edward II, and Edward III defaulted on Italian debts, Henry VIII seized monastic lands, Charles I appropriated £200,000 in coin and bullion from the London Mint in 1638 to finance a war against Scotland, and Charles II defaulted on his debts in 1672. Veitch (1986, 31) wrote: "Property confiscation and debt repudiation were common in medieval Europe." But his sole examples from England are the four concerning Edward I, Edward II, and Edward III noted above. Henry VIII and Charles I make the total six, three of which are foreign defaults. This undermines any claim of numerous English defaults or sequestrations prior to the late seventeenth century.

majority of its population had little practical access to the law. There was no major change in these circumstances until the nineteenth century.

Long-standing and well-defined rights often carried feudal obligations that constrained the growth of markets, finance, and capitalism. For example, there were numerous restrictions on landed property, known as *entails*. Some entail laws enforced primogeniture, ensuring that a landed estate passed from one generation to another through the eldest son. This limitation on a right for the living owner of the estate became an enhanced right for his future heirs. But, even when the courts limited the scope of entails in 1614, these were replaced by voluntary and widespread "strict family settlements" that had similar effects (North, Wallis, and Weingast 2009, 89–89; Allen 2012, 65). Semifeudal arrangements persisted partly because the wealthy endorsed them.

Prior to the seventeenth century, a key impediment to the rise of capitalism in England was not the lack of property rights as such but the feudal nature of an extensive system of well-established ownership rights enjoying the support of powerful interest groups. The removal of these feudal elements in property law was a long process, beginning before 1688 and continuing long afterward, with the most extensive reforming activity after 1750 (Bogart and Richardson 2011). Contrary to some claims, the British Glorious Revolution of 1688 did not lead immediately to any major changes regarding the definition or security of property rights. The Glorious Revolution did limit the power of the sovereign and enhance Parliament. And the resulting reconfiguration of the political order enabled important legal and other reforms. But it was but one of a long series of events that laid the legal foundations of modern British capitalism.

The unqualified emphasis on the role of secure property rights overlooks distinctions between different kinds of property and the fact that property rights for the rich in England were well defined and relatively secure at least from the thirteenth century. Developed capitalism requires particular kinds of property rights plus their practical extension throughout the majority of the population.[21]

---

21. Acemoglu and Robinson's (2012) concept of "inclusive institutions" and North, Wallis, and Weingast's (2009) notion of "open-access orders" rightly underline the importance of equality under the law, widespread property ownership, and nonautocratic political institutions. But North, Wallis, and Weingast (2009, 240) also claimed: "By the early 1850s, open access to political and economic organizations had been institutionalized

Also, much emphasis on secure property rights suggests that, once these were in place, the institutional structure was largely ready to support investment and entrepreneurship. This was not the case. It further required the development of key legal and financial institutions, as discussed in later chapters. Pranab Bardhan (2005) provided evidence that the development of an administrative state apparatus was also vital. Capitalism is not simply about holding property; it is also about having the supporting legal and other institutions for economic innovation and growth.

One thing required was the widespread ability to borrow money from banks or individuals, using property as collateral. Pawnbrokers have existed for millennia: they receive portable items as collateral. Before the industrial era, the most valuable property rights were in land and buildings. But land and larger items of property cannot be handed over the counter. Effective systems of property registration were required to make land usable as collateral. Furthermore, owners were disinclined to sell or mortgage buildings or land that had been in the family for generations. Loss of land meant loss of status and privileges. Capitalism requires borrowing on a large scale. It took a long time for sufficient capital to be available to finance enterprise. To progress further, capitalism needed developed financial institutions and greater social mobility as well as secure property.

4.5. Property and Contract—Summary and Conclusion

This chapter is about the twin legal concepts of property and contract. The first task has been to establish that the concepts of possession and property are different. *Possession* refers to the de facto control or ability to use an item. Much more specifically, *property* refers to a set of rights relating to tangible or intangible assets that are acknowledged by a legitimate legal authority. Different types of property right include the right to use an asset (*usus*), the right to appropriate the returns from the asset

---

in the United States." This overlooked the fact that in 1860 there were about 3.9 million slaves in the southern states of the United States, forming about 32 percent of the southern population (US Bureau of the Census 1970). Slavery existed in fifteen states as late as the Emancipation Proclamation of 1863. This large minority clearly lacked "open access to political and economic organizations."

(*usus fructus*), the right to change a good in substance or location (*abusus*), the right to the capital derived from the use of the good as collateral, the right to sell a good (*alienation*), and several other rights or limitations (Honoré 1961).

The concept of exchange is overbroadened and misused in social science. In sociology, so-called exchange theory refers to all forms of interpersonal interaction (Homans 1961; Blau 1964; Coleman 1990). But, in market societies, exchange takes a specific, contractual form. The exchange of commodities involves the contractual interchange of property or other legal rights as well as services performed, goods transferred, or money conveyed (Rau 1835; MacLeod 1878; Commons 1924). A legal contract is an agreement entered into voluntarily by two or more parties with the shared intention of creating legal obligations. These obligations are potentially enforceable through state legal authority. Whatever definitions and terms we adopt, we need sharper and historically specific concepts to identify some of the vital elements of capitalism.

But, even in a developed capitalism, full recourse to contract law is impossible. This is partly because the system and its contingent states are too varied and complex to be envisaged adequately and encapsulated in any contract. For this reason, all law relies to some degree on custom and habit, within a structure of legal rules. Judges and courts often function in reserve. They come into play when serious disputes arise.

Sometimes it is too costly to use the law. There are always cases where the cost of using lawyers or courts would exceed any expected benefit. These *legal transaction costs* help create a *zone of legal impermeability*. This does not necessarily imply illegality. In such circumstances actors may opt for relational development between the parties, to avoid contracting mishaps. For obvious reasons, the zone of legal impermeability is generally larger for the poor than for the rich. The concept of legal impermeability is important to understand the nature of firms, employment contracts, families, and civil society more generally.

Key studies of extralegal enforcement mechanisms by Greif (1989, 1993), Landa (1994), Ostrom (1990), and other authors are important to understand economic interactions in spheres where a formal legal system is absent or plays a secondary role. Such mechanisms apply to zones of legal impermeability. But it is a mistake to assume that they can apply to the whole of a developed system where the rule of law prevails.

Secure and well-defined property rights are vital for the full development of capitalism. But this is only part of the story. The transition to capitalism cannot simply involve adding security and clarity to all existing property rights. First, at least in England from the thirteenth century, property rights were relatively secure and well defined. But these rights were feudal and too restrictive to allow the development of extensive trade and investment.

Second, capitalism depends on secure property rights and also their extension throughout the population (North, Wallis, and Weingast 2009). Such an extension typically implies the removal of some preceding property rights, such as the right to own slaves. Consequently, the legal foundations of capitalism typically emerge after episodes of political struggle and social turmoil, involving the removal of some rights from rich and powerful groups. Capitalists eclipse aristocrats. Inequality in wealth and income does not disappear, but there is wider access to the law and sometimes also to the political system.

Third, capitalism is not simply about the secure tenure of property. It also involves the capacity to use that property as collateral, to obtain money to invest in projects that may revolutionize production. Capitalism requires capital and not merely property.

In the following chapter the concepts of property and contract are used to explore further the nature of exchange and markets. Step by step we move close to an understanding of the essence of capitalism.

4.6. A Note on the Ambiguity of the Term *Commodity*

The word *commodity* is used in different ways, even in economics. It derives from the Latin root *commod-* (from which words including *commodious* and *accommodate* also originate). This meant variously "appropriate," "proper measure, time, or condition," and "advantage or benefit." This same root gave rise to the Middle French *commodité*, meaning "an advantage, convenience, or benefit." *Commodity* came into use in English in the fifteenth century. Its etymology would suggest a broad definition. Hence, a commodity would be any desired thing or service. By this inclusive definition, *commodity money*, for example, would refer pleonastically to all money, unrestricted to coins or precious metals.

Against this, the definition of a commodity has been narrowed significantly in at least three different ways. One is to define a commodity as any good or service produced *intentionally* for contractual exchange. Outside slavery, most labor power is not produced intentionally for sale or hire. Parents have children for different reasons. Land may be intentionally improved or reclaimed with a view to possible sale or rental, but most terrain precedes humankind. Considerations of intentionality seem to have led Karl Polanyi (1944, 1977) to declare repeatedly that land and labor were not commodities. Polanyi (1977, 6, 10) rightly pointed out that "equating the human economy in general with its market form" was a serious error. But he went on to argue: "The crucial step was that labor and land were made into commodities; that is, they were treated *as if* they had been produced for sale. Of course, they were not actually commodities, since they were either not produced at all (like land) or, if so, not for sale (like labor)."

Intentionality is vaguely suggested by the use of the phrase *produced for sale*. But Polanyi failed to define his concept of commodity with precision or explain why intention was so crucial. The fact remains that under capitalism much land and labor power are traded or hired, whether or not they were intentionally produced for such exchange. And, contrary to Polanyi, recognition of this fact does not amount to "equating the human economy in general with its market form." Recognition of the fact of widespread trade does not mean that nontrading activities are necessarily overlooked. There are spheres of productive activity that are not organized as markets.

Perhaps Polanyi had the following in mind: because they are not created intentionally for contracted exchange, the origins of land and labor power are largely or wholly independent of the market forces of supply and demand. But again he was unclear. The important and valid point that land and labor power are not originally produced under market conditions is better made independently. It is not made effectively by attempting to narrow the definition of a commodity.

Consider another way of narrowing the definition. When economists and business people write of *commodity markets*, they typically refer to traded material substances with intrinsic use value, such as wheat or oil, rather than tokens or services. Commodities are thus seen as useful material substances that are destined for trade. This narrower meaning is reinforced by the commonplace term *commodity money*, which usually refers to money made of metal or another substance with intrinsic use value, excluding tokens or IOUs. This materiality criterion is at odds with the vital role of knowledge, especially in modern, knowledge-intensive economies.

This leads us to Marx. Unlike Polanyi, he did not require something to be intentionally produced for sale for it to qualify as a commodity. Instead, commodities were useful, with a physical presence, either as things or as operations on things. He thus admitted land and labor power as commodities. In the opening chapter of the first volume of *Capital* on commodities, Marx (1976, 125–26) beheld within capitalism an "immense collection of commodities" and wrote: "The commodity is . . . an external object, a thing which through its qualities satisfies human needs of whatever kind. . . . The usefulness of a thing makes it a use-value. But this usefulness does not dangle in mid-air. It is conditioned by the physical properties of the commodity, and has no existence apart from the latter. It is therefore the physical body of the commodity itself . . . which is the use-value or useful thing."

As noted in later chapters, this materiality criterion created problems when Marx addressed labor and money. Marx (1976, 134, 274) saw labor as the expenditure of "muscles, nerves, bones, and brains," without emphasizing the importance of knowledge. Similarly, he had to treat credit or token money as temporary surrogates for precious metals.

In a third way of narrowing the definition, some people use the term *commodity* to refer to relatively uniform and largely indistinguishable products. Hence, *commodification* means making things uniform for sale on a market. These issues of uniformity or fungibility are important but strictly unnecessary for the definition and difficult to implement in marginal cases.

All three of the above options for narrowing the definition of the commodity are unsatisfactory. Instead, the commodity is defined here broadly, as any desired thing or service (including tokens, rights, and promises) that is potentially subject to contract or trade. To avoid confusion, the terms *commodity money* and *commodity market* will be avoided where possible because these signal different and narrower definitions

CHAPTER FIVE

Commodity Exchange and Markets

The market is a place set apart where men may deceive one another. — Anarcharsis of Scythia, ca. 580 BC

To facilitate exchanges, and thereby to encourage all sorts of industry and commerce, it has been found necessary . . . to affix a public stamp upon certain quantities . . . to ascertain . . . the quantity and uniform goodness of those different commodities when brought to market. — Adam Smith, *The Wealth of Nations* (1776)

You must remember always that your business, as manufacturers, is to form the market as much as to supply it. — John Ruskin (1859)

Despite a fascination with market prices and quantities and a frequent policy preference for market solutions, economists have paid relatively little attention to the institutional structure of markets.[1] Economists often use the word *market* widely to refer to any kind of exchange, where exchange itself is sometimes defined very broadly. The market becomes the universal ether of human existence. Oliver Williamson (Williamson 1975, 20; Williamson 1985b, 143) wrote in biblical tones: "In the beginning there were markets." Instead of historically specific, human creations, markets are treated as God-given natural forces that only the unwise or ungodly would attempt to resist.

Investigation into the nature of markets has also been inhibited by disciplinary barriers between the social sciences. According to Viviana Zelizer (1993, 193), her colleagues in sociology have been obsessed "with the cash nexus, with the vision of an ever-expanding market inevitably

---

1. This chapter uses some material from Hodgson (2008b).

dissolving all social relations and corrupting culture and personal values." She went on: "Mesmerized by this vision of inexorable force, sociologists implicitly adopted an extremely simple conception of the process, making it resemble the sweeping away of landmarks by a giant flood. That left unaddressed the crucial question: How do real markets work? Markets were seldom studied as social and cultural arrangements. For if indeed the modern market neutralized social relations and homogenized cultural distinctions, there was nothing much left for sociologists to study. Thus the market was surrendered to economists."

But, while many economists have lauded markets, they have paid much less attention to their institutional character. Three Nobel laureates in economics have noted the lack of discussion of market institutions and mechanisms in the literature. George Stigler (1967, 291) wrote: "The efficacy of markets should be of great interest to the economist: Economic theory is concerned with markets much more than with factories or kitchens. It is, therefore, a source of embarrassment that so little attention has been paid to the theory of markets and that little chiefly to speculation." But his plea went largely unheard.

Ten years later, Douglass North (1977, 710) remarked: "It is a peculiar fact that the literature on economics and economic history contains so little discussion of the central institution that underlies neo-classical economics—the market." A further eleven years later Ronald Coase (1988, 7) observed: "In modern economic theory the market itself has an even more shadowy role than the firm." Economists are interested only in "the determination of market prices," whereas "discussion of the market place itself has entirely disappeared."[2]

2. But Coase's notion of the market was challengeable. Following Director (1964), Coase (1974) advocated a "market for ideas." Coase and Wang (2012, 190–207) repeated the phrase *market of ideas* about thirty times, and "the market for goods and the market for ideas . . . together in full swing" is their main policy recommendation for contemporary China, neglecting other needed institutional reforms in land tenure, corporate law, finance, or the polity (Hodgson and Huang 2013). Does their proposal for a "market for ideas" literally mean that full property rights in ideas should be established (as with goods) and that ideas should all become priced and traded on a market for money? Not so, it seems. They referred principally to the need for "freedom of speech and expression" and for "the creation and transmission of knowledge" through educational institutions. By misleadingly describing all this as a *market*, a great theorist of economics, law, and property rights thus devalued his insistence elsewhere on the importance of property and on the nonuniversality of the price mechanism. After declaring that "the delineation of property rights is a precondition for a market economy" (Coase and Wang 2012, 131), the concept of

Of course, while economics textbooks have little to say about the structure of markets, the *m* word is commonplace, and markets are classified by their degrees of competition or their numbers of buyers and sellers. But the institutional structures and detailed mechanisms of real-world markets have been widely neglected. There has been little discussion of how specific markets are structured to select and authenticate information and of how prices are actually formed. Economists refer to the forces of supply and demand and locate market equilibria at the intersection of their curves in price-commodity space, but until recently they have offered little discussion of the mechanisms through which these forces operate. Instead, the market has been treated as a relatively homogeneous and undifferentiated entity, with little consideration of different market mechanisms and structures.

Remarkably, there is no entry on markets in either the massive 1968 edition of the *Encyclopaedia of the Social Sciences* (Sills and Merton 1968) or the extensive 1987 edition of *The New Palgrave: A Dictionary of Economics* (Eatwell, Milgate, and Newman 1987). In a rare collection of essays on the history and institutional structure of markets, Mark Casson (2011, xiii) wrote that the outsider might wrongly assume that "the market as an institution . . . would now be fully understood." But, on the contrary, he declared: "While markets have expanded to cover almost every area of economic life, economics as a discipline has narrowed its horizons and become focused on a relatively narrow range of issues." The treatment of the institutional structure of markets in modern economics is partial, dominated by abstract technical models, and largely ahistorical.

Sociologists have assumed that the study of markets is the daily toil of economists. But the neglect by economists of the institutional structure of markets has left an unexplored territory at the heart of the social

---

a market was then applied to a sphere where such delineations are inevitably incomplete and in many cases impractical or even dysfunctional. Notably, Coase (1974, 384) wrote earlier: "In the market for goods, government regulation is desirable whereas, in the market for ideas, government regulation is undesirable and should be strictly limited." My main quarrel with Coase is not on these matters of regulation but on his basic concepts of property and market. What is consistent in his position, from his earliest to his latest works, is his failure to distinguish between possession and property (we *have* ideas, but we do not necessarily *own* them in a legal sense), his relative neglect of legal *rights* (beyond the capacity to impose costs or penalties on others), and his insufficient acknowledgment of the importance of corporate legal personality (see chapter 8 below).

sciences. Markets dominate the modern world economy, yet economists have had little to say about the anatomy of market institutions.

This chapter considers the historical evolution of markets as well as alternative definitions, involving different degrees of historical specificity. We need to identify the nature of market phenomena. A brief historical sketch of the evolution of the market follows, including a review of various meanings of the term *market*. This is followed by a discussion of why the anatomy of markets has been neglected by economists. Subsequently, there is a discussion of some positive contributions from economics and sociology that point to a more nuanced view of markets, recognizing different types of market mechanism or institution. A definition of the market is then offered.

5.1. A Very Brief History of Trade and Markets

Within prehistoric tribes there were frequent gifts and transfers of goods from one individual or family to another. Such transfers have occurred within human societies for hundreds of thousands of years. But the available anthropological evidence suggests that much of this internal circulation was powered by custom and tradition. It involved elements of ritual and gift giving. It typically created an obligation of future reciprocation but without exact or agreed value equivalence. Such arrangements persisted for millennia, with negotiated barter transactions remaining insignificant or confined to external transactions with strangers. Notions of contract and ownership were underdeveloped.

Within tribes, transfers of goods involved "the continuous definition, maintenance and fulfillment of mutual roles within an elaborate machinery of status and privilege" (Clarke 1987, 4). This internal circulation of goods had little to do with voluntary, contractual transfer of ownership or property rights in the modern sense. These personal, familial and kin-based exchanges were very different from modern contracts in the organized and money-driven markets of today. They had much to do with the ceremonial validation of custom and social rank.

Nevertheless, some kind of trading in goods between tribes has existed for tens of thousands of years, perhaps being as old as the capacity for abstract language that was required to facilitate it. But, as Max Weber (1927, 195) wrote, commerce did "not take place between members of the same tribe or of the same community" but was "in the oldest social communities an external phenomenon, being directed only towards foreign tribes." The proposition that trade first developed externally and between communities—rather than within them—has withstood scholarly reexamination.

With the rise of more complex societies, particularly the ancient civilizations, both external and internal trade increased substantially. Our first evidence of a market, in the sense of an organized trading forum involving multiple buyers and sellers where goods were regularly bought and sold, is in semimythological texts from ancient China. In roughly 3000 BC, it is recorded that Emperor Shennong gave permission for rows of houses in the center of his capital (in modern Shanxi Province) to be used for trading. He ruled that selling should start at noon each day. Many centuries later, during the Zhou dynasty (1046–256 BC), the shops in this same market were taxed (Wang 1936, 3–4).[3] As the economic historian Kang Chao (1986, 5) documented: "China was a market economy for more than two millennia before the 1950s." In fact, markets may have existed in China for about five millennia.[4]

Archaeological evidence of early markets in Europe and the Middle East is patchy or inconclusive. Jericho is one of the oldest cities in the world, with archaeological traces of settlement dating back to around 9000 BC. But clear evidence of an early market there has yet to be uncovered. The Greeks had trading ports on Mediterranean shores by the eighth century BC (Tandy 1997, chap. 3). The extent to which these trading zones constituted organized markets is, however, unresolved.

We have more evidence of markets in this region from around 600 BC, when it seems that the first coins outside China were in use. There are

3. In am grateful to Xueqi Zhang for finding this information. It is unclear from the sources whether barter or a form of money was used in these very early markets. By the Zhou dynasty, monetary media of exchange—first cowrie shells and then bronze coins— were in use and available for taxation.

4. This ridicules the crass description of the burgeoning Chinese economy today as an *emerging market*. China may have had markets for over two thousand years before their emergence in Europe or the Middle East. The term *emerging market* is relatively recent and was first applied to emerging *financial* markets for investment (Errunza 1983). It became an alternative to the terms *less-developed economy* and *developing economy*, which suffered from terminological loss of fashion, just as *underdeveloped* had been rejected before. By the late 1980s the term *emerging market* was applied to whole countries, including China and India, wherein markets had previously existed for millennia. The description of many other countries such as Brazil, Indonesia, South Korea, and Malaysia as *emerging markets* is also an insult to their economic and institutional history.

records of an organized marketplace (or *agora*) where goods were regularly traded according to defined rules in Athens in the sixth century BC (Polanyi 1971; North 1977).

Chapter 27 of the biblical Book of Ezekiel, written when the prophet was exiled in Babylon from 593 to 571 BC, mentions the locations of several "markets" and "fairs" in the Middle East and notes trade in metals, ivory, ebony, jewels, slaves, horses, mules, vessels, spices, embroidery, linen, wool, and other commodities. There is no other mention of a market in the Old Testament, but Genesis and Exodus report portable forms of money several times. According to modern Bible scholarship, Genesis and Exodus were also drafted in the sixth century BC (Davies 1998). Herodotus noted the introduction of coinage in the seventh century BC. Hence, Middle Eastern markets in the sixth century BC probably involved coin money.

At around the same time, also according to Herodotus, there was an annual auction market in Babylon where young women were put on display and male bidders paid money for marriage rights (Cassady 1967). Peter Temin (2002) examined recorded price data of goods from Babylon from 464 to 72 BC and concluded that the longer time series of apparently responsive and readily adjustable prices was evidence of market forces in operation.

There has been some debate on whether these ancient civilizations were predominantly market economies. Karl Polanyi and other scholars have denied this (Finley 1962; Polanyi, Arensberg, and Pearson 1957). By contrast, Temin (2001, 2006) and others have argued that the Roman Empire contained developed and interlocking markets with variable prices. But banks and money markets played a relatively small role by modern standards.[5] The existence of many other markets in ancient Rome is undeniable (Bang 2008). The dispute concerned their role in and degree of influence over the economy as a whole. The resolution of this debate depends partly on both the definition of a market and the extent to which markets dominated production and distribution. Some have estimated that three-quarters of production was directly for subsistence. Their crit-

---

5. According to Sainte Croix (1956), ancient Greece and Rome lacked double-entry bookkeeping and effective notions of debit or credit. Accounts consisted principally of inventories. Hamilton (1947, 118) noted that there was public debt in neither ancient Greece nor ancient Rome. But Cohen (1992) claimed that the banking system in ancient Greece was more sophisticated.

ics respond that markets and prices still affected the system as a whole. But, if Temin is right, this does not mean that ancient Rome was essentially a capitalist economy, at least according to acceptable definitions of capitalism that we shall entertain later in this book. Markets are a necessary but insufficient condition for capitalism. Something else must have been added to markets to make capitalism take off after 1700.

After the fall of the Western Roman Empire in AD 476, European and Mediterranean trade contracted dramatically. Intranational trade also declined, with feudal nobilities governing much economic activity in Europe. Markets for slaves existed in classical antiquity and persisted in some regions until the twentieth century. By contrast, feudal serfs were not owned as chattels, but they did not enjoy the right to choose their masters. Feudal institutions were driven by traditional obligations rather than voluntary contract.

The most important driving force behind the recovery of trade in the medieval period was mercantile activity, often over long distances. "Strange though it may seem," wrote the historian Henri Pirenne (1937, 140), "medieval commerce developed from the beginning not of local but of export trade." Trade created hubs where routes converged. These attracted settlers and sometimes gave rise to organized markets.

From the eleventh century, markets and fairs multiplied in Europe. Annual fairs often complemented the expansion of organized markets by providing outlets for longer-distance and higher-value trade (Casson and Lee 2011). In several European countries, the principal organized markets were chartered by the king. However, systematic evidence of a king enforcing his right to license all markets and fairs does not appear until the thirteenth century.

What about markets for wage labor? By the fourteenth century, bonded labor was in decline in England. A large class of potentially mobile wage laborers emerged, making up roughly half the adult male population by the seventeenth century (Lindert and Williamson 1982). But organized markets for employees, involving labor exchanges or employment agents, did not become prominent until the nineteenth century.

Financial bond markets began in Venice in 1171. The state drew a forced loan at 5 percent interest from the citizenry. The evidence of a loan, or bond, became tradable. Florence and Genoa followed by issuing their own bonds. After the development of a banking system in Venice in the thirteenth century, trade developed in government securities in several Italian cities.

In 1309 a "Beurse" was organized in Bruges in Flanders, apparently named after the Van der Beurse family, which had previously hosted regular exchanges of material goods. Soon after, similar "Beurzen" opened in Ghent and Amsterdam. In 1602 the Dutch East India Company issued the first shares on the Amsterdam Bourse or Stock Exchange. The London Stock Exchange, founded in 1801, traces its origins to 1697, when goods and stock prices began to be published in a London coffee-house. The origins of the New York Stock Exchange go back to 1792, when twenty-four stockbrokers organized a regular market for stocks in Wall Street.

Clearly, in the last five centuries, markets have expanded enormously in scope, volume, sophistication, and economic importance. Today, markets pervade internal as well as external trade and dominate the global economic system. There is international trade in countless commodities, and financial markets have become the drivers of the world economy.

Against this historical background, at least three different ways of defining markets emerge, involving different degrees of historical specificity. The broadest definition of the market refers to all forms of transfer of goods or services, including anything from customary or ceremonial transfers within tribes or households to organized markets with multiple buyers and sellers. An intermediate option would be to identify markets with all forms of voluntary trade involving discernible property rights. A third and most restrictive option is to define the market more narrowly as a sphere of organized, competitive exchange. These alternatives are now compared.

5.2. What Is a Market?

In *Human Action*, Ludwig von Mises (1949, 257) devoted an extensive chapter to the market, seeing the market economy as "the social system of the division of labour under private ownership of the means of production." In his account, the historical boundaries of the market depend on what is meant by *private ownership*. Von Mises defined ownership in terms of control of the services that derive from a good rather than in terms of legal rights. Ownership for him meant mere possession. Hence, private ownership and exchange could apply to most of human history. His conception of the market embraced all voluntary transfers of assets. Ceremonial transfers and ritualistic gift giving would be regarded as "exchanges" of "property" and within the sphere of "the market." According to von Mises, "markets" have existed for hundreds of thousands of years or more. His very broad definition of the market became possible because of his extremely wide definitions of exchange and contract.

So, if we reject the notion that markets can involve customary or ceremonial transfers without developed legal property rights, we still have further options for delineation. A dilemma emerges: whether the market is regarded as coextensive with the contractual exchange of commodities per se or whether it is given an even narrower meaning and used to refer to forms of *organized* exchange activity. At least two factors weigh in favor of the narrowest definition.

A primary consideration is the commonplace use of the word *market* and its equivalent in other languages. *Market* originally referred to a specific place where people gathered and exchanges of a particular kind occurred. The markets in China in about 3000 BC and in Athens and the Middle East in the sixth century BC involved recurrent trade organized in specific locations. Originally permitted by royal charters, medieval markets were located and regulated in specific towns. There are also permanent buildings that function as markets or exchanges for agricultural products, minerals, financial stocks, and so on. Although today it has acquired additional meanings, the term *market* still refers to places where trade is organized.

Second, there is a well-researched form of contractual exchange that takes place in different contexts and involves other considerations. In three seminal and influential works, George B. Richardson (1972), Victor P. Goldberg (1980), and Ronald Dore (1983) established that many real-world commercial transactions do not take place in competitive market arenas. Instead, firms are involved in ongoing and more intensive bilateral relationships: the parties cooperate and exchange relevant information before or after the contract itself. Such relationships are seen to enhance ongoing trust in circumstances of uncertainty where product characteristics are complex, are unusual, or involve continuous improvements. The relationship is durable, and the contract is often renewed. This is often described as *relational exchange* or *relational contracting*.[6] It is very different from the impersonal and competitive exchanges found

6. Williamson (1985b) used *relational contracting* in a different way. For him, it referred not to long-term relationships in business but to issues that can arise during the implementation of contracts that take time to run to fruition, in contrast to transactions for

in organized markets. Relational exchanges are nevertheless still contractual exchanges involving property rights. If they are distinguished by definition from market exchanges, then not all exchanges take place in markets.

Furthermore, the exchange of goods or services that are strictly unique may be regarded as a nonmarket phenomenon even if the exchange is not relational. The term *market* is then reserved for forms of exchange activity with many similar exchanges involving multiple buyers or sellers.

Consider financial markets. There are typically strict rules concerning who can trade and how trading should be conducted. Specific institutions sift information and present it to traders to help the formation of price expectations and norms (Hodgson 1988). Market institutions reduce the costs of search, negotiation, and monitoring entailed in transactions (Loasby 2000). Market institutions in other contexts monitor the quality of goods and the instruments of weight and measure. Within these structures, trading networks emerge on the basis of business connections and reputations.

Modern electronic communication has made it possible to organize markets that are unconfined by any physical location. Bidders can communicate with other traders and the market organizers over long distances as well as with many financial markets. The market*place* can itself disappear, as in the case of Internet-based markets such as eBay. The latter case nevertheless remains a market because it involves high-volume trade and is subject to codified procedures and rules.

Taking on board the arguments presented above, the market may be defined in the following terms. Markets involve multiple exchanges with multiple buyers or multiple sellers and thereby a degree of competition. A market is an institution through which multiple buyers or multiple sellers recurrently exchange rights to a substantial number of similar commodities of a particular type. Exchanges take place in a framework of law and contract enforceability. Markets involve legal and other rules that help structure, organize, and legitimize exchange transactions. They involve pricing and trading routines that help establish a consensus over prices and often help by communicating information regarding prod-

---

finished goods. He thus downplayed the role of goodwill and cooperation in these relational contexts (Earl and Potts 2011).

ucts, prices, quantities, potential buyers, or possible sellers. Markets, in short, are organized and institutionalized recurrent exchange.

But it is often difficult to draw the line between organized and relational exchange, with many possible intermediate cases. Such definitional difficulties are typical when dealing with highly varied phenomena and commonplace in some other sciences, notably biology. The difficulty of defining a species does not mean that that species should be undefined.

A question arises whether the definition of a market should involve money as opposed to barter. Clearly, there are major differences between barter and markets where money is used as the medium of exchange and store of value. Furthermore, there is surprisingly little historical evidence of economies dominated by barter (Einzig 1966; Dalton 1982; Humphrey 1985; Davies 1994; Graeber 2011). The inclusion of money exchange in the definition of a market is treated as optional here.

The operation of the law of one price is sometimes taken as an indication of the existence of a market. Of course, imperfect information and quality variations can explain price variations within a market. Nevertheless, the organized competition of the market and its associated information facilities are necessary institutional conditions for any gravitation by similar commodities to a single price level.

We may contrast the narrowest definition of the market—as an institution with multiple buyers or multiple sellers and recurrent exchanges of a specific type of commodity—with the much broader definitions raised earlier. These differences in definition do not simply affect the degree of historical specificity of market phenomena; they also sustain different theoretical frameworks and promote different questions for research.

5.3. Markets Are Institutional and Nonuniversal

Generally, the institutional character of markets has been neglected when institutions have been neglected. Among the exceptions were German historical school economists such as Gustav Schmoller and Werner Sombart (Hodgson 2001). Similarly, the British dissident economist John A. Hobson (1901, 144) wrote: "A market, however crudely formed, is a social institution." The American institutionalist John Maurice Clark (1957, 53) argued: "The mechanism of the market, which dominates the values that purport to be economic, is not a mere mechanism for neutral recording of people's preferences, but a social institution with biases of its own." Subsequently, Coase, North, and others have helped revive an interest in the institutional structure of markets that was eclipsed by developments in mainstream economics during much of the twentieth century.[7]

Vague or overly inclusive definitions of key concepts such as property, exchange, and market have not helped matters. Many economists have upheld that the principles of their subject should be as universal as possible—like physics—to the extent that substantial consideration of historically or nationally specific institutional structures is lost. Hence the idea that economics should be defined as a general "science of choice" (Robbins 1932) rather than the study of specific types of economy. Consequently, many forms of human interaction have been regarded as exchange, and summations of such exchanges are loosely described as *markets*. The market then assumes a deinstitutionalized form. Markets result neither from protracted processes of institution building nor from the full development of a specific commercial culture. Whenever free people gather together in the name of self-interest, a market somehow emerges in their midst.

Despite its emphasis on historical specificity, Marxism also treats markets as uniform entities, with a single logic based on one set of pecuniary imperatives. Marxists stress a supposed universal logic of the market system rather than specific institutional market structures or rules.

Similarly, exponents of the rational choice approach within sociology defined markets in ahistorical terms. Hence, James Coleman (1990, 35–36) saw markets as simply "transfers of rights or resources" within

---

7. Coase's (1974) use of the inappropriate term *market for ideas* has been criticized above. Similarly, despite his valid complaint (see North 1977) that economists have neglected the true nature of markets, North (1990a, 1990b) promoted an untenable and inadequately defined concept of "political market." It might refer to party competition in democracies, or perhaps any struggle between individuals or groups for political power. All such processes are poorly described as *markets*. Voting and consent to authority normally involve neither exchanges of property rights nor commercial contracts. The notion of "political market" is strangely indifferent between less-corrupt democracies and others (such as India) where the buying of popular votes and the votes of elected politicians is frequent. There may be tacit understandings between rulers and the ruled, amounting to a "social contract." But such "contracts" do not involve the exchange of rights to goods or services and cannot signal the existence of markets. A danger in the term *political market* is that it stretches the concept of the market so widely that it loses much of its meaning, particularly in relation to property and contractual exchange.

"systems of relations" or a "system of exchange." Recollect that Coleman (1990, 37) regarded exchange as a "pairwise exchange of resources"
without legal contracts or property rights. His "markets" covered a wide
range of phenomena, including taxation and gift giving.

Economists have used general equilibrium theory in their attempts
to understand markets. In the seminal model of Kenneth J. Arrow and
Gerard Debreu (1954), a complete set of markets for all present and future commodities in all possible states of the world was assumed. But
as Frank Hahn (1980, 132) pointed out: *The assumption that all inter-
temporal and all contingent markets exist has the effect of collapsing the
future into the present.*" Even here, something like the "Walrasian auc-
tioneer" and pricing rules had to be adopted in order to make the model
work. Elemental institutional structures and rules had to be assumed to
make the model function on its own terms. The limits to this project became apparent in the 1970s, when it was shown that few meaningful general conclusions could be derived. Hugo Sonnenschein (1972, 1973) and
others demonstrated that within general equilibrium theory the aggregated excess demand functions can take almost any form (Kirman 1989;
Rizvi 1994b).

The existence of "missing markets" poses a challenge for standard
general equilibrium theory (Hart 1975; Magill and Quinzii 1996). Crucially, if market institutions are too costly to establish, then some may
be missing for that reason. Furthermore, while capitalism has historically promoted market institutions, modern developed capitalism *pro-
hibits* several types of market, such as markets for slaves, children, votes,
or dangerous drugs. In particular, the development of markets for children or slaves within capitalism would undermine the egalitarian legal
principles that modern capitalism has championed.

Michael Heller (2008) pointed to the dangers of the infinite extension and subdivision of ownership in a deeply interconnected and widely
integrated economy. There is a danger of an "anticommons" where extensively parcelized rights obstruct trade and entrepreneurship. To make
markets work it is necessary that some important sources of information
are accessible with little or no cost (such as price data, legal information,
telephone directories, or the Internet). The market system itself depends
on the incompleteness of markets for information, where some crucial
data are unowned and available freely. Markets are indispensable, but
they cannot be the universal solution to every economic problem. Capitalism demonstrates this at its core.

5.4. A Revived Understanding of Markets as Institutions

After technical problems with general equilibrium theory were exposed by Sonnenschein and others, economists shifted their attention to game theory (Rizvi 1994a). By its nature, game theory tends to lead to less-general propositions and points instead to more specific rules and institutions. Game theory also became a theoretical tool for a "new institutionalist" revival in economic theory (Schotter 1981; Aoki 2001).

Further developments have helped promote the study of markets as social institutions. In economics the basic theory of auctions emerged in the 1970s and 1980s (McAfee and McMillan 1987). It was assumed that participants in an exchange had incomplete information, and it was shown that choices concerning auction forms and rules could significantly affect market outcomes. These ideas gained center stage in the 1990s with the use by governments of auction mechanisms in electricity and telecommunications deregulation, most notably in the selling of the electromagnetic spectrum for telecommunications services and subsequently with the growth of auctions on the Internet.

By simulating markets in the laboratory, experimental economists face the unavoidable problem of setting up an institutional structure. Simply calling it a *market* is not enough to provide the experimenters with sufficient structures and procedural rules. As the leading experimental economist Vernon Smith (1982, 923) wrote: "It is not possible to design a laboratory resource allocation experiment without designing an institution in all its detail." Experimental economics has underlined the importance of these specific rules.

In the real world, each market is entwined with other institutions and a particular social culture. Accordingly, there is not just one type of market but many different markets, each depending on its own inherent rules, cultural norms, and institutional makeup. Differentiating markets according to textbook typology—from perfect competition through oligopoly to monopoly—is far from the whole story. Institutions, routines, and culture have to be brought into the picture. Experimental economists have discovered an equivalent truth in laboratory settings and learned that experimental outcomes often depend on the tacit assumptions and cultural settings of participants. Different types of market institution involve different routines, pricing procedures, and so on. The notion of a single universal type of market has lost credibility (McMillan 2002).

Viktor Vanberg (1986, 75) insisted that the market "is always a system of social interaction characterized by a specific *institutional framework*, that is, by a *set of rules* defining certain restrictions on the behavior of market participants." In a definition that is similar to the one proposed in this book, the institutional economist Claude Ménard (1995, 170) recognized both the rule-governed and the recurrent character of exchange in markets: "*A* market *is a specific institutional arrangement consisting of rules and conventions that make possible a large number of voluntary transfers of property rights on a regular basis . . . implemented and enforced through a specific mechanism of regulation, the competitive price system.*"

Following the collapse of the Eastern bloc in 1989–91, some advisers presumed that markets would emerge spontaneously in the vacuum left after central planning disappeared. But capital and other markets were slow to develop, and their growth was thwarted by the lack of an institutional infrastructure. Several formerly planned economies slipped back into severe recessions. Critics such as Coase (1992, 718) spotlighted the necessary institutional foundations of a market system: "The ex-communist countries are advised to move to a market economy . . . but without the appropriate institutions, no market of any significance is possible."

Sociologists, like economists, had previously paid relatively little attention to market institutions. But, when "economic sociology" was revitalized in the 1980s, its mission was to address the social context and institutions of economic life. Leading economic sociologists such as Mark Granovetter (1985) addressed the arguments of Karl Polanyi (1944) concerning the degree of "embeddedness" of markets in social relations. But this discourse was encumbered by much vagueness as to what *social*, *economic*, and *embedded* meant. The lack of consensus on the meaning of these crucial words, and consequently whether institutions such as the family are economic or social, has undermined the key concept of embeddedness. Consequently, Neil Fligstein (1996, 656) reported that the "empirical literature has failed to clarify the precise nature of social embeddedness." Granovetter himself wrote: "I rarely use 'embeddedness' any more, because it has become almost meaningless, stretched to mean almost anything, so that it therefore means nothing" (Krippner et al. 2004, 113).

While the discourse on embeddedness reached a dead end, economic sociologists have nevertheless made a huge contribution to our understanding of the operation of financial and other markets (see Abolafia 1996; Baker 1984; Burt 1992; Fligstein 2001; Lie 1997; Swedberg 1994; and White 1981, 1988, 2002). Their works show how specific networks and social relationships structure exchanges and how cultural norms govern market operations and outcomes.

Similar issues have emerged in some empirical and simulation work by economists. This has stressed the importance of learning and previous experience in trading partner selection and in transaction decisions (Kirman and Vignes 1991; Härdle and Kirman 1995). A milestone paper by Alvin Roth (2002) challenged the view of a single universal theory of market behavior. The previous search by economists for optimal rules and institutional forms has become a will-o'-the-wisp, with the realization that assumptions concerning cognitive and information impairments have made this search difficult or impossible (Lee 1998; Mirowski 2007). Economists have begun to adopt a much more nuanced and institution-rich concept of the market (McMillan 2002). These developments now challenge the meaning and legitimacy of the boundaries between economics and sociology.

Both economists and sociologists are now paying detailed attention to the nature of specific market rules and mechanisms. An outcome is to challenge the former widespread notion—shared by many theorists from Marxists to the Austrian school—that the market is a singular type of entity entirely understandable in terms of one set of principles or laws. Markets are increasingly treated as varied and historically specific phenomena.

5.5. Concluding Remarks on Markets

There is no methodological golden rule that unfailingly points to the superiority of one definition over another. A number of options for defining a market exist. The broadest option is to regard the market as the universal ether of human interaction, depending on little more than the division of labor. A second option is to regard the market as synonymous with commodity exchange, in which case it dates at least as far back as the dawn of civilization.

Several considerations militate in favor of a third and most specific definition. Recent developments in economic theory and economic sociology also point in this direction. In this restrictive sense, markets

are organized recurrent exchange. Where they exist, they help structure, organize, and legitimize numerous exchange transactions. Pricing
and trading procedures within markets help establish a consensus over
prices and communicate information regarding products, prices, quantities, potential buyers, or possible sellers. Consequently, as André Orléan (2011, 12) put it: "Market value is not a substance . . . that predates
trade. Rather it must be considered as a sui generis creation of market
relations."[8]

With this narrow definition, as North (1977, 710) put it, "most exchanges do not take place in markets." Markets are zones of organized,
recurrent exchange. Other exchanges are more episodic, involving be-
spoke transactions or stronger trust relations. Given the organization
costs involved in the management of markets, they are unlikely to grow
to the point that they encompass all exchange. On the other hand, the
creation of numerous regional, national, and international markets for
many products and services can be a major factor in promoting competition, driving down prices, and encouraging innovation. Although far
from ubiquitous, markets are a major part of the machinery of dynamic
capitalism.

But, whether we adopt a broad or a narrow definition of markets,
their emergence cannot account for the post-1700 explosion of economic
growth portrayed in figure 1.1 above. Even by the preferred and narrower definition, markets have been important for thousands of years.
Capitalism requires markets, but markets alone do not define capitalism.

Markets are sophisticated information processors, dealing with information that comes from within and without the production system
(Hayek 1948; Mirowski 2002, 2007; Mirowski and Somefun 1998). Markets are mechanisms of collective learning, providing opportunities for
experimentation. Market prices are crude but often effective indicators
of error or success. Capitalism places markets alongside cooperation and
authority within the firm, synergizing the energies of two fundamentally
different transaction and information-signaling systems.

Variations in market rules and procedures mean that markets can
also differ substantially from one another, especially in different contexts and cultures. The markets of two thousand years ago were very
different from the electronic financial markets of today. The market is

---

8. "La valeur marchande n'est pas une substance . . . qui préexiste aux échanges. Il
faut plutôt la considérer comme une création sui generis des rapports marchands."

neither a natural datum nor an ubiquitous ether but a kind of social institution, governed by sets of rules restricting some and legitimizing other behaviors. Markets are necessarily entwined with other institutions. They can emerge spontaneously, but they are often promoted or guided by conscious design.

Crude pro- and antimarket policy stances are insensitive to the possibility of different types of market institution. Instead of recognizing the important role of different possible trading rules, many opponents and advocates of markets have focused exclusively on their general features. Marxists claim that the mere existence of markets helps encourage acquisitive, greedy behavior. This is a source of their *agoraphobia*, or fear of markets. Obversely, overenthusiastic advocates of the market claim that its benefits stem simply and unambiguously from the existence of private property and exchange, without regard to possible variations in detailed market mechanisms or cultural contexts. In a strange alliance, market opponents and advocates underestimate the degree to which all market economies are unavoidably made up of varied and interconnected social institutions.

As noted above, markets are often bolstered by the state. It underpins property, money, and contract. As noted previously, Coase (1988, 10) argued that the enforcement of contracts and market rules, with large numbers of people with very different interests, must "depend . . . on the legal system of the State." Although Karl Polanyi (1944) gave different reasons, he was right in his historical claim that liberalized markets were often engineered by the state. Some role for the state is unavoidable in even the most libertarian of market systems.

Keynesian economists have long insisted that markets are not self-righting: they can plunge into recessions from which they cannot quickly emerge unaided (Keynes 1936, 1937). An important additional point is that markets are not self-constituting: they are neither the omnipresent ether of human interaction nor entirely spontaneous institutions. Like many other crucial capitalist institutions, they involve an essential hybridity of spontaneity and design.

CHAPTER SIX

Money and Finance

With unified currency, people's faith in currency will not be divided; and where coins are exclusively issued from above, there will be no grounds for public distrust of the coinage. — Hu Jichuang, *Book of Guan Zi* (ca. 200 BC)

The necessities of the state render government upon most occasions willing to borrow upon terms extremely advantageous to the lender. The security which it grants to the original creditor is made transferable to any other creditor, and, from the universal confidence in the justice of the state, generally sells in the market for more than was originally paid for it. — Adam Smith, *The Wealth of Nations* (1776)

Furthermore it is a peculiar characteristic of money contracts that it is the State or community not only which enforces delivery, but also which decides what it is that must be delivered as lawful or customary discharge of contract which has been concluded in terms of the money of account. The State, therefore, comes in first of all as the authority of law which enforces the payment of the thing which corresponds to the name or description in the contract. — John Maynard Keynes, *A Treatise on Money* (1930)

Money is central to capitalism, but it is among its most complex and mysterious institutions. In this chapter, little new is added to the vast literature on money. My aim is more to underline some key lessons. Although courses on money and finance are commonplace in universities, students are told little about core controversies concerning its nature or about how money does not fit well into mainstream economic theory. Frank Hahn (1965, 1987, 1988) showed that general equilibrium models provided no adequate reason why rational, utility-maximizing agents should hold on to money. Token money is worthless except as a means of purchasing other goods or services. In the assumed final equilibrium, when all contracts are settled, no one would end up with money. At best, general equilibrium models resemble a barter economy.[1]

Textbooks tell us that the main functions of money are as a medium of exchange, a unit of account, and a store of value. But most mainstream accounts of money concentrate on its function as a medium of exchange: their theories of money are basically exchange based. The unit-of-account and store-of-value functions receive less attention. Rival accounts place greater relative emphasis on the role of money within a national economy as a unit of account, store of value, and means of repayment of debt.

The debate concerning the nature of money is more than two thousand years old and has yet to be resolved. Aristotle himself entertained versions of both of the two main rival accounts. In the *Politics*, he suggested that money arose spontaneously, through the process of exchange. By contrast, in the *Nicomachean Ethics*, he hinted at the "state theory" or (in modern terminology) "chartalist" view, where money is supported by law and the state.[2] The conflict between these two views of money came to a head in the final decades of the nineteenth century, within the famous *Methodenstreit* between the Austrian school theorist Carl Menger and the German historical school (Hodgson 2001).

First, I examine the spontaneous theory of money as developed by Menger. His account requires serious attention because it is explicitly an attempt to establish the essence of money. A critical discussion of Menger's account sets the stage for a brief examination of the historical development of money. Crucial innovations that immediately preceded the great expansion of capitalism were legal and institutional provisions for the sale of debt. I also address the role of the state in the creation and persistence of monetary institutions. Against the widespread conception of money as a substance it is regarded as a social institution. The basic ontology of money and its role in capitalism are outlined.

---

1. But this resemblance is partial. In general equilibrium models, everything can exchange with anything else, thus magically overcoming the problem of the lack of double coincidences of wants. Everything being universally exchangeable, every commodity in such models is like money in this respect. But this also means that no commodity has special status as money: if everyone is king, then no one is king. Money means elevating just one medium and measure and that exchanges other than for money are unlikely (Clower 1967).

2. For more on Aristotle on money, see Schumpeter (1954) and Meikle (1995, 2000).

6.1. Money as a Spontaneous Order

Against the German historical school, Menger (1871, 1883, 1892) argued that money was essentially a spontaneous outcome of interacting, self-interested individual agents. He attempted to show that it could in principle have emerged spontaneously without the state.

Under barter, there is the difficulty that, trying to swap A for B, one trader cannot always find another with the inclination to barter B for A. This lack of a "double coincidence of wants" makes barter cumbersome. Once a convenient commodity is observed as frequently traded, people will seek it out as a useful medium of exchange. This in turn will make the commodity in question even more viable as a medium of exchange. Through a process of positive feedback, it can become money. As Menger (1981, 260) argued in his *Principles* of 1871:

> As *each* economizing individual becomes increasingly more aware of his economic interest, he is led by this *interest, without any agreement, without legislative compulsion*, and *even without regard to the public interest*, to give his commodities in exchange for other, more saleable, commodities, even if he does not need them for any immediate consumption purpose. With economic progress, therefore, we can everywhere observe the phenomenon of a certain number of goods, especially those that are most easily saleable at a given time and place, becoming, under the influence of *custom*, acceptable to everyone in trade, and thus capable of being given in exchange for any other commodity.

A commodity that is seen as widely accepted in exchange will have its salability enhanced as individuals act on the basis of this perception. Emergent money becomes progressively reinforced through current perceptions and anticipations of the actions of others. Apart from the attribute of being "most marketable," which is a culmination and consequence of individual perceptions and choices, Menger (1985, 154) also suggested that the good that emerges as money may be "the most easily transported, the most durable, the most easily divisible."

Consequently, according to Menger, a commodity can emerge as money without state intervention or state decree. In Aristotelian terms, his heuristic illustration of the evolution of money thus separated what was allegedly *essential* (interactions between individuals with unintended consequences) from what he held to be *accidental* (the role of the state).

In 1883 Menger (1985, 153) accepted that "history actually offers us examples that certain wares have been declared money by law." But he saw these declarations as "the acknowledgement of an item which had already become money." Although cases of the emergence of money by agreement or legislation may be historically important, Menger (1985, 155) nevertheless argued: "The origin of money can truly be brought to our full understanding only by our learning to understand the *social* institution discussed here as the unintended result, as the unplanned outcome of specifically *individual* efforts of members of a society."

This is a powerful thought experiment. It is wrongly dismissed by many on the grounds that it does not match the historical evidence on the emergence of money. This rebuttal can be easily countered by Menger's own statement that he was not trying to describe actual historical processes. Rather than a historical account, it was a heuristic attempt to identify the essence of money.

Models and thought experiments do not have to be accurate to be useful. A primary purpose of a heuristic is to identify possible causal mechanisms. Heuristics can be useful without necessarily making good predictions or closely matching existing data. Their purpose is to establish a segment of a larger causal story without necessarily giving an adequate or complete explanation of the phenomena to which they relate. Useful heuristic models have the paradoxical feature that they are strictly unrealistic yet seem to illuminate important aspects of reality (Sugden 2000).

This raises the question of how heuristics can be appraised scientifically. If they are not realistic, then what criteria of evaluation should be used? A widely used procedure for testing a heuristic is to model it mathematically. But analytic models often become intractable. To test Menger's model, among the best options available are agent-based computer simulations. But simulations of the emergence of money have proved to be extraordinarily problematic. For example, Ramon E. Marimon, Ellen McGrattan, and Thomas J. Sargent (1990) attempted such an agent-based model. The results of their simulations were partially inconclusive. A single monetary unit did not always readily emerge. Menger's discursive analysis of an emergent convention has proved to be difficult to replicate in a computer model, at least without drastic simplification.

Menger's account of money involves a coordination game. In any such game each player has an incentive to follow the strategy chosen by others. Mutual benefits come from doing the same thing, just as communication is improved if we speak the same language. Often there can be multiple coordination equilibria. In a coordination game equilibrium, "not only does no player have any incentive to change his behavior, given the behavior of other players, but no player wishes that any other player would change either" (Schotter 1981, 22). Consequently, coordination equilibria can be self-policing and stable. For example, with language we have incentives to use, spell, and pronounce words in a way that conforms as closely as possible to the prevailing norm (Quine 1960). There are also obvious incentives (apart from avoiding legal sanctions) to stop at red traffic lights and to drive on the same side of the road as others.

Other game forms, such as the prisoner's dilemma, are different. At least in the one-shot version of the prisoner's dilemma, the incentives are not to cooperate with the other players. Once we leave the world of coordination games, self-regarding preferences are often insufficient to establish acceptable conventions. Viktor Vanberg (1994, 65) has rightly pointed out that writers in the spontaneous order tradition—from Hume and Smith through Menger to Hayek—inadequately appreciated the additional mechanisms that are required for enforcement in noncoordination games.

Many game-theoretic models of the spontaneous emergence of institutions depend on coordination games or rely on more complex mechanisms—such as the reputation of a group—to ensure that most individuals have incentives to comply with the institutional rules. But, as noted in preceding chapters, many of these mechanisms break down in complex or uncertain circumstances, especially when large numbers of actors are involved.

The causal processes identified in a heuristic model must be able to survive realistic refinements that make the model more useful for understanding reality. Returning to Menger's model, some obvious realistic modifications violate its character as a pure coordination game. Menger (1892, 255) originally assumed that everyone would recognize the emerging monetary unit and accept its value because precious metals are "easily controlled as to their quality and weight." This assumed away the possibility of undetected quality variation in the emerging monetary units and the possibilities of debasement or forgery. Without assurances and guarantees of quality, the purity and value of the emerging monetary unit may be doubted. Some actors may notice a frequently exchanged commodity but regard its quality as unreliable and avoid it as a medium of exchange.

In his later article on "Geld," Menger acknowledged that the problem of potential quality variation could be so serious that the state had to play a role. Menger (1909/1936, 42) thus wrote: "Only the state has the power to protect effectively the coins and other means of exchange which are circulated, against the issue of false coins, illegal reductions of weight and other violations that impede trade." After making the obvious and simple modification of potential quality variation, the former coordination equilibria can be undermined; in a world of imperfect information, selfish agents have incentives to forge or debase the currency. Consequently, Menger had to bring in the state. Money was no longer a spontaneous order.

Another problem is that Menger considered the emergence of money as a medium of exchange but not as a unit of account. Units of measurement do not fall from the sky (Grierson 1977). If something emerges as a medium of exchange, then a shared system of weights and measures is required. This might evolve spontaneously, but there must be some system of checking and enforcing these weights and measures, to avoid cheating. It is difficult to see this as a coordination game, with a spontaneous solution. A powerful enforcement agency of some kind seems necessary.

Menger's model of spontaneous emergence seems vulnerable to even slight improvements in its realisticness. It works in a highly simplified world where the elements that do not take the form of a coordination game are assumed away. This criticism is more devastating than the matter of historical evidence alone.

Once again it is useful to distinguish between explanations of origin and explanations of persistence. Menger's theory is weak as an explanation of origin. It is difficult to see how the difficulties of quality variation, enforcement of units of measure, and the associated threats of forgery or debasement can be overcome at the start. Although there are strong network advantages in overcoming the cost of barter by using money, these benefits are positively correlated with the extent of use of the emerging medium of exchange. But the threats of forgery and debasement are also there right at the start, when the network benefits are small. It is difficult to see how these barriers can be overcome spontaneously.[3]

3. Note Aviram's (2004) similar critique of the spontaneous emergence of private legal systems.

Historical evidence does have some bearing at this point. Given the theoretical difficulties involved in Menger's account of the emergence of money, the lack of any historical evidence of such a process provides some empirical confirmation of the theoretical critique. If such evidence were to be found, it would be important to examine more closely how the impediments were overcome. But there is none.

Nevertheless, Menger's account retains some value as an incomplete explanation of persistence. Once viable money becomes established and forgery and debasement are minimized, then people do not use money simply because it is required legal tender. They also use it because it is convenient for them to do so. Money is sustained both by state legislation and by mutual convenience.

Consequently, Menger's analysis of money retains some elements of qualified validity. To some degree, money is sustained by self-interest and convenience. This is *part* of its essence. But it is not and cannot be spontaneous (if spontaneity by definition implies the absence of involvement by the state or another powerful institution). On the contrary, such involvement is always necessary for the creation and sustenance of a monetary system.

Supporters of the state theory of money and advocates of its essential spontaneity must avoid talking past each other. Pure and exclusive formulations are mistaken. Some writing in this area is more nuanced. In his *State Theory of Money*, Georg Knapp (1924, 1) was right to declare: "Money is a creature of law." This did not mean that self-organizing and customary mechanisms were ignored.[4] Although Menger's theory of money is flawed, it would be wrong to overlook self-organizing processes in institutional evolution. To understand how economies and societies function, it is necessary to appreciate the actual processes of self-organization that typically supplement (but do not displace) state or other organizational decrees.[5]

The involvement of the state (or some other powerful institution) is crucial because money is not simply a medium of exchange but a unit of

---

4. Knapp (1924, 3) saw the evolution of money in part as "custom gradually recognised by law," thereby acknowledging the preexistence of some customary arrangements. But this insight was underdeveloped.

5. The existence and role of self-organization was given insufficient emphasis by original institutionalists such as Commons (1924, 1934, 1950). See Hodgson (2004, 301–8) for a critical discussion.

account and the integrity and measure of that unit has to be sustained by political power. Even if some thing or substance had previously emerged as money, some choice and enforcement of its units of measure would be necessary. As John Maynard Keynes (1930, 4) argued clearly, the state has historically helped enforce contracts and imposed the money unit of account by which they are settled. Money is something that will settle a legal contractual obligation. The state both enforces the laws of contract and decides what counts as money. The state may also "vary its declaration from time to time" when deemed necessary. "This right is claimed by all modern States and has been claimed for some four thousand years at least." Paul Davidson (1972, 147–48) similarly emphasized that the state claims "the right to define what is the unit of account and what thing should answer that definition." State power helps sustain the unit of account and the viability of the monetary system.[6]

But this does not mean that money is exclusively a state phenomenon. It is also bolstered by mutual convenience. Shared understandings of its role and value help establish it as a shared intersubjective convention (Searle 1995, 2005). The state alone cannot prop up money. Like several other major institutions in the capitalist firmament, it is unavoidably a combination of private and state arrangements within a legal framework. Money is neither spontaneous nor a sole creation of the state. It too has an essential hybridity.

6.2. A Very Brief History of Money

There is no evidence of a society that relied extensively on barter or of the evolution of money from a barter economy (Einzig 1966; Dalton 1982; Davies 1994; Aglietta and Orléan 1998; Ingham 2004; Graeber 2011). The anthropologist Caroline Humphrey (1985, 48) wrote: "No ex-

---

6. Clearly, this has implications for the Eurozone countries, which after 2008 began to accept that a common currency was impossible without political integration. On the flawed design of the original Euro system, see Spethmann and Steiger (2004). What about the Bitcoin, launched in 2009 as a virtual international currency? It uses an open-source cryptographic protocol that is independent of any central authority and has attracted libertarian thinkers (Brito and Castillo 2013). But it seems unable to displace national currencies. It is not a stable unit of account. It has suffered from an extremely volatile exchange rate, highly constrained supply, excessive risk of loss, computer glitches, and minimal use in trade.

ample of a barter economy, pure and simple, has ever been described, let alone the emergence from it of money; all available ethnography suggests that there never has been such a thing."

Trade in some form has existed for tens of thousands of years. Early trade was between groups of people who met each other sporadically. Transactions were often too infrequent for a common medium of exchange to be established. Exceptional cases included the cacao money of pre-Hispanic Mesoamerica and the salt money in Ethiopia (Einzig 1966, 123–26; Graeber 2011, 75).

After the Agricultural Revolution, grain and cattle became symbols of wealth and standards of value (Grierson 1977; Peacock 2006). Early units of account included the shekel, from Mesopotamia ca. 3000 BC. A shekel was a weight of barley. Bronze shekel tokens were minted, but their principal use was for religious fertility rituals. The term *pecuniary* has the Latin root *pecus*, meaning "livestock." The term *capital* derives from the Latin *capitalis*, meaning "of the head": it referred to head counts of cattle. Cattle still endure as a principal manifestation of wealth in many agricultural communities in the developing world.

Philip Grierson (1977) claimed that "social currency" long precedes commercial currency. Examples include the *wergild*: the paying of compensation for murder, injury, or theft. Grierson argued that *wergeld*-like payments have an early origin and are found in many other tribal cultures in addition to the Germanic. Such noncommercial money served as a measure of value and unit of account. Crucially, *wergeld* presupposes a system of law and perceptions of just authority.

Money of account emerged long before coins or token money. Clay accounting records from the temples and palaces of Mesopotamia as early as 3200 BC show an abstract money of account. These institutions maintained systems of weight and measurement and kept accounts of debt, including interest owed. The temple functioned as a bank, keeper of records, and state overseer (Davies 1994; Hudson and Van De Mieroop 2002; Hudson 2004; Hudson and Wunsch 2004; Graeber 2011). Credit and debt preceded coinage.

Documents from the Shang dynasty in China ca. 1380 BC mention the use of cowrie shells as money. They may have been in use much earlier. The Maldive Islands became the main source of supply of cowries, which were eventually shipped to India, China, and Africa. Spades, hoes, adzes, and knives were also used as media of exchange. Some scholars date the first Chinese minted coins (using base metals) as early as the twelfth century BC. Although there were hundreds of mints, the state supervised the issue of coinage and imposed uniformity of standards.

In the Middle East the state controlled the issue of early money. Around 2200 BC, in Cappadocia in Central Anatolia, the state supervised the purity and weight of silver ingots, thus enabling their use as money. According to Herodotus, in the seventh century BC the Lydians of Western Anatolia introduced gold and silver coins (and retail shops in permanent locations). The state quickly stepped in to control their issue. Coins appeared separately in India around the same time.

The great innovation of coinage spread rapidly east into the Persian Empire and west through the Aegean to mainland Greece and then to Greek colonies in the Mediterranean. The use of coins spread north to the Black Sea and south to Egypt. The manufacture and use of coins generally involved state supervision. As Mark Peacock (2006, 642) noted: "The state's role in the development of coinage is undisputed. . . . Coinage was not an endogenous development of the economic sphere . . . nor was it created merely in order to facilitate trade which had existed thousands of years before money."

State-minted coins were used to pay soldiers and then retrieved by requiring that taxes should be paid in the currency (Hopkins 1978; Forstater 2006; Graeber 2011). State taxation helped monetize the entire economy. As James Tobin and Steven Golub (1998, 27) put it: "By its willingness to accept a designated asset in settlement of taxes and other obligations, the government makes that asset acceptable to any who have such obligations, and in turn to others who have obligations to them."

There were also legal requirements to pay penalties or fines for injuries and other crimes in money. Eventually, systems of representative money evolved. Gold and silver merchants issued receipts to depositors that could be used to retrieve the metallic money at a later date. In time these receipts themselves became widely accepted as a means of payment and were themselves used as money.

The Chinese developed paper money from the seventh century AD, when banks issued promissory notes to depositors. Problems had arisen with the transportation of money (typically minted in copper rather than precious metals) for payments between remote locations. In the eighth century, during the Tang dynasty, Chinese merchants started using promissory notes or bills of exchange.[7] These were called *feitsyan* (flying money) and used for the safe transfer of money over long distances. The state licensed particular classes of merchant to issue *feitsyan*, and local officials received a commission for their registration. In the ninth century, the issue of *feitsyan* was placed under state control (Moshenskyi 2008, 50–52). In the tenth century, the Song dynasty, short of copper for its coins, issued the first generally circulating notes.

It is probable that bills of exchange or promissory notes spread from China to the West principally by means of Muslim traders, from the tenth to the thirteenth centuries, by land along the Silk Road and by sea via the coastal mercantile ports. Arab merchants used bills of exchange called *suftadja* and *hawala*, and these became widely established in the Middle East. The idea spread to Italy in the twelfth century and was developed systematically there from the thirteenth to the fifteenth centuries. By the sixteenth century the issue of bills of exchange or promissory notes was common practice in England.

Around that time the word *capital* appeared in English. Long separated from its bovine origins, it then signified a monetary representation of wealth and a purchasing power that transcended the intrinsic features of any particular commodity. The subsequent perversion of this term by economists and sociologists is discussed in the next chapter.

In 1661 banknotes were first issued in Europe by the Stockholms Banco, a predecessor of the Bank of Sweden. The use of banknotes, which were nominally convertible to an amount of gold, then spread through Europe.[8]

---

7. Some scholars claimed that bills of exchange had developed in ancient Rome, using writings by Cicero as evidence. But Story (1843, 7) countered: "It may be doubtful whether the contract here spoken of is that of modern Bills of Exchange. It may be said more nearly to resemble a contract for the exchange of moneys in different places, or a mandate to advance money to be repaid in another place. Certain it is, that the peculiar distinguishing quality of Bills of Exchange in modern times, their negotiable character, does not appear to have been known to the ancients, or to have found its way into the general transactions of their commercial intercourse." This issue remains controversial among historians.

8. In the United Kingdom it was not until the nineteenth century—with the Banking Acts of 1826, 1833, and 1844—that the ability of other private banks to issue their own notes was limited, thus forcing the circulation of Bank of England notes backed by gold as legal tender. In Germany banknotes did not become legal tender until 1910.

6.3. The Evolution of Capitalist Finance

Money is used for the settlement of contractual obligations. In a monetary economy, as Keynes (1930) indicated in one of this chapter's epigraphs, it is a legal requirement that contracts involving purchases are discharged through the payment of money. As the real world is never in a general equilibrium where all contracts are completed, a monetary economy necessarily implies debt. Debt is money's alter ego. Monetary economies function through the ongoing creation and discharge of debt.

In popular discourse, debt is a bad thing, to be eliminated for sound finance. On the contrary, debt is one of the driving forces of capitalist expansion. The evolution of complex financial systems based on debt played a vital role in the takeoff of capitalism in the eighteenth century. Debt is simultaneously a source of capitalism's dynamism and of its potential instability. Capitalism involves a Faustian bargain: to obtain wealth we must sanctify the sin of debt.[9]

How did financial systems based on debt evolve? In China, over a thousand years ago, the issue of bills of exchange or promissory notes was quickly regulated by the state. This regulation happened more slowly elsewhere, principally because much trade was conducted over regions under multiple sovereign authorities. In Europe the development of private banking systems followed the involvement of the state in borrowing and lending, which in turn depended on the establishment of the state itself as a singular legal entity.

Public debt first appeared in the state of Venice in the twelfth century (Hamilton 1947). By the early fourteenth century, banks and negotiable instruments such as bills of exchange were used in Venice, Florence, and elsewhere. Originally, the banks took deposits and kept 100 percent in reserve, but eventually it was realized that more could be lent on the security of these deposits and that the reserve ratio could be reduced. The expansion of lending (including to foreign governments) was curtailed in 1345 when King Edward III of England repudiated his debts. This led to catastrophic Italian bank failures. Then Italy was struck by the Black Death. Governments eventually tried to regulate the Italian banks, including requiring official licenses to operate with fractional reserves of gold. But these measures were often ineffective and undermined by cor-

9. In Sanskrit, Hebrew, and Aramaic, the same word is used to mean "debt," "guilt," and "sin" (Einzig 1966; Graeber 2011).

ruption: politicians and administrators were themselves major investors (Usher 1943).

Nevertheless, Italy prospered during the fourteenth century and the Renaissance. But it had limited access to the new Atlantic trade routes that were opened by Spain and Portugal after 1492. Ruinous wars from 1521 to 1544 on Italian territory led to economic decline. The growing power of the Ottoman Empire devastated Italy's Mediterranean trade. In 1512 the Ottoman Empire started a massive territorial expansion: by 1566 it had captured most of the eastern and southern Mediterranean coastlines. These internal and external forces brought Italian capitalist leadership to an end.

In the seventeenth century the Netherlands developed a relatively sophisticated system of public and private finance. The state was able to raise a steady supply of funds through taxation, on the basis of which the government was able to borrow. Credit was available but controlled. For over 150 years after its foundation in 1609, the Bank of Amsterdam maintained roughly a 100 percent reserve ratio on loans (Huerta de Soto 2009, 99). It also minimized state-induced deterioration of money by using bills based on the real rather than the nominal value of the precious metal in coins. With state and private support, the Dutch developed a range of innovative institutional devices for investment in trade, industry, and infrastructure. Among these were public bonds, issued by governments on national, provincial, and municipal levels, and shares in publicly traded companies such as the Dutch East India Company. Financial markets, including the Amsterdam stock exchange, facilitated investment. Stock markets permitted smaller fractional shareholdings in mercantile and manufacturing enterprises. During the seventeenth century about half of all oceangoing vessels worldwide were from the Netherlands. Taking the baton from Italy, this tiny country dominated the international capital market until successive political crises of the eighteenth century led to the collapse of the Dutch Republic in 1795 (Israel 1989; de Vries and van der Woude 1997).

Britain's Glorious Revolution of 1688 was in fact a Dutch invasion, albeit preceded by an invitation from a bishop and six members of the nobility. Once victory was certain, it received widespread popular support. The invading army of William of Orange involved 500 ships, 20,000 trained soldiers, and 20,000 mariners and support staff; it was similar in scale to the ill-fated Spanish Armada of a century earlier. This invasion shifted English allegiances from France to the Netherlands and led

to an influx of Dutch merchants and financiers as well as artists and scientists (Jardine 2008). Dutch businessmen brought knowledge of Dutch
financial institutions and helped establish London as the world's leading financial center. Among Dutch innovations in public finance was the
systematic dedication of revenues to the service and amortization of the
public debt. In the decades after 1688 the institutional infrastructure of
British finance was revolutionized.

Douglass C. North and Barry R. Weingast (1989) claimed that 1688
was a decisive moment involving a constitutional incorporation of
countervailing power. But they exaggerated the scale of constitutional
change. It was more a change in the balance of power than a rewriting of
the rules (Pincus 2009). Stephen R. Epstein (2000, 211) argued that the
constitutional restrictions on the power of the monarch were less significant than England's "belated catch up" with continental Europe's most
developed financial systems: "the result of the country's financial revolution rather than a revolution in political freedom and rights." The new
financial practices transplanted from the Netherlands were crucial (see
Powell 1915; Bagehot 1873/1919; Dickson 1967; Kindleberger 1984; Neal
1990; Roseveare 1991; and Wennerlind 2011).

Financed by London merchants, the Bank of England was formed in
1694. It issued loans to the royal treasury at 8 percent interest, the payments of which were in turn funded by taxes and custom duties. For the
Bank of England these royal debts were its monetary assets, which in
turn were buttressed by a renewed public faith in sovereign integrity.
These assets became the basis of a further massive loan issue by the
bank. Market information became more available. By 1698, stock price
quotes were regularly published in London (Morgan and Thomas 1962).
Also after 1688 "came a flurry of joint-stock company formations": "By
1695 100 new companies had been formed with a capital of £4.5 million
in all" (Kindleberger 1984, 196). During the 1690s there were several innovations in domestic financial institutions (Murphy 2009). The state
also played a role in stimulating corporate activity overseas. The crown
organized groups of creditors into companies, including the New East
India Company (1698), the United East India Company (1708), and the
South Sea Company (1708).

Gregory Clark (2007) and others are right to point out that 1688
marked no revolution in the security of legal property rights. Also, there
was no sudden fall in interest rates (Clark 2007, 149, 241–42). But the Financial Revolution was a protracted affair, lasting decades. It involved

several legislative steps and the development of new organizational structures and business habits. Taking a longer view, from 1693 to 1739, long-term interest rates fell from 14 to 3 percent (North and Weingast 1989, 824). Just thirty years later, the Industrial Revolution was visibly under way, with the beginnings of canal construction and major innovations in textile and iron production.

Much of the impetus for the heavy involvement of the state in the development of the British financial system in the eighteenth century was the need to finance wars abroad (Mann 1986, 485–86; Bowen 1995, 5). Because of its new international alliances and enemies, England was plunged into a long period of war, requiring major reform of its fiscal and administrative arrangements. The Nine Years' War (1688–97) was quickly followed by the long War of Spanish Succession (1701–13). Both the invasion of 1688 and subsequent international conflict led to major transformations of the state apparatus, including the Act of Union with Scotland in 1707. As Henry G. Roseveare (1991, 4) pointed out, accompanying the political and fiscal changes after 1688 there was "an administrative revolution—or, at least, a striking growth in the power and effectiveness of the state which manifested itself not merely in war but in the subtler tasks of peace." War was the midwife of capitalist finance.

After considering the evolution of finance in Italy, the Netherlands, and England, Geoffrey Ingham (2008, 70) concluded: "The capitalist monetary system developed from the integration of private networks of mercantile trade credit-money with public currency—that is, state money." For Ingham (and others), crucial to this system was the role of debt: "Capitalism is distinctive in that it contains a social mechanism by which privately contracted debtor-creditor relations . . . are routinely monetized" (74).

Crucial was the emergence of institutions making debt itself salable or "negotiable." A promise to pay could then be sold to another, who would then take on the legal obligation of payment. Promissory notes were first developed in China in the seventh century. An early market for debts was the French *courratier de change* in the twelfth century; it managed and regulated the debts of agricultural communities on behalf of the banks. Some Italian city-states issued tradable bonds from the twelfth century. Negotiable instruments or bills of exchange— amounting to the sale of individual debt—were used in Italy as early as the fourteenth century and in the Netherlands by the sixteenth century, although their legal basis was then underdeveloped (de Vries and van der Woude 1997). Negotiable instruments have precedents in England going back to the Jewish bankers of the twelfth and thirteenth centuries and subsequently to the *lex mercatoria* or "law merchant" courts. But again the legal underpinnings were incomplete.

The key problem is effective legal enforceability. For general negotiability, the transfer of obligations also had to be recognized and enforced by the legal system. Contracts ordinarily involve legal obligations to deliver goods or services in exchange for money. Exchanges of promissory notes involve instead the purchase of a promise, and originally this was not recognized as a valid contract in law: the selling of debt was not sanctioned by legal recognition of the transfer of the obligation to its purchaser. Major legislative changes were necessary to make this possible.

In the seventeenth century, commercial cases shifted from the law merchant courts to common law courts (Baker 1979; Berman 1983). But their "blundering attempts" (Beutel 1938, 840) to deal with the negotiability of debt led businessmen to press Parliament for robust legislation. John R. Commons (1934, 392) wrote: "It required the entire Seventeenth Century for lawyers to complete the invention of the negotiability of debts." In fact it took several more years to complete. In 1704, during the reign of William's successor, Queen Anne, Parliament passed "An Act for giving like Remedy upon Promissory Notes, as is now used upon Bills of Exchange, and for the better Payment of Inland Bills of Exchange." Significant further legislation, including another act as late as 1758, was required to consolidate negotiability (Beutel 1938; Lawrence 2002).[10] Once negotiability was established, the capitalist genie was out of the bottle. As Henry Dunning MacLeod (1872, 481) wrote: "If we were asked—Who made the discovery which has most deeply affected the fortunes of the human race? We think, after full consideration, we might safely answer—The man who first discovered that a Debt is a Saleable Commodity."[11]

10. This statute of Queen Anne did not apply automatically to the British colonies. Some of the American states adopted it, while others did not (Beutel 1940). Some states repealed all British statutes after the American Revolution and had to start from scratch, while others adopted them selectively. This lack of uniformity in US negotiability law remained until the nationwide Uniform Negotiable Instruments Act of 1896.

11. MacLeod (1858, 476–78) coined the term *Gresham's Law*. Mitchell Innes (1914, 9) credited him as the originator of the state theory of money. Commons (1934, 394) described him as "the first lawyer-economist." Schumpeter (1954, 718) judged him the only contemporary of Marx to make a systematic advance toward a credit theory of money

The use of this "discovery" required firm legal foundations and consolidation through more than one act of Parliament. But eventually, through these means, the capitalist financial system empowered economic development on a massive scale.

Capitalist finance involves a complex web of contractual obligations. Commercial banks since the fourteenth century have increasingly operated on a fractional reserve system, keeping only a fraction of their deposits in reserve as cash or gold. Fractional-reserve banking has a cumulative effect on money creation by commercial banks as it expands the money supply beyond the scale of the deposits alone. Any debt is funded by current assets or by claims owed by a third party. The purchaser of debt receives the right to an asset that itself can be used as collateral to borrow. Credit money thus feeds on itself. Commercial bank money is created endogenously (Moore 1988). But this all depends on a legal structure of enforceability, a fractional reserve system backed by private and state assurances, and sufficient confidence that debt can be redeemed. Once legal institutions supporting collateralizable property, credit money, and the sale of debt were in place, a new dynamic was unleashed.

The use of money loans to fund investment made the rate of interest crucial. Entrepreneurs with access to funds were driven by the requirement that they pay interest on loans. The need to generate a surplus over interest payments became one of the drivers of capitalist accumulation (Heinsohn and Steiger 2013, 114–15).

The whole system of credit money depends on general confidence in the future value of assets. Once this is questioned, there can be a cumulative downturn, where pessimism becomes a self-fulfilling prophecy. Defaults then have cascading negative effects. Commercial banks then become threatened by the possibility that withdrawals will exceed their fractional reserve of cash assets. A crucial institutional innovation in this regard has been the creation of national central banks. As we know from the events leading to the 2008 crash, central banks have not always been alert to the problem of excessive credit expansion, but they can be an ef-

---

(Skaggs 1997). But Marx (1978, 305) was much less complimentary: he described MacLeod as viewing "everything from the unutterably narrow standpoint of a bank clerk." Marx dismissed thinkers who regarded abstract or token money as substantive rather than epiphenomenal. Marx himself viewed money from the "narrow standpoint" of a material substance.

fective restraining force. They can intervene to stop a domino collapse of private banks. Overall, the credit-money system became more viable and empowering when it was integrated with state money and debt in politically secure states that embodied safeguards against unwarranted confiscation by governments.

If a government mismanages its economy, international markets can destabilize its currency and asset values. Trading relations with other nations can help discipline governments. Sovereign states collect revenues and pay their debts within jurisdictions where their money is legal tender. This has been an issue for centuries: medieval trade in Europe often led to the currency of one country being used for payments in another. Because of their mutual involvement in international trade, countries have to establish reputations for sound finance by keeping their debt under some control. Relations between different national economies are a major factor in the evolution of financial systems.

Different strands of the large and controversial literature on money stress the endogenous creation of money, the importance of credit, or the role of the state. It is neither possible nor necessary to review this literature here (see Mitchell Innes 1914; Knapp 1924; Keynes 1930; Lerner 1947; Schumpeter 1954; Davidson 1972; Moore 1988; Wray 1990, 1998, 2000, 2004, 2012; Lavoie 1992; Goodhart 1998; Mehrling 2000; Smithin 2000; Bell 2001; Rochon and Vernengo 2003; Ingham 2004; and Heinsohn and Steiger 2013). There are notable attempts to integrate the state, credit, and endogenous money approaches (Mitchell Innes 1914; Goodhart 1998; Wray 2000, 2004, 2012). A successful synthetic view must acknowledge that modern monetary systems require state authority and a state lender of last resort and also that money is debt, which can be created by private banks.

6.4. The Ontology of Money

Economists have had difficulty dealing with money and its relation with credit and debt. Adam Smith, David Ricardo, and Karl Marx adopted a substance view of money. Wealth meant the accumulation of things. They saw the economy as a physical system, orchestrated by human agents. The economy was a machine, involving mass and energy. Force (labor) transformed mass (things) and created value. Economics was inspired by the Newtonian vision of science and its uncovering of the laws of the physical world.

Such a physicalist social ontology has difficulty understanding money other than as a mass to be created or molded through labor and then moved and exchanged like other goods. With their substance view of money, Smith, Ricardo, and Marx treated notes and token coins as money only insofar as they were exchangeable for and represented a precious substance such as gold or silver. This shortcoming is illustrated dramatically in Marx's works.[12] Writing in 1859, Marx (1971, 64) declared: "The principal difficulty in the analysis of money is surmounted as soon as it is understood that the commodity is the origin of money. . . . [We] are only concerned with those forms of money which arise directly from the exchange of commodities, but not with forms of money, such as credit money, which belong to a higher stage of production. For the sake of simplicity gold is assumed throughout to be the money commodity."

Marx (1976, 125–26) saw a commodity as an "external object, a thing," or a "physical body." So *money commodity* referred to a material substance, such as gold. For Marx, credit money was not money as such, except insofar as it was a claim on gold or on other intrinsically valuable physical assets serving as money. But historically it is untrue that "the commodity is the origin of money" because money of account preceded any material money. Marx analyzed capitalism on the assumption that all money was gold. He downplayed the role of credit and rarely discussed it at length. In the second volume of *Capital*, Marx (1978, 192) again made the mistake of regarding credit as unimportant in the early phases of capitalist development: "Credit money played no role, or at least not a significant one, in the early period of capitalist production." On the contrary, the development of credit was crucial for early capitalism. His suggestion that credit belongs to "a higher stage" of capitalism, and hence is not part of the essence of the system, is unsubstantiated.

In the second volume of *Capital*, Marx (1978, 420–21) observed that, unlike gold and silver, credit has much lower costs of production and can alleviate the problem of producing more precious metal for circulation as capitalism expands. He continued: "This . . . disposes of the pointless

---

12. Some Marxists attempted to rescue Marx's theory of money in various ways. For a critical overview, see Dymski (1990, 2006), which stressed the divergent strands within Marx's own theory. See also de Brunhoff (1976).

question of whether capitalist production on its present scale would be possible without credit . . . i.e. with merely metallic circulation. It would clearly not be possible. It would come up against the limited scale of precious-metal production. On the other hand, we should not get any mystical ideas about the productive power of the credit system, just because this makes money capital available or fluid."

Here, Marx accepted that credit money had become vital for capitalism, at least by the nineteenth century, and that credit can help "increase capitalist wealth." But he then warned against "mystical ideas about the productive power of the credit system." There is not much more discussion of credit in the entire second volume.

Marx devoted more space to credit money in the third volume of *Capital*. But again his treatment was equivocal. Much of chapter 27 is devoted to the outcomes of credit, such as heightened speculation and the facilitation of larger joint-stock companies. But again he was reluctant to give credit its full due. In chapter 25, "Credit and Fictitious Capital," Marx (1981, 525) opened with the following words: "It lies outside the scope of our plans to give detailed analysis of the credit system and the instruments this creates (credit money, etc.). Only a few points will be emphasized here, which are necessary to characterize the capitalist mode of production in general. On this connection, we shall simply be dealing with commercial and bank credit. The connection between the development of this and the development of state credit remains outside our discussion."

Marx treated the credit system and credit money as "fictitious" and mostly outside his general analysis of the capitalist system. The role of state credit was also sidelined. On the contrary, the development of credit institutions—aided by the state—helps explain the beginnings of the growth of capitalism in the eighteenth century. Impaired by his labor-substance view of value and by his prevailing view of the economy as an ensemble of relations between agents and physical objects, Marx was unable to appreciate the institutional nature of the monetary system.

The metaphors are illuminating. Smith (1776/1976b, 289, 292, 296) saw money as "the great wheel of circulation" in the machine. Marx treated paper and credit money as shadows or representations of some produced and precious substance. Some modern economics textbooks depict money as a lubricant of a machine (Mundell 1968, 178; Samuelson and Nordhaus 2009, 40).

Crude physicalist conceptions of the economy endured after the classical and Marxist visions were abandoned. They were reinforced by further wholesale borrowings of ideas from physics. William Stanley Jevons, Francis Edgeworth, Irving Fisher, Vilfredo Pareto, and other neoclassical economists openly embraced mechanical analogies and formalisms (Mirowski 1989; Hodgson 2012, 2013a).[13] Fisher (1892, 85) even drew up a table of "mechanical analogies" where a "particle" in mechanics "corresponds to" an "individual" in economics, "Space" "corresponds to" "Commodity," "Force" to "Marginal utility or disutility," "Work" to "Disutility," and "Energy" to "Utility." Social classes disappeared; labor was no longer the sole driving force. Instead of classes there were individuals, but there still was a machine.[14]

Against the prevailing current, Thorstein Veblen (1908a, 117) insisted that money was related to debt. Capitalized wealth consisted of "negotiable securities" based on intangible as well as intangible assets. These "become a basis of credit extensions, serving to increase the aggregate claims of creditors beyond what the hypothecable material wealth of the debtors would satisfy." He noted the consequent "failure of classical theory to give an intelligent account of credit and crises." Abandoning a substance-based view of money, Veblen (1904) developed a speculation- and debt-based theory of capitalist instability and crises that was a prefiguration of the analysis of John Maynard Keynes in the *General Theory* (Vining 1939; Raines and Leathers 1996).[15]

13. Although Veblen (1900) introduced the term *neoclassical*, his usage was imprecise. Later, with Samuelson (1948), it became associated with a school of thought characterized by the utility-maximizing agents, equilibrium, and limited recognition of information problems. This school had partial equilibrium (Marshallian) and general equilibrium (Walrasian) variants and dominated economics from the 1870s to the 1990s. Lawson (2013) sidelined Samuelson's influential usage. Other writers defined neoclassical economics as a free market policy stance, despite the fact that many leading neoclassical economists (in Samuelson's sense) have been against unlimited markets.

14. Marshall is a partial exception. Instead of from the idea of a machine, his ontology drew from the evolutionism of Herbert Spencer (Moss 1990; Hodgson 1993, 2013a). The German historical and American institutionalist traditions in economics also contain reactions against reigning mechanistic views. Schäffle (1875–81) extensively developed the conception of the socioeconomic system as an organism, but his work has been forgotten. Veblen emphasized the irreducibility of pecuniary to physical phenomena, but the limitations of his conception are discussed in later chapters and in Camic and Hodgson (2011, 30–32). Commons (1924, 1934) rightly emphasized the evolution of laws and other rules but failed to provide an adequate alternative ontology (Hodgson 2004).

15. But Veblen's view of the production process remained deficient, partly because he saw production as separable from pecuniary and other incentives. See chapter 11 below.

To place money in its proper place it is necessary to abandon the physicalist ontologies that have dominated economics since the eighteenth century. It is valid but insufficient to claim that money is a social relation. Social relations and structures are ubiquitous in all socioeconomic systems. But, unless sufficient attention is paid to shared understandings and meanings, such a view can be sidelined into an agent-object view of assets and money, with a mapping between the set of physical entities and forces, on the one hand, and the set of owners, on the other. The change of ontology has to be more profound: intersubjective understandings must also be treated as fundamental.

Money cannot be understood without the concept of property, which in turn requires an ontology where legal rights and obligations are treated as basic and powerful rather than ideological or epiphenomenal. The whole system of money exchange and a fortiori the phenomena of credit money and negotiable debt depend on the possibility of legally transferable and enforceable abstract rights.[16] Money is legally enabled abstract credit rather than a material thing. It involves social relations of credit and debt, which are themselves constituted by the legal system.

An emerging rival to the physicalist view is an ontology of rules and rule systems. The emerging ontological fundamentals involve institutional structures and algorithmic learning processes involving programs or systems of rules. As Kurt Dopfer, John Foster, and Jason Potts (2004, 263) put it: "The central insight is that an economic system is a population of rules, a structure of rules, and a process of rules" (see also Arthur 2006; Dopfer 2004; Dopfer and Potts 2008; Hodgson 1997, 2004, 2007a; Hodgson and Knudsen 2004; Ostrom 2005; Parra 2005; Potts 2000; and Vanberg 2002, 2004).

John Searle's (1995, 2005) ontology of institutions in general, and money in particular, fits into this rule-based approach. For him, the mental representation of an institution is partly constitutive of that institution since an institution can exist only if people have the necessary beliefs and mental attitudes. Searle (1995, 40) elaborated: "But the truly radical break with other forms of life comes when humans, through collective intentionality, impose functions on phenomena where the function cannot be achieved solely in virtue of physics and chemistry but requires continued human cooperation in the specific forms of recogni-

---

16. This point was emphasized by the nearly forgotten "first lawyer-economist," MacLeod (1872, 1878).

tion, acceptance, and acknowledgement of a new *status* to which a *function* is assigned. This is the beginning point of all institutional forms of human culture, and must always have the structure X counts as Y in C."

The X counts as Y under conditions C formulation is a constitutive social rule that ostensibly can apply to money as well as to other institutions. Searle (1995, 46) explained: "Collective intentionality assigns a new status to some phenomenon, where that status has an accompanying function that cannot be performed solely in virtue of the intrinsic physical features of the phenomenon in question. This assignment creates a new fact, an institutional fact, a new fact created by human agreement." This agreement establishes the "X counts as Y in C" rule: "The 'counts as' locution is crucial in this formula because since the function in question cannot be performed solely in virtue of the physical features of the X element, it requires our agreement or acceptance that it be performed."

Searle was concerned with "the creation of institutional facts" (1995, 47) rather than explanations of persistence. He continued: "Where the imposition of status function according to the formula becomes a matter of general policy, the formula acquires a normative status. This is shown by the fact that the general rule creates the possibility of abuses that could not exist without the rule, such as counterfeit money" (48).

For Searle (1995, 127): "The structure of human institutions is a structure of constitutive rules."[17] His ontology is based on mutually understood information and rules. He pointed out: "Institutions are not worn out by continued use, but each use of the institution is in a sense a renewal of that institution" (57). Institutional strength is not scarce in the way that physical resources are scarce. Institutions often defy physical laws of conservation, as of energy or matter. Hence, through the sale of debt and further borrowing, additional money can be created "out of nothing" (Schumpeter 1934, 73), except for legally buttressed agreements involving property as collateral.

But Searle was more concerned with the ontological fundamentals

---

17. For Searle (1995, 7), an intention need not be conscious, but it must potentially be so. For him, "intentionality" was "that feature of representations by which they are *about* something or *directed at* something." Agreement could simply mean going along with things as they are. Searle also clarified: "People who are participating in the institutions are typically not conscious of these rules; often they have false beliefs about the nature of the institution, and even the very people who created the institution may be unaware of its structure" (127).

than with an explanation of why people come to "intend" or "agree" to the "X counts as Y in C" rules that assign status functions to entities or symbols. He assumed that this happens, somehow. For some reason he downplayed the relevant psychological concept of habit.[18] Missing too was an adequate explanation of how something becomes established as money and endures as such. He did not explain how the original convention emerged and became widely and enduringly recognized and honored.

Theories of money that embrace collective intentionality need to explain the origins of the motives behind the intention. The history and analysis of money suggest that it must be understood in part as a symbol of authority within a property-owning economy. Using money involves trust in the efficacy of political power to back money and maintain its value. As Smith suggested in one of this chapter's epigraphs, trust in money is further bolstered by perceptions of the legitimacy and just conduct of the issuing sovereign state. For money to work, it takes a sufficient number of people to respect such authority and enough others to follow their lead. Money cannot be understood without an adequate account of human motivation and supporting institutions.

6.5. Money and Capitalism: In Lieu of a Conclusion

The institutional development of finance was crucial for the takeoff of capitalism. Countervailing political powers reduced expectations of state sequestration or sovereign debt default. The growing confidence in public finances helped bolster private banks. Public and private agencies together enlarged available credit and stimulated investment. Capitalism, as the word suggests, became possible only with the emergence of money capital backed by constrained state power and collateralizable assets, including debt. These crucial changes began in England in the late sixteenth century and were consolidated in the eighteenth century. Although he did not underline the role of collateral, Joseph A. Schumpeter (1954, 78n) highlighted the importance of financial institutions: "Owing to the importance of the financial complement of capitalist production

---

18. In his development of Searle's work on institutions, Herrmann-Pillath (2012, 2013) introduced habits and proposed that rule following is grounded in acquired neural structures.

and trade, the development of the law and the practice of negotiable paper and of 'created' deposits afford perhaps the best indication we have for dating the rise of capitalism."[19]

Accordingly, this focus on these crucial institutional changes means dating the rise of capitalism in England to the eighteenth century. If we concentrate on the institutional changes of the Financial Revolution, then this precedes by a few decades the capitalist explosion as depicted in figure 1.1 above. Crucial institutional developments have now been identified that have the right historical timing.

But this does not clinch the matter. There are alternative ways of defining capitalism that might still fit the historical facts. The emphasis on finance in this chapter should not divert our attention from the technological innovations and massive expansions of productive forces that have accompanied capitalism. Just as finance has enabled these developments, expansions in production have bolstered confidence and stimulated further lending and investment.

In the eighteenth century most business activity was self-financed by retained earnings (or via borrowing from family or friends rather than from banks). British private banks were then small partnerships. Joint-stock banks did not prosper until much later.

The demand for finance is lower when transport costs or high prices limit access to markets and prevent economies of scale. The growth of the financial system was both a cause and a consequence of the successive technological and organizational revolutions after about 1780. Transport costs were greatly reduced, markets were hugely enlarged, and industry reaped massive economies of scale. In a circle of cumulative causation, finance begat industry, and industry begat finance.

The first large private financiers were the merchant banks of Baring (founded in 1762) and Rothschild (founded in 1798). They financed international trade, the Napoleonic Wars, and colonial enterprise. Partly thanks to the stimulus of war, finance grew in scale. It empowered the great expansion of British capitalism in the nineteenth century (O'Brien 1989). Productivity levels exploded as a result of technological innovations, economies of scale, and enlarged markets. The first operations

19. Schumpeter (1954, 78n) continued: "Around the Mediterranean both emerged in the course of the fourteenth century, though negotiability was not established before the sixteenth." Actually, the selling of debt and promissory notes did not receive an adequate legal foundation in Britain until the eighteenth century (Beutel 1938; Lawrence 2002).

requiring massive finance were the railways, deep coal mines, iron foundries, and shipbuilding yards.[20] There was another huge nineteenth-century expansion of banking institutions and activities in the United States.[21]

Finance is central to modern capitalism. But the capitalist financial system is vulnerable to destabilizing inflation or soaring debt. Capitalist finance depends on expectations of the future: these are inherently uncertain and prone to disturbing perceptions or rumors (Keynes 1936). Just as spiraling debt can fuel aggregate demand in a cumulative and out-of-equilibrium expansion of credit money, cumulative processes can operate in reverse with crashing demand in a slump. Hence, Hyman Minsky (1982, 1986) argued that capitalism is inherently unstable.[22]

The capitalist system of credit money has fueled a tremendous expansion of productive activity and hugely increased global average output per capita. But it has further widened inequalities of income and wealth and led to recurrent financial crises. For Keynesians, this suggests a role for the state—to regulate capitalism and try to prevent periodic financial collapse. Others disagree, but their views are often based on flawed conceptions of money and finance where the state plays no essential role.

20. From 1825 until 1850 there were more shares traded in railway companies than in all other UK companies combined (Reed 1975). The growing market for railway shares was crucial in the development of the stock market and legislation that consolidated the corporation as a legal entity (Ireland 1996).

21. In New England from 1800 there was a rapid expansion in state-level financial institutions. The number of US federal-level banks grew from 0 in 1860 to 7,518 in 1914, controlling $11.5 billion in assets (Haber 2003).

22. Reinhart and Rogoff (2009) gave eight hundred years of evidence that financial crises occur more frequently than is often believed. Minsky (1982, 1986) was more sensitive than most other economists to the legal structure of finance. For him, the stabilization of financial systems was often a matter of legislation and institutional design.

CHAPTER SEVEN

Meanings of Capital

"The question is," said Alice, "whether you can make words mean so many different things." — Lewis Carroll, *Through the Looking Glass* (1871)

It is certainly very unfortunate when a science already earnestly, even acrimoniously engaged on the solution of questions which affect society in its depths . . . is struck by a second confusion of tongues, and becomes involved in an endless wrangle as to what kind of thing it is that properly is called capital! — Eugen von Böhm-Bawerk (1890)

How complete the divorce is between the experience of daily life and the teaching of the economists can best be seen by reading, for example, Marshall's chapter on capital, with its complicated divisions into national capital, social capital, personal capital, etc. Every banker and every commercial man knows that there is only one kind of capital, and that is money. Every commercial and financial transaction is based on the truth of this proposition, every balance sheet is made out in this well-established fact. And yet every economist bases his teaching on the hypothesis that capital is not money. — Alfred Mitchell Innes (1914)

I t might reasonably be presumed that to understand capitalism we must understand *capital*. But economists have long shifted the meaning of the word and gradually widened its application. Now it no longer means very much in particular, and long ago it lost any connection with any historically specific mode of production. It has become a grand word, meaning everything and next to nothing. It has sometimes inspired ambitious empirical research programs—which have difficulties agreeing on what it is that they are trying to measure. We must consider what happened and appraise the disastrous consequences for our understanding.[1]

It would be important to explain *why* the term changed its meaning,

1. This chapter uses material from Hodgson (2014).

but that is a huge task, far beyond the scope of this chapter. As well as the changing socioeconomic context, such an account would have to examine the changes within and rivalry between the disciplines of economics and sociology. Instead, the main task of the chapter is to note some key changes and extensions of meaning and to consider their analytic implications.

The first section of this chapter locates important milestones in the historical evolution of the word *capital*. The second section addresses the broadening of the term in the notion of human capital. The third section lists some other extensions of the capital concept. The fourth section addresses social capital at length. The fifth section draws the threads together and compares the merits and demerits of different definitions.

7.1. A Brief History of the *C* Word

In the beginning, *capital* referred to head counts of cattle. But in ancient Greece and Rome the word took a broader meaning, often referring to wealth in general. But there is no need for the *c* word if the *w* word means the same. Over eight hundred years ago the word *capital* acquired a more specific meaning, one that has endured (except within economics and sociology) to this day.

Fernand Braudel (1982, 232–33) pointed out in his *Civilization and Capitalism* that the word *capitale* was in use in Italy in 1211 and is found from 1283 "in the sense of the capital assets of a trading firm." The word gradually came to mean the "*money* capital of a firm or of a merchant" and spread through Western Europe. Embryonic capitalism thus made the word its own.

A key innovation was the development of double-entry bookkeeping in Italy in the thirteenth century (Sombart 1902, 1930). This permitted a view of production and trade in terms of quantified money equivalents. There is also fourteenth-century evidence of the use of capital-discounting methods by Italian merchants (de Roover 1974). The monetary meaning of *capital* became firmly established in this mercantile and accounting context.[2]

In England in the sixteenth century the word *capital* retained its Ital-

2. Faulhaber and Baumol (1988, 583) report that some of the early methods of capital discounting were flawed. And laws against usury constrained the use of rates of interest.

ian and monetary meaning and was used by business firms in their accounting practices. Hence, in 1569 one James Peele wrote on "the art of Italian merchants accounts," described "an inventorie" of "all thinges . . . appurteyninge to trade of merchaundise," and urged a businessman to "accompte for his proper stocke or capitall" (Cannan 1921, 471). Irving Fisher (1904, 392) quoted an Italian source of 1612 that had capital as a principal advanced as a quantity of money and a French source of 1694 that referred to capital as the principal of a debt. In England in 1635 Richard Dafforne in a book on accounting instructed his readers to "booke the capitall which each partner of a joint company promiseth to bring in" (Cannan 1921, 471). The 1697 Bank of England Act of Parliament speaks of the "common" capital and "principal" stock of the company and "the said capital stock" (Cannan 1921, 473).

Fisher (1904, 393) cited English sources of 1730, 1750, and 1759 that all define capital as a sum of money advanced by a trading company or "the money which a merchant first brings into trade on his own account." According to Edwin Cannan (1921, 475), the following entry appears in 1751 in Postlethwayt's influential *Universal Dictionary of Trade and Commerce*:[3] "CAPITAL, amongst merchants, bankers, and traders, signifies the sum of money which individuals bring to make up the common stock of a partnership when it is first formed. It is also said of the stock which a merchant at first puts into trade, for his account. It signifies likewise the fund of a trading company or corporation, in which sense the word stock is generally added to it." Accordingly, from Italy from the thirteenth century to Britain in the eighteenth, the word *capital* was mostly used in the sense of the money advanced by owners or shareholders to establish a business.

But we can also find a second meaning, referring to a stock of goods or even wealth in general. Frank Fetter (1930, 187) pointed out that, in his *Dictionarie* in 1611, Randle Cotgrave defined capital as "wealth, worth; a stocke, a man's principall, or chiefe, substance." Fetter commented: "Here the idea of 'worth,' implying a valuation, is thoroughly mixed with that of substance, no doubt in the sense of material things in

---

Correct methods of capital discounting were not firmly established in Britain until the latter half of the eighteenth century.

3. Faulhaber and Baumol (1988) point out that Postlethwayt's book included authoritative tables to estimate the present value of expected future income streams using an assumed rate of interest, a calculation that to this day is referred to as *capitalization*.

possession. 'Capital' thus used is a superfluous and confusing synonym of wealth, goods and stock." But the evidence suggests that as late as the eighteenth century the monetary meaning dominated its secondary use as a "superfluous and confusing" synonym of wealth.

Then entered Adam Smith, and henceforth among economists the word *capital* decisively changed its meaning. It is not necessary here to go into all the influences on Smith, including Anne-Robert-Jacques Turgot and the Physiocrats. Inspired by the physical and natural sciences, Smith wanted to turn political economy into a rigorous discipline, where the inputs and outputs of the economic machine could be measured and explained. His vision of the economy was of the amassment of things produced and rearranged by labor. The opening preoccupation of *The Nature and Causes of the Wealth of Nations* was of the division of labor and increasing physical productivity. The "nature" of wealth was physical stuff, typically produced by other stuff. Money did not fit readily into this scheme, unless it was treated as silver or gold, with the result that it too became a thing with intrinsic value produced by labor. Capital became physical stuff. Smith wrote in several places in this book of "stock" and "capital stock," and he applied these terms to both money and goods. Eventually, he considered these terms in more depth. For Smith (1776/1976b, 282), "fixed capital, of which the characteristic is, that it affords a revenue or profit without circulating or changing masters," included machines, buildings, land, and "the acquired and useful abilities" of individuals. He continued:

> The acquisition of such talents, by the maintenance of the acquirer during his education, study, or apprenticeship, always costs a real expense, which is a capital fixed and realized, as it were, in his person. Those talents, as they make a part of his fortune, so do they likewise that of the society to which he belongs. The improved dexterity of a workman may be considered in the same light as a machine or instrument of trade which facilitates and abridges labour, and which, though it costs a certain expense, repays that expense with a profit.

Although Smith did not use the term *human capital*, he inspired the idea that the term *capital* applies to people as well as to things.[4] By extending the notion of capital to people and their labor, Smith changed

4. But the idea of valuing people in monetary terms goes back to William Petty in 1676 (Kiker 1966).

its meaning to a productive resource rather than something to do with money or money values. Cannan (1921, 480) commented on Smith's usage of the term and his "very serious departure from the conception of capital which had hitherto prevailed": "Instead of making the capital a sum of money which is to be invested, or which has been invested in certain things, Smith makes it the things themselves. Instead of being a sum of money expended on the acquisition of stock, it is part of the stock itself. But the change is not pointed out to the reader in any way."

For economics, this shift of meaning was seminal. The term *capital* acquired the twin and often mutually confused meanings of "money" and "productive goods," but often with the accent on the latter. Smith also hinted that labor power was also a form of capital, but that particular extension did not become widespread until the twentieth century.

The most important shift was to relegate the monetary connotations in favor of the physical and productive. A consequence was to conflate two different concepts: profit and interest. Interest was the reward for lending money, and profit was the return on investing money in productive resources. But, once economists adopted a physicalist view of money and capital, the two concepts began to merge and often became indistinguishable.

Although most economists followed Smith and relegated the monetary meaning, they still could not agree on the precise definition of capital. Nassau W. Senior (1836, 156) wrote: "Economists are agreed that whatever gives a profit is properly termed capital." But the agreement was illusory. John Stuart Mill (1871, 54) defined capital as the "accumulated stock of the produce of labour." For Senior, capital produced profit, but with Mill it was anything that was produced and accumulated.

Marx had the insight that capitalism was a historically specific system, where money had moved from a medium for the exchange of commodities (C–M–C) to the supreme goal of production and exchange (M–C–M′), where M′ is greater than M. Money capital thus became the driving force of the system. But otherwise Marx did not try to reverse Smith's shift to a nonmonetary meaning. He argued that the means of production become capital when they become means of exploitation of the workers. He wanted *capital* to refer to the central forms and driving processes in capitalism, including class exploitation and the production of value. Hence, Marx (1976, 933) quipped: "Capital is not a thing, but a social relation between persons, established by the instrumentality of things." Similarly, in his chapter criticizing "the trinity formula" of "capital, land, labour" in classical economics, Marx (1981, 953) argued: "But capital is not a thing, it is a definite relation of production pertaining to a particular historical social formation, which simply takes the form of a thing and gives this thing a specific social character. Capital is not the sum of the material and produced means of production. Capital . . . is the means of production monopolised by a particular section of society, the products and conditions of activity of labour-power."

Marx's addition of social relations reinstated capital as a historically specific phenomenon. But this remained remote from the everyday meaning of *capital* as money invested in production: the two foregoing quotations do not mention money. Marx was still tied to the classical vision of production in terms of physical entities and forces. Consequently, his discourse switched to and fro among relational, processual, physical, and other incompatible meanings (Ingham 2004, 61–63). Following earlier authors, he divided capital into "fixed" and "variable" forms, referring, respectively, to tangible productive resources such as machines and to labor power.

Within the German historical school there were very different usages of the term *capital*. Wilhelm Roscher (1843) followed Smith and Senior and described all productive resources as *Kapital*. But Karl Knies (1885, 40–42) narrowed the definition: "Economic goods, or economic goods in any connection, can be understood as capital, but not persons or inseparable parts of their bodies or their intellect. . . . [I]n political economy only economic goods should be understood as capital." Although this quotation appears in his *Das Geld*, Knies did not refer to capital as *money*. By contrast, Werner Sombart (1902, 2:129) recognized that capital is a phenomenon found in specific historical epochs and returned to the pre-Smithian meaning of *capital* by defining it as "the sum of exchange value which serves as the working basis of a capitalist enterprise."

Max Weber's position was similar to that of Sombart. In his *Economy and Society*—which was unpublished in his lifetime—Weber (1968, 1:91) wrote: "'Capital' is the money value of the means of profit-making available to the enterprise at the balancing of the books." Although Weber (1968, 1:94) also used the term *capital goods*, he saw capital goods as "all such goods as are administrated on the basis of capital accounting." For Weber, capital was expressed in monetary units in an era of rational accounting on the basis of monetary measurement.

The Austrian school economist Eugen von Böhm-Bawerk devoted an entire work to capital. For him, the problem of defining capital was intimately connected with the explanation of the interest rate and its magnitude. For Böhm-Bawerk (1890, 6): "Capital signifies *a complex of produced means of acquisition*—that is, a complex of goods that originate in a previous process of production, and are destined, not for immediate consumption, but to serve as means of acquiring further goods." There is no mention of money here. The focus is on physical goods that are used to produce more goods. Having demoted money, Böhm-Bawerk established a productivity theory of interest.

Worried about the conflation of money with material products, John Bates Clark (1888) made a distinction between *pure capital* and *capital goods*. The latter term became widely used, but *pure capital* referred rather vaguely to the value of the goods termed *capital*, or the fund of value somehow resident in them, and was not widely adopted. Despite Clark's attempts, *capital* took the double meaning of "money or goods." Hence, Irving Fisher (1896, 1897, 1904, 1906) influentially and more broadly defined capital as any "material" entity that produces a flow of income over time. Fisher, in contrast to Clark, regarded people as capital. He made explicit what was implicit in Smith's *Wealth of Nations*.

Against this drift, and in a work that appeared originally in 1894, John A. Hobson (1926, 26) noted that economists disputed the meaning of *capital* while "ignoring the clear and fairly constant meaning the term actually possesses in the business world around them." He pointed out that in the "business world" *capital* meant "money or the control of money, sometimes called credit," or "all forms of marketable matter which embody labour."[5]

Thorstein Veblen (1892, 1908a, 1908b, 1908c, 1908d) criticized Clark, Böhm-Bawerk, and Irving Fisher. Echoing Marx, he pointed to the failures of economists to associate capital specifically with the modern mode of production. But, diverging from Marx and many others, he argued that the sources of wealth were not simply material instruments combined with labor but also "intangible assets" or "immaterial wealth," including the common know-how in the community. In his critique of Clark, Veblen (1908d, 162–63) wrote:

5. The words *which embody labour* are overly restrictive. If someone purchases an uncultivated wilderness and uses this asset as collateral, then the wilderness could be regarded as capital—in business parlance—although it is largely untouched by labor.

In current usage, in the business community, "capital" is a pecuniary concept, of course, and is not definable in mechanical terms; but Mr. Clark, true to the hedonistic taxonomy, sticks by the test of mechanical demarcation and draws the lines of his category on physical grounds; whereby it happens that any pecuniary conception of capital is out of the question. Intangible assets, or immaterial wealth, have no place in the theory. . . . [Instead there is a] conception of capital, as a physically "abiding entity" constituted by the succession of productive goods that make up the industrial equipment.

Veblen underlined the everyday business definition of capital. Veblen (1923, 60) also wrote of the "capitalisation of the earning capacity of the property so held." He highlighted the incongruity between the notion of capital as a physical substance and the real-world cycles of boom and bust, driven by market sentiment and leading to the expansion and destruction of financial assets. Veblen (1908d, 164–66) noted the admission by economists that business crises "destroy capital in part." He continued: "The destruction in question is a matter of values; that is to say, a lowering of valuation, not in any appreciable degree a destruction of material goods. Taken as a physical aggregate, capital does not appreciably decrease through business disasters, but, taken as a fact of ownership and counted in standard units of value, it decreases. . . . It would accordingly appear that the substantial core of all capital is immaterial wealth, and that the material objects which are formally the subject of the capitalist's ownership are, by comparison, a transient and adventitious matter." Veblen (1908a, 117) thus concluded: "The failure of classical theory to give an intelligent account of credit and crises is in great part due to the habitual refusal of economists to recognize intangible assets, and Mr. Fisher's argument is, in effect, an accentuation of this ancient infirmity of the classical theory."

But Veblen's critique was inhibited by his conception of production as a largely technical and physical engineering process, resting "chiefly on the physical conditions of human life" that should be understood in terms of "Physics and the other material sciences" (Veblen 1901, 205). Hence, the structures of human organization and motivation were downplayed. He thus retained part of the reigning physicalist story of agent-object relations. Instead of denying that capital was material, he added immaterial assets. But capital is not to be understood as a mixture of the two types of asset—the material and the immaterial. It is founded on the financial system. Its essence is relational, informational, and immaterial.[6]

Despite the efforts of economists to the contrary, elsewhere in business and financial circles the term *capital* retained its monetary meaning throughout the nineteenth century and beyond.[7] For example, the relevant entry in James A. H. Murray's (1893, 98) *New English Dictionary on Historical Principles* saw "capital" as "pertaining to the original funds of a trader, company, or corporation; principal; *hence*, serving as a basis for financial and other operations." Similarly, Alfred Mitchell Innes[8] (1914, 152) noted: "Every banker and every commercial man knows that there is only one kind of capital, and that is money." Alfred Marshall (1920, 71) made a similar acknowledgment in his *Principles*: "The language of the market-place commonly regards a man's capital as that part of his wealth which he devotes to acquiring an income in the form of money. . . . This definition of capital from the business point of view is firmly established in ordinary usage."

But Marshall (1920, 78) went on to redefine capital "in harmony with the common practice of economists," which for him meant the trinity of land, labor, and capital as factors of production. In the end, he rejected the business usage; he stood with Smith and subsequent economists rather than with the heterodox minority of economist critics.

Moving further into the twentieth century, the American economist Fetter—who was influenced by both Austrian economics and the original institutionalism—was one of the few to attempt to restore an earlier meaning. Fetter (1927, 156) saw the danger in the widening of the

6. Joan Robinson (1979) rediscovered Veblen's critique of Clark's capital concept during the Cambridge capital controversies, largely stimulated by the work of Sraffa (1960). Following Veblen, the Cambridge UK side of the debate insisted that capital as finance has been confused with capital goods. But other important features of Veblen's argument were overlooked.

7. Even to this day, numerous dictionaries highlight the monetary and business meaning. For example, the *Oxford English Dictionary* defines capital as "wealth in the form of money or other assets owned by a person or organization or available for a purpose such as starting a company or investing."

8. Note that the family name here is Mitchell Innes, not Innes. Some writers are apparently unaware that English "double-barreled" surnames do not have to be hyphenated. Other nonhyphenated examples include the composer with the family name Vaughan Williams (with given name Ralph) and the biologist Maynard Smith (with given name John). But the family name of John Maynard Keynes is simply Keynes.

capital concept: "Capital is essentially an individual acquisitive, financial, investment ownership concept. It is not coextensive with wealth as physical objects, but rather with legal rights as claims to uses and incomes. It is or should be a concept relating unequivocally to private property and to the existing price system." Fetter (1930, 190) insisted that capital is both a monetary and a historically specific phenomenon: "Capital is defined as a conception of individual riches having real meaning only within the price system and the market where it originated, and developing with the spread of the financial calculus in business practice."

Within a few years another major capital debate had erupted within economics, this time between Friedrich A. Hayek (1934, 1935b, 1936) and Frank H. Knight (1934, 1935). Like J. B. Clark, Knight saw capital as a fund of value that is malleable and perpetual. For him, the rate of interest was determined entirely by the marginal productivity of capital goods, without reference to time preference. In contrast, Hayek followed Böhm-Bawerk and emphasized the heterogeneity of different capital investments with respect to their "roundaboutness" and period of production. But Hayek rejected Böhm-Bawerk's subsistence-fund theory of the interest rate (Valiente 1980; Ahmad 1991; Cohen 2003). Hayek (1941a) also criticized Arthur C. Pigou's (1941, 271) treatment of capital as an objectively measurable, "definite inventory of physical things," arguing that this took no account of subjective entrepreneurial evaluations, particularly of obsolescence. But Hayek's (1941b) view of capital was still one of physical factors of production, and it took little account of the feature of collateral. Indeed, most of Hayek's *Pure Theory of Capital* uses the abstraction of an economy without money.

What are interesting in this debate are both the points of disagreement and those of commonality. Both Hayek and Knight argued within an equilibrium framework while also hinting at its limitations. Neither saw capital as money. Both attempted to force round matters of finance into the square holes of the technical structure of production. In contrast, Joseph A. Schumpeter (1954, 322–23) insisted that the term *capital* should be applied to financial assets alone:[9]

---

9. Along the same lines, Schumpeter (1956, 174) wrote in 1917: "The capital market is the same as the phenomenon that practice describes as the money market. There is no other capital market."

> The word Capital had been part of legal and business terminology long be-
> fore economists found employment for it. With the Roman jurists and their
> successors, it denoted the "principal" of a loan as distinguished from interest
> and other accessory claims of the lender. In obvious relation with this, it later
> came to denote the sums of money or their equivalents brought by partners
> into a partnership or company, the sum total of a firm's assets, and the like.
> Thus the concept was essentially monetary, meaning either actual money, or
> claims to money, or some goods evaluated in money. . . . What a mass of con-
> fused, futile, and downright silly controversies it would have saved us, if econ-
> omists had had the sense to stick to those monetary and accounting meanings
> of the term instead of trying to "deepen" them!

This advice was not followed by economists. Notably, the Cambridge
capital controversy of the 1960s and 1970s avoided the issue raised by
Schumpeter and others. In their models, both sides of the Cambridge
controversy treated capital as physical rather than financial, with Cambridge UK insisting on the heterogeneity of capital goods and the problem of their aggregation (Sraffa 1960; Harcourt 1972; Robinson 1979;
Cohen and Harcourt 2003). The rate of profit was conflated with the rate
of interest. Money and finance were largely left out of the picture.

If Schumpeter, preceded by Hobson, Sombart, Weber, Mitchell Innes,
and Fetter, are broadly right on this question, then economists have sub-
verted a central concept. Their inability to deal adequately with capital
derives in part from a social ontology that focuses on the possession of
physical objects and in part from a reluctance to treat a core notion such
as capital as historically specific, under the illusion that economics is the
study of universal and ahistorical laws (Hodgson 2001). The German
historical school critiqued ahistorical analyses. It was no accident that
Sombart and Weber were associated with this school and that Schumpeter was deeply influenced by them (Streissler 1994; Ebner 2000; Michaelides and Milios 2009). Their key ideas were also available to Hobson, Mitchell Innes, and Fetter.

Hobson, Sombart, Weber, Mitchell Innes, Fetter, and Schumpeter insisted on a monetary and historically specific meaning. Marx and Veblen
got only part of this right. They fully understood the importance of tackling historically specific modes of production. By locating the source
of capitalist crises in speculation within the financial system, Veblen's
(1904) analysis is more persuasive than Marx's notions of undercon-
sumption or the falling rate of profit. But both economists adopted a

largely machine-like view of production. Marx's view of money was further impaired by his theory of value, where all economic value was seen as traceable to labor cost and physical effort.

What then is capital? There are two prominent options. We could follow the post-Smith trend in economics and sociology and regard it as any relatively durable thing or attribute that leads to the satisfaction of wants. According to this definition, capital has existed since the dawn of humanity, and it is not confined to any specific mode of production. Marxism offers a variant on this first definition by narrowing capital to productive factors under circumstances where workers are employees and do not own the material means of production.

A second option is to follow Hobson, Sombart, Weber, Mitchell Innes, Fetter, and Schumpeter and return to the meaning of capital that emerged in Europe by the thirteenth century in the real-world context of trading and investment. Capital is then defined as a fund of money to be invested by a person or firm in some enterprise. The word can also refer to the money value of tangible and intangible assets owned by the person or firm, which in principle can be used as collateral and serve to buy or hire resources to produce goods or services for commodity exchange. In both cases, capital is measured as an amount of money. If *capital* refers to the money value of other owned assets, then these can be used as collateral for money loans. Capital is money or the realizable money value of owned and collateralizable property. Contrary to Smith and his successors, neither wages nor wage labor can be capital—neither can act as collateral. Capital involves social relations and social institutions such as money and private property, but, contrary to Marx, it does not necessarily involve the employment of workers by capitalists.

7.2. Can Humans Be Capital?

We have seen that Smith regarded labor and skill as forms of capital, but he did not use the term *human capital*. When did the idea of labor skills as capital become prevalent, and when did the term *human capital* emerge? We have to consider both the history of the term and the history of the ideas behind it.[10]

---

10. Klaes (2001) saw merit in the history of the use of key terms in discourse, in addition to the history of the ideas that such terms may represent.

The first appearance of the term *human capital* long predates its twentieth-century exponents. Sir William Cornwallis Harris (1807–48) was an officer in the army of the East India Company. He traveled in Africa and India and was a prolific writer. Extracts from his "Report to the Secretary of the Bombay Government" (Harris 1842), which concerned the African slave trade, were published on December 2, 1844, in the British prodevelopment and antislavery journal *The Friend of the Africans*. In his report Harris addressed "African commerce" and pointed to the underdevelopment of Africa's industry and manufactures. He continued: "Few, if any, of the commodities which she barters with other countries for the rude and limited supplies that she seeks are the production of human capital, labour, or industry." This is the first known use of the term *human capital*. Its precise meaning here is unclear, particularly as the terms *human capital* and *labour* are adjacent. Ruling out the possibility of needless repetition by an accomplished writer, this suggests that for Harris these terms did not mean the same thing. Especially given the context, it is possible that by *human capital* he meant slaves.

There is a reason for this interpretation. As pointed out above, among noneconomists for centuries *capital* has had the meaning of "monetary investment in property rights to fixed assets that are unconsumed by production." This commonplace usage excludes hired labor and raw materials. But a slave, like a machine, is retained by its owner. In this sense, a slave—but not a wage laborer—can be capital. But, when thirty-eight years later the term *human capital* appeared again, there was no allusion to slavery (Donisthorpe 1880, 28). Nevertheless, five years earlier, the Scottish-born merchant, historian, statistician, and Australian politician William Westgarth (1875, 23, 64) had written in his pamphlet *The Science of Capital and Money*: "Labour can be wealth or capital . . . only when it is bonded, and thus rendered a definite subject of exchangeable value. It is in this sense that a slave is true capital, but not a free man. Labour brings wealth into being, but excepting in any of the various bonded forms I shall have occasion to allude to, it is not itself wealth. . . . A slave is a definite marketable subject, and is capital, but a free agent is not."

Westgarth (1875, 65) was not supporting slavery but protesting against the application of the term *capital* to "the mere labour possibility or labour capacity of a country, or of any of its people." I shall argue below that the issue of slavery is relevant in the discussion of the notion of human capital, but for reasons that are different from and more robust than those provided by Westgarth.[11]

The term *human capital* makes its first appearance in a prominent journal of economics in an article by Irving Fisher (1897), who proposed that all factors of production, including machines, land, and labor, should be described as *capital*. Veblen (1908a, 115) was one of the few to object to this extension of meaning: "A serviceable definition of capital, one that shall answer to the concept as it is found in practice in the habits of thought of business men, will not include persons. . . . And as for a business man's capitalizing other persons, the law does not allow it, even in the form of peonage."

Veblen thus alluded to the illegalities of enslavement, implicit in the treatment of persons as capital. But otherwise the term *human capital* met little opposition and became commonplace, especially after the seminal works of Theodore W. Schultz (1960, 1971) and Gary Becker (1964). *Human capital* therein meant "a factor of production," among other things. Its magnitude was enhanced by education and training. A key objective for economists was to estimate its value so that quantities of this labor stuff could be put into a production function alongside other inputs, in order to explain the magnitude of output, the contribution of education, the demand for education, and so on.[12]

We now turn from the history of the term *human capital* to the lineage of some of the key ideas behind it, particularly as developed in the research program of Schultz and Becker. An article by B. F. Kiker (1966) considered these precedents but neglected the history of the term. He explained that in economics there have long been broadly two approaches to the valuation of human beings. One is to estimate the cost of

11. Westgarth (1875, 28) wrote: "We must deal in economics with definite things. The unengaged labour power of a free agent is altogether an indefinite quantity, and quite outside of economic science." But, when labor became bonded by agreement or enslavement, it became "a definite subject to deal with." He suggested that the actions of a "free agent" are "indefinite" in some unclear sense. A view that all science deals solely with "definite things" might exclude powers, potentialities, and relations between things. Accordingly, with an explicit rejection of MacLeod, he adopted a substance-based view of money and denied that credit was money or capital.

12. Note the critical review of this research program by Blaug (1976). Criticizing the concept of human capital, Balibar (1994, 53) and Foucault (2008) complained of its implicit treatment of the worker as a calculating entrepreneur. But this missed the most important point: conceptions of capital in economics since Adam Smith are also flawed, for they omit the crucial attribute of collateralizability.

producing an individual in terms of care, nutrition, and so on. The other is to evaluate an individual in terms of all expected future earnings. As Kiker documented, these ideas have a long history.[13]

Sir William Petty (1690) devised a method of calculating the money value of human beings and hence the cost of life lost through diseases and wars. His method was to estimate the future wage bill in perpetuity at the market interest rate. But he did not describe labor as *capital*. His objectives were different from those of Schultz and Becker. He wished to determine the magnitude of national wealth, estimate the benefits of employing idle labor, and provide a framework for establishing just and efficient taxation.

Kiker (1966, 482) located "the first truly scientific procedure" for estimating human capital in the work of William Farr (1853). Primarily concerned with taxation, Farr argued that the present value of a person's net future earnings, which he defined as earnings less living expenses, represented wealth in the same way as did physical property and should likewise be taxed. This method of capitalizing a future net income flow was later enshrined within economics by Fisher (1907). But, unlike Fisher, Farr did not use the term *human capital* and did not imply that labor was capital. Instead, for him "the property inherent in a man" is "Inherent Property" (Farr 1853, 2). Kiker (1966, 482) commented: "Farr's work . . . suggested that since human beings are productive they should be regarded and taxed as capital. Since this would oblige people to pay tax on wealth they do not have to hand, it could lead to absurd results."

Let us probe Kiker's claim that the "capital" valuation of labor power could lead to "absurd results" because workers do not have this wealth "to hand." It is also possible that the owner of a factory and its machinery may not have "to hand" money representing the estimated value of the owned assets. Yet Kiker suggested that the capitalist is advantaged in this respect, compared to the worker. He is right, but he does not give the reason why. Both the capitalist and the worker own wealth in Farr's sense, in the form of the discounted present value of the future income streams from their assets. The unspoken difference is that the capitalist can borrow money on the basis of the collateral in his or her owned factories or machines but that the worker has no such collateral "to hand."

---

13. In *Social Capital*, Field (2003, 11–12) argued that only in the 1960s was the concept of capital expanded to include people and their capacities. This is massively inaccurate, by almost two hundred years.

Why is it unfeasible for the worker to go to the bank and borrow on similar grounds as the capitalist? A bank may offer a limited loan on the basis of expected future earnings (as with some student loans), but such offers will be relatively limited unless the worker can offer collateral. For a loan approaching the present value of the future income stream, the banker would demand collateral to cover the risk of nonpayment or of the future income being below expectations. The purpose of collateral is to safeguard the lender: if the loan is not repaid as agreed, then the banker can sue the defaulter and force the sale or gain possession of collateralized assets if necessary. The crucial point is that factories and machines can serve as collateral on a loan but that *the labor power of a wage worker cannot.* When the worker defaults on loan repayments, he or she can sell the "wealth" constituted by her future earnings *only by selling himself or herself into slavery.* To avoid the "absurd" outcome noted by Kiker and restore the symmetry between the "wealth" of the capitalist and that of the employee, the worker would have to be able to borrow money using his or her value as a slave as collateral. If the worker defaults on repayments, then he or she can be sold on the slave market to recover the debt. The symmetry in several respects would be restored, albeit at the cost of the worker's freedom. But equality under the law blocks this option. This point was briefly acknowledged by one of the seminal human capital theorists. In a rare visitation of this issue, Schultz (1972, 7) emphasized:

> Human capital has some distinctive attributes. Whatever its form, it cannot be bought and sold except where men are slaves. Whereas material capital has the legal status of property, human capital is not "protected" by this legal mantle, slavery aside. For example, the freedom of choice in acquiring educational capital is subject to the difference in the legal status of human rights and that of property. Since a person cannot indenture himself or enter into a contract that would encumber his human rights, it follows that in the case of a loan to a student for his education, the lender's property right in the capital funds that he transfers to the student cannot be covered by a mortgage on the student.

Note that this is not a matter of degree: a loan is either secured or unsecured; it is either secured by collateral, or it is not. Also, Paul Samuelson (1976, 52) wrote in his famous textbook: "Interestingly enough most of society's economic income *cannot* be capitalized into private property. Since slavery was abolished, human earning power is forbidden by law to be capitalized. A man is not even free to sell himself: he must *rent* himself at a wage." But such statements are exceptional. Samuelson and Schultz rightly noted that labor power cannot be mortgaged, that is, used as collateral. But they failed to acknowledge that the possibility of collateralization is a key part of the everyday usage of the word *capital*. If we can have human capital, then we have to find another word to describe collateralizable capital. But, instead of dealing with these conceptual problems, the literature on "human capital" moved on to address its own research program, oblivious to the conceptual limitations of treating "human capital" alongside other "capital" inputs as an array of arguments in a production function. The damage had been done.

There are two important lessons to be learned from this story. First, vital to the everyday meaning of the word *capital* is either money or the realizable money value of an asset. Realizable money value means that the asset can be *used as collateral for securing a loan*. Capital is money or money value, and it is tied up with the capitalist system of debt.

Second, and consequently, it is a major error to apply the term *capital* in this sense to assets that are not money, do not have realizable money value, or have a realizable money value only under a noncapitalist economic system. Labor power comes in under the third option. Its full money value would be realizable under a system of slavery. Westgarth (1875, 64) was right, but for the wrong reasons: "A slave is a definite marketable subject, and is capital, but a free agent is not."

The reader may object that we can define words as we wish and that the common usage of *capital* among economists is in the sense of of any productive asset. Fair enough. But, given the importance of understanding money, debt, and collateralization for even an elementary appreciation of the nature of capitalism, it is important to acknowledge that the "human capital" of a wage worker is of a very different nature from the "capital" owned by a capitalist. Both are assets, but—with slavery prohibited—only one can serve as collateral. This crucial distinction gets lost if we extend the usage of the word *capital*, at least without adding qualifying terms that preserve the vital monetary meaning and its association with collateral and debt. After Smith, economists changed their conceptual toolkit in a way that made key features of the rising capitalist order invisible to their theory. That conceptual blindness has to be rectified.

Marshall (1920, 565–69) freely acknowledged several important differences between the selling of labor and the selling of goods (see sec. 15.4 below). But he failed to note that, while goods may be used as collateral, the wage laborer cannot mortgage his or her labor power.

Marxists have also fallen short on this issue.[14] While they have generally avoided the term *human capital*, they have done so because they also use the *c* word to refer to a system of extracting surplus value from the workers rather than to a mere input into the production process. But at the same time their own usage of the term *capital*, based on a physicalist ontology and a downgrading of the legal nature of property, contract, and debt, omits the key feature of monetary collateralization.

To answer the question that heads this section, humans can be capital, but only when they are slaves. Marx sometimes misleadingly remarked that workers under capitalism were slaves (Marx and Engels 1989, 91). Mainstream economists thought differently but adopted the term *human capital* nevertheless. Neither Marx nor mainstream economists accented collateralization and the consequent crucial difference between the property of a capitalist and that of a worker.

Incidentally, the treatment of all labor resources as capital would have us ignore what was probably the greatest expropriation and liquidation of true capital in history. As Thomas Piketty (2014, 158–61) pointed out, the capital value of slaves from the founding of the United States until 1863 was about 150 percent of annual national income. With Abraham Lincoln's 1863 Emancipation Proclamation, slaves were no longer objects of alienable property. They could not be used as collateral, and they were no longer capital. As slaves were transformed into wage laborers, the owned human component of the value of total US capital assets was reduced to zero.

---

14. Nitzan and Bichler (2009) tried to develop a post-Marxist theory, complete with the ideology of class struggle and an undetailed "socialist" future, while throwing out the labor theory of value and Marx's concept of capital. They wrote that "capital is power." This is unsatisfactory, for several reasons. Power has a much longer history, so it cannot be the sole defining characteristic of capital. Without addressing the social science literature on the topic, they deployed a flawed definition of power as "*confidence in obedience*" (17). This would imply that an overconfident individual, deluded by the extent of his or her powers, was in fact powerful. Powerful people often become megalomaniacs, but megalomania is not power. More commendably, they claimed: "All capital is finance and only finance" (262).

7.3. "A Plethora of Capitals"

If the word *capital* can apply to anything that helps production or welfare, then it can apply to a huge range of material and immaterial assets.[15] *Moral capital* made a very early appearance (*Observations Relative to the Bill* 1837) and has been repeated periodically, including by
sociologists (Ross 1898, 820). Ernest Renan (1899) wrote: "An heroic
past, great men and true glory are the social capital on which the idea of
a nation is based." *Natural capital* promptly appeared as an alternative
term for land and mineral resources (Johnson 1909). Much later, Kenneth E. Boulding (1959, 121) used the term *information capital.*

But the flood came after the 1960s, prompted by the work of Schultz,
Becker, and others on human capital. It also inundated sociology. As
James N. Baron and Michael T. Hannan (1994, 1123) noted, "a minor
sociological industry" arose "to construct sociological parallels to human capital," giving rise to "a plethora of capitals." In economics, sociology, and related disciplines, this post-1960s plethora now includes the
following:

"health capital" (Grossman 1972),

"religious capital" (Azzi and Ehrenberg 1975),

"linguistic and cultural capital" and "symbolic capital" (Bourdieu 1977),

"knowledge capital" (Nelson 1982),

"reputational capital" (Veljanovski and Whelan 1983),

"social capital" (Bourdieu 1986; Coleman 1988, 1990; Putnam 1995),

"organizational capital" (Tomer 1987; Klein 1988),

"academic capital" (Bourdieu 1988),

"cultural or consumption capital" (Becker and Murphy 1988),

"cognitive capital" (Rescher 1989),

"symbolic capital" (Bourdieu 1990),

"environmental capital" (Hartwick 1991),

"self-command capital" (Lindenberg 1993),

"personal capital" (Dei Ottati 1994; Becker 1996),

"network capital" (Sik 1994),

15. Early German ventures in this direction were Roscher's (1870, 81–87) *geistige Kapital* (intellectual or spiritual capital) and the 1878 notion by Nietzsche (1996, 258) of *Geist-
und Willens-Kapital* (capital of the spirit and will).

"political, social and cultural capital" (Mouzelis 1995),

"intellectual capital" (Edvinsson and Malone 1997),

"resource capital and institutional capital" (Oliver 1997),

"spiritual capital" (Verter 2003),

"individual trust capital (relational capital)" (Castelfranchi, Falcone, and Marzo 2006),

"collective trust capital" (Castelfranchi, Falcone, and Marzo 2006),

"street capital" (Sandberg and Pedersen 2009), and even

"erotic capital" (Hakim 2011).

Given this burgeoning literature and so many different manifestations, one would have difficulty identifying what enduring entity is *not* some variety of capital. *Capital* has now acquired the broad meaning of a stock or reserve of anything of social or economic significance. Everything has become capital.

With *capital* long divested of its monetary associations, economists have made it respectable to describe any unconsumed productive resource as *capital*. Now sociologists can earn academic reputations by discovering new forms of "capital." Bourdieu started the sociological trend by his promiscuous use of the *c* word. With its meaning long degraded by economists, nothing much further stood in the way of its combination with practically anything. The reader is invited to find even more bizarre combinations. Google sometimes finds a result.[16]

Instead of critiquing each of the terms listed above, the next section focuses on the most popular, namely, the remarkable rise of research into *social capital*. Several of the critical remarks that apply to this term apply to others on the list.

7.4. Social Capital

The term *social capital* is found in all three volumes of Marx's *Capital* and in Marshall's *Principles* (Marx 1976, 1978, 1981; Marshall 1920). But in these contexts it had a different meaning: it referred to national aggre-

---

16. I would not have thought of Googling *street capital*. Then I heard it used with academic gravitas by a sociologist on a BBC radio program on February 20, 2013. It was used to refer to relations of status and credibility among street gangs. Devising your own version of capital can even get you on the radio.

gates of productive assets or wealth.[17] As Fetter (1927, 156) remarked on Marshall's usage: "Social capital is but a mischievous name for national wealth."

But a different meaning was established when the American social reformer Lyda J. Hanifan (1916, 130) defined social capital as "good will, fellowship, sympathy, and social intercourse among the individuals and families that make up a social unit." This second meaning became widely adopted when the French sociologist Pierre Bourdieu (1986), the Chicago sociologist James Coleman (1988, 1990), and the political scientist Robert Putnam (1995, 2000) used *social capital* to describe social obligations, ties, or networks that create social cohesion and help economic development. According to one count, the use of the term *social capital* increased over one hundred–fold from 1991 to 2001 (Ostrom and Ahn 2003, xii). This idea has proved enormously popular with major institutions such as the World Bank and the International Monetary Fund. But to date there is no consensus among its advocates on a clear definition of the term. It is used to refer to multidimensional social attributes, such as frequencies of interaction in different contexts, participation levels in social organizations, levels of trust, and so on.

There is no doubt that social relations, networks, and trust have economic effects. Indeed, social ties and social rules are necessary for any society and its economy to function. But a major issue of contention is whether they can generally be regarded as a form of capital. This is discussed later in this section.

Another question is whether anything new had been discovered beneath the trendy label. Sociologists had long investigated the nature and effects of such phenomena as networks, organizations, and trust, but this research was often depicted by critics as soft and secondary. Then two leading sociologists adopted the term, and the phrase took off. Long suffering from an inferiority complex vis-à-vis economists, sociologists claimed the apparent discovery of something measurable that allegedly contributed to economic performance. The term had a hard-edged economic feel while suitably underlining the importance of the social.

The term was so successful that it reentered economics with its post-

---

17. The term *public capital* appeared early in the nineteenth century (*Considerations on the Sinking Fund* 1819) and occasionally thereafter, but then the term clearly referred to money in the hands of the public. It acquired the current physical meaning of "public infrastructure" much later.

Bourdieu meaning. Economists had since the 1950s been worrying about their inability to account for much of economic growth using production functions with "capital" and "labor" as inputs.[18] Their first reaction was to regard the unexplained residual as being due to technological change. Then pioneering institutional economists such as Douglass North (1971) and Mancur Olson (1982) argued that different or changing institutions should also be taken into account. But some leading economists had long argued that institutions were the subject matter of sociology or politics, not economics. And institutional economics was treated with suspicion, at least until Oliver Williamson (1975) added the word *new*. In the search for missing ingredients to help explain economic growth, the *social capital* label worked wonders. It had connotations of yet another measurable substance that might be put into a production function, as long as the problems of its definition, heterogeneity, and measurability could be overcome. When sociologists used the term *capital* in the broad sense adopted by many twentieth-century economists (as any input that contributes to economic performance), economists could nevertheless retain their feelings of superiority. It seemed to endorse the universality of one of their favorite concepts. Extraordinarily successful in both disciplines, it was a marketing triumph (Adler and Kwon 2002).

On the positive side, *social capital* rightly suggests that production is not simply a physical process and that social relations and networks are vital. They are. But the concept, as loosely defined, is unable to distinguish between owned, unowned, and unownable factors that affect production. Companies such as Facebook, Linkedin, and Twitter own rights to Internet platforms plus their access rights to networks. When floated on the stock exchange, shares in the company that owns these rights are traded. As with the selling of machines and the hiring of labor, legal rights (of alienability, use, etc.) are exchanged. Although we speak of trading goods, in fact we are trading rights. But it is impossible to own or trade many other factors coming under the *social capital* heading, such as social trust and unowned social networks.

The term *social capital* has also attracted the criticism of both mainstream and heterodox economists (see Arrow 1999; Bowles 1999; Durlauf 1999, 2002; Solow 1999; Baron, Field, and Schuller 2000; Fine 2001; and Knorringa and van Staveren 2007). But the problems inherent in the

18. For accounts of the empirical shortcomings of growth accounting models, see King and Levine (1994), Blomstrom, Lipsey, and Zejan (1996), and Easterly and Levine (2001).

shift of meaning of *capital* from money values to things have been neglected. With the term *social capital* these previous problems are greatly
compounded. Consider some of the criticisms in more detail. Kenneth
Arrow (1999, 4) wrote: "The term 'capital' implies three aspects: (*a*) extension in time; (*b*) deliberate sacrifice in the present for future benefit;
and (*c*) alienability. The last is not true for human capital and not even
entirely true for [irreversible] physical investment. . . . But it is especially
(*b*) that fails. The essence of social networks is that they are built up for
reasons other than their economic value to the participants."

Arrow here attempted to set out three characteristics of *capital* and
measure *social capital* against them. While he rejected *social capital*, his
critique is flawed. The first characteristic (*a*) clearly applies to social capital as well, so it is unhelpful. Misleadingly, he claimed that the third characteristic (*c*) of alienability can never apply to human capital. But slaves
as human capital can be sold. And his claim that some forms of physical
investment cannot in principle be sold is perplexing. Property rights over
many irreversible or immobile investments can indeed be sold.

Arrow mentioned the nonalienability (the inability to sell) of social
capital but failed to give it sufficient weight. To do this he would also
have to reject the concept of human capital, which is not generally alienable (at least with wage labor). Failing to reject this too, he had to downgrade the importance of alienability. Instead, he ended up stressing the
second point (*b*) concerning "deliberate sacrifice . . . for future benefit."
Clearly, most of what is described as *social capital* is not built up deliberately. But, if a country were to follow the advice of the World Bank
and others and aim to build up its "social capital" with an eye toward
improving national economic performance, then Arrow's formulation
would suggest that "social capital" had also become a form of capital.
His emphasis on the second criterion is unconvincing. He should have
put more stress on the third while abandoning the concepts of "human"
as well as "social" capital.

Robert Solow (1999, 6) saw social capital as "an attempt to gain con-
viction from a bad analogy." He then wrote: "Generically 'capital' stands
for a stock of produced or natural factors of production that can be expected to yield productive services for some time. Originally anyone
who talked about capital had in mind a stock of tangible, solid, often durable things such as buildings, machinery and inventories." This additionally implies a rejection of the concept of human capital. Labor power
is generally neither "tangible" nor "solid." Solow reverted to a physical

concept of capital that has some resemblance to notions in Marx and Marshall, but his exclusion of labor or skill from the category of capital gives it an even narrower meaning than that of Smith. He concluded: "I do not see how dressing this set of issues in the language and apparatus of capital theory helps much one way or the other" (9). But his criticisms were inadequate. By claiming that originally *capital* for "anyone" meant physical assets, he seemed unaware of the term's persistent meaning outside economics.[19]

In his critique of *social capital*, Samuel Bowles (1999, 6) wrote: "'Capital' refers to a thing possessed by individuals; even a social isolate like Robinson Crusoe had an axe and a fishing net. By contrast, the attributes said to make up social capital—such as trust, commitment to others, adhering to social norms and punishing those who violate them—describe relationships *among* people." But even here there are problems. What is important about capital is not possession but legal ownership: Bowles seemed to conflate the two. He also created problems by overlooking the legal and financial institutions required to sustain capital, alongside an unhelpful reference to Robinson Crusoe. He rightly alluded to questions of alienability but weakened their punch by treating capital as things. He was right to state that social capital concerns social relations. But he also needed to focus more specifically on the historically specific social relations associated with capital more narrowly defined.

Elinor Ostrom and T. K. Ahn (2003) tried to defend the concept of social capital from the criticisms of Arrow, Solow, and others. In doing so, they concentrated on criticisms based on questions of deliberate investment, alienability, and measurement. Concerning alienability, they cited Commons (1924) on immaterial assets such as reputation and goodwill. They pointed out that, when a firm is sold, this sale may include "reputation and the list of suppliers and customers" but not "the network of suppliers and customers" (xxxii). This excludes something often described as *social capital*. Crucially, Ostrom and Ahn omitted the entire issue of collateralizability. It is significantly absent from both criticisms and defenses of the concept.[20]

In sum, economists and sociologists have vastly widened the mean-

---

19. Solow (1986) argued that natural resources should be regarded as capital, emphasizing their characteristic as a physical stock.

20. The concept of collateralizability is also absent from Sobel's (2002) survey of the literature on social capital.

ing of *capital*. Leading economists such as Arrow, Bowles, and Solow thought that *social capital* was a step too far. But Mitchell Innes, Fetter, Schumpeter, and others argued more acutely that the problems with the overstretched capital concept derive from the abandonment of its long-lasting (and still current) monetary meaning. These difficulties are compounded with the imprecise concept of "social capital." Unlike machines, land, and slaves, much of it cannot be owned, borrowed, bought, or sold. Consequently, it is generally difficult to give it a meaningful price. Crucially, because of its intrinsic elusiveness and the impossibility of owning or selling most of it, "social capital" cannot be used as collateral in order to borrow money.

Partly because of unwarranted conflation of different public and academic meanings, policies designed to build up "social capital" may employ a spurious methodology of measurability and incline with inadequate justification toward price-based instruments or market solutions. It would be all for the better if we returned to less glamorous but much more useful terms such as *institutions*, *culture*, *networks*, and *trust*.

7.5. Conclusion: Capital as Money Value

Let us take stock of the arguments. Both classical and neoclassical economists adopted physicalist ontologies where economic value was seen as deriving from physical activities, substances, or sensations, such as embodied labor time or utility (Mirowski 1989; Orléan 2011). Agents entered as possessors or controllers of these things or substances. Specific legal rights over property, such as the right to alienate or use as collateral, were downplayed. Instead of money or owned and alienable property that is convertible into money, *capital* came to mean anything lasting that contributes to the production of goods or services. With the exception of the flawed attempt by Marx to deal with this problem, capital was no longer regarded as a historically specific and monetary phenomenon associated with the capitalist epoch.

Money confounds this classical and neoclassical picture. It concerns mutual understandings and individual interactions played out on a register of symbols or material representations (Searle 1995). According to the commonplace business view, capital is either money or the money value of alienable property. This view involves legal rights and institutions as well as agent-object relations.

TABLE 7.1. **Meanings of Capital and Their Attributes**

	Types of "Capital"			
	Capital (as Finance or Collateral)	"Capital Goods" (as Physical Factors of Production)	"Human Capital"	"Social Capital"
First prominent users of the idea or concept	Medieval Italian capitalists	A. Smith had the idea	A. Smith had the idea	L. Hanifan had the idea and used the term
Social scientists who promoted the term in the designated manner	J. A. Hobson, W. Sombart, M. Weber, A. Mitchell Innes, J. A. Schumpeter	J. B. Clark	I. Fisher, G. S. Becker, T. W. Schultz	P. Bourdieu, J. Coleman
Can the use rights be owned or hired?	Yes	Yes	Yes	No
Has it a market price?	Yes	Yes—in many cases	Wage labor allows a price for use rights only	No
Can it be used as collateral?	Yes	Yes	No—except in the case of slaves	No
Can it be bought or sold (alienated)?	Yes	Yes	No—except in the case of slaves	No
Is it readily measurable in the aggregate?	Yes	No—except by assuming a list of relevant prices	No—except by assuming a list of relevant wages	No

Prominent different usages of the word *capital* and possible attributes of different forms of "capital" are summarized in table 7.1. The four notions of "capital" considered are (*a*) capital as money or collateral, (*b*) "capital goods," (*c*) "human capital," and (*d*) "social capital."

Each of these four kinds is considered in regard to five criteria: (1) Can its use rights (i.e., *usus* or *usus fructus* rights) be owned or hired? (2) Has this form of capital a price formed in the market for capital of this type? (3) Can this kind of capital be used as collateral to borrow money? (4) Can this kind of capital be sold with all rights of ownership transferred to the purchaser? (5) Is the value of this kind of capital measurable? These five criteria are self-evidently important in economic terms and reveal major differences between the different types of "capital."

The table dramatizes the contrasts between different kinds of capital, with the most extreme divergence being between "social capital" and money-oriented capital. The contrast between "human capital" and money-oriented capital is also striking. Significant but less dramatic are the differences between "capital goods" and money-oriented capital. Remarkably, the entire Cambridge UK capital controversy (Sraffa 1960; Harcourt 1972; Robinson 1979; Cohen and Harcourt 2003) focused in the lowest box in the "Capital Goods" column. While mainstream economists had treated capital as a substance, the Cambridge UK critics emphasized the heterogeneity of capital goods. Their value can be measured by assuming a price or other vector of evaluation and then aggregating according to that metric. But, because such a measure has to be assumed at the outset, there is no viable measure of capital goods that is independent of distribution or prices. This is an important point, but it is confined to one single cell in the table. The Cambridge UK critics also pointed to the unwarranted conflation of capital goods with money capital, which had been previously criticized by Veblen (Veblen 1908d, 185–86; Veblen 1908c, 121–22). But, otherwise, the famous capital controversies avoided the rest of the story in the table as a whole.

But table 7.1 does not complete the argument. It serves best to show the weaknesses of the concepts of "human capital" and "social capital." Dealing with "capital goods" is trickier, as it qualifies affirmatively on all but one criterion. The key question is what usage of the term *capital* is legitimate? Of course, there is no strict rule here because there is no law against trying to make words mean anything we wish. But I give six reasons for confining the meaning of *capital* to money investable in production or to the money value of owned, alienable, collateralizable property that is employed in production. This means rejecting the terms *human capital* (except in relation to slavery) and *social capital*. The term *capital goods* can be retained only if its meaning is changed from a factor of production to property rights to goods that can be used as collateral. The reasons are as follows.

First, capitalism is arguably a historically specific system where capital plays a dominant role. Marx, Weber, Hobson, Sombart, and Schumpeter all saw capitalism as existing from around the seventeenth century or the eighteenth. Given the data illustrated in figure 1.1 above, the explosive rise of capitalism could be dated to 1800 or thereabouts. All other forms of "capital" have a much greater longevity. Much of what goes under descriptions of "social capital"—such as networks and trust— can be found in the primates. If *human capital* means any learned capacity for labor, then this would go back to adults teaching children to make fire. With "capital goods" the use of stone tools by humanoids stretches back millions of years. By contrast, even if we regard the loans of the temple banks of Mesopotamia as capital, then the history of money capital is merely about five thousand years. We could even go further and confine capital to the second millennium of the Christian Era, noting its emergence in some Italian city states. Then the life of capital is less than a one-thousandth that of "social capital," "human capital," or "capital goods." If we consider its developed lifetime to begin in Britain around 1700, then there is an even greater contrast with its supposedly kindred concepts. Wherever the joints are carved, capital (as defined here) is much more historically specific than its purported relatives and hence is much more useful in identifying *capital*-ism.

Second, if we choose to allow *capital* to be used in more ways than its monetary meaning and to apply to other phenomena, then we need another word to describe its important, commonplace, and historically relevant monetary form. Perhaps I can persuade my economist colleagues to use the terms *money capital* or *finance capital*? But then we would have to describe the system as *money capitalism* or *finance capitalism*. Both would falsely allude to another, more basic type of capitalism when we are trying to describe the species as a whole. Further alternatives such as *collateralizable capital* are too ungainly. This leaves us with the more radical solution: to confine *capital* solely to its everyday monetary meaning.

Third, I hope that the reader is persuaded by the account in this chapter that the conjunction of the word *capital* to a large variety of very different phenomena has been at the cost of a large amount of relevant meaning. "Social capital" overturns the commonplace usage of *capital*. Serious problems remain with the ubiquitous "human capital." Problems have been caused by the conflation of "capital goods" with money-oriented capital. Best avoid such extensions of meaning.

Fourth, all words bring their own baggage. Much of this baggage is ideological. Although good economists keep a sharp lookout for ideological biases, the wider public with which economists interact is less well trained. Theories get distorted into statements of ideology. Hence, given the previous prominent designation of "capital" as a pecuniary phenom-enon, combined with the prevalence of an ideology regarding markets as the universal solution to economic and social problems, the promis-cuous associations of "capital" can give the impression that all political, cultural, social, cognitive, and ecological phenomena can be valued and traded in monetary terms and invested like finance capital. The infer-ence may be drawn that everything labeled as "capital" is tradable and has a price. Universal "commodification in discourse" may encourage practical attempts to commodify almost everything (Radin 1996; Arrow 1997). But there many things—like love, trust, and honor—that cannot be readily traded and are even degraded by attempts to give them a price (see Fox 1974; Walzer 1983; Ellerman 1992; Anderson 1993; Satz 2010; and Sandel 2012).

For example, terms such as *environmental capital* and *natural capital* may delude politicians and policymakers that all environmental assets can be, and need to be, valued properly in price terms (Rothschild 2011). But giving something a price is not the same thing as establishing the possibility of ownership and alienability. Much of nature's worth cannot be readily owned or sold. On the other hand, land and some other parts of nature may become money-valued objects of ownership and sources of pecuniary gain. But, in these cases, seeking maximum profits after privatization (especially with the degrees of complexity and uncertainty involved) does not necessarily enhance biodiversity or ecological sus-tainability (O'Neill 1993, 1997; Krall and Gowdy 2012). The terms *en-vironmental capital* and *natural capital* obscure these crucial limitations and differences.

Fifth, the issue of collateral, inherent in the monetary definition of capital, helps highlight a key difference between the assets owned by a capitalist and the labor power owned by a worker. Capitalists can use their assets as collateral and borrow more money to invest in further ventures, hence getting a double usage out of their property. By contrast, workers cannot use their labor power as collateral. This illuminates an important aspect of class inequality intrinsic to capitalism. A major source of inequality becomes capital itself. (This point is discussed fur-ther in chapter 15 below.)

Finally, especially after the Great Crash of 2008, it is time for all economists of whatever stripe to be humble. Economists have not man-aged to fit money into their highest, most general, and most prestigious theory (Hahn 1965, 1987, 1988). Most of academic monetary economics exhibits a "steadfast refusal to face facts" (Goodhart 2009) or an "unfortunate uselessness" (Buiter 2009, 821), to quote the words of two leading monetary economists. We need to sweep with a new broom. Let us also adopt a terminology that is new for us but old for the population at large. We may use the terminology of capital that prevails in the real business world. Instead of *capital goods* we may use the broader term *capital assets*, signifying the importance of immaterial or intangible as well as material property. Instead of *human capital* why not *human resources*? And instead of *social capital* why not *networks* or *social trust*? *Capital* then becomes more meaningful and special. Essentially, capital is money or property that gives access to money. It is about money valuations of property, not things themselves.

The notion of capital has generated a great deal of conceptual and theoretical controversy. Contemplate the massive intellectual effort from the 1880s to the 1970s by numerous economists devoted to debating the nature of capital and to the development of "capital theory." Consider how little this has added to our understanding of the nature or dynamics of capitalism and to the construction of practical economic policy. These debates have seen much sound and fury, but, compared with the big issues of the capitalist era, they have signified next to nothing.

What about capital as a factor of production? Here, economists have confused different questions. First, there is the need to explain how a combination of forethought, will, knowledge, organization, technology, physical inputs, and labor can create a useful output. This question applies to all production in human history and must be answered through our understanding of the socioeconomic, psychological, and physical processes involved. Some general issues concerning the nature of production are raised in chapter 11 below. In any case, labeling all things useful for production as "capital" adds nothing to the explanation of production or its output. Calling something *capital* or estimating a measure of any kind of capital does not explain what is produced, how much of it is produced, or how it is produced.

There are other questions, such as how the value of the product is explained. This can be answered only by reference to historically specific institutions that enable meaningful intersubjective valuations of cost and benefit. The marginalist question of how the valuation of output might be altered by variations in particular inputs has less relevance in a world of highly heterogeneous production factors, including physical and labor assets, especially where substitutability between individual components or types is highly limited. The Cambridge "capital" controversies showed that aggregate measures of physical assets are problematic. A described "substitution" of labor for capital is in reality a change of productive technique, not a substitution of one kind of fungible "capital" for another, with the outcome that the relative cost of labor declines. At best, aggregated or disaggregated production functions are simple heuristics or preliminary estimators. When used empirically, they may indicate some possible causal relations that need to be revealed by much deeper technological and institutional analysis.

It is important to understand the production process, but the post-Smith concept of "capital"—as anything that is useful for production—has misled research to look for aggregate fungible substances that do not exist in reality. In forlorn search of their measure, attention has been diverted from the historically specific institutions of production and distribution. It is better to regard capital as a feature of historically specific institutional arrangements involving property and money.[21]

21. Note that Piketty's (2014) definition of capital is similar to that adopted here, in the important sense that it includes the value of cash, bonds, and shares and collateralizable assets such as buildings, land, machinery, and intellectual property but excludes "social capital" and nonslave "human capital." But Piketty (2014, 46) left the door open to previous confusion when he wrote: "Capital is defined as the sum total of nonhuman assets that can be owned and exchanged on some market." By defining capital as simply assets rather than monetary valuations of property rights over assets, his formulation might retain a physicalist notion of capital as things, with the Cambridge-capital-controversy problem of how their heterogeneous sum total is to be valued. Without also rectifying the concept of property, he neglected the important issue of collateralizability. It should instead be emphasized that capital is ultimately about monetary valuations of alienable and collateralizable property. It is about the command of monetary wealth; it does not have to be about things or what matters physically in production. Also, Piketty (2014, 230–32) wrongly interpreted the Cambridge capital controversy as being about growth models: in fact, it was about the measurement of heterogeneous capital goods and the theoretical basis (if any) of aggregate production functions (Harcourt 1972; Cohen and Harcourt 2003). He failed to note that Samuelson (1966) conceded the core of the Cambridge UK argument. Nevertheless, his book is a major and hugely stimulating achievement.

CHAPTER EIGHT

Firms and Corporations

The corporation is a legal subject of right and duties. . . . If the law recognizes a distinction between a corporation and the sum of its members, it is not as a mere flight of fancy, or to indulge an inclination for metaphysics, but for the very practical and sufficient purpose of establishing the inherence of certain rights and duties which cannot be conveniently treated . . . as inhering in the members of the corporation. . . . It is the corporation (not the members) which is creditor and debtor. — W. Jethro Brown (1905)

The economic historian of the future may assign to the nameless inventor of the principle of limited liability, as applied to trading corporations, a place of honour with Watt and Stephenson, and other pioneers of the Industrial Revolution. The genius of these men produced the means by which man's command of natural resources has multiplied many times over—the limited liability company—the means by which huge aggregations of capital required to give effect to their discoveries were collected, organized and efficiently administered. — *The Economist*, Editorial (December 18, 1926)

T his chapter considers the nature of firms and corporations.[1] After a 1970s outburst of innovative research on the theory of the firm, there has been relatively little theoretical development in this area since 2000.[2] A problem is that economists cannot agree what a firm is. Different arguments for the existence and productivity of the firm often cannot readily be tested conjointly, partly because of a lack of clear definitions

---

1. See my previous discussion in Hodgson (2002). For earlier contributions emphasizing legal realities, see Masten (1991), Phillips (1994), Blair (1999), and Iwai (1999). Since 2002 several works have underlined the importance of legal personality for economic analysis (Blair 2003; Hansmann, Kraakman, and Squire 2006; Gindis 2007, 2009, 2013; Iacobucci and Triantis 2007; Spulber 2009; Pagano 2010; Robé 2011; Deakin 2012; Orts 2013).

2. Among the foremost twenty results from a Google Scholar search using "theory of the firm" (performed October 31, 2013), only four items were from 2000 or later. Only one of these four was from a leading mainstream journal of economics.

and concepts. The institutional economist Thráinn Eggertsson (1990, 158) noted that the lack of standardized vocabulary and careful definitions made it "difficult to see whether we are dealing with overlapping or competing theories." This is a chronic problem with empirical work on the theory of the firm (Carter and Hodgson 2006).

This failure to reach a consensus on definitions has multiple causes. Among them is a failure to acknowledge that property, contracts, firms, and corporations are all historically specific and relatively recent phenomena. The story of how economics transformed itself into an ahistorical discipline and elevated notions such as property, contract, and exchange into eternal verities while simultaneously eroding them of much meaning is told elsewhere (Hodgson 2001). If firms and contracts are regarded as universal to all human existence, then we are unable to treat them as outcomes of relatively recent, state-based legal systems.

Ronald Coase pioneered the modern subdiscipline of law and economics.[3] But both Coase (1937, 1988) and Oliver Williamson (1975, 1985b) made little of the legal personality of the firm. Williamson treated law as if it were akin to custom, with arrangements between parties as "private ordering," which could in principle emerge without the involvement of a state legal system. There has been insufficient acknowledgment of the role of the state in bringing corporations into existence and of how the development of company law stimulated entrepreneurial organizations that drove much of the explosive growth of capitalism in the last two hundred years.

It is argued here that firms in general (including the particular legal form of the corporation) have to be treated as legal entities, where law itself is irreducible to custom or private ordering. I use the term *firm* to apply to organizations that are functioning legal units set up to produce goods or services for sale. It can be stretched to cover individual producers as well. The *Concise Oxford English Dictionary* defines the firm as "partners carrying on business; group of persons working together." A *partnership* is one type of firm, where individuals enter into agreements to produce jointly. A *corporation* is yet another kind of firm, structured as designated under corporate law. All corporations are firms, but not all firms are corporations.[4]

3. Earlier explorations by MacLeod (1858, 1872), Commons (1924), and others of the interface between economics and law should not be overlooked.
4. In an otherwise excellent article, Robé (2011, 3) put forth a contrary view. He argued

The word *firm* derives from the Latin adjective *firmus*, meaning "strong, powerful, durable, and lasting." As a noun, the word went on to acquire the significant meaning of "a (legally binding) *signature*," and with this important connotation it survives today in some form in several Romance languages. It is reasonable to use the broad term *firm* to include both a partnership and a corporation as well as a single person employing others in production or trade. But, of course, these different types of firms all have important differences of structure, rationale, and possible behavior. Nevertheless, they can all be placed within a single taxonomic class. Within these inclusive terms, a more precise definition of the firm will be attempted later.

Sections 8.1 and 8.3 review some prominent conceptions of the firm. I am less concerned with the theories that are outlined by these authors to explain specific firm-related phenomena, such as vertical integration, firm boundaries, or firm structure. Instead, this selective survey is concerned with what leading authors mean by *firm* and whether their account of this entity is coherent or robust. Section 8.1 shows how the conception of a firm in transaction cost economics slid from a firm-market dichotomy to a firm-market continuum. Section 8.2 shows that the notion of a firm-market hybrid is untenable once we adopt the legal conception of the firm, which is missing in transaction cost economics. Section 8.3 considers some other major contributions to the theory of the firm since 1970. Section 8.4 briefly sketches the history of the corporation and other firms and considers the role of the state in this process. Section 8.5 concludes the chapter.

8.1. The Firm in Transaction Cost Economics

In his famous article Coase (1937) treated the firm and the market as two alternative ways of organizing productive activity. The firm was de-

---

that the firm and the corporation are "totally different concepts": "A corporation is a legal instrument, with a separate legal personality, which is used to legally structure the firm; a firm is an organized economic activity, corporations being used to legally structure most firms of some significance." But the idea that the firm is an "activity" is odd: most writers treat the firm as a productive organization. Robé (2011, 10) simply stated dogmatically— with little review of meanings and relevant arguments in the literature—that "it is the corporation which has legal personality and *not* the firm." He did not acknowledge that the concept of the firm is widely used in the different sense of a productive organization, of which corporations are but one example.

fined in terms of its "supersession of the price mechanism" (389). For Coase, owners of factors of production do "not have to make a series of contracts" with other factor owners in the production process: "For this series of contracts is substituted one" (391). Each factor owner makes a contract with the "entrepreneur," which was defined as "the person or persons who . . . take the place of the price mechanism in the direction of resources" (388n). "A firm . . . consists of the series of relationships which comes into existence when the direction of resources is dependent on the entrepreneur" (393).

Coase's account depends on several legal concepts, including owner, sale and contract. But his definition of the firm is defective. A major flaw is that the legal constitution and role of the (individual or collective) entrepreneur—who owns resources, makes contracts, and directs production—is incompletely specified. Unless this problem is fixed, his distinction between the firm and the market disintegrates.[5]

Coase (1937) regarded the entrepreneur as one or more people. Assume first that it is one person who enters into legal contracts with employees and suppliers of materials and that production takes place. Clearly, this firm is a legal entity, constituted by a real person with the intention of producing goods and services and with the legal capacity to make contracts. But Coase did not clearly acknowledge that the entrepreneur owns the product and has the right to the revenue from the goods or services that are produced. Instead of entrepreneurial ownership rights and potential liabilities, he concentrated on the administrative functions of the entrepreneur during the production process, including his claim that the employment contract involves flexible but limited authority over employees (1937, 391). To rectify this omission it would be necessary to augment the definition of the firm in his article quoted above.

Because Coase concentrated on the administrative functions of the entrepreneur within production, he overlooked another important issue. Who would be sued if the output of the firm proved defective or dangerous? Would it be the entrepreneur or the individual worker responsible for the defect? With a legally constituted firm it would be impossible for an outsider to sue the culpable worker directly—the firm would be sued. The legal formation of a firm establishes it as the locus of legal liability

5. A lesser problem is that Coase's concept of the market was overly spacious: one must consider relational exchange as well (as defined separately in chapter 5 above).

in trading with others. But, because Coase is insufficiently clear on the legal owner and seller of the output, he misses this point entirely.

These problems are compounded when the entrepreneur is more than one person. For instance, what are the ties or incentives that keep the entrepreneurs together as a team? Coase (1937) was again silent on this point. But there must be some legally enforceable arrangement that keeps them together and allows them as a body to make the contracts with the owners of factors of production. Employees and suppliers would not make separate contracts with each of the entrepreneurs as individuals, so with whom are they contracting? Likewise, if the firm sells a defective product, then which entrepreneur gets sued? Or are they sued as a body? In which case, how would the liability be shared between them?

If the entrepreneurs were legal partners, then they could be bound together by a legal *partnership agreement* or *articles of partnership*. This agreement would specify management responsibilities, shares of profits or losses, and mechanisms to resolve disputes between partners. Unlike a corporation, partners are jointly and severally liable for the full value of any partnership debts. Suing a partnership means suing the partners. The *glue* holding the firm together and making it a singular unit is the partnership agreement of joint responsibility. Contrary to Coase, the partnership firm is constituted not by entrepreneurial administration of a production process but by the legal presumption that those partners, who join forces to pursue entrepreneurial activities, also share the relevant responsibilities.

In a corporation, *entrepreneurs* could refer to shareholders or managers. Legal incorporation means that the state recognizes the firm as a singular legal person, with rights and duties. The corporation does not consist solely of its entrepreneurs. Neither managers nor shareholders own the corporation. The corporation itself is an owning agent. Shareholders own shares in the corporation: they do not own the corporation itself (see Marris 1964, 12; Gower 1979; Ireland 1996, 1999; Blair and Stout 1999; and Robé 2011).[6] The corporation, as a legal person, hires the workers, buys machines and raw materials, and sells the output. It can be sued if it sells defective products. It can sue others for breaches of contract. The glue binding the corporation together is the power of corporate law, the adoption of its principles by the shareholders, and the le-

6. Note that there are many corporations with only a single shareholder, including corporations owned by another corporation.

gal agreement between them. Contrary to Coase, the corporation is constituted not by entrepreneurial administration of a production process
but by the establishment of the singular legal person that can combine
the agency of multiple individual entrepreneurs.

Eventually, his neglect of the legal personality of the firm meant the
loss of a strict firm-market dichotomy. Even in his classic article, when
Coase (1937, 388) pointed out that in a department store there may be
"competitive bidding for space" or that in the Lancashire cotton industry "a weaver can rent power and shop-room and can obtain looms and
yarn on credit," these might be conceived as markets within firms, leading to "hybrid forms." But, once we conceive of the firm as a legal entity, then internal markets and hybrids disappear. A franchisee in a department store is legally separate from the franchising department store
itself, and the Lancashire weavers to which Coase referred were self-
employed producers even if they worked inside a mill owned by another
firm. Because Coase did not conceive of the firm as a legal entity, the
rot set in. Then Benjamin Klein (1983, 373) pushed against Coase's fragile framework, and previous distinctions collapsed: "Coase mistakenly
made a sharp distinction between intrafirm and interfirm transactions,
claiming that while the latter represented market contracts the former
represented planned direction. Economists now recognize that such a
sharp distinction does not exist and it is useful to consider also transactions occurring within the firm as representing market (contractual) relationships. The question what is the essential characteristic of the firm
now appears to be unimportant."

Here, Klein made an unwarranted appeal to authority and advanced
a non sequitur. Despite the mention of unnamed "economists," researchers will search with difficulty in the academic literature for any forceful
argument against the "sharp distinction" between the firm and the market. There is no known scholarly explanation why it would be "useful" to
consider transactions within the firm as "market relationships." No convincing argument has been found for abandoning the question of "the
essential characteristic of the firm." Even if the "sharp distinction between intrafirm and interfirm transactions" were untenable, this does
not mean that we can abandon the question of what the "essential characteristic of the firm" is because distinctions would still have to be made
between degrees of "firm-ness" and "market-ness." If we believe that the
firm has no clear identity, then it becomes a conceptual sponge ready to
soak up anything put in contact with it.

Then Coase (1988, 27–28) declared his revised position: "I have come across numerous examples of markets found *within* firms, but one which amused me was the discovery of a kind of market operating in the heart of a nationalized industry in England, the electricity supply industry." He quoted from a 1961 lecture given by an official of the Central Electricity Generating Board (CEGB): "The National Control Room becomes in effect an auction room, with a National Control Engineer asking the Regional Centres to quote the price at which they could supply a certain number of kilowatts at specified periods during the following day. . . . Wherever possible he accepts the lowest bid." Coase continued: "An analogous situation may, of course, be found within a privately owned firm in which separate departments or divisions may supply one another as a result . . . of what are essentially market transactions between them." The firm-market dichotomy had disappeared.

But, once we apply clear legal criteria concerning contracts and firm ownership, Coase's argument disintegrates. The UK CEGB was itself a singular legal person. It was a state-owned company, lasting from 1957 until its privatization and division into separate companies in the 1990s. The regional centers were not legally separate firms but internal divisions of the CEGB. An outside complainant would sue the CEGB, not the regional centers, just as the CEGB would sue any supplier of materials to a regional center that did not fulfill a contract. The regional centers neither owned nor sold electricity to the CEGB. Any semblance of contract between the regional centers and the CEGB would not have been recognized in law as such. It was not an exchange of property rights because ownership of the electricity remained in the hands of the CEGB throughout. Instead, the bidding and selling of electricity was an internal management mechanism to reduce costs and encourage increases in productivity.

There are often internal negotiations and transfers of resources between divisions of modern firms. These divisions may have their own accounts and profit targets. Most sizable firms use price indicators for internal accounting. But are there internal markets within firms? Again, a key test is whether these divisions have separate legal status and are recognized as legal persons. Internal transfers within the firm do not involve the exchange of legal property rights. The objects of "exchange" remain the property of the firm. These exchanges are not legally enforceable contracts of trade: they are internal transfers. If a division of the firm is delegated the power to enter into contracts with outside bodies, then the firm as a whole is legally the party to the contract. The division is merely exercising delegated powers: it acts in the name of the corporation, and the corporation as a whole is legally responsible for any liabilities under the agreed contract. Because the firm is a singular legal entity, it cannot make contracts within itself, just as our legs cannot make a legal contract with our mind to walk or run when instructed.

Williamson took much less time than Coase to slide from the dichotomy to the continuum. Although his seminal *Markets and Hierarchies* (1975) suggested a dichotomy, it was soon to disappear. Like Coase, Williamson (1981, 1538) chose to concentrate on "the internal organization of the corporation" and to downplay its legal personality. Williamson (1985b, 318) noted: "The centrality of management . . . distinguishes it from all other constituencies." Williamson (1985a, 199) further explained: "Whereas each constituent part of the enterprise strikes a bilateral deal with the firm . . . management has knowledge of and is implicated in all of the contracts." But this formulation runs into the very same problems that we have observed with Coase. What binds management, the officers and directors of a corporation, together? Being "implicated in all of the contracts" is not the same as identifying the legally responsible entity.[7]

7. Note here Williamson's peculiar use of the concept of forbearance. In law this means the intentional abstention from enforcement of a legal right. In a firm it refers to contractual flexibility, tolerance, and give and take, which is often required in such complex and changing circumstances. But Williamson (1991, 274) deployed it as follows: "The implicit contract law of internal organization is that of forbearance. Thus, whereas courts routinely grant standing to firms should there be disputes over prices, the damages to be ascribed to delays, failures of quality, and the like, courts will refuse to hear disputes between one internal division and another over identical technical issues. Access to the courts being denied, the parties must resolve their differences internally." Here, he mistakenly confused the issue of forbearance with the consequences of the singular legal personality of the firm. Although he repeatedly highlighted the term *forbearance* in the context of internal organization, Williamson (1996, 2002, 2005) failed to give it its proper legal meaning. Forbearance is not the "implicit contract law of internal organization." Internal and external contracting do not necessarily and respectively correlate with lesser and greater use of courts to settle disputes. The reason why courts "refuse to hear disputes between one internal division and another" is because these divisions are parts of a single legal person and the law cannot deal with inner disputes *within* either fictional or real persons. Courts can be used to resolve disputes between distinct legal persons only. Disputes between internal divisions of a firm are not resolved by *forbearance* because that too refers to contracts between distinct legal persons. Disputes between internal divisions of a firm are resolved by the clarification and implementation of internal rules.

More preoccupied than Coase with private ordering, Williamson (1985a, 184) wrote: "Since the efficacy of court ordering is problematic, contract execution falls heavily on the institutions of private ordering. . . . This is the world with which transaction cost economics is concerned." This suggested, rather unconvincingly, that private ordering is generally much more effective than court ordering. For this dubious reason, Williamson proposed that transaction cost economics should overlook courts and statutory law. This severe confinement of the "world with which transaction cost economics is concerned" is a serious impairment for this research program, and it is fatal for attempts to establish a clear identity for the firm.

Like Coase, Williamson treated the firm as a group of individuals, such as partners or shareholders. But this is insufficient to integrate the firm as a cohesive entity or to define its boundaries. Consequently, distinctions between the firm (or "hierarchy") and the market faded away. Williamson (1985b, 83) became "persuaded that transactions in the middle range are much more common." For Williamson (1991, 271), hierarchies (or firms) became "a continuation of market relations by other means." Instead of the firm-market dichotomy, he adopted a firm-market continuum.

Richard Langlois (1995a, 72) observed: "Much of transaction-cost economics has reached the conclusion that the distinction between firm and market is little more than semantics."[8] In transaction cost economics the theory of the firm has become a theory of different types of individual contractual arrangements and their consequences. Ironically, in the age of the large corporation, the firm as such has virtually disappeared from standard economic analysis. Typically, the firm is defined not as an entity but as a point on a continuum of possible governance and contracting structures. As Williamson (2007, 376) put it: "What defines a firm at the end of the continuum? I take the defining characteristics of governance structures to be incentive intensity, administrative

---

8. Langlois (1995b) tried to undermine a distinctive feature of the firm by arguing that firms do not and cannot plan. But his thesis depends on a very ambitious notion of planning, one involving envisaging the future and enacting appropriate responses. Few planning systems (or even individuals) could function adequately in such a visionary and proactive manner in a complex world. Planning does not have to depend on accurate and extensive prediction. With both individuals and organizations, it often involves routine repetition. Strategic decisions are often based on hunches or perceptions of past success rather than on full-blown predictive ability.

control, and the contract law regime. Firms combine relatively low powered incentives with a lot of control instruments and use hierarchy rather
than courts to settle disputes. Markets are polar opposites, and hybrids
are located in between."

As with Coase (1937), Williamson's focus was on the contractual or
administrative organization of production and its internal incentives.
Likewise absent here—seventy years after Coase's classic article—was
any notion of the contracting entity that owns the means and fruits of
that production or can be sued if its outputs are defective. Although the
research program has moved from the dichotomy to a continuum, these
sizable omissions have been thematic for Coase/Williamson-type transaction cost economics from the beginning. To their eternal credit, Coase
and Williamson opened the black box of the firm to inspect its contents.
But they forgot about the box itself.

Reinstatement of legal personality does not mean that we have to
ditch the concept of transaction costs. Indeed, legal personality and legal incorporation are vital because they can greatly reduce such costs.
When a firm is formed, the individuals involved do not have to contract
and construct anew the structure of the firm. Instead, they can adopt the
tried-and-tested legal template of a corporation, backed by the enforcement powers of the state (Robé 2011).

8.2. The Myth of the Firm-Market Hybrid

As well as within standard transaction cost economics, it became widely
popular for other economists and sociologists to argue that the boundaries of the firm were fuzzy and indistinct. Ideas emerged of "internal markets" within firms (Doeringer and Piore 1971),[9] of the "quasi firm" (Eccles 1981), and of "hybrid forms" (Ménard 1995, 1996). Arguments went
like this: the observed kind of contracting is typical of neither a market nor a firm, so it must be some kind of hybrid of the two. For example, Robert Eccles (1981, 339–40) considered "quasi firms" in the con-

---

9. Doeringer and Piore (1971, 1–2) admitted that "internal labor markets" are governed primarily not by the price mechanism but by "a set of administrative rules and procedures." Marsden (1986, 162) went further: "Internal labour markets offer quite different
transaction arrangements, and there is some doubt as to whether they fulfil the role of markets." In fact, they are not markets at all.

struction industry where "relations between the general contractor and his subcontractors are stable and continuous over fairly long periods of time and only infrequently established through competitive bidding." He overlooked the possibility that these "stable and continuous" contracting relationships may be neither markets nor (quasi) firms but examples of *relational exchange* between different legal entities (including firms), along the lines of George B. Richardson (1972), Victor P. Goldberg (1980), and Ronald Dore (1983). Eccles (1981, 342–43) went on to consider the divisions within the M-form (multi divisional) firm: "These autonomous divisions function in many ways like independent firms. Often they compete successfully with firms in the market for business with each other. Thus internal transactions in these firms can have similar characteristics to market transactions. In contrast, the inside contracting system is a set of market transactions with similar characteristics to hierarchical transactions. Most generally, pure markets and pure hierarchies are at opposite ends of a continuum of contracting modes."

In a sense it is possible that internal divisions within a firm might "compete" with each other for business. But such competition would be internal point-scoring exercises rather than contractual or market competition. If a division wins a contract with an outside firm, then the legally enforceable agreement is not between that division and the outside firm but between the firm that hosts the division and the outside firm. If separate divisions of a single firm were to compete fully for custom and contracts with a single outside company, then this would be largely self-defeating. It would be against the interests of the firm as a whole to allow its divisions to compete with each other on the price to be charged to an external customer. The key test is whether these divisions have separate legal status and are recognized as legal persons. If they are not, then competition between divisions of the same firm is neither price making nor market competition.

In a seminal article, Steven Cheung (1983, 11) also attacked the firm-market dichotomy, using this real-world example: "A landlord, who wants to build a high-rise finds a building contractor. This contractor subcontracts with a hardwood floor contractor on an agreed price per square foot—a piece count. The subcontractor, who imports the wood materials and adds finishing work to the wood on a piece-rate basis, in turn finds a sub-subcontractor, provides him wood, and offers him a price per square foot laid. Finally, the sub-subcontractor hires workers and again pays them per square foot laid."

Such complex integrations of contracts and subcontracts are very common. Cheung then saw elements of both a "firm" and a "market" in such an arrangement. Repeatedly stressing the payments per square foot, he implied that piece-rate payments mean the existence of a "market" (1983, 10). But there is no reason why the one should imply the other. Employees within a firm can be paid by the piece or by the hour. Cheung also suggested that being "vertically integrated by contracts, with transfer pricing," might suggest that "only one firm exists" (17). But being "vertically integrated by contracts" is not the same as vertical integration *within* a firm. Putting two weak arguments together, Cheung suggested that the hardwood floor example is something with the characteristics of *both* "a 'market'" and "one firm." The myth of the firm-market hybrid came of age.

Cheung's hardwood floor example involved contractual exchange between at least five legal persons: the landlord, the contractor, the subcontractor, the subsubcontracted firm, and its employees. The contracts had relational characteristics and may not have involved market contracting (in the narrower sense defined previously). Considering another example, Cheung (1983, 16–17) wrote: "If an apple orchard owner contracts with a beekeeper to pollinate his fruits, is the result one firm or two firms? The question has no clear answer. The contract involved may be a hive-rental contract, a wage contract, a contract sharing the apple yield, or, in principle, some combination of these and still other arrangements. In each case the beekeeper receives a remuneration for his service, and the orders he expects from the orchard owner vary with the form of contract."

In this case the answer to the question whether there is one firm or two depends on whether the contract involves hive rental, wage labor, or sharecropping. Cheung (1983, 17) admitted this when he wrote: "Most economists would probably opt for only one firm if the beekeeper is hired on a wage contract but for two if the hives are rented." This was a reasonable answer. The problem was not that he lacked a good answer but that he was reluctant to endorse it. He was swept along by the rhetoric of the firm-market dichotomy.

Claude Ménard (1995, 176) tried to demonstrate that *"organizations can be internally structured as quasi-markets."* Ménard considered franchising "when very strict standards are imposed on independent participants." He noted: "Classification [into markets or organizations] becomes particularly difficult when firms are interconnected by a dense

web of transactions, with strong commitments to each other and complementarities of their assets, but without formal agreements and, more-
over, with property rights on these firms clearly maintained as distinct."
He thus proposed intermediate forms between markets and hierarchies.
But, instead of focusing on the "strong commitments to each other" to
then describe them as *relational exchange*, he instead saw them as "hybrids" involving "specific combinations of markets incentives and mo-
dalities of coordination involving some form of hierarchical relationship" (175).

In fact, Ménard's example of strictly monitored and regulated franchising is an "organized" relationship between *two or more* firms or legal persons. Although the relationship has an organized or even hierarchical character, that does not mean that it constitutes a single firm.
Many contracts between separate legal persons involve ties that allocate
roles and responsibilities. This does not necessarily mean that they become a single legal entity. The fact that "property rights on these firms
[are] clearly maintained as distinct" underlines the fact that multiple
firms may be organized, just as individuals can be organized, without
necessarily creating a singular legal person or a firm. Ménard's error was
to confuse broadly defined organizational arrangements with the firm.
He also overlooked the fact that relational contracting involves different
firms but that, because of its relational character, it is not on a market. It
is thus a third option, after a market and a firm. Relational contracting
means that the firm-market dichotomy is false. It also undermines hybrids. Illusions of a firm-market hybrid disappear once we adopt the notion of the firm as a singular legal entity.

8.3. A Sample of Other Influential Views on the Firm

Armen A. Alchian and Harold Demsetz (1972) famously conflated the
firm with the market. They presented "the firm and the ordinary market
as competing types of markets" (795) and argued that market transactions were not eliminated within the firm. They declared: "The firm . . .
has no power of fiat, no authority, no disciplinary action any different in
the slightest degree from ordinary market contracting between any two
people" (777). In their view, an employer has no more authority over an
employee than a customer has over a grocer.

For Alchian and Demsetz, the principal difference between intrafirm relationships (a grocer and his employee) and ordinary market contracting (a grocer and his customer) lay in the "*team* use of inputs and a centralized position of some party in the contractual arrangements of *all* other inputs." Their challenge was to explain why, "instead of multilateral contracts among all the joint inputs' owners, a central common party to a set of bilateral contracts facilitates efficient organization of the joint inputs in team production" (1972, 794). With team production, the overall output is observable, but each individual's contribution to the output is difficult to determine. This creates an "incentive to shirk" or free-ride (780). Team members realize that their effort can be reduced without a proportional loss of their own income.

Hence, according to Alchian and Demsetz (1972, 781–82), it made sense for "someone to specialize as a monitor to check the input performance of team members," provided that the monitor has the "incentive not to shirk as a monitor." This incentive is to attribute "residual claimant status," that is, "title to the net earnings of the team, net of payment to other inputs," to the monitor.

This explanation of the nature and existence of the firm differed radically from that of Coase or Williamson, particularly by its omission of transaction costs. With Alchian and Demsetz (1972), the firm is simply the individual residual claimant who monitors the team. He or she alone reaps the profits, may sue suppliers, or be sued by customers. The firm can be only a self-employed contractor. If an attempt were made to include organizations of multiple human individuals as firms, then the alleged monitoring problem would reemerge, and one of these individuals—according to their logic—would have to become the residual claimant. The multi-individual firm would then revert back into a single-individual entity. Despite the insights in this paper, it cannot deal adequately with multi person firms or corporations.

In a highly influential article, Michael C. Jensen and William H. Meckling (1976) developed their "nexus of contracts" view of the firm.[10] Much of the article involves formal modeling, but its opening pages contain an important conceptual statement. At the outset, the authors identified a major defect in the approach of Coase and Williamson—the common failure to take into account contractual relations with custom-

10. In the citation-based study by Kim, Morse, and Zingales (2006) of "what has mattered" in economics since 1970, Jensen and Meckling's (1976) article features in third position. The Alchian and Demsetz (1972) article is in twelfth place.

ers for the firm's output. Jensen and Meckling (1976, 310) wrote: "Contractual relations are the essence of the firm, not only with employees but with suppliers, customers, creditors, and so on." They took contracts with customers into account and also stressed the role of law. In explicit terms, Jensen and Meckling (1976, 311n) acknowledged "the important role which the legal system and the law play in social organizations, especially, the organization of economic activity." They continued: "Statutory laws sets [sic] bounds on the kind of contracts into which individuals and organizations may enter without risking criminal prosecution. The police powers of the state are available and used to enforce performance of contracts or to enforce the collection of damages for non-performance."

This is a rare acknowledgment of the economic and real significance of the legal aspect of the firm. Jensen and Meckling (1976, 311) admitted that the firm can be a contracting agent. They wrote of "contracts . . . between the legal fiction (the firm) and the owners of labor, material and capital inputs and the consumers of output." Likewise, in another article, Jensen and Meckling (1983, 9) explained: "Individuals and organizations—employees, investors, suppliers, customers, etc.—contract with each other in the name of a fictional entity—the corporation." Here again it was suggested that organizations as well as individuals can contract—and "in the name of" the corporation. This seemed to admit the possibility of corporate legal personality. But ultimately this was denied.

Although Jensen and Meckling noted "the artificial construct under the law which allows certain organizations to be treated as individuals" (1976, 310n), they argued that this is simply a "legal fiction which serves as a nexus for contractual relationships." "Viewing the firm as the nexus of a set of contracting relationships among individuals," they warned: "The personalization of the firm . . . is seriously misleading. *The firm is not an individual*" (311). As Jensen (1983, 327) elaborated elsewhere: "The nexus of contracts view of organizations helps to dispel the tendency to treat organizations as if they were persons. Organizations do not have preferences, and they do not choose in the conscious and rational sense that we attribute to people. . . . [T]he behavior of the organization is like the equilibrium behavior of the market. . . . [T]he individual agent is the elementary unit of analysis."

There are several points of contention here. One concerns the meaning of *legal fiction*. Another concerns the claim that organizations cannot be treated as agents, contrary to many other writers.

Addressing the latter point first, of course organizations do not have their own separate minds or brains. But whether organizations have *preferences* or are *rational* depends on the adopted meanings of those terms.[11] The variability of behavior that Jensen and Meckling observed in organizations is also found in individuals. We can procrastinate or change our minds. There is also the hypothesis of "multiple selves" (Elster 1986a). The differences between individuals and organizations are real, but not entirely as Jensen and Meckling claimed. At root of their argument was a refusal to admit that, when there are clear procedures for resolving internal conflicts and making decisions, organizations can be treated for some purposes as singular agents. This does not imply that individuals are unimportant or dispensable or that organizations are themselves conscious entities.[12]

The position of Jensen and Meckling on "legal fictions" was also problematic. *Legal fictions are not false* (Fuller 1967). They are devices used in legal reasoning to transfer principles that have been established in one context to another. For example, once an order of child adoption is entered, the biological parents become legally unrelated to the child and lose their parental rights. The adoptive parents are legally considered to be the parents of the adopted child. A new birth certificate may be issued. It is a legal fiction. But, as with other legal fictions, it is backed by the power of the law. It is real.

In the case of the corporation, the legal fiction involves a transfer of rights and liabilities concerning ownership and contracting from individuals to registered corporate organizations. This does not necessarily mean that the law grants corporations all the rights that it grants to individuals. Important here are rights to own assets, to enter into contracts, to sue, and to be sued. But other legalities are different: people who terminate a corporation are not charged with murder.

---

11. Could an organization have a preference function? In much analysis, consistency of behavior is the main qualifying criterion. Given such consistency, standard analysis would also describe such a behavioral entity as *rational* (Gintis 2009). As Posner (1980, 5) wrote: "Rationality . . . is a matter of consequences, not states of mind." So, if organizational behavior is consistent, then, by widely accepted criteria, an organization can be given a preference function and regarded as rational. I do not share this standard view (Hodgson 2013b), but Jensen and Meckling (1976) do not even consider it.

12. Coleman (1982), Hindess (1989), and North, Wallis, and Weingast (2009) all argue that under restrictive conditions organizations can be treated as agents. For an excellent philosophical discussion, see List and Pettit (2011).

Jensen and Meckling (1976) failed to acknowledge these nuances. Viewing the firm simply as "a set of contracting relationships among individuals" (311), they failed to show how this "nexus" itself forms a contract with suppliers or customers if it is no longer deemed to be a singular legal entity. They did not consider how the problem of how to deal with the death, bankruptcy, or insanity of one of the individuals making up the nexus. In short, they evaded the issue of how the firm survives the legally operational lives of the individuals in the nexus. Corporations themselves can face critical life-and-death events, such as the merger, acquisition, or liquidation of the entity. These differ from simple contractual relations between individuals.

The key point of contention is whether an organization, as well as a human individual, can itself enter into contracts and have ownership rights. Terms such as *legal person*, *legal personality*, or *legal fiction* should not mislead us into thinking that anything else of major importance is necessarily at stake here. When the law sees the firm as a person, it means no more than that the law treats the firm as a point of imputation for legal rights and duties. Legal "personality" involves an analogy. In his discussion of corporate personality, John Dewey (1926, 656) pointed out that, when we describe a wine as *dry*, we do not mean that it is no longer a liquid—we have merely followed conventional usage and taken this word from one context and applied it to another.

Jensen and Meckling (1976, 311) also blurred the distinction between a firm and a market. They wrote: "The firm is . . . a legal fiction which serves as a focus for a complex process in which the conflicting objectives of individuals . . . are brought into equilibrium within a framework of contractual relations. In this sense the 'behavior' of the firm is like the behavior of a market, that is, the outcome of a complex equilibrium process." On the contrary, a corporation need not be in equilibrium. All that is required of it is the capacity to establish a coherent and legally recognizable position, through appropriate legal procedures, when making any contract with another legal entity. Although bound by their past contracts, organizations, like humans, can change policies back and forth. They can—and sometimes do—develop incoherent or unstable strategies. Although individual contracts may lead to the formation of a firm—as with a partnership contract—they are not contracts to which the firm itself is a party. Negotiations and votes that take place at meetings of boards of directors or shareholders are neither markets nor legal contracts. They are decisionmaking processes within an already-established framework of legal and internal rules. The claim that the firm is like a market is illogical and ungrounded.

Jensen and Meckling (1983, 10) hinted at a different source for their anxiety and an alternative account of the origin of the corporation: "The corporation is *neither* the creature of the state *nor* the object of special privileges extended by the state. . . . [T]he corporation requires for its existence only freedom of contract. Corporate vitality is in no way dependent on *special* dispensation from the authorities. Limited liability, for example, is not an idea specialized to corporations. Non-profit organizations, partnerships, and individual proprietorships, for example, all exhibit various forms of limited liability. . . . Freedom of contract surely encompasses the right of parties to prescribe limits to liability in contracts." Their argument here was not against corporate legal personality as such but against the idea that corporate vitality and limited liability are necessarily creations of the state. They suggested that these arrangements can emerge spontaneously. All that is required is "freedom of contract." This is again redolent of previous debates over the nature of law and money, as visited in preceding chapters. The possibility of spontaneous corporate arrangements is discussed below.

The final case study in this section is the "new property rights theory" of Sanford J. Grossman, Oliver D. Hart, and John H. Moore (Grossman and Hart 1986; Hart 1989, 1995; Hart and Moore 1990; Moore 1992). This approach builds on several preceding theories but is critical of their limitations. Hart (1989, 1764) argued: "The nexus of contracts approach does less to resolve the questions of what a firm is than to shift the terms of the debate." Moore (1992, 494n) wrote similarly: "One can . . . sidestep the issue entirely, by arguing that everything is contractual, and that firms are a mirage. . . . This is the view proposed by Jensen and Meckling. . . . But if firms are a mirage, it is difficult to explain the enormous resources that firms expend merging and breaking up."

Grossman and Hart (1986, 692–93) "define the firm as being composed of the assets (e.g., machines, inventories) that it owns": "We define a firm to consist of those assets that it owns or over which it has control." Or, more crudely, the firm was viewed "as a collection of physical assets" (Hart and Moore 1990, 1121). But a pile of physical assets is insufficient to constitute a firm. Ironically, by focusing solely on control, Grossman and Hart eviscerated the term *property rights*, which they used to describe their theory. In general, an entity cannot be defined solely in terms of what it controls.

Grossman and Hart (1986, 693) saw as a major problem in previous theories the lack of "a sufficiently clear definition of integration." They were right in their identification of a key problem but deficient in terms of its solution. They explained integration in terms of owned nonhuman assets, including machines, buildings, contracts, and patents. These allegedly hold firms together and explain how their managements exert effective powers of authority over employees. In their theory the firm owns these assets and holds rights of control over them as well as the rights to the residual income of the enterprise. Workers require use of those assets and may have few alternative options, especially if they require specialist equipment. Consequently: "Authority over assets translates into authority over people" (Hart and Moore 1990, 1150). As Hart (1995, 57–59) argued: "A firm's nonhuman assets . . . simply represent the glue that keeps the firm together. . . . If such assets do not exist, then it is not clear what keeps the firm together. . . . One would expect firms without at least some significant nonhuman assets to be flimsy and unstable entities, constantly subject to the possibility of break-up or dissolution."

This formulation is inadequate, on at least two counts. First, a collection of assets cannot "simply represent the glue that keeps the firm together." Even in Hart's own terms it is *ownership* or *control* of these collections of assets that provides the firm with power over employees and suppliers. These powers are backed by law. As Scott Masten (1991, 208) insisted: "Ownership itself is a condition sustained by legal rules and remedies." Yet Grossman, Hart, and Moore paid even less attention to the legal nature of the firm than did some of the competing theorists. Hart (2011, 102) asked: "Is a firm circumscribed by its legal status or by its economic activities?" This is a false and misleading dichotomy. The "economic" activities of the firm become possible because the firm has a legal status and powers enshrined in law. As Simon Deakin (2006, 2012) explained, legally recognized capacities define conditions of access to the market—the capacity to own assets and enter contractual relations. As Edward M. Iacobucci and George G. Triantis (2007, 518) put it: "Legal persons may vindicate their ownership rights in court, and they may be defendants against whose property creditors may enforce their claims. Accordingly, only a legal person has the capacity to contract—that is, to make a legally enforceable pledge of its assets to the performance of its promise."

A collection of assets without a legal person as their owner is no more a firm than a collection of bones, flesh, and blood is a human being.

Once the legal and ownership aspects of the problem are fully acknowledged, we face the question of how the firm establishes itself as a unitary
legal entity and becomes more than a collection of contracting individuals. Bengt Holmström (1999, 87) thus wrote: "Individual ownership of
assets does not offer a theory of organizational identities unless one as-
sociates individuals with firms." He concluded: "Property rights theory,
as articulated in Hart and Moore (1990) and other representative pieces,
says very little about the firm. The problem is that there are really no
firms in these models, just representative entrepreneurs" (100).[13]

If nonhuman assets are insufficient to keep the firm together, are they
necessary? Raghuram G. Rajan and Luigi Zingales (2000, 2001) argued
that they are not, pointing out that many modern firms are highly labor
and knowledge intensive. This puts more bargaining power in the hands
of the highly skilled knowledge worker and relatively less in the hands
of the owner of physical assets (Hodgson 1999). According to this argument, the relative importance of ownership of physical assets is diminishing in modern capitalism. There are knowledge-intensive firms such
as software producers that rely on relatively inexpensive hardware. And
there are so-called hollow corporations—such as Benetton or Marks and
Spencer—that subcontract out much of their manufacturing; their corporate identity and competences are more to do with image and marketing
than material assets.

These puzzles concerning the nature and identity of the firm are
solved once we treat it as a legal entity. The glue that holds the firm together consists of the contracts or articles that bind the parties into one
legal entity with its own legal rights and obligations. The organization
becomes a firm when it acquires a legal personality; its ownership of assets is secondary. In the case of the corporation, the glue can outlast the
lifetimes of the individual members involved. Some corporations are
hundreds of years old. Their individuals and assets have changed many
times over, but the corporations live on.

Crucially, the firm is distinct from any or all of its human constitu-
ents, contrary to views of the firm as a coalition of owners, and it is distinct from any and all of its nonhuman assets, contrary to the new property rights theory of Grossman, Hart, and Moore. A coalition of owners

13. See Foss and Foss (2001) for a critique of the concept of ownership in the new
property rights economics. Khalil (1997, 523–24) makes related points in critiques of Hart
and Moore (1990) and Marx.

may create a firm. Firms typically own nonhuman assets. But the firm is not the same thing as a coalition of individuals or a collection of assets.

There is no good reason for economists to relinquish a legally grounded definition of the firm or corporation. All major theories of the firm depend on legal concepts—particularly ownership—despite the neglect of the firm itself as a legal entity. Legal specifications and frameworks are vital for the firm to operate. Legal relations are an unavoidable part of the definition, alongside other factors. This argument is strengthened, not undermined, by the real growth of other economically significant entities such as business units, conglomerates, *keiretsu*, strategic alliances, supplier networks, relational contracting, and so on. Each of these entities makes use of legal forms, including contracts and property rights. Indeed, the growth of a diversity of business and industrial structures makes it imperative to develop clear, distinct definitions of the different entities involved and to understand their legal structure. A muddled reality is no excuse for muddled definitions. Likewise, a mutable reality is no justification for elastic ideas. To describe or understand a tangled reality we need clear concepts and careful definitions to guide us.

8.4. On the History of Firms and the Importance of Legal Incorporation

An aim of this section is to sketch the evolution of the corporate form and related entities and to locate the period when they became widely established. The possibility that corporate arrangements could have arisen spontaneously is then considered in light of this brief historical account.

Paul VerSteeg (2000, 184) claimed that the temples of ancient Mesopotamia, nearly four millennia ago at the time of the Code of Hammurabi, were in some respects like corporations. Vikramaditya S. Khanna (2006) argued that corporate entities were present in ancient India as early as the ninth century BC and were more developed than such entities were in ancient Rome. Sir William Blackstone's *Commentaries on the Laws of England* (1765–69) followed Plutarch by claiming that protocorporations were invented by the Romans in the seventh century BC. The Roman corporations (*societates*) had a singular legal identity, but they were often set up to do business with the state that was denied to private contractors (Silver 2007–8). Paul Vinogradoff (1922, 120–23) provided evidence of corporate entities in ancient Athens in the sixth century BC. In all these cases the state was involved in their formation, registration, or regulation.

Sea-trading partnership firms appeared in Venice and Amalfi in the ninth century of the Christian era to finance single voyages. Apparently, they were modeled on the legal form of the Islamic *muqarada* (Micklethwait and Wooldridge 2003, 17). The terms *company* and *corporation* are medieval in origin. Companies emerged in Florence and Genoa in the twelfth century, when several individuals—typically from one family—agglomerated their capital by establishing a partnership with unlimited and joint liability (Greif 1996). Each partner invested some capital in the company and took a share of any profits in proportion to his investment. Italian-style partnership companies were imitated in parts of Northern Europe. The word *company* comes from the medieval Latin *compagnia*–shared bread. It notified the bringing in of an outside partner to share in a family business. But partnerships are always vulnerable the death or exit of one of the partners.

In the twelfth and thirteenth centuries, new legal systems were developed in England, France, Germany, Sweden, Poland, and the Netherlands, under the influence of the new canon law of the church and the discovery of Justinian Roman law (Berman 1983, 2003). These states began to recognize some organizations as "corporate persons"—which could endure in perpetuity and survive the death or exit of an individual member. These developments were most advanced in England. Towns, charities, religious communities, universities, and guilds became corporations. They were set up by royal charter and regulated by the state, with privileges and immunities. Most of these were not business institutions, and they did not evolve into modern business corporations (Hessen 1979, 1987). The legal terms *corporation* and *act of incorporation* date from this time, with the connotation of a grant of rights from the state to a relatively autonomous organization. Elements of this legal framework of incorporation were later applied to business firms.

Chartered companies emerged in England in the sixteenth and seventeenth centuries, including the Muscovy Company (1555), the East India Company (1600), and the Hudson's Bay Company (1670), the latter still in existence today. Until the Glorious Revolution of 1688, companies had to obtain a royal charter of incorporation. The Dutch East India Company was formed in 1602. Unlike many preceding English chartered companies, it was structured in such a way that shareholders extended their membership beyond one voyage. It instituted a form of limited liability and traded shares on a stock exchange from 1611 (Micklethwait and Wooldridge 2003, 28). The institutional ancestors of the modern business corporation were the joint-stock companies that grew in England from the seventeenth century.[14]

After the collapse of the South Sea Bubble in 1720, new legal restrictions impaired the formation of companies in England. But these were often circumvented by mechanisms such as the legal partnership or legal trust. Legally chartered corporations continued to exist alongside unincorporated firms, which often adopted a similar organizational structure (Du Bois 1938).

During the Industrial Revolution the advantages of corporate organization in raising and investing large amounts of capital became apparent. As transactions became more complex and extensive, the difficulties of dealing with unincorporated firms and partnerships became more burdensome. In the case of contract default, for example, it was necessary to litigate against all partners, thus incurring high legal costs. In his 1837 UK Parliamentary report on the limitations of partnership arrangements, the esteemed lawyer Henry Bellenden Ker bemoaned the impracticality of litigating simultaneously against numerous partners in cases of dispute (Arruñada 2012, 98). By contrast, with a corporation, there is only one legal person to litigate against.

France established a corporate form in 1807 and Sweden in 1848. Connecticut in 1837 allowed corporations to be formed by registration rather than legal enactment. This legislation was copied by the other US states (Handlin and Handlin 1945; Hessen 1979, 1987). Corporations in the United States grew massively in number and size. Alfred Chandler (1977, 50–65, 204) reported that, before 1840, few US firms employed over 50 workers but that by 1891 the Pennsylvania Railroad Company alone employed over 110,000 persons.[15]

In Britain, prior to the company legislation of 1844, the emerging

14. It is estimated that in 1760 joint-stock companies represented 15 percent of England's net reproducible stock and that by 1840 this figure had risen to over 24 percent (Harris 2000, 193–98).

15. Roy (1997) showed that the government underwrote and promoted some of the major infrastructural and other projects that led to the first sizable US corporations after 1870.

industrial economy was dominated by joint-stock companies, partnerships, and family firms. Many operated in legal terms as partnerships but with freely transferable shares (Ireland 1984, 1996, 2010). But a few large-scale, pre-1844 firms—notably railway companies[16]—were individually incorporated by acts of Parliament.

The UK Joint Stock Companies Act of 1844 made explicit in law the distinction between a partnership and a joint-stock company. Partners are mutual agents, able to establish contracts with others that are binding on all partners. By contrast, shareholders are not mutual agents; they cannot themselves act in the name of the firm. The 1844 act created the Register of Joint Stock Companies and made it much easier to form a company. The Limited Liability Act of 1855 established the general rights of a legal corporation and allowed limited liability to companies of more than twenty-five shareholders (Du Bois 1938; Hunt 1935a, 1935b). By 1862, UK corporate legislation had clearly established three key principles: a single legal personality, multiple shareholding, and limited liability. By the end of the nineteenth century, many countries in Europe had adopted limited liability legislation for corporations.

The UK company legislation from 1844 to 1862 removed an "important limitation on the growth and ultimate size of the business firm when it destroyed the connection between the extent and nature of a firm's operations and the personal financial position" of the shareholders (Penrose 1959, 6). But as late as 1885 the limited companies were relatively few in number and confined to larger firms in the shipping, iron and steel, and cotton industries. Family businesses still dominated British industry (Payne 1967, 520). Corporate registration took off toward the end of the nineteenth century. Between 1893 and 1897 the annual registrations of new limited companies more than doubled, from 2,515 to 5,149. In 1905, of the forty-five largest manufacturing, extractive, and agricultural processing companies with capital over £2,000,000, only four were registered before 1880, and thirty-two were registered in 1890 or after (Payne 1967, 527, 539–40). While the most important developments in corporate law—in the United States, the United Kingdom, and other

16. Railway companies required parliamentary enactment of legal powers of compulsory land purchase. As noted in chapter 6 above, from 1825 until 1850 the railway companies played a huge role on the UK stock markets and outweighed the share volume of all other companies combined (Reed 1975). The burgeoning market in railway shares prompted the legislation that buttressed the corporation as a legal entity (Ireland 1996).

countries—were in the nineteenth century, corporate capitalism was more a twentieth-century phenomenon.

The nineteenth-century corporate law reforms in Britain, America, and elsewhere facilitated the formation and operation of business corporations and provided them with the protection of limited liability. As John Micklethwait and Adrian Wooldridge (2003, 60) put it in their historical study: "No matter how much modern businessmen may presume to the contrary, the company was a political creation."

A problem with the claim that corporate personality and legal liability could emerge spontaneously is that we have no historical example of them doing so. Theories of the spontaneous emergence of money rely on the fact that, once money gets partially established, it becomes convenient for others to adopt it. But the formation of a company is not necessarily more advantageous simply because others are formed. Company formation does not involve the network externalities or coordination advantages that are claimed for money. Forming a company is one option among several. By the 1860s, in developed countries, businesspeople had the choice of numerous legal options. Partnership agreements and corporate articles of association were also flexible. Yet many opted for the state-registered company. One reason for this is obvious: official registration provided a ready-made and tested legal template, saving the cost and bother of drawing up something different. But, for this template to be there, the state first had to establish the legal framework.

As noted above, Jensen and Meckling (1983, 10) proposed that limited liability could emerge spontaneously through "freedom of contract." Voluntarily contracts would be drawn up to limit liability when agreed. But, if a firm established a policy of limited liability, this limitation would have to be inserted in every one of its contracts, and every partner or shareholder would have to check every single contract with every contractor or employee to ensure that his or her assets were not unlimitedly liable, in case the firm were sued (Robé 2011). Especially with large and complex organizations this is highly impractical. The transaction costs are too high. It is difficult to see how such arrangements could emerge and spread spontaneously. It is more feasible to establish the status of limited liability, backed by law. This underlines the importance of firm registration and a standard procedure for legal incorporation.

According to some accounts, some towns and monasteries in medieval Europe established a corporate legal personality without the legal approval of their sovereign states (Berman 1983, chap. 12; Pirenne 1925,

121–51). But these towns and monasteries were effectively local monopolies, and any trader might have faced a costly journey of several days to find an alternative legal arrangement.

Otherwise, it is difficult to see how corporate legal personality could emerge and spread by mutual agreement. Assume that a group of traders thinks that the legal fiction of the corporation is a good idea and attempts to set up one or more corporations. Everyone who does business with these corporations must accept that they are making contracts not with partners or shareholders but with the corporation itself. Furthermore, the courts must universally recognize this in the case of any dispute. A single court judgment that strayed from this rule would upset the applecart. Occasional recognition would not necessarily establish a general rule. It would be difficult to see how the law would be changed to recognize corporate legal personality without the traders forming the group getting involved in the politics of the sovereign state of which they are citizens and pushing through legislation providing the option of legal incorporation and its basic rules. If they were successful, that state would then have to establish a register of corporations. It would no longer be a spontaneous process in the sense of being separate (or separable) from the state. Such business pressure on legislatures in fact happened during the nineteenth century.

Legal personality has clear advantages in regard to uncertainties and complexities surrounding any long-standing contract. It provides flexibility in the face of an unpredictable future. Jean-Philippe Robé (2011, 16–17) put it clearly:

> In a situation where it is difficult or even impossible to agree details in advance in a complete contract, parties . . . will *not* choose to write an incomplete contract and see what happens. . . . They would be foolish to put themselves in a position where they know in advance events will occur forcing them to revise the contract, on which they will most likely disagree . . . which will put them in the hands of a third party to resolve their dispute. Businessmen acting in such a way go bankrupt. Rather, a solution is (*a*) to create a separate juridical entity to own or control the key assets used in the firm's operations and (*b*) to specify (in the articles of incorporation and bylaws, or even via a side shareholders' agreement) the *procedures* which will be followed to operate the venture. And if the procedures provided for in the articles of incorporation and bylaws are incomplete, corporate law and general contract law will specify the rights and obligations of the parties. One of the key ad-

vantages of creating a juridical person owning or controlling the assets used in the business is precisely that it avoids having to agree in advance on detailed contracts among the shareholders to specify who will do what in what circumstances and get what in return. All the rights, including the residual control rights in connection with the various assets contributed to the business, are now owned by the "artificial" juridical person, not by any of the contracting parties. The so-called "legal fiction" of the corporation, far from being negligible in economic analysis, *is actually central to it.*

There are further reasons for the economic effectiveness of the corporation. Margaret Blair (1999, 2003) argued that legal entity status protects corporate property by "locking-in capital" so that it can be neither retrieved by the shareholders nor taken away by lawsuits from creditors. Similarly, Henry Hansmann, Reinier Kraakman, and Richard Squire (2006) wrote of the "entity shielding" function of the corporation, which protects corporate assets from the personal creditors of its shareholders and, conversely, the shareholders' creditors from those of the corporation. These reasons explain why ownership rights to assets are vested in the corporation itself and why contracts are made with corporations rather than with their shareholders.

8.5. Conclusion: Defining the Firm

Although *firm* is used here in the broad sense of a legally recognized unit set up for the purposes of producing and selling goods or services, there are other productive entities that are different from firms and also have to be defined. For example, P. Sargant Florence (1957) considered matters of control and possible oligopolistic concentrations of power. He argued: "To economists, more directly interested in degrees of competition and monopoly than in industrial location, the firm, the unit of control, is more important than the plant, the physical unit" (244). In this context, he placed more emphasis on the "unit of control" than on the legally defined entity of the firm. The problem was how to deal statistically with subsidiary companies that legally were separate firms but were managed and controlled by their parent companies. Florence endorsed the practice of the UK Census of Production, which used the term *business unit* to refer to a parent company together with any subsidiary companies of which it owned more than 50 percent. Hence, a business unit was not the same as a single company in the legal sense. Neither would it include subsidiaries in which the interest of the parent company was in practice sufficient for managerial control but did not amount to as much as 50 percent. Florence made it clear that firms and business units were different things and required different definitions.

Fritz Machlup (1967, 26) argued differently. He listed no less than ten "concepts of the firm employed in the literature of business and economics" and suggested that even more were in use. He argued that the firm had been regarded as an organization, a decisionmaking system, a collection of assets and liabilities, a juridical person, a business unit under a single management, and much more besides. He then concluded: "This exercise should have succeeded in showing how ludicrous the efforts of some writers are to attempt *one* definition of the firm in economic analysis. . . . I hope that there will be no argument about which concept of the firm is the most important or the most useful. Since they serve different purposes, such an argument would be pointless" (28).

But clearly this is a non sequitur. The fact that several different conceptions of the firm exist does not imply that the formulation and promotion of one best definition should be abandoned. On the contrary, it could be argued that the very confusion itself calls out for a single, commonly accepted definition. Machlup rightly pointed out that these different concepts "serve different purposes." But it did not occur to him that these different definitions might also point to different things. A (legal) firm is not the same thing as a business unit, or a collection of assets, or a production plant. These are not simply different *concepts*: they are different *entities*. Accordingly, we require a plurality of concepts to refer to a plurality of real arrangements.

Cheung (1983, 17) argued that any definition of the firm is subjective and arbitrary: "According to one's view a 'firm' may be as small as a relationship between two input owners or, if the chain of contracts is allowed to spread, as big as the whole economy." He then concluded: "Thus it is futile to press the issue of what is or is not a firm" (18). Cheung's argument was basically this: because different definitions of X are possible, it is futile to define X. But this too is a non sequitur. If different definitions exist, then to communicate we have to make clear the one we have chosen rather than abandon definitions altogether.

No good argument has been presented to abandon a legal conception of the firm. It is also important to adopt additional concepts such as business unit, production plant, and conglomerate to describe other important structures in the business world. Multiple concepts are required to describe multiple real entities. Instead, it is repeatedly proclaimed that all attempts to define the firm are fruitless. This licensed imprecision promotes habits of conceptual vagueness and terminological sloppiness that have marred the literatures in economics and business studies ever since. It is no wonder that progress in the theory of the firm has virtually ground to a halt.

Claims that the boundaries of the firm have broken down and that there is no essential distinction between firms and markets are misconceived. Internal markets within firms prove to be chimerical. Alleged cases of firm-market hybrids turn out to be interlocking relations or networks between multiple and distinct legal firms or legal persons rather than an encompassing firm or hybrid form.

Recognition of the absence of markets and commodity exchange inside firms is important for several reasons. It dispenses with confused terms such as *internal market, continuum,* and *hybrid.* It also helps underline the relevance of the boundaries of the firm and the vital interface between nonmarket and market modes of coordination. Any analysis of the formation and role of these boundaries has vital implications for corporate and public policy. A neglect of legal realities impairs any attempt by the social scientist to give advice on appropriate legal structures to enhance economic performance.

Furthermore, without attention to legal relations, social scientists are ill equipped to intervene in the long debate concerning the limitation of abuses of corporate power. They will be less able to evaluate the conditions involved in any legal incorporation of a firm by the state and the nature of the quid pro quo for society in return for the legal privilege of limited liability. Without attention to these features, social scientists may become dangerously indifferent to policies that extend or diminish the scope of corporate power or the real market. They will be unable to engage effectively in important debates concerning corporate law reform and the development of corporate structures that are more conducive to social welfare.

The firm has at least two fundamental features: (1) it is set up with resources and capabilities to produce goods or services for sale; and (2) in owning assets, contracting inputs, and selling outputs it acts as a single legal person. As a legal person, the firm has legal ownership of the goods as property up to the point that they are exchanged with the customer, the legal right to obtain contracted remuneration for the produced services, and the potential liability to be sued for nonfulfillment of contracts with suppliers or customers.

Consider a third possible condition: (3) a firm is an organization of two or more people. This condition would rule out the possibility of single-person firms. A person acting as a sole trader with the aim of producing goods or services would not be a firm in this case. There are arguments for and against condition (3).[17] The main argument in favor is that by *firms* people often mean organizations. Single-person firms lack intraorganizational relations that are grist to the mill of business practice, industrial relations, and organization studies.

A strong argument against condition (3) is that it is possible for a single-person business to become a corporation. Although one person only is involved, incorporation separates the liabilities of the individual from those of the business. A corporation is a single legal person, and it matters less whether one or more individuals are involved behind the corporate veil. Furthermore, in countries where businesses have to be officially registered, single-person units are typically included.

If we treat the firm as always an organization, then we raise the familiar problems of organizational boundaries. A classic problem is distinguishing, in both law and practice, between an employment contract and a contract for services.[18] With a contract for services, the worker is not an employee of the firm in question. He or she may be a contracted employee of another firm or a self-employed consultant selling a service. One might conclude that an employee would be inside the organization while the worker working under a contract for services would be outside. Hence, with condition (3), a single entrepreneur employing an office cleaner would be a firm, whereas that same entrepreneur contracting the services of that same cleaner as a nonemployee would not be a firm. This anomaly militates against condition (3).

If we drop condition (3) and retain conditions (1) and (2), then the notion of the boundaries of the firm has diminished meaning. Following Jensen, Meckling, and others, the firm is more a *nexus* than a bounded

17. In earlier works (Hodgson 2002), condition (3) was integral to my definition of the firm. I have since been persuaded—principally by David Gindis—to abandon it.

18. This difference "has taxed the ingenuity of judges" (Wedderburn 1971, 53). See also Kahn-Freund (1983), Wedderburn (1993), and Deakin and Morris (1995). It is not suggested here that the distinction between an employment contract and a contract for services is unreal or unimportant.

zone. But condition (1) sharpens this nexus from being any contracting agent or individual, to give the firm the distinct purpose of production for exchange. This makes it *more* than a nexus: it is a functional entity. Furthermore, the vital stipulation of legal personality in condition (2) constitutes the nexus and provides the missing person that is absent in much of the theory of the firm (Gindis 2013).

An individual trader is a nexus of contracts but has mind, body, memory, expectations, and intentions as well. A firm is also a nexus of contracts but similarly is more than that. All firms have the capacity to produce and sell a product. When the firm is an organization, it also has structure, managers, routines, capabilities, strategies, and much more.

The principal structural bonds that keep the multi-person firm together are fixed by the founding agreement of association, to be altered infrequently rather than through everyday renegotiation. These bonds are very different from market relationships. The firm is a distinct legal entity. It owns its products and sells or hires them to others. It enters into contracts with its workforce and its customers. Accordingly, its external relations involve contracts and sometimes markets. But neither markets nor exchange can exist *inside* the single legal entity of the firm. To engage in production, firms manage their owned or hired resources by administrative control rather than via markets and exchange.

Coase (1937) started a long debate on the nature of the firm that is still unresolved. The argument in this chapter is that theorists have basically been looking in the wrong direction. They have looked to managing and contracting in production as the portal to an understanding of the nature of the firm. Instead, the firm is constituted by its relations with society more broadly, including the state. External relations and legal powers provide the glue that holds the firm together. They may bind partners together with durable contracts, or they may constitute the firm as a corporate entity. The firm is an institution made not by private ordering but through the interactions of business with the established rules of contract and company law. Even if the legal notion of a firm tells us little of how production is or can be organized, it is vital to understand how a firm interacts with suppliers and customers. Production comes in as a condition and purpose of its existence, as a means to create goods and services to trade with the outside world.

CHAPTER NINE

Labor and Employment

When we leave this sphere of simple circulation or the exchange of commodities . . . a certain change takes place, or so it appears, in the physiognomy of our *dramatis personae*. He who was previously the money-owner now strides out in front as a capitalist; the possessor of labour-power follows as his worker. The one smirks self-importantly and is intent on business; the other is timid and holds back, like someone who has brought his own hide to market and now has nothing else to expect but—a tanning. — Karl Marx (1867)

But in our society, labor is one of the few productive factors that cannot legally be bought outright. Labor can only be rented, and the wage rate is really a rental. — Paul A. Samuelson (1976)

This chapter has three primary aims. The first is to consider the nature of the employment relationship. An employment contract is different from a sales contract or a contract for services. The employment contract has evolved from feudal beginnings and adapted to deal with severe problems of complexity, uncertainty, and unpredictability in production. Nevertheless, much of the interaction between employees and managers cannot be reduced to the detail of contractual agreements and relies on additional mechanisms of motivation and control.

The second aim is to consider the consequences of practical and legal limitations on contracts for future employment. Although employment became a predominant social relation within capitalism and capitalism is associated with the spread of commodity exchange, contracting possibilities for future employment are severely limited. Employees cannot be tied down for life: they quit after serving a period of notice. Hence, there are inevitable "missing markets" at the core of capitalism. Employers have to address the problem of expenditure on training and how trained

employees in a firm can be retained. The risk of an employee quitting di-
minishes employer incentives for training workers.

Third, I consider Marx's claim that the employment relationship is a
foremost characteristic of capitalism. This is questioned on the basis of
historical evidence and its defining features. One section of this chapter
is devoted to each of these three questions.

9.1. The Nature of the Employment Relationship

As does law in most other developed countries today, English law makes
a distinction between a *contract of service* (employment) and a *contract
for services* (sales contract). A servant or employee "is any person who
works for another upon the terms that he is subject to the control of that
other person as to the *manner* in which he shall do his work" (James
1966, 322–23). In contrast, with a contract for services, the worker is an
independent contractor and not an employee of the person purchasing
the services. The law "of master and servant" applies to an employment
contract where the master has "the right to control the servant's work":
"It is this right of control or interference . . . which is the dominant characteristic in this relation and marks off the servant from an independent
contractor" (Batt 1929, 6).

The economist Herbert Simon (1951, 294) recognized that the employment contract differs "fundamentally from a sales contract—the
kind of contract that is assumed in ordinary formulations of price theory." In a sales contract a "completely specified commodity" is exchanged for an agreed amount. In contrast, in the employment contract
the worker agrees to perform one of several roles or assignments and allows the employer to select and allocate the tasks from a known set. In
addition, the worker accepts the authority of the employer to choose the
work to be performed and supervise the details of its execution.

A distinctive feature of the employment relationship is the *potential*
power of employer control over the manner and pattern of work. Because of the uncertainties and complexities involved, these powers of
control cannot be specified in detail. But there are legal and contractual
limits to what the employer can require of the employee. In return, the
employer agrees to pay the worker by the hour, day, week, or month or
by the quantity of output produced.

In contrast, if we hire a window cleaner, typically we are not employing that person; instead, we are purchasing window-cleaning services. The person cleaning the windows may be self-employed or employed by a window-cleaning company. In neither case are we employing the window cleaner. To make the window cleaner our employee we would have to assume the right of detailed control and interference in the manner and pattern of work.

Control test refers to consideration of who is in control of the manner of work as the means of discriminating between the two types of contract. But in legal practice this is often inconclusive. Additional criteria are often used, particularly whether the worker owns or provides the instruments of work and whether the worker is genuinely working "on his or her own account" or is part of an organization (Wedderburn 1971, 1993; Kahn-Freund 1983; Deakin and Morris 1995). But, despite the real-world muddle, the demarcation of legal ideal types is a necessary means of dealing with an enduringly important distinction.

A contract for services can be offered by both a self-employed worker and a firm with employees. Marxists refer to a society of self-employed producers as *simple* or *petty* commodity production, and they distinguish this from the capitalist mode of production. This acknowledges the importance of the difference between employment and self-employment.

A key feature of Simon's (1951) model is the fact that the outcomes (such as costs, profits, or work satisfaction) for each pattern of work are not known precisely at the time of contracting. Simon formalizes this by considering the probabilities of outcomes for each possible pattern of work. At the time of contracting both employer and employee are assumed to know the relevant probabilities but not the precise outcomes. But, if this were the case, then there would be no need for an employment contract. A detailed contract for services specifying what would happen in all contingencies could be negotiated. Parties to the contract would know the expected costs and benefits for all possible eventualities. In reality, neither the possibilities nor the probabilities are known to the extent that Simon surmised. His model did not adequately encapsulate the ignorance, complexity, unpredictability, and uncertainty (in the sense of Frank Knight [1921] or John Maynard Keynes [1937]) that are associated with production processes, especially in modern capitalism. Such complexity, uncertainty, or ignorance makes the meaningful calculation of probabilities impossible.

Armen A. Alchian and Harold Demsetz (1972) downplayed the difference between firms and markets and dissolved the distinction between an employment contract and a contract for services. For Alchian and Demsetz (1972, 777), the authority of an employer over an employee was no different than other legal powers of enforcement in other contracts: "Telling an employee to type this letter rather than to file that document is like my telling a grocer to sell me this brand of tuna rather than that brand of bread." But this overlooked an important difference between an employment contract and a sales contract (or contract for services). The consumer has little power over the *manner of execution* of a sales contract. It would be like the customer asking the grocer to smile when passing the tuna and to consider dressing more smartly in the future. Such commands can have legal force with an employment contract but not within a sales contract. It is the power of detailed control over the manner of work that is crucial.

Alchian and Demsetz assumed that, when control over the detailed manner of work is being exercised in an employment contract, the contract is (implicitly) being "continuously renegotiated."[1] But this is not the case. Unless the employee or the employer raises the question of renegotiation explicitly, it will generally not be recognized in law. It is bad theory and dangerous policy to assume that people are negotiating and coming to agreements when they are themselves aware of no such thing.[2]

It is true that "custom and practice" can be recognized by legal authority as a modification of the contract itself. But there are often legal requirements that these changes have to be brought to the attention of those involved. Under British law, for example, employers have "an obligation to report those terms and conditions of employment that have been either individually agreed, incorporated into individual contracts from collective agreements, or implied from some other source such as

---

1. Commons (1924, 285) wrote: "The labor contract is not a contract, it is a continuing renewal of a contract at every successive moment, implied simply from the fact that the laborer keeps at work and the employer accepts his product." But his conclusion does not follow. Consider a slave who "keeps at work" and a slave owner who "accepts his product." This is not a "continuing renewal of a contract" between master and slave. Furthermore, the accepted performance of a worker who "keeps at work" is hardly evidence of renegotiation. It might mean that both employer and employee are satisfied with an enduring contractual arrangement.

2. Dangers of reckless attribution of "implicit contracts" are dramatized by the claims of the Reverend Seabury (1861), a defender of slavery during the American Civil War. He argued that there was an implicit legal contract between slave owner and slave, evidenced by the failure of some slaves to flee when they had an opportunity.

custom or practice" (Brown, Deakin, Nash, and Oxenbridge 2000, 623). Although implicit ("implied-in-fact") contracts are sometimes recognized in law, they are subject to legal tests. The evolved contract must itself be legal, and the conduct of the parties must show tacit understanding concerning relevant details.

Production processes depend vitally on dispersed, uncodifiable, and tacit knowledge. The complexity and inaccessibility of much of this knowledge means that no worker or manager can know fully what is going on. Furthermore, all production involves learning, and in principle we do not know what is yet to be learned in the future. There can be innovations in organization or technology, and these are by definition unpredictable. Production processes are often complex to the degree that precise analysis and prediction are confounded. They involve human actors, who can be capricious or unpredictable. They are vulnerable to uncertain shocks and disturbances from the outside world. Overall, key outcomes are uncertain, in the Keynesian and Knightian sense.

Consequently, in many circumstances, employment contracts can have productive advantages over contracts for services.[3] By their nature, employment contracts rely on authority and are imperfectly and incompletely specified. The terms of the contract cannot be spelled out in full detail because of the complexity of the work process and the unpredictability of key outcomes. Problems of complexity and uncertainty are found to some degree in other contracts, but with contracts relating to the production process they are particularly severe. Employment contracts are always messy and incomplete. They typically rely on trust and give and take rather than complete or strict legal specification (Fox 1974). Often, they involve intensive social interaction and rely acutely on cultural and noncontractual norms.

The impossibility of completely specified employment contracts has profound implications for economic theory and policy. Output depends not simply on the contract and the capabilities of those involved but on the motivation of the workers. This motivation is at best partly contractible. The literature on "efficiency wages" proposes that workers may increase productivity without contractual obligation, in response to higher

---

3. There is a moral case against employment contracts, with the proposed alternative being democratic worker cooperatives (Ellerman 1992). By some criteria, producer cooperatives can be of superior efficiency (Pagano 1985; Bonin, Jones, and Putterman 1993; Zamagni and Zamagni 2010). Cooperatives are discussed later in this book.

wages or better working conditions (Hobson 1901; Akerlof and Yellen 1986; Stiglitz 1987; Weiss 1991).

The limits to contract and the dependence on informal norms are widely accepted in organization theory (Levitt and March 1988; Powell and DiMaggio 1991). As a result, one of the most subversive instruments that can be used by employees in disputes with employers is "working to rule." The contract is followed in pedantic rather than conciliatory mode, tediously observing each letter and detail of its specification, and violating unwritten cultural norms that are the fabric of cooperation and goodwill. With these informal supports removed, formalities of the contract become more an encumbrance than an asset.

Accordingly, a potentially counterproductive managerial practice is to attempt to specify an employment contract in every detail. Such measures often fail, partly because of the degree of complexity and unpredictability of the phenomena they attempt to describe and control. Furthermore, they can undermine trust and cooperation and create a punitive and corrosive atmosphere of litigation within the firm.[4]

Hence, the employment contract is imperfectly bounded, containing a sizable zone of legal impermeability. Again, one is reminded of Émile Durkheim's argument that "in a contract not everything is contractual." There are additional and unavoidable factors, not reducible to the intentions or agreements of individuals, that have regulatory and binding functions for the contract itself.

Given the limits of formal contract, employment relationships must rely on the cultural cement of loyalty, trust, duty, and moral obligation (Fox 1974; Minkler 2008; Hodgson 2013b). In an analysis of hierarchy, Gary Miller (1992) suggests that firms succeed insofar as they transcend narrow, individual opportunism by an ethic of mutual cooperation. As Joseph A. Schumpeter (1942, 423) pointed out, capitalist production depends on "those loyalties and those habits of super- and subordination that are nevertheless essential for the efficient working of the institutionalized leadership of the producing plant."

Living and working in cooperative social groups for millions of years,

---

4. Jacoby (1990, 334) observed: "As industrial studies have repeatedly shown, the presumption of innate opportunism is fatal to trust. . . . It leads to a proliferation of control structures—supervision, rules, and deferred rewards—intended to inhibit opportunism. These create resentment and distrust among employees, who correctly perceive the controls as expressions of their employer's distrust."

humans have evolved dispositions to cooperate and respect authority (Darwin 1871; Milgram 1974; Bowles and Gintis 2011; Krebs 2011;
Nowak and Highfield 2011; Hodgson 2013b). Our prehistoric social world
was not one of freely negotiated contracts between individuals enjoying
equal legal rights. Instead, there was cooperation with others on the basis of customary rules and conventions, within hierarchies of power and
authority. Until very recently, in the terms of Henry Maine (1861), human society has had much more to do with status than with contract.

The capitalist firm harnesses our genetically and culturally inherited
impulses to cooperate and respect authority. Although capitalism itself
is a very recent social formation, the humans that live and work within it
have evolved both genetically and culturally over a much longer period
of time. Capitalism is obliged to use, and marginally adapt, our evolved
human nature.

Law in general and property and contract in particular are core institutions of the capitalist order. But law cannot encapsulate everything.
The employment relation is the perfect illustration: it is irreducible to
contract alone. The exercise of power, even in a contract-ridden economy, is largely a result of noncontractual phenomena such as taking
things for granted or of conformism to established custom and accepted
authority. Such matters cannot be understood adequately in terms of explicit disputes over the details of any contractual agreement. Marx (1976,
280) emphasized that the "silent compulsion of economic relations sets
the seal on the domination of the capitalist over the worker." John Commons (1934, 701) noted that on those rare occasions "when customs
change . . . it is realized that the compulsion of custom has been there
all along, but unquestioned and undisturbed." As John Westergaard and
Henrietta Resler (1976, 144) put it: "Power is to be found more in un-
eventful routine than in conscious and active exercise of will."

Capitalism retains zones of legal impermeability in the sphere of production. Historically, these have often meant the servitude of the worker
and the arbitrary power of the employer, where the employee has had
limited practical recourse to the law to protect his or her rights. But this
noncontractarian zone has also been the site of enhanced cooperation; it
draws on the evolved dispositions in our human nature both to respect
authority and to cooperate with others.

Part of the unwitting genius of capitalism is to harness these noncontractarian elements in the sphere of production while giving fuller reign
to property and contract in the spheres of financing, innovation, invest-

ment, marketing, and distribution. For millions of years, rivalry between human groups has given the advantage to those communities that cohere and cooperate. Cultural group selection among competing groups has honed dispositions to cooperate with others in the same group. As Darwin (1871) explained, intergroup competition is the spur for intragroup cooperation.[5]

Such an evolutionary perspective challenges both the individualist depiction of the economy as a self-interested struggle of each against all and the rose-tinted ultraleftist utopia of unbounded amity and cooperation with little need for structures or incentives. Although not necessarily optimal, modern capitalism exhibits a creative tension between organizational cooperation and market competition. Competition and cooperation are synergetic phenomena.

This does not mean that capitalism is natural or the supreme expression of human nature. The synergy of cooperation and competition has worked in different kinds of social structure before. Capitalism is but one possible expression of this synergy. Furthermore, like other social arrangements, it has glitches and anomalies. A major congenital limitation of capitalism is discussed in the next section.

9.2. Capitalism and the Inevitability of Missing Markets

General equilibrium theory, as developed by Kenneth J. Arrow and Gerard Debreu (1954), assumed that markets exist for all commodities, in all possible states of the world, for all points of time in the future. Similarly, a contractarian ideology associated with capitalism might suggest that everything, under any condition, at any time, is—or should be—subject to trade. But, if one of these commodity-, state-, and time-dependent markets is missing, then the absence of key information concerning prices on that missing market can cascade through the system and affect the overall outcome. The efficiency of other markets can be spoiled.

Oliver Hart (1975, 442) showed that in "an economy with incomplete

5. Because of intergroup migration in primate groups and hunter-gatherer human tribes (De Waal 2006; Hill et al. 2011), this group selection process has probably been stronger at the cultural than at the genetic level. See Henrich (2004) for an explanation of the difference between genetic and cultural group selection and Boyd and Richerson (1985), Bowles and Gintis (2011), and Hodgson (2013b) for discussions.

markets . . . the usual continuity and convexity assumptions are not sufficient to ensure the existence of equilibrium" and that in such circumstances a market equilibrium may be Pareto suboptimal. Furthermore:
"If we start off in a situation where markets are incomplete, opening
new markets may make things worse rather than better. In this respect,
an economy with incomplete markets is like a typical second best situation." In their more extensive discussion of models with incomplete
markets, Michael Magill and Martine Quinzii (1996) show that missing
markets can mean that equilibria are absent or indeterminate. *All these
conclusions apply inevitably to capitalism because markets therein are
unavoidably incomplete.*

Under capitalism there can never be a complete set of markets for labor power. Although capitalism has meant a huge extension of property
and markets, it has also, by freeing labor from servitude, created *missing* markets for labor futures. For there to be full futures markets for
labor, all workers must be able to enter into contracts for every future
instant in their expected working life. Such a complete curtailment of future discretion would be tantamount to voluntary bondage. The uncertainties involved in the system, from the perspective of both employer
and employee, make such extensive future contracting impractical. Unlike some other missing markets—as with externalities–there is in principle no satisfactory contractarian solution within capitalism to missing
markets for labor power. Enforcing detailed and extended property and
contracting rights would limit the freedom of workers to quit their employment. Typically, workers are employed under a contract that allows
exit, subject to notice of a few months maximum. The limitation of extended futures markets for labor is an important safeguard of the freedom of the employee.

There is some future contracting for labor, particularly when a student receives financial support for studies from a company in return for
a commitment to work for some years in the firm. But the time period is
typically a few years, amounting to a small fraction of the student's future working life. Also, in modern, knowledge-intensive capitalism there
are sometimes noncompete agreements with skilled employees that prevent them leaving a firm and working for a rival for a while. These restrictive agreements are still far short of lifetime contracts.

Also, the future supply of labor power is not something that can be
contracted at source because babies cannot legally be farmed and sold
as commodities within developed capitalism. Human infants and their

future labor power are not themselves produced under capitalist conditions. If they were, it would not be capitalism. Consequently, under capitalism there are unavoidable missing markets for the original production of human resources.[6]

Generally, under capitalism, there can be no complete set of futures markets for the labor of existing or future workers.

This creates a problem for the employer with the existing workforce. If the employer spends money on employee training and skill development, then this investment is lost when workers leaves. As a result, without compensatory arrangements, employers might underinvest in human learning and education. As Alfred Marshall (1920, 565) pointed out: "We meet the difficulty that whoever may incur the expense of investing capital in developing the abilities of the workman, these abilities will be the property of the workman himself: and thus the virtue of those who have aided him must remain for the greater part its own reward." He argued that the development of skills in the capitalist enterprise must depend "in great measure on the unselfishness of the employer."

This system shortfall has a number of possible remedies. With due credit to Marshall, relying on employer unselfishness is hardly a viable solution because employers face competition from other firms and obligations to make profits. Could employers retain workers by offering wages at above the market rate? This might lead to an arms race of employee compensation, each firm trying to improve on the wages offered by the others in attempts to retain and attract skilled workers. Employers might create a more participatory corporate culture that engenders worker commitment and loyalty to encourage "voice" rather than "exit" when grievances arise (Hirschman 1970). But again other firms are likely to compete with similar strategies to retain and attract workers.

The likelihood of worker exit can also be reduced by distributing shares in the company to employees (Poole and Whitfield 1994; Pen-

---

6. Sometimes babies are adopted in return for payment. But as Posner (1994, 410) rightly pointed out: "The term *baby selling* . . . is misleading. A mother who surrenders her parental rights for a fee is not selling her baby; babies are not chattels, and cannot be bought and sold. She is selling her parental rights." In contrast, Becker (1991, 362ff.) wrote imprecisely of babies being sold when in fact he meant the sale of parental rights. Note that Posner's valid argument depends on a distinction between property and possession that he otherwise failed to sustain. Parents may control and thereby possess their babies, but they do not own them.

dleton, Wilson, and Wright 1998; Hubbick 2001; Robinson and Zhang 2005). There may be an additional role for state aid for training. Governments have subsidized employee training (with some success) in some countries and in some US states (Holzer, Block, Cheatham, and Knott 1993; Van Horn and Fichtner 2003; Thelen 2004).

The very imperfections of the market system can also come to the rescue here. If workers face high transaction costs in moving from one job to the other, or if labor markets are local and limited, or if employees are tied to one job owing to family or other circumstances, then they are less likely to exit the firm.

The problem of incentivizing investment in training and retaining workers in the firms in which they have been trained is intrinsic to capitalism. Yet this central problem in the system has received remarkably little attention by economists since Marshall, with a few exceptions, such as John Maurice Clark (1923), Kenneth Arrow (1962a), and Donald Stabile (1996). In a major mainstream text, missing markets are treated generally as outcomes of the limitations of the human psyche (Magill and Quinzii 1996) rather than the consequence of historically specific social structures. Precious few students of economics are taught that capitalism must unavoidably entail missing markets, precisely because of the legal freedoms granted to workers, and consequently the fundamental theorems of welfare economics do not apply (Christ 1975; Ellerman 1992, 102).

It is possible within a market economy to circumvent the problem by replacing employee firms by self-employed producers or by worker cooperatives. Self-employed workers have obvious incentives to train themselves in relevant skills. Workers in cooperative firms are shareholders; consequently, they are less likely to quit, and there are stronger incentives to provide training. Would a market economy dominated by self-employed producers or worker cooperatives still be capitalism? This question is considered in the next section.

9.3. Is Wage Labor a Defining Characteristic of Capitalism?

Marx saw wage labor as a defining feature of capitalism. For example, in the first volume of *Capital*, Marx (1976, 291–92) saw the "capitalist firm" as an institution where "the worker works under the control of the capitalist" and "the product is the property of the capitalist and not that of the worker." In the third volume of *Capital*, Marx (1981, 1019) identified wage labor as a "characteristic trait" of the system.

Consider the explosion of capitalist growth that started in about 1800 and is illustrated in figure 1.1 above. Was there a significant and rapid growth of wage labor that preceded this explosion? Marx (1976, 875–76) dated the rise of wage labor in England to the sixteenth century: "The starting point of the development that gave rise to the wage-labourer and to the capitalist, was the enslavement of the worker. The advance consisted in a change in the form of this servitude, in the transformation of feudal exploitation into capitalist exploitation. To understand the course taken by this change, we need not go back very far at all. Although we come across the first sporadic traces of capitalist production as early as the fourteenth or fifteenth centuries in certain towns of the Mediterranean, the capitalist era dates from the sixteenth century."

Even if we forgive Marx's inaccurate description of wage labor as enslavement, he also downplayed the extent of wage labor before the sixteenth century. For example, in some areas in Italy and Flanders in the fourteenth century the employment relationship was well established. In Florence—one of the foremost industrial cities in Europe at that time— there were factories with more than two hundred waged workers, regulated by a communal bell striking the hour. A reawakened Florentine knowledge of Roman law was reflected in a documented distinction between an employment contract (*locatio operarum*) and a contract for services (*locatio operis*). In England, rural labor for day wages was common after the rapid decline of serfdom in the fourteenth century (Postan 1972; Epstein 1991).

The character of wage labor has also to be taken into account. Peter H. Lindert and Jeffrey G. Williamson (1982, 393) estimate, from data provided by Gregory King, that in 1688 about 57 percent of heads of families were "laboring people and . . . servants," "cottagers and paupers," or "vagrants." Estimates rise to 64 percent if those employed in the armed forces are included. But most of this 1688 wage labor was agricultural and often conducted in or around the family residence. Accurate timekeeping and payment of wages by the hour were restricted before the widespread use of clocks or watches (Allen 2012, 42). It took the Industrial Revolution to make timekeeping devices widely available.

Although he identified the sixteenth century as the turning point, Marx wrote more in *Capital* of large-scale employment in mills, mines, and factories. Marx (1973a, 585) wrote in his *Grundrisse*: "Productive capital, or the mode of production corresponding to capital, can be present in only two forms: manufacture and large-scale industry." The use of wage labor as a criterion to help date the birth of capitalism might depend on the relative emphases placed on industrial employment, or employment separated from the family household, vis-à-vis other forms of wage labor.

The difference is dramatic. While rural wage labor dates from medieval times, widespread industrial wage labor emerged much later. As late as about 1803, when the Industrial Revolution was under way, industrial laborers (excluding agriculture, services, and the armed forces) made up about 21 percent of heads of households (Lindert and Williamson 1982, 400). Estimates for 1817 put the number of industrial laborers (excluding agriculture, services, and the armed forces) as 41 percent of males aged over twenty years. In the same year, the figure for male agricultural employment was 40 percent, according to the same study (Kitson et al. 2012, 137).[7]

Marx's vision of a large industrial proletariat was first realized in England in the nineteenth century. But why should the demarcation criterion focus solely on *industrial* wage labor? Apart from the arbitrariness of this narrower criterion, it hit problems in the last quarter of the twentieth century, when capitalism in several countries began to deindustrialize, services played a much more prominent role, and industrial employees eventually became a minority of the workforce (Rowthorn and Wells 1987).

Another factor to be taken into account is the changing nature of the employment relationship as it evolved from quasi-feudal servitude to a contract with parties enjoying nominally equal legal rights. Even in Britain, the legal definition of the employment contract as a free exchange between consenting parties is a relatively recent phenomenon. Wedderburn (1971, 76) quoted a legal authority who observed: "Ideas which had come down from the days of serfdom and villeinage lingered on, so that a master was regarded as having a proprietary right in his servant." In his major study of nineteenth-century employment relations in Britain, Robert Steinfeld (2001) vividly documented the quasi-feudal master-servant relationship, including forms of industrial bondage that severely limited the rights and powers of workers to quit or seek redress.

---

7. Estimating female employment prior to the late nineteenth century is even more difficult. See Shaw-Taylor (2007) for calculations based on the 1851 UK census.

For most of the nineteenth century, employers could use heavy pecuniary and legal sanctions. In Britain until 1875, breach of a labor contract was a criminal rather than a civil offence. This put enormous power in the hands of employers. Premature exit of an employment relationship could be punished by fines, imprisonment, whipping, or transportation. The 1823 Master and Servant Act used "broad language that could be read to cover the overwhelming majority of manual wage workers" and allowed British employers to "have their workmen sent to the house of correction and held at hard labor for up to three months for breaches of their labor agreements" (Steinfeld 2001, 47–48). These were not idle proclamations. Between 1858 and 1875 there were over ten thousand Master and Servant prosecutions per year across Britain—more than for petty larceny (Naidu and Yuchtman 2011). Employment relations then were very different from those prevailing today.

It was the rising trade union movement that led to the termination of criminal sanctions against laborers. But in Britain trade unions were insecure prior to the Trade Union Act of 1871. Trade union rights, combined with the prior extensions of the male franchise, gave organized labor the power to press for reform. The Employers and Workmen Act of 1875 removed criminal sanctions from employment law. But, as late as the early twentieth century, master-servant relations entailing wage labor were often framed and understood in terms of *legal service, established status*, and *traditional obligation*. These terms were more reminiscent of the distant feudal past than the consensual transactions of modern contract law (Kahn-Freund 1977). In the United States similar legal freedoms for workers were not achieved until the early twentieth century, when legal strictures were put in place to limit employers' ability to impose contracts that in practice severely limited the power of the workers to quit.

Labor contracts of six months or a year were commonplace during the nineteenth century. Subject to tolerable working conditions, employees often preferred longer-period contracts because of the increased security of employment and income. Much of the impetus to reduce the term of employment contracts came from employers.

An employment contract involving voluntary agreement akin to trade did not become firmly established in Britain until well into the twentieth century. Even the term *employee* did not become widespread until after 1900. It took the National Insurance Act of 1946 to consolidate the general position and belatedly to extend the terminology of employment law to professional workers such as doctors, lecturers, and administrators (Deakin 1998). Yet the key feature of employer control over the manner and pattern of work is common to both the earlier notion of "service" and the modern contractual formulation.

Ironically, the free exchange of labor power, where the worker met the employer with some semblance of legal equality, was not a product of the classical liberal era of expanding markets and private enterprise. Freer labor markets, where both sides of the employment contract had recourse to legal remedies, came about through the combined strength of trade unions, enlarged democracy, widening taxation, and the twentieth-century welfare state (Deakin 1998, 2001).

These historical facts question any straightforward association between the rise of the employment contract and the economic takeoff of capitalism around 1800. Wage labor existed in England on a large scale much earlier. But these early employment relations were as much remnants of feudal compulsion as examples of free contract. The 1823 Master and Servant Act codified punitive hangovers from the feudal past. Further developments in UK employment law occurred as late as 1875 and 1946. On the one hand, the appearance of wage labor long precedes 1800, but, on the other, other important changes come much later. So where do we draw the line?

Restricting the criterion to *industrial* employment might bring us closer to 1800, but less than half of all male workers were employed in industry at that time. And why focus on industry alone?

The complexities of the employment relationship and its long evolution over several centuries make it a loose historical measure for the life of capitalism. But all is not lost. The importance of the employment relationship can be shown by comparing it with alternatives.

Wage labor differs from both slavery and serfdom: it involves an extension of legal rights that were not enjoyed by serfs or slaves. Slave societies were remarkably slow in developing new technologies. By contrast there was more innovation under feudalism, where serfs had some incentives to improve productivity. But the increases of productivity unleashed under employment contracts have been much greater, owing to their flexibility and their compatibility with restless innovation and rapidly developing, large-scale production.

Imagine a society where every worker is self-employed. Workers may own their own means of production, or they may rent them from others. All self-employed workers would trade outputs or services with others. Markets and private ownership would still exist. But there would no longer be an employment relation.[8] Is a system with self-employed commodity producers fundamentally different from a private enterprise economy in which most workers are employed? Some characteristics would be very different. A community of self-employed commodity producers would face the extended transaction costs of exchanging their commodity outputs with one another, and this would limit technological possibilities as well as affecting the organization and character of the production process. Working for oneself is very different from working for a boss.

Consider a second scenario where all firms are transformed into worker cooperatives. The workers would own all the shares in their own enterprises. Their outputs would be sold collectively, creating revenue for the cooperative as a whole. Such a system could allow large-scale production and cooperation, but its inner dynamic, the character of industrial relations, and the motivations of the workers could differ radically from a system that relied instead on contracts of employment.[9] This could remain true even if there were a financial sector run along capitalist lines on which many cooperatives depended for their finance.

The points outlined above underline the distinctive importance of the employment relationship, even if its development does not closely match the spectacular rise of capitalism from the eighteenth century. Hence, there are grounds for considering the employment relationship as an essential feature of capitalism even if it is relatively unhelpful in providing a criterion to identify and date the rise of that system. The inclusion of this criterion will be considered further in the following chapter, where I bring the important definitional characteristics together.

8. In his supplement to vol. 3 of Marx's *Capital*, Engels introduced the term *simple commodity production* to describe such an arrangement, suggesting that it had preceded capitalism historically (Marx 1981, 1037). But apparently Marx never used the terms *simple* or *petty commodity production*.

9. The dynamics of such a system and its differences from both capitalism and traditionally defined socialism have been analyzed by numerous writers, including Ward (1958, 1967), Vanek (1970, 1972), Estrin (1983), Meade (1986, 1989), and Ellerman (1992).

CHAPTER TEN

A Definition of Capitalism

[At] the very roots of the capitalist mode of production, [is] the self-valorization of capital . . . by means of the "free" purchase and consumption of labour-power. — Karl Marx (1867)

"Credit" operations . . . affect the capitalist engine—so much so as to become an essential part of it without which it cannot be understood at all. — Joseph A. Schumpeter (1954)

Capitalism is better viewed as a "historical formation," distinguished from formations that have preceded it . . . both by a core of central institutions and by the motion these institutions impart to the whole. Although capitalism assumes a wide variety of appearances from period to period and place to place . . . these core institutions and distinctive movements are discoverable in all of them, and allow us to speak of capitalism as a historical entity. — Robert L. Heilbroner (1987)

This chapter brings together several threads from earlier chapters and attempts to define capitalism. The origins of the word are explored. Many dictionary definitions focus on private property and markets, but—in line with both Karl Marx and Joseph Schumpeter—it is argued that such definitions are too broad and unspecific.

The second section considers the notion of "state capitalism." It is argued that the term *state capitalism* might usefully be applied to state-dominated varieties of capitalism that also involve private property, exchange, and a developed financial sector but that it does not usefully apply to Soviet-style systems that lack extensive private ownership of the means of production, widespread commodity markets, and financial markets. The third section proposes a six-condition definition of capitalism with two optional variants.

10.1. *Capitalism* and Its Usage

According to Fernand Braudel (1982, 234): "The word capitalist probably dates from the seventeenth century." It was taken to mean an owner of much money or wealth. In French, A. R. J. Turgot used *capitaliste* in his 1774 "Reflections on the Formation and Distribution of Wealth." William Godwin used the word *capitalist* in his *Enquiry concerning Political Justice* (1793). David Ricardo used it several times in his *Principles* of 1817.

The person most widely credited with the invention of the word *capitalisme* is the socialist Louis Blanc in his *Organisation du travail*. Absent from at least the first five editions (from 1839 to 1848), it appears in the ninth, where Blanc (1850, 161) wrote of the "fallacy" of the "usefulness of capital" being "perpetually confused with what I call capitalism, that is to say the appropriation of capital by some, to the exclusion of others."[1] In 1849 the word *capitalism* appeared in an English translation of an article by Blanc, written while he was in exile in London. Blanc (1849, 117) wrote: "The suppression of capitalism cannot, then, have anything to do with the suppression of *capital*."[2] Shortly afterward, Pierre-Joseph Proudhon (1851, 271) used the term *capitalisme*, and its usage slowly widened in both English and French. William Makepeace Thackeray wrote of "capitalism" in his 1855 novel *The Newcomes*. Karl Marx wrote frequently of the "capitalist mode of production" and of "capitalists." But he rarely used the term *capitalism*. It appears only twice in the first volume of *Capital* (1867) and nine times in the following two volumes. Its frequency in German was boosted greatly by the publication of *Kapitalismus und Sozialismus* by the nonsocialist, historical school economist Albert Schäffle in 1870.

Having dealt with the origins of the word, we now turn to its current meanings. Definitions proliferate. Most dictionaries stress private ownership and markets; many add the profit motive.[3] The entry in *The*

1. "Ce sophisme consiste à confondre perpétuellement l'utilité du *capital* avec ce que j'appellerai le *capitalisme*, c'est-à-dire l'appropriation du capital par les uns, à l'exclusion des autres."

2. It is unclear whether this is the first appearance of *capitalism* or *capitalisme* or whether it is preceded in an undiscovered 1848 or 1849 edition of *Organisation du travail*.

3. These include the *Compact Oxford English Dictionary*, *Webster's New World College Dictionary*, the *Webster Dictionary of the English Language*, *Chambers 21st Century*

New Encyclopaedia Britannica (1998, 2:831) is typical: "Capitalism, also called free market economy, or free enterprise economy: economic system . . . in which most of the means of production are privately owned and production is guided and income distributed largely through the operation of markets."

But, if we consider systems based largely on private ownership, the profit motive, and markets, we can find many examples before the medieval era. As noted in previous chapters, trade has existed for tens of thousands of years, markets may have appeared as long as five millennia ago in China, and they were evident in several locations in the eastern Mediterranean and the Middle East around 600 BC. Private ownership, the pecuniary calculus, and the profit motive have similarly played a prominent role in leading economic regions for thousands of years. Hence, prominent dictionary definitions of capitalism make it a system that has lasted for multiple millennia. If we adopt such definitions, then we need to find another word to describe the institutional structures that were consolidated in the eighteenth century and gave rise to spectacular economic growth and ongoing technological innovation.

Marx took a different approach. While he emphasized the roles of private property, markets, and profit, he also highlighted wage labor and the employment relationship.[4] Marx (1976, 291–92) saw wage labor as a defining feature of the capitalist mode of production. More fully, Marx (1981, 1019–20) wrote:

> Two characteristic traits mark the capitalist mode of production right from the start. *Firstly*. It produces its products as commodities. The fact that it produces commodities does not in itself distinguish it from other modes of production; but that the dominant and determining character of its product is the

---

Dictionary, and the *Cambridge Dictionary of American English*. Other definitions stress private ownership and markets, such as in the *Merriam-Webster Third New International Unabridged Dictionary*, the *Merriam-Webster Collegiate Dictionary*, the *Merriam-Webster Online Dictionary*, *The American Heritage Dictionary of the English Language*, *The New Dictionary of Cultural Literacy*, the *Newbury House Dictionary*, and *The Wordsmyth Educational Dictionary-Thesaurus*.

4. Hobson (1926, 1) also made employment central to his definition: "Capitalism may provisionally be defined as the organization of business upon a large scale by an employer or company of employers possessing an accumulated stock of wealth wherewith to acquire raw materials and tools, and hire labour, so as to produce an increased quantity of wealth which shall constitute growth."

commodity certainly does so. This means, first of all, that . . . labour generally appears as wage-labour . . . [and] the relationship of capital to wage-labour determines the whole character of the mode of production. . . . The *second* thing that particularly marks the capitalist mode of production is the production of surplus-value as the direct object and decisive motive of production.

When describing the capitalist mode of production, Marx emphasized private property, widespread commodification, and markets, including the hiring of labor power and wage labor (Khalil 1992). Hence, the Marxist writer Ernest Mandel (1967) described capitalism as "generalized commodity production." Marx and Mandel made it clear that labor power and money were also commodities. With a slight modification of Marx's position, the term *M-capitalism* is used here to refer to a definition of capitalism in terms of the following five characteristics:

1. A legal system supporting widespread individual rights and liberties to own, buy, and sell private property
2. Widespread commodity exchange and markets involving money
3. Widespread private ownership of the means of production by firms producing goods or services for sale in the pursuit of profit
4. Much of production organized separately and apart from the home and family
5. Widespread wage labor and employment contracts

Most dictionary and encyclopedia definitions emphasize conditions (1), (2), and (3), albeit often without emphasis on the legal system. More than Marx, the notion of M-capitalism emphasizes the legal system and individual rights.[5] Regarding condition (4), the separation of much production from the family and the domestic sphere was emphasized by Weber (1968) and is implicit in Marx's writings. Weber rightly argued that this separation was important to subject production to systems of rational accounting and pecuniary motivation. Marx emphasized condition (5) because it flows from the nature of capitalism as generalized commodity production and encapsulates the driving antagonism between the employing class and the working class. With this awesome concep-

---

5. Marx's account of capitalism emphasized money (condition [2]), but he laid no stress on collateralization, credit money, or the selling of debt (see condition [6] in the definition of S-capitalism below).

tual schema, Marx linked the free market, possessive individualism of the classical liberal era with the class struggle and the promise of its transformation into collective property under proletarian rule.

A problem, as noted in the previous chapter, is that the addition of condition (5), widespread wage labor, to the preceding four does not effectively demarcate modern industrial capitalism from the four preceding centuries when wage labor was widespread in rural England. M-capitalism, as specified above, gives us a better-than-average definition, but not one that is sufficiently sharp in terms of historical specificity.

Further problems of historical demarcation arise with the first four conditions. As noted in section 4.4 above, the idea that secure property rights were first established in England in the seventeenth century is a myth. Furthermore, money, markets, and private ownership have existed for millennia. The fourth condition is helpful but hardly sufficient as an explanation of massive expansion of capitalism around 1800. The five conditions are inadequate to demarcate historically the explosion of capitalist productivity even if they are necessary for that system.

In search of help we turn to Joseph A. Schumpeter, who emphasized the development of financial institutions. Schumpeter (1934, 126) saw the money markets as the "headquarters" of capitalism. Schumpeter (1939, 223) wrote: "Capitalism is that form of private property economy in which innovations are carried out by means of borrowed money, which in general . . . implies credit creation." Schumpeter (1954, 78n) also thought that "the development of the law and the practice of negotiable paper and of 'created' deposits afford perhaps the best indication we have for dating the rise of capitalism." For him, the "capitalist engine" could not be understood without reference to its credit operations and a distinctive monetary system, involving the creation of money by banks through the selling of debt (Schumpeter 1954, 318–20). This inspires a definition of S-capitalism; it involves the following:[6]

1. A legal system supporting widespread individual rights and liberties to own, buy, and sell private property
2. Widespread commodity exchange and markets involving money

---

6. But note that, while he emphasized the role of the financial sector, Schumpeter made little of the distinction between property and possession and the role of collateralization. As with Marx and M-capitalism, we are crediting Schumpeter with slightly more than his due.

3. Widespread private ownership of the means of production by firms producing goods or services for sale in the pursuit of profit
4. Much of production organized separately and apart from the home and family.
5. [No condition specified]
6. A developed financial system with banking institutions, the widespread use of credit with property as collateral, and the selling of debt

The addition of condition (6) takes seriously the monetary definition of capital and institutions promoting collateralization and the salability of debt. Capitalism is thus marked by "the predominance of 'capital'" (Sombart 1930, 196).[7] This definition points to the development of institutions of clearer historical specificity. According to this definition, the emergence of capitalism in England is marked by developments in financial institutions in the eighteenth century.

Note that condition (1) in the definitions of M-capitalism and S-capitalism rules out (at least widespread) slavery. Consequently, both M-capitalism and S-capitalism involve missing futures markets for labor. With S-capitalism, there may be self-employment or worker cooperatives but not extensive slave labor. M-capitalism rules out an economy with predominant self-employment or worker cooperatives.

But there is a cost to the exclusion of condition (5) from this definition. As argued in the preceding chapter, the advantage of retaining the employment contract in the definition of capitalism is that it demarcates the system from economies involving self-employed producers or worker cooperatives. Furthermore, the introduction of wage labor gave important incentives for labor-saving innovations and led to increases in productivity. Consequently, the definition of capitalism that is favored here—and described simply as *capitalism*, without any prefix—involves all six of the above conditions.

---

7. Note the money-based definition of capital developed in chapter 7 above. Both Sombart (1902, 1930) and Weber (1904–5/1930, 1968) defined capitalism partly in terms of its rational, pecuniary, and entrepreneurial *Geist*, "spirit" or "economic outlook." But Commons criticized Weber and Sombart for giving ideas and spirit—instead of property and other relations—too much weight. Commons (1934, 732–34) noted their "failure to start economic theory upon the *economic bond* which ties individuals together, such as transactions, debts, property rights." For Commons, ideas were important, but social and legal relations were also fundamental. See Hodgson (2001) for further criticisms of the concept of *Geist*.

Nevertheless, as with all definitions, there is no finality. That may exasperate the lover of mathematical proofs. But mathematics and reality are different worlds. The beautiful finalities of the former are not found in analytic engagements with the latter. The virtues of different definitions of capitalism are a matter for ongoing debate.

10.2. State Capitalism?

From the late nineteenth century, some Marxist writers (including V. I. Lenin and Wilhelm Liebknecht) and non-Marxist writers proposed that state ownership and management of a large part of a market economy would amount to *state capitalism*. But subsequently the term was applied to planned economies. By the 1940s some Marxists (such as Amadeo Bordiga and Raya Dunayevskaya) were describing the Soviet Union as *state capitalist*.

Accordingly, Tony Cliff (1955), Ernesto Screpanti (1997, 2001), and others proposed that private ownership is not a defining feature of capitalism; instead, it is control by a minority of the labor process, as in the employment contract. Unimpeded by any definitional reference to private ownership of the means of production or to the existence of money capital or capital markets, all twentieth-century systems, from the market-driven West to planned systems under Stalin and Mao, were described as *capitalist*.[8]

---

8. Ultrarevolutionaries, describing all modern and some other social formations as *capitalist*, conveniently blacken everything. It removes the need to identify any positive features of any system. By contrast, those who approvingly describe the former Soviet Union, Mao's China, or North Korea as *socialist* are obliged either to ignore the famines, prison camps, mass executions, and purges or to perform acrobatic acts of apology. Trotsky's (1937) description of these regimes as "transitional" and "degenerated workers' states" is also unsatisfactory, partly because the workers never controlled the state. A fourth option for a Marxist is to describe these systems as *bureaucratic collectivist* (or similar) with a "new class" in control (Shachtman 1940). These dilemmas can be avoided by ditching the Marxist notion that systems are defined by a class in power. Instead, systems can be defined by the social and legal relations that dominate and regulate the production and distribution of their wealth. *State-planned economy* is a possible label for a Soviet-type system. But non-Marxists on the Left still have the problem that the word *socialism* has been historically associated with central planning, as found in the aforementioned totalitarian regimes. Perhaps the Left has to abandon the term *socialism* as well, possibly in favor of *social democracy* (with its post-1959 and Bad Godesberg meaning).

There are arguments against this preeminent definitional emphasis on control. First, owners have significant legal and real powers over the managers even if these powers are not exercised daily. The separation of ownership from control in modern capitalism (Berle and Means 1932) does not imply that ownership is unimportant or does not carry with it significant powers. Second, ownership of the means of production is a means of obtaining property income *even if* direct control of the labor process is not exercised. Third, the employment contract itself always involves some form of (public or private) *ownership* of the means of production and in particular the *private ownership* of labor power itself. Fourth, the employment contract does not involve *absolute* control and typically is accompanied by a significant zone of autonomy and discretion for the workers (Littler and Salaman 1982; Nelson 1981b).

More generally, the argument for retaining notions of property in the definition of capitalism is that property and contract are key elements of the modern system of production and distribution. Removing these and other legal terms from the definition would fail to identify major features of the modern social order, including the roles played by commodity exchange, financial markets, and the collateralization of private property.

As well as recognizing that significant power does emanate from ownership, one of the advantages of retaining both private ownership of the means of production and the existence of an employment relationship in the definition of capitalism is that such a denotation differentiates the former Eastern Bloc countries from capitalism. This conceptual differentiation underlines the major structural and ideological contrasts between East and West that dominated the world scene from 1917 to 1989. After 1989 these economies faced the huge tasks of building markets and capitalist financial institutions. The switch of their economic "headquarters" from their central planning bureaus to their financial markets involved massive institutional changes of enormous significance. The understanding of *capital* as money, depending on a web of legal and financial institutions, means that neither the Soviet Union nor Maoist China was *capital*-ist. Capitalism is still reasonably defined in terms of private ownership of the means of production, the ubiquity of the employment relationship, and the dominance of financial institutions.

Following Lenin and Liebknecht, a better use of the term *state capitalism* is to describe state-dominated versions of capitalism as that system is defined here. This might include the reformed Chinese system, which since 1978 has involved a combination of markets, private and state enterprise, with state management and coordination of much of the economy (Naughton 2007; Huang 2008; Bremmer 2010; Coase and Wang 2012; Hodgson and Huang 2013; Peck and Zhang 2013; Wu 2013). Hence, there is a case for describing post-1980 China as *state capitalist*.

But the large financial sector in China is restrictive and structurally inflexible. Banking in China is largely dominated by the state, and favorable access to the state bureaucracy is often a condition for obtaining capital for business investment (Boyreau-Debray and Wei 2005). The Chinese legal system is also underdeveloped by Western standards. China is clearly a socioeconomic system in transition. The classical institutions of capitalism are incompletely developed. Once again, it is a question of drawing the line and determining on what side of it China should sit. I leave this issue open for future debate.

10.3. In Summary: Defining Capitalism

For the reasons given above, capitalism is defined here as a system of production with the following six characteristics:

1. A legal system supporting widespread individual rights and liberties to own, buy, and sell private property
2. Widespread commodity exchange and markets involving money
3. Widespread private ownership of the means of production by firms producing goods or services for sale in the pursuit of profit
4. Much of production organized separately and apart from the home and family
5. Widespread wage labor and employment contracts
6. A developed financial system with banking institutions, the widespread use of credit with property as collateral, and the selling of debt

This six-condition definition is given two further variants. *M-capitalism* (broadly after Marx) is a social system defined by conditions (1), (2), (3), (4), and (5). *S-capitalism* (after Schumpeter) is a social system defined by conditions (1), (2), (3), (4), and (6). To adapt a lapsed advertising slogan from a famous British retail company, capitalism is "not just" markets and private property but *M&S-capitalism*—or *capitalism* for short. Conditions (5) and (6) serve as fuzzy historical bookends, together demarcating capitalism from preceding systems and possible successors.

As noted in chapter 1 above, a definition is neither an analysis nor an adequate description. All sorts of vital things are missing from the six-point definition. For example, capitalism involves human beings that must eat to survive. While human nutrition is needed for capitalism to survive, it is not part of the essence because it does not demarcate this system from others. Similarly, the definition of capitalism does not have to point out that a social system depends on shared meanings, culture, habits, or whatever. Likewise, there are all sorts of complex and analytic issues—such as the nature of property or money and the sources of its dynamism—that do not have to enter into the definition of capitalism because they are defined or analyzed elsewhere.

For example, why is technological innovation absent from the definition? Again, things that are vital to the system do not necessarily have to be included in a definition. If we listed everything that was important, then a definition would be many pages long. A definition of a system is different from an analysis of how a system works. Definitions are about demarcation, not analysis. Arguably, technological innovation is a possible behavioral consequence of the core capitalist institutions, and some forms of capitalism have been relatively stagnant technologically.

As another example, why is the organization and diffusion of knowledge absent from the definition of capitalism? Again, the organization and diffusion of knowledge are clearly vital for this system. But they play a fundamental role in any economy involving communication and cooperation between agents. Hence, the organization and diffusion of knowledge does not demarcate capitalism from other systems, and, hence, it is not part of its definition.

Explicit reference to social class is also absent from the definition offered above. In his review of different definitions of capitalism, Michael Merrill (1995) argued that capitalism is much more than simply a market economy. He was right about that. But he wanted to define capitalism as "a market economy ruled by, or in the interests of, capitalists" (322). A problem, as noted in chapter 2 above, is that the basis of class itself has to be defined, and Marx and Engels were obliged to use legal terms such as *ownership* to do so. Being a capitalist or a worker is not a congenital attribute: it is the occupation of a social role that is determined in part by legal relations. Class-related legal terms appear in all points above, except condition (4).

Marxists have abused class-centered definitions of capitalism. They see class struggle, where the destiny of one class is to seize control of the system from another. But, notwithstanding the power of capitalists over workers, capitalists do not control capitalism: it is more the other way round. Such large and complex systems cannot be fully controlled, as if from a single chamber of power. This point is relevant to the debate between capitalism and socialism and the issues raised in the following two chapters.

PART II

Capitalism and Beyond

CHAPTER ELEVEN

Conceptualizing Production

Economic development . . . is essentially a knowledge process . . . but we are still too much obsessed by mechanical models, capital-income ratios, and even input-output tables, to the neglect of the study of the learning process which is the real key to development. — Kenneth Boulding (1966)

The neoclassical . . . production function . . . does not describe production as a process, that is, an ordered sequence of operations. It is more like a recipe for a bouillabaisse where ingredients are dumped in a pot (K, L) heated up, $f(\cdot)$, and output, X, is ready. This abstraction from the sequencing of tasks . . . is largely responsible for the well-known fact that neoclassical production theory gives us no clue to how production is actually organized. — Axel Leijonhufvud (1986)

Science cannot be conducted without metaphors. Yet, at the same time, these metaphors hold science in an eternal grip and prevent us from taking directions and solving problems that lie outside their scope. — Richard C. Lewontin (1996)

This chapter focuses on the nature and organization of production in highly general terms. It does not focus on a specific type of economic system, and it applies to most human history. But it raises issues that are important to understand capitalism and the viability of alternative systems. Underlying the analysis of any economic system are conceptions of the nature of production and distribution that guide the vision of the institutions and activities involved. These notions are covert and rarely discussed. Investigations into them reveal deep-rooted metaphors that affect analytic language and guide the development of theory and mathematical models (see Black 1962; Hesse 1966, 1980; Lakoff 1987; Mirowski 1989, 2002).

Discussions in previous chapters of property and money have revealed problems in treating an economic system as a physical machine where individuals relate primarily to objects and rearrange physical matter. Often neglected are agent-to-agent interactions that involve shared interpretations, meanings, understandings, rules, and institutional facts (Searle 1995).

Mechanistic and physical metaphors have misled economists, at least from the days of Adam Smith and Karl Marx. Even after Thorstein Veblen diagnosed their negative influence and pointed to an alternative, he was still under their sway when he addressed the process of production. Particular versions of physics have also dominated neoclassical economics (Mirowski 1989).

Mechanical and physical metaphors inhibit our understandings of such concepts as property, right, and collateral. We need to find alternative ways of thinking about economic systems. The argument in the present chapter is that mechanistic or substance-oriented metaphors should be replaced by a richer narrative that derives from modern informational conceptions of evolution. As well as dealing with communication and meaning, this informational metaphor is much more capable of dealing with key institutional features of capitalism, involving law, property, and contract.

The following section highlights mechanistic and physical conceptions of production and shows their influence over a selection of key authors, including Adam Smith, John Stuart Mill, Karl Marx, and Thorstein Veblen. Alfred Marshall is identified as a partial exception.

The second and final section of this chapter briefly sketches an alternative view of the production process using informational metaphors. These allow the introduction of the key features of knowledge, incentives, and organization into the sphere of production.

11.1. The Production Process as Depicted by Some Leading Economists

Once apprenticed as a surgeon, the French Physiocrat François Quesnay used the metaphor of the economy as a body, with wealth as circulating blood (Foley 1973, 1976). Influenced by Quesnay, Smith was swept up by the Newtonian vision of science and the growth of the physical and natural sciences. Generally, the classical economists saw the economy as a physical system where material things were produced by machine-aided physical labor.

While Smith recognized that the organization of production also mattered, it was primarily through a finer division of labor and via increased
manual dexterity through learning by doing. For Smith, labor was primarily a physical and mechanical process rather than one based on cognition, knowledge, or information. In the *Wealth of Nations*, the words
machine, machines, and *machinery* appear sixty-five times in all and *tool*
and *tools* twenty-three times in all. The words *judgment* and *knowledge*
appear only eight and four times, respectively, in the context of labor
or production despite Smith's devotion of great attention to that sphere.
The words *intelligence* and *intelligent* appear at best three times in all in
relation to production. The word *information* appears in the book but
never in the context of labor or production.

Compare the writings of John Stuart Mill in the following century.
In the *Principles of Political Economy* he gave detailed and instructive
attention to some institutions. The word *knowledge* appears fifty-five
times in the context of labor and production. But a physical conception
of production remained. This is most clear where Mill (1871, 199–200)
famously distinguished production radically from distribution:

> The laws and conditions of the production of wealth, partake of the character
> of physical truths. There is nothing optional, or arbitrary in them. Whatever
> mankind produce, must be produced in the modes, and under the conditions,
> imposed by the constitution of external things, and by the inherent proper-
> ties of their own bodily and mental structure. Whether they like it or not,
> their productions will be limited by the amount of their previous accumula-
> tion, and, that being given, it will be proportional to their energy, their skill,
> the perfection of their machinery, and their judicious use of the advantages of
> combined labour. . . . But howsoever we may succeed in making for ourselves
> more space within the limits set by the constitution of things, we know that
> there must be limits. We cannot alter the ultimate properties either of mat-
> ter or mind, but can only employ those properties more or less successfully,
> to bring about the events in which we are interested. It is not so with the Dis-
> tribution of Wealth. That is a matter of human institution solely. The things
> once there, mankind, individually or collectively, can do with them as they
> like. They can place them at the disposal of whomsoever they please, and on
> whatever terms.

Mill argued that production is governed by natural laws while the distribution of wealth is a matter of human discretion, relations of power,

and social institutions. This frames views of capitalist and postcapitalist possibilities. But Mill's formulation is subject to a number of criticisms.

First, the fact that production is governed by the laws of nature does not mean that there is no discretion over the "modes . . . and . . . conditions" under which production takes place. There are choices regarding how tools are used and the sequences of operations, for example. There *is* something optional about them. Against this, it may be argued that there is only one best way of doing things. Yet what is best is variable and dependent on context, costs, knowledge, and so on. So the actual or perceived best technique may frequently change.

Second, if we accept that "productions will be limited by the amount of their previous accumulation," this does not mean that production cannot innovate, expand in scale, or change in the detailed composition of its output. "Previous accumulation" may limit but does not sufficiently determine the nature and composition of output in current and future periods: this too is to a large extent a matter of human discretion. A level of "previous accumulation" provides an *output possibility frontier* for future production. Within this frontier there are multiple options where individuals within institutions may decide the next steps. Hence, production is also a matter of institutions, power, and choice.

Third, motivation and performance depend partly on ownership and organization of the firm and not simply on Smithian learning by doing through a division of labor. Workers' motivation is affected by perceptions of their place in the scheme of things. For example, there is evidence that partial or complete employee ownership of the firm can affect productivity (see Jones 1987; Bonin, Jones, and Putterman 1993; Poole and Whitfield 1994; Doucouliagos 1995; Pendleton, Wilson, and Wright 1998; Hubbick 2001; Robinson and Zhang 2005; Gagliardi 2009; Birchall 2011). Workers are not simply machines, but Mill sometimes seemed to treat them as such. Elsewhere in the *Principles*, from the third edition of 1852 on, Mill (1971, 698, 772–73) showed some support for worker cooperatives and acknowledged that they can enhance productivity. In doing so he undermined his own suggestion that output was wholly governed by physical laws.

Fourth, motivation can also be dependent on wage levels. A large literature confirms the efficiency wage argument that higher wages can induce workers to increase the quantity or quality of their output (Akerlof and Yellen 1986; Stiglitz 1987; Weiss 1991). As noted in chapter 9 above, an employment contract is not (and cannot be) fully specified and involves a good deal of discretion on both sides. This zone of discretion allows scope for various inducements, including the possibility that workers may work more than the contractual minimum. Again, output may depend on more than "previous accumulation" or "mental structure."

Fifth, "the inherent properties of their own . . . mental structure" can change through time and be dependent on circumstances within the sphere of production and elsewhere. This does not overturn Mill's argument that "productions will be limited by the amount of their previous accumulation," but it challenges their unqualified depiction in terms of simple "physical truths."

Sixth, the organization of production involves *social relations* between people and not simply "things" and "mental structures." Mill might have rightly claimed that any adjustments to organization would depend on physical resources and mental capacities, but they depend on previous *organizational structures* as well. His use of terms such as *things* and *physical truths* diverts attention from social relations and structures.

Marx (1973a, 832) regarded this passage from Mill as "highly absurd" and argued: "The 'laws and conditions of the production of wealth' and the laws of the 'distribution of wealth' are the same laws under different forms, and both change, undergo the same historic process; are as such only moments of a historic process." But, although Marx emphasized relations of production and struggles between employers and employees, his conception of production was still dominated by physical entities such as muscles and machines, downplaying knowledge and information.

A textual analysis confirms this. In the first volume of *Capital*, which is the one most devoted to production, the words *machine, machines,* and *machinery* appear 824 times in all and *tool* and *tools* 92 times in all. *Knowledge* appears only about 3 times in the context of labor or production. The words *intelligence* and *intelligent* appear only 8 times in all in the context of labor or production. The word *information* never appears in such a context. Marx wrote more than once in this volume of labor as the expenditure of "muscles, nerves, bones, and brains." But "brains" are not linked explicitly with intelligence or knowledge.

This textual analysis underlines that fact that for Marx the labor process was primarily physical, involving the expenditure of muscle and the use of tools and machines. As noted above, Marx (1971, 21) wrote in 1859 of "the material transformation of the economic conditions of production, which can be determined with the precision of natural science." In *Capital*, Marx (1976, 284) wrote: "The simple elements of the labour process are (1) purposeful activity, that is work itself, (2) the object on which that work is performed, and (3) instruments of that work." There was little mention of knowledge, information, or intelligence in such contexts.

Early neoclassical writers such as William Stanley Jevons (1871) and Irving Fisher (1906) also paid scant attention to information and knowledge when they discussed productive activity. They explicitly embraced mechanical metaphors and analogies (Mirowski 1989).

But Marshall, the great synthesizer of neoclassical theory, was a striking exception to this trend. In his *Principles* (eighth ed. of 1920), the words *machine, machines,* and *machinery* appear 296 times in all and *tool* and *tools* 17 times in all. Words like *knowledge, judgment,* and *intelligence* appear quite frequently—about 55, 30, and 16 times, respectively—in the context of production, labor, or industry. Notably, Marshall diverged from other neoclassical writers with his preference for biological and evolutionary metaphors over those taken from mechanics (Hodgson 2013a). Perhaps by diminishing the use of mechanical metaphors he made space for information and knowledge in the context of production.

Similarly the Austrian school—from Carl Menger to Friedrich Hayek —generally rejected mechanical metaphors and focused on information and knowledge. But its adherents paid relatively little attention to the production process, often treating the firm as an individual entrepreneur (Ciepley 2004; Hodgson 2005a). Consequently, their ontology of production is unclear.

Thorstein Veblen was a contemporary of Marshall, and he likewise paid much attention to evolutionary ideas from biology. In the large anthology *Essential Writings of Thorstein Veblen*, containing items originally published from 1882 to 1914 (Camic and Hodgson 2011), the words *machine, machines,* and *machinery* appear forty-two times in all and tool and *tools* thirty-five times in all. Words like *knowledge, information, intelligence,* and *judgment* appear ninety, twelve, twelve, and two times, respectively, in the context of labor or production. As noted previously, Veblen also emphasized "intangible assets" and the fact that capital was not essentially a physical entity. Evolutionary ideas from biology seemed to make a positive difference.

But, on the other hand, Veblen's view of production was still deficient. He distinguished "pecuniary" or "business" employments (to do with the pursuit of money or profit) from "industrial" activity aimed at the production of material wealth. Redolent of Mill's demarcation between production and distribution, Veblen (Veblen 1899a, 114; Veblen 1901, 206) explained that this distinction between "industrial" and "pecuniary" employments "marks the difference between workmanship and bargaining." For him, industrial employment involved labor or management leading to production. Pecuniary employment related to the valuation, marketing, and distribution of that which is produced.

The aim of this distinction was "to indicate the different economic value of the aptitudes and habits of thought fostered by the one and the other class of employments" (Veblen 1899a, 113). As Veblen admitted, this dichotomy had precursors in the classical distinction between productive and unproductive labor. Veblen (1899a, 115) referred approvingly to Mill's claim that production—in contrast to distribution—must be understood in terms of the laws of physical nature. According to Veblen (1899a, 114), pecuniary employments "rest on the institution of private property," while industrial employments "rest chiefly on the physical conditions of human life." Similarly, Veblen (1901, 205) suggested that, while "business" centers on the "higgling of the market," by contrast "industrial" employments are aimed at "the shaping and guiding of material things and processes." Industry is "primarily occupied with . . . material serviceability . . . rather than . . . exchange value" and is to be understood in terms of "Physics and the other material sciences."[1]

A problem here is that industrial output depends on and is affected by the organization of the firm. Even if we avoid extreme versions of social constructivism, there is a large literature testifying to the interaction and inseparability of technology and organization (see Suchman 1987, 2007; Button 1993; Star 1995; Collins and Kusch 1998; Latour 2005; and Orlikowski 2010). Technology is not an exogenous force. The uses and developments of technology are interpretative and contingent (Faulkner and Runde 2009). Hence, social production is necessarily institutional and cannot be grounded on physical conditions without the inclusion of organizational, perceptual, and motivational matters as well.

Veblen (1901, 205–6) admitted that pecuniary and industrial activi-

---

1. Veblen's (1921) technological and engineering view of production explained his sympathy for of time-and-motion and "engineering efficiency" methods in line with Taylor's (1911) "scientific management." But Veblen (1923, 280) wrote: "The technological system is an organisation of intelligence, a structure of intangibles and imponderables, in the nature of habits of thought. It resides in the habits of thoughts of the community and comes to a head in the habits of thought of the technicians." This might have opened the door to the idea that technology is inextricably entwined with social relations.

ties interact and that "business activity may . . . effect an enhancement of the aggregate material wealth of the community, or the aggregate serviceability of the means at hand." He acknowledged that particular business arrangements often lead to greater industrial output. He went so far as to admit: "Shrewd business management is a requisite to success in any industry that is carried on within the scope of the market. Pecuniary failure carries with it industrial failure. . . . In this way industrial results are closely dependent upon the presence of business ability" (209–10).

But this admission had two defects. First, variations in output due to different "business arrangements" were explained by the "business ability" of individuals. Despite his institutionalism, Veblen omitted the nature and structure of business institutions. Second, he treated the organization of industry within "the scope of the market" as an option but avoided the questions of how industry could be organized otherwise and whether a greater or lesser industrial output would result. While he was normatively disposed toward nonmarket solutions, he did not explain in detail what they are or how they would work. He simply suggested that, without any market, most "business" activities will be dispensable. Veblen (1914, 24n) also wrote that the "all-pervading modern institution of private property appears to have . . . grown out of the self-regarding bias of men in their oversight of the community's material interests." This suggested that "the community's material interests" are not served by private property. But he failed to give an account of how an alternative society could be organized without private property or markets— how knowledge would be tapped and used, how decisions would be delegated and made, how people would be incentivized to work effectively, and how the rewards of production would be distributed. Hence, the institutional economist John Maurice Clark (1925, 57) objected: "As for the technical processes, neither Veblen nor anyone else has ever shown how social efficiency can be organized on a technical basis alone. . . . Veblen's antithesis [between business and industry], valuable as it is as a challenge to orthodoxy, cannot serve the purposes of a constructive search for the line of progress. This calls for an evolution of our scheme of values, not for a 'technocracy' which ignores value."

Veblen (1921, 100) declared: "Twentieth-century technology has outgrown the eighteenth-century system of vested rights." But he did not describe the system of economic organization and coordination that was appropriate for twentieth-century technology. He never gave a detailed picture of an alternative mode of organization of modern industrial society, other than his vague references to a "Soviet of engineers" or an "industrial directorate" of experts (Veblen 1921, 144). With his insufficiently grounded presumption that private property and markets are entirely dispensable in complex, large-scale economic systems, he here converged with Marxism despite other analytic differences with that doctrine. He depicted markets and private ownership as an unwarranted intrusion into the sphere of industry, which otherwise could be organized on the basis of technological expertise alone.[2] As Sidney Plotkin and Rick Tilman (2011, 103) put it: "Veblen believed that left alone, without political direction from on high, people tend to work, unobtrusively, with and for one another. They routinely perform the tasks necessary to keep their community going. The apologetics of power notwithstanding, ordinary people do not need to be reminded or commanded to work in order to live."

In response, it must be admitted that self-motivated and cooperative activity may be possible in small groups. Survey data reveal that much unpaid work is performed in modern capitalism, in the household and the wider community (Gershuny 2000). There is copious evidence that individuals and groups can get much done, even with voluntary effort.[3]

---

2. Veblen's confidence in the capacity of people to sustain adequate productive activity was bolstered by his notion of an evolved "instinct of workmanship" (Veblen 1898b, 1914). In Hodgson (2004, chap. 9), I criticized Veblen's argument. He claimed that workshirking "economic man" would not have survived because work is necessary for survival. But, more accurately, neoclassical economists argued that the individual would avoid work *unless forced or induced to do so.* The marginal disutility of labor can be countered by payments of sufficient utility to induce work. Veblen belittled the role of compensating inducements and incentives. He also overlooked the possibility of the evolutionary survival of an aversion to labor. Such an aversion could be favored in evolution because it reduced expenditure of energy and effort. Economies of effort bestow greater fitness by reducing energy inputs or exhaustion. Accordingly, animals have inherited dispositions for rest and sleep. Of course, a life consisting *wholly* of repose would lead to extinction. There must be inducements to occasional productive activity, triggered by hunger or whatever. Hence, the existence of an aversion to energetic activity would not mean that individuals would always avoid work. For this reason, and contrary to Veblen, any species can evolve a "consistent aversion" to energetic activity, as long as a compensating productive behavior is triggered when survival is at risk.

3. Ostrom's (1990) superb account of how communities manage common-pool resources, without recourse to commodity exchange, private property rights, or central direction, shows what can be possible in relatively small, well-defined groups where close interpersonal monitoring is feasible. But such governance mechanisms cannot readily be extended to large-scale complex societies. Her useful additional discussion of polycentric

But no one has shown how such undirected cooperation would be possible in a large-scale economy with a complex division of labor. The baker has somehow to be assured that he or she will in some way receive adequate supplies of flour and fuel from suppliers remote and personally unknown to him or her. We live no longer in a world of small groups, relying on custom or face-to-face interaction. Especially on this larger scale, questions of how to organize and incentivize production and distribution become immensely relevant. "Routinely" organized production might inhibit innovations in techniques or technologies, especially when their benefits at the beginning are unclear and their scope and development require outlay and experimentation.

If, after the passing of feudalism, nations had relied simply on primitive dispositions to work and cooperate, then our species would have survived, but we would be stuck with little more than medieval technology. We would lack not simply trains and planes but also much of modern medicine and health-care technology. We would have greater incapacitation through illness and lower average life expectancy. All these things have required incentivized innovation, a highly developed division of labor, and large-scale investment.

Production is inseparable from organization and motivation: we have to face the question of organizational and other incentives. No one has yet provided an adequately detailed and viable account of how a large, innovative, modern economy can be organized without some private property and some commodity exchange or markets. Adequate incentives might be maintained in a mixed economy, where some (partial or indicative) planning is performed by the state, as found in modern capitalism. There is also planning inside firms. But getting rid of private property, contracts, and exchange altogether in such modern circumstances is unviable. Sadly, on such matters, and despite his much greater emphasis on the role of knowledge in production, Veblen is of as little help as Marx. Both pointed to a private-property-less, market-free economy, without showing us how it would work in a modern, large-scale context.

Their explanations of the explosions in productivity that have accompanied the rise of capitalism since the eighteenth century are also flawed. Failing to give adequate recognition of the roles of private prop-

---

governance in larger systems introduces legal, property, and contractual relations that are absent at the smaller-scale community level.

erty, contracts, exchange, and capitalist finance in facilitating entrepre-neurship and innovation, Marx and Veblen had to fall back on largely technological explanations of the capitalist takeoff, with Marx empha-sizing productive conglomeration and Veblen extolling the role of the machine. Although Veblen attended more than Marx to legal and other institutions, they were still insufficiently emphasized.

In their *Communist Manifesto* panegyric on the role of the "bour-geoisie" in creating "more massive and more colossal productive forces than have all preceding generations together," Marx and Engels de-picted a social class as the agent of the process rather than incentivized individuals acting within capitalist institutions. According to them, such spectacular rises in productivity were not a consequence of these institu-tions but largely a result of an "agglomerated population" and the asso-ciated "centralized" clustering of the means of production. They asked: "What earlier century had even a presentiment that such productive forces slumbered in the lap of social labour?" (Marx 1973b, 72).[4]

Of course, the enlargement and conglomeration of production facili-tated an ever-finer division of labor and was an ongoing part of capitalist development. But one has to explain the institutional arrangements that enabled and incentivized that process. The circumstances under which technological innovators and entrepreneurs were motivated and aided have to be understood.

Marx saw labor as the source of all value and hence regarded prof-its and rents as robbery from the working class. But this assumed what he wanted to prove. Labor may be necessary to produce value, but this does not mean that organization and incentives are any less necessary for a dynamic system. Capitalists have always sought to limit wages and increase profits, but that does not necessarily mean that capitalism and its institutions become a removable burden on a production process that otherwise would be more innovative and dynamic.

Clearly, the nature (or ontology) of production has important impli-cations for the assessment of capitalism and the possibility of alterna-

---

4. Marx's *social labor* referred to a general, ahistorical notion of production as a so-cial process (Khalil 1990). For Marx, capitalism does not stop labor from being social, but it brings production together on a wider scale, both ("chaotically") through the market and (more "rationally") through the enlargement of firm organization. Marx's (1973b, 87) aim was to extend the "rational" organization of production to the national system as a whole, in "a vast association of the whole nation."

tive economic systems. Incentives or disincentives, stemming from the institutional structure of society as a whole, positively or negatively affect the motivations and modes of activity of those engaged in production. Ontologies of production that regard it primarily as a mechanical process involving physical effort, downplaying the distribution and organization of knowledge or taking for granted the incentives for work and innovation, are ill equipped for an evaluation of the merits and demerits of capitalism.

11.2. Toward an Evolutionary and Informational Ontology of Production

Although modern economists typically treat production as a black box, summarized by a production function where factors of production are mysteriously transformed into an output, there have been attempts on the sidelines to deal with production in a more detailed manner, taking more account of real processes, operations, and inputs (see, e.g., Chenery 1949; Georgescu-Roegen 1970, 1971; Winter 1982; Saviotti and Metcalfe 1984; Leijonhufvud 1986; Morroni 1992; Baldwin and Clark 2000; Buenstorf 2004; and Lipsey, Carlaw, and Bekar 2005).[5]

Some narratives treat production as a purely technological or engineering process. Other accounts differ on the amount of knowledge taken as given and on degrees of emphasis on organized learning, problem solving, knowledge creation, and knowledge transformation. But, while production is clearly all these things, many accounts end up focusing on either technological details or epistemic considerations, without adequately combining them both.

In a prescient passage, Alfred Marshall (1920, 138–39) wrote: "Knowledge is our most powerful engine of production. . . . Organization aids knowledge; it has many forms. . . . [I]t seems best sometimes to reckon organization apart as a distinct agent of production." But subsequent neoclassical economics took little heed of knowledge and organization and adopted mechanical analogies. Similarly, while Veblen played great attention to knowledge, he treated production as largely a technological or engineering matter. But there were strong evolutionary elements

---

5. Padgett, Lee, and Collier (2003) pioneered the notion that production is comparable to chemistry (Padgett and Powell 2012).

in Marshall's and Veblen's systems of thought that signal a way forward today. Abstract formulations of Darwinian theory have since made considerable progress, with interpretations that stress that evolutionary processes in complex systems are very much about the selection, retention, and development of complex information (see, e.g., Wicken 1987; Clark 1991; Plotkin 1994; Dennett 1995; Fenzl and Hofkirchner 1997; Adami, Ofria, and Collier 2000; Crutchfield and Schuster 2003; Beinhocker 2006, 2011; and Hodgson and Knudsen 2010).

An underlying problem here is the conceptual reconciliation of the world of ideas with the material and physical world. This problem has been prominent in philosophy and social theory since the ancient Greeks. The material side of the story, guided by physical metaphors and notions of the conservation and scarcity of matter or energy, sits awkwardly alongside the realm of knowledge and learning, where ideas replicate and multiply with little physical input and seemingly without limit (Nelson 1959; Arrow 1962b).

A related impairment is an ontology of separateness: "an ontology of separate things that need to be joined together" (Suchman 2007, 257). But, ever since humans used simple tools, we have thought and acted with and through things. *Situated cognition* means that knowing is inseparable from doing and from its material setting (Lave and Wenger 1991; Hutchins 1995; Lane, Maxfield, and Orsenigo 1996; Clark 1997a, 1997b). The processes of learning and doing are both social and material.

The pragmatist approach in philosophy and psychology is also of value here. Inspired by the Darwinian evolutionary agenda, pragmatists such as William James (1890) and John Dewey (1922) bridged the material and ideal worlds with their concept of habit. Habits are repositories of skills and knowledge. They are propensities to think or behave in particular ways in response to stimuli or cues. Individuals brought together in organizations interact and can trigger each other's habits, thus creating emergent complex dispositions for sequential behaviors, known as *routines* (Cohen and Bacdayan 1994; Hodgson 2008a). Relevant habits are acquired and developed in a social and material context.

Habits and routines take the form of information in the broad and basic (Shannon and Weaver 1949) sense of some conditional dispositions, data, or coding that can be transmitted to other entities and cause a response. Information is the underlying metaphor. Of course, ideas and knowledge have other key features, particularly concerning meanings and interpretations. It is necessary to bring these into the picture. Us-

ing conceptual frameworks and categories that we develop through human interaction, we selectively interpret our sense data and give them
meaning.

Knowledge is meaningful information that has been acquired through
social interaction, placed in an interpretative framework, and ingrained
in habits. It involves a tacit or codified rule structure involving triggers
and stimuli: it is an adaptation to circumstances (Plotkin 1994). Organizational knowledge is an emergent property in groups with individual
knowledge, where some of that knowledge is shared. It depends on the
existence of routines that can trigger behaviors as a result of interactions
with the group. Just as individuals develop knowledge to deal with adaptive problems, organizations too are problem-solving entities. They are
"epistemic communities" and "machineries of knowing."[6]

Production is a goal-oriented process involving purposeful individuals organized as "machineries of knowing" in the sense outlined above.
Even manual labor involves the development of habits and is thus an informational as well as a physical process. All production is subject to an
informational metaphor, encompassing knowledge and organization, as
Marshall realized. The management of production is organized in terms
of hierarchies (unitary or multidivisional) to process, filter, and screen
large amounts of information (see Nonaka and Takeuchi 1995; Nooteboom 2000; Nonaka, von Krogh, and Voelpel 2006; Knudsen, Puranam,
and Raveendran 2012).

Production involves the processing of information that is stored and
encoded in arrangements of physical matter—in brains and material objects. It is purposeful, problem-solving, and informational, played out on
the register of material things.

This view of production as a materially grounded information system
dovetails with the role of key institutions in the economy—such as property and contract—that function as information registries of what is produced and owned and when and how those things are allocated. In ear-

6. The quoted phrases are from Haas (1992) and Knorr-Cetina (1981), respectively.
For a selection of the large relevant literature on several themes relevant to this paragraph,
see Blumer (1969), DiMaggio and Powell (1983), Rogoff and Lave (1984), Suchman (1987),
Lave (1988), Brown and Duguid (1991), Donald (1991), Lave and Wenger (1991), Boisot
(1995), Hutchins (1995), Nonaka and Takeuchi (1995), Hendriks-Jansen (1996), Clark
(1997a, 1997b), Wenger (1998), Nooteboom (2000), Keijzer (2001), Lorenz (2001), Goldstein and Gigerenzer (2002), Nelson and Nelson (2003), Todd and Gigerenzer (2003), Nonaka, von Krogh, and Voelpel (2006), Luo, Baldwin, Whitney, and Magee (2012).

lier societies, custom and tradition would play these roles. Any complex economy is a structure of organization and suborganization, each subsystem playing its role in storing and processing information in habits, customs, and routines.

This information metaphor admits an evolutionary perspective, using generalized Darwinian principles of variation, selection, and inheritance synthesized with notions of entropy and negentropy taken from thermodynamics and with insights from the study of complexity (see Wicken 1987; Plotkin 1994; Beinhocker 2006, 2011; Hodgson and Knudsen 2010; Mayfield 2013; Wallast 2013). Complex economic systems contain multiple organizations. These host routines and habits and compete with other organizations for locally scarce resources.

At the international level, military conflict between states is one form of such competition. The development of a legal system involving property and contract was historically a major transition within nations, often itself imposed through military force, but allowing competition to also occur through trade and markets (Hodgson and Knudsen 2010, chap. 8). While adapting and problem solving at a new level, legal institutions bestowed new rights, incentives, and constraints. The production system became tied up with a set of institutions adjudicating property and other rights.[7]

Under specific conditions this type of evolutionary process has the potential to create greater complexity (Hodgson and Knudsen 2010, chap. 6). Complexity can be measured in terms of negentropy—the creation of order and information out of chaos. Eric Beinhocker (2006, 317) suggested that negentropy is the ultimate measure of social wealth:

> Economic wealth and biological wealth are thermodynamically the same sort of phenomena, and not just metaphorically. Both are systems of locally low entropy, patterns of order that evolved over time under the constraint of fitness functions. . . . In physics, order is the same thing as information, and thus we can also think of wealth as fit information; in other words, *knowledge*. . . .

---

7. Coase (1960, 43–44) identified in much of economics a "faulty concept of a factor of production": "This is usually thought of as a physical entity which the businessman acquires and uses (an acre of land, a ton of fertilizer) instead of as a right to perform certain (physical) actions." His mention of rights is to be applauded. But many rights depend on historically specific legal institutions. Production predates law. It is more accurate to say that generally we must also be concerned with information and rules and that at least in modern capitalism we must also be concerned with legal rights.

The origin of wealth is knowledge. Yet rather than treating knowledge as an assumption, an exogenous input, a mysterious process outside the bounds of economics, the complexity-based view . . . puts the creation of knowledge at the endogenous heart of the economy.

Consequently, the emerging evolutionary paradigm combines Darwinian principles with the concept of entropy and places the growth of information and knowledge at the center. In this manner, inspired also by theorists such as Nicholas Georgescu-Roegen (1971) and Friedrich Hayek (1948, 1988), we can develop a metaphor for production that is both informational and evolutionary, realizing Veblen's goal of an "evolutionary" and "post-Darwinian" economics. In modern capitalism, markets adjoin production to create an enhanced, polycentric, and dynamic information-processing system (Hayek 1948; Mirowski 2002, 2007; Mirowski and Somefun 1998). Yet knowledge is vital from the beginning: all economies are knowledge based. The "knowledge economy" has existed since the caves. Likewise, production always involves matter and energy. But as economic systems develop they become increasingly knowledge intensive. Knowledge and learning are the paths of progress.[8]

Why is a knowledge-based perspective important? Consider past predictions of a dramatic shortening of the average working day. For example, in a 1930 lecture, Keynes (1931, 325) imagined ongoing exponential economic growth and remarked: "Think of this in terms of material things—houses, transport, and the like." After having "solved" the "economic problem" of providing for human material needs, Keynes predicted that his hypothetical grandchildren might have to work only fifteen hours a week. More than half a century later, contemplating growing automation, André Gorz (1985) and Jeremy Rifkin (1995) predicted "the end of work."

It is true that the average number of working hours has decreased in developed countries, but to nowhere near the levels envisaged by Keynes

---

8. In a neglected book, Scott (1989) questioned the standard definition of investment in terms of tangible assets and argued that investment should include research and development, the creation of new production-related institutional structures, and the formation of new management teams. He argued that economic growth is predominately a cognitive, learning process in which the scope for learning is progressively extended by gross investment.

and others. Working time previously spent with tools and machines is now spent on computers and "smart machines" (Zuboff 1988). If past futurologists had understood the production of wealth as an information-processing, cognitive, and judgmental—as well as a physical—process, then they would have been less disposed to forecast dramatic reductions in working hours. The increased variety of produced goods and services and the growing complexity of economic systems mean that these knowledge-based, judgmental tasks and possibilities have increased enormously.

Work has changed, and is changing, more dramatically in character than quantity, with waves of innovation in information technology with huge impacts on patterns of employment (Brynjolfsson and McAfee 2012). This presents a massive challenge for economic policy–makers. It also undermines conventional measures of economic activity and output. The conventional methods of measuring and accounting for economic output are deficient not simply because they underestimate the natural environment and some forms of important activity. They are also inadequate in their appreciation of the roles of information and knowledge.

Among other things, the great debate between capitalism and socialism has to take the nature and organization of production into account. This debate is the subject of the following chapter.

CHAPTER TWELVE

Socialism, Capitalism, and the State

We regard the state as an educational and ethical agency whose positive aid is an indispensable condition of human progress. — Original platform of the American Economic Association (Ely 1886)

It is the character rather than the volume of government activity that is important. — Friedrich A. Hayek (1960)

In 1827 in the *Co-Operative Magazine*—published in London by followers of Robert Owen—the word *socialist* emerged in English for the first time. It appeared in the *Poor Man's Guardian* in 1833 and moved into wider usage from thereafter (Bestor 1948). Owen and his followers saw socialism as the abolition of private property. In 1848 in the *Communist Manifesto*, Marx and Engels—like Owen—called for the abolition of private property. They wished for an economic order in which "capital is converted into common property, into the property of all members of society." They wanted the abolition of the "free selling and buying" of all commodities (Marx 1973b, 80–81). They welcomed efforts "to centralize all instruments of production in the hands of the state" and looked forward to a time when "all production has been concentrated in the hands of a vast association of the whole nation" (Marx 1973b, 86–87).

From the 1830s, definitions of socialism in terms of the abolition of private property and some form of common ownership were dominant (Beer 1940; Landauer 1959). This central motif pervaded the writings of socialists as diverse as the Continental revolutionary communists, German state socialists, and British Fabians. Hostility toward both markets and private property was thematic for socialism as a whole. As Noel Thompson (1988, 281) put it: "The market was anathematised by

almost all nineteenth century socialist writers." Among the few exceptions were John Ruskin and some of the Christian socialists, who sought
to rid the market system of its excesses. Even Fabian socialists had an
"ultimate vision of a fully planned and consciously controlled socialist
economy" where all markets and private ownership of the means of production were gradually marginalized to insignificance (see, e.g., Webb
and Webb 1920). The market was condemned for fostering competition,
encouraging greed, and generating inequality and exploitation. Socialists believed that markets could be abolished and replaced by collective
planning, often with an insistence on democratic control. The word *socialism* endured until the 1950s with these collectivist and antimarket
connotations.

When Oskar R. Lange (Lange 1936–37; Lange and Taylor 1938) adopted a notion of market socialism, it was an attempt to *simulate* aspects of price adjustment in a *planned* economy. He did not intend the
introduction of private firms, contractual exchange, or true markets.
When Abba Lerner (1944, 1)—who had developed Lange's theoretical
approach—wrote that the "fundamental aim of socialism is not the abolition of private property but rather the extension of democracy," he
was on his own intellectual journey away from the goal of collectivized
property that almost all socialists had embraced from the 1830s to the
1940s. The reconciliation of a sizable wing of the socialist movement to
the market, private enterprise, and a mixed economy came with the publication of *The Future of Socialism* by C. Anthony Crosland in 1956 and
the decision of the (West) German Social Democratic Party at its Bad
Godesberg conference in 1959—jolted by the division of Germany with
collectivism in its East—to abandon the goal of widespread common
ownership. The word *socialism* began to mutate in meaning.

Since the 1950s, most influential political parties that formally were
socialist have abandoned blanket opposition to private ownership and
markets. For example, Deng Xiaoping, the leader of China's post-Mao
reform movement within its Communist Party, shifted the meaning of
socialism away from its original opposition to private property and markets. Treating planning and markets as means, not ends, Deng (1992) declared: "The essence of socialism is liberation and development of the
productive forces, elimination of exploitation and polarization, and the
ultimate achievement of prosperity for all." If that is socialism, then perhaps we are all socialists now.

Yet blanket hostility to markets persists among some prominent academics. For example, the MIT-educated economist Michael Albert (2004) wrote: "I am a market abolitionist. I know markets are going to be with us for some time to come, but I also know—or hope—that in time we will replace them entirely." His coauthor, the Harvard-educated economist Robin Hahnel (2007, 1157), similarly upheld a vision of a marketless economy: "I do not believe that markets have any role to play in a truly desirable economy. . . . [O]ur long run goal should be to replace markets entirely with some kind of democratic planning."[1]

As another illustration, the influential "critical realist" philosophers Roy Bhaskar and Andrew Collier (1998, 392) supported "a form of socialism which is neither a market economy nor a command economy nor a mix of the two, but a genuine extension of pluralistic democracy into economic life." We are not told how this market-free system would work, particularly in terms of the organization of complex, large-scale production and incentives to work and innovate.

After an interesting discussion of the socialist calculation debates and a sophisticated ethical analysis of markets, John O'Neill (1998, 176–77) claimed to "puncture the case for a market economy" and argued for the moneyless, nonmarket, international associationism as sketched in outline by the socialist philosopher Otto Neurath. He outlined the ethical limitations of the market, but without detailing any plausible alternative. Even if markets were ethically flawed, without a viable and humane alternative we are obliged to tolerate them. We should have learned that nonmarket alternatives can be much worse ethically.

The statements reported above are extreme in outlawing any form of market arrangement, even at the fringes of an otherwise planned economy. Their unqualified use of the term *market* means a prohibition of all contractual exchanges of goods of services and the wholesale abolition of the right to alienate property, if not the abolition of all private property rights. Despite debates on the possibility of such arrangements and the repressive outcomes of "socialist" experiments in the twentieth century, an intolerant *agoraphobia* (fear of markets) is still evident in some intellectual quarters.

---

1. Albert and Hahnel (1978, 265–66) warned that, "if one insists on maintaining markets," this will lead to "a modified continuation of capitalist characteristics." Here, markets, which have existed for thousands of years, are mistakenly treated as embodiments of capitalism, which has existed for only a few hundred years. Both advocates and opponents of capitalism make this error.

But in other quarters there is a vibrant *kratophobia*—a fear of government or of the state. Both states and markets create problems, but neither is expendable in a large-scale complex economy. Alongside the need for markets, this book upholds the indispensability of the state in the constitution and regulation of capitalism. This chapter addresses the possibility (or otherwise) of socialism, at least as it has been historically defined, before its meaning shifted in the 1950s.

One of the most important controversies in the history of economics—known as the *socialist calculation debate*—was initiated by the Austrian school economist Ludwig von Mises (1920, 1935, 1949) and continued by Friedrich Hayek (1935a, 1944, 1948, 1988). At the peak of the controversy, Hayek criticized neoclassical economists, such as Oskar R. Lange and Henry Dickenson, who used general equilibrium theory to model their socialist proposals. But, while the Austrian school economists effectively undermined general equilibrium theory and successfully rebutted socialism as originally defined, several of their arguments were inadequate, including, ironically, their defense of capitalism.

For example, many Austrian school writers treated markets in a de-institutionalized manner, as the ether of all meaningful human interaction. On the other side, many socialists depicted market forces as the main enemy of democracy or human emancipation. Neither side paid adequate attention to historically specific institutional, legal, and statutory arrangements that make property, contracts, and hence markets possible. Neither group probed sufficiently the structures and institutions of capitalism.

Section 12.1 outlines the debates on socialism and reiterates important reasons why private property and commodity exchange are unavoidable in any large-scale complex economy. Section 12.2 criticizes both Austrian school and socialist economists for neglecting the role of state and law in constituting any viable modern economic system. The Austrian school conflated property with possession and regarded exchange as a universal and ahistorical phenomenon. Both sides overlooked key aspects of capitalism, paying insufficient attention to the peculiarities of employment contracts and the capitalist financial system. Section 12.3 addresses crucial institutions—such as corporations and networks—that must span the individual and the state in a modern complex economy. These too were largely overlooked in the socialist calculation debates. They challenge both statist and individualistic visions and can also pose problems for democratic governance. Section 12.4 extends the Austrian school emphasis on the importance of information and knowledge in an economic system but also argues that information and knowledge challenge a simple contractarian framework. Paradoxically, an effective market economy requires much information to be obtainable at very little cost. While many socialists have now accepted the market, the ironic section 12.5 considers the claim by some pro–von Mises libertarians that Hayek was a social democrat.

Overall, this chapter reconsiders past debates on the feasibility of socialism in light of the institutional analysis developed in previous chapters. It addresses disputes that involved impractical versions of socialism and inadequate conceptions of capitalism. It is about the failure of one side to propose a feasible alternative system while the other side had an insufficiently clear vision of what it was defending. Possible alternatives to capitalism are postponed to a later chapter.

12.1. Past Debates on the Possibility of Socialism

Despite their importance, accounts of the socialist calculation debates appear rarely in economics textbooks. Even worse, the remarkable earlier contribution of Albert Schäffle has been almost entirely ignored, even by historians of economic thought.[2]

In a series of works, Schäffle (1870, 1874, 1885, 1892, 1908) explored the limitations of socialism. The first of these was fifty years before von Mises's seminal article. Unlike some leading members of the Austrian school, Schäffle did not argue that socialism was impossible. Instead, he focused on the difficulties of organizing and planning a collectivist system. He identified problems concerning individual incentives for work and innovation within large groups and how shirking could be minimized. Schäffle (1908, 57) considered a society with a million workers: "My income from my social labour is conditional upon my 999,999 co-operating comrades being as industrious as I. . . . Socialism would have to give the individual at least as strong an interest in the collective work as he has under the liberal system of production."

This problem of incentives with large numbers haunts any social-

---

2. Discussions of rare instances where Schäffle's critique of socialism has been mentioned, plus some reasons for the widespread neglect of his contribution, appear in Hodgson (2010a).

ist scheme of large-scale cooperation. If everything is shared, then incentives for extra individual effort or innovation can be much less than likely rewards. This point was later illustrated dramatically in post-Mao China when from about 1978 peasant farmers began to withdraw from large collective farms and take responsibility for production and revenue from output at the household level. China's explosive economic growth began with those changes (Zhou 1996; Oi 1999; Coase and Wang 2012).

Schäffle (1908) also contended that a system based on calculations concerning labor time faced intractable problems, including the heterogeneity of labor and the inaccessibility of relevant data. Measuring labor inputs in this way would also undermine individual incentives to increase productivity.

Schäffle (1885, 1892) argued that a state collectivist system of production could minimize these severe and large-scale incentive and monitoring problems only by the exercise of central authority, thus undermining any egalitarian or democratic distribution of power. Hence, he saw socialism administered by democratic means as unfeasible. As Schäffle (1892, 37) wrote in 1885, "collective production without firm hands to govern it, and without immediate individual responsibility, or material interests on the part of the participators," is "impossible for all time." Schäffle (1892, 73) elaborated: "Without a sufficiently strong and attractive reward for individual or corporate preeminence, without strongly deterrent drawbacks and compensatory obligations for bad and unproductive work, a collective system of production is inconceivable, or at least any system that would even distantly approach in efficiency the capitalistic system of today. But democratic equality cannot tolerate such strong rewards and punishments."

Schäffle thus presented socialists with a severe dilemma: they must choose between socialism and democracy. They cannot have both. With the benefit of hindsight, after the twentieth-century attempts to establish socialism in Russia, China, Eastern Europe, and elsewhere, Schäffle's stance on the relationship between central planning and democracy is highly prescient. In no case has an adequate democracy prevailed within a centrally planned economy. In this and other vital respects, his neglected analysis has stood the test of time.

That economic analysis was not as sophisticated as the later efforts of von Mises and Hayek. Nevertheless, it is unduly neglected. Amazingly, Schäffle (1892, 416–19) predicted the likely survival of a regulated capitalism with democratic political institutions beyond the year 2000. In that respect his analysis is superior to von Mises's (1949, 259) declaration that a mixed economy involving markets and state regulation is impossible and to Hayek's (1944, 31) contestable claim that such a mixture of "competition and central direction" would "become poor and inefficient. . . . [N]either will really work and . . . the result will be worse than if either system had been consistently relied upon."

Much evidence endorses Schäffle rather than the Austrians. Mixed economies are everywhere. Different forms of production and allocation coexist within capitalism. Despite their critique of any mixture of market with central direction, von Mises and Hayek did not propose that family households should be transformed into markets with the result that sexual, household, and caring services should be traded between the individuals within them or that large corporations should be broken up into one-person firms. The impressive dynamism of several capitalist systems shows that, while markets are necessary for economic innovation and vitality, modern economies also benefit from some economic intervention by the state (see Nelson 1981a, 2003; Johnson 1982; Amsden 1989; Lazonick 1991; Kenworthy 1995; Chang and Rowthorn 1995; Chang 1997, 2002a, 2002b; Bardhan 2005; Vogel 2006; Reinert 2007; Martinez 2009; and Mazzucato 2013).[3]

In their contribution to the socialist calculation debate, the Austrian school underlined the nature and role of knowledge, especially in regard to incentives, innovation, and entrepreneurship. Lange, Dickenson, and others sidelined these issues. Reevaluations of the debate have overturned the preceding consensus that von Mises and Hayek were on the losing side. Lange and his followers did not adequately answer the criticisms of von Mises and Hayek in the debate, and they failed to provide a satisfactory outline of a workable and dynamic socialist system.[4]

---

3. This does not mean that state intervention is always beneficial (Olson 1982; Scully 1992). But further evidence suggests that the relationship is nonlinear and that marginal increases in government expenditure may be more beneficial at lower levels of development (Yavas 1998). A possible reason for this could be that private systems of finance and investment are less reliable at lower levels of development with underdeveloped means of collateralization. The state then becomes a relatively more viable economic investor. Positing an inverted-U relation between government size and growth, some recent estimates of "the optimal size of government" put it at about 37 percent in the European Union as a whole and as high as 43 percent in the United Kingdom, while estimates for the United States are generally lower (Forte and Magazzino 2010).

4. See Vaughn (1980), Murrell (1983), Lavoie (1985a, 1985b), and Steele (1992) for

Consider the problem of managerial incentives. How are managers to be encouraged to take some risks but not to be too reckless? Dickenson (1939) proposed a system of managerial bonuses to reward competent entrepreneurs. But Hayek (1948, 199) rightly pointed out: "Managers will be afraid of taking risks if, when the venture does not come off, it will be somebody else who will afterward decide whether they have been justified in embarking on it." Bureaucrats often eschew risk taking, minimize personal exposure to responsibility, and stick to established routine. For Hayek (1948, 194), Lange and Dickenson were "deplorably vague" about key issues, including how competent managers were to be selected.

Hayek showed that these authors had a naive view of knowledge in socioeconomic systems. They assumed that all relevant technical and economic information would be readily available to the decisionmakers. As Dickenson (1939, 9, 191) wrote: "All organs of the socialist economy will work, so to speak, within glass walls." As a result, the central planning authority would be the "omnipresent, omniscient organ of the collective economy." Similarly, writing in 1942, Lange (1987, 23) argued that under socialism all relevant information concerning production would be widely available, with the result that "everything done in one productive establishment would and should also be done by the managers of each productive establishment."

Lange and Dickenson acquired this flawed view of information and knowledge from the neoclassical theory they had embraced. Criticizing the neoclassical approach, Hayek (1948, 46, 33) concluded that, by depicting "economic man" as "a quasi-omniscient individual," economics has hitherto neglected the problem that should be its major concern, that is, "how knowledge is acquired and communicated." The general equilibrium models proposed by Lange and others did not deal adequately with this central problem of knowledge. Tacit knowledge held by work-

---

good discussions of the debate. Until the 1980s the consensus was with Lange. Schumpeter (1942, 167) asked: "Can socialism work?" He echoed contemporary widespread opinion: "Of course it can. . . . There is nothing wrong with the pure theory of socialism" (172). For Schumpeter (1954, 989n), von Mises and Hayek were "definitely wrong." Much later, Shleifer and Vishny (1994, 166) could still opine in a prestigious journal that the objections of von Mises and Hayek to socialism "were effectively rebutted by Lange." But others at that time, such as Blaug (1993) and Stiglitz (1994), understood the severe limitations of Lange-type models.

ers and managers was ignored. The assimilation of new technical knowledge was assumed to be unproblematic.[5]

In reality, and contrary to Lange and Dickenson, it would be impossible for managers to calculate marginal costs accurately or for central planners to make fully rational investment decisions on this basis. In a complex, dynamic world we are obliged to deal with an uncertain future. Such uncertainty (in the Knightian or Keynesian sense) rules out the possibility of any reliable calculation of probabilities or expected returns. Instead, we have to rely on intuition and judgment concerning the future. As Hayek (1948, 198) argued: "In no sense can costs during any period be said to depend solely on prices during that period. They depend as much on whether these prices have been correctly foreseen as on the views that are held about future prices. Even in the very short run costs will depend on the effects which current decisions will have on future productivity. . . . [A]lmost every decision on how to produce . . . now depends at least in part on the views held about the future."

Innovation also depends on hunches about the future. Successful innovation takes into account local, tacit, and other knowledge concerning circumstances and possibilities. Much of this knowledge involves complex details and contexts and cannot all be brought together and utilized by a central committee or planning authority.

The Austrian school emphasized market competition. Although prices were formed in Lange-type models, they neither performed a competitive function nor acted as a spur to innovation, as in a private enterprise economy. As Hayek (1948, 196) argued: "The force which in a competitive society brings about the reduction of price to the lowest cost at which the quantity salable at that cost can be produced is the oppor-

---

5. Roemer (1994, 1996) also used general equilibrium analysis to develop his version of socialism. Addressing the problem of unequal wealth under capitalism, he proposed the replacement of the capitalist stock market by a coupon stock market. All citizens would be given an equal endowment of coupons to be used to buy shares in conventional firms. Coupons would not be exchangeable for cash, and they would be sold at death, with revenues returning to the state. But his critics (in Roemer 1996; Burczak 2006, 127–29) have pointed to major flaws in this proposal, several of which derive from the unrealistic information assumptions in general equilibrium models. Given that information is assumed to be freely available, there would be little need or scope for entrepreneurship. In advocating state-controlled banks, Roemer overlooked the problem that government officials may have limited knowledge of investment opportunities.

tunity for anybody who knows a cheaper method to come in at his own risk and to attract customers by underbidding the other producers. But, if prices are fixed by the authority, this method is excluded."

Thus, for Hayek (1948, 78–79), the "economic problem of society is . . . not merely a problem of how to allocate 'given' resources . . . [but] a problem of the utilization of knowledge which is not given to anyone in its totality." In his 1974 Nobel lecture, Hayek (1989, 4) expanded on this point. He considered the "relative prices and wages that will form themselves on a well-functioning market." He argued: "Into the determination of these prices and wages there will enter the effects of particular information possessed by every one of the participants in the market process—a sum of facts which in their totality cannot be known to the scientific observer, or to any other single brain. It is indeed the source of the superiority of the market order . . . that in the resulting allocation of resources more of the knowledge of particular facts will be utilized which exists only dispersed among uncounted persons, than any one person can possess."

Hayek and other Austrian school theorists saw the market as an indispensable information-processing and knowledge-transmission system. In large, complex economies the market deals with the otherwise insurmountable problems of dispersed and tacit knowledge, which cannot be gathered together adequately by single individuals or organizations.

Hayek regarded government interference as generally a distortion of the free market information-processing system. Even if we were to disagree and acknowledge some economic and regulatory roles for the state, the market is still vital to coordinate vast amounts of complex, dispersed, and tacit information. There is no known viable alternative. Proposals for planning that overly limit or even remove the role of the market overlook this fact.

For example, in their proposal for "democratic planning," Fikret Adaman and Pat Devine (1994, 1996, 1997; Devine 1988) greatly underestimated the problem of the enduring tacitness and inaccessibility of much relevant knowledge. Adaman and Devine (1996, 531–32) argued that through "democratic participatory planning . . . tacit knowledge is discovered and articulated and, on the basis of that knowledge, economic decisions are consciously planned and coordinated." Accordingly, for Adaman and Devine, tacit knowledge was something that can eventually be "discovered and articulated" and thereby used for conscious planning.[6]

On the contrary, in principle tacit knowledge is both prior to and beyond the reach of explicit articulation. In his classic text on the topic, Michael Polanyi (1967, 4) wrote: "*We can know more than we can tell.*" Tacit knowledge is a necessary foundation to all knowledge. Just as logically we cannot adequately define every single word in the dictionary in terms of the other words, generally we must rely on intuitions or tacit meanings. There is evidence that some tacit knowledge can be communicated, but without articulation or full awareness (Reber 1993). Although the boundary between the tacit and the explicit may shift, such as when our detailed understanding improves, *it cannot be all brought up to a visible level where everything is rendered explicit.*[7]

Tacit knowledge is social knowledge, in the sense that it is acquired and developed through interaction with others.[8] Hayek (1944, 165) wrote: "[The] interaction of individuals, possessing different knowledge and different views, is what constitutes the life of thought. The growth of reason is a social process based on the existence of such differences."

Polanyi (1967, 19) showed that the foundation of all knowledge must remain inexplicit: all codifiable knowledge is necessarily an emergent property of underlying and tacit rudiments. Accordingly: "The ideal of eliminating all personal elements of knowledge would, in effect, aim at the destruction of all knowledge. . . . [T]he process of formalizing all knowledge to the exclusion of any tacit knowledge is self-defeating." Indeed, for Polanyi, to attempt to dispense with tacitness and subject *all* human affairs to open reason and discussion would be dangerous and destructive. It is thus a serious misunderstanding of the concept of tacit

6. Adaman and Devine (1997, 75) wrote similarly: "A process of cooperation and negotiation . . . would enable tacit knowledge to be articulated."

7. The boundary between tacit and codifiable knowledge is in a constant state of movement. While much knowledge is unavoidably tacit, organizations constantly encode the uncodified so that others can learn (Ioannides 1992; Nonaka and Takeuchi 1995).

8. Wainwright (1994, 58, 169) mistakenly claimed that the concept of tacit knowledge is individualistic. Having rightly noted that knowledge is a social product, she wrongly concluded that tacitness can be overcome. She envisaged the possibility of "social action to share information and extend the knowledge of individuals through associating for the purpose." But, while the development of knowledge does require social interaction, this does not negate tacitness: social production does not necessarily imply shared epistemic accessibility. See Sciabarra (1995, 110–16) for a critical discussion of Wainwright's argument.

knowledge to treat it as something that eventually and generally can be articulated.

Tacit knowledge forms the indissoluble core of all skills. All skillful human activity involves the use of rules and principles that are not known openly to the person involved. For example, we may be unable to articulate the rules of grammar, but in our use of language we largely conform to them. We may be able to ride a bicycle or fly an airplane, but we shall be unable to communicate anything but the barest principles of these activities in codifiable form. Indeed, all productive human activity has these features: we use rules, but we are unable to make many of them explicit. The tacit realm is basic and indispensable. As Richard Nelson and Sidney Winter (1982, 81–82) argued: "Much operational knowledge remains tacit because it cannot be articulated fast enough, because it is impossible to articulate all that is necessary to a successful performance, and because language cannot simultaneously serve to describe relationships and characterize the things related." Giovanni Dosi (1988, 1131) noted similarly: "In each technology there are elements of *tacit and specific* knowledge that are not and *cannot* be written down in a 'blueprint' form, and cannot, therefore, be entirely diffused either in the form of public or proprietary information."

Knowledge is contextual; it is rooted in practice. For it to be accessible, conceptions and practices have to be shared. But there are limits to the amount of shared or widely accessible knowledge. Learning depends on repeated practice and ingrained familiarity. For this reason—and contrary to the views of socialists such as Owen and Marx—in any complex society people have no alternative but to be specialists. There must be some division of labor. There are limits to the amount of knowledge that can be understood by any individual or group.

As Polanyi explained, all scientific advances and technological innovations are bound up with tacit knowledge. They rely on accumulated skills and habits implanted in individuals and institutions. Creative sparks come typically from the striking of intuition on flint stones of tacit skill rather than by logical deduction or rational deliberation (Margolis 1994).

The unavoidable tacitness of much knowledge is one problem. Processing the huge amounts of accessible knowledge is another. In their schemes to bring all knowledge together into the hands of planners, advocates of comprehensive planning overlook the time involved in gathering and dealing with available information. Also, they give inadequate consideration to how innovations are to be incentivized, tested, and promoted. These problems would be massively confounded if all decisions were subject to widespread democratic discussion.

Adaman and Devine (1996, 1997) argued that the market should be confined to the allocation of the "output of existing capacity" only. The remainder of the economy would be run by hierarchies of committees where everyone would participate in the decisionmaking (Devine 1988, 190–91).[9] Their proposal would somehow confine markets to exchanges of the "output of existing capacity" only, without being clear how "existing capacity" can be clearly demarcated. (Consider a machine repaired by replacing an old component with a new part with a slightly improved design. Is that existing capacity or new investment?) A massive bureaucracy would be required to police this fuzzy line of demarcation, with powers to prohibit private contracts on one side of the supposed boundary. On the "democratic planning" side of the fence, where "all would participate," countless meetings would be required. With innumerable meetings, would much work get done? Oscar Wilde was right: socialism is impossible because it would take too many meetings.

Going further than Adaman and Devine, Albert and Hahnel (1978) wished to abolish the market in its entirety. They argued that all production should be governed by democratic worker and consumer councils through an iterative democratic process of evaluation, plan reconciliation, and adjustment (Albert and Hahnel 1978, 269–74; Albert 2003). Similarly, Sidney and Beatrice Webb (Webb and Webb 1920) proposed a collectivized economy run by a maze of democratic councils and committees. None of these authors considered the problems of tacit knowledge and the unfeasibility of the enormous number of meetings required.

Albert (2003, 9) proposed: "Workers and consumers would develop and express their desires via democratic councils with . . . influence over decisions in proportion to the degree he or she will be affected by them." But how, and by whom, would the degrees of affect be assessed? Instead of individual or collective bargaining power, Albert proposed that remuneration for work would be "in tune with how hard we have worked,

---

9. The feasibility of their proposal for "democratic planning" has been debated elsewhere (Adaman and Devine 2001, 2002; Hodgson 1999, 2005b). The suggestion by Cockshott and Cottrell (1993) that computers can replace markets also suffers from a fatal disregard of the problem of dispersed and tacit knowledge. Computerized socialism is criticized in Hodgson (1999).

how long we have worked, and how great a sacrifice we have made in our work" (2003, 10). But how would the amount of effort be assessed? And who would assess it? Imagine endless quarrels over these decisions. Overwhelmed by endless parleying and conferring, the economy would at best achieve a routine and minimal performance. With such an over-burdened and dysfunctional democracy, a grave danger would be that a good part of the population would begin to yearn for dictatorship. An overloaded democracy, with too many problems and decisions, could collapse or be overturned.

Another fateful problem for such schemes is the stifling of innovation. According to Adaman and Devine, innovators should not be allowed free access to the market. Any proposed innovation must be considered by the democratic planning committees within a "single participatory process" (Adaman and Devine 2002, 352). After due experimentation and testing, the most useful innovations will be chosen: "The criteria and interests involved in selecting across the innovations that emerge will determine the outcome of the innovation process" (Adaman and Devine 2001, 235). But there would be a high likelihood of error. For in-stance, when the first digital electronic computer was developed in Man-chester in the 1940s, it was thought by a majority of experts to be so pow-erful that only one model would be required in the whole country. No one fully appreciated the wider possible uses of the computer beyond its function as a numeric calculator. There is no reason to suppose that a more democratic and participatory decisionmaking system would have reached a superior decision.

Novelty, by its nature, challenges established belief. Accordingly, a socioeconomic system that fosters innovation must allow eccentric in-ventors and entrepreneurs to develop ideas that may seem implausible or far-fetched. Systems based on private property and contracts allow en-trepreneurs to test the demand for new innovations by bringing them to the market. It is an imperfect system. But there is no known viable alter-native in a large-scale economy.

Does the existence of planning within large corporations swing the argument back in favor of socialism? There is an important difference. While large, centrally planned economies face relatively little exposure to markets, most corporations have to deal with national or international competition from other businesses. Corporations typically respond by building devolved and flexible internal structures and by learning from other organizations. The removal of the market can remove competition and thwart incentives, thus condemning an isolated planned system to virtual stasis. The synergy of corporate planning and market competition provides modern capitalism with much of its innovative vigor.[10]

Whatever the limitations of a market system, it has the supreme advantage that it does not require everyone to agree on everything before a decision can be made to produce or distribute a good or service. Private property and contracts permit zones of partial autonomy within an interrelated system; agents attempt to enact their decisions through negotiated contracts with others. It is thus possible for many technological or institutional innovations to be pioneered without the prior agreement of committees or bureaucrats. The former Soviet-type economies in Russia and China lacked the devolved autonomy secured by private ownership and largely failed to innovate.[11]

The arguments of von Mises and Hayek point decisively in favor of substantial private ownership and market competition. Von Mises underlined the importance of meaningful prices to make allocative decisions. Hayek's powerful epistemic critique highlighted the impossibility of bringing all knowledge together to make a comprehensive plan.

Schäffle's earlier arguments also remain important. In particular, he outlined the problem of incentivizing individuals in large-scale operations. We have ample evidence that people can cooperate together in relatively small groups, especially when they know each other personally. Our capacities for cooperation in small groups are helped by our evolution over millions of years in tribal units of roughly 150 in number (Dunbar 1993, 2011; Richerson and Boyd 1999, 2001). Socialism of a kind might work on such a small scale, albeit lacking in the high output and technological dynamism of large-scale capitalism. If socialist societies were any larger, individual incentives for effort and innovation would be gravely diminished, and compensatory, interpersonal, trust-based mech-

---

10. As noted in chapter 8 above, some economists put firms on a continuum with markets. This might seem to circumvent the problem of explaining the existence of planning within capitalism. But also it degrades of meaning concepts such as exchange and market. Langlois (1995b) questioned the notion of planning within firms. Contrary to his account, planning does not necessarily rely on the capacity to predict the future. If it did, very little planning would be possible. Much planning in bureaucracies involves the ongoing implementation and adaptation of routines. In that sense there is planning within firms.

11. Murrell (1991) showed empirically that the former "Communist" countries were apparently no less efficient in allocating resources than are capitalist societies. Where they lagged was in terms of dynamic efficiency: the ability to innovate.

anisms to sustain cooperation would be less effective. Consequently, externally imposed discipline would be necessary to sustain production, and larger-scale socialism would engender authoritarianism and bureaucracy. Twentieth-century evidence supports this conclusion.

12.2. Capitalism versus Socialism:
The Neglect of Law and the State

Having sided (mostly) with the Austrian school in the great debate over socialism, I now criticize some aspects of its adherents' position. They developed a powerful critique of comprehensive central planning but offered little detailed practical advice for reform or development within capitalism, other than to privatize public enterprises, encourage competition, minimize regulation, and shrink the scale and powers of the state to the practical minimum. They failed to consolidate their victory in the socialist calculation debate and develop the foundations of practical policy. By refusing a mixed economy or any other intermediate position, they shifted to an extreme, playing an ideological rather than a detailed practical role for policymakers or politicians. In pursuing market imperatives without restraint, they failed to explain why nonmarket organizations such as the family should be retained.[12]

Ironically, such Austrian writers share with many Marxists a failure to elaborate the details of practical economic policy for the here and now. Both extremes have more in common than either would care to admit.

Von Mises and Hayek argued for a system based on private property and exchange. But remarkably their depiction of these vital institutional features was inadequate. As noted above, they failed to distinguish be-

---

12. In noting important changes in the family since medieval times, the Austrian school economist Horwitz (2007, 26) made "the dual claim that the market is a key reason why the family has changed the way it has in recent years and that such changes are good." Yet he was silent on the question of whether the family represents a distinct mode of production and distribution, different from the market or planning. And (assuming it were a distinct system) he was silent on the questions of the practicality or desirability of turning the family into a market system with legal contracts and exchanges between the individuals involved. If the market is such an unalloyed good thing, then why should it not dominate the family as well? Sex tonight dear? That will cost you $50. My invoice for the child care this week is $200. And so on. We require an explanation why the family is not, and perhaps should not be, a market.

tween property and possession. Property involves legal rights established by legislative and judicial institutions. Austrian writers downplay the capacity for individuals to make distinctions between matters of *want* and matters of *right*, and the role of the state in a large-scale economy, which is required as a "superior authority" (Commons 1924, 87) to sustain legal rights.

Austrian economists have adopted extremely wide notions of market or exchange. For example, as noted above, von Mises (1981, 27) saw ownership as de facto having something or control of the services that derive from a good, thus removing the issue of legal rights from the notion of property. Von Mises (1949, 97) saw all action, even by an isolated individual, as exchange, thus removing any notion of the exchange of these rights. Accordingly, von Mises (1949, 257) adopted a near-universal definition of the market as "the social system of the division of labour under private ownership of the means of production." Consequently, his conception of the market embraced all forms of trade or exchange with assets under private control. He described any economy with a division of labor where production was vaguely under some private control as a *market* economy. These loose criteria could apply to almost all social formations in human history.

Overall, the Austrian economists' positive case for private property and markets was weakened by a serious dilution in meaning of those terms. The concepts of property, exchange, and market were eviscerated. Their near ubiquity robbed them of much meaning. At least until Hayek's *Constitution of Liberty* (1960), relatively little attention was given to the detailed institutional arrangements that are necessary to sustain real property, exchange, and markets.

Again the Austrians were almost a mirror image of their socialist antagonists. Neither side invested the concepts of property and exchange with sufficient institutional texture and historical specificity. Neither side adequately appreciated the role of the state and its legal system in sustaining and enforcing the rights of property and contract. Similar deficiencies are evident in later debates concerning the privatization of state-managed services. The institutional thinness of traditional positions in debates over state versus private provision was pinpointed by Elinor Ostrom (1990, 22):

> Both the centralizers and the privatizers frequently advocate oversimplified, idealized institutions—paradoxically, almost "institution-free" institutions.

An assertion that central regulation is necessary tells us nothing about the way a central agency should be constituted, what authority it should have, how the limits on its authority should be maintained, how it will obtain information, or how its agents should be selected, motivated to do their work, and have their performances monitored and rewarded or sanctioned. An assertion that the imposition of private property rights is necessary tells us nothing about how that bundle of rights is to be defined, how the various attributes of the goods involved will be measured, who will pay for the costs of excluding nonowners from access, how conflicts over rights will be adjudicated, or how the residual interests of the right-holders in the resource system itself will be organized.

Von Mises and Hayek pointed to private property and markets as the unavoidable solution to economic problems. Although this allowed a more sophisticated institutional perspective than the unworkable schemes of their socialist opponents, it remained little more than an indication. As Gunnar Heinsohn and Otto Steiger (2013, 12) argued, the crucial difference between property and possession was overlooked by both sides: "The common dichotomy emphasized by economists that links freedom, law and economic prosperity with the private individual, and blames the collective for the lack or deficiency of this trinity, suffers from a simplified view of property rights as rights of . . . possession. This view misses the critical importance of the rights of ownership altogether. In a similar way, economists who emphasize the . . . contrast between *private* ownership and *state* ownership miss the correct dichotomy between ownership and . . . possession."

Such vital matters were overlooked by both sides in the socialist calculation debates. The lack of precision when it comes to such key concepts such as property diverted the Austrian side into an untenable market absolutism that was both vague and impractical. While driving home key arguments concerning incentives and knowledge, much of the remaining structure of mainstream economic theory, with its weak concepts of property and exchange, remained intact.

Ironically, by failing to acknowledge the difference between law and custom, Austrian school thinkers have inadvertently diminished the importance of the separation of powers within the state itself. Hayek's evolutionary portrayal of law as an experimental search for universal principles of justice downplayed its actual institutional features and its reliance on countervailing power. Hayek relied too often on exhortations for individual freedom and the rule of law, with inadequate attention to the power relations and institutional structures that are necessary for their preservation.[13]

If law were mere custom, then its efficacy against any delinquent developments in a modern state—with all its powers of propaganda and force—would be weak and fragile. To be legitimate and effective, law has to rely on countervailing power *within the state machine* as well from outside interest groups. It has to be legitimate even in the eyes of the state and sufficiently independent and powerful to be enforced, even against the erring rich and mighty in politics or business. This in turn is an argument for democratic government with checks and balances—to legitimate government power and to increase the probability that powerful vested minority interests can be effectively scrutinized and checked.

On the other side, Marxists have regarded laws as serving the ruling class and urged their abolition on the victory of the proletariat.[14] Suspicion of law is understandable, especially in circumstances where the poor have little or no means to protect or enforce their legal rights. But that does not mean that we should throw all law overboard. Christine Synopwich (1990) argued that contempt for law in socialist theory has led to a contemptible form of socialist legality in practice. The "socialist" experiments in Russia and China did not simply abolish private property rights. By regarding law as a cynical political instrument of a ruling class rather than a potential safeguard of human rights, they ditched the very notion of the rule of law and undermined personal rights and civil liberties. The human cost was massive.

In the great twentieth-century debate on capitalism versus socialism, both sides gave insufficient attention to legal rules and structures and

---

13. In a powerful critique, Burczak (2006, 59–66) used the "legal realist" arguments of Frank (1930, 1949) and Llewellyn (1960) to counter Hayek's view of law as a potentially neutral process by which apolitical rules of justice are established. Legal realists emphasize that law unavoidably depends on interpretations of facts, by judges, witnesses, and other participants, that are selected and colored by preconceptions and prejudices. Legal judgments can thus be swayed by political and ideological circumstances.

14. Writing in 1918, Lenin (1967, 3:49) advocated Marx's "dictatorship of the proletariat" in these terms: "Dictatorship is rule base directly upon force and unrestricted by any laws. The revolutionary dictatorship of the proletariat is rule won and maintained by the use of violence by the proletariat against the bourgeoisie, rule that is unrestricted by any laws." This principle of legally unrestrained class struggle was shared by Marxist-Leninists worldwide, including Stalinists, Trotskyists, and Maoists.

failed to characterize the rival systems adequately. The proponents of socialism played with general equilibrium models that were supposed to fit
all worlds and ignored key institutional features and specificities of both
capitalism and socialism. The Austrian school inadequately specified
the nature of private property and exchange, rendering them as near-
universal phenomena. Hence, they omitted key historically specific features of capitalism. Neither side considered the more specific institutions
that helped bring about the dramatic takeoff of capitalism around 1800.

Consider the six definitional features of capitalism that were developed in chapter 10 above. The Austrian arguments underline the importance of private property rights, widespread commodity exchange and
markets, and widespread private ownership of the means of production,
partly corresponding to the first three conditions. But their notions of
property and exchange were inadequate. The Austrian economists had
little to say about the sphere of production—conditions (4) and (5)—
including the employment contract. Although they mentioned money
many times, they paid insufficient attention to the use of property as collateral or to the selling of debt—condition (6). Their theory of money
downplays the vital constitutive role of the state. At best, they stressed
three of the six conditions only. The first three conditions are insufficient to identify the institutions of the capitalist system that were responsible for the explosive production of wealth in the last three hundred
years.

12.3. Crucial Institutions That Span
the Individual and the State

For different reasons, both sides in the socialist calculation debates neglected the importance for capitalism of countervailing institutions and
its system of law. Generally, the Austrian school stressed market competition, believing that individual and market forces are the remedy. Austrian school writers have been generally hostile to trade unions and have
complained that their power has led to market distortions and unemployment. Concerning corporations, von Mises (1949, 307) regarded the
separation of ownership and control as inefficient, anticompetitive, and
the result of hostile intrusion by government: "A successful corporation
is ultimately never controlled by hired managers. The emergence of an
omnipotent managerial class is not a phenomenon of the unhampered

market economy. It was, on the contrary, an outgrowth of the interventionist policies consciously aiming at an elimination of the influence of the shareholders and at their virtual expropriation."

But requiring all shareholders to be managers would greatly limit the possibilities of financing large-scale production. Hayek (1948, 116) similarly blamed much corporate corpulence on the state. With their small-scale, individualistic view of entrepreneurship and economic activity, Austrian school economists have never adequately come to grips with the modern corporation and the dynamic role it has often played in the development of capitalism and modern technology. Corporations within capitalism have helped enable massive investment and economies of scale.

The socialist side of the debate assumed neoclassical models of "perfect" market competition that assumed away any oligopolistic or monopoly power. Both in their theoretical models and in their ideology, socialists have often promoted an ideal, homogenized economic system.

At least in their economic theories, neither side acknowledged the possibility that counterbalancing agglomerations of economic or political power could have positive as well as negative outcomes in terms of economic dynamism and sociopolitical progress. The emergence and enduring dynamism of capitalism depended on effective countervailing power and layers of organization between the individual and the state (North, Wallis, and Weingast 2009).

As a negative historical illustration, consider an attempt to eliminate all large organizations in civil society between the individual and the state.[15] In prerevolutionary France under Louis XIV there were numerous corporations, closely tied up with royal power and bureaucracy, that spanned the worlds of business and politics (Lamoreaux and Rosenthal 2005; Guinnane, Harris, Lamoreaux, and Rosenthal 2007). The sale of corporate offices provided an important source of royal revenues. In return, numerous corporations and guilds received privileges from the

---

15. The term *civil society* is ambiguous and has historically gone through several changes of meaning (Kocka 2004). Here, it refers to the aggregate of nonstate institutions and networks, including families, private firms, business associations, social networks, churches, and numerous other organizations, whether for profit or otherwise. The important role of civil society has been downplayed by both sides in former debates between socialism and politicoeconomic individualism. By contrast, Crouch (2011, 179) referred to the "quadrilateral of forces . . . needed to make a good society: state, market, corporation, civil society."

king. This era of "Colbertism" involved bureaucratic meddling, regulation, nepotism, and corruption.

In search of an individualistic utopia, and against the despised institutions of the ancien régime, the French revolutionary authorities enacted laws from 1791 that prohibited organizations of workers, professionals, and entrepreneurs and ended much state regulation of business. Business coalitions, guilds, and even business corporations were abolished (North, Wallis, and Weingast 2009, 206–7). Individuals were free to pursue their business interests but forbidden to join together for business purposes. Generally, apart from local chambers of commerce composed of individual traders, organized intermediate forms between the individual and the state were banned.

But there were no regulations or institutions to ensure product quality or guarantee professional competence. The legislators proposed that the market would take care of these problems. But, after the prohibition of professional and business associations, the only option for airing commercial grievances, instituting standards, or establishing codes of conduct was for individuals to lobby the state. In the absence of other channels, the state became by default the only grievance forum and sole regulatory authority, against the spirit of the laissez-faire doctrine of the time. In the absence of substantial intermediate organizations, the very legislation designed to minimize state meddling in business created paradoxically a monopoly of state regulation and interference. Consequently, this revolutionary experiment in market individualism was short-lived (Kuisel 1981; Hirsch 1989, 1991; Hirsch and Minard 1998; Minard 2005).

Corporations were later reinstated under Napoléon and enshrined in his legal code. But the statist response to the laissez-faire atomization of business left enduring marks on French economic institutions. Laissez-faire individualism removed intermediate institutions between individuals and the state, which in turn fed the state bureaucracy that laissez-faire was designed to disempower. France's reputation for dirigisme and bureaucracy has some roots in its free market market individualism of the 1790s.

This illuminates the potentially positive role of organized, countervailing, and intermediate institutions between the individual and the state. The corporation itself is such an intermediate institution. Although its creation depends on recognition and registration by the state, it has considerable autonomy regarding its internal organization and rules. This autonomy helps account for large-scale investment and the dynamic adaptability of capitalism. But the very existence of the corporation means that competition is not just between individuals: it is between multiple legal entities with vastly different powers and resources. The corporate form permits large concentrations of resources with enduring nodes of ownership that can outlast the life of an individual.

As another illustration, Timur Kuran (2004, 2010) argued that the medieval Islamic legal prohibition of the corporate form, with the requirement that human individuals alone could own property, combined with inflexible inheritance laws that divided estates, helped explain why the Islamic world failed to develop beyond its impressive cultural and scientific achievements in medieval times and accumulate sufficient capital to enable large-scale industrial and other developments. The medieval Islamic world had extensive mercantile trade and well-enforced property rights, but it failed to develop a capitalist system before the rise of West. Lacking legally grounded and economically dynamic intermediate layers of power, the vacuum was filled by clans and religious factions.

The role of business networks in modern capitalism has been studied extensively, from the *chaebols* in Korea, and the *keiretsu* in Japan, to business associations in Europe and North America. These networks have inspired a range of empirical studies and elaborate theoretical speculations. Most scholars agree that they often have knowledge-sharing, knowledge-development, and political-lobbying functions (see Granovetter 1982; Baker 1990; Powell 1990; Grabher 1993; Sik 1994; Boisot and Child 1996; Hage and Alter 1997; Cohendet, Kern, Mehmanpazir, and Munier 1999; Rauch and Casella 2001; White 2002; Thompson 2003; Nooteboom 2004; and Padgett and Powell 2012).[16] These studies illustrate the powerful role that organizations and coalitions play as mediators between the individual and state in modern capitalism.

So important are these constellations of economic power that attempts at deregulation are often thwarted. In an empirical study of attempted deregulation in the United Kingdom, the United States, France,

---

16. But the concept of a network has lost much analytic precision, being stretched toward the point that it may seem to "explain everything" but "end up explaining nothing" (Thompson 2003, 2). In particular, theories of networks typically overlook the legal rules and structures of business, including property, contract, and corporate law. Unless that void is filled, the idea (held by some) that networks offer a new vision of a future beyond markets and central planning will remain shallow and unconvincing.

Germany, and Japan, Steven K. Vogel (1996) showed that regulations have often increased rather than diminished. In attempting to establish freer competition, new rules are necessary to encourage new entrants and promote competition. Proponents of liberalization sometimes make the mistake of the French revolutionaries of the 1790s and some Eastern Bloc reformers of the 1990s: they assume that the retreat of the state will automatically lead to competitive markets. They overlook the likely and sometimes useful concentrations of power in civil society and the inevitability of rules, including rules framed by governments. The global movement for deregulation in fact led to reregulation in various forms.

These examples of intermediate organization suggest that, as long as we are trapped in the Tweedledum-and-Tweedledee debate between planning and markets, we shall be unable to appreciate the intermediating networks and institutions that have played a vital role in the development of modern capitalism. Experience reveals the limitations of both wholesale socialism and atomized individualism. Along with individual property rights, all successful capitalisms have embraced corporate organization and other intermediate layers of organized power as well as varying measures of state intervention. These are important for both its emergence and its vitality.

But, while intermediate organization is necessary, it is insufficient. It guarantees neither dynamism, democracy, nor legality. The experience of fascism in the twentieth century shows that big business can connive with autocracy against democracy and liberty (Turner 1985). As US president Franklin D. Roosevelt (1938/1941) argued: "The liberty of a democracy is not safe if the people tolerate the growth of private power to a point where it becomes stronger than their democratic state itself." Excessive corporate or military power can also undermine or constrain democracy (Galbraith 1952, 1969; Lindblom 1977; Dahl 1982; Crouch 2004, 2011). Countervailing power has to balance rather than overwhelm other legitimate authority. The maintenance of politicoeconomic systems with their counterbalanced powers requires constant vigilance.

12.4. Information, Knowledge, and Limits to the Market

The Austrian school economists emphasized that knowledge is localized, is often tacit and dispersed, and cannot readily be communicated to a large collective body. They had a much more sophisticated appreciation of the nature of knowledge than did their neoclassical opponents. But the Austrians failed to note that similar knowledge problems also apply to large corporations. Corporations face the ongoing problem of accessing and sharing knowledge within their organizations (Nonaka and Takeuchi 1995).

Furthermore, not all assets are physical. Rights to access, use, and sell information can also be owned. Addressing intellectual property such as patents and trademarks, Hayek (1948, 114–15) pointed to limitations of the contractual framework in this area. But, as capitalism becomes more and more knowledge intensive, the limits to contract when dealing with information and knowledge become more serious, for reasons that I shall now summarize.

Unlike other commodities, the contractual transfer of information has some curious features that challenge the standard contractarian framework (Nelson 1959; Arrow 1962b). First, once acquired, codifiable information can often be easily reproduced in multiple copies by its buyer and possibly sold to others. This places the seller at a disadvantage. Accordingly, there may be licenses, patents, or other restrictions to prevent the buyer from selling it on to others.

Second, codifiable information has the peculiar property that, once it is sold, it also remains in the hands of the seller. Information is not a normal commodity that changes hands from seller to buyer when it is purchased. US president Thomas Jefferson allegedly likened knowledge to the light of a candle: its flame may be used to light another, but its own light is not weakened. Information is a *club good*: its use is nonrivalrous, but it is potentially excludable (through copyright laws etc.).

Third, Arrow (1962b, 616) wrote: "There is a fundamental paradox in the determination of demand for information: its value for the purchaser is not known until he has the information, but then he has in effect acquired it without cost." If we knew what we were going to buy, then we would no longer need to buy it.

Consequently, in an economy involving substantial flows of information, it is sometimes problematic or counterproductive to follow Hayek's (1948, 18) advice and establish clear "rules which, above all, enable man to distinguish between mine and thine." Information challenges the bounds of exclusive and individual property. What is possessed cannot always be clearly defined because to define it fully is to give it away. It is often unclear as to who owns what information. It is not always possible or efficient to break up information into discrete pieces and give each one an ownership tag. It is often difficult to determine who discovered the information in the first place or who can claim legal title to its ownership. An information-rich society challenges the meaning and boundary of what is mine and what is thine.

Hayek rightly emphasized the importance and unavoidable inaccessibility of much tacit knowledge, something that his socialist opponents had ignored. But he wrote as if an appreciation of tacit and inaccessible knowledge clinched the matter in favor of a system based on private property and markets. He overlooked the differences between information and physical commodities, as itemized by Nelson and Arrow.

As Arrow (1996, 651) pointed out, firms share much technical and managerial knowledge. He continued: "Information is the basis of production, production is carried on in discrete legal entities, and yet *information is a fugitive resource*, with limited property rights." He envisaged an "increasing tension" between legal relations based on private ownership and the information-intensive economy.

Information is a nonrival good that often can be easily shared (its use by one person does not diminish its usability by another). But private ownership of intellectual assets involves exclusive concentrations of rights and a massive general denial of readily available user rights to others. But such exclusive property rights are necessary for informational assets to be used as collateral. If followed fully, the logic of a knowledge-intensive capitalist economy requires knowledge to be privatized. The resulting denial of the cheaply acquired benefits of the shared possession of nonrivalrous informational assets can generate remarkable inefficiencies. Furthermore, the infinite extension and subdivision of ownership in a densely interconnected knowledge economy can create an anticommons where extensively divided and interconnected rights—in a real world with positive transaction costs—obstruct investment and trade. This problem applies particularly to patents and other intellectual property and has become more severe in an increasingly knowledge-intensive economy (Heller 2008; Pagano 2014). The ubiquitous imposition of legal rules "to distinguish between mine and thine" (Hayek 1948, 18) can deprive many people of information that is vital for their work or well-being. Capitalism is challenged by increasing knowledge intensity: it must limit its own use of private property and the market mechanism to survive.

The huge productivity growth associated with modern capitalism has been partly empowered by science and technology. Yet the development of science has traditionally depended on commitments to the pursuit and distribution of truth as well as to profit (Hagstrom 1965). Some scholars have argued that the wholesale commercialization of science could threaten its viability (Mirowski and Sent 2002; Buenstorf 2009).

To his credit Hayek (Hayek 1944, 38; Hayek 1979, 44) accepted that government should provide "channels of information" plus "standards of measure, and . . . many kinds of information ranging from land registers, maps, and statistics to the certification of the quality of some goods or services." As capitalism has become more complex, these informational needs have become much greater, implying a greater need for public provision. While much information and knowledge cannot be shared (because of tacitness, interpretative difficulty, or inaccessibility), much else can, and this can be of huge productive value. Consequently, the benefits of private and contractual provision of this information may be much less than the overall opportunity costs of charging a price for its use. A healthy market system itself depends on the incompleteness of markets for information; some crucial data must be unowned and available freely.

Consider the phenomenal growth of the Internet. In the early 1990s, CERN (the European Organization for Nuclear Research) developed key elements of the Internet infrastructure. They were released to the public for free to ensure that the information technology would become widespread. Similarly, many software programs and even operating systems are available free of charge. The Internet has vastly stimulated markets, but not all its components or enablers were marketed. Modern capitalism has reduced the marginal cost of many additional informational goods and services to near zero, making profitability less viable as the main spur of production (Rifkin 2014).

Especially in a technologically complex capitalism, effective consumer choice often requires some scientific and technical knowledge in order to evaluate what is being bought. Consequently, informed choice in a market economy requires effective public education in science. This problem was addressed by liberal thinkers such as John Dewey, who saw roles for education and democracy in facilitating public debate about science and its objectives (see Dewey 1916, 1935, 1938, 1939; Ryan 1995; Evans 2000; Hodgson 2013b, chap. 10).

It was argued in the preceding chapter that the economy might be conceived as an information-processing system, in contrast to the machine-like visions of classical, Marxian, or neoclassical economics. To their credit, the Austrian school economists promoted a nonmechanistic view of the economy where information and knowledge are paramount. But they paid insufficient attention to different types of information or knowledge, their different degrees of accessibility, their different strategic roles, and the limitations of information contracting. These points lead us away from a pure market utopia toward an economy that combines markets with state and nonstate organizations.

The Austrians and others have rightly pointed to the limits of state intervention and the inherent difficulties of government involvement in a modern complex economy. But that does not mean that the state should have no economic role. As some Austrian writers concede, the constitutive roles of law and the state imply that some state involvement is unavoidable. While state intervention in the economy is often confounded by problems of complexity and distributed knowledge, the state can sometimes intervene effectively as a coordinator, enabler, information processor, and strategic leader (Nelson 1981a, 2003; Chang 1997, 2002a; Mazzucato 2013).

12.5. Ironic Digression: Was Hayek a Social Democrat?

It is hugely ironic that, according to some interpreters, the great twentieth-century debate on socialism ends up with an important convergence of opinion. Consider the socialist side first. In its historic retreat from socialism as originally defined, the 1959 Bad Godesberg program of the German Social Democratic Party included the following passage: "Totalitarian control of the economy destroys freedom. The Social Democratic Party therefore favours a free market wherever free competition really exists. . . . As much competition as possible—as much planning as necessary."[17]

By the 1980s, most large socialist parties throughout the world had adopted a similar position or were moving visibly in that direction. Today, socialists who think otherwise are a small minority within all sizable political parties that describe themselves as *Labor*, *Social Democratic*, *Socialist*, or even *Communist*.

From about 1916 to 1924, Hayek sympathized with the gradualist socialism of the Fabians (Ebenstein 2001, 36–40). But his deepening relationship with von Mises pushed him toward extreme liberalism. Still, his

17. http://en.wikipedia.org/wiki/Godesberg_Program.

growing distrust of the state is unsurprising given his location in Europe
and the political events in his youth, including the conflagration of world
war, imperial collapse, rising nationalism, the advance of Bolshevism,
and the upsurge of fascism. Others turned toward socialism in those tu-
multuous years. Hayek took a different but understandable road.

From the 1940s to the 1980s, Hayek still acknowledged the necessary
role of government in several spheres. But for some libertarian writers
this was too much. Hans-Hermann Hoppe (1994, 67) opined: "Hayek's
view regarding the role of market and the state cannot systematically be
distinguished from that of a modern social democrat." Hayek thought
that the state should do more than protect private property rights and
defend the nation from attack.[18]

In *The Road to Serfdom*, Hayek (1944, 37) endorsed several government interventions in the economy, including the enactment of legislation to limit working hours. Generally, Hayek (1979, 41) believed that
"in an advanced society government ought to use its power of raising
funds by taxation to provide a number of services which for various reasons cannot be provided, or cannot be provided adequately, by the market." Among these are public goods and services where, by definition,
because of cost or practicality, nonpayers cannot be excluded from the
benefits. Accordingly, Hayek (1944, 111) wrote of needed services "such
as sanitary and health measures . . . which could not possibly be provided
by the market for the obvious reason that . . . it is not possible to confine
the benefits to those who are willing or able to pay for them." For Hayek
(1944, 121), additional roles for government included assistance in the
case of "such 'acts of God' as earthquakes and floods" where individuals are unable to make provision. Hayek (1979, 44) also saw government
as providing "protection against . . . epidemics, or such natural forces as
floods and avalanches, but also many of the amenities which make life in
modern cities tolerable, most roads (except some long-distance highways
where tolls can be charged), the provision of standards of measure, and

18. Block (1996, 365) also bemoaned "Hayek's interventionistic views." But Rodrigues
(2012) applauded them. While supporting the Austrian school arguments against comprehensive planning, Steele (1992, 22) wrote: "Contrary to what Mises and some of his followers have occasionally seemed to imply, it is perfectly reasonable for a welfare-statist or interventionist to accept the economic calculation argument in its entirety. No inconsistency
is entailed in this." Burczak (2006) went further by trying to rescue a form of market "socialism" (with genuine markets and worker cooperatives) from the jaws of defeat by the
Austrian school while accepting key arguments from Hayek and others.

of many kinds of information ranging from land registers, maps, and statistics to the certification of the quality of some goods or services offered
on the market."

Hayek argued that government provision of these collective or public
goods was necessary because they were unlikely to be supplied via markets. Hayek (1944, 120–21) also proposed state assistance for social and
health insurance, justifying this in terms of the uncertainties involved
and the fact that such assistance would not typically diminish incentives
to avoid sickness or accident:

> Nor is there any reason why the state should not assist the individuals in pro-
> viding for those common hazards of life against which, because of their un-
> certainty, few individuals can make adequate provision. Where, as in the case
> of sickness and accident, neither the desire to avoid such calamities nor the
> efforts to overcome their consequences are as a rule weakened by the provi-
> sion of assistance, where, in short, we deal with genuinely insurable risks, the
> case for the state helping to organise a comprehensive system of social insur-
> ance is very strong. There . . . is no incompatibility in principle between the
> state providing greater security in this way and the preservation of individ-
> ual freedom.

Hayek (1979, 62) argued that government should finance education
and research as well as enforcing "building regulations, pure food laws,
the certification of certain professions, the restriction on the sale of certain dangerous goods (such as arms, explosives, poisons and drugs),
as well as some safety and health regulations for the processes of production and the provision of such public institutions as theatres, sports
grounds, etc." His approval of government support for health care and
education could open the door for the provision of other services on
the basis of need rather than the ability to pay (Doyal and Gough 1991;
Hodgson 2013b).

Hayek (1944, 120) also saw a need for "the security of a minimum
income" to provide "security against severe physical privation" and establish "the certainty of a given minimum of sustenance for all." Hayek
(1979, 55) reiterated this guaranteed basic income proposal, which would
give "the assurance of a certain minimum for everyone." He also agreed
to legislation for a maximum number of hours at work, if "not carried
too far."

Hayek (1994, 111) also advocated government activity to protect and

preserve market competition, which "requires a good deal of government activity directed toward making it effective and toward supple-
menting it where it cannot be made effective."

In remarkable Keynesian flourishes, Hayek (1944, 121) also addressed
"the supremely important problem of combating general fluctuations of
economic activity and the recurrent waves of large-scale unemployment
which accompany them." While urging that government countermea-
sures should not undermine market competition, he nevertheless established a role for them. Hayek (1979, 59) proposed a countercyclic government strategy to "distribute its expenditure over time in such a manner
that it will step in when private investment flags."

It does not end there. Hayek's own arguments can be turned around
to counter his strong personal opposition to trade unions. Torsten
Niechoj (2008) argued that a Hayekian emphasis on locally available
knowledge, plus acknowledgment of the role of trade unions in channeling information and developing rules for conflict resolution, can justify
moderate trade union activity.

But Hayek was remote from social democracy by one major criterion. Most social democrats support redistributive tax measures to reduce inequalities in wealth and income. By contrast, Hayek (1994, 108)
worried that a redistributive welfare state would "ultimately lead to the
same result" as central planning. Likewise, in *The Constitution of Liberty*, Hayek (1960, chap. 20) argued against redistributive income taxes.
But earlier Hayek (1948, 118) had accepted the possibility that "inheritance taxes could, of course, be made an instrument toward greater social mobility and greater dispersion of property and, consequently, may
have to be regarded as important tools of a truly liberal policy." While
generally rejecting redistributive income taxes, he left the door ajar for a
tax on inherited wealth. But inequality is not a major theme of his work.
He promoted a competitive market economy with small producers and
blamed the state for concentrations of capital and corporate power. He
never came to grips with the real sources of inequality under capitalism.

12.6. Hayek versus Von Mises

Nevertheless, Hayek adopted a number of key policies that are prominent among modern social democrats. For this reason, some libertarians
became critical of him and transferred their foremost allegiance to von

Mises (Hoppe 1994; Block 1996). Others noted differences in the theoretical approaches of the two Austrians (Salerno 1993). For Hayek (1994, 72), von Mises's limitation was that he "remained in the end a rationalist-utilitarian." But also consider their contrasting conceptions of exchange, property, and markets. Although Hayek insufficiently acknowledged the essential role of the state in sustaining the legal system, he did at least pay much attention to legal aspects of a market economy. By contrast, von Mises argued that legal concepts could be largely sidelined from economics and sociology. His rationalism and utilitarianism involved ahistorical and individualist concepts deemed "independent of social relations between men" (Mises 1981, 27).

As already noted, von Mises (1949, 97) saw all human action as exchange. Von Mises (1981, 27) considered property as "purely a physical relationship of man to the goods, independent of social relations between men or of a legal order." This would extend the meaningful life of these broadly defined concepts, from the few centuries of capitalism's existence, to long before the few thousand years of extensive trade and market activity, and through millions of years of our ape-like evolution. Consequently, while undermining comprehensive central planning and all schemes to abolish markets in their entirety, von Mises's defense of property, exchange, and markets does not promote a clearly defined socioeconomic system. It is not even specific to human society. His defense of private property is no more than an argument for private possession. His discourse was too blunt to defend real historical exchange or markets. Consequently, as a defense of capitalism in institutional detail, especially as it has emerged from the eighteenth century, it is weak and ineffective.

Hayek was more of an institutionalist than was von Mises. He provided his core concepts with greater legal and historical specificity even if his moves in that direction were inadequate. Furthermore, by giving more detailed attention to matters of practical policy, he realized that government had to retain a significant role in the economic sphere. By contrast, von Mises and his followers showed unwittingly that an ahistorical universality of concepts, combined with an ideological purism, can lead to practical ineffectiveness. It means so little to defend an exchange economy when exchange is defined as no more than action. It is a weak case for private property when it is defined simply as that which we can access or use, irrespective of any legal rights to do so. Von Mises's attempts to render these concepts universal denuded them of much meaning and thereby eviscerated his policy recommendations.

Neither Hayek nor von Mises adequately came to grips with some of the great institutional structures that help define modern capitalism. They played down the place of debt in the constitution of money and largely overlooked its salability as a driver of capitalist advance. They gave no emphasis to the role of property as collateral for securing money for investment. They greeted the corporation with caution, regretting the establishment of limited liability while yearning for a lost world of individual entrepreneurs. The defects of the corporation were largely blamed on the state. The market economy that they defended had more to do with an economy of self-employed producers and small-scale production than with the real capitalist world of large oligopolistic corporations.

The great debate between capitalism and socialism has been plagued by purists on both sides. Capitalism has been let down by its supporters, who have failed to identify adequately its key features. But it has also been fortunate in its enemies, who have generally failed to articulate a feasible alternative. With a deeper analysis of its fundamental institutions, and with an acknowledgment of the vital role of the state in a capitalist economy, we now have a chance of reaching a richer understanding of the system, its potential, and its limitations.

CHAPTER THIRTEEN

How Does Capitalism Evolve?

[We] are apt to look at progress as the normal rule in human society; but history refutes this. — Charles Darwin (1871)

We live in a world of emergent evolution; of problems whose solutions, if they are solved, beget new and deeper problems. — Karl Popper (1982)

*E*volution is a trendy but vague and ambiguous word. It can mean an alternative to revolution. It can connote any form of change. In some disciplines—such as evolutionary psychology—it signifies a biologically grounded account of origins and change in species. Yet modern evolutionary economics has made little reference to biology or human origins (Nelson and Winter 1982). It is often unclear whether *evolution* refers to the development of a single entity or changes over generations in a population. Terms such as *evolution* and *coevolution* are often used in the social sciences with gravitas, as if they signify something important. But without further specification they actually mean very little. One is repeatedly left asking what kind of evolutionary theory or framework is intended.

Etymologically, both *evolution* and *development* come from the Latin verbs *volvere* and *evolvere*, meaning "to roll" and "to unroll." Unrolling is a specifically directional and predestined operation applied to one object; the scroll is unrolled to reveal that which is already written within. Also, *evolution* has widespread connotations of predestination, teleology, or improvement that help explain why Charles Darwin used it very sparingly. In modern biology the word is typically used to apply to populations rather than single objects.

Instead of attempting to give this ambiguous word a specific meaning, it is better to consider the nature of the phenomena that are changing. It must be made clear whether we are referring to a single entity or to a population. For example, while important in terms of understanding individual development, prominent views of evolution as self-organization or spontaneous order clearly become insufficient when they apply to populations: they cannot explain the differential survival of multiple entities that have evolved (Hodgson 2011b; Hodgson and Knudsen 2010, 2012).

Even when populations are acknowledged, evolution is sometimes treated as stages in the progression of a typical entity, which is then scaled up to apply to the whole population, regarding some entities as more advanced along this fixed road than others. Much writing on the evolution of capitalism is the attempted enumeration of predetermined stages of development, as if the word *evolution* was used in its original sense of "unrolling." This idea of evolution as a series of stages is found in G. W. F. Hegel's notion of evolution, the German historical school, much of Marxism, and the once-popular work of Walt W. Rostow (1960). Every country is deemed to follow a similar, preordained developmental path.

But this underestimates interactions between countries at different levels of development. The more advanced countries may accelerate, delay, or divert the latecomers, which may then forge paths and pass through stages that are different from those previously taken by the more advanced countries. Consequently, an account of the evolution of capitalism in terms of fixed stages is at most appropriate for the global totality. Even this requires us to explain these global stages in terms of the interactions between individual, varied capitalisms.

Has global capitalism passed through various stages, such as the mercantile, imperialistic, industrial, and financial? Even here it is difficult to establish clear zones and divisions between one stage and another. For example, finance was central to emergent capitalism in Italy and the Netherlands, right at the beginning. Stages theories are typically ex post classifications. Describing changes historically is one thing, but showing that one stage necessarily leads to its successor is another. It is possible that the global development of capitalism is a result more of the rise and decline of different capitalist countries than of immanent mechanisms within the system as such.

Obviously, the development of major individual capitalist economies has global consequences. The rise of Britain as an imperial hegemon in the eighteenth and nineteenth centuries established a global trading and financial system. Its legal and administrative institutions were cloned in North America, Australia, and elsewhere. Britain's loss of its hegemonic position after the First World War and the absence of a willing successor was a major factor in the breakdown of world trade in the 1930s (Kindleberger 1973). A new world order based on US hegemony arose after 1945, initially based on the global financial institutions established in Bretton Woods. A larger and less-regulated global financial system followed from the 1980s (Glyn 2006; Rodrik 2011). A big question for the twenty-first century is the impact of China's rapid growth. But the global impact of China's rise cannot be understood without a detailed appraisal of developments within its economy and other major economies. To understand the evolution of global capitalism, just as to understand the evolution of biological species, it is necessary to understand the forces acting on relevant entities at individual and other levels.

With populations of varied, interacting entities we are obliged to address at least three basic explanatory problems. First, how does variation occur, and how is it sustained within a population? Second, how does one explain that some members of the population survive and replicate while others are less successful or expire? Third, how is the retention of features and their transmission from one entity to another explained? These three explanatory requirements, concerning variation, selection, and inheritance, are central to Darwinism and are thematic to the long, final paragraph of the *Origin of Species* (1859).

Global capitalism presents us with populations of entities at multiple levels. First, there is a population of national capitalist systems. Second, within each capitalist system there are further populations of organizations competing for resources and within markets. Third, every capitalist system is made up of a number of human individuals, each of whom requires the means of survival. At every level, these entities face problems of immediate local scarcity of resources.[1] Important information is transmitted from one entity to another. In every one of these populations, the three Darwinian questions concerning the explanation of

---

1. The concept of scarcity is ambiguous. Some things, like oil and iron, are physically limited and *globally scarce*. Global scarcity is not universal because some assets, like trust and honor, are not physically limited. But *local scarcity* is universal for agents in the sense that the use of any physical or informational resource requires energy and effort, whether cognitive or physical, even if that resource is globally abundant or unlimited.

variation, differential success, and the transmission of information remain vital.

The core Darwinian principles operate as a metatheoretical framework rather than as an adequate theory that is generally capable of explaining details (Hodgson and Knudsen 2006, 2010; Aldrich et al. 2008). Friedrich Hayek (1952, 74) made a useful distinction between explanation in principle and explanation in detail. Generalized Darwinism fits into the former but not the latter category.

In addition to the three Darwinian principles, a distinction is made between (1) the *entities* that compete for locally scarce resources and (2) the *information* useful for survival that is transmitted from one entity to another. Using David Hull's (1988) terminology, the entities themselves are termed *interactors*, and program-like sequences of information that are transmitted from one interactor to another are termed *replicators*. Hull (1988, 408) defined an interactor as "an entity that directly interacts as a cohesive whole with its environment in such a way that this interaction *causes* replication to be differential." This definition is refined in Hodgson and Knudsen (2010, 239–40). A replicator is not a separate thing but an information-carrying mechanism within an interactor. Replication (synonymous with *inheritance*) is a process where replicator-held information is passed from one interactor to another.

There are cases where one interactor gives rise to another (including new replicators within the new interactors), such as the formation of a new political state by the secession of a region or component nation, or a new company by a spinoff, or a new human by sexual reproduction. There is a different kind of replication, termed *diffusion*, where no new interactor is formed but replicators are copied from one interactor to another. Examples of diffusion include the copying of laws or policies by states, the copying of routines by firms, and the transmission of habits from one individual to another, such as when we learn a skill from a teacher. Diffusion is much more common in socioeconomic than in biological evolution.

These ideas provide a preliminary framework for analyzing the evolution of capitalism. This framework is necessary but insufficient for analysis or prediction. I concentrate on some general features of capitalist evolution rather than exploring variations and multiple scenarios. The following chapter discusses whether there is likely to be convergence between different types of capitalism.

Section 13.1 addresses the evolutionary concept of selection and its relevance. Section 13.2 discusses processes involving the diffusion of rules and routines and gives several examples. Section 13.3 considers how an evolving system builds on survivals from the past. This dovetails with research concerning institutional complementarities in modern capitalist systems. Section 13.4 considers the dramatic increase of complexity within capitalism.

13.1. Selection and the Evolution of Capitalism

Evolutionary selection seems a simple idea, but it is conceptually tricky. Following the work of George Price (1995), we may distinguish between *subset selection* and *successor selection*. *Subset selection* refers straightforwardly to the elimination of some interactors in a population and the survival of others. *Successor selection* is more complex. It involves differential replication, novel interactors, and a changed distribution of population properties, such as through the creation of a new generation of offspring. Both types of selection involve some notion of fitness (Hodgson and Knudsen 2010). The objects of selection, on which selection operates directly, are interactors such as biological phenotypes or social organizations. The pool of genotypes, or other replicators, changes indirectly as a result of selection.

Consider the three types of population mentioned above, starting at the individual level. When the interactors are human individuals, both subset and successor selection can occur. Subset selection occurs when individuals die. Successor selection comes about through the creation of new offspring. But the evolution of socioeconomic systems is much more than the selection of individuals.

At the organizational level within capitalism, among the most important organized entities below the state are business firms. Subset selection occurs when firms go bankrupt. This can lead to the extinction of some types of organizational routine (replicators) within the population of firms. Successor selection occurs when there are spinoffs from existing firms. In both cases the *objects* of selection are firms and the *outcomes* of selection include a changed pool of organizational routines within the population as a whole.

Multiple-level evolution complicates the competitive functions of markets. Sometimes the conditions for improvement of efficiency at one level conflict with those at another. For example, competition between firms could be more effective if individual competition and mobility in the workforce were reduced—to nurture enhanced teamwork, coopera- tion, and learning—thereby advancing interorganizational competition (Campbell 1994).

There are theoretical and empirical reasons to suggest that compe- tition between firms does not always favor those with higher efficiency or productivity (Winter 1964, 1971; Boyd and Richerson 1980; Schaf- fer 1989; Hodgson 1993, 1994). Markets lead to efficient or optimal out- comes under special circumstances only (Stiglitz 1991). In the natural world the environment of selection is also changeable, but selection of specific organizations in socioeconomic systems is often not repeated sufficiently to make strong fitness enhancement likely (Van Parijs 1981).

Firms that do well in one institutional context may do badly in an- other (see Pagano 1991, 2001; Amable 2000, 2003; Aoki 2001, 2010; Hall and Soskice 2001; Boyer 2005a, 2005b; Gagliardi 2009; Belloc and Pa- gano 2009, 2013; Hall and Thelen 2009; and Sturn 2013). Both business firms and natural organisms sometimes alter their own environments through niche creation. Fitness is always context dependent. Under capi- talism, government is partly responsible for that context, including work- able institutions of property and contract on which markets depend.

Contrary to a widespread misunderstanding, Darwinism does not suggest that competition is the royal road to perfection. Darwinism nei- ther favors or disfavors a predominantly free market ideology nor fa- vors or disfavors the possibility of effective state intervention (Hodgson 1999, 2006a; Singer 1999; Beinhocker 2006). Competition is manifestly a powerful force in capitalism, especially as markets increase in size and extend globally. It promotes cost cutting and innovation (Joffe 2011). But competition between business firms guarantees neither progress nor ef- ficiency. There can be limitations and failures owing to externalities or imperfect information. Hence, supplementary government intervention is commonplace in modern economies. There is no guarantee that gov- ernments will intervene for the better. But neither evolutionary theory nor skepticism of government imply that we should (or can) leave every- thing to the market.

At the level of a population of states, selection processes are haphaz- ard and imperfect. Subset selection could occur through national uni- fication, the invasion of a defeated country, or imperial conquest more generally. Successor selection must involve the birth of a new state, such as through secession or decolonization.

Pseudoscientific evolutionary rhetoric has been used to justify war between states, notably during the First World War (Hodgson and Knudsen 2010, 102–3). But there is no foundation for nationalism or racism in Darwin's writings. The outcome of an evolutionary process of selection is not necessarily moral or just. Military defeat does not imply the inferiority of a whole nation. Genghis Khan invaded much of Asia and established the largest contiguous empire in history, largely because of superior Mongol military tactics and numbers. This did not mean that Mongol social organization or culture was more advanced. Furthermore, given the haphazardness of selection as a process, even a long conflict between two military blocs is hardly decisive as an experiment.

States clearly adapt and evolve. But much of this change does not result from selection. As with business organizations, both development and selection are possible. Most peaceful change among political systems is through development rather than selection. But, as with business organizations, political structures and routines are often difficult to alter. Accordingly, much political development involves an interaction between outcomes of relatively inert structures and routines and their changing environment. Notably, studies by political scientists of the evolution of modern states have concentrated almost entirely on developmental rather than selection processes (Steinmo 2010).

What is as important in the evolution of states is the threat rather than the reality of military defeat. This selection pressure can lead to major internal change, including replicator manipulation of state routines and the selection of firms through competition within national markets. For example, as Robert Neild (2001) has elaborated, fear of military defeat in the eighteenth century and the early nineteenth prompted the development of more efficient national administrations and reductions in public corruption in European states. Military rivalry with Russia and China from 1894 to 1905 was a key factor in the modernization of the Japanese state and the development of its industry and infrastructure (Yamamura 1977).

Generally, socioeconomic processes of selection are relatively haphazard and have limited efficacy. This means not that the core Darwinian principles are inapplicable but that they have to be supplemented by consideration of additional mechanisms peculiar to or more prominent in this domain.

As in the biological world, change does not come through selection alone. Equally important is the development of the individual entity.

The processes of selection and development are entwined, as established in the "evo-devo" debate in biology (Gilbert, Opitz, and Raff 1996; Baguñà and Garcia-Fernàndez 2003). The biological development (ontogeny) of individual organisms is the result of their (mostly fixed) genetic inheritance and interaction with the environment. The development of a social organization is an outcome of its (more plastic) routines and the habits of individuals. Routines are sometimes altered in response to organizational difficulties (Nelson and Winter 1982).

13.2. The Diffusion of Rules and Routines

A central mechanism of change in global capitalism is diffusion. Diffusion is the copying of replicators from one interactor to another. It occurs at the individual level through learning when skillful habits are passed from one individual to another. Technological diffusion from one enterprise to another is also an important case (Rogers 1962; Rogers and Shoemaker 1971; Rosenberg 1976; Basalla 1989). But there are equally important and plentiful examples of the institutional diffusion of rules and routines at the levels of firms and states.

Several institutional diffusions, important for the evolution of capitalism, have been mentioned above, such as the influence of Islamic institutions on medieval European commerce and law. For example, the sea-trading partnerships of Venice and Amalfi in the ninth century were apparently modeled on the legal form of the Islamic *muqarada* (Micklethwait and Wooldridge 2003, 17). It is likely that the Chinese innovation of bills of exchange was spread west into Europe by Muslim traders. The twelfth-century reforms of the English legal system by King Henry II may also have had Islamic inspirations, leading to the adoption of the jury system (which replaced trial by ordeal) and English charity and corporate law (Cattan 1955, 213–18; Badr 1978; Boisard 1980; Gaudiosi 1988; Makdisi 1999).

Diffusions have also occurred within countries, from one organization to another, and from one sphere of activity to another. Consider the influence of military hierarchy on factory organization. Prior to industrial capitalism, armies were among the few institutions where large numbers of people were brought together for some time and placed under an authority structure involving roles and rules. The diffusion of organizational structures and practices from military to industrial contexts is thus unsurprising. In a polemical statement holding a historical truth, Karl Marx and Frederick Engels wrote in 1848: "Masses of labourers, crowded into the factory, are organized like soldiers. As privates in the industrial army they are placed under the command of a perfect hierarchy of officers and sergeants" (Marx 1973b, 74). Max Weber (1968, 3:1155) argued: "The discipline of the army gives birth to all discipline." Lewis Mumford (1934, 92) noted: "The psychology of the new industrial order appeared upon the parade ground before it came, fully fledged, into the workshop." John U. Nef (1950), William H. McNeill (1980), and others have charted multiple military influences on social organizations. As Barton C. Hacker (1993, 2) wrote: "Corporate management, patterns of professionalization in related fields, the very process of [nineteenth-century] industrialization drew on military models and battened on military funding." The developing factory system was influenced by military structures and routines.

In turn, structures and rules found in factory organization spread to other spheres of life. Noting the early Victorian development of a "great proliferation in the techniques of social control" in the hospitals, asylums, and workhouses, the historians Robert Dingwall, Anne Marie Rafferty, and Charles Webster (1988, 26) observed: "The factory itself offered one model in its idea of collecting people in one, physically-bounded location for a common purpose, and then minutely classifying them according to their role in the division of labour . . . where they might learn habits of order and discipline."

Diffusions of legal rules and practices have been conspicuous throughout the history of capitalism. Laws allowing and regulating the sale of debt spread intermittently from England to other countries from the eighteenth century. Legal forms for the joint stock company and eventually the corporation also spread internationally. The modern limited liability corporation was developed in France, Britain, and the United States in the first half of the nineteenth century and then rapidly copied throughout Europe and elsewhere.

Established patterns of industrial organization and management practice often disperse within and between countries. These organizational and managerial diffusions are just as important as diffusions of technology. A few of them have attracted attention, such as the development of the multidivisional corporation, its spread within the United States, and its replication in other countries (Chandler 1962; Fligstein 1985). There are celebrated recent examples of the international diffusion of organizational and managerial methods, such as the spread of flat hierarchies, just-in-time strategies, and quality circles from Japan in the 1980s (Abo 1994).

Military force has sometimes promoted institutional diffusion, either directly by invasion or indirectly by political influence. The Dutch invasion of Britain in 1688 brought financial practices from the Netherlands, resulting in a major reconfiguration of British finance and administration. The growth of the British Empire spread common law systems to many countries. The arrival of American warships in Tokyo Bay led to the Meiji Restoration of 1868 and Japan's abrupt transition from feudalism to a Western-inspired capitalist society. Japan then imported Western management and administrative know-how, particularly from Germany after 1881 and from the United States after Germany's defeat in 1945.

The American and French Revolutions of the eighteenth century promoted ideals of legal rights and democratic government that spread globally in the following centuries. From 1792 French armies occupied some European countries and reformed their institutions. After Napoléon seized power in 1799, his influence spread into the heart of Germany, and the Napoleonic legal code was widely adopted. Radical reforms included the imposition of a civil legal code, the abolition of surviving remnants of feudalism, the introduction of equality before the law, and the undermining of aristocratic privileges. Prussia and some other states retained these reforms after 1815. This massive institutional replication of legal rules and procedures extended from France into continental Europe and has had lasting effects on political life and economic performance.[2]

Consider some general observations. First, while diffusion is a prominent mechanism in all social evolution and has become increasingly important in eras of imperialism and globalization, the diffusion of information and know-how is not easy. Detailed studies of the diffusion of technologies and management practices show that the successful transmission of knowledge depends on recipient institutions being adaptive enough to absorb it. Given the tacit knowledge involved, effective diffusion requires a good deal of organized repetition and experimentation.[3]

---

2. See Acemoglu, Cantoni, Johnson, and Robinson (2011) for econometric evidence of lasting positive economic effects in those countries that retained the Napoleonic code.

3. In practice the transfer of routines from one context to another is often problem-

Second, even when diffusion takes place, it does not necessarily lead to greater efficiency or productivity. What works in one context does not necessarily operate as effectively in another. In particular, if the required complementary institutions are lacking, then the diffusion of institutional knowledge or rules may lead to deleterious outcomes.

Third, in biological evolution, diffusion is much less important, and the forces of selection promote relatively adapted outcomes, often in relatively stable environments, typically over long periods of time. In social evolution the time period is often shorter and the environment less stable. Selection pressure is episodic and less reliable. Consequently, diffusion can be inadequately honed by competition and selection through time.

Finally, the importance of diffusion decisively undermines the Marx-Schumpeter notion that evolution is the unfolding of a system exclusively from within (Marx 1976, 91; Schumpeter 1934, 63; Schumpeter 1954, 391). While internal development is vitally important, the transmission of information from entity to entity in a population is also a vital feature in social evolution. The persistence today of the from-within claim is sustained by the ambiguity of the word *evolution* and a lack of clarity as to whether it refers to a single entity or to a population of entities (Hodgson 2011b). Marxists should learn that revolutions are never purely internal matters and have generally involved the interference of outside powers (Skocpol 1979).

13.3. Complementarities and Rudimentary Survivals

Evolution in populations, in both nature and human society, involves complex entities with interdependent subsystems. Evolution proceeds incrementally. It cannot redesign the whole configuration when a subsystem becomes redundant or undergoes a change in function. It is path dependent: it builds on its own legacy. Noting the way that evolution builds on its own past, Darwin (1871, 1:211) wrote: "The same part appears often to have been modified first for one purpose, and then long afterwards for some other and quite distinct purpose; and thus all the parts

---

atic and can lead to substandard outcomes (Teece 1976; Florida and Kenney 1991; Kogut and Zander 1992, 1993; Lincoln, Kerbo, and Wittenhagen 1995; Grant 1996; Szulanski 1996; Szulanski and Winter 2002).

are rendered more and more complex. But each organism will still retain the general type of structure of the progenitor from which it was aboriginally derived."

Here, Darwin built on the laws of development outlined by the Baltic-German embryologist Karl Ernst von Baer (Gould 1977). Von Baer argued that specialist characteristics are developed from those of more general function, thus increasing the degrees of both complexity and specialization in the organism. His laws have been refined by the biologists Jeffrey Schank and William Wimsatt (Schank and Wimsatt 1987; Wimsatt 1986) and by the psychologist Arthur Reber (1993, 85), who proposed: "Once successful forms are established, they tend to become fixed and serve as foundations for emerging forms." In addition: "Earlier appearing, successful, and well-maintained forms and structures will tend towards stability, showing fewer successful variations than later appearing forms." In other words, once established, the more basic structures become less changeable than the layers that are built on them.[4]

These von Baerian principles counter the view that evolution is necessarily a road to perfection. Evolution always builds on sufficiently successful but imperfect survivals from the past. It is unable to rebuild everything to a near-optimal arrangement. It is not an expert redesigner, somehow understanding the complex interconnections between each part of the system. Such a degree of detailed, complicated, and fortuitous reengineering is unlikely to happen in the haphazard turmoil of change. Evolution is obliged to use the vestigial organs or modules of the past. As Stephen Jay Gould (1985, 210) remarked: "Evolution cannot achieve engineering perfection because it must work with inherited parts available from previous histories in different contexts." In their evolution, complex systems carry the baggage of their own history.

In complex human societies, because of the tangled, interlocking relationship between social substructures, the processes of adaptation are typically confined to incremental and partial adjustments within an existing configuration. Competitive forces alone cannot often achieve radical, overall redesign. Institutional and technoinstitutional complementarities can make such options difficult, if not impossible. If more efficient configurations of technology and property relations exist, then social evolution will often be unable to find them. Research on varieties

---

4. Reber (1993, 85) advised: "These general principles should be viewed as heuristics. . . . [T]hey are not laws in any strict sense and should not be seen as inviolable."

of capitalism and institutional complementarities underlines the importance of these phenomena in modern socioeconomic systems. This undermines the notion of a single, optimal path of evolution.

13.4. Capitalism and Increasing Complexity

There has been a long debate whether Darwinian evolutionary processes necessarily increase systemic complexity (Gould 1977; Saunders and Ho 1976, 1981). Disagreement also surrounds what definitions and measures of complexity to use when such claims are assessed (Adami 2002; Adami, Ofria, and Collier 2000). Consistent with mathematical information theory, Christoph Adami (2002) upholds that the essence of *complexity for an evolving entity is the amount of information that it stores about the environment in which it evolves.* Complexity is thus measured as negentropy. It is the difference between the theoretical maximum amount of information about an environment and the actual entropy (disorder) present in the relevant organizational habits and routines. As this difference increases, the habits and routines exhibit less disorder and more complexity and contain more useful information about the environment. By contrast, if there is a diminishing difference between the maximum amount of information and actual entropy (of replicators), then the habits and routines lose track of the environment and exhibit less physical complexity.

Some evolutionary processes in biology can be rapid, such as mutations in viruses. But, if we were to travel back ten thousand years, we would be familiar with most of the plants and animal species that we found on Earth despite significant changes of climate and species distribution. By contrast, technology would be rudimentary compared to today, and human institutions would be relatively primitive. Especially since about 1750, social and economic change has been dramatic. Institutions and technology have become much more sophisticated. Complexity has grown rapidly in the socioeconomic sphere. Capitalism is by far the most dynamic and complex economic system in human history.

What are the drivers of rapidly increasing complexity within capitalism? One major factor is the expansion and diversification of markets. As Adam Smith argued, the growth of markets can enable an ever-finer division of labor, which in turn can fuel greater productivity, reduce costs, and enable a further enlargement of markets. Allyn Young (1928,

537) argued in a classic article that "industrial differentiation . . . remains the type of change characteristically associated with the growth of production." He also underlined "the increase in the complexity of the apparatus of living, as shown by the increase in the variety of goods offered in consumers' markets," plus an allegedly greater "diversification of intermediate products."

As capitalism expands, corporations seek ever-new opportunities for trade and gain. As competition intensifies within particular markets, profit-seeking corporations innovate and diversify their products, in the unceasing pursuit of new market niches (Chamberlin 1933; Abernathy and Clark 1985; Rueschemeyer 1986; Metcalfe 1998). Firms in competition continuously face the choice of sticking with the same products and trying to drive down costs or innovating and finding new niches. Many firms invest in new technology or new skills. In this quest for innovation, the frontiers of science and technology are advanced, leading to new fields of knowledge and inquiry. New products are created and marketed. Improved global communications and increased mobility give a further impetus to product diversification and greater complexity. New and varied organizational forms are devised to increase productivity and to manage an exponentially expanding number of products and processes. Accordingly, there is a long-run tendency in capitalist economic systems toward greater complexity, driven by powerful economic forces both caused by and causing the widening of markets and leading to innovation and greater product diversification (Warsh 1985; Pryor 1996).

Complexity and variety grew in preceding socioeconomic systems, particularly when there was expanding trade and growing markets. What additional conditions promoted the spectacular rise of productivity in capitalism after 1800? Michael Joffe (2011) emphasizes the manner in which corporate structures and the employment relationship increased adaptive flexibility, innovation capacity, economies of scale, and the size of the market that can be supplied. Schumpeter and others were right to point also to the role of the financial sector and its capacity to bankroll corporate innovation and expansion. In the leading capitalist countries these necessary conditions set off a process of positive feedback where corporate innovation fed markets and markets fed innovation. Economies grew remarkably in both scale and complexity.

Capitalism has created a cornucopia of different outputs. Eric Beinhocker (2006, 9, 456–57) estimated that there may be about ten billion distinct goods for sale in New York City. There were far fewer in the year 1800. By investigating the diversity and pattern of exported products, César A. Hidalgo and Ricardo Hausmann (2009) measured the complexity levels of several national economies. They showed that these measures of complexity are correlated with a country's level of income, further indicating that capitalist economic development is strongly associated with both a growth of knowledge and a growth of complexity (Hausmann et al. 2011).

Although a growth in complexity and a rise in average levels of skill are not the same thing, they are likely to be correlated. Continuous innovation requires retraining and adaptability. We can consider an alternative scenario where computers displace human ingenuity and the remaining work of humans would become routine and inflexible (Hodgson 1999, 186–89, 235–70). But computer algorithms cannot replace much human intuition and tacit judgment (Dreyfus and Dreyfus 1986). At least for the foreseeable future, growing complexity is more likely to depend on rising levels of human skill, especially skills involving information technology (Zuboff 1988; Levy and Murnane 1996).

This is contrary to Marx's prognosis that capitalism would lead to the deskilling of the workforce. Marx's (1976, 549, 788) claim was based on his mechanistic view of production, where any specialized skill held by a worker "vanishes as an infinitesimal quantity in the face of the science, the gigantic natural forces, and the mass of social labour embodied in the system of machinery." Accordingly, the development of capitalism "enables the capitalist . . . to set in motion more labour . . . as he progressively replaces skilled workers by less skilled." This deskilling thesis was later elaborated by Harry Braverman (1974).

The deskilling hypothesis is confounded by both evidence and argument. As Marshall (1920, 263) pointed out, machines first replace the most monotonous and muscular labor. Other forms of work, involving adaptive skills and judgment, are less readily replaceable by machines. There are greater and cheaper possibilities for creating machines to do simple and repetitive work, compared with getting machines to carry out sophisticated analytic and creative tasks. Because capitalism is a restless and turbulent system, there are limits to what can be routinized or foreseen. Ongoing requirements of adaptability and oversight provide opportunities for skilled human judgment and intervention.

The prediction of widespread deskilling has failed to materialize. Historical evidence shows that machines can enhance skills rather than always reducing them. At least throughout the twentieth century, in many major sectors of modern capitalist economies, skill levels have increased rather than decreased. Citing further evidence against general deskilling, Frederic L. Pryor (1996, 55) concluded: "Although deskilling in terms of substantive skills has occurred in certain industries, the notion of a general deskilling process for the economy as a whole represents a triumph of ideology over common sense. The fears about a fall in levels of substantive skills arising from the shift into services also are groundless. On the contrary, the evidence shows clearly that the entire job structure is shifting toward work requiring more data analysis, more general education, and also more specific vocational preparation."

Empirical evidence over the lifetime of capitalism confirms the strong overall trends toward higher complexity and increasing levels of skill. While there are examples of deskilling in some spheres, the dynamic core of capitalism has become ever more complex and knowledge intensive. General deskilling is possible in principle but neither realized nor inevitable (see Attewell 1992; Wood 1982, 1989; Rubery and Wilkinson 1994; Ashton and Green 1996; and Goldin and Katz 1996).[5]

Is deskilling more prevalent in less-developed economies? Does globalized capitalism mean the raising of skill levels in the core and the lowering of them elsewhere? Such an eventuality is possible in principle, and there is some evidence that exports from richer to poorer nations can have deskilling effects in the less-developed economies (Auer 2010). On the other hand, economies such as China and India, which have taken much manufacturing and exporting activity away from Europe and North America, show scant evidence of general deskilling. Overall, levels of education and training are increasing in these rapidly growing countries (OECD 2012).

But the growth of complexity in capitalism is not preordained. Capitalism has existed for a few hundred years. We cannot generalize from such a short period. We can conceive of long periods of crisis or stagnation, with slower rates of innovation. Nuclear conflict, pandemics, ecological catastrophes, or natural disasters may drag capitalism back to a lower level of development. With increasing dependence on electronic

---

5. By contrast, Head (2005) provides extensive evidence of the use of information technology to simplify the work of middle- and lower-level employees and set up digital monitoring to make sure that management rules are obeyed. Scenarios are possible where the rising skill levels that marked the twentieth century are arrested and reversed (Hodgson 1999).

information networks and greater vulnerability to cyberattacks and crashes, the integration and complexity of global capitalism has itself become a problem that could endanger its survival.

It is also clear that the past dynamism of capitalism has depended on a delicate institutional arrangement of political, legal, cultural, and other conditions. These institutions can unravel. The massive growth of variety and complexity in capitalism, exhibited especially in the second half of the twentieth century, may not be as rapid in the twenty-first. Prediction, especially with complex systems, is highly fallible. Some possible futures for global capitalism are considered in the next chapter.

CHAPTER FOURTEEN

The Future of Global Capitalism

The economic history of the last century, and especially of the years since World War II, has its own examples of rise and decline. They are not so melodramatic as some accounts of ancient civilizations, but they are no less mysterious, and the rises and declines are probably more rapid. — Mancur Olson (1982)

Instead of focusing on relatively recent events, such as the growth of neoliberalism since the 1970s and the international financial crises of 1987, 1997, 2000, and 2008, this chapter takes a longer view, looking forward until about the middle of the twenty-first century. Its themes are the ongoing globalization of capitalism and the rising challenges to US economic leadership and political hegemony.

Although his predictions of a deskilled working class and the demise of capitalism have not been realized, Marx was right about increasing globalization, which has been a prominent tendency in capitalism since the beginning and has acquired a new momentum. As Marx (1973a, 408) wrote in the *Grundrisse* in 1857–58: "The tendency to create the *world market* is directly given in the concept of capital itself."

There is an enormous and controversial literature on globalization, and it cannot be even summarized here (see, e.g., Boyer and Drache 1996; Hirst and Thompson 1996; Dunning 1997; Thompson 2000; Stiglitz 2002; Amable 2003; Bordo, Taylor, and Williamson 2003; Michie 2003; Glyn 2006; and Rodrik 2007, 2011). The word *globalization* has several meanings. Here, it refers to the greater frequency and scale of international business connections between individuals and firms, including exchanges of information and mobility of money, people, and goods, all involving legal contracts across national boundaries. A key question is whether the march of globalization will lead to greater institutional and policy homogenization across different countries or whether globalization is compatible with enduring varieties of capitalism.

I first consider whether the accelerated post-1980 global diffusion of institutions and technology will lead to the rise of a new economic leader or hegemon, such as China. Various future growth estimates are addressed alongside problems in institutional development. There is evidence that higher levels of capitalist development are related to the rule of law, open government, and lower levels of corruption. It is also argued that global capitalism is likely to maintain some diversity, including in levels of inequality and public social expenditure, despite the creation of an increasingly integrated world economy. The chapter concludes with a brief discussion of major problems for future global development, including financial instability and threats to the global ecosystem.

14.1. Will the Great Global Diffusion Lead to a New Economic Hegemon?

Angus Maddison's (2001, 2003, 2007) historical data reveal a remarkable politicoeconomic correlation. In any epoch, the country with the highest GDP per capita is typically a leading or dominant global power. The locus of advanced capitalism was in Italy in the fifteenth and sixteenth centuries, which then had the highest GDP per capita. It shifted to the Netherlands in the seventeenth century, to Britain in the nineteenth century, and to the United States in the twentieth century (see fig. 1.1 above). Exceptions include Spain and Portugal, which were global powers from the sixteenth century to the eighteenth but were not among the leaders in terms of productivity or capitalist development. Each transition from one hegemon to another involved war, enabling the rising leviathan to extend its grip over global trade.

The existence of leaders and followers can mean some diffusion of technology and institutions from the advanced to the less-advanced economies. As Alexander Gerschenkron (1962) and Stanislav Gomulka (1971) argued, the interaction of advanced and relatively backward countries creates the potential for catch-up and real convergence in productivity and real income per head. These authors emphasized technological diffusion in this catching-up process. Given the importance of the institutional preconditions for development, due emphasis should be given to possible institutional diffusion as well. Productivity is not a matter of technology alone. The country in question must also develop its institutions to support high levels of skill, innovation, and consumption. Robert J. Barro and Xavier Sala-i-Martin (1992, 2003) provided evidence to support a notion of diffusion with "conditional convergence": once we control for other determinants of growth, growth rates do exhibit a tendency to decline with rising relative levels of GDP per capita.

The global financial and political settlement after the Second World War facilitated a long economic boom that lasted until the 1971 crisis in the Bretton Woods system and the oil crisis of 1973. During this boom there was a diffusion of technological and institutional knowledge from North America and Western Europe to other parts of the world economy. But it was partial and uneven, with lesser effects on the Soviet Bloc and the Third World. From 1950 to 1973 global GDP per capita grew at an average annual rate of 2.9 percent. But Latin America, Africa, and much of Asia (excluding Japan) grew at lesser overall rates.[1] The gap widened between North America and Europe, on one side, and much of the rest of the world, on the other.

Nevertheless, during this period, a few countries were able to absorb sufficient knowledge from the West to narrow the gap dramatically. Japan rose from a lesser to a major economic power. Its GDP per capita grew at an average annual rate of 1.5 percent from 1870 to 1913 and 0.9 percent from 1913 to 1950. Then it took off. While sheltering under US military hegemony, adopting a Western-style political system, imitating Western know-how, and developing new organizational and manufacturing techniques, it saw its per capita GDP explode from 1950 to 1973 at an average annual rate of 8.1 percent. It moved into the ranks of the developed economies. In 1950 its GDP per capita was 20 percent of that in the United States. In 1990 it reached 81 percent of the US level (Maddison 2007, 337, 383). But then the collapse of the Japanese asset bubble ended its period of rapid growth.

South Korea and Taiwan—both former colonies of Japan—also grew rapidly. But unlike Japan they did not falter in the 1990s. From 1950 to 2001 their average growth rates of GDP per capita were 5.9 and 5.8 percent, respectively (Maddison 2003, 562). In 1950 the absolute GDP per

---

1. From 1950 to 1973 the average annual per capita GDP growth was 2.8 percent in Mao's China and 3.3 percent in the Soviet Union. Growth data are from Maddison (2007, 383).

capita of South Korea and Taiwan was 8 and 10 percent, respectively, of that of the United States (Maddison 2003, 466, 562). In 2012 it reached 64 and 78 percent, respectively, of the US level.[2]

Japan, South Korea, and Taiwan narrowed their gap with the United States in a spectacular manner. Although many other countries have since enjoyed rapid growth rates since 1950, few have moved from 20 percent or less of the GDP per capita level of the lead country to over 60 percent. The Japanese, South Korean, and Taiwanese cases are thus very important in developmental terms, particularly when we consider the prospects for other countries that have experienced rapid growth from low levels of GDP per capita up to levels close to those of the leading country.

Another phase of global development began with China's transition from a planned to a market economy after 1978. The expansion of internal markets and the opening up of China brought a fifth of the world's population into the global trading system. The fall of the Berlin Wall in 1989 and the collapse of the Soviet Union in 1991 completed the process worldwide, save for the Cuban and North Korean outliers. From 1990 a new great global diffusion of technology and capitalist institutions was under way. China, India, Vietnam, South Korea, Indonesia, and several other less-developed countries all entered a prolonged period of rapid growth.

The global financial crash in 2008 pushed most developed countries into recession. But China, India, Brazil, and others continued to grow. What will happen in the next few decades? Projections suggest that around 2020 China will become the largest economy in the world in terms of GDP. Will it then become the new global economic hegemon?

China has previously been the world's largest economy. Around 1500 it overtook India in terms of overall GDP. It remained the world's largest economy until it was overtaken by the United States in the 1880s (Maddison 2001, 261; Maddison 2003, 462, 548). Yet it was far from being a world power from 1500 to 1880, when it was nominally ahead in terms of overall GDP. The largest economy is not necessarily a world hegemon in economic terms. But, of course, military prowess is a different matter: China could greatly enhance its already-burgeoning military strength.

---

2. All 2012 GDP per capita figures in this section are averaged from World Bank, International Monetary Fund, and US Central Intelligence Agency data, all calculated at purchasing power parity (PPP). Singapore is another example of an East Asian country that developed rapidly in this period.

Now compare China in terms of GDP per capita. In 2012 Chinese GDP per capita was about 18 percent of that in the United States. Despite extremely rapid post-1950 growth, Japan failed to catch up with the United States in forty years. In terms relative to contemporary US GDP per capita, China in 2012 was in a worse position than Japan was in 1950.

Many countries tipped as actual or potential high-growth performers are much poorer than China. These include India, Bangladesh, Vietnam, Indonesia, and the Philippines. No country in sub-Saharan Africa has a higher GDP per capita than China except Equatorial Guinea (whose economy is dominated by oil production) and South Africa.

Both Brazil and Russia have also been tipped as actual or potential high-growth countries. In 2012 Brazil's and Russia's GDP per capita (PPP) were, respectively, about 24 and 39 percent of that of the United States.

Two notable attempts to estimate future growth rates for these countries are by Maddison (2007, 337, 345)—writing before the 2008 economic crash—and Willem H. Buiter and Ebrahim Rahbari (2011). Some of their estimates of per capita GDP growth are summarized in table 14.1. An illustrative guesstimate or scenario by the present author has been added.

Actual country rankings for 2012 are given in the first two columns of table 14.1. Smaller countries—including high-performing Singapore, Taiwan, South Korea, and Hong Kong—are excluded. The European Union is considered as an economic unit on the grounds that it is undergoing further integration—especially in the core Euro area—and that common regulations and monetary union promote a high degree of internal diffusion. The European Union was the largest global economy in 2012 in terms of overall GDP.

In all three projections, the European Union is overtaken by the United States in GDP terms. This is largely because the population of the United States is expected to increase more rapidly than that of the European Union, assuming no further major enlargement of the latter. All the projections have China overtaking the United States and the European Union before 2030 in terms of absolute GDP and remaining in the lead at least until 2050. All 2030 projections for overall GDP put China first, followed by the United States and then the European Union.

Table 14.1 also exhibits some concordance between future estimates in other areas. All projections concur that the United States will remain the lead country in terms of GDP per capita until at least 2050. It will

TABLE 14.1. **Conjectured Reorderings of Economic Power by 2030 and 2050**

	Actual Data		Maddison's (2007) Estimates			Buiter and Rahbari's (2011) Estimates					An Alternative Scenario			
	2012 GDP (PPP) per Capita Rank	2012 GDP (PPP) Rank	2003–30 GDP per Capita Growth % per Annum	2030 GDP per Capita Rank	2030 GDP Rank	2010–30 Real GDP per Capita Growth % per Annum	2030 GDP per Capita Rank[a]	2030 GDP Rank[b]	2010–50 Real GDP per Capita Growth % per Annum	2050 GDP per Capita Rank[c]	2010–50 Real GDP per Capita Growth % per Annum	2050 GDP Rank[d]	2050 GDP per Capita Rank	2050 GDP Rank
United States	1	2	1.7	1	2	1.7	1	2	1.7	1	1.8	3	1	2
European Union[e]	2	1	1.7	2	3	1.6	4	3	1.8	4	1.7	4	2	3
Japan	3	5	1.3	3	5	1.5	2	5	1.2	5	1.2	9	3	6
Russia	4	6	3.5	4	6	3.7	3	7	3.7	2	2.2	8	4	7
Brazil	5	7	1.5	6	7	3.5	6	6	3.5	6	3.0	7	6	5
China	6	3	4.5	5	1	6.6	5	1	6.1	3	4.2	1	5	1
India	7	4	4.5	7	4	7.7	7	4	6.4	7	4.3	2	7	4

[a]Rankings calculated using Buiter and Rahbari's (2011) real GDP per capita growth estimates. Some predicted high-GDP-per-capita performers, including Canada and smaller East Asian countries (Singapore, Taiwan, South Korea, and Hong Kong), are omitted.

[b]Buiter and Rahbari's (2011) rankings, with the inclusion of the European Union.

[c]Rankings calculated using Buiter and Rahbari's (2011) real GDP per capita growth estimates. Some predicted high-GDP-per-capita performers, including Canada, Saudi Arabia, and smaller East Asian countries (Singapore, Taiwan, South Korea, and Hong Kong), are omitted.

[d]Buiter and Rahbari's (2011) rankings with the inclusion of the European Union. Buiter and Rahbari rank Indonesia and Nigeria after the European Union and before Brazil, Russia, and Japan.

[e]Maddison's (2007) and Buiter and Rahbari's (2011) projections for individual countries were used to estimate their implicit EU outcomes.

remain the locus of advanced capitalism, with the European Union and Russia not far behind. Capitalism will retain a strong European–North American locus while also powering ahead in East and South Asia.

But table 14.1 shows that the estimates by Buiter and Rahbari for 2030 differ from those by Maddison in crucial respects. Buiter and Rahbari are much more optimistic about the GDP per capita growth prospects for China, India, Brazil, and a number of African countries. They are also slightly more hopeful than Maddison about growth in Japan and Russia. Consequently, the 2030 GDP per capita rankings are different: Buiter and Rahbari put the United States, Japan, and Russia ahead of the European Union in GDP per capita terms.

The more optimistic GDP per capita growth rates assumed by Buiter and Rahbari make a radical difference to the rankings by 2050. According to Buiter and Rahbari, excluding small countries, by 2050 the United States and Russia will be global leaders in terms of GDP per capita. And China will become the third-highest-ranking large country in terms of GDP per capita as well as that boasting the largest GDP overall.[3]

14.2. The Rule of Law and Economic Development

I shall briefly make the case for my lower growth projections in Russia, Brazil, China, and India (and for other large countries, including Indonesia, Nigeria, and Mexico). Buiter and Rahbari underestimate the institutional changes required in these countries to reach high levels of GDP per capita.

We need to be extremely cautious when using growth extrapolations or aggregate production functions to estimate future growth rates. One major reason for this is that, as countries grow, their service sectors tend to increase as a proportion of GDP and of employment. Yet rates of growth of productivity in services tend to be much lower than in manufacturing or even agriculture (Rowthorn and Wells 1987). GDP growth rates are likely to slow down as a result of structural development in any economy (Rodrik 2013).

---

3. Even more optimistically, the Nobel laureate Robert W. Fogel (2010) predicted that China's GDP will grow at an average annual rate of over 8 percent until 2040, by which time its GDP per capita would be twice that projected for Europe and similar to that in the United States.

There is another important reason why the Buiter-Rahbari and other growth estimates may be excessive. China, India, Brazil, Russia, Indonesia, Nigeria, and Mexico all suffer from high levels of deeply rooted corruption. Ranked on a scale from 0 to 100, where lower figures refer to higher levels of corruption, Transparency International's (2012) corruption-perception indices were 27 for Nigeria, 28 for Russia, 32 for Indonesia, 34 for Mexico, 36 for India, 39 for China, and 43 for Brazil. By comparison, Belgium, Canada, France, Germany, Japan, the Netherlands, the United States, and the United Kingdom all scored in the 71–84 range. Scandinavian countries have even higher scores and hence even lower perceptions of corruption.

There is strong evidence that corruption is an impediment to economic growth. Although there are problems with standard definitions of corruption that focus on public-sector corruption alone (Hodgson and Jiang 2007; Hodgson 2013b), there is widespread agreement that corruption inhibits investment and undermines politicoeconomic stability (Shleifer and Vishny 1993; Mauro 1995; Jain 2001; Mo 2001; Aidt 2003; Pellegrini and Gerlagh 2004).[4] Organizational corruption involves collaboration to break rules, thereby undermining operational goals and often making (public or private) organizations less effective or efficient. Rule-breaking behavior and weak enforcement can spread contagiously throughout society. General organizational effectiveness is vital for any developed economy.

Other institutional factors to be taken into account are democracy and open government. A number of databases attempt to measure aspects of democracy, including openness of government, extent of the franchise, frequency of elections, and regularity of government changeover. Although economic growth is not a major cause of democracy (Acemoglu and Robinson 2000), there is some evidence for causality in a reverse direction: democracy may help a country innovate and grow. But, in less-developed circumstances, democracy can lead to division and conflict (Weingast 2005), and a strong, unimpeded state may be a force for growth in the early stages. Such complications result in some studies

4. Admittedly, measures of corruption are crude and imperfect, but the systematic evidence is so strong that only the blinkered can deny its importance. Some development scholars mistakenly downplay the impact of corruption because they dislike anticorruption policies that promote privatization (Bukovansky 2006; Khan 2006). But the dubiousness of the medicine does not negate the reality of the disease.

showing a mixed or inconclusive relationship between democracy and development. But recent analyses have overcome some of these problems to show that democracy can help promote economic growth. Furthermore, the extension of democracy appears to have a greater impact on economic growth when moving from lower relative levels to higher levels of development (Baum and Lake 2003; Gerring, Bond, Barndt, and Moreno 2005; Butkiewicz and Yanikkaya 2006).

Figure 14.1 shows a simple test of the relationship between a composite index of the rule of law and the level of nonoil GDP per capita. It is well-known that resource endowments, particularly oil, can negatively affect economic performance (Ross 2012). Removing oil revenues from GDP per capita establishes a stronger statistical relationship with the variables on the rule of law.

Data on the rule of law were taken from a World Justice Project Report (Agrast, Botero, Martinez, and Pratt 2013). This study scores several component variables on scales between zero and unity. With nonoil GDP per capita as the dependent variable, separate regressions were performed with the eight summary factor variables and forty-four subfactor variables. The results of these simple tests are dramatic. Two summary factors—namely, absence of corruption and open government—explain about 76 percent of the variance in nonoil GDP per capita, with both variables being highly statistically significant.

Five of the subfactor variables proved to be highly significant in explaining nonoil GDP per capita. These variables measured the degree to which "freedom from arbitrary interference with privacy is effectively guaranteed," "the laws are publicized and accessible," "official information is available on request," "alternative dispute resolutions are accessible, impartial, and effective," and "correctional system is effective in reducing criminal behavior." These five rule-of-law variables explain about 80 percent of the variance in nonoil GDP per capita, with each variable being highly statistically significant.

Brazil, China, and India could conceivably double their nonoil-GDP-per-capita levels without much improvement in their rule of law and remain within the spread of variation of existing countries. But all three countries will eventually have to tackle corruption and the rule of law if they are to develop much further. This implies that—without improvement in their rule of law—GDP per capita growth rates in the 4–8 percent range are conceivable in Brazil, China, and India until about 2025 but that then the institutional shortcomings would make further growth

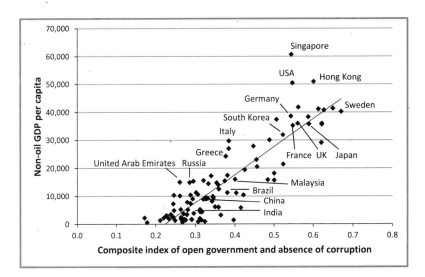

FIGURE 14.1. The rule of law and nonoil GDP per capita.

Data source: IMF GDP (PPP) 2012 per capita data were used, after deducting my estimate of 2012 oil revenue per capita, using *CIA World Factbook* data. Indices concerning the rule of law are from Agrast, Botero, Martinez, and Pratt (2013). Two the eight summary factors were found to be significant in the following regression: "absence of corruption" (Uncorrupt) and "open government" (Open_Gov). Other summary factors from Agrast, Botero, Martinez, and Pratt (2013) were eliminated as insignificant at the 10 percent level. The composite index is 0.27812 Uncorrupt + 0.43286 Open_Gov, where the coefficients were derived from the following regression (standard errors in brackets):

$$\text{Non-Oil\_GDP\_per\_Capita} = -22{,}365 + 27{,}812 \text{ Uncorrupt} + 43{,}286 \text{ Open\_Gov}$$
$$(2{,}393) \quad (6{,}491) \quad\quad\quad (8{,}311)$$
$$N = 97, R^2 = 0.764, \text{ Adjusted } R^2 = 0.759$$

A second regression (not illustrated here) was performed on the forty-four subfactors from Agrast, Botero, Martinez, and Pratt (2013). In the following regression (standard errors in brackets), the five significant subfactors are "freedom from arbitrary interference with privacy is effectively guaranteed" (Privacy), "the laws are publicized and accessible" (Laws_Pub), "official information is available on request" (Off_Info), "alternative dispute resolutions are accessible, impartial, and effective" (ADR), and "correctional system is effective in reducing criminal behavior" (Cor_Crim):

$$\text{Non-Oil\_GDP\_per\_Capita} =$$
$$-32{,}137 + 13{,}266 \text{ Privacy} + 26{,}258 \text{ Laws\_Pub} + 17{,}275 \text{ Off\_Info} + 17{,}795 \text{ ADR} + 13{,}479 \text{ Cor\_Crim}$$
$$(3{,}939) \quad (4{,}697) \quad\quad (6{,}849) \quad\quad\quad (5{,}684) \quad\quad\quad (6{,}702) \quad\quad (4{,}627)$$
$$N = 97, R^2 = 0.799, \text{ Adjusted } R^2 = 0.788$$

at such rates more difficult. Russia has much less scope for immediate improvement without tackling these institutional problems.

Clearly, there is a need for more in-depth empirical research here, but these results suggest that it is difficult for any country to reach a high level of development when there is weak rule of law, corruption, injustice, and secretive government.

The scenario in the three rightmost columns in table 14.1 takes account of the problems of corruption, lack of open government, and limited rule of law in the aforementioned developing economies. The growth guesstimate for China of 4.2 percent in GDP per capita from 2012 to 2050 may seem particularly low, especially after spectacular growth rates averaging about 9 percent from 1990 to 2012. But China's demographic problems are more severe than those in India. The number of children plus old people per person of working age is set to increase dramatically in China, while in India it will decrease.

The impressive growth in China and several other developing countries has been from low levels. The lack of adequate legal institutions is likely to slow down future expansion, particularly when it comes to raising internal capital for investment (Arner, Booth, Lejot, and Hsu 2007). The Chinese *hukou* (internal passport) system restricts the skill development of rural registrants. Reform of the law and the ramshackle system of land tenure is a major priority (Ho 2005). Despite its rapid growth, contemporary China lacks adequate, uncorrupt, and impartial legal mechanisms for finance and private business. There is instead a reliance on personal and political connections, appeals to personal honor while shaming defaulters, the use of networks fostering reciprocity, and recourse to local political officials (Wank 1999). Yasheng Huang (2008) noted that several prominent "Chinese" corporations are in fact registered in Hong Kong (where a system of English law survives). Because the corporate legal system in mainland China is underdeveloped, China itself has yet to produce many world-class, mainland-registered firms (see Nolan 2004, 20; Naughton 2007, 325; Huang 2008; and Hodgson and Huang 2013).

Given its impending institutional and demographic problems and its high levels of discontent and protest over pollution and land allocation, China could even enter a period of political instability before 2050.[5]

---

5. Inspired by the Marxist world-systems approach of Wallerstein (1979), Li (2008) assumed that capitalism implies a global search for cheap labor. Li argued that, as China expands and its workers push for higher wages, one of the last major global reserves of low-

This could exacerbate international tensions and even lead to war. For all these reasons it is unlikely that China will be able to maintain a growth rate of over 5 percent until 2050. Rather than a firm prediction, 4.2 percent is a possible scenario taking these factors into account. Compared with Buiter and Rahbari (2011), considerations of corruption and the weak rule of law also account for lower guesstimates of average GDP per capita growth for Brazil, India, and Russia up to 2050.

Sustained growth in the European Union would partly depend on its ability to overcome problems in its monetary system. Its success will hinge on further political and institutional integration, which is likely to be achieved gradually in the coming decades. A slightly higher growth estimate for the United States does not imply an underestimation of its problems: from patchy health care to poor schooling and political gridlock.

Significantly, Japan, South Korea, and Taiwan are among the few countries that have moved rapidly from low to high levels of development since 1950. All three countries developed democratic institutions and reduced corruption in that period. High rates of growth may be compatible with corruption and totalitarian regimes at a relatively low level of development. But the route to higher levels of prosperity seems to require lower corruption and the effective rule of law.[6]

14.3. The Persistence of Varieties of Capitalism

It has already been noted that the persistence of varieties of capitalism challenges both traditional Marxist and procapitalist natural-state doctrines. The global diffusion of institutions and technology may be too

---

waged employment will be exhausted, thus shaking capitalism at its foundations. Large corporations and Western consumers have definitely benefited from low wage costs in China and elsewhere. But, even if reserves of low-cost labor are globally exhausted, this does not imply the demise of capitalism, as Li opined. Labor productivity and automation are also increasing rapidly in China, and these provide a means for capitalism's continuance. What matters for profits is not simply the hourly cost of labor but its productivity—the labor cost of a unit of output. Hourly wage costs can rise while the labor cost of a unit of output falls.

6. See Neild (2001) for a fascinating account of the circumstances that led to the decline of public corruption in Britain, France, Germany, and the United States in the eighteenth and nineteenth centuries. Neild argued that wars involving mass mobilization against a common enemy helped reduce corruption, but the technology of modern warfare has reduced such potentially rectifying effects of national conflict.

weak to ensure gravitation to one natural state or developmental track. There are also major internal barriers to convergence, including institutional complementarities.[7]

There are several ways of classifying different varieties of modern capitalism. In the influential collection of essays edited by Peter A. Hall and David Soskice (2001), the most basic distinction is between "liberal market" capitalisms (such as the United States) and "coordinated market" capitalisms (such as Germany). Contributors to the volume detailed complementary institutions for each type. Institutional variations and complementarities included central bank independence (or otherwise), which was related to the degree of coordination of wage bargaining. Different social insurance schemes were related to skill levels and job security. The data presented on economic performance show that countries of one type (such as liberal market economies) did not consistently outperform others. Instead, each institutional configuration performed differently in different circumstances. Consequently, economic policies must be tailored to their institutional contexts: what serves well in one circumstance may be less effective or even dysfunctional in another.[8]

The Hall and Soskice (2001) classification into liberal market versus coordinated market ideal types has been questioned. But problems of taxonomy do not negate institutional complementarities and path dependence in the evolution of capitalism. Many countries have undergone major transformations in recent decades—via the global spread of commodification, privatization, and market liberalization—but this does not mean that historical, cultural, ideological, and institutional specificities have little effect or generally can be overcome. Global convergence toward one model is not inevitable. Some convergence is happening, but significant variety is likely to be maintained.

The very fact that countries are at different levels of development and are experiencing different rates of growth means that variety will

7. On varieties of capitalism, see Albert (1993), Hodgson (1995, 1996), Berger and Dore (1996), Boyer (1999, 2005a, 2005b), Whitley (1999), Dore (2000), Amable (2000, 2003), Streeck and Yamamura (2001), Coates (2005), Crouch (2005), Elsner and Hanappi (2008), and many others. More particularly, on institutional complementarities, see Pagano (1991, 2001, 2007), Amable (2000, 2003), Aoki (2001, 2010), Hall and Soskice (2001), Boyer (2005a, 2005b), Gagliardi (2009), Belloc and Pagano (2009, 2013), Hall and Thelen (2009), and Sturn (2013).

8. Kesting and Nielsen (2008) and Streeck (2011) provide useful summaries of Hall and Soskice (2001) and of the subsequent critical literature and debates surrounding the book.

be preserved. For example, firms may adopt routines that are profitable in times of boom but much less so when market demand is static or falling. Some evidence (see above) suggests that the state can play a more effective economic role in the early stages of development. But democracy and the rule of law become relatively more important in more sophisticated economies. Generally, institutional modifications are adaptions to peculiar local circumstances as well as global influences. Forcing countries to fit one mold may inhibit development rather than enhancing it. Institutions and other structures that are necessary for higher growth rates are different from those that are suitable for more gradual change. Fast-growing economies require much higher proportions of GDP devoted to infrastructure and other fixed assets. Consequently, the global dynamics of development are forever uneven.[9]

Consider some selected indicators of variety within modern capitalism, including data on different measures of economic inequality and of public social expenditure. Capitalism has generally been an unequal system, but we should not overlook differences between and within countries in degrees of inequality. Consider inequalities of wealth first.

The data are patchy, and countries differ in terms of whether wealth inequality is measured using adults, families, or households as the basic units. One of the most comprehensive and up-to-date sources available (Credit Suisse Research Institute 2012, 15) shows significant differences, with the richest 1 percent owning 34.8 percent of the wealth in Switzerland, 34.1 percent in the United States, 15.5 percent in Canada, and 12.5 percent in the United Kingdom, for example.

9. Trotsky's "law of uneven and combined development" underlined both the global integration and the separate development of different capitalisms. But there are important differences from what is being argued in the present text. First, as Elster (1986b), Rosenberg (2010), and others have pointed out, this "law" might amount to little more than the weak empirical claim that development is both connected and uneven. Trotsky's (Trotsky 1934, 22; Trotsky 1936, 19) vivid but imprecise explanations highlighted episodes of individual countries "skipping a whole series of intermediate stages" where capitalism "gains mastery only gradually over the inherited unevenness." Trotsky continued to explain: "[Capitalism] constantly aims at . . . the surmounting of economic differences. . . . Thereby it brings about their *rapprochement* and equalizes the economic and cultural levels of the most progressive and the most backward countries." By contrast, the notion of global and uneven development promoted in the present work upholds that countries may never equalize or converge. Rather than skipping stages down one route, they may forge substantially different developmental paths. It seems that Trotsky retained Marx's natural-state conception of capitalism (see sec. 1.2 above).

TABLE 14.2. **Distributions of Wealth in Selected Countries**

	Year (for Share Data)	Unit (for Share Data)	Share of Top (%)					Gini
			20	10	5	2	1	
Australia	2010	Household	61.8	...	...	...	...	.622
Brazil	...	...	...	...	...	...	...	.784
Canada	2005	Family	69.0	50.4	35.8		15.5	.688
China	2002	Person	59.3	41.4	...	...	...	.550
France	2010	Adult	...	62.0	...	...	24.0	.730
Germany	2007	Household	61.1	...	...	...	...	.667
India	2002	Household	69.9	52.9	38.3		15.7	.669
Italy	2010	Household	62.6	45.7	32.9	21.0	14.8	.609
Japan	1999	Household	57.7	39.3	...	...	...	.547
Netherlands	2008	Household	78.5	62.7	...	...	...	.650
Norway	2004	Household	80.1	65.3	...	...	...	.633
Russia	...	...	...	...	...	...	...	.699
South Korea	2011	Household	63.9	...	...	...	...	.579
Spain	2008	Household	61.3	45.0	32.6	21.7	16.5	.570
Sweden	2007	Adult	...	67.0	49.0	...	24.0	.742
Switzerland	1997	Family	...	71.3	58.0	...	34.8	.803
UK	2008	Adult	62.8	44.3	30.5	...	12.5	.697
USA	2010	Family	86.7	74.4	60.9	44.8	34.1	.801

Sources: Gini coefficients (all household-based estimates for the year 2000) are from Davies, Sandström, Shorrocks, and Wolff (2009); other data are from Credit Suisse Research Institute (2012).

Table 14.2 shows additional data for the distribution of wealth. Few developed countries are as unequal as the United States. Switzerland is a notable exception. Several developed countries—notably Japan, South Korea, and Spain—have been much more equal in terms of their distributions of wealth, although this is not to claim that they are egalitarian.

Table 14.3 shows data for household distributions of income, using Gini coefficients for 1970 and 2000. The most unequal countries in the table for the year 2000 were Brazil, India, and Russia. Among the more developed countries, the United States, Canada, and Spain were the most unequal in terms of household income. The table also shows big rises in the degree of inequality from 1970 to 2000 in several countries, including India, Russia, and the United Kingdom, all of which have largely abandoned socialist or social-democratic commitments to income redistribution.[10] The increases in inequality are much smaller in other countries. Italy, Spain, and South Korea—which were among the most unequal in

10. Korpi and Palme (1998) provide evidence showing that welfare states can reduce income inequality.

TABLE 14.3. **Gini Coefficients for Distributions of Income in Selected Countries**

	1970	2000	Change
Australia	31.93	37.17	+5.24
Brazil	. . .	46.66	. . .
Canada	35.11	38.19	+3.08
France	. . .	36.42	. . .
Germany (W)	32.35	36.48	+4.13
India	35.68	49.28	+13.6
Italy	39.44	36.31	−3.13
Japan	35.47	36.51	+1.04
Netherlands	34.32	35.10	+.78
Norway	31.55	33.68	+2.13
Russia	25.31	45.16	+19.85
South Korea	42.12	37.60	−4.52
Spain	41.21	39.25	−1.96
Sweden	28.62	28.96	+.34
United Kingdom	26.78	36.77	+9.99
United States	35.08	38.28	+3.20

Source: Gini coefficients are from the University of Texas Inequality Project, Estimated Household Income Inequality Data Set: http://utip.gov .utexas.edu/data.html. Brazil's "2000" figure is actually for 1995, and Japan's "2000" figure is for 1993. Data for China and Switzerland are not on this database for 1970, 2000, or nearby years.

1970—have decreased their levels of income inequality. Accordingly, the variance in the sample decreased slightly from 1970 to 2000, but it remained high. Globalization has far from eradicated differences.

Branko Milanovic (2011) showed that the level of global income inequality has increased since the early nineteenth century, reaching a high level in about 1950, with slower growth since.[11] He found that, in the early nineteenth century, most global income inequality between individuals in the world was due to differences *within* countries. But, by the early twenty-first century, most global income inequality was due to differences *between* countries. Accordingly, much of the change in global inequality in the next few decades could result from economic growth in large and relatively low-income countries, including China, India, and Brazil. Furthermore, variations between developed countries and the changes between 1970 and 2000 indicate that there is further scope for reductions as well as increases in inequality within capitalism. In short, all capitalist countries are unequal, but some are more unequal than others.

11. Milanovic (2011, table 3) estimated the global Gini coefficients to be 53.2 in 1850, 64.0 in 1950, and 65.4 in 2002.

TABLE 14.4. **Public Social Spending as a Percentage of GDP in Selected Countries**

	1980	2005	Change
Australia	10.3	16.5	+6.2
Austria	22.4	27.1	+4.7
Belgium	23.5	26.5	+3.0
Canada	13.7	16.9	+3.2
Denmark	24.8	27.7	+2.9
Finland	18.1	26.2	+8.1
France	20.8	·30.1	+9.3
Germany	22.1	27.3	+5.2
Italy	18.0	24.9	+6.9
Japan	10.2	18.5	+8.3
Netherlands	24.8	20.7	−4.1
Norway	16.9	21.6	+4.7
Portugal	9.9	23.0	+13.1
Spain	15.5	21.1	+5.6
Sweden	27.1	29.1	+2.0
Switzerland	13.8	20.2	+6.4
United Kingdom	16.5	20.5	+4.0
United States	13.2	16.0	+2.8

Source: OECD data are from http://stats.oecd.org/Index.aspx?
datasetcode=SOCX_AGG.

As a final dimension of variety, I examine differences and changes in public social spending in different developed countries. Again, this shows enduring capitalist divergence. Table 14.4 shows social expenditure as percentages of GDP for selected countries from 1980 to 2005. The principal components of public social spending include health services, old age benefits, unemployment benefits, incapacity-related benefits, family support, active labor market public programs, and housing benefits. Most countries increased this percentage during a period when the ideology of privatization was resurgent. The Netherlands is an exception—there, the percentage allocation to public social spending has declined. The differences between countries in the changes and absolute values remain substantial. The 2005 figures range from below 17 percent for Australia, Canada, and the United States to above 27 percent for Austria, Denmark, France, Germany, and Sweden.[12]

In conclusion, although there may have been a slight convergence be-

---

12. Note that unemployment payments are a relatively small proportion of public social spending. As percentages of GDP from 1980 to 2005, the OECD data show few marked average national increases in unemployment payments.

tween countries in recent decades, capitalist systems around the world remain highly varied, at least in terms of degrees of inequality and levels of social spending. Capitalist development is always uneven, thus harboring and creating more variety despite a massive and growing global diffusion of institutions and technologies.

14.4. Conclusion: Capitalism into the New Millennium

Economists are often too focused on making predictions, yet the complexities and uncertainties involved typically thwart accurate or meaningful forecasting. We can discern global trends of development, but these can be diverted or arrested by catastrophic events.

But some shifts and tensions can be highlighted. First, despite different estimates of growth, there is a consensus that the center of gravity of the global economy is going to shift to the east, especially with the rise of China and India. This new configuration of economic power will lift still more millions out of poverty, but it will also bring the threat of economic imbalance and political instability. Furthermore, the development processes within these countries may precipitate internal disturbances that fuel belligerent nationalism and exacerbate international tensions.

Modern Anglo-American capitalism was born after the Anglo-French wars of 1756–63 and baptized in the Napoleonic wars of 1803–15. The twentieth century saw two barbaric world wars and many other armed conflicts. There is no guarantee that the twenty-first century will be free of global war. But the remarkable fact remains that few wars have been fought between substantially democratic states, although the causal relationship between democracy and peace remains disputed (Maoz 1997; Mousseau, Hegre, and Oneal 2003; Gartze 2007). This raises the question of China's political as well as its economic development. Would a democratic China reduce the chances of global war?

Second, capitalism is a highly dynamic and complex system that is vulnerable to financial instability. Since the breakup of the Bretton Woods system in the 1970s, world capitalism has experience greater financial turbulence, including the stock market crash of 1987, the Asian financial crisis of 1997, the bursting of the dot-com bubble in 2000, and the Great Crash of 2008. Subsequent reform of international financial arrangements, to help create greater stability, has been minimal, and the institutional and political bases for such measures are frayed.[13] Another major global financial crash in the next fifty years is more likely than not.

Third, global human population is still rising rapidly, the world is facing shortages of usable water and other important physical resources, pollution in some countries is rising to spectacular levels, and the possibility of dramatic climate change brings the threat of large-scale population movements, famines, and severe sociopolitical disruption. It has proved extremely difficult to establish sufficient global political agreement over substantive measures to deal with these problems.

These problems interact with each other. The risk of war, for example, could be exacerbated by an economic depression following another financial collapse. Protests in developing countries against high levels of pollution could also destabilize regimes. Crop failures and population movements caused by climate change could trigger financial crises.

Dani Rodrik (2011, xviii) posed an interesting politicoeconomic problem for the future. He established a "fundamental political trilemma of the world economy": "We cannot simultaneously pursue democracy, national determination, and economic globalization. If we want to push globalization further, we have to give up either the nation state or democratic politics." He rejected "hyperglobalization" in favor of the other two.[14] *Hyperglobalization* means pushing the integration of world markets even further, progressively reducing tariffs and eliminating protectionism. Rodrik argued that further gains along this dimension would be puny and, on the downside, that developing nations would be less able to establish and develop young industries in the face of fierce price competition from powerful global corporations. He also argued that further development of institutions of global governance would be difficult. History is with him on this: new global hegemonic orders are rarely established except via war. Europe adds a further wrinkle to the argument. National determination by component European states is also unviable, especially if Europe is to develop further. A feasible scenario is that the global economy becomes dominated by the large economies of the United States, Europe, China, India, and Japan.

Capitalism is by far the most innovative economic system in hu-

---

13. See Admati and Hellwig (2013) and Tymoigne and Wray (2013) on the need for further financial reform after the 2008 crash.

14. See also van de Klundert (2013) on the "fragile" relationship between capitalism and democracy.

man history, and there is a chance that some of these problems—such as global warming—could be alleviated by technological developments. But technology is not the great savior. Capitalism's own history shows that political and other institutions are also crucial. Political developments in the largest economies will have major effects. International cooperation to extend global institutions for politicoeconomic order and human development is vital.

CHAPTER FIFTEEN

Addressing Inequality

The contrast of affluence and wretchedness continually meeting and offending the eye, is like dead and living bodies chained together. — Thomas Paine (1797)

We can accept the outcome of a competitive process as fair only when the participants have equality in basic capabilities; the fact that no one is allowed to have a head start does not make the race fair if some contestants have only one leg. — Ha-Joon Chang (2010)

At least nominally, capitalism embodies and sustains an Enlightenment agenda of freedom and equality. Typically, there is freedom to trade and equality under the law, meaning that most adults—rich or poor—are formally subject to the same legal rules. But, with its inequalities of power and wealth, capitalism darkens this legal equivalence. As Anatole France (1894) noted ironically: "The law, in its majestic equality, forbids the rich as well as the poor to sleep under bridges, to beg in the streets, and to steal bread." But this does not mean that legal equality is unreal or unimportant. On the contrary, legal systems enshrining such equality have been beacons of prosperity.

Evidence gathered by Richard Wilkinson and Kate Pickett (2009) shows multiple deleterious effects of inequalities of income and wealth. Using data from twenty-three developed countries and from the separate states of the United States, they observed negative correlations between inequality and physical health, mental health, education, child well-being, social mobility, trust, and community life. They also found positive correlations between inequality and drug abuse, imprisonment, obesity, violence, and teenage pregnancies. They suggested, but did not establish in detail, that inequality creates adverse outcomes through psychosocial stresses generated through interactions in an unequal society.

A massive literature—too extensive to review here—examines the relationship between inequality and economic performance (Galbraith
and Berner 2001). Some argue that inequality is a necessary foundation
for capital accumulation. But Robert J. Barro (2000) found that, after
introducing controls for education, fertility, and investment, there is no
significant correlation between inequality and economic growth. While
some inequality provides high-powered incentives for entrepreneurs and
other highfliers, an unequal society also wastes the talent of many on
middle and lower incomes who have less access to high-quality education, subcultural support, and financial backing.[1]

What are the mechanisms within capitalism that exacerbate inequalities of income or wealth? The following section considers possible types
of exploitation within capitalism and factor asymmetries between labor
power and capital assets. The second section considers the sources of
inequality. The final section briefly reviews some recent proposals for
dealing with the problem of inequality.

15.1. Factor Asymmetry and Exploitation under Capitalism

Against its agenda of legal and political equality, does exploitation—in
some sense—exist under capitalism? This, of course, depends on the definition of exploitation. There are many possible meanings. *Exploitation*
connotes disadvantages or injustices that apply to one group rather than
another. We are concerned in this context with groups or classes that
own different types of production factor, including labor power, machinery, and land. We are particularly interested in possible exploitation that
can lead to cumulative divergences in income or wealth between rich
and poor.

Marx traced the source of exploitation—leading to the concentration of wealth in the hands of the rich—to the extraction of surplus value
from the workers in the sphere of production. He presumed that labor is
the sole source of all value. It is then observed that much value is not re-

---

1. An additional problem with the increasing concentration of income in the top few
percent is that overall savings rates increase because those with the highest incomes tend
to save more. "The relationship is straightforward and ironclad: as more money becomes
concentrated at the top, aggregate demand goes into a decline" (Stiglitz 2012a). This can
lead to further unemployment and stagnation (Palley 2012).

turned to labor. The "surplus value" retained by the capitalists is thus exploitation. But there is no good reason to assume that labor is the source of all value. This approach assumes what it has to prove.

As David P. Ellerman (1992) explained, defenders of the Marxian notion of exploitation conflate different questions. Asking who (or what) is *responsible* for an output is not the same as asking what (in part) causally *determines* an output or its value. Responsibility here is taken in the more restrictive sense of being personally accountable for the outcome. In this manner we attribute responsibility to persons rather than objects. Intentional agents are held responsible for their acts: the person, not the gun, murders the victim; the driver, not the vehicle, was responsible for the crash. Similar arguments apply to the production process. As the Austrian school economist Friedrich von Wieser (1930, 79) wrote in 1889: "Land and capital have no merit that they bring forth fruit; they are dead tools in the hand of man; and a man is responsible for the use he makes of them."

Within production, the owners of land, buildings, and machines do nothing: it is the workers alone who are responsible for the output. But this overlooks the responsibility of the owners of land, buildings, and machines in agreeing to the use of their property for productive purposes. Similarly, the criminal who knowingly lent the killer a gun is also responsible for the murder. Distribution matters as well as production. For a more adequate picture it is necessary to consider other possible forms of exploitation.

We may define bargaining exploitation as an asymmetry of bargaining power between agents in the sphere of exchange.[2] But, although employers often have much greater bargaining power, combinations of workers can sometimes exert strong bargaining power over employers. There is nothing in the definition of capitalism that implies that, by this measure, capitalists will always have the upper hand in this regard. Bargaining exploitation typically exists under capitalism, but strictly it is not necessary for its existence. Although commonplace, asymmetries of bargaining power are not part of the essence of capitalism, simply because it

---

2. In Hodgson (1982), I noted Chamberlain's (1951) measure of bargaining power: bargaining power of A = (cost to B of disagreement with A)/(cost to B of agreement with A). In Marshall's (1920, 565–69) discussion of the "peculiarities" of labor, as opposed to other agents of production, he saw these peculiarities as a source of labor's "disadvantage in bargaining," which "wherever it exists is likely to be cumulative in its effects" (569).

is conceivable that capitalism could exist with relatively little bargaining asymmetry, particularly if employees are organized in strong unions.[3]

Consider the asymmetrical authority established in the employment contract and exercised in the sphere of production. A crucial feature of the employment contract is the potential power (within limits) of employers over employees regarding the manner of work. This asymmetric authority may be regarded as a form of exploitation, and I previously called it *authority exploitation* (Hodgson 1982). Ellerman (1992) called for the abolition of asymmetric authority and for the replacement of employment by shared, democratic authority, as found in worker cooperatives. But, while the renting of individuals may have ethical limitations, I argue in the following chapter that the complete abolition of all employment contracts is neither advisable nor a priority.

There are other dimensions of exploitation. The political philosopher Thomas Green (1888, 373) wrote: "Labour, the economist tells us, is a commodity exchangeable like other commodities. This is in a certain sense true, but it is a commodity which attaches in a peculiar manner to the person of man. Hence restrictions may need to be placed on the sale of this commodity which would be unnecessary in other cases, in order to prevent labour from being sold under conditions which make it impossible for the person selling it ever to become a free contributor to social good in any form." Marshall (1920, 566) echoed this: "When a person sells his services, he has to present himself where they are delivered. It matters nothing to the seller of bricks whether they are to be used in building a palace or a sewer: but it matters a great deal to the seller of labour." Hobson (1929, 209) wrote similarly: "[A] disabling element in the sale of labour-power is that it is not detachable in the conditions of its delivery from the human factors of personality." Compared with the capitalist who makes his property available and may reap a reward without actually being present on the job, workers and their labor power are inseparable (Dow 2003). I called this *corporeal exploitation* (Hodgson 1982).

---

3. Some economists identified a source of asymmetrical bargaining power in the "perishability" of labor power (Marshall 1920, 567; Hobson 1929, 208–9). If unemployed this hour, then that labor is lost forever. Here, perishability relates to opportunities for use. Hence, as Marshall (1920, 567) concedes and Hutt (1930) emphasizes, land and machines are also perishable in this sense. A machine unused is also an opportunity lost forever. Labor power is not unique in this respect.

Corporeal exploitation is present in any mode of production involving labor and incomes from other separately owned factors of production. The problem is the disadvantage that that inseparability bestows on labor, compared with the owners of other factors. Given that capitalists can delegate the tasks of management to others and obtain rewards simply from their ownership of nonlabor assets, they are placed at an advantage. They can use their time for trading and other entrepreneurial ventures while simultaneously their property reaps rewards. Hence, corporeal exploitation is likely to have cumulative effects, creating a widening division between one social class and another. Workers have less time to devote to their education or training or to searching for alternative opportunities.

The differences between factors of production in this regard can be ended by eradicating the capacity to reap a reward from the private ownership of nonlabor assets. This might happen through wholesale nationalization or by creating an economy with self-employed producers or worker cooperatives. None of these solutions overcome the inseparability of laboring activity from the worker: at best they deal with labor's disadvantage by abolishing incomes from the separate ownership of other factors of production.

Alleviation of the problem of corporeal exploitation can result from the reduction of the working day, which would give workers more time apart from their work. But the fundamental difference—noted by Green, Marshall, and Hobson—between the inseparability of labor from its agency and the separability of other assets from their proprietors will always remain within capitalism.

Another vital dimension of possible exploitation was missing from my 1982 account. One of the most important issues in the present book is the centrality of the collateralization of property to the functioning of capitalism. Outside economics and sociology, the concept of capital has meant property that can be used as collateral for securing monetary loans. Differential collateralizability leads us to another dimension of exploitation and a powerful engine of cumulative inequality. Employees are not slaves, and selling oneself into slavery is prohibited. Hence, capitalism limits the possibility of mortgaging labor power. Banks may lend money on the basis of expected future earnings. But, if the loan is not repaid, they cannot seize the earner and sell him or her as a slave. Freedom from enslavement denies the employee opportunities for obtaining loans using labor assets as collateral. This is *exploitation through unequal collateralizability.*[4]

Unequal access to collateral is a major source of further inequality. Unless they have other property, workers cannot obtain sizable loans. By contrast, the capitalist receives income from property that can also be used as collateral to borrow more money and invest still more in profitable enterprises. Capitalism thus follows the biblical maxim: "For whosoever hath, to him shall be given, and he shall have more abundance: but whosoever hath not, from him shall be taken away even that he hath" (Matt. 13:12; see also Mark 4:25, Luke 8:18, and Luke 19:26.).

I have identified several factor asymmetries and types of exploitation, but two are particularly important under capitalism. They are inherent sources of inequality within capitalist societies. These are *corporeal* exploitation and exploitation through *unequal collateralizability.* Further sources of inequality and possible remedies are addressed in the following sections.

15.2. Sources of Inequality within Capitalism

Some inequality results from individual differences in talent or skill. But this cannot explain the huge gaps between rich and poor in many countries. Much of the inequality of wealth found within capitalist societies results from inequalities of inheritance (Bowles and Gintis 2002; Credit Suisse 2012). Some children are born into much more fortunate circumstances than others. The process is cumulative: inequalities of wealth often lead to differences in education, economic power, and further inequalities in income.

To what extent can inequalities of income or wealth be attributed to the fundamental institutions of capitalism rather than a residual landed aristocracy or other surviving elites from the precapitalist past? Much inherited wealth may originate from former eras. So we must focus on possible sources of inequality from within capitalism itself.

A familiar mantra (which I have previously repeated) is that markets

---

4. This does not mean that slaves are free of exploitation. They suffer the loss of legal rights and are exploited in different ways. The forms of exploitation discussed here are the ones most relevant to capitalism.

are the source of inequality under capitalism.[5] Is this true? Noting the "scant attention" paid to this issue and a "dearth of studies" in this area, Christopher Kollmeyer (2012, 400) analyzed data from eighteen advanced capitalist countries over several decades and found "a strong and positive link between the size of consumer markets and income inequality." Other studies have found that inequality has increased markedly in formerly Soviet-type countries in their transitions from planned to market economies after 1989 (Bandelj and Mahutga 2010). So can markets be blamed for inequality?

Kollmeyer (2012, 401) argued: "Economic activity in consumer markets is based on competition and the pursuit of private gain, which should create abundant opportunities for individual differentiation and hence relatively high levels of income inequality." By contrast: "[The] public sector is oriented toward the fulfilment of social need using resources obtained through progressive taxation." But markets and "the pursuit of private gain" are simply assumed to be the source of inequality, without any demonstration of the mechanisms involved. Another error is the presumption that the public sector is necessarily oriented toward the egalitarian fulfilment of social need. Nationalization does not necessarily turn an industry into a public benefit. Some state-run systems have generated catastrophic famines or degraded the natural environment. Kollmeyer suggested that markets in modern economies should be dramatically diminished in scope. But he presumed rather than demonstrated the benefits of public provision. Both the argument and the policy conclusion are challengeable. Kollmeyer's claims are based on a statistical correlation with no explanation of causation.

In his hard-hitting analysis of growing inequality in the United States, Joseph E. Stiglitz (2012b, xiii) wrote: "Markets, by themselves, even when they are stable, often lead to high levels of inequality." But he then modified this claim: "Market forces played a role, but it was not market forces alone" (28). The subtle shift from "markets" to "market forces" should be noted. Blaming market forces is not necessarily the same thing as blaming markets. Such forces could be inequalities of power and wealth that operate within markets. In this case, the main fac-

---

5. Note that Marx (1976) did not regard markets as the source of inequality. Instead, he located it historically in the "primitive accumulation" that separated the workers from the means of production and in the ongoing expropriation of surplus value in the sphere of production.

tors involved in the explanation resemble the inequality that we are trying to explain. Then, in his chapter on "markets and inequality," Stiglitz
blamed not markets as such but how they are "shaped" along with other
possible causes of inequality, including technological changes, advances
in productivity, international shifts in comparative advantage, and other
important factors that are not strictly markets as such. Despite the rhetoric, Stiglitz did not show that markets can be blamed for inequality.

In reality, of course, no market is perfectly competitive. When a seller
has sufficient salable assets to affect prices, then strategic market behavior is possible to drive out competitors. Many economists see greater
competition as the remedy. If markets per se are to be blamed for inequality, then it has to be shown that competitive markets also have this
outcome. Unless we can demonstrate their culpability, blaming competitive markets for inequalities of success or failure might be like blaming the water for drowning a weak swimmer. To demonstrate that competitive markets are a source of inequality we would have to start from
an imagined world where there was initial equality in the distribution of
income and wealth and then show how the use of markets (or commodity exchange) alone led to inequality. I know of no such theoretical explanation. Markets involve voluntary exchange, where both parties to an
exchange expect benefits. One party to the exchange may benefit more
than the other, but there is no reason to assume that individuals who
benefit more or benefit less will generally do so.

Of course, there can be strong positive feedbacks where the rich get
richer, as in Daniel Rigney's (2010) "parable of the Monopoly game." But
the sources of the resulting inequalities are not the acts of trading themselves. They are combinations of luck and strategy that lead to small differences in wealth that get exaggerated as the game unfolds. Random
effects or slight skill differences become cumulatively exaggerated via
positive feedbacks. Here, the multiplication of effects is to blame for almost all the inequality, not the markets themselves.

Those who blame markets for inequality sometimes overlook their
institutional character and isolate them from their institutional integu-
ment. Markets are institutionally constructed and not natural phenomena. The level of inequality under capitalism is then a function of a complex of diverse institutions often involving different types of market.

What about globalization? The globalization of markets has important consequences but does not necessarily increase inequality. According to the empirical study by Branko Milanovic (2011), global income in-

equality has not increased much since 1950. Furthermore, most global income inequality is due to differences *between* countries rather than differences within countries. Accordingly, as less-developed countries grow, global inequality could *decrease*.

It is theoretically possible for inequality to increase within every country while global inequality decreases (Milanovic 2005). This would be an example of the well-known Simpson's paradox, or the Yule-Simpson effect, in which a pattern that is ubiquitous in different individual cases is absent or reversed when the data are aggregated. Consider this intuitively. About one-fifth of the world's population is Chinese. In 1950, most people in China were desperately poor. These many millions were at the bottom of the global prosperity rankings. Since 1980, China has become more unequal, but most of its population has become much better off. As China moves up the country rankings in terms of average wealth or income, it affects global distribution and the global degree of inequality. Many ordinary Chinese move from the bottom of the global prosperity league, which amounts to a significant global redistribution of income and wealth. Depending on countervailing forces, this can in principle mean a reduction in global inequality. This helps explain why globalization does not necessarily lead to greater global inequality despite high and growing inequality within many countries.

This is not an apology for globalization. There is a case for protecting infant industries in developing countries (List 1841; Chang 2002a, 2002b; Fletcher 2011).[6] I am also sympathetic to Rodrik's (2011) arguments against "hyperglobalization." My point here is different: there is

---

6. Critics of the infant-industry argument pointed out that competitive capital markets can ensure that new firms can borrow money to invest sufficiently to overcome initial problems of workforce training and production scale and thereby reach the levels of efficiency required to compete internationally (Meade 1955; Baldwin 1969). This capital market argument overlooks the Keynesian or Knightian type of uncertainties involved. Furthermore, even if the lenders had a sound positive appraisal of future benefits once the industry had matured, they still might be deterred from lending to an infant firm under capitalism because of missing futures markets for labor and the possibility that trained workers may quit the emerging firm or industry. As Hart (1975) showed, with missing (e.g., labor) markets there is no guarantee that their incremental extension (e.g., for finance capital) will improve efficiency. Of course, there is no guarantee that tariffs to protect infant industries will work either, and there are clear downside risks with such a policy. But it does mean that any infant industry protection must be combined with interventionist measures to incentivize the training and retention of workers by firms.

no forceful argument to suggest that the globalization of markets necessarily leads to greater global inequality.

So, if markets per se are not the root cause of inequality under capitalism, then what is? A clear answer to this question is vital if effective policies to counter inequality are to be developed. Capitalism builds on inherited inequalities of class, ethnicity, and gender. By affording more opportunities for the generation of profits, it may also exaggerate differences due to location or ability. Partly through the operation of markets, it can also enhance positive feedbacks that further magnify these differences. But its core sources of inequality lie elsewhere.

The answer has been foreshadowed in the preceding section. *The foremost generator of inequality under capitalism is not markets but capital.*[7] This may sound Marxist, but it is not. I define capital differently from Marx and most other economists (excepting Fetter, Hobson, Mitchell Innes, Schumpeter, Sombart, and Weber). Capital is money, or the realizable money value of owned and collateralizable property. Precisely because waged employees are not slaves, they cannot use their lifetime capacity for work as collateral to obtain money loans. The very commercial freedom of workers denies them the possibility to use their labor assets or skills as collateral. By contrast, capitalists may use their property to make profits and as collateral to borrow money, invest, and make still more money. Differences become cumulative, between those with and without collateralizable assets, and between different amounts of collateralizable wealth. Even when workers become homeowners with mortgages, the wealthier can still race ahead.

Labor cannot be collateralized because workers are not owned: there are missing futures markets for labor. A further consequence—as noted above—is that employers have diminished incentives to invest in the skills of their workforce. Especially as capitalism becomes more knowledge intensive, unless compensatory measures are put in place, this can create an unskilled and low-paid underclass and further exacerbate inequality. A socially excluded underclass is observable in several developed capitalist countries.

Another source of inequality results from the inseparability of the worker from the work itself. By contrast, the owners of other factors of

7. Piketty (2014) provided historical data and rich empirical vindication of this claim. He showed that the main driver of inequality is the tendency of returns on capital to exceed the rate of economic growth.

production are free to trade and seek other opportunities while their property makes money or yields other rewards. As Green, Marshall, and Hobson recognized, this puts workers at a disadvantage. As noted above, even slight disadvantages can have cumulative effects.

None of these core drivers of inequality can be diminished by extending markets or increasing competition. These drivers are congenital to capitalism and its system of wage labor. If capitalism is to be retained, then the compensatory arrangements required to counter inequality cannot simply be extensions of markets or private property rights.

By misdefining capital and overlooking these asymmetries, both orthodox and heterodox economists have neglected the true sources of inequality under capitalism. Improved definitions begin to reveal these core asymmetries. Good definitions are vital for empirical discovery and policy development.

15.3. Alleviating Inequality

Primarily through concentrations of self-expanding capital (collateralizable property), capitalism has developed rich elites sustained via inherited wealth and in many ways more powerful than the landed aristocracy that preceded them.[8]

Let us briefly turn the clock back to an earlier age, when the inheritance of land was the primary mechanism of inequality. Allow me to introduce the Anglo-American radical Thomas Paine. Over two hundred years ago he proposed a one-off, state-funded distribution "to every person, when arrived at the age of twenty-one years, the sum of fifteen pounds sterling, as a compensation in part, for the loss of his or her natural inheritance, by the introduction of the system of landed property" (Paine 1797).[9] The effect of this benefit would be to provide every adult with an amount of wealth that could be used to invest in property

8. Piketty and Zucman (2013) and Piketty (2014) showed that wealth-to-income ratios in rich countries have been increasing since the 1970s and are returning to pre-1900 levels. As they put it: "Capital is making a comeback." Because wealth is very concentrated, high wealth-to-income ratios imply that inequalities of wealth—and potentially of inherited wealth—matter more. Policies of progressive capital and inheritance taxation move up the agenda (Ackerman and Alstott 1999; Bowles and Gindis 1999; Piketty and Saez 2013; Piketty 2014).

9. In terms of purchasing power in 2011, £15 converts to roughly £1,300 or $2,000. But,

or personal development, irrespective of the income or status of his or her parents.

Rare among thinkers, Paine is admired by moderate socialists, social democrats, and free market libertarians. Robert Lamb (2010) showed that Paine's analysis of property rights is a distinct and underestimated contribution to political theory. Paine combined a libertarian defense of private ownership with a redistributive egalitarianism, founded on the individual right to both property and personal development. Instead, the socialist movement from the 1830s made the abolition of private property and commodity exchange the priority, believing that this was the only way to deal with inequality. By contrast, Paine understood that an essential source of prosperity in modern society was devolved ownership; its abolition would reduce incentives and the size of the cake to be shared. Private ownership of many assets, protected by the law, is necessary to guarantee individual autonomy and the vibrancy of civil society. Policies that might address inequality—like wholesale collectivization— would be counterproductive if they baffled incentives and reduced overall output. For over a century, socialists took the wrong road. Many have since tried to find the way back. Perhaps we should return to Paine and move forward from there.[10]

Today, we face problems of inequality even greater than those addressed by Paine. Land and buildings are immobile and can be readily assessed and taxed. But capital is fleet-footed and covert: it can be easily moved around the world or hidden in foreign accounts.

Bruce Ackerman and Anne Alstott (1999) took up similar themes in their proposal for a "stakeholder society." They stressed progressive taxes on wealth rather than on income. Echoing Paine, they proposed a large cash grant to all citizens when they reach the age of majority, around the benchmark cost of taking a bachelor's degree at a private university in the United States. This grant would be repaid into the national treasury at death. They argued: "Property is so important to the

---

as a fraction of 1797 UK GDP, £15 converts to about £79,000 or $120,000 as an equivalent share of 2011 UK GDP.

10. The protosocialist Thomas Spence proposed in the 1770s that land should be owned in common at the parish level instead of being nationalized. He attacked Paine's 1797 proposal on the grounds that it retained individual ownership of land (Bonnett 2007). Evidence suggests that common ownership or participatory management can work on a smaller scale, as with cooperatives and some common-pool resources (Ostrom 1990; Bonin, Jones, and Putterman 1993).

free development of individual personality that everybody ought to have some" (191). To further advance redistribution, they argued for the gradual implementation of an annual wealth tax of 2 percent on a person's net worth above a threshold of $80,000. Like Paine, they argued that every citizen has the right to share in the wealth accumulated by preceding generations. A redistribution of wealth, they proposed, would bolster the sense of community and common citizenship.

Samuel Bowles and Herbert Gintis (1999) also advocated wealth redistribution. They addressed problems of asymmetrical information in enterprises, schools, and elsewhere and proposed redistributions of property in order to align the incentives of owners more closely with the incentives of users. While they proposed no ban on capitalist enterprises, they favored workplace democracy and government provision of credit to worker cooperatives.

As modern capitalist economies become more knowledge intensive, access to education to develop skills becomes all the more important. Those deprived of such education suffer a degree of social exclusion, and, unless it is addressed, this problem is likely to get worse (Cowen 2013). Widespread skill-development policies are needed, alongside integrated measures to deal with job displacement and unemployment (Ashton and Green 1996; Crouch, Finegold, and Sako 1999; Acemoglu and Autor 2011, 2012).

The need for ongoing education is one argument for a basic income guarantee. Such a basic income would be paid to everyone out of state funds, irrespective of other income or wealth and whether people are working or not (Van Parijs 1992, 1995; Corning 2011). It is justified on the grounds that individuals require a minimum income to function as free and choosing agents. Everyone has the right to the means of survival so that they can make use of their liberty, have some autonomy, function as effective citizens, and participate in civil society. These are conditions of adequate and educated inclusion in the market world of choice and trade.

A basic income would also reward caring work to help the sick or elderly, which is typically performed within families. But it is typically undervalued and uncompensated monetarily (Folbre 1994; Folbre and Nelson 2000; Nussbaum 2000; Jochimsen 2003). A basic income would also encourage new entrepreneurs and creative artists and reduce migration from the countryside to the cities in search of work. There would also be a huge saving in administration costs of often complex social security and welfare schemes.

Some forms of unconditional basic income have been pledged or introduced in several localities, including Alaska and Brazil. Several developed countries have legal minimum income entitlements. In 1968, James Tobin, Paul A. Samuelson, John Kenneth Galbraith, and another twelve hundred economists signed a document calling for the US Congress to introduce a system of income guarantees and supplements. Winners of the Nobel Prize in economics who fully support a basic income include Milton Friedman, Friedrich Hayek, James Meade, Herbert Simon, and Robert Solow. This idea cuts across the political spectrum.

A key challenge for modern capitalist societies, alongside the needs to protect the natural environment and enhance the quality of life, is to retain the dynamic of innovation and investment while ensuring that the rewards of the global system are not returned largely to the richer owners of capital. As Paine (1797) put it long ago: "All accumulation, therefore, of personal property, beyond what a man's own hands produce, is derived to him by living in society; and he owes on every principle of justice, of gratitude, and of civilization, a part of that accumulation from whence the whole came."

But the benefits of "living in society" are not simply through the advantages of cooperation or the division of labor. Modern societies have developed complex institutions that have empowered innovations and massive expansions of wealth. The ultimate and indivisible accumulation is not simply of things but of knowledge, relations, and rules guarded by law within an adaptable and pluralist polity.

CHAPTER SIXTEEN

After Capitalism?

The struggle between the opponents and defenders of capitalism is a struggle between innovators who do not know what innovation to make and conservatives who do not know what to conserve. — Simone Weil (1937/1986)

L eading economists, including Karl Marx and Joseph A. Schumpeter, argued that capitalism carries the seeds of its own destruction. They saw capitalism as being replaced by classical socialism, with the abolition of private property, although they disagreed on the desirability of this outcome. In chapter 12 it was argued that classical socialism is inconsistent with a large-scale, dynamic economy with a democratic polity. But the other issue remains: Are there tendencies within capitalism that lead to its supersession? Given the unfeasibility of marginalizing or abolishing markets and private property in a modern complex economy, are there different postcapitalist possibilities that are consistent with human freedom and flourishing? What are the least desirable features of capitalism that need to be alleviated, either within or beyond its boundaries? Clearly, strong normative as well as definitional and analytic issues are involved here. But any normative suggestions must be made within the space of developmental possibilities and based on an adequate analysis of the nature of the system.

Answers to these questions depend on the definition of capitalism. Consider the six-point definition of capitalism proposed in chapter 10 above. Conditions (1), (2), and (4)—involving widespread private property, markets, money, and the separation of much production from the home and family—are unlikely to change greatly; some detailed reforms are important, but more radical abolitions do not seem feasible or desirable.

Turning to condition (6) of the definition of capitalism (a developed financial system based on debt and collateralization), the future of the financial sector is uncertain, and feasible alternatives to current arrangements are under debate. But in any case it is doubtful that a modern, large-scale dynamic economy will be able to dispense with a banking system based on collateralization and debt. It is possible that there may be more state involvement in the financial system and even some limited "socialisation of investment," as Keynes (1936, 378) vaguely put it. The more immediate focus is on regulatory reforms and measures to restrain speculative bubbles, such as the proposed "Tobin tax" (Tobin 1978). While reform of international financial institutions is urgent, the first departures from capitalism—if and when they happen—are more likely to be across a different frontier.

More scope for fundamental change in the coming decades surrounds conditions (3) (profit-seeking private firms) and (5) (wage labor and employment contracts). It is important to note that, given the definition of capitalism, if any one of the six criteria is unfulfilled, then the system is not capitalist.

On condition (3), replacements for profit-seeking private firms could include publicly owned firms (which may or may not be profit seeking), worker-owned cooperatives (which may seek objectives other than profit), or not-for-profit private enterprises. The system might remain capitalist, where profit-seeking private firms dominate a smaller cooperative or not-for-profit sector. For capitalism to expire by these means, profit-seeking private firms would have to be marginalized. Alternatively, capitalism could be terminated by widespread nationalization in response to a catastrophic financial crisis, war, or some other major disaster.

A massive expansion of worker-producer cooperatives or worker self-employment could lead to the breach of condition (5). But, as argued below, the employment contract could gradually change its form and content so that employer power and authority are significantly reduced. This too could spell the end of capitalism, at least in the forms in which we have known it for the last two hundred years and as it was described by Marx.

This chapter has four sections. Section 16.1 considers the employment relationship: Is its abolition a priority? Section 16.2 considers feasible developments within capitalism that might lead to the fundamental transformation of this relationship, at least in some areas of work. The aim here is not to make predictions about the future, or to make a claim about desirability, but to consider a possible path of development that takes modern economies beyond capitalism, as defined in this book. Section 16.3 considers possible changes of institutional and legal structure of business corporations. Section 16.4 concludes the chapter.

16.1. Is the Abolition of the Employment Relationship a Priority?

According to Marx, many others, and the definition of capitalism adopted here, the employment relationship is a central defining feature of capitalism. In an employment contract the worker agrees, within limits, to work under the authority of an employer. There is potential employer control over the manner and pattern of work. This control typically concerns the manner and specification of the work to be performed.

Marx argued in *Capital* that the power of capital is exercised precisely at this point, within the sphere of production, where surplus value is allegedly generated. Hence, for Marxists, the abolition of the employment relationship is one of their foremost political objectives (Screpanti 2001; Wolff 2012).

From a non-Marxist viewpoint, David Ellerman (1992) criticized the employment relationship: he saw it as partial slavery. The slave owner has control rights over the slave. An employee rents his or her capacities for a limited period of time and grants control rights for that period to an employer. Ellerman argued that, just as slavery is immoral and illegal, employment likewise should be condemned and prohibited. Voluntary agreement to an employment contract is not a valid counterargument. There are prohibitions in most countries on many consensual activities: individuals are not allowed to sell banned drugs, their votes, or themselves into slavery. According to Ellerman, entering into an employment contract, thereby conceding authority to an employer, means an abdication of individual rights and responsibilities and should be outlawed. His alternative is a system of worker cooperatives where decisions are taken jointly and democratically by the workforce and no one is strictly an employee. Following Jaroslav Vanek (1970, 1972) and others, he pro-

posed the abolition of all capitalist firms and their replacement by autonomous worker cooperatives, each able to enter into contracts and trade
on markets.

Possible advantages of such a system of worker cooperatives are discussed below. But is the abolition of employment a priority? There is an
opposing case for being less absolutist and more lenient. This would permit wider experimentation with different forms, including modified capitalist firms and corporations.

But Ellerman and others would protest: for them this is a matter of
principle. There can be no compromise with this modern version of servitude: people should be neither rented nor sold. But the real world is
more complex. Just as in practice the line is often difficult to draw between an employment contract and a contract for services, authority and
responsibility each come in fifty shades of gray.

In some practical cases the exercise of authority by employers is extremely limited. For example, with knowledge-intensive employment,
close, detailed supervision is often dysfunctional or impossible. Often,
the knowledge worker has more specialist knowledge than his or her
line manager. But it is also the case with other professions. An employed
truck driver is told what load to pick up and when and where it should
be delivered. Otherwise, there is little close supervision of the activity.
The pattern and nature of the work would not be changed hugely if the
driver owned the truck and was self-employed. Self-employment has advantages but also the disadvantages that the driver has greater responsibility for the upkeep of the truck and increased financial anxieties. The
choice is not black versus white.

Authority of a kind exists in a cooperative setup. The inevitable division of labor leads to different roles and identities. Within groups,
leaders typically emerge. Although individuals in the group may nominally have equal rights and votes, studies of group dynamics show internal group differentiation, subgroup formation, differential influence,
and the emergence of hierarchies of power (Hogg and Terry 2000; Keltner, Van Kleef, Chen, and Kraus 2008). While workers in a cooperative
cannot be threatened with dismissal in the same way as employees, other
threats and sanctions operate within groups.

A worker shareholder in a cooperative has ties and responsibilities
that may not suit everyone. Majority rule in a democratic collective can
compromise the needs or rights of minorities. For example, pressure

may be put on all workers to put in the same hours, thus sidelining part-time or flexible work patterns. The difficulty of shareholder exit is a serious problem in worker cooperatives. Workers may not be able to sell or obtain the full value of their share. The employment relationship is typically easier and less costly to terminate. Many people are willing to accede to some authority in the workplace in return for greater flexibility in dealing with the rest of their lives.

Finally, submission to political authority in any large society is unavoidable. Modern states involve monopolies of legitimate force and complex legal systems to which, even in a democracy, no one has consented in detail. The abolition of all authority is the pipe dream of anarchism. The practical focus instead should be on checks, balances, legal limitations, and democratically accountable oversight.

Consequently, the emphasis should be on improving the rules and conditions governing the employment relationship rather than abolishing it entirely. This would involve both general legislation and employee negotiation with particular employers. The general policy approach toward the organization of enterprise should be experimental, trying different types of firms, including cooperatives and other structures. Find what works best, in regard to individual satisfaction and human flourishing as well as profitability or revenue. Then experiment anew.

16.2. Specialization, Knowledge Intensification, and Employment

Elsewhere (Hodgson 1999), I considered the implications of specialization and growing knowledge intensity in a capitalist economy. That account is summarized and updated in this section. It involves possible scenarios rather than predictions: it is an exercise in "what if?" Other outcomes are possible, including mass automation and consumption without human cultural enrichment or an economy where information technology results in increased surveillance rather than the development of skills (Head 2005; Brynjolfsson and McAfee 2012).

One possible path of capitalist development may undermine the employment relationship within capitalism. The scenario explored here concerns the most knowledge-intensive core of the world capitalist system rather than every sector or recess. This does not rule out the persistence of a substantial underclass of unskilled or unemployed workers, in both developed and developing countries.

Employment involves potential control and supervision by others. But, as Peter Drucker (1993, 107) pointed out, the knowledge-intensive organization "is increasingly composed of specialists, each of whom knows more about his or her own specialty than anybody else in the organization." If the worker has highly specific and idiosyncratic skills, then proficient supervision and control depend also on the possession of relevant capabilities by the supervisor. As complexity and specialization increase, these particular capabilities may become increasingly scarce. Close and highly evaluative supervision, based on a hierarchy of command, would be less viable, simply because the nominal supervisors will not know the best way of doing the job or even its precise purpose. The worker will know better (Cornuelle 1976; Zuboff 1988).

In a complex, evolving, knowledge-intensive system, agents require sophisticated cognitive abilities. Workers and managers have to learn, adapt, and create anew (see Marquand 1989; Senge 1990; Drucker 1993; Fransman 1994; Boisot 1995; Nonaka and Takeuchi 1995; and Choo 1998). A knowledge-intensive economy involves the dematerialization of much production and the shift from physical to intellective skills. As Shoshana Zuboff (1988, 71) put it in her classic study: "Immediate physical responses must be replaced by an abstract thought process in which options are considered, and choices are made and then translated into the terms of the information system." The growing knowledge intensity of work means a shift from physical power and dexterity to the processing and evaluation of ideas. All human activity involves the use of both muscle and brain. But, as the balance shifts radically from muscle to intellect and from the manipulation of materials to the interpretation and processing of symbols, work undergoes a fundamental transformation.

Computers can mimic some aspects of intelligent behavior with their immense data-processing powers. But (at least so far) they cannot replicate key features of human intelligence. Crucially, they lack intuition and sophisticated judgment (Dreyfus and Dreyfus 1986). Insofar as computers can take over some functions, the overall, net outcome in terms of the balance of skills in the workforce is not necessarily toward deskilling.

Computers may free up skilled workers for tasks of a more evaluative and judgmental character. Critical judgment involves asking questions and saying no when things do not seem right. But questioning established procedures can be inimical to managerial authority. As Zuboff (1988, 291, 308) elaborated:

> Obedience has been the axial principle of task execution in the traditional environment of imperative control. . . . When tasks require intellective effort, however, obedience can be dysfunctional and can impede the exploitation of information. Under such conditions, internal commitment and motivation replace authority as the primary bond between the individual and the task. . . . The explication of meaning that is so central to the development of intellective skills requires that people become their own authorities. . . . Without the consensual immediacy of a shared action context, individuals must construct interpretations of the information at hand and so reveal what they believe to be significant. In this way, authority is located in the process of creating and articulating meaning, rather than in a particular position or function.

The shift from physical to intellectual work can undermine supervisory powers. With physical work, managers can observe the activity and its output and make judgments concerning the efficiency and aptitude of the worker. But, with intellective skills, meaningful supervision is less viable. It is impossible to see what is going on in someone's head. *Consequently, as the complexity and knowledge intensity of production processes increase, the key characteristic in the employment contract of detailed managerial control is increasingly bounded and impaired.*

On the other hand, developments in information technology increase possibilities for workforce surveillance (Head 2005). But such oversight would mainly concern the detectable aspects of work and less the quality of judgment and the workings of the mind. If managers cannot know what their workers know, then neither can technology. The installation of surveillance systems can also undermine the culture of trust and cooperation that is necessary for the full development of the knowledge-intensive economy.

Well before the end of the twentieth century the possibilities for detailed monitoring were limited. As Richard Nelson (1981b, 1038) pointed out: "Management cannot effectively 'choose' what is to be done in any detailed way, and has only broad control over what is done, and how well. Only a small portion of what people actually do on a job can be monitored in detail." As complexity, specialization, and knowledge intensity increase, detailed managerial direction will become less viable and productive. Workers have always possessed some tacit and other skills beyond the reach of managerial comprehension. But in modern, complex, knowledge-intensive capitalism the predicament has become immensely more compounded and severe. What were formerly regarded as exclusively managerial, administrative, or organizational capabilities are increasingly being expected of other workers. The old distinctions between the conception of a task and its execution, as elaborated in the "scientific management" of Frederick Winslow Taylor (1911), have long been eroded (Vroom and Deci 1970).

A further consequence of an increasing reliance on advanced skills and knowledge would be that these become relatively more important, compared with the physical instruments of work, such as tools and machines. This shifting balance would be expressed in changes in relative costs. Insofar as the physical means of production become relatively less important, the question of who owns them becomes less consequential to a similar degree. Accordingly, the possession of useful knowledge and skills by the worker increases in relative significance, compared to the tangible instruments of work. It is not being suggested that we should disregard the question of who owns the means of production. What is being argued is that the changing balance between intangible and tangible assets and the growing reliance on knowledge and skills mean that the relative bargaining power of the skilled employee increases and that the gap in this respect between the skilled and the unskilled worker widens. These differences lead to growing differences of income and possible shortages of skilled labor, compared with possible mass unemployment of unskilled labor.

As more workers would be in possession of a valuable set of conceptual, analytic, administrative, and other skills, then the notion of proletarians—meaning literally that they possess nothing but their children—becomes even more of an exaggeration. But this does not mean the abolition of divisions between social classes or necessarily a reduction in material inequality.

These developments create increasing practical problems for the legal distinction between employment contracts and contracts for services. The legal system has already experienced severe difficulties in identifying whether a worker is under the detailed supervisory control of another person. Hence, as noted above, the provision or otherwise of the physical instruments of work is often used as a surrogate criterion. But knowledge is intangible, so this legal test faces severe difficulties. Self-employed experts and consultants are widely used in modern capitalism, yet their provision of physical instruments of work is insignificant.

As the boundary between manager and employee breaks down, a kind of quasi self-employment may develop. By owning part of the intangible means of production, in the form of specialist knowledge, and having a considerable degree of control over his or her work process, in some respects the employee will resemble a self-employed worker. On the other hand, the employing corporation will retain ownership of the goods or services that are produced, of the physical means of production, and of some of the crucial mechanisms of knowledge accreditation. For these reasons the worker does not become fully self-employed, in either a de facto or a de jure sense. Nevertheless, the possession of highly specialist knowledge and the control of the work process by the employee can give the worker some practical autonomy. We can find examples of this quasi self-employment today in many public and private universities and in some research units in large, knowledge-intensive capitalist corporations.

As Charles Handy (1984) pointed out, with the increase in the relative and absolute cost of specialist skills, there may be more cases of employment contracts being replaced by de facto and de jure self-employment, where the skilled worker contracts explicitly for specific services, not hours of work. The relatively high cost of skilled labor provides a strong push toward the hiring of the services of skilled, professional individuals or groups on the basis of a contract for services rather than an employment contract.

With the increasing role of specialist and idiosyncratic knowledge and the emergence of real and quasi self-employment, the stipulation of a number of hours to be worked would lose much of its operational significance and meaning. Even if they remain formally employees, knowledge workers may require periods of contemplation, reading, research, or study that cannot always be confined to official office hours. By its nature, knowledge work means a shift from time-keeping to normative control, permitting indefinite extension and intensification. Work will be taken home, to be performed in an unsupervised environment. The boundary between work and leisure becomes blurred. These developments bring severe dangers, such as overwork and a deprived family life, as well as benefits, such as self-supervision and autonomy.

With all these developments, the meaning of the employment contract would be stretched to the limit, creating normative and legal tensions that may suggest its radical reformulation. This bodes the end of the classical employment relationship, the transformation of the capitalist firm, and definitionally the demise of capitalism itself.

These developments are detectable in some areas of work, even in profit-hungry capitalist corporations. It remains to be seen whether this scenario will become more widespread or whether different futures will unfold. While employment contracts have a long history going back to medieval times, the nature of the employment contract has changed radically over the centuries, from quasi-feudal servitude, through centuries where employees faced the sanctions of criminal law, to the degree of autonomy and self-motivation found in some areas of modern employment today. Further fundamental changes cannot be ruled out.

Marx (1976, 1019–38) made a distinction between the "formal" and the "real subsumption of labour under capital." He argued that "formal subsumption" occurred in a precapitalist state of affairs when businessmen took ownership of the means of handicraft or peasant production but work carried on, outsourced and dispersed as before. "Real subsumption" came later, when these moneyed interests directly or indirectly took control of and organized the labor process in larger units. According to Marx, it is only with the real subsumption of labor and the control of work by an employer that capitalism proper became established.

But in some respects the historical sequence outlined by Marx may be reversed. In some knowledge-intensive and specialist spheres the real subsumption of labor is being undermined while formal subsumption survives. The basic formalities of employment law and the employment contract remain. But actual or possible control of the manner of work by the employer becomes increasingly difficult and even counterproductive. The relationship becomes closer to that in a contract for services rather than an employment contract. If formal subsumption is ended as well by the transformation of the employment contract into something different, then this signals—according to Marx's own conception—the end of the capitalist system.

It has also been noted in preceding chapters that attempts to establish widespread private ownership of information, thus making vital nonrivalrous resources excludable, can have inegalitarian and dysfunctional consequences. More broadly than in the employment contract, to a significant degree the growing knowledge intensity of capitalism challenges the universal claims of private property. Attempts to overextend rights of ownership of information can challenge the vitality of capitalism at its core (Pagano 2014).

This would be especially the case in a knowledge-intensive economy where the accumulation of capital (i.e., collateralizable property) required much knowledge to be privatized. This denial of shared possession of nonrival assets would constrain the growth of knowledge-intensive capitalism. This could lead to political challenges to the system.

16.3. The Capitalist Corporation and Beyond

From about 1880, advanced capitalism has been powered increasingly by large-scale finance and large corporations coordinated by global markets. These structures and organizations have led to huge economies of scale, rapid technological development, massive increases in productivity, and growing average personal incomes. Any attempt to reform or replace capitalism must take account of these facts. As cited above, some academic writers still believe in the complete abolition of markets, private property, and money. They overlook the perils of their abolition, as illustrated by ruinous experiments in the twentieth century, from Stalin and Mao to Pol Pot. We have to understand capitalism, the roots of its success, and the *feasible* possibilities for reform and progress.

Large corporations can have disbenefits as well as benefits. Corporations can act as powerful lobbies for rich and established interests. Unless there is effective countervailing legislation, corporate power can distort democracy and mislead public opinion. The political financing, lobbying, and media powers of large corporations should be on the agenda of capitalist reform (Galbraith 1969; Lindblom 1977; Dahl 1982; Crouch 2004, 2011).

Legal structures such as the joint-stock company and the limited liability corporation have facilitated large agglomerations of capital to reap the economies of scale involved in mass production. But that does not mean that corporations should be left as they are. Because legal structures are often overlooked or downgraded in social science, critics of capitalism have paid insufficient attention to the possibilities for the reform of corporate law.

Friedrich Hayek (1948, 116) worried about corporate legal personhood and limited liability, rightly blaming the state for their existence, but wrongly assuming that the clock could be turned back to the eighteenth century. The abolition of both corporate legal personhood and limited liability would tear apart the institutional fabric of modern capitalism. Such a radical move would counter Hayek's own doctrine of cautious experimentalism. Such reverses could hobble the system, especially in the sphere of large-scale production.

The concept of corporate social responsibility has arisen after concerns about alleged malpractices against the public interest. But declarations of intent by corporations and voluntary self-regulation do not amount to structural reforms of the corporation itself. "It is hardly surprising," wrote Paddy Ireland (2010, 853), that the idea of corporate social responsibility "has been warmly embraced by so many corporations." But another survey suggests that there is scope to push this agenda further (Werther and Chandler 2011). An important question is whether renewed corporate law reform could reverse the trend toward making corporate directors responsible for the maximization of shareholder value rather than more diverse objectives, including serving the public interest (Hutton 1995, 1997).

Margaret Blair (1995) provided a deeper analysis of the corporation and made apposite and feasible recommendations. She argued that there is no guarantee that the interests of the public at large and the shareholders of the corporation will coincide. The model of the firm in mainstream economics focuses on residual risks taken by shareholders. But residual risks are also taken by long-term employees with firm-specific skills, especially in knowledge-intensive contexts. Having been trained to work on highly skilled tasks peculiar to one firm, they would have difficulty finding equivalent remuneration elsewhere. Shareholders do not bear all the residual risks. Furthermore, shareholders do not generally have day-to-day contact with the firm. Hence, compared with employees, shareholders are often in a weaker position to exercise all the responsibilities of ownership. Among other policy proposals, Blair suggested the issue of shares in corporate equity to workers.

The question of limited liability is also important. The legal incorporation of a firm by the state should involve a quid pro quo for society in return for the legal privilege of limited liability. Some nineteenth-century campaigners proposed decoupling limited liability from rights of control by separating special shareholders who had rights of control and unlimited liability from general shareholders with limited liability but no rights of managerial control (Ireland 2010, 852). Rather than abolish limited liability in its entirety—perhaps to replace it with liability insurance (Toporowski 2010)—this separation proposal has been modernized in favor of a statutory principle of unlimited liability for the corporation as a whole while retaining limited liability for shareholders (Muchlinski 2010). There is scope for experimentation in this area too.

Further corporate reforms are possible. The idea of extending employee shareholding has surfaced several times in the history of capitalism, but in recent years—at least in the United States—the practice has spread widely. The US-based National Center for Employee Ownership (2012) reported that in 2009–11 about 10,900 enterprises, involving 10.3 million workers, were part of employee-ownership, stock bonus, or profit-sharing schemes, with assets estimated at about $869 billion. In 1975 only 1,600 US enterprises were in such schemes. Employee ownership ostensibly increases incentives, personal identification with the enterprise, and job satisfaction for workers. The evidence suggests that, when employee-ownership schemes and employee participation in decisionmaking are combined, greater increases in profitability and productivity can be obtained (see Jones 1987; Bonin, Jones, and Putterman 1993; Poole and Whitfield 1994; Doucouliagos 1995; Pendleton, Wilson, and Wright 1998; Hubbick 2001; Robinson and Zhang 2005; and Birchall 2011). If implemented more widely and forcefully, employee-ownership schemes or management buyouts could lead to workers owning a major proportion of the shares of large corporations.

Not all private enterprises are profit driven. In recent decades there has been a growth in social enterprises, defined broadly as organizations that have the explicit aim of improving well-being rather than maximizing profits for shareholders (Borzaga and Defourny 2001; Nyssens 2006; Birchall 2011). Social enterprises can be charities or nonprofit corporations, depending on the legal framework in which they operate.

According to the six-point definition of capitalism in this book, a frontier would be crossed into a different system if the economy were dominated either by self-employment ("petty" or "simple" commodity production) or by worker cooperatives. In most capitalist countries a sizable minority of the workforce is self-employed. These numbers might be sustained or even increased, but self-employment is unlikely to become dominant because of the dependence in many sectors of a modern economy on large-scale production and associated economies of scale.

There are some large-scale worker cooperatives, such as Chèque Déjeuner and Acome in France and the Mondragón Cooperative in Spain. There are numerous smaller cooperatives in most capitalist countries. The evidence suggests that worker cooperatives can be relatively efficient in particular circumstances and that they are not generally inferior in efficiency to capitalist corporations (see Bonin, Jones, and Putterman 1993; Dow 2003; Gagliardi 2009; and Zamagni and Zamagni 2010).[1]

Cooperatives are not anachronistic hangovers from a fading socialist ideology. A key factor in favor of worker cooperatives is that they address the inevitably incomplete markets for future labor power in a nonslave economy. Because workers are free to quit the capitalist firm, the employer has insufficient incentive to invest fully in the skills of employees (Marshall 1920, 565). A capitalist employer must bear the risk that investment in training will be lost because the trained worker can readily leave the firm after a finite contracted period. But in a worker cooperative the workers are shareholders, with an interest in training workers with relevant skills. Prominent proofs of the alleged suboptimality of cooperatives are based on static efficiency models that do not consider ongoing learning and overlook this advantage (Ward 1958, 1967; Vanek 1970, 1972). Learning is basically an out-of-equilibrium process, and, once we consider dynamic efficiency, then the prominent suboptimality proofs become irrelevant (Hodgson 1999).

Henry Hansmann's (1996) transactional analysis focused on ownership and contracting costs in cooperatives in general (including cooperatives formed by separate firms, such as farmers' cooperatives) rather than worker cooperatives in particular, so he did not underline the skill-training advantages of worker cooperatives. But his arguments concerning the costs and benefits of collective decisionmaking are clearly relevant to worker cooperatives. They are typically more successful with

---

1. Cooperatives have not always been embraced by socialists. In the mid-nineteenth century, Philippe Buchez, a follower of Saint-Simon, proposed autonomous worker cooperatives linked by contracts and markets (Reibel 1975, 44–45). Similarly, Pierre-Joseph Proudhon suggested a system of "mutualist associations" involving groups of workers who would pool their labor and their property, holding and using these resources in common, and entering into contractual relations with others. But in accord with most socialists and communists of that time, Marx and Engels proposed that all the means of production should be owned by society as a whole, not by autonomous communes or associations. In 1864 Marx (1974, 80) praised the established producer cooperatives, but argued that they should be quickly nationalized and consolidated into one national unit. In 1875, Marx (1974, 353–54) described Buchez's ideas as "reactionary," "sectarian," opposed to the workers' "class movement," and contrary to the true revolutionary aim of "cooperative production . . . on a national scale." See also Jossa (2005).

a group of worker-owners with shared aims and similar backgrounds. Problems with worker cooperatives include limited adaptability, dealing with a wide range of products, and changing the workforce through recruitment or exit. Nevertheless, it is quite possible that worker cooperatives could play a large role. If they ever become dominant, then such an economy would no longer be predominantly capitalist.

16.4. Conclusion—Beyond Left and Right

The French Revolution gave us the political terms *Left* and *Right*. They originated from the seating in the National Convention of 1789, with monarchists on the right and the republicans on the left. In the two centuries since their origins, the political labels have shifted their meanings. Originally, *Left* meant opposition to monarchy, aristocracy, church institutions, state monopolies, and privilege. It meant liberty (including the freedom to earn, own, and trade in a free market), equality (under the law), and fraternity (in the community). These legal and political rights helped unleash great engines of economic development in Europe and elsewhere. But, while average incomes increased, inequality widened, revealing Dickensian vistas of destitution. Private ownership and markets were blamed for deprivation and social injustice. Consequently, by the late nineteenth century, the term *Left* had been appropriated by advocates of common ownership of the means of production, thereby losing the freedom-to-trade part of its original meaning.

The first half of the twentieth century saw global devastations from militant nationalism and fascism. This delayed a major shift in the term *Right*: as late as the 1960s it still had strong associations with traditionalism, nationalism, and fascism. But then it too shifted, from nationalist and traditionalist apologies for the privileges of aristocracy to the defense of free markets and private ownership, which ironically had been the territory of the original Left of the 1790s. By the 1970s, and delayed by a century or more, the Right took hold of much of the ground vacated by the original Left.

The collapse of major "socialist" experiments in China and the Soviet Bloc in the 1980s meant a further seismic shift. Promoters of nationalization and comprehensive planning on the contemporary Left were no longer seen as the dynamic movement of the future. In the circumstances of this transition, members of the promarket Right were not reactionary defenders of a doomed social order. Within the Eastern Bloc countries, the freedom-to-trade Right became radical and anticonservative. This bewildered 1960s radicals from the West, who discovered in the 1990s that the Eastern European radicals and revolutionaries were libertarian advocates of free enterprise and private property (Wainwright 1994).

We need to invent new political labels. I do not argue that libertarian promarketeers should simply be relabeled *Left* (Lavoie 1985a). This would be an attempt to revert to original meanings without an adequate challenge to prevailing conceptions. A foremost aim of this book is to show that capitalism is not simply a market system: unavoidably, it contains different subsystems of governance, production, distribution, and exchange. Its very dynamism springs from a special, synergetic combination of dissimilar parts. Too few on the *Left* or the *Right* have come to grips with this.

The socialist movement got it wrong by prioritizing the abolition of private property and markets. It failed to understand that significant private property, protected by law, is a condition of liberty and devolved power. Obversely, many promarket libertarians exaggerate the capacities of markets to deal with systemic problems. A new agenda must arise where the limitations of both doctrines are acknowledged and understood. This agenda spans the concerns of both the *Left* and the *Right*.

Markets, commodity exchange, and private ownership existed for thousands of years before capitalism, and they will continue to exist if capitalism is eclipsed by new ways of organizing the production and distribution of wealth. Would-be reformers have to accept markets and much private property. To do otherwise is to ignore the twentieth-century lessons of devastating socialist failure. But, from an acceptance of markets and private property, radical avenues can still be found. Some of these may lead beyond capitalism.

A system of commodity exchange devolves crucial decisionmaking onto individuals and requires them to enter into contracts with others. The individual has to carry out numerous transactions and act responsibly. But people cannot function effectively in a system of contracts and markets if they are deprived of food, shelter, basic education, or fruitful social interaction. Through engagement in a social culture, people acquire the education and capabilities to deliberate effectively and serve their autonomous goals. These are conditions for social inclusion (see Gray 1993, 306–14; and O'Neill 1998, chaps. 5–7).

Hence, it is possible to promote a welfare state using libertarian political principles. James Sterba (1985) established the need for welfare provision to ensure that the poor can exercise their (libertarian) rights to life and property. Justifying taxation, Michael Davis (1987) argued that beneficiaries of state services (such as public health programs that reduce epidemics and police services that improve personal security) have the duty to pay for them.

Markets need to operate in accord with an ethic of individual rights and social inclusion. The limits to markets also have to be understood. Capitalism itself celebrates the business corporation, which is not a market and is organized on different principles. Detailed arguments concerning externalities and other problems suggest that health care, education, and protection of the natural environment are not best served by giving markets unrestricted reign (Reisman 1993; Davis 2001; Vatn 2005; Winston 2006; Hodgson 2013b).

Among both opponents and critics, few appreciate that capitalism cannot in principle be a 100 percent market system, no matter how far it tries to move in that direction. By pushing back slavery and widening wage labor, capitalism limited markets at its core: it disallowed complete futures markets for labor power. In addition, within capitalism, future labor power is not produced under capitalist conditions: babies are neither owned nor produced for profit. Capitalism unavoidably involves missing markets. Capitalism inescapably implies limits to the scope of markets and commodity exchange. We may obtain complete markets only by fully enslaving and dehumanizing all providers of labor power.

The birth of capitalism was stimulated by Enlightenment ideas of individual liberty and equality under the law. But rightly we lack the liberties to enslave others, trade in slaves, or enslave ourselves. We have equal legal rights to use property to produce more wealth. But the owner of labor power is placed at two indelible disadvantages, compared with the owner of nonlabor assets. Because of the ban on slavery, he or she cannot be used as collateral for obtaining loans and cannot separate himself of herself from the deployment of his or her labor in production. The congenital and unavoidable "contradictions" of capitalism are neither mass immiseration in a world of wealth, impelled clashes of class against class, nor capital accumulation undermining the rate of profit. They are systemic limitations to the Enlightenment principles of liberty and equality that are embedded in its being.

Key policies arise from an agenda that addresses the springs of capitalist prosperity and appreciates the system's limitations; they include universal education, a welfare state, a guaranteed basic income, the promotion of worker cooperatives, corporate law reform, and inheritance taxation. These policies find supporters across the now mislabeled *Left* and *Right*. They help consolidate the Enlightenment principles of human flourishing, autonomy, and liberty that emerged with capitalism at its inception.

Glossary

This is a selection of key definitions of terms used in this book. They are proposed for wider use.

Capital: The meaning adopted here is the one that had emerged in Europe by the thirteenth century in the context of trading and investment. This same meaning is widely used in business and financial circles today. Capital is a fund of money to be invested in some enterprise. It can also refer to the money value of tangible or intangible property usable as collateral. As Schumpeter (1954, 322) put it, capital is "essentially monetary, meaning either actual money, or claims to money, or some goods evaluated in money." Capital is money or the realizable money value of collateralizable property. Contrary to Adam Smith and many other economists, waged labor cannot be capital because (unlike slaves) it is not owned and cannot be used as collateral. Capital involves social relations and social institutions such as money and private property. But, contrary to Marx, it does not necessarily involve the employment of workers by capitalists.

Capitalism: Capitalism is defined as a socioeconomic system with the following six characteristics:

1. A legal system supporting widespread individual rights and liberties to own, buy, and sell private property
2. Widespread commodity exchange and markets involving money
3. Widespread private ownership of the means of production by firms producing goods or services for sale in the pursuit of profit
4. Much of production organized separately and apart from the home and family
5. Widespread wage labor and employment contracts
6. A developed financial system with banking institutions, the widespread use of credit with property as collateral, and the selling of debt

M-capitalism (after Marx) is a social system defined by conditions (1), (2), (3), (4), and (5), hence omitting condition (6). *S-capitalism* (after Schumpeter) is a social system defined by conditions (1), (2), (3), (4), and (6), hence omitting condition (5). (See *capital, commodity, contract, employment, exchange, firm, market, money, production, property.*)

Commodity: A commodity is here defined broadly as any owned asset (including goods, services, tokens, rights, and promises) that is potentially subject to contractual exchange or hire. By this definition—in apparent contrast to Karl Polanyi (1944, 1977)—a commodity might not be *intentionally* produced for exchange: what matters is its potential exchangeability. Furthermore, the term is not restricted to tangible materials of intrinsic use value, as in the terms *commodity market* or *commodity money*. With the inclusive definition adopted here, all markets involve commodities, and all forms of money are commodity money. (See *exchange, market, money.*)

Contract: A legal contract is an agreement entered into voluntarily by two or more parties with the shared intention of creating legal obligations. It may be made in writing, verbally, or by other signaled assent. A contract may involve the delivery of services or the exchange of goods. (See *exchange, law.*)

Customs: Customs are dispositions in cohesive groups to energize rule-bound patterns of behavior and interaction, involving conditional and sequential responses to cues that are partly dependent on social positions in the group. Rituals, ceremonies, and work routines are examples of customs. Customs are rule systems and thus can be classed as a kind of institution. (See *institutions, law, routines, social position.*)

Definition: Definitions list a minimum number of essential properties of a type of entity, sufficient to demarcate it from other types. (See *essence.*)

Diffusion: Diffusion is a type of replication (or inheritance) that involves the copying of *replicators* but not of *interactors*. Diffusion is common in the social domain, particularly in regard to ideas, rules, and technologies. In these cases, associated habits, customs, or routines are copied from one interactor to another. (See *habits, interactor, replicator, routine, rules.*)

Employment: In an employment contract the worker agrees, within limits, to work under the authority of an employer for a period of time. A distinctive feature of the employment relationship is the *potential* power of employer control over the manner, specification, and pattern of the work performed under all sorts of contingencies. (See *contract, exchange, firm, property.*)

Essence: The essence of a type of entity is the minimal set of properties that members of that type must have to be an object of that kind and thus differentiate one kind of entity from another. Descriptions of an essence may include some but not all properties that are necessary for the existence of an entity of a particular type. (See *definition, natural state model*.)

Essentialism: Essentialism has many ascribed meanings, but it is taken here to mean the (valid) claim that essences are real. (See *definition, essence*.)

Evolution: *Evolution* is a vague word that is used to refer to change in a single entity or change in a population of entities. It has diverse connotations and usages. Except when explicitly noted, no attempt here is made to give it a more specific meaning. (See *population thinking*.)

Exchange: *Exchange* here refers to the process of completion of a contract involving an agreed transfer of goods or services and an assignment of property or other legal rights. An employment contract qualifies as an exchange despite its involving asymmetric authority. Exchanges do not have to be equal or fair to qualify as exchanges. But they do have to be legal and (with some legal exceptions) voluntary. (See *commodity, contract, employment, law, property*.)

Exploitation: *Exploitation* has many possible meanings. The term can be usefully applied to asymmetries between labor power and other factors of production. Some of these asymmetries play a part in the generation of inequalities of income and wealth. Four types of exploitation have been identified in this book:

1. *Bargaining exploitation*. This arises from asymmetries of bargaining power between agents in the sphere of exchange. Bargaining exploitation often exists under capitalism, but strictly it is unnecessary for its existence.

2. *Authority exploitation*. This is another way of referring to the asymmetrical authority relationship found in the employment contract, where the employer has potential power, within limits, over the employee concerning the manner of the work performed.

3. *Corporeal exploitation*. The peculiarity that labor power, unlike other factors of production, is inseparable from its owner was noted by Thomas Green (1888), Alfred Marshall (1920), and John A. Hobson (1929). Corporeal exploitation is present in any mode of production involving labor. The problem is not so much its existence but the relative disadvantage that inseparability bestows on labor compared with the owners of other factors of production.

4. *Exploitation through unequal collateralizability*. This refers to the fact that waged employees cannot use themselves as collateral in obtaining loans. To do this would involve possible enslavement if the loan were not repaid, and this is widely prohibited under capitalism.

The last two forms of exploitation are major generators of further inequalities of income and wealth within capitalism. (See *capital, capitalism, employment*.)

Firm: A firm has two fundamental features: (1) it is set up with resources and capabilities to produce goods of services for sale, and (2), in owning assets, contracting inputs, and selling outputs, it acts as a legal person. As a legal person, the firm has legal ownership of goods or services up to the point that they are delivered to the customer, the legal right to obtain contracted remuneration for the produced services, and the potential liability to be sued for nonfulfillment of contracts with suppliers or customers. By this simpler definition—contrary to Hodgson (2002)—a firm is not necessarily an organization, although it often entails one.

Habits: A habit is a disposition to engage in previously adopted or acquired behavior (including patterns of thought) that is triggered by an appropriate stimulus or context. Habits are influenced by prior activity and have durable, self-sustaining qualities. Although formed through repetition of action or thought, habits themselves are not behaviors. If we acquire a habit, we do not necessarily use it all the time. Habits are the basis of both reflective and nonreflective behaviors. (See *institutions, replicator, rules*.)

Impurity principle: The impurity principle is the proposition that every socioeconomic system must rely on at least one partially integrated and structurally dissimilar subsystem to function.

Information: Information is defined here in the broad and basic (Shannon and Weaver 1949) sense of some conditional dispositions, data, or coding that can be transmitted to other entities and hence cause a response. This omits key features of ideas and knowledge in the human domain, particularly meanings and interpretations. When we consider social evolution, it is vital to bring these into the picture. Because this concept is at a high level of generality, spanning both social and biological evolution, information cannot be defined more narrowly. (See *knowledge*.)

Institutions: *Institution* is a broad term that covers systems of social rules of many different types. Institutions are systems of established and prevalent social rules that structure social interactions. The term *rule* is broadly understood as an injunction or disposition that in circumstances X do Y. A rule can be constitutive or regulative and include norms of behavior and social conventions as well as legal or formal rules. By their nature, institutions must involve some shared conceptions in order to make rules operative. Systems of language, money, law, weights and measures, traffic conventions, table manners, and firms (and all other organizations) are all institutions. All institutions are social structures, but not all social structures are institutions (e.g., demographic or gender structures). *Organizations* are an important subclass of institutions. Their component routines are also rule systems and can thus also be classed as institutions (but not as organizations). (See *organizations, routines, rules, social structure, spontaneous institutions*.)

Interactor: David Hull (1988, 408) defined an interactor as "an entity that directly interacts as a cohesive whole with its environment in such a way that this interaction *causes* replication to be differential." This definition is refined and given more technical detail in Hodgson and Knudsen (2010, 239–40). (See *diffusion, replicator.*)

Knowledge: Our minds receive sense data. Using conceptual frameworks and categories, we selectively interpret these data and provide meaning. Knowledge is meaningful information that has been placed in an interpretative framework and ingrained in habits. It is a tacit or codified rule structure involving triggers to selected stimuli. It constitutes an adaptation to circumstances. Organizational knowledge is a possible emergent property of groups with individual knowledge. It depends on the existence of customs or routines that can trigger behaviors as a result of interactions within the group. (See *habits, information, routines.*)

Law: Definitions of law are controversial, some being so broad as to include any custom. But a number of legal scholars treat it more narrowly as a set of codifiable rules in an institutional system involving courts with arbitrators or judges who hear evidence, decide on responsibility, and assess damages or punishments. These courts are subject to a sovereign political power and its constitutional rules. By contrast, custom involves norms or rules about the ways in which people should behave to sustain nonjudicial social institutions. Laws may derive from customs and depend on them, but they also involve judicial institutions subject to a sovereign power. All laws depend on a state monopoly of organized force. (See *customs, institutions, rules.*)

Legal impermeability: Legal impermeability occurs when the expected costs of using the legal system exceed the expected benefits, where perceived costs and benefits may include nonpecuniary considerations. Legal impermeability does not necessarily imply illegality, but one party to a contract may perceive a breach of the law for which is too costly to seek redress. Instead, there may be a reliance on relational development between the parties to avoid future mishaps in repeated contracting. (See *law.*)

Market: Markets involve multiple exchanges with multiple buyers or multiple sellers and thereby a degree of competition. A market is an institution through which multiple buyers or multiple sellers recurrently exchange rights to a substantial number of similar commodities of a particular type. Exchanges themselves take place in a framework of law and contract enforceability. Markets involve legal and other rules that help to structure, organize, and legitimize exchange transactions. They involve pricing and trading routines that help establish a consensus over prices and often help by communicating information regarding products, prices, quantities, potential buyers, or possible sellers. Markets, in short, are organized and institutionalized recurrent exchange. (See *contract, exchange, institutions, law*.)

Money: Money is a generally accepted means, involving a shared unit of account, of payment for goods, services, or debts. It is not a thing but a set of shared rules and understandings that constitute an owned, socially acknowledged asset that acts as a potential claim on and measure of the value of goods or services. It hence serves as a unit of account and store of value within a sovereign authority. (See *institutions, rules*.)

Natural state model: This Aristotelian idea presumes a distinction between the natural state of a kind of entity and those states that are not natural. The latter are always seen to be produced by subjecting the entity to an interfering force. Hence, variability within nature or society is regarded as a deviation from what is natural. Darwin's ontological assumptions overturned the natural state model by treating variation as inherent to the essence of a type of entity. (See *definition, essence, population thinking*.)

Organizations: An organization is a special type of *institution* involving (*a*) criteria to establish its boundaries and to distinguish its members from its nonmembers, (*b*) principles of sovereignty concerning who is in charge, and (*c*) a structure delineating responsibilities within the organization. These conditions imply the existence of social roles or positions that have properties irreducible to those who occupy them. (See *institutions, social position, social structure*.)

Population thinking: In population thinking, variation is all important. It is a key feature of any species, and it is the evolutionary fuel for natural selection. Consequently, the essence of any species cannot be understood without encompassing that variation. This applies to social as well as biological entities. Population thinking implies a rejection of the *natural state model* but not of *essentialism*.

Possession: *Possession* refers simply to the de facto control of or ability to use an item. It differs from property in that possession may not be legally recognized, and it does not necessarily entail or lead to rights. (See *law, property*.)

Production: Production is the *intentional* creation of a good or service for use or sale by one or more human beings using appropriate knowledge, skills, organization, tools, machines, and materials. Production may or may not serve human needs, and its outputs can be ceremonial or practical.

Property: *Property* refers to a set of rights relating to an asset that are formally acknowledged by a legitimate legal authority. Different types of property right include the right to use a tangible or intangible asset (*usus*), the right to appropriate the returns from the asset (*usus fructus*), the right to change a good in substance or location (*abusus*), the right to the capital derived from the use of the good as collateral, the right to sell a good (and thus transmit other rights), and several other rights or limitations. (See *law, possession*.)

Replicator: Replication is a process whereby replicators are copied under the following conditions:

1. *Causal implication.* The source must be causally involved in the production of the copy, at least in the sense that without the source the particular copy would not be created.

2. *Similarity.* The copy must be like its source in relevant respects.

3. *Information transfer.* During its creation, the copy must obtain the information that makes the copy similar to its source from that same source.

A replicator is a material structure hosted by the entity that is causally involved in the replication process and carries the information in condition (3) above. All replicators are hosted by *interactors*. Replication and inheritance are synonymous. (See *diffusion, interactor*.)

Routines: Routines are organizational dispositions to energize conditional patterns of behavior and interaction within *organizations* and involve rule-bound, sequential responses to cues that are partly dependent on social positions in the organization. The term *routine* is typically applied to business and military organizations, whereas *custom* is a term applied more broadly to other organizations. *Ritual* and *ceremony* apply to specific organizational contexts and functions. Routines are rule systems and thus can be classed as a kind of institution. Routines, customs, rituals, and ceremonies typically qualify as *replicators*. (See *customs, institutions, organizations, replicator, social position*.)

Rules: As a first approximation, we may understand a rule as a learned and mutually understood injunction or disposition that in circumstances X do Y. In turn, "do Y" must be interpreted broadly, to include prohibitions as well as obligations. Rules can be constitutive (where "do Y" is short for "take to mean or be Y") or regulative ("carry out actions Y"). The rules that make up institutions must be more than mere declarations by some authority. They must be rules in actual or potential use in a community and not merely rules in form. Even if the rule is never violated, it must act as a real constraint. Rules must also involve some commitment in the community to follow the rule. Rules are potentially codifiable so that breaches can become subjects of discourse. (See *institutions, routines*.)

Socialism: The term *socialism* originally appeared in the 1830s and originally referred to schemes for the abolition of private property and the replacement of all markets and commodity exchange by some form of comprehensive planning at a national or more local level. Marx promoted the term in this strong sense, with an emphasis on national ownership. It was not until the 1950s that the term widely acquired alternative meanings. Many socialists abandoned the goals of complete common ownership and comprehensive planning and accepted a significant role for markets and private enterprise. The focus instead was shifted to questions of economic equality and social justice. Today, in more moderate versions, "socialism" does not even require the abolition of capitalism. An alternative term today for a reformed capitalism is *social democracy*. (See *capitalism*.)

Social position: A social position is a designated social role within a social structure. A social position is a specified social relationship with other individuals or social positions (such as priest, prime minister, production manager, or sales representative) that might in principle be occupied by alternative individuals. When an individual occupies a social position, he or she brings his or her own qualities or powers and acquires additional qualities, powers, and obligations associated with that position. (See *organizations, social structure*.)

Social structure: A social structure is a set of social relations between interacting individuals in a social system. Although social structures always depend on individuals and would not exist if all individuals ceased to exist, a social structure is more than the sum of the individuals involved because it includes social relations between individuals. Furthermore, social structures may exist and endure separately from each individual *taken severally*. But they cannot be external to human individuals as a whole. All institutions are social structures, but some social structures—such as demographic structures or gender ratios—that are not systems of rules are not institutions (See *institutions*.)

Spontaneous institutions: Spontaneous institutions are here defined as institutions that emerge without the intervention of the state, such as language. Spontaneous institutions may be designed by a nonstate authority or undesigned. (See *institutions*.)

References

Abercrombie, Nicholas, Stephen Hill, and Bryan S. Turner. 2000. *The Penguin Dictionary of Sociology*. 4th ed. London: Penguin.

Abernathy, William J., and K. B. Clark. 1985. "Innovation: Mapping the Winds of Creative Destruction." *Research Policy* 14:3–22.

Abo, Tetsuo. 1994. *Hybrid Factory: The Japanese Production System in the United States*. Oxford: Oxford University Press.

Abolafia, Mitchel Y. 1996. *Making Markets: Opportunism and Restraint on Wall Street*. Cambridge, MA: Harvard University Press.

Acemoglu, Daron, and David H. Autor. 2011. "Skill, Tasks and Technologies: Implications for Employment Earnings." In *The Handbook of Labor Economics* (4 vols. to date), ed. Orley Ashenfelter and David E. Card, 4b:1043–72. Amsterdam: Elsevier.

———. 2012. "What Does Human Capital Do? A Review of Goldin and Katz's *The Race between Education and Technology*." *Journal of Economic Literature* 50, no. 2 (June): 426–63.

Acemoglu, Daron, Davide Cantoni, Simon Johnson, and James A. Robinson. 2011. "The Consequences of Radical Reform: The French Revolution." *American Economic Review* 101, no. 7 (December): 3286–3307.

Acemoglu, Daron, and Simon Johnson. 2005. "Unbundling Institutions." *Journal of Political Economy* 113, no. 5 (October): 949–95.

Acemoglu, Daron, Simon Johnson, and James A. Robinson. 2005a. "Institutions as a Fundamental Cause of Long-Run Growth." In *Handbook of Economic Growth* (1 vol. to date), ed. Philippe Aghion and Steven N. Durlauf, 1A:385–472. Amsterdam: Elsevier.

———. 2005b. "The Rise of Europe: Atlantic Trade, Institutional Change and Economic Growth." *American Economic Review* 95, no. 3 (June): 546–79.

Acemoglu, Daron, and James A. Robinson. 2000. "Why Did the West Extend the Franchise? Democracy, Inequality and Growth in Historical Perspective." *Quarterly Journal of Economics* 115, no. 4:1167–99.

――――. 2012. *Why Nations Fail: The Origins of Power, Prosperity, and Poverty.* New York: Random House; London: Profile.

Ackerman, Bruce, and Anne Alstott. 1999. *The Stakeholder Society.* New Haven, CT: Yale University Press.

Adaman, Fikret, and Patrick Devine. 1994. "Socialist Renewal: Lessons from the 'Calculation Debate.'" *Studies in Political Economy*, no. 43 (Spring): 63–77.

――――. 1996. "The Economic Calculation Debate: Lessons for Socialists." *Cambridge Journal of Economics* 20, no. 5 (September): 523–37.

――――. 1997. "On the Economic Theory of Socialism." *New Left Review*, no. 221 (January–February): 54–80.

――――. 2001. "Participatory Planning as a Deliberative Democratic Process: A Response to Hodgson's Critique." *Economy and Society* 30, no. 2 (May): 229–39.

――――. 2002. "A Reconsideration of the Theory of Entrepreneurship: A Participatory Approach." *Review of Political Economy* 14, no. 3 (July): 329–55.

Adami, Christoph. 2002. "What Is Complexity?" *BioEssays* 24, no. 12:1085–94.

Adami, Christoph, Charles Ofria, and Travis C. Collier. 2000. "Evolution of Biological Complexity." *Proceedings of the National Academy of Sciences* 97, no. 9:4463–68.

Address to the Proprietors of India Stock, on the Late Transactions at the East India College at Haileybury, in Hertfordshire. 1823. London: Sherwood, Jones.

Adler, Paul S., and Seok-Woo Kwon. 2002. "Social Capital: Prospects for a New Concept." *Academy of Management Review* 27:17–40.

Admati, Anat, and Martin Hellwig. 2013. *The Bankers' New Clothes: What's Wrong with Banking and What to Do about It.* Princeton, NJ: Princeton University Press.

Aglietta, Michel, and André Orléan. 1998. *La monnaie souveraine.* Paris: Odile Jacob.

Agrast, Mark D., Juan C. Botero, Joel Martinez, and Christine S. Pratt. 2013. *World Justice Project Rule of Law Index, 2012–2013.* Washington, DC: World Justice Project. Downloadable with data set from http://worldjusticeproject.org/rule-of-law-index.

Ahmad, Syed. 1991. *Capital in Economic Theory: Neo-Classical, Cambridge and Chaos.* Aldershot: Edward Elgar.

Aidt, Toke S. 2003. "Economic Analysis of Corruption: A Survey." *Economic Journal* 113, no. 8 (November): F632–F652.

Akerlof, George A. 1991. "Procrastination and Obedience." *American Economic Review: Papers and Proceedings* 81, no. 2 (May): 1–19.

Akerlof, George A., and Janet L. Yellen, eds. 1986. *Efficiency Wage Models of the Labor Market.* Cambridge: Cambridge University Press.

Albert, Michael. 2003. *Parecon: Life After Capitalism*. London: Verso.

———. 2004. "Market Madness." *Znet*, http://zcomm.org/znetarticle/market
-madness-by-michael-albert-1.

Albert, Michael, and Robert Hahnel. 1978. *Unorthodox Marxism: An Essay on
Capitalism, Socialism and Revolution*. Boston: South End.

Albert, Michel. 1993. *Capitalism against Capitalism*. Translated from the 1991
French ed. by Paul Haviland. London: Whurr.

Alchian, Armen A. 1965. "Some Economics of Property Rights." *Il politico*
30:816–29. Reprinted in Armen A. Alchian, *Economic Forces at Work* (Indianapolis: Liberty Press, 1977), 127–49.

———. 1977. "Some Implications of Recognition of Property Right Transaction Costs." In *Economics and Social Institutions: Insights from the Confer-
ences on Analysis and Ideology*, ed. Karl Brunner, 234–55. Boston: Martinus
Nijhoff.

Alchian, Armen A., and Harold Demsetz. 1972. "Production, Information
Costs, and Economic Organization." *American Economic Review* 62, no. 4
(December): 777–95.

Aldrich, Howard E., Geoffrey M. Hodgson, David L. Hull, Thorbjørn Knudsen,
Joel Mokyr, and Viktor J. Vanberg. 2008. "In Defence of Generalized Darwinism." *Journal of Evolutionary Economics* 18, no. 5 (October): 577–96.

Alesina, Alberto, Reza Baquir, and William Easterly. 1999. "Public Goods and
Ethnic Divisions." *Quarterly Journal of Economics* 114, no. 4 (November):
1243–84.

Allen, Douglas W. 1991. "What Are Transaction Costs?" *Research in Law and
Economics* 14:1–18.

———. 2012. *The Institutional Revolution: Measurement and the Economic
Emergence of the Modern World*. Chicago: University of Chicago Press.

———. 2014. "The Coase Theorem: Coherent, Logical, and Not Dis-
proved." *Journal of Institutional Economics*, February 28. DOI: 10.1017/
S1744137414000083.

Althusser, Louis. 1969. *For Marx*. Translated from the 1965 French ed. by Ben
Brewster. London: Allen Lane.

Amable, Bruno. 2000. "Institutional Complementarity and Diversity of Social
Systems of Innovation and Production." *Review of International Political
Economy* 7, no. 4 (Winter): 645–87.

———. 2003. *The Diversity of Modern Capitalism*. Oxford: Oxford University
Press.

Amable, Bruno, and Stefano Palombarini. 2009. "A Neorealist Approach to Institutional Change and the Diversity of Capitalism." *Socio-Economic Review*
7, no. 1 (January): 123–43.

Amsden, Alice H. 1989. *Asia's Next Giant: South Korea and Late Industrialization*. Oxford: Oxford University Press.

Anderson, Elizabeth. 1993. *Value in Ethics and Economics.* Cambridge, MA: Harvard University Press.

Andreoni, James. 1995. "Cooperation in Public Goods Experiments: Kindness or Confusion?" *American Economic Review* 85, no. 4 (December): 891–904.

Aoki, Masahiko. 2001. *Toward a Comparative Institutional Analysis.* Cambridge, MA: MIT Press.

———. 2010. *Corporations in Evolving Diversity: Cognition, Governance, and Institutions.* Oxford: Oxford University Press.

Archer, Margaret S. 1995. *Realist Social Theory: The Morphogenetic Approach.* Cambridge: Cambridge University Press.

Aristotle. 1956. *Metaphysics.* Edited and translated by John Warrington, with an introduction by W. David Ross. London: Dent.

Armour, John, Simon Deakin, Prabirjit Sarkar, Mathias Siems, and Ajit Singh. 2009. "Shareholder Protection and Stock Market Development: An Empirical Test of the Legal Origins Hypothesis." *Journal of Empirical Legal Studies* 6, no. 2:343–80.

Arner, Douglas W., Charles D. Booth, Paul Lejot, and Berry Fong Chung Hsu. 2007. "Property Rights, Collateral, Creditor Rights, and Insolvency in East Asia." *Texas International Law Journal* 42 (August): 515–59.

Arrow, Kenneth J. 1962a. "The Economic Implications of Learning by Doing." *Review of Economic Studies* 29, no. 2 (June): 155–73.

———. 1962b. "Economic Welfare and the Allocation of Resources to Invention." In *The Rate and Direction of Inventive Activity: Economic and Social Factors,* ed. Richard R. Nelson, 609–25. Princeton, NJ: Princeton University Press.

———. 1994. "Methodological Individualism and Social Knowledge." *American Economic Review: Papers and Proceedings* 84, no. 2 (May): 1–9.

———. 1996. "Technical Information and Industrial Structure." *Industrial and Corporate Change* 5, no. 2:645–52.

———. 1997. "Invaluable Goods." *Journal of Economic Literature* 35, no. 2 (June): 757–65.

———. 1999. "Observations on Social Capital." In *Social Capital: A Multifaceted Perspective,* ed. Partha Dasgupta and Ismail Serageldin, 3–5. Washington, DC: World Bank.

Arrow, Kenneth J., and Gerard Debreu. 1954. "Existence of an Equilibrium for a Competitive Economy." *Econometrica* 22, no. 3:265–90.

Arruñada, Benito. 2012. *Institutional Foundations of Impersonal Exchange: Theory and Policy of Contractual Registries.* Chicago: University of Chicago Press.

Arthur, W. Brian. 2006. "Out-of-Equilibrium Economics and Agent-Based Modeling." In *Handbook of Computational Economics,* vol. 2, *Agent-Based Computational Economics,* ed. Kenneth L. Judd, Leigh Tesfatsion, Michael D. Intriligator, and Kenneth J. Arrow, 1551–64. Amsterdam: North-Holland.

Ashby, W. Ross. 1952. *Design for a Brain*. New York: Wiley.

———. 1956. *An Introduction to Cybernetics*. New York: Wiley.

Ashton, David, and Francis Green. 1996. *Education, Training and the Global Economy*. Cheltenham: Edward Elgar.

Assiter, Alison. 1996. *Enlightened Women: Modernist Feminism in a Postmodern Age*. London: Routledge.

Attewell, Paul. 1992. "Skill and Occupational Changes in U.S. Manufacturing." In *Technology and the Future of Work*, ed. Paul Adler, 46–88. Oxford: Oxford University Press.

Auer, Raphael Anton. 2010. "Are Imports from Rich Nations Deskilling Emerging Economies? Human Capital and the Dynamic Effects of Trade." Working Paper no. 2010-18. Zurich: Swiss National Bank.

Aviram, Amitai. 2004. "A Paradox of Spontaneous Formation: The Evolution of Private Legal Systems." *Yale Law and Policy Review* 22, no. 1:1–68.

Ayres, Clarence E. 1921. "Instinct and Capacity I: The Instinct of Belief-in-Instincts." *Journal of Philosophy* 18, no. 21 (October 13): 561–65.

———. 1958. "Veblen's Theory of Instincts Reconsidered." In *Thorstein Veblen: A Critical Appraisal*, ed. Douglas F. Dowd, 25–37. Ithaca, NY: Cornell University Press.

Azzi, Corry, and Ronald Ehrenberg. 1975. "Household Allocation of Time and Church Attendance." *Journal of Political Economy* 38, no. 1 (February): 27–56.

Badr, Gamal Moursi. 1978. "Islamic Law: Its Relation to Other Legal Systems." *American Society of Comparative Law* 26, no. 2 (February): 187–98.

Baechler, Jean. 1975. *The Origins of Capitalism*. Translated from the 1971 French ed. by Barry Cooper. Oxford: Basil Blackwell.

Bagehot, Walter. 1873/1919. *Lombard Street: A Description of the Money Market*. London: Murray.

Baguñà, Jaume, and Jordi Garcia-Fernàndez. 2003. "Evo-Devo: The Long and Winding Road." *International Journal of Developmental Biology* 47:705–13.

Baker, J. H. 1979. "The Law Merchant and the Common Law Before 1700." *Cambridge Law Journal* 38, no. 2 (November): 295–322.

Baker, Wayne E. 1984. "The Social Structure of a National Securities Market." *American Journal of Sociology* 89, no. 4:775–811.

———. 1990. "Market Networks and Corporate Behavior." *American Journal of Sociology* 93, no. 3:589–625.

Baldwin, Carliss Y., and Kim B. Clark. 2000. *Design Rules*. Vol. 1, *The Power of Modularity*. Cambridge, MA: MIT Press.

Baldwin, Robert E. 1969. "The Case against Infant-Industry Tariff Protection." *Journal of Political Economy* 77, no. 3 (May–June): 295–305.

Balibar, Étienne. 1994. *Masses, Classes, Ideas: Studies on Politics and Philosophy Before and After Marx*. New York: Routledge.

Bandelj, Nina, and Matthew C. Mahutga. 2010. How Socio-Economic Change Shapes Income Inequality in Post-Socialist Europe." *Social Forces* 88, no. 5: 2133–62.

Banerjee, Abhijit, and Lakshmi Iyer. 2005. "History, Institutions, and Economic Performance: The Legacy of Colonial Land Tenure Systems in India." *American Economic Review* 95, no. 4 (September): 1190–1213.

Bang, Peter Fibiger. 2008. *The Roman Bazaar: A Comparative Study of Trade and Markets in a Tributary Empire.* Cambridge: Cambridge University Press.

Bardhan, Pranab K. 2005. "Institutions Matter, but Which Ones?" *Economics of Transition* 13, no. 3:499–532.

Baron, James N., and Michael T. Hannan. 1994. "The Impact of Economics on Contemporary Sociology." *Journal of Economic Literature* 32, no. 3 (September): 1111–46.

Baron, Stephen, John Field, and Tom Schuller, eds. 2000. *Social Capital: Critical Perspectives.* Oxford: Oxford University Press.

Barro, Robert J. 1997. *Determinants of Economic Growth: A Cross-Country Empirical Study.* Cambridge, MA: MIT Press.

———. 2000. "Inequality and Growth in a Panel of Countries." *Journal of Economic Growth* 7, no. 1 (March): 5–32.

Barro, Robert J., and Xavier Sala-i-Martin. 1992. "Convergence." *Journal of Political Economy* 100, no. 2 (April): 223–51.

———. 2003. *Economic Growth.* 2nd ed. New York: McGraw-Hill.

Barthes, Roland. 1972. *Mythologies.* Translated from the 1957 French ed. New York: Hill & Wang.

Bar-Yosef, Ofer. 1998. "The Natufian Culture in the Levant: Threshold to the Origins of Agriculture." *Evolutionary Anthropology* 6, no. 5:159–77.

———. 2001. "From Sedentary Foragers to Village Hierarchies: The Emergence of Social Institutions." In *The Origin of Human Social Institutions,* ed. Walter Garry Runciman, 1–38. Oxford: Oxford University Press.

Barzel, Yoram. 1994. "The Capture of Wealth by Monopolists and the Protection of Property Rights." *International Review of Law and Economics* 14, no. 4:393–409.

———. 1997. *Economic Analysis of Property Rights.* 2nd ed. Cambridge: Cambridge University Press.

Basalla, George. 1989. *The Evolution of Technology.* Cambridge: Cambridge University Press.

Batt, Francis Raleigh. 1929. *The Law of Master and Servant.* New York: Pitman.

Baum, Matthew A., and David A. Lake. 2003. "The Political Economy of Growth: Democracy and Human Capital." *American Journal of Political Science* 42, no. 2 (April): 333–47.

Bechara, Antoine, and Antonio R. Damasio. 2005. "The Somatic Marker Hypothesis: A Neural Theory of Economic Decision." *Games and Economic Behavior* 52, no. 2:336–72.

Beck, Anthony. 1994. "Is Law an Autopoietic System?" *Oxford Journal of Legal Studies* 14, no. 3:401–18.

Becker, Gary S. 1964. *Human Capital: A Theoretical Analysis with Special Reference to Education.* New York: Columbia University Press.

———. 1991. *A Treatise on the Family.* 2nd ed. Cambridge, MA: Harvard University Press.

———. 1996. *Accounting for Tastes.* Cambridge, MA: Harvard University Press.

Becker, Gary S., and Kevin M. Murphy. 1988. "A Theory of Rational Addiction." *Journal of Political Economy* 96, no. 4:675–700.

Becker, Markus C. 2001. "Managing Dispersed Knowledge: Organizational Problems, Managerial Strategies, and Their Effectiveness." *Journal of Management Studies* 38, no. 7 (November): 1037–51.

Beer, Max. 1940. *A History of British Socialism.* 2 vols. London: Allen & Unwin.

Beer, Stafford. 1972. *Brain of the Firm.* London: Allen Lane.

Beinhocker, Eric D. 2006. *The Origins of Wealth: Evolution, Complexity, and the Radical Remaking of Economics.* New York: Random House.

———. 2011. "Evolution as Computation: Integrating Self-Organization with Generalized Darwinism." *Journal of Institutional Economics* 7, no. 3 (September): 393–423.

Bell, Stephanie A. 2001. "The Role of the State and the Hierarchy of Money." *Cambridge Journal of Economics* 25, no. 2 (March): 149–63.

Bellemare, Marc F. 2013. "The Productivity Impacts of Formal and Informal Land Rights: Evidence from Madagascar." *Land Economics* 89, no. 2:272–90.

Belloc, Marianna, and Ugo Pagano. 2009. "Co-Evolution of Politics and Corporate Governance." *International Review of Law and Economics* 29, no. 2 (December): 106–14.

———. 2013. "Politics-Business Co-Evolution Paths: Workers' Organization and Capitalist Concentration." *International Review of Law and Economics* 33, no. 1 (March): 23–66.

Belnap, Nuel D. 1993. "On Rigorous Definitions." *Philosophical Studies* 72, nos. 2/3 (December): 115–46.

Ben-Ner, Avner, and Louis Putterman. 2000. "Some Implications of Evolutionary Psychology for the Study of Preferences and Institutions." *Journal of Economic Behavior and Organization* 43, no. 1 (September): 91–99.

Benson, Bruce L. 1989. "Enforcement of Property Rights in Primitive Societies: Law without Government." *Journal of Libertarian Studies* 9 (Winter): 1–22.

Berger, Suzanne, and Ronald Dore, eds. 1996. *National Diversity and Global Capitalism.* Ithaca, NY: Cornell University Press.

Berle, Adolf A., and Gardiner C. Means. 1932. *The Modern Corporation and Private Property.* New York: Commerce Clearing House.

Berman, Harold J. 1983. *Law and Revolution: The Formation of the Western Legal Tradition*. Cambridge, MA: Harvard University Press.

———. 2003. *Law and Revolution II: The Impact of the Protestant Reformations on the Western Legal Tradition*. Cambridge, MA: Harvard University Press.

Bernstein, Lisa. 1992. "Opting Out of the Legal System: Extralegal Contractual Relations in the Diamond Industry." *Journal of Legal Studies* 21, no. 1:115–57.

———. 2001. "Private Commercial Law in the Cotton Industry: Creating Cooperation through Rules, Norms, and Institutions." *Michigan Law Review* 99:1724–88.

Bestor, Arthur E., Jr. 1948. "The Evolution of the Socialist Vocabulary." *Journal of the History of Ideas* 9, no. 3 (June): 259–302.

Beutel, Frederick K. 1938. "The Development of Negotiable Instruments in Early English Law." *Harvard Law Review* 51, no. 5:813–45.

———. 1940. "The Development of State Statutes on Negotiable Paper Prior to the Negotiable Instruments Law." *Columbia Law Review* 40:836–65.

Bhaskar, Roy. 1975. *A Realist Theory of Science*. Leeds: Leeds Books.

Bhaskar, Roy, and Andrew Collier. 1998. "Introduction: Explanatory Critiques." In *Critical Realism: Essential Readings*, ed. Margaret S. Archer, Roy Bhaskar, Andrew Collier, Tony Lawson, and Alan Norrie, 385–94. London: Routledge.

Birchall, Johnston. 2011. *People-Centred Businesses: Co-Operatives, Mutuals and the Idea of Membership*. London: Palgrave Macmillan.

Black, Max. 1962. *Models and Metaphors: Studies in Language and Philosophy*. Ithaca, NY: Cornell University Press.

Blackstone, William. 1765–69. *Commentaries on the Laws of England*. 4 vols. Oxford: Clarendon.

Blair, Margaret M. 1995. *Ownership and Control: Rethinking Corporate Governance for the Twenty-First Century*. Washington, DC: Brookings Institution.

———. 1999. "Firm-Specific Human Capital and Theories of the Firm." In *Employees and Corporate Governance*, ed. Margaret M. Blair and Mark Roe, 58–89. Washington, DC: Brookings Institution.

———. 2003. "Locking in Capital: What Corporate Law Achieved for Business Organizers in the Nineteenth Century." *UCLA Law Review* 51, no. 2:387–455.

Blair, Margaret M., and L. A. Stout. 1999. "A Team Production Theory of Corporate Law." *Journal of Corporation Law* 24, no. 4:751–806.

Blake, Peter R., and Paul L. Harris. 2009. "Children's Understanding of Ownership Transfers." *Cognitive Development* 24, no. 2 (April): 133–45.

Blanc, Louis. 1849. "The New World." *Monthly Review: The New World of Politics, Arts, Literature, and Sciences*, no. 1 (July): 5–172.

———. 1850. *Organisation du travail*. 9th ed. Paris: Sociétée de l'industrie fraternelle.

Blanton, Richard E., and Lane F. Fargher. 2008. *Collective Action in the Formation of Pre-Modern States*. New York: Springer.

Blass, Thomas. 1991. "Understanding Behavior in the Milgram Obedience Experiment: The Role of Personality, Situations, and Their Interactions." *Journal of Personality and Social Psychology* 60, no. 3 (March): 398–413.

Blau, Peter. 1964. *Exchange and Power in Social Life*. New York: Wiley.

Blaug, Mark. 1976. "The Empirical Status of Human Capital Theory: A Slightly Jaundiced Survey." *Journal of Economic Literature* 14, no. 3 (September): 827–55.

———. 1993. Review of *From Marx to Mises*, by D. R. Steele. *Economic Journal* 103, no. 6 (November): 1570–71.

———. 1997. "Ugly Currents in Modern Economics." *Options politiques* 18, no. 17 (September): 3–8. Extended and revised in *Fact and Fiction in Economics: Models, Realism and Social Construction*, ed. Uskali Mäki (Cambridge: Cambridge University Press, 2002), 35–56.

———. 1998. "Disturbing Currents in Modern Economics." *Challenge* 41, no. 3 (May–June): 11–24.

Block, Walter. 1996. "Hayek's Road to Serfdom." *Journal of Libertarian Studies* 12, no. 2 (Fall): 339–65.

Blomstrom, Magnus, Richard E. Lipsey, and Mario Zejan. 1996. "Is Fixed Investment the Key to Economic Growth?" *Quarterly Journal of Economics* 111, no. 1 (February): 269–76.

Blumer, Herbert. 1969. *Symbolic Interactionism: Perspective and Method*. Chicago: University of Chicago Press.

Boehm, Christopher. 1999. *Hierarchy in the Forest: The Evolution of Egalitarian Behavior*. Cambridge, MA: Harvard University Press.

———. 2000. "The Origin of Morality as Social Control." *Journal of Consciousness Studies* 7, nos. 1–2:149–83.

Bogart, Dan, and Gary Richardson. 2011. "Property Rights and Parliament in Industrializing Britain." *Journal of Law and Economics* 54, no. 2 (May): 241–74.

Bogdan, Radu. 2000. *Minding Minds: Evolving a Reflexive Mind in Interpreting Others*. Cambridge, MA: MIT Press.

Bohannan, Paul. 1965. "The Differing Realms of the Law: Pt. 2, The Ethnography of Law." *American Anthropologist*, n.s., 67, no. 6 (December): 33–42.

Böhm, Franz. 1980. *Freiheit und Ordnung in der Marktwirtschaft*. Edited by E.-J. Mestmäcker. Baden Baden: Nomos.

Boisard, Marcel A. 1980. "On the Probable Influence of Islam on Western Public and International Law." *International Journal of Middle East Studies* 11, no. 4 (July): 429–50.

Boisot, Max H. 1995. *Information Space: A Framework for Learning in Organizations, Institutions and Culture*. London: Routledge.

Boisot, Max H., and John Child. 1996. "From Fiefs to Clans and Network Capitalism: China's Emerging Economic Order." *Administrative Science Quarterly* 41, no. 4:600–628.

Bonin, John P., Derek C. Jones, and Louis Putterman. 1993. "Theoretical and Empirical Studies of Producer Cooperatives: Will Ever the Twain Meet?" *Journal of Economic Literature* 31, no. 3 (September): 1290–1320.

Bonnett, Alastair. 2007. "The Other Rights of Man: The Revolutionary Plan of Thomas Spence." *History Today* 57, no. 9:42–48.

Bordo, Michael D., Alan M. Taylor, and Jeffrey G. Williamson, eds. 2003. *Globalization in Historical Perspective*. Chicago: University of Chicago Press.

Borzaga, Carlo, and Jacques Defourny, eds. 2001. *The Emergence of Social Enterprise*. London: Routledge.

Boulding, Kenneth E. 1959. "National Images and International Systems." *Journal of Conflict Resolution* 3, no. 2 (June): 120–31.

———. 1966. "The Economics of Knowledge and the Knowledge of Economics." *American Economic Review: Papers and Proceedings* 56, no. 1 (March): 1–13.

Bourdieu, Pierre. 1977. *Outline of a Theory of Practice*. Translated by Richard Nice. Cambridge: Cambridge University Press.

———. 1986. "The Forms of Capital." In *Handbook of Theory and Research for the Sociology of Education*, ed. John G. Richardson, 241–58. New York: Greenwood.

———. 1988. *Homo Academicus*. Stanford, CA: Stanford University Press.

———. 1990. *The Logic of Practice*. Translated from the 1980 French ed. by Richard Nice. Stanford, CA: Stanford University Press; Cambridge: Polity.

Bowen, Huw V. 1995. "The Bank of England during the Long Eighteenth Century: 1694–1815." In *The Bank of England*, ed. Richard Roberts and David Kynaston, 1–18. Oxford: Oxford University Press.

Bowles, Samuel. 1999. "'Social Capital' and Community Governance." *Focus: Newsletter for the Institute for Research on Poverty* 20, no. 3:6–10.

———. 2009. "Did Warfare among Ancestral Hunter-Gatherer Groups Affect the Evolution of Human Social Behaviors?" *Science* 324, no. 5932:1293–98.

Bowles, Samuel, and Herbert Gintis. 1999. *Recasting Egalitarianism: New Rules for Markets, States, and Communities*. London: Verso.

———. 2002. "The Inheritance of Inequality." *Journal of Economic Perspectives* 16, no. 3 (Summer): 3–30.

———. 2011. *A Cooperative Species: Human Reciprocity and Its Evolution*. Princeton, NJ: Princeton University Press.

Boyd, Robert, Herbert Gintis, Samuel Bowles, and Peter J. Richerson. 2003. "Evolution of Altruistic Punishment." *Proceedings of the National Academy of Sciences* 100, no. 6 (March): 3531–35.

Boyd, Robert, and Peter J. Richerson. 1980. "Sociobiology, Culture and Economic Theory." *Journal of Economic Behavior and Organization* 1, no. 1 (March): 97–121.

———. 1985. *Culture and the Evolutionary Process.* Chicago: University of Chicago Press.

———. 1992. "Punishment Allows the Evolution of Cooperation (or Anything Else) in Sizable Groups." *Ethology and Sociobiology* 13:171–95.

Boyer, Robert. 1999. "The Variety and Dynamics of Capitalism." In *Institutions and the Evolution of Capitalism: Implications of Evolutionary Economics,* ed. John Groenewegen and Jack J. Vromen, 122–40. Cheltenham: Edward Elgar.

———. 2005a. "Coherence, Diversity, and the Evolution of Capitalisms—the Institutional Complementarity Hypothesis." *Evolutionary and Institutional Economics Review* 2, no. 1 (October): 43–80.

———. 2005b. "How and Why Capitalisms Differ." *Economy and Society* 34, no. 4:509–57.

Boyer, Robert, and Daniel Drache, eds. 1996. *States against Markets: The Limits of Globalization.* London: Routledge.

Boyreau-Debray, Genevieve, and Shang-Jin Wei. 2005. "Pitfalls of a State-Dominated Financial System: The Case of China." Working Paper no. 11214. Cambridge, MA: National Bureau of Economic Research.

Bradley, Joseph P. 1884/1902. "Lecture on 'Law, Nature and Office: Bond and Basis of Civil Society.'" In *Miscellaneous Writings of the Late Hon. Joseph P. Bradley,* 224–66. Newark, NJ: Hardham.

Braudel, Fernand. 1982. *Civilization and Capitalism, 15th–18th Century.* Vol. 2, *The Wheels of Commerce.* London: Collins.

———. 1984. *Civilization and Capitalism, 15th–18th Century.* Vol. 3, *The Perspective of the World.* London: Collins.

Braverman, Harry. 1974. *Labor and Monopoly Capital: The Degradation of Work in the Twentieth Century.* New York: Monthly Review Press.

Bremmer, Ian. 2010. *The End of the Free Market: Who Wins the War between States and Corporations?* New York: Portfolio.

Brito, Jerry, and Andrea Castillo. 2013. *Bitcoin: A Primer for Policymakers.* Fairfax, VA: Mercatus Center, George Mason University.

Brown, John Seely, and Paul Duguid. 1991. "Organizational Learning and Communities of Practice: Toward a Unified View of Working, Learning and Innovation." *Organizational Science* 2, no. 1:40–57.

Brown, W. Jethro. 1905. "The Personality of the Corporation and the State." *Law Quarterly Review* 21:365–79. Reprinted in *Journal of Institutional Economics* 4, no. 2 (August 2008): 255–73.

Brown, William, Simon Deakin, David Nash, and Sarah Oxenbridge. 2000. "The Employment Contract: From Collective Procedures to Individual Rights." *British Journal of Industrial Relations* 38, no. 4 (December): 611–29.

Brynjolfsson, Erik, and Andrew McAfee. 2012. *Race against the Machine: How the Digital Revolution Is Accelerating Innovation, Driving Productivity, and Irreversibly Transforming Employment and the Economy*. Lexington, MA: Digital Frontier.

Buenstorf, Guido. 2004. *The Economics of Energy and the Production Process: An Evolutionary Approach*. Cheltenham: Edward Elgar.

———. 2009. "Is Commercialization Good or Bad for Science? Individual-Level Evidence from the Max Planck Society." *Research Policy* 38:281–92.

Buiter, Willem H. 2009. "The Unfortunate Uselessness of Most 'State of the Art' Academic Monetary Economics." *Financial Times*, March 3. http://blogs.ft.com/maverecon/2009/03/the-unfortunate-uselessness-of-most-state-of-the-art-academic-monetary-economics.

Buiter, Willem H., and Ebrahim Rahbari. 2011. "Global Growth Generators: Moving beyond 'Emerging Markets' and 'BRIC.'" *Citigroup Global Economics View*, February 21. http://www.willembuiter.com/Citi20.pdf.

Bukovansky, Mlada. 2006. "The Hollowness of Anti-Corruption Discourse." *Review of International Political Economy* 13, no. 2 (May): 181–209.

Burczak, Theodore. 2006. *Socialism After Hayek*. Ann Arbor: University of Michigan Press.

Burr, Vivien. 1995. *An Introduction to Social Constructivism*. London: Routledge.

Burt, Ronald S. 1992. *Structural Holes: The Social Structure of Competition*. Cambridge, MA: Harvard University Press.

Bush, Winston C., and Lawrence S. Mayer. 1974. "Some Implications of Anarchy for the Distribution of Property." *Journal of Economic Theory* 8, no. 4:401–12.

Butkiewicz, James L., and Halit Yanikkaya. 2006. "Institutional Quality and Economic Growth: Maintenance of the Rule of Law of Democratic Institutions, or Both?" *Economic Modelling* 23, no. 4 (July): 648–61.

Button, Graham, ed. 1993. *Technology in Working Order: Studies of Work, Interaction and Technology*. London: Routledge.

Byock, Jesse L. 1988. *Medieval Iceland: Society, Sagas, and Power*. Berkeley and Los Angeles: University of California Press.

Camic, Charles, and Geoffrey M. Hodgson, eds. 2011. *Essential Writings of Thorstein Veblen*. London: Routledge.

Campbell, Donald T. 1994. "How Individual and Face-to-Face Group Selection Undermine Firm Selection in Organizational Evolution." In *Evolutionary Dynamics of Organizations*, ed. Joel A. C. Baum and Jitendra V. Singh, 23–38. New York: Oxford University Press.

Cannan, Edwin. 1921. "Early History of the Term Capital." *Quarterly Journal of Economics* 35, no. 3 (May): 469–81.

Carneiro, Robert L. 1970. "A Theory of the Origin of the State." *Science* 169:733–38.

Carpenter, Jeffrey P., and Peter Hans Matthews. 2009. "What Norms Trigger Punishment?" *Experimental Economics* 12, no. 3 (September): 272–88.

Carpenter, Jeffrey P., Peter Hans Matthews, and Okomboli Ong'ong'a. 2004. "Why Punish? Social Reciprocity and the Enforcement of Prosocial Norms." *Journal of Evolutionary Economics* 14, no. 4 (October): 407–29.

Carter, James Coolidge. 1907. *Law: Its Origin, Growth and Function.* New York: Putnam's.

Carter, Richard, and Geoffrey M. Hodgson. 2006. "The Impact of Empirical Tests of Transaction Cost Economics on the Debate on the Nature of the Firm." *Strategic Management Journal* 27, no. 5 (May): 461–76.

Cassady, Ralph. 1967. *Auctions and Auctioneering.* Berkeley: University of California Press.

Casson, Mark C., ed. 2011. *Markets and Market Institutions: Their Origin and Evolution.* Cheltenham: Edward Elgar.

Casson, Mark C., and John S. Lee. 2011. "The Origin and Development of Markets: A Business History Perspective." *Business History Review* 85, no. 1 (Spring): 9–37.

Castelfranchi, Cristiano, Rino Falcone, and Francesca Marzo. 2006. "Being Trusted in a Social Network: Trust as Relational Capital." *Lecture Notes in Computer Science* 3986:19–32.

Cattan, Henry. 1955. "The Law of Waqf." In *Law in the Middle East,* vol. 1, *Origin and Development of Islamic Law,* ed. Majid Khadduri and Herbert J. Liebesny, 203–20. Washington, DC: Middle East Institute.

C-EM. 2011. "Why Occupy Wall Street?" http://www.c-em.com/?p=1712 (now defunct; see instead http://www.salem-news.com/articles/october122011/why _occupy_ws_dj.php).

Chamberlain, Neil W. 1951. *Collective Bargaining.* New York: McGraw-Hill.

Chamberlin, Edward H. 1933. *The Theory of Monopolistic Competition: A Re-Orientation of the Theory of Value.* Cambridge, MA: Harvard University Press.

Chandler, Alfred D., Jr. 1962. *Strategy and Structure: Chapters in the History of the Industrial Enterprise.* New York: Doubleday.

———. 1977. *The Visible Hand: The Managerial Revolution in American Business.* Cambridge, MA: Harvard University Press.

Chang, Ha-Joon. 1997. "The Economics and Politics of Regulation: A Critical Survey." *Cambridge Journal of Economics* 21, no. 6 (November): 703–28.

———. 2002a. "Breaking the Mould: An Institutionalist Political Economy Alternative to the Neo-Liberal Theory of the Market and the State." *Cambridge Journal of Economics* 26, no. 5 (September): 539–59.

———. 2002b. *Kicking Away the Ladder: Development Strategy in Historical Perspective*. London: Anthem.

———. 2010. "We Lost Sight of Fairness in the False Promise of Wealth." *Guardian*, August 30. http://www.theguardian.com/commentisfree/2010/aug/30/fairness-inequality-free-market-growth.

Chang, Ha-Joon, and Robert E. Rowthorn, eds. 1995. *The Role of the State in Economic Change*. Oxford: Clarendon.

Chao, Kang. 1986. *Man and Land in Chinese History: An Economic Analysis*. Stanford, CA: Stanford University Press.

Chenery, Hollis B. 1949. "Engineering Production Functions." *Quarterly Journal of Economics* 63:507–31.

Cheung, Steven N. S. 1983. "The Contractual Nature of the Firm." *Journal of Law and Economics* 26, no. 2 (April): 1–21.

Choo, Chun Wei. 1998. *The Knowing Organization: How Organizations Use Information*. Oxford: Oxford University Press.

Christ, Carl F. 1975. "The Competitive Market and Optimal Allocative Efficiency." In *Competing Philosophies in American Political Economics*, ed. John Elliott and John Cownie, 332–38. Pacific Palisades, CA: Goodyear.

Ciepley, David. 2004. "Authority in the Firm (and the Attempt to Theorize It Away)." *Critical Review* 16, no. 1:81–115.

Cipolla, Carlo M. 1965. *Guns, Sails and Empires: Technological Innovation and the Early Phases of European Expansion, 1400–1700*. New York: Pantheon.

Clark, Andy. 1997a. *Being There: Putting the Brain, Body and World Together Again*. Cambridge, MA: MIT Press.

———. 1997b. "Economic Reason: The Interplay of Individual Learning and External Structure." In *The Frontiers of the New Institutional Economics*, ed. John N. Drobak and John V. C. Nye, 269–90. San Diego, CA: Academic.

Clark, John Bates. 1888. "Capital and Its Earnings." *Publications of the American Economic Association* 3, no. 2 (May): 9–69.

Clark, John Maurice. 1923. *Studies in the Economics of Overhead Costs*. Chicago: University of Chicago Press.

———. 1925. "Problems of Economic Theory—Discussion." *American Economic Review: Papers and Proceedings* 15, no. 1, suppl. (March): 56–58.

———. 1957. *Economic Institutions and Human Welfare*. New York: Knopf.

Clark, Gregory. 2007. *A Farewell to Alms: A Brief Economic History of the World*. Princeton, NJ: Princeton University Press.

Clark, Norman G. 1991. "Organization and Information in the Evolution of Economic Systems." In *Evolutionary Theories of Economic and Technological Change: Present Status and Future Prospects*, ed. Pier Paolo Saviotti and J. Stanley Metcalfe, 88–107. Reading: Harwood.

Clarke, David L. 1987. "Trade and Industry in Barbarian Europe till Roman

Times." In *The Cambridge Economic History of Europe*, vol. 2, *Trade and Industry in the Middle Ages* (2nd ed.), ed. Michael M. Postan and Edward Miller, 1–70. Cambridge: Cambridge University Press.

Clay, Karen. 1997. "Trade without Law: Private-Order Institutions in Mexican California." *Journal of Law, Economics and Organization* 13, no. 1 (April): 202–31.

Cliff, Tony. 1955. *Stalinist Russia: A Marxist Analysis*. London: Michael Kidron. Reprinted and enlarged as *Russia: A Marxist Analysis* (London: International Socialism, n.d.).

Clower, Robert W. 1967. "A Reconsideration of the Microfoundations of Monetary Theory." *Western Economic Journal* 6:1–9.

Coase, Ronald H. 1937. "The Nature of the Firm." *Economica*, n.s., 4 (November): 386–405.

———. 1960. "The Problem of Social Cost." *Journal of Law and Economics* 3, no. 1 (October): 1–44.

———. 1974. "The Market for Goods and the Market for Ideas." *American Economic Review: Papers and Proceedings* 64, no. 2 (May): 384–91.

———. 1984. "The New Institutional Economics." *Journal of Institutional and Theoretical Economics* 140, no. 1:229-31.

———. 1988. *The Firm, the Market, and the Law*. Chicago: University of Chicago Press.

———. 1992. "The Institutional Structure of Production." *American Economic Review* 82, no. 4 (September): 713–19.

Coase, Ronald H., and Ning Wang. 2012. *How China Became Capitalist*. London: Palgrave Macmillan.

Coates, David, ed. 2005. *Varieties of Capitalism: Varieties of Approaches*. London: Palgrave Macmillan.

Cockshott, W. Paul, and Allin F. Cottrell. 1993. *Towards a New Socialism*. Nottingham: Spokesman.

Cohen, Avi J. 2003. "The Hayek/Knight Capital Controversy: The Irrelevance of Roundaboutness or Purging Processes in Time?" *History of Political Economy* 35, no. 3 (Fall): 469–90.

Cohen, Avi J., and Geoffrey C. Harcourt. 2003. "Whatever Happened to the Cambridge Capital Theory Controversies?" *Journal of Economic Perspectives* 17, no. 1 (Winter): 199–214.

Cohen, Edward E. 1992. *Athenian Economy and Society: A Banking Perspective*. Princeton, NJ: Princeton University Press.

Cohen, Michael D., and Paul Bacdayan. 1994. "Organizational Routines Are Stored as Procedural Memory—Evidence from a Laboratory Study." *Organization Science* 5, no. 4 (November): 554–68.

Cohen, Michael D., Roger Burkhart, Giovanni Dosi, Massimo Egidi, Luigi Marengo, Massimo Warglien, and Sidney Winter. 1996. "Routines and Other

Recurring Action Patterns of Organizations: Contemporary Research Issues." *Industrial and Corporate Change* 5, no. 3:653–98.

Cohendet, Patrick, Francis Kern, Babak Mehmanpazir, and Francis Munier. 1999. "Knowledge Coordination, Competence Creation and Integrated Networks in Globalised Firms." *Cambridge Journal of Economics* 23, no. 2 (March): 225–41.

Coleman, James S. 1982. *The Asymmetric Society.* Syracuse, NY: Syracuse University Press.

———. 1988. "Social Capital in the Creation of Human Capital." *American Journal of Sociology* 94, suppl.:S95–S120.

———. 1990. *Foundations of Social Theory.* Cambridge, MA: Harvard University Press.

Collins, Harry, and Martin Kusch, eds. 1998. *The Shape of Actions—What Humans and Machines Can Do.* Cambridge, MA: MIT Press.

Commons, John R. 1900. "A Sociological View of Sovereignty VI." *American Journal of Sociology* 5, no. 6 (May): 814–25. Reprinted in John R. Commons, *A Sociological View of Sovereignty*, ed. and with an introduction by Joseph Dorfman (New York: Augustus Kelley, 1965), 75–86.

———. 1924. *Legal Foundations of Capitalism.* New York: Macmillan.

———. 1925. "Marx To-Day: Capitalism and Socialism." *Atlantic Monthly*, November, 682–93.

———. 1934. *Institutional Economics—Its Place in Political Economy.* New York: Macmillan.

———. 1950. *The Economics of Collective Action.* Edited by K. H. Parsons. New York: Macmillan.

Considerations on the Sinking Fund. 1819. London: Hatchard & Son.

Coquillette, Daniel R. 1987. "Legal Ideology and Incorporation IV: The Nature of Civilian Influence on Modern Anglo-American Commercial Law." *Boston University Law Review* 67:877–970.

Corning, Peter A. 2011. *The Fair Society: The Science of Human Nature and the Pursuit of Social Justice.* Chicago: University of Chicago Press.

Cornuelle, Richard. 1976. *De-Managing America.* New York: Vintage.

Costanza, Robert, Ida Kubiszewski, Enrico Giovannini, Hunter Lovins, Jacqueline McGlade, Kate E. Pickett, Kristín Vala Ragnarsdóttir, Debra Roberts, Roberto De Vogli, and Richard Wilkinson. 2014. "Time to Leave GDP Behind." *Nature* 505, no. 16 (January): 283–85.

Cotterrell, Roger. 1999. *Emile Durkheim: Law in a Moral Domain.* Edinburgh: Edinburgh University Press.

Cowen, Tyler. 2013. *Average Is Over: Powering America beyond the Age of the Great Stagnation.* New York: Dutton.

Crawford, Sue E. S., and Elinor Ostrom. 1995. "A Grammar of Institutions." *American Political Science Review* 89, no. 3 (September): 582–600.

Credit Suisse Research Institute. 2012. *Credit Suisse Global Wealth Databook, 2012*. Zurich: Credit Suisse Research Institute.

Crockett, Sean, Vernon L. Smith, and Bart J. Wilson. 2009. "Exchange and Specialisation as a Discovery Process." *Economic Journal* 119, no. 539 (July): 1162–88.

Crosland, C. Anthony R. 1956. *The Future of Socialism*. London: Jonathan Cape.

Crouch, Colin. 2004. *Post-Democracy*. Cambridge: Polity.

——. 2005. *Capitalist Diversity and Change*. Oxford: Oxford University Press.

——. 2011. *The Strange Non-Death of Neoliberalism*. Cambridge: Polity.

Crouch, Colin, David Finegold, and Mari Sako. 1999. *Are Skills the Answer? The Political Economy of Skill Creation in Advanced Industrial Countries*. Oxford: Oxford University Press.

Crutchfield, James P., and Peter Schuster. 2003. *Evolutionary Dynamics: Exploring the Interplay of Selection, Accident, Neutrality, and Function*. Oxford: Oxford University Press.

Dahl, Robert A. 1982. *Dilemmas of Pluralist Democracy*. New Haven, CT: Yale University Press.

Dahlman, Carl J. 1979. "The Problem of Externality." *Journal of Law and Economics* 22, no. 1 (April): 141–62.

Dalton, George B. 1982. "Barter." *Journal of Economic Issues* 16, no. 1 (March): 181–90.

Darwin, Charles R. 1859. *On the Origin of Species by Means of Natural Selection; or, The Preservation of Favoured Races in the Struggle for Life*. London: Murray.

——. 1871. *The Descent of Man, and Selection in Relation to Sex*. 2 vols. London: Murray; New York: Hill.

Davidson, Paul. 1972. *Money and the Real World*. London: Macmillan.

Davies, Glyn. 1994. *A History of Money: From Ancient Times to the Present Day*. Cardiff: University of Wales Press.

Davies, Graham I. 1998. "Introduction to the Pentateuch." In *Oxford Bible Commentary*, ed. John Barton and John Muddiman, 12–38. Oxford: Oxford University Press.

Davies, James B., Susanna Sandström, Anthony B. Shorrocks, and Edward N. Wolff. 2009. "The Level and Distribution of Global Household Wealth." Working Paper no. 15508. Cambridge, MA: National Bureau of Economic Research.

Davis, John B., ed. 2001. *The Social Economics of Health Care*. London: Routledge.

Davis, Michael. 1987. "Nozick's Argument *for* the Legitimacy of the Welfare State." *Ethics* 97 (April): 576–94.

Deakin, Simon. 1998. "The Evolution of the Contract of Employment, 1900–

1950: The Influence of the Welfare State." In *Governance, Industry and Labour Markets in Britain and France: The Modernising State in the Mid-Twentieth Century*, ed. Noel Whiteside and Robert Salais, 213–30. London: Routledge.

———. 2001. "The Contract of Employment: A Study in Legal Evolution." *Historical Studies in Industrial Relations* 11:1–36.

———. 2006. "*Capacitas*: Contract Law and the Institutional Foundations of a Market Economy." *European Review of Contract Law* 2, no. 3:317–41.

———. 2009. "Legal Origin, Juridical Form and Industrialization in Historical Perspective: The Case of the Employment Contract and the Joint-Stock Company." *Socio-Economic Review* 7, no. 1 (January): 35–65.

———. 2012. "The Juridical Nature of the Firm." In *The Sage Handbook of Corporate Governance*, ed. Thomas Clarke and Douglas Branson, 113–35. London: Sage.

Deakin, Simon, David Gindis, Geoffrey M. Hodgson, Kainan Huang, and Katharina Pistor. In press. "Legal Institutionalism: Capitalism and the Constitutive Role of Law." *Journal of Comparative Economics*.

Deakin, Simon, and Gillian S. Morris. 1995. *Labour Law*. London: Butterworth.

Deaton, Angus. 2013. *The Great Escape: Health, Wealth, and the Origins of Inequality*. Princeton, NJ: Princeton University Press.

de Brunhoff, Suzanne. 1976. *Marx on Money*. New York: Urizen.

Dei Ottati, Gabi. 1994. "Trust, Interlinking Transactions and Credit in the Industrial District." *Cambridge Journal of Economics* 18, no. 6 (December): 529–46.

Demsetz, Harold. 1967. "Toward a Theory of Property Rights." *American Economic Review: Papers and Proceedings* 57, no. 2 (May): 347–59.

Deng, Xiaoping. 1992. "Exerpts from Talks Given in Wuchang, Shenzhen, Zhuhai, and Shanghai." *People's Daily*, January 18–February 21. http://english.peopledaily.com.cn/dengxp/v013/text/d1200.html. Also available in Deng Xiaoping, *Selected Works* (Chinese ed.) (Beijing: People's Publishing House, 1993), 3:360.

Dennett, Daniel C. 1995. *Darwin's Dangerous Idea: Evolution and the Meanings of Life*. London: Allen Lane; New York: Simon & Schuster.

Dequech, David. 2002. "The Demarcation between the 'Old' and the 'New' Institutional Economics: Recent Complications." *Journal of Economic Issues* 36, no. 2 (June): 565–72.

de Roover, Raymond A. 1974. *Business, Banking, and Economic Thought in Late Medieval and Early Modern Europe*. Chicago: University of Chicago Press.

De Soto, Hernando. 2000. *The Mystery of Capital: Why Capitalism Triumphs in the West and Fails Everywhere Else*. New York: Basic.

Devine, Patrick. 1988. *Democracy and Economic Planning: The Political Economy of a Self-Governing Society.* Cambridge: Polity.

Devlin, Patrick. 1965. *The Enforcement of Morals.* Oxford: Oxford University Press.

de Vries, Jan, and Ad van der Woude. 1997. *The First Modern Economy: Success, Failure, and Perseverance of the Dutch Economy, 1500–1815.* Cambridge: Cambridge University Press.

De Waal, Frans B. M. 1982. *Chimpanzee Politics: Power and Sex among Apes.* New York: Harper & Row; London: Jonathan Cape.

———. 1996. *Good Natured: The Origin of Right and Wrong in Humans and Other Animals.* Cambridge, MA: Harvard University Press.

———. 2006. *Primates and Philosophers: How Morality Evolved.* Princeton, NJ: Princeton University Press.

Dewey, John. 1916. *Democracy and Education.* New York: Macmillan.

———. 1922. *Human Nature and Conduct: An Introduction to Social Psychology.* New York: Holt.

———. 1926. "The Historic Background of Corporate Legal Personality." *Yale Law Journal* 35, no. 6 (April): 655–73.

———. 1929. *The Quest for Certainty: A Study of the Relation of Knowledge and Action.* New York: Minton, Balch.

———. 1935. *Liberalism and Social Action.* New York: Putnam's.

———. 1938. *Logic: The Theory of Enquiry.* New York: Holt.

———. 1939. *Theory of Valuation.* Chicago: University of Chicago Press.

Diamond, A. S. 1935. *Primitive Law.* London: Watts.

Diamond, Jared. 1997. *Guns, Germs and Steel: A Short History of Everybody for the Last 13,000 Years.* London: Jonathan Cape.

Dickenson, Henry D. 1939. *Economics of Socialism.* Oxford: Oxford University Press.

Dickson, Peter G. M. 1967. *The Financial Revolution in England: A Study in the Development of Public Credit, 1688–1756.* London: Macmillan.

DiMaggio, Paul J., and Walter W. Powell. 1983. "The Iron Cage Revisited: Institutional Isomorphism and Collective Rationality in Organizational Fields." *American Sociological Review* 48, no. 2 (April): 147–60.

Dingwall, Robert, Anne Marie Rafferty, and Charles Webster. 1988. *The Social History of Nursing.* London: Routledge.

Director, Aaron. 1964. "The Parity of the Economic Market Place." *Journal of Law and Economics* 7 (October): 1–10.

Dixit, Avinash K. 2004. *Lawlessness and Economics: Alternative Modes of Governance.* Princeton, NJ: Princeton University Press.

Doeringer, Peter B., and Michael J. Piore. 1971. *Internal Labor Markets and Manpower Analysis.* Lexington, MA: Heath.

Donald, Merlin. 1991. *Origins of the Modern Mind: Three Stages in the Evolution of Culture and Cognition.* Cambridge, MA: Harvard University Press.

Doner, Richard F. 1992. "Limits of State Strength: Towards an Institutionalist View of Economic Development." *World Politics* 44, no. 3 (April): 398–431.

Donisthorpe, Wordsworth. 1880. *The Claims of Labour; or, Serfdom, Wagedom, and Freedom.* London: Samuel Tinsley.

Dopfer, Kurt. 2004. "The Economic Agent as Rule Maker and Rule User: *Homo sapiens oeconomicus.*" *Journal of Evolutionary Economics* 14, no. 2 (May): 177–95.

———, ed. 2005. *The Evolutionary Foundations of Economics.* Cambridge: Cambridge University Press.

Dopfer, Kurt, John Foster, and Jason Potts. 2004. "Micro-Meso-Macro." *Journal of Evolutionary Economics* 14, no. 3 (July): 263–79.

Dopfer, Kurt, and Jason Potts. 2008. *The General Theory of Economic Evolution.* London: Routledge.

Dore, Ronald. 1983. "Goodwill and the Spirit of Market Capitalism." *British Journal of Sociology* 34, no. 4:459–82.

———. 2000. *Stock Market Capitalism: Welfare Capitalism: Japan and Germany versus the Anglo Saxons.* Oxford: Oxford University Press.

Dosi, Giovanni. 1988. "The Sources, Procedures, and Microeconomic Effects of Innovation." *Journal of Economic Literature* 26, no. 3 (September): 1120–71.

Doucouliagos, Chris. 1995. "Worker Participation and Productivity in Labor-Managed and Participatory Capitalist Firms: A Meta-Analysis." *Industrial and Labor Relations Review* 49, no. 1 (October): 58–77.

Douglas, Mary T. 1986. *How Institutions Think.* London: Routledge & Kegan Paul; Syracuse, NY: Syracuse University Press.

Dow, Gregory K. 2003. *Governing the Firm: Workers' Control in Theory and Practice.* Cambridge: Cambridge University Press.

Doyal, Leonard, and Ian Gough. 1991. *A Theory of Human Need.* London: Macmillan.

Dreyfus, Hubert L., and Stuart E. Dreyfus. 1986. *Mind over Machine: The Power of Human Intuition and Expertise in the Era of the Computer.* New York: Free Press.

Drucker, Peter F. 1993. *Post-Capitalist Society.* Oxford: Butterworth-Heinemann.

Du Bois, Armand B. 1938. *The English Business Company After the Bubble Act, 1720–1800.* New York: Commonwealth Fund.

Dunbar, Robin I. M. 1993. "Coevolution of Neocortical Size, Group Size, and Language." *Behavioral and Brain Sciences* 16:681–94.

———. 2011. "Constraints on the Evolution of Social Institutions and Their Implications for Information Flow." *Journal of Institutional Economics* 7, no. 3 (September): 345–71.

Dunning, John H., ed. 1997. *Governments, Globalization and International Business.* Oxford: Oxford University Press.

Durkheim, Émile. 1984. *The Division of Labour in Society.* Translated from the 1893 French ed. London: Macmillan.

Durlauf, Steven D. 1999. "The Case 'against' Social Capital." *Focus* 20, no. 3:1–5.

———. 2002. "On the Empirics of Social Capital." *Economic Journal* 112 (November): F459–F479.

Dymski, Gary A. 1990. "Money and Credit in Radical Political Economy: A Survey of Contemporary Perspectives." *Review of Radical Political Economics* 22, nos. 2–3:38–65.

———. 2006. "Money and Credit in Heterodox Theory: Reflections on Lapavitsas." *Historical Materialism* 14, no. 1:49–73.

Earl, Peter E., and Jason Potts. 2011. "A Nobel Prize for Governance and Institutions: Oliver Williamson and Elinor Ostrom." *Review of Political Economy* 23, no. 1 (January): 1–24.

Easterly, William, and Ross Levine. 1997. "Africa's Growth Tragedy: Policies and Ethnic Divisions." *Quarterly Journal of Economics* 112:1203–50.

———. 2001. "It's Not Factor Accumulation: Stylized Facts and Growth Models." *World Bank Economic Review* 15, no. 2:177–219.

Eatwell, John, Murray Milgate, and Peter Newman, eds. 1987. *The New Palgrave Dictionary of Economics.* 4 vols. London: Macmillan.

Ebenstein, Alan O. 2001. *Friedrich Hayek: A Biography.* Chicago: University of Chicago Press.

Ebner, Alexander. 2000. "Schumpeter and the 'Schmollerprogramm': Integrating Theory and History in the Analysis of Economic Development." *Journal of Evolutionary Economics* 10, no. 3:355–72.

Eccles, Robert G. 1981. "The Quasifirm in the Construction Industry." *Journal of Economic Behavior and Organization* 2:335–57.

Edvinsson, Leif, and Michael S. Malone. 1997. *Intellectual Capital: Realizing Your Company's True Value by Finding Its Hidden Brainpower.* New York: Harper.

Edwards, Jeremy, and Sheilagh Ogilvie. 2008. "Contract Enforcement, Institutions and Social Capital: The Maghribi Traders Reappraised." Working Paper no. 2254. Munich: CESifo.

Eggertsson, Thráinn. 1990. *Economic Behavior and Institutions.* Cambridge: Cambridge University Press.

Einzig, Paul. 1966. *Primitive Money in Its Ethnological, Historical and Economic Aspects.* 2nd ed. Oxford: Pergamon.

Elder-Vass, Dave. 2010. *The Causal Power of Social Structures.* Cambridge: Cambridge University Press.

Ellerman, David P. 1992. *Property and Contract in Economics: The Case for Economic Democracy.* Oxford: Basil Blackwell.

Ellickson, Robert C. 1991. *Order without Law: How Neighbors Settle Disputes.* Cambridge, MA: Harvard University Press.

Elsner, Wolfram, and Hardy Hanappi, eds. 2008. *Varieties of Capitalism and New Institutional Deals: Regulation, Welfare and the New Economy.* Cheltenham: Edward Elgar.

Elster, Jon. 1986a. *The Multiple Self.* Cambridge: Cambridge University Press.

———. 1986b. "The Theory of Combined and Uneven Development: A Critique." In *Analytical Marxism*, ed. John Roemer, 54–63. Cambridge: Cambridge University Press.

Ely, Richard T. 1886. "Report on the Organization of the American Economic Association." *Publications of the American Economic Association* 1, no. 1 (March): 5–32.

Engel, Christoph. 2008. "Learning the Law." *Journal of Institutional Economics* 4, no. 3 (December): 275–97.

Engels, Frederick. 1902. *Origin of the Family, Private Property and the State.* Translated from the 1884 German ed. by Ernest Untermann. Chicago: Charles Kerr.

Epstein, Stephen R. 1991. *Wage Labor and Guilds in Medieval Europe.* Chapel Hill: University of North Carolina Press.

———. 2000. *Freedom and Growth: The Rise of States and Markets in Europe, 1300–1750.* London: Routledge.

Errunza, Vihang. 1983. "Emerging Markets: A New Opportunity for Improving Global Portfolio Performance." *Financial Analysts Journal* 39, no. 5 (September–October): 51–58.

Espejo, Raul, and Roger Harnden, eds. 1989. *The Viable System Model: Interpretations and Applications of Stafford Beer's VSM.* Chichester: Wiley.

Estrin, Saul. 1983. *Self-Management: Economic Theory and Yugoslav Practice.* Cambridge: Cambridge University Press.

Evans, Karen G. 2000. "Reclaiming John Dewey: Democracy, Inquiry, Pragmatism, and Public Management." *Administration and Society* 32, no. 3 (July): 308–28.

Everest-Phillips, Max. 2008. "The Myth of 'Secure Property Rights': Good Economics as Bad History and Its Impact on International Development." SPIRU Working Paper no. 23. London: Overseas Development Institute.

Farnsworth, E. Allan. 1969. "The Past of Promise: An Historical Introduction to Contract." *Columbia Law Review* 69, no. 4 (April): 576–607.

Farr, William. 1853. "The Income and Property Tax." *Journal of the Royal Statistical Society* 16, no. 1 (March): 1–45.

Faulhaber, Gerald R., and William J. Baumol. 1988. "Economists as Innovators: Practical Products of Theoretical Research." *Journal of Economic Literature* 26, no. 2 (June): 577–600.

Faulkner, Philip, and Jochen Runde. 2009. "On the Identity of Technological

Objects and User Innovations in Function." *Academy of Management Review* 34, no. 3 (July): 442–62.

Fehr, Ernst, and Simon Gächter. 2000a. "Cooperation and Punishment in Public Goods Experiments." *American Economic Review* 90, no. 4 (December): 980–95.

———. 2000b. "Fairness and Retaliation: The Economics of Reciprocity." *Journal of Economic Perspectives* 14, no. 3 (Summer): 159–81.

———. 2002. "Altruistic Punishment in Humans." *Nature* 415, no. 10 (January): 137–40.

Fehr, Ernst, and Herbert Gintis. 2007. "Human Motivation and Social Cooperation: Experimental and Analytical Foundations." *Annual Review of Sociology* 33:3.1–3.22.

Felin, Teppo, and Nicolai J. Foss. 2009a. "Performativity of Theory, Arbitrary Conventions, and Possible Worlds: A Reality Check." *Organization Science* 20, no. 3 (May): 676–78.

———. 2009b. "Social Reality, the Boundaries of Self-Fulfilling Prophecy, and Economics." *Organization Science* 20, no. 3 (May): 654–68.

Fenzl, Norbert, and Wolfgang Hofkirchner. 1997. "Information Processing in Evolutionary Systems: An Outline Conceptual Framework for a Unified Information Theory." In *Self-Organization of Complex Structures: From Individual to Collective Dynamics*, ed. Frank Schweitzer, 59–70. London: Gordon & Breach.

Fetter, Frank A. 1927. "Clark's Reformulation of the Capital Concept." In *Economic Essays Contributed in Honor of John Bates Clark*, ed. Jacob H. Hollander, 136–56. New York: Macmillan.

———. 1930. "Capital." In *Encyclopaedia of the Social Sciences* (15 vols.), ed. Edwin R. A. Seligman and Alvin Johnson, 3:187–90. New York: Macmillan.

Field, Alexander J. 1979. "On the Explanation of Rules Using Rational Choice Models." *Journal of Economic Issues* 13, no. 1 (March): 49–72.

———. 1981. "The Problem with Neoclassical Institutional Economics: A Critique with Special Reference to the North/Thomas Model of Pre-1500 Europe." *Explorations in Economic History* 18, no. 2 (April): 174–98.

———. 1984. "Microeconomics, Norms and Rationality." *Economic Development and Cultural Change* 32, no. 4 (July): 683–711.

———. 1991. "Do Legal Systems Matter?" *Explorations in Economic History* 28, no. 1:1–35.

———. 2001. *Altruistically Inclined? The Behavioral Sciences, Evolutionary Theory, and the Origins of Reciprocity.* Ann Arbor: University of Michigan Press.

Field, John. 2003. *Social Capital.* London: Routledge.

Fine, Ben. 2001. *Social Capital versus Social Theory: Political Economy and Social Science at the Turn of the Millennium.* London: Routledge.

Finley, Moses I., ed. 1962. *Second International Conference of Economic History*. Vol. 1, *Trade and Politics in the Ancient World*. New York: Arno.

Fisher, Irving. 1892. *Mathematical Investigations in the Theory of Value and Prices*. New Haven, CT: Yale University Press.

———. 1896. "What Is Capital?" *Economic Journal* 6, no. 4 (December): 509–34.

———. 1897. "Senses of 'Capital.'" *Economic Journal* 7, no. 2 (June): 199–213.

———. 1904. "Precedents for Defining Capital." *Quarterly Journal of Economics* 18, no. 3 (May): 386–408.

———. 1906. *The Nature of Capital and Income*. New York: Macmillan.

———. 1907. *The Rate of Interest: Its Nature, Determination and Relation to Economic Phenomena*. New York: Macmillan.

Fleetwood, Steve. 2008. "Institutions and Social Structures." *Journal for the Theory of Social Behaviour* 38, no. 3:241–65.

Fletcher, Ian. 2011. *Free Trade Doesn't Work: What Should Replace It and Why*. Washington, DC: US Industry and Business Council.

Fligstein, Neil. 1985. "The Spread of the Multidivisional Form among Large Firms, 1919–1979." *American Sociological Review* 50, no. 3:377–91.

———. 1996. "Markets as Politics: A Political-Cultural Approach to Market Institutions." *American Sociological Review* 61, no. 4 (August): 656–73.

———. 2001. *The Architecture of Markets: An Economic Sociology of Twenty-First Century Capitalist Societies*. Princeton, NJ: Princeton University Press.

Florence, P. Sargant. 1957. "New Measures of the Growth of Firms." *Economic Journal* 67, no. 2 (June): 244–48.

Florida, Richard, and Martin Kenney. 1991. "Organisation vs. Culture: Japanese Automotive Transplants in the US." *Industrial Relations Journal* 22, no. 3:181–96.

Fogel, Robert W. 2004. *The Escape from Hunger and Premature Death, 1700–2100: Europe, America, and the Third World*. Cambridge: Cambridge University Press.

———. 2010. "$123,000,000,000,000: China's Estimated Economy by 2040. Be Warned." *Foreign Policy*, January–February. http://www.foreignpolicy.com/articles/2010/01/04/123000000000000.

Folbre, Nancy. 1994. *Who Pays for the Kids? Gender and the Structures of Constraint*. London: Routledge.

Folbre, Nancy, and Julie A. Nelson. 2000. "For Love or Money—or Both?" *Journal of Economic Perspectives* 14, no. 4 (Fall): 123–40.

Foley, Vernard. 1973. "An Origin of the Tableau Oeconomique." *History of Political Economy* 5, no. 2 (Summer): 121–50.

———. 1976. *The Social Physics of Adam Smith*. West Lafayette, IN: Purdue University Press.

Forstater, Mathew. 2006. "Tax-Driven Money: Additional Evidence from the History of Thought, Economic History, and Economic Policy." In *Complex-*

ity, Endogenous Money, and Exogenous Interest Rates, ed. Mark Setterfield, 202–20. Cheltenham: Edward Elgar.

Forte, Francesco, and Cosimo Magazzino. 2010. "Optimal Size of Government and Economic Growth in EU-27." Working Paper no. 4/2010. Rome: Centro di Ricerca Interdipartimentale di Economia delle Istituzioni.

Foss, Kirsten, and Nicolai Juul Foss. 2001. "Assets, Attributes and Ownership." *International Journal of the Economics of Business* 8, no. 1:19–37.

Foucault, Michel. 2008. *The Birth of Biopolitics: Lectures at the Collège de France, 1978–1979*. London: Palgrave Macmillan.

Fox, Alan. 1974. *Beyond Contract: Work, Power and Trust Relations*. London: Faber & Faber.

France, Anatole. 1894. *Le lys rouge*. Paris: Calmann Lévy.

Frank, Jerome. 1930. *Law and the Modern Mind*. New York: Brentano's.

———. 1949. *Courts on Trial: Myth and Reality in American Justice*. Princeton, NJ: Princeton University Press.

Fransman, Martin. 1994. "Information, Knowledge, Vision and Theories of the Firm." *Industrial and Corporate Change* 3, no. 3:713–57.

Fried, Barbara H. 1998. *The Progressive Assault on Laissez Faire: Robert Hale and the First Law and Economics Movement*. Cambridge, MA: Harvard University Press.

Friedman, David D. 1979. "Private Creation and Enforcement of Law: A Historical Case." *Journal of Legal Studies* 8, no. 2:399–415.

Friedman, Milton. 1999. "Conversation with Milton Friedman." In *Conversations with Leading Economists: Interpreting Modern Macroeconomists*, ed. Brian Snowdon and Howard Vane, 122–44. Cheltenham: Edward Elgar.

Friedman, Ori. 2008. "First Possession: An Assumption Guiding Inferences about Who Owns What." *Psychonomic Bulletin and Review* 15, no. 2: 290–95.

Fukuyama, Francis. 1992. *The End of History and the Last Man*. New York: Free Press.

Fuller, Lon L. 1967. *Legal Fictions*. Stanford, CA: Stanford University Press.

———. 1969a. "Human Interaction and the Law." *American Journal of Jurisprudence* 14:1–36.

———. 1969b. *The Morality of Law*. Rev. ed. New Haven, CT: Yale University Press.

Furubotn, Eirik G., and Svetozar Pejovich. 1972. "Property Rights and Economic Theory: A Survey of Recent Literature." *Journal of Economic Literature* 10, no. 4 (December): 1137–62.

———, eds. 1974. *The Economics of Property Rights*. Cambridge, MA: Ballinger.

Fuss, Diana. 1989. *Essentially Speaking: Feminism, Nature and Difference*. London: Routledge.

Fustel De Coulanges, Numa Denis. 1864/1980. *The Ancient City: A Study of the*

Religion, Laws, and Institutions of Greece and Rome. Translated from the 1864 French ed. Baltimore: Johns Hopkins University Press.

Gagliardi, Francesca. 2009. "Financial Development and the Growth of Cooperative Firms." *Small Business Economics* 32, no. 4 (April): 439–64.

Galanter, Marc. 1981. "Justice in Many Rooms: Courts, Private Ordering and Indigenous Law." *Journal of Legal Pluralism* 19, no. 1:1–47.

Galbraith, James K., and Maureen Berner, eds. 2001. *Inequality and Industrial Change: A Global View*. Cambridge: Cambridge University Press.

Galbraith, John Kenneth. 1952. *American Capitalism: The Concept of Countervailing Power*. Boston: Houghton Mifflin.

———. 1969. *The New Industrial State*. Harmondsworth: Penguin.

———. 1987. *Economics in Perspective: A Critical History*. Boston: Houghton Mifflin.

Gartzke, Erik. 2007. "The Capitalist Peace." *American Journal of Political Science* 51, no. 1:166–91.

Gat, Azar. 2006. *War in Human Civilization*. Oxford: Oxford University Press.

Gaudiosi, Monica M. 1988. "The Influence of the Islamic Law of Waqf on the Development of the Trust in England: The Case of Merton College." *University of Pennsylvania Law Review* 136, no. 4 (April): 1231–61.

Georgescu-Roegen, Nicholas. 1970. "The Economics of Production." *American Economic Review* 60, no. 2 (May): 1–9.

———. 1971. *The Entropy Law and the Economic Process*. Cambridge, MA: Harvard University Press.

Geras, Norman. 1983. *Marx and Human Nature: Refutation of a Legend*. London: Verso.

Gerring, John, Philip J. Bond, William T. Barndt, and Carola Moreno. 2005. "Democracy and Growth: A Historical Perspective." *World Politics* 57, no. 3 (April): 323–64.

Gerschenkron, Alexander. 1962. *Economic Backwardness in Historical Perspective: A Book of Essays*. Cambridge, MA: Belknap Press of Harvard University Press.

Gershuny, Jonathan. 2000. *Changing Times: Work and Leisure in Post-Industrial Society*. Oxford: Oxford University Press.

Gilbert, Alan. 2002. "On the Mystery of Capital and the Myths of Hernando De Soto: What Difference Does Legal Title Make?" *International Development Planning Review* 24, no. 1 (February): 1–19.

Gilbert, Margaret. 1989. *On Social Facts*. London: Routledge.

———. 2001. "Social Rules as Plural Subject Phenomena." In *On the Nature of Social and Institutional Reality*, ed. Eerik Lagerspetz, Heikki Ikäheimo, and Jussi Kotkavirta, 1–31. Jyväskylä: SoPhi Academic.

Gilbert, Scott F., John M. Opitz, and Rudolf A. Raff. 1996. "Resynthesizing

Evolutionary and Developmental Biology." *Developmental Biology* 173, no. 2 (February): 357–72.

Gindis, David. 2007. "Some Building Blocks for a Theory of the Firm as a Real Entity." In *The Firm as an Entity: Implications for Economics, Accounting and Law*, ed. Yuri Biondi, Arnaldo Canziani, and Thierry Kirat, 266–91. London: Routledge.

———. 2009. "From Fictions and Aggregates to Real Entities in the Theory of the Firm." *Journal of Institutional Economics* 5, no. 1 (April): 25–46.

———. 2013. "The Nexus Paradox: Legal Personality and the Theory of the Firm." Ph.D. diss., University of Hertfordshire.

Gintis, Herbert. 2000. "Strong Reciprocity and Human Sociality." *Journal of Theoretical Biology* 206:169–79.

———. 2007. "The Evolution of Private Property." *Journal of Economic Behavior and Organization* 64, no. 1 (September): 1–16.

———. 2009. *The Bounds of Reason: Game Theory and the Unification of the Behavioral Sciences*. Princeton, NJ: Princeton University Press.

Gintis, Herbert, Samuel Bowles, Robert Boyd, and Ernst Fehr, eds. 2005. *Moral Sentiments and Material Interests: The Foundations of Cooperation in Economic Life*. Cambridge, MA: MIT Press.

Glaeser, Edward L., and Andrei Shleifer. 2002. "Legal Origins." *Quarterly Journal of Economics* 117, no. 4 (November): 1193–1229.

Gluckman, Max. 1967. *The Judicial Process among the Barotse of Northern Rhodesia*. 2nd ed. Manchester: Manchester University Press.

Glyn, Andrew. 2006. *Capitalism Unleashed: Finance, Globalization, and Welfare*. Oxford: Oxford University Press.

Goldberg, Victor P. 1980. "Relational Exchange: Economics and Complex Contracts." *American Behavioral Scientist* 23, no. 3:337–52.

Goldin, Claudia, and Lawrence F. Katz. 1996. "Technology, Skill, and the Wage Structure: Insights from the Past." *American Economic Review: Papers and Proceedings* 86, no. 2 (May): 252–57.

Goldstein, Daniel G., and Gerd Gigerenzer. 2002. "Models of Ecological Rationality: The Recognition Heuristic." *Psychological Review* 109, no. 1:75–90.

Gomulka, Stanislaw. 1971. *Inventive Activity, Diffusion, and the Stages of Economic Growth*. Aarhus: Aarhus Institute of Economics.

Goodhart, Charles A. E. 1998. "The Two Concepts of Money: Implications for the Analysis of Optimal Currency Areas." *European Journal of Political Economy* 14 (March): 407–32.

———. 2009. "The Continuing Muddles of Monetary Theory: A Steadfast Refusal to Face Facts." *Economica* 76 (October): 821–30.

Gorz, André. 1985. *Paths to Paradise: On the Liberation from Work*. London: Pluto.

Gould, Stephen Jay. 1977. *Ontogeny and Phylogeny.* Cambridge, MA: Harvard University Press.

——. 1985. *The Flamingo's Smile.* New York: Norton.

Gower, Laurence C. B. 1979. *Principles of Modern Company Law.* 4th ed. London: Sweet & Maxwell.

Grabher, Gernot, ed. 1993. *The Embedded Firm: On the Socioeconomics of Industrial Networks.* London: Routledge.

Graeber, David. 2011. *Debt: The First 5,000 Years.* New York: Melville House.

Granovetter, Mark. 1982. "The Strength of Weak Ties: A Network Theory Revisited." In *Social Structure and Network Analysis,* ed. P. Marsden and N. Lin, 105–31. Beverly Hills, CA: Sage.

——. 1985. "Economic Action and Social Structure: The Problem of Embeddedness." *American Journal of Sociology* 91, no. 3 (November): 481–510.

Grant, Robert M. 1996. "Toward a Knowledge-Based Theory of the Firm." Special issue, *Strategic Management Journal* 17 (Winter): 109–22.

Gray, John. 1993. *Post-Liberalism.* London: Routledge.

Graybiel, Ann M. 2008. "Habits, Rituals and the Evaluative Brain." *Annual Review of Neuroscience* 31, no. 1:359–87.

Green, Thomas H. 1888. *Philosophical Works.* Vol. 3. London: Longmans, Green.

Greif, Avner. 1989. "Reputations and Coalitions in Medieval Trade: Evidence on the Maghribi Traders." *Journal of Economic History* 49, no. 4 (December): 857–82.

——. 1993. "Contract Enforceability and Economic Institutions in Early Trade: The Maghribi Traders' Coalition." *American Economic Review* 83, no. 3 (June): 525–48.

——. 1994. "On the Political Foundations of the Late Medieval Commercial Revolution: Genoa during the Twelfth and Thirteenth Centuries." *Journal of Economic History* 54, no. 2 (June): 271–87.

——. 1996. "The Study of Organizations and Evolving Organizational Forms through History: Reflections from the Late Medieval Family Firm." *Industrial and Corporate Change* 5, no. 2:473–501.

——. 2006. *Institutions and the Path to the Modern Economy: Lessons from Medieval Trade.* Cambridge: Cambridge University Press.

——. 2008. "Contract Enforcement and Institutions among the Maghribi Traders: Refuting Edwards and Ogilvie." Typescript, Stanford University.

——. 2009. "The Curious Commentary on the Citation Practices of Avner Greif." *Public Choice* 141:273–75.

Greif, Avner, Paul Milgrom, and Barry R. Weingast. 1994. "Coordination, Commitment, and Enforcement: The Case of the Merchant Guild." *Journal of Political Economy* 102, no. 4 (August): 745–76.

Greif, Avner, and Guido Tabellini. 2010. "Cultural and Institutional Bifurcation:

China and Europe Compared." *American Economic Review: Papers and Proceedings* 100, no. 2 (May): 135–40.

———. 2012. "The Clan and the City: Sustaining Cooperation in China and Europe." Typescript, Stanford University.

Grierson, Philip. 1977. *The Origins of Money*. London: Athlone.

Griffiths, John. 1986. "What Is Legal Pluralism?" *Journal of Legal Pluralism* 24; no. 1:1–55.

Groenewegen, John, Frans Kerstholt, and Ad Nagelkerke. 1995. "On Integrating the New and Old Institutionalisms: Douglass North Building Bridges." *Journal of Economic Issues* 29, no. 2 (June): 467–75.

Grossman, Michael. 1972. "On the Concept of Health Capital and the Demand for Health." *Journal of Political Economy* 80, no. 2 (March–April): 223–55.

Grossman, Sanford J., and Oliver D. Hart. 1986. "The Costs and Benefits of Ownership: A Theory of Vertical and Lateral Integration." *Journal of Political Economy* 94, no. 4 (August): 691–719.

Guinnane, Timothy W., Ron Harris, Naomi R. Lamoreaux, and Jean-Laurent Rosenthal. 2007. "Putting the Corporation in Its Place." *Enterprise and Society* 8, no. 3:687–779.

Guzmán, Ricardo Andrés, Carlos Rodriguez-Sicken, and Robert Rowthorn. 2007. "When in Rome, Do as the Romans Do: The Coevolution of Altruistic Punishment, Conformist Learning, and Cooperation." *Evolution and Human Behavior* 28:112–17.

Haas, Peter M. 1992. "Introduction: Epistemic Communities and International Policy Coordination." *International Organization* 46, no. 1:1–35.

Haber, Stephen H. 2003. "Political Institutions and Banking Systems: Lessons from the Economic Histories of Mexico and the United States, 1790–1914." Working Paper no. 163. Stanford, CA: Center for Research on Economic Development and Policy Reform, Stanford University.

Hacker, Barton C. 1993. "Engineering a New Order: Military Institutions, Technical Education, and the Rise of the Industrial State." *Technology and Culture* 34, no. 1 (January): 1–27.

Hacking, Ian. 1999. *The Social Construction of What?* Cambridge, MA: Harvard University Press.

Hadfield, Gillian K., and Barry R. Weingast. 2012. "What Is Law? A Coordination Account of the Characteristics of Legal Order." *Journal of Legal Analysis*, July 29. DOI: 10.1093/jla/las008.

Hage, Jerald, and Catherine Alter. 1997. "A Typology of Interorganizational Relationships and Networks." In *Contemporary Capitalism: The Embeddedness of Institutions*, ed. J. Rogers Hollingsworth and Robert Boyer, 94–125. Cambridge: Cambridge University Press.

Hagstrom, Warren O. 1965. *The Scientific Community*. New York: Basic.

Hahn, Frank H. 1965. "On Some Problems of Proving the Existence of an Equilibrium in a Monetary Economy." In *The Theory of Interest Rates*, ed. Frank H. Hahn and Frank P. R. Brechling, 126–35. London: Macmillan.

———. 1980. "General Equilibrium Theory." Special issue, *Public Interest*, 123–38.

———. 1987. "The Foundations of Monetary Theory." In *Monetary Theory and Economic Institutions*, ed. Marcello de Cecco and Jean-Paul Fitoussi, 21–43. London: Macmillan.

———. 1988. "On Monetary Theory." *Economic Journal* 98, no. 4 (December): 957–73.

Hahnel, Robin. 2007. "The Case against Markets." *Journal of Economic Issues* 41, no. 3 (December): 1139–59.

Haidt, Jonathan, and Craig Joseph. 2004. "Intuitive Ethics: How Innately Prepared Intuitions Generate Culturally Variable Virtues." *Daedalus* 133, no. 4 (Fall): 55–66.

———. 2007. "The Moral Mind: How Five Sets of Innate Intuitions Guide the Development of Many Culture-Specific Virtues, and Perhaps Even Modules." In *The Innate Mind*, vol. 3, *Foundations and the Future*, ed. Peter Carruthers, Stephen Laurence, and Stephen Stich, 367–444. Oxford: Oxford University Press.

Hakim, Catherine. 2011. *Honey Money: The Power of Erotic Capital*. London: Allen Lane.

Hale, Robert Lee. 1952. *Freedom through Law*. New York: Colombia University Press.

Hall, Peter A., and David Soskice, eds. 2001. *Varieties of Capitalism: The Institutional Foundations of Comparative Advantage*. Oxford: Oxford University Press.

Hall, Peter A., and Kathleen Thelen. 2009. "Institutional Change in Varieties of Capitalism." *Socio-Economic Review* 7, no. 1 (January): 7–34.

Hallowell, A. Irving. 1943. "The Nature and Function of Property as a Social Institution." *Journal of Legal and Political Sociology* 1, nos. 3–4:115–38.

Hamilton, Earl J. 1947. "The Origin and Growth of the National Debt in Western Europe." *American Economic Review: Papers and Proceedings* 37, no. 2 (May): 118–30.

Hamilton, William D. 1964. "The Genetical Evolution of Social Behavior, I and II." *Journal of Theoretical Biology* 7, no. 1 (July): 1–32.

Handlin, Oscar, and Mary F. Handlin. 1945. "Origins of the American Business Corporation." *Journal of Economic History* 5, no. 1 (May): 1–23.

Handy, Charles B. 1984. *The Future of Work: A Guide to a Changing Society*. Oxford: Basil Blackwell.

Hanifan, Lyda J. 1916. "The Rural School Community Center." *Annals of the American Academy of Political and Social Science* 67:130–38.

Hansmann, Henry. 1996. *The Ownership of Enterprise*. Cambridge: Cambridge University Press.

Hansmann, Henry, Reinier Kraakman, and Richard Squire. 2006. "Law and the Rise of the Firm." *Harvard Law Review* 119, no. 5 (March): 1333–1403.

Harcourt, Geoffrey C. 1972. *Some Cambridge Controversies in the Theory of Capital*. Cambridge: Cambridge University Press.

Härdle, Wolfgang K., and Alan P. Kirman. 1995. "Nonclassical Demand: A Model-Free Examination of Price Quantity Relations in the Marseille Fish Market." *Journal of Econometrics* 67, no. 1:227–57.

Harré, Rom, and Edward H. Madden. 1975. *Causal Powers: A Theory of Natural Necessity*. Oxford: Basil Blackwell.

Harré, Rom, and Charles R. Varela. 1996. "Conflicting Varieties of Realism: Causal Powers and the Problems of Social Structure." *Journal for the Theory of Social Behavior* 26, no. 3 (September): 313–25.

Harris, Ron. 2000. *Industrializing English Law: Entrepreneurship and Industrial Organization, 1720–1844*. Cambridge: Cambridge University Press.

Harris, William Cornwallis. 1842. "Report to the Secretary of the Bombay Government: Slave-Trade of Abyssinia, Embassy to Shoa, Etc." Extracted in *The Friend of the Africans* 2, no. 19 (December 2, 1844): 101–6.

Hart, Herbert L. A. 1961. *The Concept of Law*. Oxford: Oxford University Press.

Hart, Oliver D. 1975. "On the Optimality of Equilibrium When the Market Structure Is Incomplete." *Journal of Economic Theory* 11, no. 3 (December): 418–43.

———. 1989. "An Economist's Perspective on the Theory of the Firm." *Columbia Law Review* 89, no. 7:1757–74.

———. 1995. *Firms, Contracts, and Financial Structure*. Oxford: Oxford University Press.

———. 2011. "Thinking about the Firm: A Review of Daniel Spulber's *The Theory of the Firm*." *Journal of Economic Literature* 49, no. 1:101–13.

Hart, Oliver D., and John H. Moore. 1990. "Property Rights and the Nature of the Firm." *Journal of Political Economy* 98, no. 6 (December): 1119–58.

Hartwick, John. 1991. "Degradation of Environmental Capital and National Accounting Procedures." *European Economic Review* 35, nos. 2–3 (April): 642–49.

Hasnas, John. 2005. "Hayek, the Common Law, and the Fluid Drive." *NYU Journal of Law and Liberty* 1:79–110.

Hausmann, Ricardo, César A. Hidalgo, Sebastián Bustos, Michele Coscia, Sarah Chung, Juan Jimenez, Alexander Simoes, and Muhammed A. Yildirim. 2011. *The Atlas of Economic Complexity: Mapping Paths to Prosperity*. Cambridge, MA: Harvard University HKS/CDI—MIT Media Lab.

Hayek, Friedrich A. 1934. "On the Relationship between Investment and Output." *Economic Journal* 44, no. 2 (June): 207–31.

———, ed. 1935a. *Collectivist Economic Planning*. London: Routledge.

——. 1935b. "The Maintenance of Capital." *Economica* 2, no. 3 (August): 241–76.

——. 1936. "The Mythology of Capital." *Quarterly Journal of Economics* 50, no. 2 (February): 199–228.

——. 1941a. "Maintaining Capital Intact: A Reply." *Economica*, n.s., 8, no. 31 (August): 276–80.

——. 1941b. *The Pure Theory of Capital.* London: Macmillan.

——. 1944. *The Road to Serfdom.* London: Routledge.

——. 1948. *Individualism and Economic Order.* London: Routledge; Chicago: University of Chicago Press.

——. 1952. *The Counter-Revolution of Science: Studies on the Abuse of Reason.* Glencoe, IL: Free Press.

——. 1960. *The Constitution of Liberty.* London: Routledge & Kegan Paul; Chicago: University of Chicago Press.

——. 1967. "Notes on the Evolution of Systems of Rules of Conduct." In *Studies in Philosophy, Politics and Economics,* 66–81. London: Routledge & Kegan Paul.

——. 1973. *Law, Legislation and Liberty.* Vol. 1, *Rules and Order.* London: Routledge & Kegan Paul.

——. 1976. *Law, Legislation and Liberty.* Vol. 2, *The Mirage of Social Justice.* London: Routledge & Kegan Paul.

——. 1979. *Law, Legislation and Liberty.* Vol. 3, *The Political Order of a Free People.* London: Routledge & Kegan Paul.

——. 1988. *The Fatal Conceit: The Errors of Socialism.* Vol. 1 of *The Collected Works of Friedrich August Hayek,* ed. William W. Bartley III. London: Routledge.

——. 1989. "The Pretence of Knowledge." *American Economic Review* 79, no. 6 (December): 1–7.

——. 1994. *Hayek on Hayek: An Autobiographical Dialogue.* Edited by Stephen Kresge and Leif Wenar. London: Routledge; Chicago: University of Chicago Press.

Head, Simon. 2005. *The New Ruthless Economy: Work and Power in the Digital Age.* Oxford: Oxford University Press.

Hédoin, Cyril. 2013. "Collective Intentionality in Economics: Making Searle's Theory of Institutional Facts Relevant for Game Theory." *Erasmus Journal for Philosophy and Economics* 6, no. 1 (Spring): 1–27. http://ejpe.org/pdf/6-1 -art-1.pdf.

Hegel, Georg Wilhelm Friedrich. (1821) 1942. *Philosophy of Right.* Translated from the 1821 German ed. Oxford: Oxford University Press.

Heilbroner, Robert L. 1987. "Capitalism." In *The New Palgrave: A Dictionary of Economics,* vol. 1, ed. John Eatwell, Murray Milgate, and Peter Newman, 347–53. London: Macmillan.

Heinsohn, Gunnar, and Otto Steiger. 2000. "The Property Theory of Interest and Money." In *What Is Money?* ed. John Smithin, 67–100. London: Routledge.

———. 2013. *Ownership Economics: On the Foundations of Interest, Money, Markets, Business Cycles and Economic Development.* Translated and edited by Frank Decker. London: Routledge.

Heller, Michael A. 2008. *The Gridlock Economy: How Too Much Ownership Wrecks Markets, Stops Innovation, and Costs Lives.* New York: Basic.

Hendriks-Jansen, Horst. 1996. *Catching Ourselves in the Act: Situated Activity, Interaction, Emergence, Evolution and Human Thought.* Cambridge, MA: MIT Press.

Henrich, Joseph. 2004. "Cultural Group Selection, Coevolutionary Processes and Large-Scale Cooperation." *Journal of Economic Behavior and Organization* 53, no. 1 (February): 3–35.

Henrich, Joseph, and Robert Boyd. 1998. "The Evolution of Conformist Transmission and the Emergence of between Group Differences." *Evolution and Human Behavior* 19:215–42.

———. 2001. "Why People Punish Defectors: Why Conformist Transmission Can Stabilize Costly Enforcement of Norms in Cooperative Dilemmas." *Journal of Theoretical Biology* 208, no. 1:79–89.

Henrich, Joseph, Jean Ensminger, Richard McElreath, Abigail Barr, Clark Barrett, Alexander Bolyanatz, Juan Camilo Cardenas, Michael Gurven, Edwins Gwako, Natalie Henrich, Carolyn Lesorogol, Frank Marlowe, David Tracer, and John Ziker. 2010. "Markets, Religion, Community Size, and the Evolution of Fairness and Punishment." *Science* 327, no. 5972:1480–84.

Henrich, Joseph, and Francisco J. Gil-White. 2001. "The Evolution of Prestige: Freely Conferred Deference as a Mechanism for Enhancing the Benefits of Cultural Transmission." *Evolution and Human Behavior* 22, no. 3:165–96.

Henrich, Joseph, Richard McElreath, Abigail Barr, Jean Ensminger, Clark Barrett, Alaexander Bolyanatz, Juan Camilo Cardenas, Michael Gurven, Edwins Gwako, Natalie Henrich, Carolyn Lesorogol, Frank Marlowe, David Tracer, and John Ziker. 2006. "Costly Punishment across Human Societies." *Science* 312, no. 5781:1767–70.

Herrmann-Pillath, Carsten. 2012. "Institutions, Distributed Cognition and Agency: Rule-Following as Performative Action." *Journal of Economic Methodology* 19, no. 1 (March): 21–42.

———. 2013. *Foundations of Economic Evolution: A Treatise on the Natural Philosophy of Economics.* Cheltenham: Edward Elgar.

Hesse, Mary B. 1966. *Models and Analogies in Science.* Notre Dame, IN: University of Notre Dame Press.

———. 1980. *Revolutions and Reconstructions in the Philosophy of Science.* Brighton: Harvester.

Hessen, Robert. 1979. *In Defense of the Corporation*. Stanford, CA: Hoover Institute.

——. 1987. "Corporations." In *The New Palgrave Dictionary of Economics*, vol. 1, ed. John Eatwell, Murray Milgate, and Peter Newman, 675–77. London: Macmillan.

Hidalgo, César A., and Ricardo Hausmann. 2009. "The Building Blocks of Economic Complexity." *Proceedings of the National Academy of Sciences of the United States of America* 106, no. 26 (June 30): 10570–75.

Hill, Kim R., Robert S. Walker, Miran Božičević, James Eder, Thomas Headland, Barry Hewlett, A. Magdalena Hurtado, Frank Marlowe, Polly Wiessner, and Brian Wood. 2011. "Co-Residence Patterns in Hunter-Gatherer Societies Show Unique Human Social Structure." *Science* 331, no. 6022 (March 11): 1286–89.

Himma, Kennet Einar. 2009. "Philosophy of Law." *Internet Encyclopedia of Philosophy*. http://www.iep.utm.edu/law-phil.

Hindess, Barry. 1987. *Freedom, Equality and the Market*. London: Tavistock.

——. 1989. *Political Choice and Social Structure: An Analysis of Actors, Interests and Rationality*. Aldershot: Edward Elgar.

Hindriks, Frank, and Francesco Guala. In press. "Institutions, Rules, and Equilibria: A Unified Theory." *Journal of Institutional Economics*.

Hirsch, Jean-Pierre. 1989. "Revolutionary France, Cradle of Free Enterprise." *American Historical Review* 94, no. 5 (December): 1281–89.

——. 1991. *Les deux rêves du commerce: Entreprise et institution dans la région lilloise, 1780–1860*. Paris: EHESS.

Hirsch, Jean-Pierre, and Philippe Minard. 1998. "'Libérez-nous, Sire, protégez-nous beaucoup': Pour une histoire des pratiques institutionelle dans l'industrie française, XVIIIe–XIXe siècles." In *La France n'est elle-pas douée pour l'industrie?* ed. Louis Bergeron and Patrice Bourdelais, 135–58. Paris: Belin.

Hirschman, Albert O. 1970. *Exit, Voice, and Loyalty: Responses to Decline in Firms, Organizations, and States*. Cambridge, MA: Harvard University Press.

Hirschon, Renée. 1984. *Women and Property: Women as Property*. London: Croom Helm.

Hirst, Paul Q. 1975. *Durkheim, Bernard and Epistemology*. London: Routledge & Kegan Paul.

Hirst, Paul Q., and Grahame F. Thompson. 1996. *Globalization in Question: The International Economy and the Possibilities of Governance*. Cambridge: Polity.

Ho, Peter. 2005. *Institutions in Transition: Land Ownership, Property Rights and Social Conflict in China*. Oxford: Oxford University Press.

Hobson, John A. 1901. *The Social Problem: Life and Work*. London: James Nisbet.

———. 1926. *The Evolution of Modern Capitalism: A Study of Machine Production*. Rev. ed. London: Walter Scott; New York: Scribner's.

———. 1929. *Wealth and Life: A Study in Values*. London: Macmillan.

Hodgson, Geoffrey M. 1982. *Capitalism, Value and Exploitation: A Radical Theory*. Oxford: Martin Robertson.

———. 1984. *The Democratic Economy: A New Look at Planning, Markets and Power*. Harmondsworth: Penguin.

———. 1988. *Economics and Institutions: A Manifesto for a Modern Institutional Economics*. Cambridge: Polity; Philadelphia: University of Pennsylvania Press.

———. 1993. *Economics and Evolution: Bringing Life Back into Economics*. Cambridge: Polity; Ann Arbor: University of Michigan Press.

———. 1994. "Optimisation and Evolution: Winter's Critique of Friedman Revisited." *Cambridge Journal of Economics* 18, no. 4 (August): 413–30.

———. 1995. "Varieties of Capitalism from the Perspectives of Veblen and Marx." *Journal of Economic Issues* 29, no. 2 (June): 575–84.

———. 1996. "Varieties of Capitalism and Varieties of Economic Theory." *Review of International Political Economy* 3, no. 3 (Autumn): 381–434.

———. 1997. "The Ubiquity of Habits and Rules." *Cambridge Journal of Economics* 21, no. 6 (November): 663–84.

———. 1999. *Economics and Utopia: Why the Learning Economy Is Not the End of History*. London: Routledge.

———. 2001. *How Economics Forgot History: The Problem of Historical Specificity in Social Science*. London: Routledge.

———. 2002. "The Legal Nature of the Firm and the Myth of the Firm-Market Hybrid." *International Journal of the Economics of Business* 9, no. 1 (February): 37–60.

———. 2003. "The Enforcement of Contracts and Property Rights: Constitutive versus Epiphenomenal Conceptions of Law." *International Review of Sociology* 13, no. 2 (July): 373–89.

———. 2004. *The Evolution of Institutional Economics: Agency, Structure and Darwinism in American Institutionalism*. London: Routledge.

———. 2005a. "Knowledge at Work: Some Neoliberal Anachronisms." *Review of Social Economy* 63, no. 4 (December): 547–65.

———. 2005b. "The Limits to Participatory Planning: A Reply to Adaman and Devine." *Economy and Society* 31, no. 1 (February): 141–53.

———. 2006a. *Economics in the Shadows of Darwin and Marx: Essays on Institutional and Evolutionary Themes*. Cheltenham: Edward Elgar.

———. 2006b. "Instinct and Habit Before Reason: Comparing the Views of John Dewey, Friedrich Hayek and Thorstein Veblen." *Advances in Austrian Economics* 9:109–43.

———. 2006c. "What Are Institutions?" *Journal of Economic Issues* 40, no. 1 (March): 1–25.

———. 2007a. "Evolutionary and Institutional Economics as the New Mainstream?" *Evolutionary and Institutional Economics Review* 4, no. 1 (September): 7–25.

———. 2007b. "*The Impossibility of Social Democracy* by Albert E. F. Schäffle." *Journal of Institutional Economics* 3, no. 1 (April): 113–25.

———. 2008a. "The Concept of a Routine." In *Handbook of Organizational Routines*, ed. Markus C. Becker, 3–14. Cheltenham: Edward Elgar.

———. 2008b. "Markets." In *The Elgar Companion to Social Economics*, ed. John B. Davis and Wilfred Dolfsma, 251–66. Cheltenham: Edward Elgar.

———. 2008c. "Prospects for Economic Sociology." *Philosophy of the Social Sciences* 38, no. 1 (March): 133–49.

———. 2009. "On the Institutional Foundations of Law: The Insufficiency of Custom and Private Ordering." *Journal of Economic Issues* 43, no. 1 (March): 143–66.

———. 2010a. "Albert Schäffle's Critique of Socialism." In *Economic Theory and Economic Thought: Essays in Honour of Ian Steedman*, ed. John Vint, J. Stanley Metcalfe, Heinz D. Kurz, Neri Salvadori, and Paul A. Samuelson, 296–315. London: Routledge.

———. 2010b. "Choice, Habit and Evolution." *Journal of Evolutionary Economics* 20, no. 1 (January): 1–18.

———. 2010c. Review of *An Engine, Not a Camera: How Financial Models Shape Markets* and *Material Markets: How Economic Agents Are Constructed*, by Donald MacKenzie. *Socio-Economic Review* 8, no. 2:399–406.

———. 2011a. "The Eclipse of the Uncertainty Concept in Mainstream Economics." *Journal of Economic Issues* 45, no. 1 (March): 159–75.

———. 2011b. "A Philosophical Perspective on Contemporary Evolutionary Economics." In *The Elgar Companion to Recent Developments in Economic Methodology*, ed. John B. Davis and D. Wade Hands, 299–318. Cheltenham: Edward Elgar.

———, ed. 2012. *Mathematics and Modern Economics*. Cheltenham: Edward Elgar.

———. 2013a. "Come Back Marshall, All Is Forgiven? Complexity, Evolution, Mathematics and Marshallian Exceptionalism." *European Journal of the History of Economic Thought* 20, no. 6 (December): 957–81.

———. 2013b. *From Pleasure Machines to Moral Communities: An Evolutionary Economics without Homo Economicus.* Chicago: University of Chicago Press.

———. 2014. "What Is Capital? Economists and Sociologists Have Changed Its Meaning—Should It Be Changed Back?" *Cambridge Journal of Economics* 38, no. 5 (September): 1063–86.

Hodgson, Geoffrey M., and Kainan Huang. 2013. "Brakes on Chinese Economic Development: Institutional Causes of a Growth Slowdown." *Journal of Economic Issues* 47, no. 3 (September): 599–622.

Hodgson, Geoffrey M., and Shuxia Jiang. 2007. "The Economics of Corruption and the Corruption of Economics: An Institutionalist Perspective." *Journal of Economic Issues* 41, no. 4 (December): 1043–61.

Hodgson, Geoffrey M., and Thorbjørn Knudsen. 2004. "The Complex Evolution of a Simple Traffic Convention: The Functions and Implications of Habit." *Journal of Economic Behavior and Organization* 54, no. 1:19–47.

———. 2006. "Why We Need a Generalized Darwinism: And Why a Generalized Darwinism Is Not Enough." *Journal of Economic Behavior and Organization* 61, no. 1 (September): 1–19.

———. 2008. "The Emergence of Property Rights Enforcement in Early Trade: A Behavioral Model without Reputational Effects." *Journal of Economic Behavior and Organization* 68, no. 1:48–62.

———. 2010. *Darwin's Conjecture: The Search for General Principles of Social and Economic Evolution.* Chicago: University of Chicago Press.

———. 2012. "Generalized Darwinism and Evolutionary Economics: From Ontology to Theory." *Biological Theory* 6, no. 4:326–37.

Hoebel, Edward Adamson. 1964. *The Law of Primitive Man: A Study in Legal Dynamics.* Cambridge, MA: Harvard University Press.

Hoffmann, Johann Gottfried. 1840. *Die Lehre von den Steuern.* Berlin: Nicolai.

Hogg, Michael A., and Deborah I. Terry. 2000. "Social Identity and Self-Categorization Processes in Organizational Contexts." *Academy of Management Review* 25, no. 1 (January): 121–40.

Hohfeld, Wesley Newcomb. 1919. *Fundamental Legal Conceptions as Applied in Judicial Reasoning.* Edited by Walter W. Cook. New Haven, CT: Yale University Press.

Holmström, Bengt. 1999. "The Firm as a Subeconomy." *Journal of Law, Economics, and Organization* 15:74–102.

Holmwood, John. 1996. *Founding Sociology? Talcott Parsons and the Idea of General Theory.* London: Longman.

Holzer, Harry J., Richard N. Block, Markus Cheatham, and Jack H. Knott. 1993. "Are Training Subsidies for Firms Effective? The Michigan Experience." *Industrial and Labor Relations Review* 46, no. 4 (July): 625–36.

Homans, George C. 1961. *Social Behaviour: Its Elementary Form.* London: Routledge & Kegan Paul.

Honoré, Antony M. 1961. "Ownership." In *Oxford Essays in Jurisprudence*, ed. Anthony G. Guest, 107–47. Oxford: Oxford University Press.

Hook, J. 1993. "Judgments about the Right to Property from Preschool to Adulthood." *Law and Human Behavior* 17, no. 1:135–46.

Hopkins, Keith. 1978. *Conquerors and Slaves.* Cambridge: Cambridge University Press.

Hoppe, Hans-Hermann. 1994. "F. A. Hayek on Government and Social Evolution: A Critique." *Review of Austrian Economics* 7, no. 1:67–93.

Horwitz, Steven. 2007. "Capitalism and the Family." *The Freeman*, July–August, 26–30.

Huang, Yasheng. 2008. *Capitalism with Chinese Characteristics: Entrepreneurship and the State*. Cambridge: Cambridge University Press.

Hubbick, Elizabeth. 2001. *Employee Share Ownership*. London: Chartered Institute of Personnel and Development.

Hudson, Michael. 2004. "The Archaeology of Money: Debt versus Barter Theories of Money's Origins." In *Credit and State Theories of Money: The Contributions of A. Mitchell Innes*, ed. L. Randall Wray, 99–127. Cheltenham: Edward Elgar.

Hudson, Michael, and Marc Van De Mieroop, eds. 2002. *Debts and Economic Renewal in the Ancient Near East*. Baltimore: CDL.

Hudson, Michael, and Cornelia Wunsch, eds. 2004. *Record-Keeping, Standardization and the Development of Accounting in the Ancient Near East*. Baltimore: CDL.

Huerta de Soto, Jesús. 2009. *Money, Bank Credit, and Economic Cycles*. Auburn, AL: Ludwig von Mises Institute.

Hull, David L. 1965. "The Effect of Essentialism on Taxonomy: 2000 Years of Stasis." *British Journal for the Philosophy of Science* 15:314–16; 16:1–18.

———. 1988. *Science as a Process: An Evolutionary Account of the Social and Conceptual Development of Science*. Chicago: University of Chicago Press.

Humphrey, Caroline. 1985. "Barter and Economic Disintegration." *Man* 20, no. 1 (March): 48–72.

Hunt, Bishop C. 1935a. "The Joint-Stock Company in England, 1800–1825." *Journal of Political Economy* 43, no. 1 (February): 1–33.

———. 1935b. "The Joint-Stock Company in England, 1830–1844." *Journal of Political Economy* 43, no. 3 (June): 331–64.

Huntington, Samuel P. 1968. *Political Order in Changing Societies*. New Haven, CT: Yale University Press.

Hutchins, Edwin. 1995. *Cognition in the Wild*. Cambridge, MA: MIT Press.

Hutchinson, Allan C. 2005. *Evolution and the Common Law*. Cambridge: Cambridge University Press.

Hutt, William H. 1930. *The Theory of Collective Bargaining*. London: King.

Hutton, Will. 1995. *The State We're In*. London: Jonathan Cape.

———. 1997. *The State to Come*. London: Vintage.

Iacobucci, Edward M., and George G. Triantis. 2007. "Economic and Legal Boundaries of Firms." *Virginia Law Review* 93, no. 3:515–70.

Ingham, Geoffrey. 1996. "Money Is a Social Relation." *Review of Social Economy* 54, no. 4 (Winter): 507–29.

———. 2004. *The Nature of Money*. Cambridge: Polity.

———. 2008. *Capitalism*. Cambridge: Polity.

Ioannides, Stavros. 1992. *The Market, Competition and Democracy: A Critique of Neo-Austrian Economics*. Aldershot: Edward Elgar.

Ireland, Paddy W. 1984. "The Rise of the Limited Liability Company." *International Journal of the Sociology of Law* 12:239–60.

———. 1996. "Capitalism without the Capitalist: The Joint Stock Company Share and the Emergence of the Modern Doctrine of Separate Corporate Personality." *Journal of Legal History* 17, no. 1 (April): 40–72.

———. 1999. "Company Law and the Myth of Shareholder Ownership." *Modern Law Review* 62, no. 1 (January): 32–57.

———. 2010. "Limited Liability, Shareholder Rights and the Problem of Corporate Irresponsibility." *Cambridge Journal of Economics* 34, no. 5 (September): 837–56.

Israel, Jonathan I. 1989. *Dutch Primacy in World Trade, 1585–1740*. Oxford: Oxford University Press.

Iwai, Katsuhito. 1999. "Persons, Things and Corporations: The Corporate Personality Controversy and Comparative Corporate Governance." *American Journal of Comparative Law* 47, no. 4 (Autumn): 583–632.

Jacoby, Sanford M. 1990. "The New Institutionalism: What Can It Learn from the Old?" *Industrial Relations* 29, no. 2 (Spring): 316–59.

Jahnsen, D. Bruce. 1986. "The Formation and Protection of Property Rights among the Southern Kwakiutl Indians." *Journal of Legal Studies* 17, no. 1 (January): 41–67.

Jain, Arvind K. 2001. "Corruption: A Review." *Journal of Economic Surveys* 15, no. 1 (February): 71–120.

James, Philip S. 1966. *Introduction to English Law*. 6th ed. London: Butterworths.

James, William. 1890. *The Principles of Psychology*. 2 vols. New York: Holt; London: Macmillan.

Jardine, Lisa. 2008. *Going Dutch: How England Plundered Holland's Glory*. London: Harper.

Jary, David, and Julia Jary, eds. 1991. *The Harper Collins Dictionary of Sociology*. New York: Harper Collins.

Jaworski, Taylor, and Bart J. Wilson. 2013. "Go West Young Man: Self-Selection and Endogenous Property Rights." *Southern Economic Journal* 79, no. 4 (April): 886–904. DOI: http://dx.doi.org/10.4284/0038-4038-2011.249.

Jensen, Michael C. 1983. "Organization Theory and Methodology." *Accounting Review* 58, no. 2 (April): 323–29.

Jensen, Michael C., and William H. Meckling. 1976. "Theory of the Firm: Managerial Behavior, Agency Costs and Ownership Structure." *Journal of Financial Economics* 3, no. 4 (October): 305–60.

———. 1983. "Reflections on the Corporation as a Social Invention." *Midland Corporate Finance Journal* 1, no. 3 (Autumn): 1–21.

Jevons, William Stanley. 1871. *The Theory of Political Economy*. London: Macmillan.

Jochimsen, Maren A. 2003. *Careful Economics: Integrating Caring Activities and Economic Science*. Boston: Kluwer.

Joffe, Michael. 2011. "The Root Cause of Economic Growth under Capitalism." *Cambridge Journal of Economics* 35, no. 5 (September): 873–96.

Johnson, Allen W., and Timothy K. Earle. 2000. *The Evolution of Human Societies: From Foraging Group to Agrarian State*. Stanford, CA: Stanford University Press.

Johnson, Alvin S. 1909. *Introduction to Economics*. Boston: Heath.

Johnson, Chalmers. 1982. *MITI and the Japanese Miracle: The Growth of Industrial Policy, 1925–1975*. Stanford, CA: Stanford University Press.

Jones, Derek C. 1987. "Alternative Sharing Arrangements: A Review of the Evidence of Their Effects and Some Policy Implications for the U.S." *Economic and Industrial Democracy* 8:489–516.

Jones, Eric. 1981. *European Miracle: Environments, Economies and Geopolitics in the History of Europe and Asia*. Cambridge: Cambridge University Press.

Jossa, Bruno. 2005. "Marx, Marxism and the Cooperative Movement." *Cambridge Journal of Economics* 29, no. 1 (January): 3–18.

Joyce, Richard. 2006. *The Evolution of Morality*. Cambridge, MA: MIT Press.

Kahn-Freund, Otto. 1977. "Blackstone's Neglected Child: The Contract of Employment Law." *Law Quarterly Review* 93:508–28.

———. 1983. *Labour and the Law*. 3rd ed. Edited by P. Davies and M. Freedland. London: Stevens.

Kanngiesser, Patricia, Nathalia Gjersoe, and Bruce M. Hoo. 2010. "The Effect of Creative Labor on Property-Ownership Transfer by Preschool Children and Adults." *Psychological Science* 21, no. 9 (September): 1236–41.

Kay, Neil M. 1984. *The Emergent Firm: Knowledge, Ignorance and Surprise in Economic Organization*. London: Macmillan.

Keeley, Lawrence H. 1996. *War Before Civilization: The Myth of the Peaceful Savage*. Oxford: Oxford University Press.

Keijzer, Fred. 2001. *Representation and Behavior*. Cambridge, MA: MIT Press.

Kelsen, Hans. 1967. *Pure Theory of Law*. Translated from the German by Max Knight. Berkeley, CA: University of California Press.

Keltner, Dacher, Gerben A. Van Kleef, Serena Chen, and Michael W. Kraus. 2008. "A Reciprocal Influence Model of Social Power: Emerging Principles and Lines of Inquiry." *Advances in Experimental Social Psychology* 40:151–91.

Kennedy, David. 2011. "Some Caution about Property Rights as a Recipe for Economic Development." *Accounting, Economics, and Law* 1, no. 1, article 3.

Kenworthy, Lane. 1995. *In Search of National Economic Success: Balancing Competition and Cooperation*. Thousand Oaks, CA: Sage.

Kesting, Stefan, and Klaus Nielsen. 2008. "Varieties of Capitalism: Theoretical Critiques and Empirical Observations." In *Varieties of Capitalism and New Institutional Deals: Regulation, Welfare and the New Economy*, ed. Wolfram Elsner and Hardy Hanappi, 23–51. Cheltenham: Edward Elgar.

Keynes, John Maynard. 1930. *A Treatise on Money.* Vol. 1, *The Pure Theory of Money.* London: Macmillan.

———. 1931. *Essays in Persuasion.* London: Macmillan.

———. 1936. *The General Theory of Employment, Interest and Money.* London: Macmillan.

———. 1937. "The General Theory of Employment." *Quarterly Journal of Economics* 51, no. 1 (February): 209–23.

Khalil, Elias L. 1990. "Rationality and Social Labor in Marx." *Critical Review* 4, nos. 1–2 (Winter–Spring): 239–65.

———. 1992. "Marx's Understanding of the Essence of Capitalism." *History of Economics Review* 17, no. 1 (Winter): 19–32.

———. 1995. "Organizations versus Institutions." *Journal of Institutional and Theoretical Economics* 151, no. 3:445–66.

———. 1997. "Is the Firm an Individual?" *Cambridge Journal of Economics* 21, no. 4 (July): 519–44.

Khan, Mushtaq. 2006. "Corruption and Governance." In *The New Development Economics: After the Washington Consensus*, ed. S. Kwame Jomo and Ben Fine, 200–221. London: Zed; New Dehli: Tulika.

Khanna, Vikramaditya S. 2006. "The Economic History of the Organizational Entities in Ancient India." Michigan Law and Economics Research Paper no. 05-014, updated version. University of Michigan.

Kiker, B. F. 1966. "The Historical Roots of the Concept of Human Capital." *Journal of Political Economy* 74, no. 5 (October): 481–99.

Kim, E. Han, Adair Morse, and Luigi Zingales. 2006. "What Has Mattered to Economics since 1970." *Journal of Economic Perspectives* 20, no. 4 (December): 189–202.

Kimbrough, Erik O., Vernon L. Smith, and Bart J. Wilson. 2010. "Exchange, Theft, and the Social Formation of Property." *Journal of Economic Behavior and Organization* 74, no. 3:206–29.

Kindleberger, Charles P. 1973. *The World in Depression, 1929–1939.* London: Allen Lane.

———. 1984. *A Financial History of Western Europe.* London: Allen & Unwin.

King, Robert J., and Ross Levine. 1994. "Capital Fundamentalism, Economic Development and Economic Growth." *Carnegie-Rochester Conference Series on Public Policy* 40 (June): 259–92.

Kirman, Alan P. 1989. "The Intrinsic Limits of Modern Economic Theory: The Emperor Has No Clothes." *Economic Journal (Conference Papers)* 99:126–39.

——. 1992. "Whom or What Does the Representative Individual Represent?" *Journal of Economic Perspectives* 6, no. 2 (Spring): 117–36.

Kirman, Alan P., and Annick Vignes. 1991. "Price Dispersion: Theoretical Considerations and Empirical Evidence from the Marseilles Fish Market." In *Issues in Contemporary Economics: Proceedings of the Ninth World Congress of the International Economic Association*, ed. Kenneth J. Arrow, 160–85. New York: New York University Press.

Kitson, Peter M., L. Shaw-Taylor, E. A. Wrigley, R. S. Davies, G. Newton, and A. E. M. Satchell. 2012. "The Creation of a 'Census' of Adult Male Employment for England and Wales for 1817." Working paper. Cambridge: Cambridge University, Cambridge Group for the History of Population and Social Structure.

Klaes, Matthias. 2001. "*Begriffsgeschichte*: Between the Scylla of Conceptual and the Charybdis of Institutional History of Economics." *Journal of the History of Economic Thought* 23, no. 2:153–79.

Klein, Benjamin. 1983. "Contracting Costs and Residual Claims: The Separation of Ownership and Control." *Journal of Law and Economics* 26:367–74.

——. 1988. "Vertical Integration as Organizational Ownership: The Fisher Body–General Motors Relationship Revisited." *Journal of Law, Economics, and Organization* 4, no. 1 (Spring): 199–213.

Kley, Roland. 1994. *Hayek's Social and Political Thought*. Oxford: Clarendon.

Knapp, Georg F. 1924. *The State Theory of Money*. Translated and abridged from the 1923 (4th) German ed. (1st ed. 1905). London: Macmillan.

Knies, Karl. 1885. *Das Geld: Darlegung der Grundlehren von dem Gelde*. 2nd ed. Berlin: Weidmann.

Knight, Frank H. 1921. *Risk, Uncertainty and Profit*. New York: Houghton Mifflin.

——. 1934. "Capital, Time and the Interest Rate." *Economica* 1, no. 3 (August): 257–86.

——. 1935. "Professor Hayek and the Theory of Investment." *Economic Journal* 45, no. 1 (March): 77–94.

Knight, Jack. 1992. *Institutions and Social Conflict*. Cambridge: Cambridge University Press.

Knorr-Cetina, Karin D. 1981. *The Manufacture of Knowledge: An Essay on the Constructivist and Contextual Nature of Science*. Oxford: Pergamon.

Knorringa, Peter, and Irene van Staveren. 2007. "Beyond Social Capital: A Critical Approach." *Review of Social Economy* 65, no. 1 (March): 1–9.

Knudsen, Thorbjørn, Phanish Puranam, and Marlo Raveendran. 2012. "Organization Design: The Epistemic Interdependence Perspective." *Academy of Management Review* 37, no. 3:419–40.

Kocka, Jürgen. 2004. "Civil Society in Historical Perspective." *European Review* 12, no. 1:65–79.

Kogut, Bruce, and Udo Zander. 1992. "Knowledge of the Firm, Combinative Capabilities, and the Replication of Technology." *Organization Science* 3:383–97.

———. 1993. "Knowledge of the Firm and the Evolutionary Theory of the Multinational Corporation." *Journal of International Business Studies* 24, no. 4:625–45.

Kollmeyer, Christopher. 2012. "Consumer Markets and National Income Inequality: A Study of 18 Advanced Capitalist Countries." *International Journal of Comparative Sociology* 53, nos. 5–6 (October/December): 400–418.

Korpi, Walter, and Joakim Palme. 1998. "The Paradox of Redistribution and Strategies of Equality: Welfare State Institutions, Inequality, and Poverty in the Western Countries." *American Sociological Review* 63, no. 5:661–87.

Krall, Lisi, and John M. Gowdy. 2012. "An Institutional and Evolutionary Critique of Natural Capital." In *Toward an Integrated Paradigm for Heterodox Economics*, ed. Julien-François Gerber and Rolf Steppacher, 127–46. London: Palgrave Macmillan.

Kramer, Matthew H. 1999. *In Defense of Legal Positivism: Law without the Trimmings*. Oxford: Oxford University Press.

Krebs, Dennis. 2011. *The Origins of Morality: An Evolutionary Account*. Oxford: Oxford University Press.

Kripke, Saul. 1972. "Naming and Necessity." In *Semantics of Natural Languages*, ed. D. Davidson and G. Harman, 253–355, 763–69. Dordrecht: Reidel.

Krippner, Greta, Mark Granovetter, Fred Block, Nicole Biggart, Tom Beamish, Youtien Hsing, Gillian Hart, Giovanni Arrighi, Margie Mendell, John Hall, Michael Burawoy, Steve Vogel, and Sean O'Riain. 2004. "Polanyi Symposium: A Conversation on Embeddedness." *Socio-Economic Review* 2, no. 1 (January): 109–35.

Krueger, Anne O. 1991. "Report of the Commission on Graduate Education in Economics." *Journal of Economic Literature* 29, no. 3 (September): 1035–53.

Krugman, Paul R. 2009. "How Did Economists Get It So Wrong?" *New York Times*, September 2. http://www.nytimes.com/2009/09/06/magazine /06Economic-t.html.

Kuisel, Richard F. 1981. *Capitalism and the State in Modern France*. Cambridge: Cambridge University Press.

Kuran, Timur. 2004. "Why the Middle East Is Economically Underdeveloped: Historical Mechanisms of Institutional Stagnation." *Journal of Economic Perspectives* 18, no. 3 (Summer): 71–90.

———. 2010. *The Long Divergence: How Islamic Law Held Back the Middle East*. Princeton, NJ: Princeton University Press.

Laclau, Ernesto, and Chantal Mouffe. 1985. *Hegemony and Socialist Strategy: Towards a Radical Democratic Politics*. London: Verso.

Lakoff, George. 1987. *Women, Fire and Other Dangerous Things: What Categories Reveal about the Mind.* Chicago: University of Chicago Press.

Lamb, Robert. 2010. "Liberty, Equality, and the Boundaries of Ownership: Thomas Paine's Theory of Property Rights." *Review of Politics* 72, no. 3 (Summer): 483–511.

Lamoreaux, Naomi R., and Jean-Laurent Rosenthal. 2005. "Legal Regime and Contractual Flexibility: A Comparison of Business's Organizational Choices in France and the United States during the Period of Industrialization." *American Law and Economics Review* 7, no. 1:28–61.

Landa, Janet. 1994. *Trust, Ethnicity, and Identity: Beyond the New Institutional Economics of Ethnic Trading Networks, Contract Law, and Gift Exchange.* Ann Arbor: University of Michigan Press.

———. 1999. "Bioeconomics of Some Nonhuman and Human Societies: New Institutional Economics Approach." *Journal of Bioeconomics* 1, no. 1:95–113.

Landauer, Carl A. 1959. *European Socialism: A History of Ideas and Movements from the Industrial Revolution to Hitler's Seizure of Power.* 2 vols. Berkeley: University of California Press.

Lane, David, Franco Malerba, Robert Maxfield, and Luigi Orsenigo. 1996. "Choice and Action." *Journal of Evolutionary Economics* 6, no. 1:43–76.

Lange, Oskar R. 1936–37. "On the Economic Theory of Socialism: Parts One and Two." *Review of Economic Studies* 4, no. 1:53–71; 4, no. 2:123–42. Reprinted in Lange and Taylor (1938).

———. 1967. "The Computer and the Market." In *Capitalism, Socialism and Economic Growth: Essays Presented to Maurice Dobb*, ed. C. Feinstein, 158–61. Cambridge: Cambridge University Press.

———. 1987. "The Economic Operation of a Socialist Society." *Contributions to Political Economy* 6:3–24. Two lectures delivered in 1942.

Lange, Oskar R., and Frederick M. Taylor. 1938. *On the Economic Theory of Socialism.* Edited by Benjamin E. Lippincot. Minneapolis: University of Minnesota Press.

Langlois, Richard N. 1984. "Internal Organization in a Dynamic Context: Some Theoretical Considerations." In *Communication and Information Economics: New Perspectives*, ed. Meherhoo Jussawalla and Helene Ebenfield, 23–49. Amsterdam: North-Holland.

———. 1995a. "Capabilities and Coherence in Firms and Markets." In *Resource-Based and Evolutionary Theories of the Firm: Towards a Synthesis*, ed. Cynthia A. Montgomery, 71–100. Boston: Kluwer.

———. 1995b. "Do Firms Plan?" *Constitutional Political Economy* 6:247–61.

La Porta, Rafael, Florencio Lopez-de-Silanes, and Andrei Shleifer. 2008. "The Economic Consequences of Legal Origins." *Journal of Economic Literature* 46, no. 2 (June): 285–332.

Lascaux, Alex. 2008. "Trust and Uncertainty: A Critical Re-Assessment." *International Review of Sociology* 18, no. 1 (March): 1–18.

La Torre, Massimo. 1993. "Institutionalism Old and New." *Ratio Juris* 6, no. 2 (July): 190–201.

Latour, Bruno. 2005. *Reassembling the Social: An Introduction to Actor-Network-Theory.* Oxford: Oxford University Press.

Lave, Jean. 1988. *Cognition in Practice: Mind, Mathematics, and Culture in Everyday Life.* Cambridge: Cambridge University Press.

Lave, Jean, and Etienne Wenger. 1991. *Situated Learning: Legitimate Peripheral Participation.* Cambridge: Cambridge University Press.

Lavoie, Donald. 1985a. *National Economic Planning: What Is Left?* Cambridge, MA: Ballinger.

———. 1985b. *Rivalry and Central Planning: The Socialist Calculation Debate Reconsidered.* Cambridge: Cambridge University Press.

Lavoie, Marc. 1992. "Jacques Le Bourva's Theory of Endogenous Credit-Money." *Review of Political Economy* 4, no. 4 (October): 436–46.

Lawrence, William H. 2002. *Understanding Negotiable Instruments and Payment Systems.* Newark, NJ: Matthew Bender.

Lawson, Tony. 1997. *Economics and Reality.* London: Routledge.

———. 2013. "What Is This 'School' Called Neoclassical Economics?" *Cambridge Journal of Economics* 37, no. 5 (September): 947–98.

Lazaric, Nathalie. 2000. "The Role of Routines, Rules and Habits in Collective Learning: Some Epistemological and Ontological Considerations." *European Journal of Economic and Social Systems* 14, no. 2:157–71.

Lazonick, William. 1991. *Business Organization and the Myth of the Market Economy.* Cambridge: Cambridge University Press.

LeBlanc, Steven A. 2003. *Constant Battles.* New York: St. Martin's.

Lee, Ruben. 1998. *What Is an Exchange? The Automation, Management, and Regulation of Financial Markets.* Oxford: Oxford University Press.

Leeson, Peter T. 2009. *The Invisible Hook: The Hidden Economics of Pirates.* Princeton, NJ: Princeton University Press.

Leijonhufvud, Axel. 1986. "Capitalism and the Factory System." In *Economics as a Process: Essays in the New Institutional Economics*, ed. Richard N. Langlois, 203–23. Cambridge: Cambridge University Press.

Lenin, Vladimir Ilyich. 1967. *Selected Works in Three Volumes.* London: Lawrence & Wishart.

Lerner, Abba P. 1944. *The Economics of Control: Principles of Welfare Economics.* New York: Macmillan.

———. 1947. "Money as a Creature of the State." *American Economic Review* 37, no. 2 (June): 312–17.

Levins, Richard, and Richard C. Lewontin. 1985. *The Dialectical Biologist.* Cambridge, MA: Harvard University Press.

Levitt, Barbara, and James G. March. 1988. "Organizational Learning." *Annual Review of Sociology* 14:319–40.

Levy, Frank, and Richard J. Murnane. 1996. "With What Skills Are Computers a Complement?" *American Economic Review: Papers and Proceedings* 86, no. 2 (May): 258–62.

Lewin, Shira B. 1996. "Economics and Psychology: Lessons for Our Own Day from the Early Twentieth Century." *Journal of Economic Literature* 34, no. 3 (September): 1293–1323.

Lewontin, Richard C. 1996. "Evolution as Engineering." In *Integrative Approaches to Molecular Biology*, ed. Julio Collado-Vides, Boris Magasanik, and Temple F. Smith, 1–10. Cambridge, MA: MIT Press.

Li, Minqi. 2008. *The Rise of China and the Demise of the Capitalist World Economy*. London: Pluto; New York: Monthly Review Press.

Lie, John. 1997. "Sociology of Markets." *Annual Review of Sociology* 23:341–60.

Lincoln, James R., Harold R. Kerbo, and Elke Wittenhagen. 1995. "Japanese Companies in Germany: A Case Study in Cross-Cultural Management." *Industrial Relations* 34, no. 2:417–40.

Lindblom, Charles E. 1977. *Politics and Markets: The World's Political-Economic Systems*. New York: Basic.

Lindenberg, Siegwart. 1993. "Club Hierarchy, Social Metering and Context Instruction: Governance Structures in Response to Varying Self-Command Capital." In *Interdisciplinary Perspectives on Organization Studies*, ed. Siegwart Lindenberg and Hein Schreuder, 195–220. Oxford: Pergamon.

Lindert, Peter H., and Jeffrey G. Williamson. 1982. "Revising England's Social Tables, 1688–1812." *Explorations in Economic History* 19, no. 4 (October): 385–408.

Lipsey, Richard G., Kenneth I. Carlaw, and Clifford T. Bekar. 2005. *Economic Transformations: General Purpose Technologies and Long Term Economic Growth*. Oxford: Oxford University Press.

List, Christian, and Philip Pettit. 2011. *Group Agency: The Possibility, Design, and Status of Corporate Agents*. Oxford: Oxford University Press.

List, Friedrich. 1841. *Das nationale System der politischen Ökonomie*. Stuttgart and Tübingen: J. G. Cotta. Translated as *The National System of Political Economy* (London: Longmans, Green, 1904).

Littler, Craig R., and Graeme Salaman. 1982. "Bravermania and Beyond: Recent Theories of the Labour Process." *Sociology* 16, no. 2 (May): 251–69.

Llewellyn, Karl N. 1960. *The Bramble Bush: On Our Law and Its Study*. New York: Oceana.

Lloyd, Dennis. 1964. *The Idea of Law*. Harmondsworth: Penguin.

Loasby, Brian J. 1976. *Choice, Complexity and Ignorance: An Enquiry into Economic Theory and the Practice of Decision Making*. Cambridge: Cambridge University Press.

———. 2000. "Market Institutions and Economic Evolution." *Journal of Evolutionary Economics* 10, no. 3:297–309.

Lorenz, Edward H. 2001. "Models of Cognition, the Development of Knowledge and Organisational Theory." *Journal of Management and Governance* 5:307–30.

Ludwig, Arnold M. 2002. *King of the Mountain: The Nature of Political Leadership*. Lexington: University Press of Kentucky.

Lueck, Dean, and Thomas J. Miceli. 2007. "Property Law." In *Handbook of Law and Economics* (2 vols.), ed. A. Mitchell Polinsky and Steven Shavell, 1:183–257. Amsterdam: Elsevier.

Luhmann, Niklas. 1985. *A Sociological Theory of Law*. Translated by E. King. Edited by M. Albrow. London: Routledge & Kegan Paul.

———. 1993. *Das Recht der Gesellschaft*. Frankfurt a.M.: Suhrkamp. Translated as *Law as a Social System* (Oxford: Oxford University Press, 2004).

Luo, Jianxi, Carliss Y. Baldwin, Daniel E. Whitney, and Christopher L. Magee. 2012. "The Architecture of Transaction Networks: A Comparative Analysis of Hierarchy in Two Sectors." *Industrial and Corporate Change* 21, no. 6:1307–35.

Macaulay, Stewart. 1963. "Non-Contractual Relations in Business: A Preliminary Study." *American Sociological Review* 28, no. 1:55–67.

MacCormick, D. Neil. 1998. "Laws, Institutions, and Facts." *Law and Philosophy* 17, no. 3 (May): 301–45.

———. 2007. *Institutions of Law: An Essay in Legal Theory*. Oxford: Oxford University Press.

Macfarlane, Alan. 1978. *The Origins of English Individualism*. Oxford: Basil Blackwell.

Machlup, Fritz. 1967. "Theories of the Firm: Marginalist, Behavioral, Managerial." *American Economic Review* 57, no. 1 (March): 1–33.

MacKenzie, Donald. 2006. *An Engine, Not a Camera*. Cambridge MA: MIT Press.

MacLeod, Christine. 2002. *Inventing the Industrial Revolution: The English Patent System, 1660–1800*. Cambridge: Cambridge University Press.

MacLeod, Henry Dunning. 1858. *Elements of Political Economy*. London: Longmans Green.

———. 1872. *The Principles of Economic Philosophy*. 2nd ed. London: Longmans Green.

———. 1878. *The Elements of Banking*. 4th ed. London: Longmans Green.

Maddison, Angus. 2001. *The World Economy: A Millennial Perspective*. Paris: OECD.

———. 2003. *The World Economy: Historical Statistics*. Paris: OECD.

———. 2007. *Contours of the World Economy, 1–2030 AD: Essays in Macro-Economic History*. Oxford: Oxford University Press.

Magill, Michael, and Martine Quinzii. 1996. *Theory of Incomplete Markets.* 2 vols. Cambridge, MA: MIT Press.

Maine, Henry Sumner. 1861. *Ancient Law, Its Connection with the Early History of Society, and Its Relation to Modern Ideas.* London: Murray.

Makdisi, John A. 1999. "The Islamic Origins of the Common Law." *North Carolina Law Review* 77, no. 5 (June): 1635–1739.

Malthus, Thomas Robert. 1827. *Definitions in Political Economy.* London: John Murray.

Mandel, Ernest. 1967. *An Introduction to Marxist Economic Theory.* New York: YSA.

Mann, Michael. 1986. *The Sources of Social Power.* Vol. 1, *A History of Power from the Beginning to A.D. 1760.* Cambridge: Cambridge University Press.

Mantzavinos, Chris. 2001. *Individuals, Institutions and Markets.* Cambridge: Cambridge University Press.

Maoz, Zeev. 1997. "The Controversy over the Democratic Peace: Rearguard Action or Cracks in the Wall?" *International Security* 22, no. 1 (Summer): 162–98.

Margolis, Howard. 1994. *Paradigms and Barriers: How Habits of Mind Govern Scientific Beliefs.* Chicago: University of Chicago Press.

Marimon, Ramon E., Ellen McGrattan, and Thomas J. Sargent. 1990. "Money as a Medium of Exchange in an Economy with Artificially Intelligent Agents." *Journal of Economic Dynamics and Control* 14:329–73.

Marquand, Judith. 1989. *Autonomy and Change: The Sources of Economic Growth.* Hemel Hempstead: Harvester Wheatsheaf.

Marris, Robin. 1964. *The Economic Theory of "Managerial" Capitalism.* London: Macmillan.

Marsden, David. 1986. *The End of Economic Man? Custom and Competition in Labour Markets.* Brighton: Wheatsheaf.

Marshall, Alfred. 1919. *Industry and Trade.* London: Macmillan.

———. 1920. *Principles of Economics: An Introductory Volume.* 8th ed. London: Macmillan.

Marshall, Gordon, ed. 1998. *Oxford Dictionary of Sociology.* Oxford: Oxford University Press.

Martinez, Mark A. 2009. *The Myth of the Free Market: The Role of the State in a Capitalist Economy.* Sterling, VA: Kumarian.

Marx, Karl. 1867. *Das Kapital: Kritik der politischen Ökonomie.* Vol. 1. Hamburg: Meissner.

———. 1971. *A Contribution to the Critique of Political Economy.* Translated from the 1859 German ed. London: Lawrence & Wishart.

———. 1973a. *Grundrisse: Foundations of the Critique of Political Economy.* Harmondsworth: Penguin.

———. 1973b. *The Revolutions of 1848: Political Writings—Volume 1*. Edited and with an introduction by David Fernbach. Harmondsworth: Penguin.

———. 1974. *The First International and After: Political Writings—Volume 3*. Edited and with an introduction by David Fernbach. Harmondsworth: Penguin.

———. 1975. *Early Writings*. Harmondsworth: Penguin.

———. 1976. *Capital*. Vol. 1. Translated from the 1890 (4th) German ed. Harmondsworth: Pelican.

———. 1978. *Capital*. Vol. 2. Translated from the 1893 German ed. Harmondsworth: Pelican.

———. 1981. *Capital*. Vol. 3. Translated from the 1894 German ed. Harmondsworth: Pelican.

Marx, Karl, and Frederick Engels. 1976. *Karl Marx and Frederick Engels, Collected Works*. Vol. 5, *Marx and Engels: 1845–47*. London: Lawrence & Wishart.

———. 1989. *Karl Marx and Frederick Engels, Collected Works*. Vol. 24, *Marx and Engels: 1874–1883*. London: Lawrence & Wishart.

Masten, Scott E. 1991. "A Legal Basis for the Firm." In *The Nature of the Firm: Origins, Evolution, and Development*, ed. Oliver E. Williamson and Sidney G. Winter, 196–212. Oxford: Oxford University Press.

Masten, Scott E., and Jens Prüfer. 2011. "On the Evolution of Collective Enforcement Institutions: Communities and Courts." Discussion Paper no. 2001-074. Tilburg: Tilburg University.

Mauro, Paolo. 1995. "Corruption and Growth." *Quarterly Journal of Economics* 110, no. 3 (August): 681–712.

Mayfield, John E. 2013. *The Engine of Complexity: Evolution as Computation*. New York: Columbia University Press.

Mayr, Ernst. 1963. *Animal Species and Evolution*. Cambridge, MA: Harvard University Press.

———. 1976. *Evolution and the Diversity of Life: Selected Essays*. Cambridge, MA: Harvard University Press.

———. 1982. *The Growth of Biological Thought: Diversity, Evolution, and Inheritance*. Cambridge, MA: Harvard University Press.

———. 1988. *Toward a New Philosophy of Biology: Observations of an Evolutionist*. Cambridge, MA: Harvard University Press.

Mazzucato, Mariana. 2013. *The Entrepreneurial State: Debunking Public vs. Private Sector Myths*. London: Anthem.

McAfee, R. Preston, and John McMillan. 1987. "Auctions and Bidding." *Journal of Economic Literature* 25, no. 2 (June): 699–738.

McCloskey, Deirdre N. 2010. *Bourgeois Dignity: Why Economics Can't Explain the Modern World*. Chicago: University of Chicago Press.

———. In press. *The Treasured Bourgeoisie: How Markets and Innovation Became Virtuous, 1600–1848, and Then Suspect*. Chicago: University of Chicago Press.

McCloskey, Donald N. 1991. "Economic Science: A Search through the Hyperspace of Assumptions?" *Methodus* 3, no. 1 (June): 6–16.

McMillan, John. 2002. *Reinventing the Bazaar: A Natural History of Markets.* New York: Norton.

McMillan, John, and Christopher Woodruff. 1999. "Dispute Prevention without Courts in Vietnam." *Journal of Law, Economics, and Organization* 15 (October): 637–58.

———. 2000. "Private Order under Dysfunctional Public Order." *Michigan Law Review* 98:2430–35.

McNeill, William H. 1980. *The Pursuit of Power: Technology, Armed Force, and Society since A.D. 1000.* Chicago: University of Chicago Press.

Meade, James E. 1955. *Trade and Welfare.* Oxford: Oxford University Press.

———. 1986. *Different Forms of Share Economy.* London: Public Policy Centre.

———. 1989. *Agathotopia: The Economics of Partnership.* Aberdeen: Aberdeen University Press.

Mehrling, Perry G. 2000. "Modern Money: Fiat or Credit?" *Journal of Post Keynesian Economics* 22, no. 3 (Spring): 397–406.

Meikle, Scott. 1985. *Essentialism in the Thought of Karl Marx.* London: Duckworth.

———. 1995. *Aristotle's Economic Thought.* Oxford: Oxford University Press.

———. 2000. "Aristotle on Money." In *What Is Money?* ed. John N. Smithin, 157–73. London: Routledge.

Ménard, Claude. 1995. "Markets as Institutions versus Organizations as Markets? Disentangling Some Fundamental Concepts." *Journal of Economic Behavior and Organization* 28, no. 2:161–82.

———. 1996. "On Clusters, Hybrids, and Other Strange Forms: The Case of the French Poultry Industry." *Journal of Institutional and Theoretical Economics* 152, no. 1 (March): 154–83.

Menger, Carl. 1871. *Grundsätze der Volkwirtschaftslehre.* Tübingen: J. C. B. Mohr. Translated into English as Menger (1981).

———. 1883. *Untersuchungen über die Methode der Sozialwissenschaften und der politischen Ökonomie insbesondere.* Tübingen: J. C. B. Mohr. Translated into English as Menger (1985).

———. 1892. "On the Origins of Money." *Economic Journal* 2, no. 2 (June): 239–55.

———. 1909/1936. "Geld." In *The Collected Works of Carl Menger,* vol. 4, *Schriften über Geldtheorie und Währungspolitik,* 1–116. London: London School of Economics. Reprinted as "Money," in *Carl Menger and the Evolution of Payments Systems,* ed. Michael Latzer and Stefan Schmitz (Cheltenham: Edward Elgar, 2002), 25–107.

———. 1981. *Principles of Economics.* New York: New York University Press. English translation of Menger (1971).

———. 1985. *Investigations into the Method of the Social Sciences with Special Reference to Economics.* New York: New York University Press. English translation of Menger (1883).

Merriam-Webster. 2012. "Words of the Year 2012." http://www.merriam-webster.com/info/2012words.htm.

Merrill, Michael. 1995. "Putting 'Capitalism' in Its Place: A Review of Recent Literature." *William and Mary Quarterly*, 3rd ser., 52, no. 2 (April): 315–26.

Merry, Sally Engle. 1988. "Legal Pluralism." *Law and Society Review* 22, no. 5:869–96.

Mesoudi, Alex. 2011. *Cultural Evolution: How Darwinian Evolutionary Theory Can Explain Human Culture and Synthesize the Social Sciences.* Chicago: University of Chicago Press.

Metcalfe, J. Stanley. 1988. "Evolution and Economic Change." In *Technology and Economic Progress*, ed. Aubrey Silberston, 54–85. Basingstoke: Macmillan.

———. 1998. *Evolutionary Economics and Creative Destruction.* London: Routledge.

Michaelides, Panayotis G., and John G. Milios. 2009. "Joseph Schumpeter and the German Historical School." *Cambridge Journal of Economics* 33, no. 3 (May): 495–516.

Michie, Jonathan, ed. 2003. *The Handbook of Globalisation.* Cheltenham: Edward Elgar.

Micklethwait, John, and Adrian Wooldridge. 2003. *The Company: A Short History of a Revolutionary Idea.* New York: Modern Library.

Milanovic, Branko. 2005. *Worlds Apart: Measuring International and Global Inequality.* Princeton, NJ: Princeton University Press.

———. 2011. "A Short History of Global Inequality: The Past Two Centuries." *Explorations in Economic History* 48, no. 4 (December): 494–506.

Milgram, Stanley. 1974. *Obedience to Authority: An Experimental View.* New York: Harper & Row; London: Tavistock.

Milgrom, Paul R., Douglass C. North, and Barry R. Weingast. 1990. "The Role of Institutions in the Revival of Trade: The Law Merchant, Private Judges and the Champagne Fairs." *Economics and Politics* 2, no. 1 (March): 1–23.

Milhaupt, Curtis J., and Katharina Pistor. 2008. *Law and Capitalism: What Corporate Crises Reveal about Legal Systems and Economic Development around the World.* Chicago: University of Chicago Press.

Mill, John Stuart. 1871. *Principles of Political Economy with Some of Their Applications to Social Philosophy.* 7th ed. London: Longman, Green, Reader & Dyer.

Miller, Gary J. 1992. *Managerial Dilemmas: The Political Economy of Hierarchy.* Cambridge: Cambridge University Press.

Minard, Philippe. 2005. "Norms, Institutions and Economic Liberalism." Typescript, Université Paris 8.

Minkler, Lanse P. 2008. *Integrity and Agreement: Economics When Principles Also Matter.* Ann Arbor, MI: University of Michigan Press.

Minsky, Hyman P. 1982. *Can "It" Happen Again? Essays in Instability and Finance.* Armonk, NY: M. E. Sharpe.

———. 1986. *Stabilizing an Unstable Economy.* New Haven, CT: Yale University Press.

Mirowski, Philip. 1989. *More Heat Than Light: Economics as Social Physics, Physics as Nature's Economics.* Cambridge: Cambridge University Press.

———. 2002. *Machine Dreams: Economics Becomes a Cyborg Science.* Cambridge: Cambridge University Press.

———. 2007. "Markets Come to Bits: Evolution, Computation and Markomata in Economic Science." *Journal of Economic Behavior and Organization* 63, no. 2 (June): 209–42.

———. 2013. *Never Let a Serious Crisis Go to Waste: How. Neoliberalism Survived the Financial Meltdown.* London: Verso.

Mirowski, Philip, and Edward Nik-Khah. 2007. "Markets Made Flesh: Callon, Performativity and the FCC Spectrum Auctions." In *Do Economists Make Markets? On the Performativity of Economics,* 190–224. Princeton, NJ: Princeton University Press.

Mirowski, Philip, and Esther-Mirjam Sent, eds. 2002. *Science Bought and Sold: Essays on the Economics of Science.* Chicago: University of Chicago Press.

Mirowski, Philip, and Koye Somefun. 1998. "Markets as Evolving Computational Entities." *Journal of Evolutionary Economics* 8, no. 4:329–56.

Mitchell Innes, Alfred. 1914. "The Credit Theory of Money." *Banking Law Journal* 31 (December–January): 151–68.

Mnookin, R. H., and L. Kornhauser. 1979. "Bargaining in the Shadow of the Law: The Case of Divorce." *Yale Law Journal* 88:950–97.

Mo, Pak Hung. 2001. "Corruption and Economic Growth." *Journal of Comparative Economics* 29, no. 1 (March): 66–79.

Mokyr, Joel. 2003. *The Gifts of Athena: Historical Origins of the Knowledge Economy.* Princeton, NJ: Princeton University Press.

———. 2010. *The Enlightened Economy: An Economic History of Britain, 1700–1850.* New Haven, CT: Yale University Press.

Montgomery, Jonathan. 1988. "Children as Property?" *Modern Law Review* 51, no. 3 (May): 323–42.

Moore, Barrington, Jr. 1966. *Social Origins of Dictatorship and Democracy: Lord and Peasant in the Making of the Modern World.* London: Allen Lane.

Moore, Basil J. 1988. *Horizontalists and Verticalists: The Macroeconomics of Credit Money.* Cambridge: Cambridge University Press.

Moore, John H. 1992. "The Firm as a Collection of Assets." *European Economic Review* 36, nos. 2–3:493–507.

Morgan, E. Victor, and W. A. Thomas. 1962. *The Stock Exchange: Its History and Functions*. London: Elek.

Morroni, Mario. 1992. *Production Process and Technical Change*. Cambridge: Cambridge University Press.

Moshenskyi, Sergii. 2008. *History of the Weksel: Bill of Exchange and Promissory Note*. Bloomington, IN: Xlibris.

Moss, Laurence S. 1990. "Evolutionary Change and Marshall's Abandoned Second Volume." *Economie appliquée* 43, no. 1:85–98.

Mousseau, Michael, Håvard Hegre, and John R. Oneal. 2003. "How the Wealth of Nations Conditions the Liberal Peace." *European Journal of International Relations* 9, no. 4:277–314.

Mouzelis, Nicos. 1995. *Sociological Theory: What Went Wrong? Diagnosis and Remedies*. London: Routledge.

Muchlinksi, Peter. 2010. "Limited Liability and Multinational Enterprises: A Case for Reform." *Cambridge Journal of Economics* 34, no. 5 (September): 915–28.

Mumford, Lewis. 1934. *Technics and Civilization*. New York: Harcourt, Brace & World; London: Routledge.

Mundell, Robert A. 1968. *International Economics*. New York: Macmillan.

Murphy, Anne L. 2009. *The Origins of English Financial Markets: Investment and Speculation Before the South Sea Bubble*. Cambridge: Cambridge University Press.

Murphy, James Bernard. 1994. "The Kinds of Order in Society." In *Natural Images in Economic Thought: "Markets Read in Tooth and Claw,"* ed. Philip Mirowski, 536–82. Cambridge: Cambridge University Press.

Murray, James A. H. 1893. *A New English Dictionary on Historical Principles*. Vol. 2. Oxford: Clarendon.

Murrell, Peter. 1983. "Did the Theory of Market Socialism Answer the Challenge of Ludwig von Mises? A Reinterpretation of the Socialist Controversy?" *History of Political Economy* 15, no. 1 (Spring): 92–105.

———. 1991. "Can Neoclassical Economics Underpin the Reform of Centrally Planned Economies?" *Journal of Economic Perspectives* 5, no. 4 (Fall): 59–76.

Myrdal, Gunnar. 1978. "Institutional Economics." *Journal of Economic Issues* 12, no. 4 (December): 771–84.

Nagel, Thomas. 2002. *Concealment and Exposure and Other Essays*. Oxford: Oxford University Press.

Naidu, Surech, and Noam Yuchtman. 2011. "Coercive Contract Enforcement: Law and the Labor Market in 19th Century Industrial Britain." Working Paper no. 17051. Cambridge, MA: National Bureau of Economic Research.

National Center for Employee Ownership. 2012. "A Statistical Profile of Employee Ownership." http://www.nceo.org/articles/statistical-profile-employee -ownership.

Naughton, Barry. 2007. *The Chinese Economy: Transitions and Growth*, Cambridge, MA: MIT Press.

Neal, Larry. 1990. *The Rise of Financial Capitalism: International Capital Markets in the Age of Reason*. Cambridge: Cambridge University Press.

Nee, Victor, and Sonja Opper. 2013. *Capitalism from Below: Markets and Institutional Change in China*. Cambridge, MA: Harvard University Press.

Nef, John U. 1950. *War and Human Progress: An Essay on the Rise of Industrial Civilization*. Cambridge, MA: Harvard University Press.

Neild, Robert R. 2001. *Public Corruption: The Dark Side of Social Evolution*. London: Anthem.

Nelson, Katherine, and Richard R. Nelson. 2003. "The Cumulative Advance of Human Know-How." *Philosophical Transactions of the Royal Society of London: Mathematical, Physical and Engineering Sciences* 361, no. 1809 (August): 1635–53.

Nelson, Richard R. 1959. "The Simple Economics of Basic Scientific Research." *Journal of Political Economy* 67, no. 3 (June): 297–306.

———. 1981a. "Assessing Private Enterprise: An Exegesis of Tangled Doctrine." *Bell Journal of Economics* 12, no. 1:93–111.

———. 1981b. "Research on Productivity Growth and Productivity Differences: Dead Ends and New Departures." *Journal of Economic Literature* 29, no. 3 (September): 1029–64.

———. 1982. "The Role of Knowledge in R&D Efficiency." *Quarterly Journal of Economics* 97, no. 3 (August): 453–70.

———. 1991. "Why Do Firms Differ, and How Does It Matter?" Special issue, *Strategic Management Journal* 12 (Winter): 61–74.

———. 2003. "On the Complexities and Limits of Market Organization." *Review of International Political Economy* 10, no. 4 (November): 697–710.

Nelson, Richard R., and Sidney G. Winter. 1982. *An Evolutionary Theory of Economic Change*. Cambridge, MA: Harvard University Press.

———. 2002. "Evolutionary Theorizing in Economics." *Journal of Economic Perspectives* 16, no. 2 (Spring): 23–46.

The New Palgrave: A Dictionary of Economics. 1987. Edited by John Eatwell, Murray Milgate, and Peter Newman. 4 vols. London: Macmillan.

Niechoj, Torsten. 2008. "Hayek vs. Hayek: A Defence of Moderate Trade Union Activity." *Explorations in Austrian Economics* (Advances in Austrian Economics, vol. 11), ed. Roger Koppl, 123–41. Amsterdam: Elsevier.

Nietzsche, Friedrich. 1996. *Human, All Too Human: A Book for Free Spirits*. Translated from the 1878 German ed. by R. J. Hollingdale. Cambridge: Cambridge University Press.

Nitzan, Jonathan, and Shimshon Bichler. 2009. *Capital as Power: A Study of Order and Creorder*. London: Routledge.

Nivette, Amy E. 2011. "Violence in Non-State Societies." *British Journal of Criminology*. DOI: 10.1093/bjc/azr008.

Nolan, Peter. 2004. *China at the Crossroads*. Cambridge: Polity.

Nonaka, Ikujiro, and Hirotaka Takeuchi. 1995. *The Knowledge-Creating Company: How Japanese Companies Create the Dynamics of Innovation*. Oxford: Oxford University Press.

Nonaka, Ikujiro, Groeg von Krogh, and Sven Voelpel. 2006. "Organizational Knowledge Creation Theory: Evolutionary Paths and Future Advances." *Organization Studies* 27, no. 8:1179–1208.

Nooteboom, Bart. 2000. *Learning and Innovation in Organizations and Economies*. Oxford: Oxford University Press.

———. 2002. *Trust: Forms, Foundations, Failures and Figures*. Cheltenham: Edward Elgar.

———. 2004. *Inter-Firm Collaboration, Learning and Networks: An Integrated Approach*. London: Routledge.

Nooteboom, Bart, and Frédérique Six, eds. 2003. *The Trust Process in Organizations: Empirical Studies of the Determinants and the Process of Trust Development*. Cheltenham: Edward Elgar.

North, Douglass C. 1971. "Institutional Change and Economic Growth." *Journal of Economic History* 31, no. 1 (March): 118–25.

———. 1977. "Markets and Other Allocation Systems in History: The Challenge of Karl Polanyi." *Journal of European Economic History* 6, no. 3 (Winter): 703–16.

———. 1990a. *Institutions, Institutional Change and Economic Performance*. Cambridge: Cambridge University Press.

———. 1990b. "A Transactions Cost Theory of Politics." *Journal of Theoretical Politics* 2, no. 4 (October): 355–67.

———. 1991. "Institutions." *Journal of Economic Perspectives* 5, no. 1 (Winter): 97–112.

———. 1994. "Economic Performance through Time." *American Economic Review* 84, no. 3 (June): 359–67.

———. 2002a. Letter to G. M. Hodgson dated September 10, 2002. Extracted in Hodgson (2006c).

———. 2002b. Letter to G. M. Hodgson dated October 7, 2002. Extracted in Hodgson (2006c).

———. 2005. *Understanding the Process of Economic Change*. Princeton, NJ: Princeton University Press.

North, Douglass C., John J. Wallis, and Barry R. Weingast. 2009. *Violence and Social Orders: A Conceptual Framework for Interpreting Recorded Human History*. Cambridge: Cambridge University Press.

North, Douglass C., and Barry R. Weingast. 1989. "Constitutions and Commitment: The Evolution of Institutions Governing Public Choice in Seventeenth-Century England." *Journal of Economic History* 49, no. 4 (December): 803–32.

Nowak, Martin A., and Roger Highfield. 2011. *Super Cooperators: Evolution, Altruism and Human Behaviour (or Why We Need Each Other to Succeed)*. London: Penguin.

Nozick, Robert. 1974. *Anarchy, State, and Utopia*. New York: Basic.

Nussbaum, Martha C. 1992. "Human Functioning and Social Justice: In Defense of Aristotelian Essentialism." *Political Theory* 20, no. 2 (May): 202–46.

———. 2000. *Women and Economic Development: The Capabilities Approach*. Cambridge: Cambridge University Press.

Nyssens, Marthe, ed. 2006. *Social Enterprise: At the Crossroads of Market, Public Policies and Civil Society*. London: Routledge.

O'Brien, Patrick K. 1989. "The Impact of the Revolutionary and Napoleonic Wars, 1793–1815, on the Long Run Growth of the British Economy." *Review Fernand Braudel Center* 12:335–83.

———. 1993. "Political Preconditions for the Industrial Revolution." In *The Industrial Revolution and British Society*, ed. Patrick K. O'Brien and R. Quinault, 124–55. Cambridge: Cambridge University Press.

———. 1994. "Central Government and the Economy, 1688–1815." In *The Economic History of Britain since 1700*, vol. 1, *1700–1815* (2nd ed.), ed. R. Floud and D. McCloskey, 205–41. Cambridge: Cambridge University Press.

Observations Relative to the Bill Introduced in the Last Session of Parliament, for the Abolition of Arrest, and Imprisonment for Debt: With Remarks on the Pamphlet of B. Hawes Esq. MP, by a Conservative Reformer. 1837. London: J. Shackell.

O'Donnell, John M. 1985. *The Origins of Behaviorism: American Psychology, 1870–1920*. New York: New York University Press.

Oi, Jean C. 1999. *Rural China Takes Off: Institutional Foundations of Economic Reform*. Berkeley and Los Angeles: University of California Press.

Oliver, Christine. 1997. "Sustainable Comparative Advantage: Combining Institutional and Resource-Based Views." *Strategic Management Journal* 18, no. 9 (October): 697–713.

Olson, Mancur, Jr. 1982. *The Rise and Decline of Nations: Economic Growth, Stagflation and Social Rigidities*. New Haven, CT: Yale University Press.

———. 2000. *Power and Prosperity: Outgrowing Communist and Capitalist Dictatorships*. New York: Basic.

O'Neill, John. 1993. *Ecology, Policy and Politics: Human Wellbeing and the Natural World*. London: Routledge.

———. 1997. "Managing without Prices: The Monetary Valuation of Biodiversity." *Ambo* 26, no. 8:546–50.

———. 1998. *The Market: Ethics, Knowledge and Politics*. London: Routledge.

———. 2001. "Essences and Markets." In *The Economic World View: Studies in the Ontology of Economics*, ed. Uskali Mäki, 157–73. Cambridge: Cambridge University Press.

Oppenheimer, Stephen. 2004. *The Real Eve*. New York: Carroll & Graf. Published in the United Kingdom as *Out of Eden* (London: Constable & Robinson, 2003).

Oregon Tea Party. 2011. "Oregon Tea Party PAC—Mission." http://www.oregon teapartypac.org/about/mission.

Organisation for Economic Co-Operation and Development (OECD). 2012. *Education Indicators in Focus*. Paris: OECD.

Orléan, André. 2011. *L'empire de la valeur*. Paris: La Seuil.

Orlikowski, Wanda J. 2010. "The Sociomateriality of Organisational Life: Considering Technology in Management Research." *Cambridge Journal of Economics* 34, no. 1 (January): 125–41.

Orts, Eric W. 2013. *Business Persons: A Legal Theory of the Firm*. Oxford: Oxford University Press.

Ostrom, Elinor. 1990. *Governing the Commons: The Evolution of Institutions for Collective Action*. Cambridge: Cambridge University Press.

———. 2000. "Collective Action and the Evolution of Social Norms." *Journal of Economic Perspectives* 14, no. 3 (Summer): 137–58.

———. 2004. "The Ten Most Important Books." *Tidsskriftet Politik* 4, no. 7 (December): 36–48.

———. 2005. *Understanding Institutional Diversity*. Princeton, NJ: Princeton University Press.

Ostrom, Elinor, and T. K. Ahn. 2003. Introduction to *Foundations of Social Capital*, ed. Elinor Ostrom and T. K. Ahn, xi–xxxix. Cheltenham: Edward Elgar.

Ouellette, Judith A., and Wendy Wood. 1998. "Habit and Intention in Everyday Life: The Multiple Processes by Which Past Behavior Predicts Future Behavior." *Psychological Bulletin* 124:54–74.

Outhwaite, William, and Tom Bottomore. 1994. *The Blackwell Dictionary of Twentieth Century Thought*. Oxford: Basil Blackwell.

Padgett, John F., Doowan Lee, and Nick Collier. 2003. "Economic Production as Chemistry." *Industrial and Corporate Change* 12, no. 4 (August): 843–77.

Padgett, John F., and Walter W. Powell, eds. 2012. *The Emergence of Organizations and Markets*. Princeton, NJ: Princeton University Press.

Pagano, Ugo. 1985. *Work and Welfare in Economic Theory*. Oxford: Basil Blackwell.

———. 1991. "Property Rights, Asset Specificity, and the Division of Labour under Alternative Capitalist Relations." *Cambridge Journal of Economics* 15, no. 3 (September): 315–42.

———. 2001. "The Origin of Organisational Species." In *The Evolution of Eco-*

nomic Diversity, ed. Antonio Nicita and Ugo Pagano, 21–48. London: Routledge.

———. 2007. "Legal Positions and Institutional Complementarities." In *Legal Orderings and Economic Institutions*, ed. Fabrizio Cafaggi, Antonio Nicita, and Ugo Pagano, 54–83. London: Routledge.

———. 2010. "Marrying in the Cathedral: A Framework for the Analysis of Corporate Governance." In *The Law and Economics of Corporate Governance*, ed. Alessio M. Pacces, 264–89. Cheltenham: Edward Elgar.

———. 2011. "Interlocking Complementarities and Institutional Change." *Journal of Institutional Economics* 7, no. 3 (September): 373–92.

———. 2014. "The Crisis of Intellectual Monopoly Capitalism." *Cambridge Journal of Economics* 38, no. 6 (November): 1409–29.

Paine, Thomas. 1797. *Agrarian Justice: Opposed to Agrarian Law and to Agrarian Monopoly*. Philadelphia: Folwell.

Palley, Thomas I. 2012. *From Financial Crisis to Stagnation: The Destruction of Shared Prosperity and the Role of Economics*. Cambridge: Cambridge University Press.

Parisi, Francesco. 1995. "Toward a Theory of Spontaneous Law." *Constitutional Political Economy* 6, no. 3 (October): 211–31.

Parra, Carlos M. 2005. "Rules and Knowledge." *Evolutionary and Institutional Economics Review* 2, no. 1 (October): 81–111.

Payne, P. L. 1967. "The Emergence of the Large-Scale Company in Great Britain, 1870–1914." *Economic History Review* 20, no. 3 (December): 19–42.

Peacock, Mark S. 2006. "The Origins of Money in Ancient Greece: The Political Economy of Coinage and Exchange." *Cambridge Journal of Economics* 30, no. 4 (July): 637–50.

Peck, Jamie, and Jun Zhang. 2013. "A Variety of Capitalism . . . with Chinese Characteristics?" *Journal of Economic Geography* 13:357–96.

Peirce, Charles Sanders. 1878. "How to Make Our Ideas Clear." *Popular Science Monthly* 12 (January): 286–302. Reprinted in Peirce (1923, 32–60).

———. 1923. *Chance, Love, and Logic*. Edited by M. R. Cohen. New York: Harcourt, Brace.

Pejovich, Svetozar. 1990. *The Economics of Property Rights: Towards a Theory of Comparative Systems*. Boston: Kluwer.

———, ed. 1997. *The Economic Foundations of Property Rights: Selected Readings*. Cheltenham: Edward Elgar.

Pelikan, Pavel. 2003. "Bringing Institutions into Evolutionary Economics: Another View with Links to Changes in Physical and Social Technologies." *Journal of Evolutionary Economics* 13, no. 3 (August): 237–58.

Pellegrini, Lorenzo, and Reyer Gerlagh. 2004. "Corruption's Effect on Growth and Its Transmission Channels." *Kyklos* 57, no. 3:429–56.

Pendleton, Andrew, Nicholas Wilson, and Mike Wright. 1998. "The Perception and Effects of Share Ownership: Empirical Evidence from Employee Buy-Outs." *British Journal of Industrial Relations* 36, no. 1 (March): 99–123.

Penner, James E. 1996. "The 'Bundle of Rights' Picture of Property." *University of California Law Review* 43:711–41.

———. 1997. *The Idea of Property in Law*. Oxford: Oxford University Press.

Penrose, Edith T. 1959. *The Theory of the Growth of the Firm*. Oxford: Basil Blackwell.

Petty, William. 1690. *Political Arithmetick*. London: Clavel & Mortlock. Reprinted in *The Economic Writings of Sir William Petty* (2 vols.), ed. Charles H. Hull (Cambridge: Cambridge University Press, 1899), 1:233–313.

Phillips, Michael J. 1994. "Reappraising the Real Entity Theory of the Corporation." *Florida State University Law Review* 21, no. 4:1061–1123.

Pigou, Arthur C. 1941. "Maintaining Capital Intact." *Economica*, n.s., 8, no. 31 (August): 271–75.

Piketty, Thomas. 2014. *Capital in the Twenty-First Century*. Cambridge, MA: Belknap Press of Harvard University Press.

Piketty, Thomas, and Emmanuel Saez. 2013. "A Theory of Optimal Inheritance Taxation." *Econometrica* 81, no. 5 (September): 1851–86.

Piketty, Thomas, and Gabriel Zucman. 2013. "Capital Is Back: Wealth-to-Income Ratios in Rich Countries, 1700–2010." Discussion Paper no. 9588. Washington, DC: Center for Economic Policy Research.

Pincus, Steven C. A. 2009. *1688: The First Modern Revolution*. New Haven, CT: Yale University Press.

Pipes, Richard. 1999. *Property and Freedom*. New York: Knopf.

Pirenne, Henri. 1925. *Medieval Cities: Their Origins and the Revival of Trade*. Princeton, NJ: Princeton University Press.

———. 1937. *Economic and Social History of Medieval Europe*. New York: Harcourt Brace.

Plotkin, Henry C. 1994. *Darwin, Machines and the Nature of Knowledge: Concerning Adaptations, Instinct and the Evolution of Intelligence*. Harmondsworth: Penguin.

Plotkin, Sidney, and Rick Tilman. 2011. *Political Ideas of Thorstein Veblen*. New Haven, CT: Yale University Press.

Polanyi, Karl. 1944. *The Great Transformation: The Political and Economic Origins of Our Time*. New York: Rinehart.

———. 1971. *Primitive and Modern Economics: Essays of Karl Polanyi*. Edited and with an introduction by George Dalton. Boston: Beacon.

———. 1977. *The Livelihood of Man*. Edited by Harry W. Pearson. New York: Academic.

Polanyi, Karl, Conrad M. Arensberg, and Harry W. Pearson, eds. 1957. *Trade and Market in the Early Empires*. Chicago: Henry Regnery.

Polanyi, Michael. 1967. *The Tacit Dimension*. London: Routledge & Kegan Paul.

Pollock, Frederick, and Frederic William Maitland. 1898. *The History of English Law Before the Time of Edward I.* 2nd ed. 2 vols. Cambridge: Cambridge University Press.

Poole, Michael, and Keith Whitfield. 1994. "Theories and Evidence on the Growth and Distribution of Profit Sharing and Employee Shareholding Schemes." *Human Systems Management* 13, no. 3:209–20.

Popper, Karl R. 1945. *The Open Society and Its Enemies.* 2 vols. London: Routledge & Kegan Paul.

———. 1960. *The Poverty of Historicism.* London: Routledge & Kegan Paul.

———. 1963. *Conjectures and Refutations.* London: Routledge & Kegan Paul.

———. 1972. *Objective Knowledge: An Evolutionary Approach.* Oxford: Oxford University Press.

———. 1982. *The Open Universe: An Argument for Indeterminism.* London: Hutchinson.

———. 1990. *A World of Propensities.* Bristol: Thoemmes.

Porpora, Douglas V. 1989. "Four Concepts of Social Structure." *Journal for the Theory of Social Behaviour* 19, no. 2:195–211.

Posner, Richard A. 1980. "A Theory of Primitive Society, with Special Reference to Law." *Journal of Law and Economics* 23, no. 1:1–53.

———. 1994. *Sex and Reason.* Cambridge, MA: Harvard University Press.

Postan, Michael M. 1972. *The Medieval Economy and Society: Economic History of Britain, 1100–1500.* Harmondsworth: Penguin.

Potts, Jason. 2000. *The New Evolutionary Microeconomics: Complexity, Competence and Adaptive Behaviour.* Cheltenham: Edward Elgar.

Powell, Ellis T. 1915. *The Evolution of the Money Market (1385–1915): An Historical and Analytical Study of the Rise and Development of Finance as a Centralised, Co-Ordinated Force.* London: Financial Press.

Powell, Walter W. 1990. "Neither Market nor Hierarchy: Network Forms of Organization." *Research in Organizational Behavior* 12:295–336.

Powell, Walter W., and Paul J. DiMaggio, eds. 1991. *The New Institutionalism in Organizational Analysis.* Chicago: University of Chicago Press.

Price, George R. 1995. "The Nature of Selection." *Journal of Theoretical Biology* 175:389–96.

Price, Michael E., Leda Cosmides, and John Tooby. 2002. "Punitive Sentiment as an Anti-Free-Rider Device." *Evolution and Human Behavior* 23:203–31.

Proudhon, Pierre-Joseph. 1851. *Les confessions d'un révolutionnaire.* Paris: Garnier.

———. (1840) 1890. *What Is Property? An Inquiry into the Principle of Right and Government.* Translated from the 1840 French ed. New York: Humbold.

Pryor, Frederic L. 1996. *Economic Evolution and Structure: The Impact of Complexity on the U.S. Economic System.* Cambridge: Cambridge University Press.

Putnam, Hilary. 1975. "The Meaning of 'Meaning.'" In *Mind, Language and Reality*, 215–71. Cambridge: Cambridge University Press.

Putnam, Robert D. 1995. "Tuning in, Tuning Out: The Strange Disappearance of Social Capital in America." *PS: Political Science and Politics* 28, no. 4:664–83.

———. 2000. *Bowling Alone: The Collapse and Revival of American Community.* New York: Simon & Schuster.

Quine, Willard van Orman. 1951. "Two Dogmas of Empiricism." *Philosophical Review* 60, no. 1 (January): 20–43.

———. 1960. *Word and Object.* Cambridge, MA: Harvard University Press.

———. 1966. *The Ways of Paradox and Other Essays.* New York: Random House.

Radcliffe-Brown, Arthur R. 1933. "Law: Primitive." In *Encyclopaedia of the Social Sciences*, 9:202–6. New York: Macmillan.

Radin, Margaret Jane. 1996. *Contested Commodities.* Cambridge, MA: Harvard University Press.

Radin, Margaret Jane, and R. Polk Wagner. 1999. "The Myth of Private Ordering: Rediscovering Legal Realism in Cyberspace." *Chicago-Kent Law Review* 73, no. 4:1295–1317.

Raines, J. Patrick, and Charles G. Leathers. 1996. "Veblenian Stock Markets and the Efficient Markets Hypothesis." *Journal of Post Keynesian Economics* 19, no. 1 (Fall): 137–51.

Rajan, Raghuram G., and Luigi Zingales. 2000. "The Governance of the New Enterprise." In *Corporate Governance: Theoretical and Empirical Perspectives*, ed. Xavier Vives, 201–27. Cambridge: Cambridge University Press.

———. 2001. "The Influence of the Financial Revolution on the Nature of Firms." *American Economic Review* 91, no. 2 (May): 203–11.

Rasmussen, Douglas B. 1984. "Quine and Aristotelian Essentialism." *New Scholasticism* 58, no. 5 (Summer): 316–35.

Rau, Karl Heinrich. 1835. "Ueber den Nutzen, den gegenwärtigen Zustand und die neueste Literatur der Nationalökonomie." *Archiv der politischen Oekonomie und Polizeiwissenschaft* (Heidelberg) 1 (Winter): 1–43.

Rauch, James E., and Alessandra Casella, eds. 2001. *Networks and Markets.* New York: Sage.

Ravaisson, Félix. 2008. *Of Habit (De l'habitude).* Translated from the 1838 French ed. New York: Continuum.

Rawls, John. 1964. "Legal Obligation and the Duty of Fair Play." In *Law and Philosophy*, ed. Sidney Hook, 3–18. New York: New York University Press.

Reber, Arthur S. 1993. *Implicit Learning and Tacit Knowledge: An Essay on the Cognitive Unconscious.* Oxford: Oxford University Press.

Redfield, Robert. 1950. "Maine's *Ancient Law* in the Light of Primitive Societies." *Western Political Quarterly* 3, no. 4 (December): 574–89.

———. 1957. *The Primitive World and Its Transformations*. Ithaca, NY: Cornell University Press.

Reed, M. C. 1975. *Investment in Railways in Britain, 1820–1844*. Oxford: Oxford University Press.

Reibel, R. 1975. "The Workingman's Production Association; or, The Republic in the Workshop." In *Self-Management: The Economic Liberation of Man*, ed. Jaroslav Vanek, 39–46. Harmondsworth: Penguin.

Reinert, Erik S. 2007. *How Rich Countries Got Rich . . . and Why Poor Countries Stay Poor*. London: Constable.

Reinhart, Carmen, and Kenneth S. Rogoff. 2009. *This Time Is Different: Eight Centuries of Financial Folly*. Princeton, NJ: Princeton University Press.

Reisman, David. 1993. *The Political Economy of Health Care*. London: Macmillan.

Renan, Ernest. 1899. "Nation." In *Cyclopedia of Political Science, Political Economy, and the Political History of the United States* (3 vols.), ed. Joseph Lalor, 2:932–33. New York: Maynard, Merril.

Rescher, Nicholas. 1989. *Cognitive Economy: The Economic Dimension of the Theory of Knowledge*. Pittsburgh: University of Pittsburgh Press.

Resnick, Stephen A., and Richard D. Wolff. 1987. *Knowledge and Class: A Marxian Critique of Political Economy*. Chicago: University of Chicago Press.

Ricardo, David. 1817. *Principles of Political Economy and Taxation*. London: John Murray.

Richards, R. D. 1926. "Early History of the Term Capital." *Quarterly Journal of Economics* 40, no. 2 (February): 329–38.

Richardson, George B. 1972. "The Organisation of Industry." *Economic Journal* 82:883–96.

Richerson, Peter J., and Robert Boyd. 1999. "Complex Societies: The Evolutionary Origins of a Crude Superorganism." *Human Nature* 10:253–89.

———. 2001. "Institutional Evolution in the Holocene: The Rise of Complex Societies." In *The Origin of Human Social Institutions*, ed. Walter Garry Runciman, 197–234. Oxford: Oxford University Press.

———. 2004. *Not by Genes Alone: How Culture Transformed Human Evolution*. Chicago: University of Chicago Press.

Richerson, Peter J., Robert Boyd, and Robert L. Bettinger. 2001. "Was Agriculture Impossible during the Pleistocene but Mandatory during the Holocene? A Climate Change Hypothesis." *American Antiquity* 66:387–411.

Rifkin, Jeremy. 1995. *The End of Work: The Decline of the Global Labor Force and the Dawn of the Post-Market Era*. New York: Putnam.

———. 2014. *The Zero Marginal Cost Society: The Internet of Things, the Collaborative Commons, and the Eclipse of Capitalism*. New York: Palgrave Macmillan.

Rigney, Daniel. 2010. *The Matthew Effect: How Advantage Begets Further Advantage*. New York: Columbia University Press.

Riley, James C. 2001. *Rising Life Expectancy: A Global History.* Cambridge: Cambridge University Press.

Rizvi, S. Abu Turab. 1994a. "Game Theory to the Rescue?" *Contributions to Political Economy* 13:1–28.

———. 1994b. "The Microfoundations Project in General Equilibrium Theory." *Cambridge Journal of Economics* 18, no. 4 (August): 357–77.

Robbins, Lionel. 1932. *An Essay on the Nature and Significance of Economic Science.* London: Macmillan.

Robé, Jean-Philippe. 2011. "The Legal Structure of the Firm." *Accounting, Economics, and Law* 1, no. 1, article 5.

Robinson, Andrew M., and Hao Zhang. 2005. "Employee Share Ownership: Safeguarding Investments in Human Capital." *British Journal of Industrial Relations* 43, no. 3 (September): 469–88.

Robinson, Joan. 1979. *Collected Economic Papers.* Vol. 5. Oxford: Basil Blackwell.

Robinson, Paul H., Robert Kurzban, and Owen D. Jones. 2007. "The Origins of Shared Intuitions of Justice." *Vanderbilt Law Review* 60, no. 6:1633–88.

Robinson, Richard. 1950. *Definition.* Oxford: Clarendon.

Rochon, Louis-Philippe, and Matias Vernengo. 2003. "State Money and the Real World; or, Chartalism and Its Discontents." *Journal of Post Keynesian Economics* 26, no. 1 (Fall): 57–67.

Rodrigues, João. 2012. "Where to Draw the Line between the State and the Market?" *Journal of Economic Issues* 46, no. 4 (December): 1007–33.

Rodrik, Dani. 2007. *One Economics, Many Recipes: Globalization, Institutions, and Economic Growth.* Princeton, NJ: Princeton University Press.

———. 2011. *The Globalization Paradox: Why Global Markets, States, and Democracy Can't Coexist.* Oxford: Oxford University Press.

———. 2013. "The Perils of Premature Deindustrialization." *Project Syndicate*, October 11. http://www.project-syndicate.org/commentary/developing -economies—missing-manufacturing-by-dani-rodrik.

Roemer, John E. 1994. *A Future for Socialism.* Cambridge, MA: Harvard University Press.

———, ed. 1996. *Equal Shares: Making Market Socialism Work.* London: Verso.

Rogers, Everett M. 1962. *Diffusion of Innovations.* New York: Free Press.

Rogers, Everett M., and Floyd F. Shoemaker. 1971. *Communication of Innovations: A Cross-Cultural Approach.* New York: Free Press.

Rogers, James Steven. 1995. *The Early History of the Law of Bills and Notes: A Study of the Origins of Anglo-American Commercial Law.* Cambridge: Cambridge University Press.

Rogoff, E., and Jean Lave. 1984. *Everyday Cognition: Development in Social Context.* Oxford: Oxford University Press.

Roosevelt, Franklin D. 1938/1941. "Recommendations to the Congress to Curb

Monopolies and the Concentration of Economic Power." In *The Public Papers and Addresses of Franklin D. Roosevelt*, ed. Samuel I. Rosenman, 7:305–15. New York: Macmillan.

Rorty, Richard. 1979. *Philosophy and the Mirror of Nature*. Princeton, NJ: Princeton University Press.

Roscher, Wilhelm. 1843. *Grundriss zu Vorlesungen über die Staatswirtschaft nach geschichtlicher Methode*. Göttingen: Dieterich.

———. 1870. "Die romantische Schule der Nationalökonomie in Deutschland." *Zietschrift für die gesamte Staatswissenschaft* 26:57–105.

Rose-Ackerman, Susan. 1999. *Corruption and Government: Causes, Consequences and Reform*. Cambridge: Cambridge University Press.

Rosenberg, Justin. 2010. "Basic Problems in the Theory of Uneven and Combined Development, Pt. 2: Unevenness and Political Multiplicity." *Cambridge Review of International Affairs* 23, no. 1:165–89.

Rosenberg, Nathan. 1976. *Perspectives on Technology*. Cambridge: Cambridge University Press.

Roseveare, Henry G. 1991. *The Financial Revolution, 1660–1760*. Harlow: Longman.

Ross, Edward Alsworth. 1898. "Social Control XIII: The System of Social Control." *American Journal of Sociology* 3, no. 6 (May): 809–28.

Ross, Michael L. 2012. *The Oil Curse: How Petroleum Wealth Shapes the Development of Nations*. Princeton, NJ: Princeton University Press.

Rostow, Walt W. 1960. *The Stages of Economic Growth: A Non-Communist Manifesto*. Cambridge: Cambridge University Press.

Roth, Alvin E. 1988. "Laboratory Experiments in Economics: A Methodological Overview." *Economic Journal* 98, no. 4 (December): 974–1031.

———. 2002. "The Economist as Engineer: Game Theory, Experimentation, and Computation as Tools for Design Economics." *Econometrica* 70, no. 4 (July): 1341–78.

Rothschild, Emma. 2011. "Maintaining (Environmental) Capital Intact." *Modern Intellectual History* 8, no. 1 (April): 193–212.

Rowthorn, Robert E., and John R. Wells. 1987. *De-Industrialization and Foreign Trade*. Cambridge: Cambridge University Press.

Roy, William G. 1997. *Socializing Capital: The Rise of the Large Industrial Corporation in America*. Princeton, NJ: Princeton University Press.

Rubery, Jill, and Frank Wilkinson, eds. 1994. *Employer Strategy and the Labour Market*. Oxford: Oxford University Press.

Rueschemeyer, Dietrich. 1986. *Power and the Division of Labor*. Stanford, CA: Stanford University Press; Cambridge: Polity.

Runciman, Walter Garry. 1982. "Origins of States: The Case of Ancient Greece." *Comparative Studies in Society and History* 24, no. 3:351–77.

———. 2001. "From Nature to Culture, from Culture to Society." In *The Origin of Human Social Institutions*, ed. Walter Garry Runciman, 235–54. Oxford: Oxford University Press.

———. 2002. "Heritable Variation and Competitive Selection as the Mechanism of Sociocultural Evolution." In *The Evolution of Cultural Entities*, ed. Michael Wheeler, John Ziman, and Margaret A. Boden, 9–25. Oxford: Oxford University Press.

———. 2005. "Stone Age Sociology." *Journal of the Royal Anthropological Institute* 11, no. 1 (March): 129–42.

Ruskin, John. 1859. *The Two Paths*. London: Smith & Elder.

Ruttan, Vernon W. 1997. "Induced Innovation, Evolutionary Theory and Path Dependence: Sources of Technical Change." *Economic Journal* 107, no. 5 (September): 1520–29.

———. 2003. *Social Science Knowledge and Economic Development: An Institutional Design Approach*. Ann Arbor: University of Michigan Press.

———. 2006. "Social Science Knowledge and Induced Institutional Innovation: An Institutional Design Perspective." *Journal of Institutional Economics* 2, no. 3 (December): 249–72.

Ryan, Alan. 1995. *John Dewey and the High Tide of American Liberalism*. New York: Norton.

Sainte Croix, Geoffrey E. M. de. 1956. "Greek and Roman Accounting." In *Studies in the History of Accounting*, ed. A. C. Littleton and B. S. Yamey, 14–74. Homewood, IL: Irwin.

Salerno, Joseph T. 1993. "Mises and Hayek Dehomogenized." *Review of Austrian Economics* 6, no. 2:13–46.

Samuels, Warren J. 1989. "The Legal-Economic Nexus." *George Washington Law Review* 57, no. 6 (August): 1556–78.

Samuelson, Paul A. 1948. *Economics*. 1st ed. New York: McGraw-Hill.

———. 1966. "A Summing Up." *Quarterly Journal of Economics* 80, no. 4 (November): 568–83.

———. 1976. *Economics*. 10th ed. New York: McGraw-Hill.

Samuelson, Paul A., and William D. Nordhaus. 2009. *Economics*. 18th ed. New York: McGraw-Hill.

Sandberg, Sveinung, and Willy Pedersen. 2009. *Street Capital: Black Cannabis Dealers in a White Welfare State*. Bristol: Policy.

Sandel, Michael. 2012. *What Money Can't Buy: The Moral Limits of Markets*. London: Allen Lane.

Satz, Debra. 2010. *Why Some Things Should Not Be for Sale: The Moral Limits of Markets*. Oxford: Oxford University Press.

Saunders, Peter T., and Mae-Wan Ho. 1976. "On the Increase in Complexity in Evolution." *Journal of Theoretical Biology* 63:375–84.

———. 1981. "On the Increase in Complexity in Evolution II: The Relativity of Complexity and the Principle of Minimum Increase." *Journal of Theoretical Biology* 90:515–30.

Saviotti, Pier Paolo, and J. Stanley Metcalfe. 1984. "A Theoretical Approach to the Construction of Output Indicators." *Research Policy* 13:141–51.

Sayer, Andrew. 1997. "Essentialism, Social Constructivism and Beyond." *Sociological Review* 45, no. 3 (August): 453–87.

Schaffer, Mark E. 1989. "Are Profit-Maximisers the Best Survivors? A Darwinian Model of Economic Natural Selection." *Journal of Economic Behavior and Organization* 12, no. 1 (March): 29–45.

Schäffle, Albert E. F. 1870. *Kapitalismus und Sozialismus: Mit besonderer Riicksicht auf Geschäfts und Vermögensformen*. Tübingen: Laupp.

———. 1874. *Quintessenz des Sozialismus*. Gotha: Perthes.

———. 1885. *Die Aussichtslosigkeit der Socialdemokratie: Drei Briefe an einen Staatsmann zur Ergänzung der "Quintessenz des Sozialismus."* Tübingen: Laupp.

———. 1892. *The Impossibility of Social Democracy: Being a Supplement to "The Quintessence of Socialism."* Translated from the 4th German ed. of Schäffle (1885) by A. C. Morant, with a preface by Bernard Bosanquet. London: Swan Sonnenschein; New York: Scribner's. Excerpted in Hodgson (2007b, 118–25).

———. 1893. *The Theory and Policy of Labour Protection*. Translated by A. C. Morant. London: Swan Sonnenschein.

———. 1908. *The Quintessence of Socialism*. Translated from the 8th German ed. of Schäffle (1874) under the supervision of Bernard Bosanquet. London: Swan Sonnenschein; New York: Scribner's.

Schank, Jeffrey C., and William C. Wimsatt. 1987. "Generative Entrenchment and Evolution." In *PSA 1986: Proceedings of the Meeting of the Philosophy of Science Association* (vol. 7), ed. A. Fine and P. Machamer, 33–60. East Lansing, MI: Philosophy of Science Association.

Schotter, Andrew R. 1981. *The Economic Theory of Social Institutions*. Cambridge: Cambridge University Press.

Schultz, Theodore W. 1960. "Capital Formation by Education." *Journal of Political Economy* 68, no. 4 (December): 571–83.

———. 1971. *Investment in Human Capital: The Role of Education and of Research*. New York: Free Press.

———. 1972. "Human Capital: Policy Issues and Research Opportunities." In *Economic Research: Retrospect and Prospect*, vol. 6, *Human Resources*, ed. Theodore W. Schultz, 1–84. New York: National Bureau of Economic Research.

Schultz, Walter J. 2001. *The Moral Conditions of Economic Efficiency*. Cambridge: Cambridge University Press.

Schumpeter, Joseph A. 1934. *The Theory of Economic Development: An Inquiry into Profits, Capital, Credit, Interest, and the Business Cycle*. Translated from the 1926 (2nd) German ed. by Redvers Opie. Cambridge, MA: Harvard University Press.

———. 1939. *Business Cycles: A Theoretical Statistical and Historical Analysis of the Capitalist Process.* 2 vols. New York: McGraw-Hill.

———. 1942. *Capitalism, Socialism and Democracy.* London: Allen & Unwin.

———. 1954. *History of Economic Analysis.* Oxford: Oxford University Press.

———. 1956. "Money and the Social Product." Translated from the 1917 German ed. by A. W. Marget. *International Economic Papers,* no. 6:148–211.

Sciabarra, Chris Matthew. 1995. *Marx, Hayek, and Utopia.* Albany, NY: State University of New York Press.

Scott, Bruce R. 2009. *The Concept of Capitalism.* Berlin: Springer.

———. 2011. *Capitalism: Its Origins and Evolution as a System of Governance.* Berlin: Springer.

Scott, Maurice Fitzgerald. 1989. *A New View of Economic Growth.* Oxford: Oxford University Press.

Screpanti, Ernesto. 1997. "Towards a General Theory of Capitalism: Suggestions from Chapters 23 and 27." In *Marxian Economics: A Reappraisal: Essays on Volume III of Capital* (2 vols.), ed. Riccardo Bellofiore, 1:110–24. London: Macmillan.

———. 2001. *The Fundamental Institutions of Capitalism.* London: Routledge.

Scully, Gerald B. 1992. *Constitutional Environments and Economic Growth.* Princeton, NJ: Princeton University Press.

Seabury, Samuel. 1861. *American Slavery Justified by the Law of Nature.* New York: Mason.

Seagle, William. 1941. *The Quest for Law.* New York: Knopf.

Searle, John R. 1995. *The Construction of Social Reality.* London: Allen Lane.

———. 2005. "What Is an Institution?" *Journal of Institutional Economics* 1, no. 1 (June): 1–22.

Sekine, Thomas T. 1975. *"Uno-Riron:* A Japanese Contribution to Marxian Political Economy." *Journal of Economic Literature* 8, no. 4 (December): 847–77.

Sened, Itai. 1997. *The Political Institution of Private Property.* Cambridge: Cambridge University Press.

Senge, Peter M. 1990. *The Fifth Discipline: The Art and Practice of the Learning Organization.* New York: Doubleday.

Senior, Nassau W. 1836. *An Outline of the Science of Political Economy.* London: Clowes & Sons.

Shachtman, Max. 1940. "The Soviet Union and the World War." *New International* 6, no. 3 (April): 68–72. http://www.marxists.org/archive/shachtma/1940/04/ussrwar.htm.

Shannon, Claude E., and Warren Weaver. 1949. *The Mathematical Theory of Communication.* Urbana: University of Illinois Press.

Shaw-Taylor, Leigh. 2007. "Diverse Experiences: The Geography of Adult Female Employment and the 1851 Census." In *Women's Work in Industrial*

England: Regional and Local Perspectives, ed. Nigel Goose, 51–75. Hatfield: University of Hertfordshire Press.

Sheleff, Leon Shaskolsky. 1997. *Social Cohesion and Legal Coercion: A Critique of Weber, Durkheim, and Marx.* Amsterdam: Rodopi.

Shleifer, Andrei, and Robert W. Vishny. 1993. "Corruption." *Quarterly Journal of Economics* 108, no. 3 (August): 599–617.

———. 1994. "The Politics of Market Socialism." *Journal of Economic Perspectives* 8, no. 2 (Spring): 165–76.

Sik, Endre. 1994. "Network Capital in Capitalist, Communist and Post-Communist Societies." *International Contributions to Labour Studies* 4: 73–93.

Sills, David L., and Robert K. Merton, eds. 1968. *International Encyclopaedia of the Social Sciences.* 17 vols. New York: Macmillan.

Silver, Morris. 2007–8. "Fiscalism in the Emergence and Extinction of *Societates Publicanorum.*" *Pomoerivm* 6:46–71.

Simmel, Georg. 2004. *The Philosophy of Money.* Translated from the 1907 (2nd) German ed. by Tom Bottomore and David Frisby. London: Routledge.

Simon, Herbert A. 1951. "A Formal Theory of the Employment Relationship." *Econometrica* 19 (July): 293–305.

———. 1979. "Rational Decision Making in Business Organizations." *American Economic Review* 69, no. 4 (September): 493–513.

———. 1981. *The Sciences of the Artificial.* 2nd ed. Cambridge, MA: MIT Press.

Simpson, S. Rowton. 1976. *Land Law and Registration.* London: William Clowes.

Singer, Peter. 1999. *A Darwinian Left: Politics, Evolution and Cooperation.* London: Wiedenfeld & Nicholson; New Haven, CT: Yale University Press.

Skaggs, Neil T. 1997. "Henry Dunning Macleod and the Credit Theory of Money." In *Money, Financial Institutions and Macroeconomics*, ed. Avi J. Cohen, Harald Hagemann, and John N. Smithin, 109–23. Boston: Kluwer.

Skocpol, Theda. 1979. *States and Social Revolutions: A Comparative Analysis of France, Russia, and China.* Cambridge: Cambridge University Press.

Smith, Adam. 1759/1976a. *The Theory of Moral Sentiments.* Edited by D. D. Raphael and A. L. MacFie. Oxford: Clarendon.

———. 1776/1976b. *An Inquiry into the Nature and Causes of the Wealth of Nations.* Edited by Roy H. Campbell and Andrew S. Skinner. 2 vols. London: Methuen.

Smith, Henry E. 2012. "Property as the Law of Things." *Harvard Law Review* 125:1691–1726.

Smith, Michael E. 2004. "The Archaeology of Ancient State Economies." *Annual Review of Anthropology* 33:73–102.

Smith, Peter B., and Michael Harris Bond. 1993. *Social Psychology across Cultures: Analysis and Perspectives.* Needham Heights, MA: Allyn & Bacon; Brighton: Harvester Wheatsheaf.

Smith, Vernon L. 1982. "Microeconomic Systems as an Experimental Science." *American Economic Review* 72, no. 5 (December): 923–55.

———. 2013. "Adam Smith: From Propriety and Sentiments to Property and Wealth." *Forum for Social Economics* 42, no. 4:283–97.

Smithin, John, ed. 2000. *What Is Money?* London: Routledge.

Sobel, Joel. 2002. "Can We Trust Social Capital?" *Journal of Economic Literature* 40, no. 1 (March): 139–54.

Sober, Elliott. 1980. "Evolution, Population Thinking and Essentialism." *Philosophy of Science* 47, no. 3 (September): 350–83.

Sober, Elliott, and David Sloan Wilson. 1998. *Unto Others: The Evolution and Psychology of Unselfish Behavior.* Cambridge, MA: Harvard University Press.

Solow, Robert M. 1986. "On the Intergenerational Allocation of Natural Resources." *Scandinavian Journal of Economics* 88, no. 1 (March): 141–49.

———. 1999. "Notes on Social Capital and Economic Performance." In *Social Capital: A Multifaceted Perspective,* ed. Partha Dasgupta and Ismail Serageldin, 6–10. Washington, DC: World Bank.

Sombart, Werner. 1902. *Der moderne Kapitalismus: Historisch-systematische Darstellung des gesamteuropäischen Wirtschaftslebens von seinen Anfängen bis zur Gegenwart.* 1st ed. 2 vols. Munich and Leipzig: Duncker & Humblot.

———. 1930. "Capitalism." In *Encyclopaedia of the Social Sciences* (15 vols.), ed. Edwin R. A. Seligman and Alvin Johnson, 3:195–208. New York: Macmillan. Reprinted in Werner Sombart, *Economic Life in the Modern Age,* ed. and with an introduction by Nico Stehr and Reiner Grundmann (New Brunswick, NJ: Transaction, 2001), 3–29.

Somek, Alexander. 2006. "Stateless Law: Kelsen's Conception and Its Limits." *Oxford Journal of Legal Studies* 26, no. 4:753–74.

Sonnenschein, Hugo F. 1972. "Market Excess Demand Functions." *Econometrica* 40, no. 3:549–63.

———. 1973. "Do Walras's Identity and Continuity Characterize the Class of Community Excess Demand Functions?" *Journal of Economic Theory* 6, no. 4:345–54.

Spethmann, Dieter, and Otto Steiger. 2004. "The Four Achilles's Heels of the Eurosystem: Missing Central Monetary Institution, Different Real Rates of Interest, Nonmarketable Securities, and Missing Lender of Last Resort." *International Journal of Political Economy* 34, no. 2 (Summer): 46–68.

Spulber, Daniel F. 2009. *The Theory of the Firm: Microeconomics with Endogenous Entrepreneurs, Firms, Markets, and Organizations.* Cambridge: Cambridge University Press.

Sraffa, Piero. 1960. *Production of Commodities by Means of Commodities: Prelude to a Critique of Economic Theory.* Cambridge: Cambridge University Press.

Stabile, Donald R. 1996. *Work and Welfare: The Social Cost of Labor in the History of Economic Thought*. Westport, CT: Greenwood.

Stadermann, Hans-Joachim. 2002. *Das Geld der Ökonomen*. Tübingen: Mohr Siebeck.

Stake, Jeffrey Evans. 2004. "The Property Instinct." *Philosophical Transactions of the Royal Society of London B* 359, no. 1451 (November): 1763–74.

Star, Susan Leigh, ed. 1995. *Ecologies of Knowledge: Work and Politics in Science and Technology*. Albany: State University of New York Press.

Steele, David Ramsay. 1992. *From Marx to Mises: Post-Capitalist Society and the Challenge of Economic Calculation*. La Salle, IL: Open Court.

Steiger, Otto, ed. 2008. *Property Economics: Property Rights, Creditor's Money and the Foundations of the Economy*. Marburg: Metropolis.

Stein, Peter. 1980. *Legal Evolution: The Story of an Idea*. Cambridge: Cambridge University Press.

Steinfeld, Robert J. 2001. *Coercion, Contract, and Free Labor in the Nineteenth Century*. Cambridge: Cambridge University Press.

Steinmo, Sven. 2010. *The Evolution of Modern States: Sweden, Japan and the United States*. Cambridge: Cambridge University Press.

Sterba, James P. 1985. "A Libertarian Justification for the Welfare State." *Social Theory and Practice* 11, no. 3 (Fall): 285–306.

Stigler, George J. 1967. "Imperfections in the Capital Market." *Journal of Political Economy* 75, no. 3 (June): 287–92.

Stiglitz, Joseph E. 1987. "The Causes and Consequences of the Dependence of Quality on Price." *Journal of Economic Literature* 25, no. 1 (March): 1–48.

———. 1991. "The Invisible Hand and Modern Welfare Economics." In *Information, Strategy and Public Policy*, ed. David Vines and Andrew Stevenson, 12–50. Oxford: Basil Blackwell.

———. 1994. *Whither Socialism?* Cambridge, MA: MIT Press.

———. 2002. *Globalization and Its Discontents*. New York: Norton.

———. 2012a. "The 1 Percent's Problem." *Vanity Fair*, May 31. www.vanityfair.com/politics/2012/05/joseph-stiglitz-the-price-on-inequality.

———. 2012b. *The Price of Inequality: How Today's Divided Society Endangers Our Future*. New York: Norton.

Story, Joseph. 1843. *Commentaries on the Law of Bills of Exchange, Foreign and Inland, as Administered in England and America; with Occasional Illustrations from the Commercial Law of the Nations of Continental Europe*. 2nd ed. Boston: Little, Brown.

Streeck, Wolfgang. 2011. "E Pluribus Unum? Varieties and Commonalities of Capitalism." In *The Sociology of Economic Life* (3rd ed.), ed. Mark Granovetter, 419–55. Boulder, CO: Westview.

Streeck, Wolfgang, and Kozo Yamamura, eds. 2001. *The Origins of Neoliberal*

Capitalism: Germany and Japan in Comparison. Ithaca, NY: Cornell University Press.

Streissler, Erich W. 1994. "The Influence of German and Austrian Economics on Joseph A. Schumpeter." In *Schumpeter in the History of Ideas*, ed. Yuichi Shionoya and Mark Perlman, 13–38. Ann Arbor: University of Michigan Press.

Sturn, Simon. 2013. "Are Corporatist Labour Markets Different? Labour Market Regimes and Unemployment in OECD Countries." *International Labour Review* 152, no. 2:237–54.

Suchman, Lucy A. 1987. *Plans and Situated Actions: The Problem of Human-Machine Communication*. Cambridge: Cambridge University Press.

———. 2007. *Human-Machine Reconfigurations: Plans and Situated Actions*. Cambridge: Cambridge University Press.

Sugden, Robert. 1986. *The Economics of Rights, Co-Operation and Welfare*. Oxford: Basil Blackwell.

———. 2000. "Credible Worlds: The Status of Theoretical Models in Economics." *Journal of Economic Methodology* 7, no. 1 (March): 1–31.

Swedberg, Richard. 1994. "Markets as Social Structures." In *Handbook of Economic Sociology*, ed. Neil J. Smelser and Richard Swedberg, 255–82. Princeton, NJ: Princeton University Press.

Synopwich, Christine. 1990. *The Concept of Socialist Law*. Oxford: Clarendon.

Szulanski, Gabriel. 1996. "Exploring Internal Stickiness: Impediments to the Transfer of Best Practice within the Firm." Special issue, *Strategic Management Journal* 17 (Winter): 27–43.

Szulanski, Gabriel, and Sidney G. Winter. 2002. "Getting It Right the Second Time." *Harvard Business Review* 80, no. 1:62–69.

Tamanaha, Brian Z. 1993. "The Folly of the 'Social Scientific' Concept of Legal Pluralism." *Journal of Law and Society* 20, no. 2 (Summer): 192–217.

Tandy, David W. 1997. *Warriors into Traders: The Power of the Market in Early Greece*. Berkeley and Los Angeles: University of California Press.

Taylor, Frederick Winslow. 1911. *The Principles of Scientific Management*. New York: Harper.

Teece, David J. 1976. *The Multinational Corporation and the Resource Cost of International Technology Transfer*. Cambridge, MA: Ballinger.

Teece, David J., and Gary Pisano. 1994. "The Dynamic Capabilities of Firms: An Introduction." *Industrial and Corporate Change* 3, no. 3:537–56.

Temin, Peter. 2001. "A Market Economy in the Early Roman Empire." *Journal of Roman Studies* 91:169–81.

———. 2002. "Price Behavior in Ancient Babylon." *Explorations in Economic History* 39, no. 1:46–60.

———. 2006. "The Economy of the Early Roman Empire." *Journal of Economic Perspectives* 20, no. 1 (Spring): 133–51.

Tett, Gillian. 2009. *Fool's Gold: How Unrestrained Greed Corrupted a Dream, Shattered Global Markets and Unleashed a Catastrophe*. New York: Free Press; London: Little, Brown.

Teubner, Gunther, ed. 1988. *Autopoietic Law*. Berlin: De Gruyter.

———. 1993. *Law as an Autopoietic System*. Oxford: Oxford University Press.

Thelen, Kathleen. 2004. *How Institutions Evolve: The Political Economy of Skills in Germany, Britain, the United States and Japan*. Cambridge: Cambridge University Press.

Thompson, Grahame F. 2003. *Between Hierarchies and Markets: The Logic and Limits of Network Forms of Organization*. Oxford: Oxford University Press.

Thompson, Noel. 1988. *The Market and Its Critics: Socialist Political Economy in Nineteenth Century Britain*. London: Routledge.

Thompson, William R. 2000. *The Emergence of the Global Political Economy*. London: Routledge.

Tilly, Charles, ed. 1975. *The Formation of National States in Western Europe*. Princeton, NJ: Princeton University Press.

Tobin, James. 1978. "A Proposal for International Monetary Reform." *Eastern Economic Journal* 4, nos. 3–4 (July–October): 153–59.

Tobin, James, and Steven Golub. 1998. *Money, Credit, and Capital*. Boston: Irwin McGraw-Hill.

Todd, Peter M., and Gerd Gigerenzer. 2003. "Bounding Rationality to the World." *Journal of Economic Psychology* 24, no. 2:143–65.

Tomasello, Michael. 2008. *Origins of Human Communication*. Cambridge, MA: MIT Press.

Tomasello, Michael, with Carol Dweck, Joan Silk, Brian Skyrms, and Elizabeth Spelke. 2009. *Why We Cooperate*. Cambridge, MA: MIT Press.

Tomer, John F. 1987. *Organizational Capital: The Path to Higher Productivity and Well-Being*. New York: Praeger.

Tomlinson, James. 1982. *The Unequal Struggle? British Socialism and the Capitalist Enterprise*. London: Methuen.

Toporowski, Jan. 2010. "Corporate Limited Liability and the Financial Liabilities of Firms." *Cambridge Journal of Economics* 34, no. 5 (September): 885–93.

Torstensson, Johan. 1994. "Property Rights and Economic Growth: An Empirical Study." *Kyklos* 47, no. 2:231–47.

Transparency International. 2012. *Corruption Perceptions Index 2012*. Berlin: Transparency International. http://www.transparency.org/cpi2012/in_detail.

Trotsky, Leon D. 1934. *The History of the Russian Revolution*. London: Gollancz.

———. 1936. *The Third International After Lenin*. New York: Pioneer.

———. 1937. *The Revolution Betrayed: What Is the Soviet Union and Where Is It Going?* London: Faber & Faber.

Tullock, Gordon. 1994. *The Economics of Non-Human Societies*. Tuscon, AZ: Pallas.

Turner, Henry A. 1985. *German Big Business and the Rise of Hitler*. Oxford: Oxford University Press.

Turunen, Olli. 2009. "Ideas of Social Capital in Early German Historical Economics." *Essays in Economic and Business History* 27:47–60.

Tyler, Tom R. 1990. *Why People Obey the Law*. New Haven, CT: Yale University Press.

Tymoigne, Éric, and L. Randall Wray. 2013. *The Rise and Fall of Money Manager Capitalism: Minsky's Half Century from World War Two to the Great Recession*. London: Routledge.

Umbeck, John. 1981. "Might Makes Rights: A Theory of the Formation and Initial Distribution of Property Rights." *Economic Inquiry* 19, no. 1 (January): 38–59.

Uno, Kozo. 1980. *Principles of Political Economy: Theory of a Purely Capitalist Society*. Translated from the 1964 Japanese ed. by Thomas T. Sekine. Brighton: Harvester.

US Bureau of the Census. 1970. *Historical Statistics of the United States*. Collected in "Historical Demographic, Economic and Social Data: The United States, 1790–1970" (ICPSR 3). http://www.icpsr.umich.edu/icpsrweb/ICPSR /studies/3.

Usher, Abbott P. 1943. *The Early History of Deposit Banking in Mediterranean Europe*. Cambridge, MA: Harvard University Press.

Valiente, Wilfredo Santiago. 1980. "Is Frank Knight the Victor in the Controversy between the Two Cambridges?" *History of Political Economy* 12, no. 1:41–64.

Vanberg, Viktor J. 1986. "Spontaneous Market Order and Social Rules: A Critique of F. A. Hayek's Theory of Cultural Evolution." *Economics and Philosophy* 2 (June): 75–100.

———. 1994. *Rules and Choice in Economics*. London: Routledge.

———. 2002. "Rational Choice versus Program-Based Behavior: Alternative Theoretical Approaches and Their Relevance for the Study of Institutions." *Rationality and Society* 14, no. 1 (Summer): 7–53.

———. 2004. "The Rationality Postulate in Economics: Its Ambiguity, Its Deficiency and Its Evolutionary Alternative." *Journal of Economic Methodology* 11, no. 1 (March): 1–29.

van de Klundert, Theo C. M. J. 2013. *Capitalism and Democracy: A Fragile Alliance*. Cheltenham: Edward Elgar.

Vanek, Jaroslav. 1970. *The General Theory of Labor-Managed Market Economies*. Ithaca, NY: Cornell University Press.

———. 1972. *The Economics of Workers' Management*. London: Allen & Unwin.

Van Horn, Carl E., and Aaron R. Fichtner. 2003. "An Evaluation of State-Subsidized, Firm-Based Training: The Workforce Development Partnership Program." *International Journal of Manpower* 24, no. 1:97–111.

Van Parijs, Philippe. 1981. *Evolutionary Explanations in the Social Sciences: An Emerging Paradigm*. London: Tavistock.

———, ed. 1992. *Arguing for Basic Income: Ethical Foundations for a Radical Reform*. London: Verso.

———. 1995. *Real Freedom for All: What (If Anything) Can Justify Capitalism?* Oxford: Clarendon.

Vatiero, Massimiliano. 2013. "Positional Goods and Robert Lee Hale's Legal Economics." *Journal of Institutional Economics* 9, no. 3:351–62.

Vatn, Arild. 2005. *Institutions and the Environment*. Cheltenham: Edward Elgar.

Vaughn, Karen I. 1980. "Economic Calculation under Socialism: The Austrian Contribution." *Economic Inquiry* 18:535–54.

Veblen, Thorstein B. 1892. "Böhm-Bawerk's Definition of Capital and the Source of Wages." *Quarterly Journal of Economics* 6:247–52. Reprinted in Camic and Hodgson (2011, 77–79).

———. 1897. Review of *Die marxistische Socialdemokratie* by Max Lorenz. *Journal of Political Economy* 6, no. 1 (December): 136–37. Reprinted in Camic and Hodgson (2011, 115–16).

———. 1898a. "The Beginnings of Ownership." *American Journal of Sociology* 4, no. 3 (November): 352–65. Reprinted in Camic and Hodgson (2011, 169–78).

———. 1898b. "The Instinct of Workmanship and the Irksomeness of Labor." *American Journal of Sociology* 4, no. 2 (September): 187–201. Reprinted in Camic and Hodgson (2011, 158–68).

———. 1898c. "Why Is Economics Not an Evolutionary Science?" *Quarterly Journal of Economics* 12, no. 3 (July): 373–97. Reprinted in Camic and Hodgson (2011, 143–57).

———. 1899a. "Mr. Cummings's Strictures on 'The Theory of the Leisure Class.'" *Journal of Political Economy* 8, no. 1 (December): 106–17. Reprinted in Camic and Hodgson (2011, 271–79).

———. 1899b. "The Preconceptions of Economic Science: II." *Quarterly Journal of Economics* 13, no. 4 (July): 121–50. Reprinted in Camic and Hodgson (2011, 206–25).

———. 1899c. *The Theory of the Leisure Class: An Economic Study in the Evolution of Institutions*. New York: Macmillan.

———. 1900. "The Preconceptions of Economic Science: III." *Quarterly Journal of Economics* 14, no. 2 (February): 240–69. Reprinted in Camic and Hodgson (2011, 225–43).

———. 1901. "Industrial and Pecuniary Employments." *Publications of the American Economic Association*, ser. 3, 2, no. 1 (February): 190–235. Reprinted in Camic and Hodgson (2011, 281–306).

———. 1904. *The Theory of Business Enterprise*. New York: Scribner's.

———. 1908a. "Fisher's Capital and Income." *Political Science Quarterly* 23, no. 1 (March): 112–28. Reprinted in Camic and Hodgson (2011, 492–506).

———. 1908b. "On the Nature of Capital I: The Productivity of Capital Goods." *Quarterly Journal of Economics* 22, no. 4 (August): 517–42. Reprinted in Camic and Hodgson (2011, 441–57).

———. 1908c. "On the Nature of Capital II: Investment, Intangible Assets, and the Pecuniary Magnate." *Quarterly Journal of Economics* 23, no. 1 (November): 104–36. Reprinted in Camic and Hodgson (2011, 457–77).

———. 1908d. "Professor Clark's Economics." *Quarterly Journal of Economics* 22, no. 2 (February): 147–95. Reprinted in Camic and Hodgson (2011, 410–40).

———. 1909. "The Limitations of Marginal Utility." *Journal of Political Economy* 17, no. 9 (November): 620–36. Reprinted in Camic and Hodgson (2011, 513–24).

———. 1914. *The Instinct of Workmanship, and the State of the Industrial Arts.* New York: Macmillan.

———. 1919. *The Place of Science in Modern Civilization and Other Essays.* New York: Huebsch.

———. 1921. *The Engineers and the Price System.* New York: Harcourt, Brace & World.

———. 1923. *Absentee Ownership and Business Enterprise in Recent Times.* New York: Huebsch.

———. 1925. "Economic Theory in the Calculable Future." *American Economic Review: Papers and Proceedings* 15, no. 1 (March): 48–55.

Veitch, John M. 1986. "Repudiations and Confiscations by the Medieval State." *Journal of Economic History* 46, no. 1 (March): 31–36.

Veljanovski, C. G., and C. J. Whelan. 1983. "Professional Negligence and the Quality of Legal Services: An Economic Perspective." *Modern Law Review* 46, no. 6 (November): 700–718.

VerSteeg, Russ. 2000. *Early Mesopotamian Law.* Durham, NC: Carolina Academic.

Verter, Bradford. 2003. "Spiritual Capital: Theorizing Religion with Bourdieu against Bourdieu." *Sociological Theory* 21, no. 2 (June): 150–74.

Vining, Rutledge. 1939. "Suggestions of Keynes in the Writings of Veblen." *Journal of Political Economy* 47, no. 5 (October): 692–704.

Vinogradoff, Paul. 1922. *Outlines of Historical Jurisprudence.* Vol. 2, *The Jurisprudence of the Greek City.* Oxford: Oxford University Press.

Vogel, Steven K. 1996. *Freer Markets, More Rules: Regulatory Reform in Advanced Industrial Countries.* Ithaca, NY: Cornell University Press.

———. 2006. *Japan Remodelled: How Government and Industry Are Reforming Japanese Capitalism.* Ithaca, NY: Cornell University Press.

von Böhm-Bawerk, Eugen. 1890. *Capital and Interest: A Critical History of Economical Theory.* Translated from the 1889 German ed. by William Smart. London: Macmillan.

von Mises, Ludwig. 1920. "Die Wirtschaftsrechnung im sozialistischen Gemein-wesen." *Archiv für Sozialwissenschaften und Sozialpolitik* 47, no. 1 (April): 86–121.

———. 1935. "Economic Calculation in the Socialist Commonwealth." In *Collectivist Economic Planning*, ed. Friedrich A. Hayek, 87–130. London: George Routledge. A translation by S. Adler of von Mises (1920).

———. 1949. *Human Action: A Treatise on Economics*. London: William Hodge; New Haven, CT: Yale University Press.

———. 1981. *Socialism: An Economic and Sociological Analysis*. Translated from the 2nd (1932) German ed. of von Mises's *Die Gemeinwirtschaft* by J. Kahane. Indianapolis: Liberty Classics.

Vroom, Victor H., and E. L. Deci, eds. 1970. *Management and Motivation*. Harmondsworth: Penguin.

Wainwright, Hilary. 1994. *Arguments for a New Left: Answering the Free-Market Right*. Oxford: Basil Blackwell.

Wallast, Len H. 2013. *Evolvodynamics—the Mathematical Theory of Economic Evolution: A Coherent Way of Interpreting Time, Scarceness, Value and Economic Growth*. Berlin: Springer.

Wallerstein, Immanuel. 1979. *The Capitalist World-Economy*. New York: Cambridge University Press.

Walzer, Michael. 1983. *Spheres of Justice: A Defense of Pluralism and Equality*. New York: Basic.

Wang, Xiaotong. 1936. *Zhongguo Shangye Shi* (History of Chinese commerce [in Chinese]). Beijing: Commerce Press.

Wank, David L. 1999. "Producing Property Rights: Strategies, Networks, and Efficiency in Urban China's Nonstate Firms." In *Property Rights and Economic Reform in China*, ed. Jean C. Oi and Andrew G. Walder, 248–72. Stanford, CA: Stanford University Press.

Ward, Benjamin. 1958. "The Firm in Illyria: Market Syndicalism." *American Economic Review* 48, no. 4 (September): 566–89.

———. 1967. *The Socialist Economy: A Study of Organizational Alternatives*. New York: Random House.

Warsh, David. 1985. *The Idea of Economic Complexity*. New York: Viking.

Wasylenko, Michael. 1997. "Taxation and Economic Development: The State of the Economic Literature." *New England Economic Review*, March/April, 37–52.

Webb, Sidney J., and Beatrice Webb. 1920. *A Constitution for the Socialist Commonwealth of Great Britain*. London: Longmans Green.

Weber, Max. 1904–5/1930. *The Protestant Ethic and the Spirit of Capitalism*. London: Allen & Unwin.

———. 1927. *General Economic History*. Translated from the 1923 German ed. by Frank H. Knight. London: Allen & Unwin.

———. 1949. *Max Weber on the Methodology of the Social Sciences.* Translated and edited by Edward A. Shils and Henry A. Finch. Glencoe, IL: Free Press.

———. 1968. *Economy and Society: An Outline of Interpretative Sociology.* Translated from the 1921–22 German ed. by G. Roth and C. Wittich. 2 vols. Berkeley: University of California Press.

———. 1978. *Max Weber: Selections in Translation.* Edited and with an introduction by W. G. Runciman. Cambridge: Cambridge University Press.

Wedderburn, Kenneth W. 1971. *The Worker and the Law.* 2nd ed. Harmondsworth: Penguin.

———. 1993. *Labour Law and Freedom: Further Essays in Labour Law.* London: Lawrence & Wishart.

Weil, Simone. 1937/1986. "The Power of Words." In *Simone Weil: An Anthology,* ed. Siân Miles, 218–38. New York: Grove.

Weingast, Barry R. 2005. "The Constitutional Dilemma of Economic Liberty." *Journal of Economic Perspectives* 19, no. 3 (Summer): 89–108.

Weiss, Andrew. 1991. *Efficiency Wages: Models of Unemployment, Layoffs, and Wage Dispersion.* Oxford: Clarendon.

Weissman, David. 2000. *A Social Ontology.* New Haven, CT: Yale University Press.

Wells, Alan F. 1970. *Social Institutions.* London: Heinemann.

Wenger, Etienne. 1998. *Communities of Practice: Learning, Memory and Identity.* Cambridge: Cambridge University Press.

Wennerlind, Carl. 2011. *Casualties of Credit: The English Financial Revolution, 1620–1720.* Cambridge, MA: Harvard University Press.

Werther, William B., Jr., and David Chandler, eds. 2011. *Strategic Corporate Social Responsibility: Stakeholders in a Global Environment.* Thousand Oaks, CA: Sage.

Westergaard, John, and Henrietta Resler. 1976. *Class in a Capitalist Society: A Study of Contemporary Britain.* Harmondsworth: Penguin.

Westgarth, William. 1875. *The Science of Capital and Money: With Prefatory Remarks on Commercial and Financial Crises in Their Past and Present Features, and on Paper Issues and the Bank Act.* London: T. W. Nicholson.

White, Harrison C. 1981. "Where Do Markets Come From?" *American Journal of Sociology* 87, no. 3:517–47.

———. 1988. "Varieties of Markets." In *Social Structure: A Network Approach,* ed. Barry Wellman and S. D. Berkowitz, 261–303. Cambridge, MA: Harvard University Press.

———. 2002. *Markets from Networks: Socioeconomic Models of Production.* Princeton, NJ: Princeton University Press.

White, Nicholas P. 1972. "Origins of Aristotle's Essentialism." *Review of Metaphysics* 26, no. 1:57–85.

Whitley, Richard. 1999. *Divergent Capitalisms: The Social Structuring and Change of Business Systems.* Oxford: Oxford University Press.

Wible, James R. 1998. *The Economics of Science: Methodology and Epistemology as If Economics Really Mattered.* London: Routledge.

Wicken, Jeffrey S. 1987. *Evolution, Thermodynamics, and Information: Extending the Darwinian Paradigm.* Oxford: Oxford University Press.

Wieser, Friedrich von. 1930. *Natural Value.* Translated from the 1889 German ed. New York: G. E. Stechert.

Wiessner, Polly. 2005. "Norm Enforcement among the Ju/'hoansi Bushmen: A Case of Strong Reciprocity?" *Human Nature* 16, no. 2:115–45.

Wilkins, John S. 2009. *Species: A History of the Idea.* Berkeley and Los Angeles: University of California Press.

———. 2012. "Did Popper and Quine Invent 'Aristotelian Essentialism'?" *Evolving Thoughts,* February 7. http://evolvingthoughts.net/2012/02/did-popper -and-quine-invent-aristotelian-essentialism/#more-6024.

Wilkinson, Richard, and Kate Pickett. 2009. *The Spirit Level: Why More Equal Societies Almost Always Do Better.* London: Allen Lane.

Williams, Raymond. 1976. *Keywords: A Vocabulary of Culture and Society.* Glasgow: Fontana.

Williamson, Oliver E. 1975. *Markets and Hierarchies: Analysis and Anti-Trust Implications: A Study in the Economics of Internal Organization.* New York: Free Press.

———. 1981. "The Modern Corporation: Origins, Evolution, Attributes." *Journal of Economic Literature* 19, no. 4 (December): 1537–68.

———. 1985a. "Assessing Contract." *Journal of Law, Economics, and Organization* 1, no. 1 (Spring): 177–208.

———. 1985b. *The Economic Institutions of Capitalism: Firms, Markets, Relational Contracting.* London: Macmillan.

———. 1991. "Comparative Economic Organization: The Analysis of Discrete Structural Alternatives." *Administrative Science Quarterly* 36, no. 2:269–96.

———. 1996. *The Mechanisms of Governance.* Oxford: Oxford University Press.

———. 1999. "Strategy Research: Governance and Competence Perspectives." *Strategic Management Journal* 20, no. 12 (December): 1087–1108.

———. 2000. "The New Institutional Economics: Taking Stock, Looking Ahead." *Journal of Economic Literature* 38, no. 3 (September): 595–613.

———. 2002. "The Lens of Contract: Private Ordering." *American Economic Review: Papers and Proceedings* 92, no. 2 (May): 438–43.

———. 2005. "Why Law, Economics, and Organization?" *Annual Review of Law and Social Science* 1:369–96.

———. 2007. "An Interview with Oliver Williamson." *Journal of Institutional Economics* 3, no. 3 (December): 373–86.

Wilson, Bart J., Taylor Jaworski, Karl E. Schurter, and Andrew Smyth. 2012.

"The Ecological and Civil Mainsprings of Property: An Experimental Economic History of Whalers' Rules of Capture." *Journal of Law, Economics and Organization* 28, no. 4:617–56.

Wilson, David Sloan, and Edward O. Wilson. 2007. "Rethinking the Theoretical Foundations of Sociobiology." *Quarterly Review of Biology* 82, no. 4 (December): 327–48.

Wimsatt, William C. 1986. "Developmental Constraints, Generative Entrenchment, and the Innate-Acquired Distinction." In *Integrating Scientific Disciplines*, ed. W. Bechtel, 185–208. Dordrecht: Martinus Nijhoff.

Winston, Clifford. 2006. *Government Failure versus Market Failure: Microeconomics Policy Research and Government Performance*. Washington, DC: Brookings Institute.

Winter, Sidney G., Jr. 1964. "Economic 'Natural Selection' and the Theory of the Firm." *Yale Economic Essays* 4, no. 1:225–72.

———. 1971. "Satisficing, Selection and the Innovating Remnant." *Quarterly Journal of Economics* 85, no. 2 (May): 237–61.

———. 1982. "An Essay on the Theory of Production." In *Economics and the World Around It*, ed. Saul H. Hymans, 55–91. Ann Arbor: University of Michigan Press.

Wittgenstein, Ludwig. 1960. *Blue Book*. Oxford: Basil Blackwell.

Wolff, Richard D. 2012. *Democracy at Work: A Cure for Capitalism*. New York: Haymarket.

Wood, Stephen, ed. 1982. *The Degradation of Work? Skill, Deskilling and the Labour Process*. London: Hutchinson.

———, ed. 1989. *The Transformation of Work? Skill, Flexibility and the Labour Process*. London: Unwin Hyman.

Wood, Wendy, and David T. Neal. 2007. "A New Look at Habits and the Habit-Goal Interface." *Psychological Review* 114, no. 4 (October): 843–63.

Wray, L. Randall. 1990. *Money and Credit in Capitalist Economies: The Endogeneous Money Approach*. Aldershot: Edward Elgar.

———. 1998. *Understanding Modern Money: The Key to Full Employment and Price Stability*. Cheltenham: Edward Elgar.

———. 2000. "Modern Money." In *What Is Money?* ed. John Smithin, 42–66. London: Routledge.

———, ed. 2004. *Credit and State Theories of Money: The Contribution of A. Mitchell Innes*. Cheltenham: Edward Elgar.

———. 2012. *Modern Money Theory: A Primer on Macroeconomics for Sovereign Monetary Systems*. London: Palgrave Macmillan.

Wu, Jinglian. 2013. *Wu Jinglian: Voice of Reform in China*. Edited and with an introduction by Barry Naughton. Cambridge, MA: MIT Press.

Yamamura, Kozo. 1977. "Success Illgotten? The Role of Meiji Militarism in

Japan's Technological Progress." *Journal of Economic History* 37, no. 1 (March): 113–35.

Yavas, Abdulla. 1998. "Does Too Much Government Investment Retard Economic Development of a Country?" *Journal of Economic Studies* 25, no. 4: 296–308.

Yoffee, Norman. 2005. *Myths of the Archaic State: Evolution of the Earliest Cities, States, and Civilizations.* Cambridge: Cambridge University Press.

Young, Allyn A. 1928. "Increasing Returns and Economic Progress." *Economic Journal* 38, no. 4 (December): 527–42.

Zamagni, Stefano, and Vera Zamagni. 2010. *Cooperative Enterprise: Facing the Challenge of Globalisation.* Cheltenham: Edward Elgar.

Zelizer, Viviana A. 1993. "Making Multiple Monies." In *Explorations in Economic Sociology*, ed. Richard Swedberg, 193–212. New York: Sage.

Zhou, Kate Xiao. 1996. *How the Farmers Changed China.* Boulder, CO: Westview.

Zuboff, Shoshana. 1988. *In the Age of the Smart Machine: The Future of Work and Power.* Oxford: Heinemann.

Index

Abercrombie, Nicholas, 54
Abernathy, William J., 328
Abo, Tetsuo, 324
Abolafia, Mitchel Y., 144
abstraction, 10, 19, 42–46, 59, 182, 265
accidental properties, 27, 29, 34–35, 149–50
Acemoglu, Daron, 17, 110, 120–23, 324, 339, 364
Ackerman, Bruce, 362–64
Adaman, Fikret, 291–95
Adami, Christoph, 277, 327
Adler, Paul S., 194
Admati, Anat, 350
Africa, 77, 96, 155, 185, 334, 336
agoraphobia, 146, 284
Agrast, Mark D., 340–41
Agricultural Revolution, 155
Ahmad, Syed, 182
Ahn, T. K., 193, 196
Aidt, Toke S., 15, 339
Akerlof, George A., 70, 240, 268
Alaska, 365
Albert, Michael, 284, 294–95, 344
Albert, Michel, 33
Alchian, Armen A., 8–9, 106–7, 216–17, 237–38
Aldrich, Howard E., 318
Alesina, Alberto, 96
Allen, Douglas W., 107, 112–13, 118, 123, 246
Alstott, Anne, 362–64
Alter, Catherine, 304
Althusser, Louis, 28–29
altruism, 68–69, 73

Amable, Bruno, 33, 320, 332, 344
American Economic Association, 282
American Revolution, 162, 324
Amsden, Alice H., 288
Amsterdam, 159
Amsterdam Bourse, 136
Anarcharsis of Scythia, 129
Anatolia, 156
Anderson, Elizabeth, 201
Andreoni, James, 69
Anne, Queen of England, 120, 162
anthropology, 7, 30, 52, 67–68, 83, 91, 154
antiessentialism, 11, 26–31
antirealism, 26
Aoki, Masahiko, 33, 45, 85, 142, 320, 344
Archer, Margaret S., 42, 55
Arensberg, Conrad M., 134
Aristotle, 25–28, 32–33, 47, 50, 54, 148–49, 390
Armour, John, 83
Arner, Douglas W., 104, 342
Arrow, Kenneth J., 53, 56, 141, 194–97, 201, 242, 245, 277, 306–7
Arruñada, Benito, 104, 109, 113, 226
Arthur, W. Brian, 168
Ashby, W. Ross, 40
Ashton, David, 330, 364
Assiter, Alison, 30
Athens, 83, 134, 137, 225
Attewell, Paul, 330
auctions, 134, 142
Auer, Raphael Anton, 330
Australia, 185, 317, 346–48
Austria, 348

Austrian school economists, 6, 21, 105, 144, 148, 179, 270, 285–91, 297–310, 354
authority, 3, 9, 13–14, 19, 54, 58, 65, 70–78, 84–103, 106, 108, 113–14, 119, 124–25, 140, 145, 155, 164, 170, 207, 209, 216, 222, 236–41, 287, 298–99, 305, 322, 355, 367–72, 386–92; in employment contracts, 65, 113, 222, 236–41, 355, 367–72, 386–87; evolved dispositions to obey, 14, 99, 240–41
Aviram, Amitai, x, 83–84, 88, 152
Ayres, Clarence E., 48
Azzi, Corry, 191

Bad Godesberg conference, 257, 283, 309
Badr, Gamal Moursi, 94, 322
Baechler, Jean, 16
Bagehot, Walter, 39, 160
Baguñà, Jaume, 322
Baker, J. H., 77, 162
Baker, Wayne E., 144, 304
Baldwin, Carliss Y., 276
Baldwin, Robert E., 360
Balibar, Étienne, 186
Bandelj, Nina, 358
Banerjee, Abhijit, 104
Bang, Peter Fibiger, 134
Bangladesh, 336
banking, 17–20, 61, 115, 124, 134–35, 156–64, 170–72, 188, 200, 255–56, 259, 290, 367, 385
Bank of England, 39, 157, 160, 175
bankruptcy, 220, 229, 319
Bardhan, Pranab K., 124, 288
Barndt, William T., 340
Baron, James N., 191
Baron, Stephen, 194
Barro, Robert J., 110, 334, 353
barter, 132–33, 139, 148–49, 152–55
Barthes, Roland, 28
Bar-Yosef, Ofer, 91
Barzel, Yoram, 14, 107–9
base and superstructure, 8, 62, 74
basic income guarantee, 311, 364–65, 383
Batt, Francis Raleigh, 236
Baum, Matthew A., 340
Baumol, William J., 174–75
Bechara, Antoine, 82
Beck, Anthony, 81
Becker, Gary S., 186–87, 191, 198, 244

Becker, Markus C., 49
Beer, Max, 282
Beer, Stafford, 40
Beinhocker, Eric D., 277, 279, 320, 328
Bekar, Clifford T., 276
Bell, Stephanie A., 78, 164
Bellemare, Marc F., 104
Belloc, Marianna, 320, 344
Belnap, Nuel D., 46
Ben-Ner, Avner, 69
Benson, Bruce L., 83–84
Berger, Suzanne, 33, 344
Berle, Adolf A., 258
Berman, Harold J., 16, 77, 83–84, 162, 225, 228
Berner, Maureen, 353
Bernstein, Lisa, 84
Bettinger, Robert L., 69
Beutel, Frederick K., 162, 171
Bhaskar, Roy, 48, 284
Bible, 134, 357
Bichler, Shimshon, 50, 190
bills of exchange, 157–58, 161–62, 322
biology, 11, 30–31, 139, 270, 315, 322, 327
Birchall, Johnston, 268, 378
Bitcoin, 154
Black, Max, 156, 158, 265
Blackstone, William, 224
Blair, Margaret M., 78, 204, 208, 230, 377
Blake, Peter R., 101
Blanc, Louis, 252
Blanton, Richard E., 91
Blass, Thomas, 70
Blau, Peter, 112, 125
Blaug, Mark, 5, 186, 289
Block, Richard N., 245
Block, Walter, 310, 313
Blomstrom, Magnus, 194
Blumer, Herbert, 278
Boehm, Christopher, 70
Bogart, Dan, 122–23
Bogdan, Radu, 56
Bohannan, Paul, 52, 97
Böhm, Franz, 80
Boisard, Marcel A., 94, 322
Boisot, Max H., 278, 304, 371
Bond, Michael Harris, 70
Bond, Philip J., 340
Bonin, John P., 239, 268, 363, 378–79
Bonnett, Alastair, 363

Booth, Charles D., 104, 342
Bordiga, Amadeo, 257
Bordo, Michael D., 332
Borzaga, Carlo, 378
Botero, Juan C., 340–41
Bottomore, Tom, 55
Boulding, Kenneth E., 191, 265
Bourdieu, Pierre, 191–94, 198
Bowen, Huw V., 161
Bowles, Samuel, 68–69, 73, 90, 96, 194–97, 241–42, 357, 362, 364
Boyd, Robert, 67, 69–70, 90, 242, 296, 320
Boyer, Robert, 33, 320, 332, 344
Boyreau-Debray, Genevieve, 259
Bradley, Joseph P., 76
Braudel, Fernand, 17, 174, 252
Braverman, Harry, 329
Brazil, 133, 335–40, 343, 346–47, 365
Bretton Woods agreement, 317, 334, 349
Britain, 10, 18, 20, 39, 51, 120–23, 159–62, 171, 174–75, 200, 226–28, 247–48, 259, 282, 316–17, 323–24, 333, 343
British Empire, 121, 162, 316–17, 324
Brito, Jerry, 154
Brown, John Seely, 278
Brown, William, 239
Brown, W. Jethro, 204
Brunhoff, Suzanne, 165
Brynjolfsson, Erik, 281, 370
Buchez, Philippe, 379
Buenstorf, Guido, 276, 308
Buiter, Willem H., 202, 336–39, 343
Bukovansky, Mlada, 339
Burczak, Theodore, 290, 300, 310
Burke, Edmund, 80
Burr, Vivien, 30
Burt, Ronald S., 144
Bush, Winston C., 108
Butkiewicz, James L., 340
Button, Graham, 271
Byock, Jesse L., 95

Cambridge, 181, 183, 199, 203
Camic, Charles, 15, 67, 167, 270
Campbell, Donald T., 320
Canada, 337, 339, 345–48
Cannan, Edwin, 175, 177
Cantoni, Davide, 324
capital, ix, 2, 4, 6, 18–19, 65, 74, 122–26, 157, 160, 166, 173–204, 218, 225–27, 244, 247, 252, 256–59, 304, 332, 342, 353–54, 363, 365, 376, 382, 390; academic, 191; business view of, 173–75, 179–86, 197, 202; collateral and, 104–5, 125, 170, 201, 356, 362, 376; cultural, 191–92; definition of, 20, 50, 175, 179, 181, 184, 186, 195–200, 203, 256, 361, 385; degraded concepts of, 3–4, 10–11, 20, 173–203, 362; and emancipation of slaves, 190; environmental, 191, 201; erotic, 192; evolution of term, 174; health, 191; historical specificity of, 182–84, 196–200; human, 10–11, 174, 176, 184–91, 195, 198–200; intellectual, 191; knowledge, 191; locking in, 230; markets, 143, 159; Marx's view of, 177–78, 190, 251, 254, 368, 375; as money, 180–90, 197–99, 256; natural, 196, 201; organizational, 191; origins of term, 155, 174–75; physicalist views of, 175–84, 195–96, 270; as power, 50, 190; public, 193; religious, 191; slaves as, 185–90; social, 10, 11, 173–74, 191–203; spiritual, 192; street, 192; symbolic, 191; trust, 192
capital controversies, 181–83, 199, 202–3
capital goods, 178–83, 198–203
capitalism, ix, 1–7, 11–12, 18–21, 25, 33, 38–41, 53–54, 59–64, 74, 76, 79, 100–101, 110, 114, 116, 120, 125–28, 145, 170, 202, 223, 237, 241–61, 265–66, 273–76, 279–80, 285, 296, 301–8, 314, 320, 322, 327–31, 351, 357, 360–62, 366–67, 374–78, 386; British, 123, 171, 255, 333, 349; capital and, 11, 19–20, 104, 124, 126, 147, 173, 189, 199, 256; corporate, 227–28, 323, 328, 376–78, 383; definition of, 2–3, 7, 10, 19–20, 26, 35–39, 50, 135, 171, 245, 250–60, 284, 301, 354, 366–68, 378, 381, 385–86; democracy and, 350; deskilling and, 329–30; Dutch, 159, 333; evolution of, 6, 21, 50, 77, 96, 122, 126, 148, 165, 170, 200, 205, 246, 249, 255, 274–75, 316–23, 328, 344–45; exploitation within, 353–57, 387; finance and, 158, 163, 167, 170–72, 183, 200, 255–56, 275, 285, 314, 356, 376; firms and, 302; flawed concepts have impaired the understanding of, ix, 3, 11, 18, 21, 189–90; German, 344; globalization of, 5–6, 17, 21, 136, 316–24, 330–35, 342–50, 359–

capitalism (*continued*)
61, 376; historical specificity of, 10, 37–
38, 65, 75, 177, 190, 199, 250–55, 259,
313, 330, 381; impurities within, 29, 39–
41, 51, 288, 296; increase of complexity
within, 319, 327–30; inequality within,
116, 201, 290, 312, 345, 347, 352–62,
382–83, 387; instability of, 167, 172, 183,
329, 349–50; Italian, 159, 333; knowledge intensive, 243, 330, 361, 364, 370–
76; liberal-democratic, 33, 41; literacy
and the rise of, 16; Marx's view of, 6,
38–41, 51, 165–66, 236, 245–46, 253–
55, 260, 275, 329, 332; missing markets
within, 4, 5, 18, 41, 125, 141, 241–45,
256, 360–61, 379, 382; more than an ideology, 59–62, 73–74; not a reflection of
human nature, 10, 54, 101, 242; origins
of, 16–18, 123, 166, 171, 174, 246–47,
256, 333, 382; origins of term, 252; regulation of, 7, 13, 95, 131, 142, 172, 274,
285, 287; religion and the rise of, 16;
role of the state within, 6–18, 21, 40, 51,
65–66, 91, 94, 101, 110, 124–25, 146–48,
154, 172, 205–8, 213, 218, 221, 228–29,
232, 234, 245, 259, 274, 282, 285, 288,
291, 297–305, 309–14, 320, 345, 362,
364, 367, 376–77, 381–83; secure property rights and, 120–26; separation of
ownership and control within, 258; skill
development within, 4, 5, 186, 235–36,
244–45, 329–30, 360, 379; slavery prohibited within, 243, 387; social classes
within, 6–8, 64–66, 74, 111, 177, 254–55,
260–61, 275, 332, 353, 356, 361, 371, 373,
382; versus socialism, 8, 21, 273–76, 281,
285–305, 313–14, 366, 392; stages theory
of, 316; state, 251, 257–59; survival of,
331, 342–43, 366–68, 375, 380; United
States, 333, 338, 349; varieties of, 6, 11,
19–21, 32–34, 39–42, 50, 251, 316, 326–
27, 333, 343–49; wage labor and, 38, 127,
190, 235–36, 243–50, 253–55, 368
capital markets, 182, 257, 360
capital taxation, 362
capital theory, 196, 202
caring work, 364
Carlaw, Kenneth I., 276
Carneiro, Robert L., 91
Carpenter, Jeffrey P., 69

Carroll, Lewis, 173
Carter, James C., 80
Carter, Richard, 205
Casella, Alessandra, 304
Cassady, Ralph, 134
Casson, Mark C., 131, 135
Castelfranchi, Cristiano, 192
Castillo, Andrea, 154
Catholicism, 16
Cattan, Henry, 94, 322
causality, 48–49, 55, 150–51, 354
causal powers, 48, 55
Chamberlain, Neil W., 354
Chamberlin, Edward H., 328
Chandler, Alfred D., 226, 323
Chandler, David, 377
Chang, Ha-Joon, 288, 309, 352, 360
Chao, Kang, 133
charities, 94, 322
Charles I of England, 122
Charles II of England, 122
chartalism, 20, 78, 148
Cheatham, Markus, 245
Chen, Serena, 369
Cheung, Steven N. S., 214–15, 231
Child, John, 304
China, ix, 1, 19, 95, 110, 119, 130, 133, 137,
155–58, 161, 253, 259, 287, 296, 300, 317,
321, 322, 330, 333–50, 360, 380; Mao-
ist, 257–58, 334; post-Maoist, 258–59,
283, 287
Choo, Chun Wei, 371
Christ, Carl F., 245
Christians, 96, 283
Cicero, 157
Ciepley, David, 270
Cipolla, Carlo M., 17
civil society, 119, 125, 302, 305, 363–64
Clark, Andy, 37, 277–78
Clark, Gregory, 122, 160
Clark, John Bates, 34, 179–82, 198
Clark, John Maurice, 139, 245, 272
Clark, Kim B., 276, 328
Clark, Norman G., 277
Clarke, David L., 132
classes, definition of social, 8, 64–66, 74, 111
class struggle, 6, 8, 94, 190, 254–55, 260–61,
275, 300, 382
Clay, Karen, 84, 155
Cliff, Tony, 257

climate change, 351
Clower, Robert W., 148
Coase, Ronald H., 15, 67, 88–89, 110, 119,
    130–31, 140, 143, 146, 205–13, 217, 234,
    259, 279, 287
Coates, David, 33, 344
Cockshott, W. Paul, 294
cognition, 57, 82, 101, 267; situated, 37, 277
Cohen, Avi J., 182–83, 199, 203
Cohen, Edward E., 134
Cohen, Michael D., x, 49, 277
Cohendet, Patrick, 304
coinage, 126, 133, 147, 152, 155–59, 165
Coleman, James S., 43, 112, 125, 140–41,
    191, 193, 198, 219
collateral, 2, 4, 6, 20, 104–5, 108, 124–26,
    163, 169–70, 179, 182, 184, 187–90, 197–
    203, 254–59, 266, 288, 301, 307, 314,
    356–57, 361–62, 367, 376, 382, 385, 387,
    390–91; slaves as, 189–90, 382, 385
Collier, Andrew, 284
Collier, Nick, 276
Collier, Travis C., 277, 327
Collins, Harry, 55, 271
commodity, 65, 103, 111, 125–29, 137–39,
    141, 148–49, 152, 157, 165–67, 177, 242–
    43, 254, 273, 306, 381, 386; ambiguity of
    term, 126–28; definition of, 126–28; in-
    formation as a, 306–7; Marx's concept
    of, 128, 165; origins of term, 126; Po-
    lanyi's view of, 127
commodity exchange, 4, 18, 20, 40, 113,
    144, 184–85, 232–36, 251, 254–55, 258–
    59, 274, 285, 301, 355, 359, 363, 381–82,
    385, 389; abolition of, 272–74, 282–84,
    363, 391
commodity fetishism, 111
commodity markets, 127
commodity money, 127–28, 386
commodity production, 250, 253; general-
    ized, 254; simple, 237, 250, 378
common-pool resources, 119, 273–74, 363
Commons, John R., 7, 12, 15–16, 79, 91–94,
    99–100, 103, 113, 125, 153, 162, 167, 196,
    205, 238, 241, 256, 298
companies, joint-stock, 160, 166, 226–27
competition, 1, 15, 74, 131, 138–42, 145, 214,
    230, 242, 244, 279, 283, 288, 290, 295–
    97, 301–5, 309, 312, 320–21, 325, 328,
    350, 358–59, 362, 389

complexity, 1, 5, 12–14, 21, 26, 29, 40–41,
    50, 60–62, 66–73, 76–83, 88–92, 97, 99,
    102, 113–20, 125, 133, 137, 151, 163, 193,
    201, 211–15, 220, 226, 228, 235–40, 260–
    61, 273–74, 277–81, 284–85, 290–93,
    308–9, 319, 325–31, 349, 359, 365–66,
    369–73; evolution of, 279, 327; growth
    within capitalism, 319, 327–30
conformist transmission, 69
Confucius, 25
Congo, Democratic Republic of, 95
Connecticut, 226
constructivism, 79–80
contracts, 3, 10, 20, 39, 56, 60–66, 73, 75,
    77, 79, 81, 85–88, 93–94, 101–28, 132,
    135–41, 146–47, 154, 157–58, 161–63,
    188, 190, 205–43, 246–50, 254–59, 266–
    69, 273–79, 283–85, 295–98, 301, 304,
    306, 308, 320, 332, 355, 367, 369, 372–
    75, 379, 381, 385–89; degraded concepts
    of, 3, 112, 137; Durkheim on, 115–16;
    employment, 4, 8, 19–20, 35, 39, 64–66,
    112–13, 119, 121, 125, 135, 184, 207–8,
    222, 233–59, 268–71, 285, 301, 328, 342–
    43, 355, 367–75, 379, 385–87; futures,
    4, 360, 379, 382; historical specificity
    of, 15; implicit, 3, 211, 238–39; informa-
    tion, 309; limits to, 115–16; mortgage,
    113–14; nexus of, 217–21, 234; partner-
    ship, 220, 227–28, 234; prohibition of,
    294; relational, 137–38, 215–16, 224;
    sales, 65, 235–38; for services, 65, 138,
    145–47, 162, 184, 205, 207, 230–39, 246,
    254, 256, 259, 284, 311, 355, 369, 373–
    75, 385–90
cooperation, 66–69, 73, 86, 88, 91, 119, 145,
    168, 241–42, 250, 260, 274, 287, 292,
    296–97, 320, 351, 365
cooperatives, 239, 245, 250, 256, 268, 310,
    355–56, 363–64, 367–70, 378–80, 383
coordination games, 150–52
Corning, Peter A., 364
Cornuelle, Richard, 371
corporate capitalism, 227–28, 323, 328,
    376–78, 383
corporations, 7, 17, 20, 78, 109, 172, 175,
    181, 204–13, 217–30, 233, 285, 288, 295,
    301–6, 314, 323, 328, 342–43, 350, 368–
    69, 374–79, 382; historical specific phe-
    nomena, 205; nonprofit, 378

corruption, ix, 14–15, 18, 114, 158–59, 303,
    321, 333, 339–43
Cosmides, Leda, 69
Costanza, Robert, 35
Cotgrave, Randle, 175
Cotterrell, Roger, 79–80
Cottrell, Allin F., 294
countervailing power, 10, 17–18, 160, 170,
    299–305, 376; origins of term, 17; in
    work of J. K. Galbraith, 17
Cowen, Tyler, 364
Crawford, Sue E. S., 45, 58
credit, 20, 115, 128, 134, 147, 155, 159–72,
    179–80, 186, 204, 209, 213, 218, 222,
    230, 251, 254–56, 259, 364, 385; Marx's
    view of, 165–66
Crockett, Sean, 102
Crosland, C. Anthony, 283
Crouch, Colin, 2, 33, 302, 305, 344, 364, 376
Crusoe, Robinson, 56, 112, 113, 196
Crutchfield, James P., 277
Cuba, 335
cultural relativism, 30
Cultural Revolution, 95
culture, 11, 30, 33, 57, 67–74, 78, 82, 85, 90,
    96–99, 130, 142, 144–46, 155, 191–92,
    201, 239–42, 304, 331, 344–45, 353, 370
cumulative causation, 171
custom, 8, 15, 19, 76–83, 90–102, 106, 116–
    18, 125, 132, 149, 153, 160, 205, 214,
    238–41, 274, 279, 299–300, 389–91

Dafforne, Richard, 175
Dahl, Robert A., 305, 376
Dahlman, Carl J., 4, 118
Dalton, George B., 139, 154
Damasio, Antonio R., 82
Darwin, Charles R., 31–32, 42, 68–69, 72,
    90, 98, 241–42, 315, 317, 321, 325–26, 390
Darwinism, 34, 50, 67, 72, 75, 80–81, 277–
    80, 317–18, 321, 327
Davidson, Paul, 154, 164
Davies, Glyn, 139, 154–55
Davies, Graham I., 134
Davies, James B., 346
Davis, John B., x, 382
Davis, Michael, 382
Deakin, Simon, x, 12, 78, 83–84, 204, 222,
    233, 237, 239, 249
Deaton, Angus, 36

Debreu, Gerard, 141, 242
debt, 20, 38, 122, 134, 148, 155, 158, 160–72,
    175, 188–90, 254–56, 259, 301, 314, 323,
    367, 385; negotiability of, 162–63
Deci, E. L., 373
definitions, ix, 2, 3, 8, 10–11, 18–21, 25–27,
    34–39, 42–52, 54–65, 74, 106, 108, 120,
    125, 128, 132, 135, 137, 140, 174, 204–
    5, 224, 231, 251–57, 260, 282, 327, 339,
    362, 385–86, 389; do not imply similar-
    ity, 51; generally ill-based on behaviors,
    51, 54, 106
Defourny, Jacques, 378
deindustrialization, 338
Dei Ottati, Gabi, 191
democracy, 1, 10, 21, 33, 79, 99, 122, 239,
    249, 283–87, 291, 294–95, 300, 305, 308,
    324, 339–40, 343, 345, 349–50, 355, 364,
    366, 369–70, 376; socialism and, 287,
    295; war and, 349
Demsetz, Harold, 106, 216–17, 237–38
Deng, Xiaoping, 283
Denmark, 95, 348
Dennett, Daniel C., 277
Dequech, David, 15
de Roover, Raymond A., 174
deskilling, 329–32, 371
De Soto, Hernando, 104
Devine, Pat, 291–95
de Vries, Jan, 159, 161–62
De Waal, Frans B. M., 69, 70, 72, 90, 242
Dewey, John, 27–28, 82, 220, 277, 308
Diamond, A. S., 92
Diamond, Jared, 91
Dickenson, Henry D., 285, 288–90
Dickson, Peter G. M., 39, 160
dictatorship of the proletariat, 300
diffusion, 318, 324–25, 334, 336, 386; the
    great global, 335; institutional, 88, 94,
    318–19, 322–25, 333–43, 349, 386; of
    knowledge, 260, 324–25, 334; technolog-
    ical, 36, 322–24, 333–35, 343, 349, 386
DiMaggio, Paul J., 240, 278
Dingwall, Robert, 323
distribution of income, 4, 21, 35, 89, 109,
    134, 199, 203, 252, 258, 265, 267, 271,
    274, 346–47, 354, 359–60, 381
distribution of wealth, 4, 21, 35, 89, 109,
    134, 199, 203, 252, 257, 258, 265, 267,
    269, 271, 274, 346, 354, 359–60, 364, 381

division of labor, 91, 113, 144, 176, 267–68, 274–75, 293, 298, 327, 365, 369
Dixit, Avinash K., 83, 85
Doeringer, Peter B., 213
Donald, Merlin, 278
Donisthorpe, Wordsworth, 185
Dopfer, Kurt, 168
Dore, Ronald, x, 33, 137, 214, 344
double-entry bookkeeping, 134, 174
Doucouliagos, Chris, 268, 378
Douglas, Mary T., 56
Dow, Gregory K., 355
Drache, Daniel, 332
Dreyfus, Hubert L., 329, 371
Dreyfus, Stuart E., 329, 371
Drucker, Peter F., 371
Du Bois, Armand B., 226–27
Duguid, Paul, 278
Dunayevskaya, Raya, 257
Dunbar, Robin I. M., 296
Dunning, John H., 101, 113, 162, 332
Duranton, Alexandre, 109
Durkheim, Émile, 80, 93, 115–16, 240
Durlauf, Steven D., 194
Dymski, Gary A., x, 165

Earl, Peter E., 137–38
Earle, Timothy K., 70
Easterly, William, 96, 194
Eatwell, John, 131
Ebenstein, Alan O., 309
Ebner, Alexander, 183
Eccles, Robert G., 213–14
economics, ix, 3–15, 20, 31, 34, 42, 48, 56–57, 61–63, 67–70, 74–75, 99, 105–12, 126–32, 139–46, 157, 166–68, 172–206, 209, 212–17, 224, 230–32, 245, 266, 276, 279–80, 285–86, 289, 296–302, 305, 308, 313, 355–56, 359–62, 365–66, 377, 385; classical, 166–67, 178–80, 197, 266, 271, 308; evolutionary, 46, 315; law and, 12, 15, 162, 168, 205; neoclassical, 130, 167, 190, 197, 265–66, 270, 273, 276, 285, 289, 302, 306–8; new institutional, 15, 66–67, 108, 142; of property rights, 105–10, 221–23; welfare, 245
Edgeworth, Francis Y., 167
education, 5, 56, 176, 186, 188, 244, 308, 311, 330, 352–57, 364, 381–83
Edvinsson, Leif, 192

Edward I of England, 122
Edward II of England, 122
Edward III of England, 122, 158
Eggertsson, Thráinn, 205
Egypt, 156
Ehrenberg, Ronald, 191
Einstein, Albert, 26
Einzig, Paul, 139, 154–55, 158
Elder-Vass, Dave, 55
Ellerman, David P., 78, 201, 239, 245, 250, 354–55, 368, 369
Ellickson, Robert C., 83–84
Elsner, Wolfram, 33, 344
Elster, Jon, 219, 345
Ely, Richard T., 282
embeddedness, 143
emotions, 70, 72, 78, 90, 97, 101, 118
employee training, 4, 5, 186, 235–36, 244–45, 330, 356, 360, 379
employment contracts, 4, 8, 19–20, 35, 39, 64–66, 112–13, 119–21, 125, 135, 184, 207–8, 222–43, 246–50, 253–59, 268–71, 285, 301, 328, 355, 367–75, 379, 385–87; abolition of, 355, 367–70, 375; removal of criminal sanctions from, 248
Engel, Christoph, x, 82
Engels, Frederick, 63–66, 94, 109, 190, 250, 260, 275, 282, 323, 379
England, 17, 33, 37–38, 77, 83–84, 94, 120–23, 126, 135, 157–62, 170–75, 210, 224–26, 246–49, 255–56, 322–23
Enlightenment, 18, 352, 382–83; Scottish, 83–84
entails, 123
enterprises. See firms
entrepreneurs, 43, 182, 186, 205–9, 223, 233, 256, 270, 275, 289, 295, 303, 314, 353, 356, 364
entropy, 279–80, 327
environmental capital, 191, 201
epistemology, 28–30
Epstein, Stephen R., 160, 246
Equatorial Guinea, 336
equilibrium, 34, 45, 57, 85–88, 131, 147, 151–52, 167, 172, 182, 218, 220, 242–43, 289, 379
Errunza, Vihang, 133
Espejo, Raul, 40
essential hybridity, 100, 146, 154
essentialism, 11, 26–34, 50, 387

essential properties, 19–20, 25–29, 32–35, 46, 50–51, 65, 78, 100, 106, 146, 149, 154, 386
Estrin, Saul, 250
Ethiopia, 155
Eucken, Walter, 80
Eucleides of Megara, 47, 54
Europe, 2, 17–18, 35, 39–40, 50, 77, 96, 122, 133, 135, 154, 157–60, 164, 174, 184, 225–28, 246, 287–88, 304, 310, 321–24, 330, 334, 336, 338, 350, 380–81
European Union, 154, 288, 336, 343
Evans, Karen G., 308
Everest-Phillips, Max, 122
evolution from within, 6, 18, 94, 145, 325
exchange, ix, 3–4, 12, 15, 18–21, 42, 102–3, 107, 111–13, 117, 125–29, 133, 136–49, 152–59, 162, 165, 168, 177–78, 184, 205, 210, 215, 226, 232–35, 247, 249, 251, 254–55, 258–59, 271–75, 283, 285, 297–301, 313, 354, 359, 363, 381–82, 385–91; degraded concepts of, 3, 112, 137, 141, 296, 313
explanations of origin, 88, 152
explanations of persistence, 88, 152–53, 169
exploitation, 92, 177, 246, 283, 353–57, 372, 387; authority, 355, 387; bargaining, 354, 387; corporeal, 355–57, 387; through unequal collateralizability, 356–57, 387

Fabians, 282–83, 309
factors of production, 5, 181–86, 194–95, 198–99, 202, 207–8, 235, 276, 279, 353, 356–57, 361–62, 387
factory organization, 322–23
Falcone, Rino, 192
falsifiability, 40
families, 9, 20, 39, 58, 68, 93, 113–14, 119, 123–25, 132, 136, 143, 171, 181, 193, 225, 227, 245–47, 254, 256, 259, 288, 297, 302, 345–48, 364, 366, 374, 385
Fargher, Lane F., 91
Farnsworth, E. Allan, 93
Farr, William, 187
fascism, 79, 305, 310, 380
Faulhaber, Gerald R., 174, 175
Faulkner, Philip, 271
Fehr, Ernst, 69
Felin, Teppo, 61
feminism, 30

Fenzl, Norbert, 277
Fetter, Frank A., 175, 181–84, 193, 197, 361
feudalism, 40, 77, 123, 126, 135, 235, 246–49, 274, 324, 375
Fichtner, Aaron R., 245
Field, Alexander J., 57, 69, 84–85, 88
Field, John, 187, 194
finance, 1, 2, 5–6, 11, 18, 20, 35–39, 50–51, 61, 101, 104, 108, 122–24, 130, 133, 136–38, 144–47, 158–64, 170–73, 180–83, 190, 196, 198, 200–201, 225, 227, 243, 250–51, 255–59, 275, 285, 288, 311, 316–17, 324, 328, 332–35, 342, 349–50, 353, 360, 367, 369, 376, 385
financial markets, instability of, 164, 167, 172, 183
Financial Revolution, in UK, 160–61, 171
Fine, Ben, 194
Finley, Moses I., 134
firm-market hybrids, 213–16
firms, 3, 4, 9, 15, 19–20, 32, 43–47, 58, 110, 115, 119, 125, 130, 137, 145, 159, 175, 204–45, 250, 254, 256, 259, 268–71, 274, 283, 288–90, 296–97, 302, 307, 318–22, 328, 332, 345, 357, 360, 364, 367–70, 377–79, 385–88; Chinese, 342; definition of, 204, 207, 212, 230–34, 387–88; distinguished from markets, 207–11, 214–16, 221; origin of term, 206
First World War, 317, 321
Fisher, Irving, 112, 167, 175, 179–80, 186–87, 198, 270
Flanders, 136, 246
Fleetwood, Steve, x, 55–56
Fletcher, Ian, 360
Fligstein, Neil, 143–44, 323
Florence, 135, 158, 225, 246
Florence, P. Sargant, 230–31
Florida, Richard, 324
Fogel, Robert W., 36, 338
Folbre, Nancy, 364
Foley, Vernard, 266
forbearance, 118, 211
Forstater, Mathew, 156
Forte, Francesco, 288
Foss, Kirsten, 223
Foss, Nicolai J., x, 61, 223
Foster, John, 168
Foucault, Michel, 186
foundationalism, 28

Fox, Alan, 116, 119, 201, 239–40
France, 28, 83–84, 109, 126, 159, 161, 175, 193, 225–26, 252, 266, 302–5, 323–24, 339, 343, 346–49, 378–80
France, Anatole, 352
Fransman, Martin, 371
Freiburg school, 80
French Revolution, 303, 305, 324, 380
Fried, Barbara H., 99
Friedman, David, x, 83–84, 95
Friedman, Milton, 5, 365
Friedman, Ori, 101
Fukuyama, Francis, 33
Fuller, Lon L., 79, 87, 117, 219
functionalism, 40
Furubotn, Eirik G., 108
Fuss, Diana, 30, 31
Fustel De Coulanges, Numa Denis, 80, 99

Gagliardi, Francesca, x, 268, 320, 344, 379
Galanter, Marc, 96
Galbraith, James K., 353
Galbraith, John Kenneth, 11, 17, 305, 365, 376
game theory, 45, 53, 57, 85–86, 89, 111, 142, 151
Garcia-Fernàndez, Jordi, 322
Gartze, Erik, 349
Gat, Azar, 96
Gaudiosi, Monica M., 94, 322
GDP, limitations as a measure, 35
general equilibrium theory, 3, 56, 141–42, 147–48, 158, 167, 242, 285, 290, 301
generalized commodity production, 254
Genghis Khan, 321
Genoa, 135, 225
Georgescu-Roegen, Nicholas, 276, 280
Geras, Norman, 54
Gerlagh, Reyer, 15, 339
German historical school, 7, 10, 78, 139, 148–49, 178, 183, 316
German Social Democratic Party, 283, 309
Germany, 7, 33, 63–64, 83–84, 148, 155, 157, 167, 191, 225, 252, 282–83, 304–5, 324, 326, 339, 343–44, 346–48
Gerring, John, 340
Gerschenkron, Alexander, 333
Gershuny, Jonathan, 273
Ghent, 136
Gigerenzer, Gerd, 278

Gilbert, Margaret, 58, 104
Gilbert, Scott F., 322
Gil-White, Francisco J., 69
Gindis, David, x, 12, 78, 204, 233–34, 362
Gintis, Herbert, 68–70, 73, 90, 102, 219, 241–42, 357, 364
Gjersoe, Nathalia, 101
Glaeser, Edward L., 83
globalization, 1, 5, 17, 21, 136, 317, 320, 322, 324, 330–35, 344–50, 359–61, 376
global warming, 351
Glorious Revolution, 123, 159–60, 225, 324
Gluckman, Max, 77
Glyn, Andrew, 317, 332
Godwin, William, 252
Goldberg, Victor P., 137, 214
Goldin, Claudia, 330
Goldstein, Daniel G., 278
Golub, Steven, 156
Gomulka, Stanislav, 333
Goodhart, Charles A. E., x, 164, 202
Gorz, André, 280
Gould, Stephen Jay, 326–27
Gowdy, John M., 201
Gower, Laurence C. B., 208
Graeber, David, 139, 154–56, 158
Granovetter, Mark, 68, 143, 304
Grant, Robert M., 324
Gray, John, 381
Graybiel, Anne M., 82
Greece, 83, 120, 133–34, 137, 156, 174, 225, 277
greed, 9, 14, 74, 146, 283
Green, Francis, 330, 364
Green, Thomas H., 355–56, 362, 387
Greif, Avner, x, 77, 83–85, 87, 114, 119, 125, 225
Grierson, Philip, 152, 155
Griffiths, John, 96
Groenewegen, John, 15
Grossman, Michael, 191
Grossman, Sanford J., 106, 221–23
group selection, 71, 242
Guala, Francesco, 45
guilds, 77, 84, 225, 302–3
Guinnane, Timothy W., 302
Guzmán, Ricardo Andrés, 69

Haas, Peter M., 278
Haber, Stephen H., 172

habits, 10, 14, 48–49, 59, 61, 67, 71–72, 82,
    87–90, 97–99, 125, 161, 170, 186, 232,
    240, 260, 271, 277–79, 293, 318, 322–23,
    327, 386–89; conformist, 72; of obei-
    sance, 71–72
Hacker, Barton C., 323
Hacking, Ian, 27
Hadfield, Gillian K., 86–87
Hage, Jerald, 304
Hahn, Frank, 3, 141, 147, 201
Hahnel, Robin, 284, 294
Haidt, Jonathan, 14, 71, 87, 90
Hakim, Catherine, 192
Hale, Robert Lee, 99
Hall, Peter A., 33, 320, 344
Hallowell, A. Irving, 103
Hamilton, Earl J., 134, 158
Hamilton, William D., 69
Hanappi, Hardy, 33, 344
Handlin, Mary F., 226
Handlin, Oscar, 226
Handy, Charles B., 374
Hanifan, Lyda J., 193, 198
Hannan, Michael T., 191
Hansmann, Henry, 78, 204, 230, 379
Harcourt, Geoffrey C., 183, 199, 203
Härdle, Wolfgang K., 144
Harnden, Roger, 40
Harré, Rom, 48, 55
Harris, Paul L., 101
Harris, Ron, 226, 302
Harris, William Cornwallis, 185
Hart, Herbert L. A., 79, 86–87, 99
Hart, Oliver D., 106, 141, 221–23, 242–
    43, 360
Hartwick, John, 191
Hasnas, John, 77, 83–84
Hausmann, Ricardo, 329
Hayek, Friedrich A., ix, 5–6, 62, 77–84,
    145, 151, 182, 270, 280, 282, 285–92,
    296–302, 306–14, 318, 365, 376–77
Head, Simon, 330, 370, 372
Hédoin, Cyril, 111
Hegel, G. W. F., 41, 316
Hegre, Håvard, 349
Heilbroner, Robert L., 251
Heinsohn, Gunnar, 103–4, 163–64, 299
Heller, Michael A., 141, 307
Hellwig, Martin, 350
Hendriks-Jansen, Horst, 278

Henrich, Joseph, 69, 71, 242
Henry II of England, 94, 322
Henry VIII of England, 122
Herodotus, 134, 156
Herrmann-Pillath, Carsten, 170
Hesse, Mary B., 265
Hessen, Robert, 225–26
heuristics, 149–51, 203, 326
Hidalgo, César A., 329
Highfield, Roger, 241
Hill, Kim R., 242
Hill, Stephen, 54
Himma, Kennet Einar, 87
Hindess, Barry, 29, 43, 219
Hindriks, Frank, 45
Hirsch, Jean-Pierre, 303
Hirschman, Albert O., 244
Hirst, Paul Q., 88, 332
historical specificity, 2–3, 10, 15, 19, 37–
    38, 53, 62, 65, 75, 99, 107, 112, 125, 129,
    132, 136, 139–40, 144, 173, 177–78, 182–
    83, 197–205, 245, 251–56, 259, 279, 285,
    298, 301, 313, 330, 381
Ho, Mae-Wan, 327
Ho, Peter, 110, 342
Hobbes, Thomas, 25
Hobson, John A., 139, 179, 183–84, 198–99,
    240, 253, 355–56, 361–62, 387
Hoebel, Edward Adamson, 92
Hoffmann, Johann Gottfried, 76
Hofkirchner, Wolfgang, 277
Hogg, Michael A., 369
Hohfeld, Wesley Newcomb, 104
Holmström, Bengt, 223
Holzer, Harry J., 245
Homans, George C., 112, 125
Hong Kong, 336–37, 342
Honoré, Antony M., 101, 103–4, 109, 125
Hoo, Brian M., 101
Hook, J., 101
Hopkins, Keith, 156
Hoppe, Hans-Hermann, 310, 313
Horwitz, Steven, 297
Hsu, Berry Fong Chung, 104, 342
Hu, Jichuang, 147
Huang, Kainan, x, 12, 130, 259, 342
Huang, Yasheng, 259, 342
Hubbick, Elizabeth, 245, 268, 378
Hudson, Michael, 155, 225
Huerta de Soto, Jesús, 159

Hull, David L., 31, 318, 389
human capital, 10, 11, 174, 184–91, 195,
    198–203; first appearance of term, 185;
    first use of term in economics, 186
Hume, David, 80, 83, 84, 151
Humphrey, Caroline, 139, 154
Hunt, Bishop C., 227
Huntington, Samuel P., 14
Hutchins, Edwin, 37, 277–78
Hutchinson, Allan C., 81
Hutt, William H., 355
Hutton, Will, 377

Iacobucci, Edward M., 78, 204, 222
Iceland, 83, 95
ideology, 2, 8, 59–62, 73, 190, 200–201, 242,
    302, 320, 330, 348, 379
immaterial assets, 180–81, 191, 196
impurity principle, 40–42, 51, 388
incentives, 5, 18, 36, 42, 67, 73, 80, 85, 89,
    105, 108, 116, 120, 122, 151–52, 167, 208,
    213, 216, 236, 242, 245, 249, 256, 266,
    273–76, 279, 284–89, 296, 299, 311, 353,
    361–64, 378
income, distribution of, 4, 21, 35, 89, 109,
    134, 199, 203, 252, 258, 265, 267, 271,
    274, 346–47, 354, 359–60, 381
India, 1, 17, 133, 136, 140, 155–56, 159–60,
    185, 224–25, 330, 335–40, 342–43, 346–
    47, 349–50
individualism, 66, 242, 285, 292, 302–5, 313;
    possessive, 255
Indonesia, 133, 335–39
Industrial Revolution, 38, 161, 204, 226,
    246, 247
inequality, 1, 4, 21, 201, 283, 312, 333, 345–
    49, 352–63, 373, 380; global, 359–61
infant-industry argument, 360
Ingham, Geoffrey, x, 78, 154, 161, 164, 178
innovation, 6, 7, 17–18, 36–37, 50, 116, 124,
    145, 156, 163, 174, 241, 249, 253, 260,
    268, 274–76, 281, 284, 286–90, 295–96,
    320–22, 328–30, 334, 339, 350, 365–66
instincts, 48, 67–73, 81–82, 89–90, 97, 100–
    102, 273; conformist, 72; of obeisance,
    78; of workmanship, 273
institutionalism, 313; legal, ix, 12–16; new
    economic, 15, 66–67, 108, 142; origi-
    nal American, 7, 10, 15–16, 48, 139, 153,
    167, 181, 272

institutions, ix, 1–21, 35–45, 53–67, 74–85,
    89–94, 97–100, 104–18, 123–24, 130–
    35, 138–48, 151, 154–55, 160–63, 166–
    72, 184, 193–97, 202–3, 212, 225, 241,
    251, 255–60, 265–68, 272, 275–79, 285–
    87, 293, 298, 301–5, 311, 314, 317, 320–
    27, 331–35, 342–45, 349–51, 357, 359,
    365, 367, 380, 385, 388–92; definition of,
    43–45, 58
intangible assets, 15, 103, 124, 167, 179–80,
    184, 270
intellective skills, 371–72
interactors, 318–19, 386, 391
International Monetary Fund, 193, 335
Internet, 95, 138, 141–42, 194, 308
Ioannides, Stavros, 292
Ireland, Paddy W., 172, 208, 227, 377
Islam, 94, 96, 225, 304, 322
Israel, Jonathan I., 159
Italy, 10, 20, 35, 93–94, 101, 120, 122, 134–
    35, 157–61, 174–75, 198, 200, 224–25,
    246, 316, 333, 346–48
Iwai, Katsuhito, 78, 204
Iyer, Lakshmi, 104

Jacoby, Sanford M., 240
Jahnsen, D. Bruce, 84
Jain, Arvind K., 15, 339
James, Philip S., 236
James, William, 48, 82, 277
Japan, 41, 304–5, 321, 324, 334–39, 343,
    346–48, 350
Jardine, Lisa, 160
Jary, David, 55
Jary, Julia, 55
Jaworski, Taylor, 102
Jensen, Michael C., 217–21, 228, 233
Jericho, 133
Jevons, William Stanley, 167, 270
Jews, 96, 122, 162
Jiang, Shuxia, 15, 339
Jochimsen, Maren A., 364
Joffe, Michael, 320, 328
Johnson, Allen W., 70
Johnson, Alvin S., 191
Johnson, Chalmers, 288
Johnson, Simon, 17, 110, 120, 122, 324
joint-stock companies, 160, 166, 226, 227
Jones, Derek C., 239, 268, 363, 378–79
Jones, Eric, 17

Jones, Owen D., 72
Joseph, Craig, 14, 71, 87, 90
Jossa, Bruno, 379
jury system, 94, 322
justice, 9, 14, 25, 72, 75, 91, 95, 100–101,
    108–9, 147, 155, 299–300, 365, 392

Kahn-Freund, Otto, 233, 237, 248
Kanngiesser, Patricia, 101
Katz, Lawrence F., 330
Kay, Neil M., 4
Keeley, Lawrence H., 96
Keijzer, Fred, 278
Kelsen, Hans, 79, 99
Keltner, Dacher, 369
Kennedy, David, 121
Kenney, Martin, 324
Kenworthy, Lane, 288
Ker, Henry Bellenden, 226
Kerbo, Harold R., 324
Kern, Francis, 304
Kerstholt, Frans, 15
Kesting, Stefan, 344
Keynes, John Maynard, ix, 3, 5, 7, 78, 146–
    47, 154, 158, 164, 167, 172, 181, 237, 239–
    90, 312, 360, 367
Khalil, Elias L., 42, 223, 254, 275
Khan, Mushtaq, 339
Kiker, B. F., 176, 186–88
Kim, E. Han, 217
Kimbrough, Erik O., 102
Kindleberger, Charles P., 39, 160, 317
King, Gregory, 246
King, Robert J., 194
Kirman, Alan P., 31, 141, 144
Kitson, Peter M., 247
Klaes, Matthias, 184
Klein, Benjamin, 191, 209
Kley, Roland, 81
Knapp, George F., 78, 153, 164
Knies, Karl, 178
Knight, Frank H., 4, 182, 237, 239, 290, 360
Knight, Jack, 13, 45, 88–89, 100, 106, 120
Knorr-Cetina, Karin D., 278
Knorringa, Peter, 194
Knott, Jack H., 245
knowledge, ix, 6, 16, 28, 30, 40, 48, 69, 86,
    127–30, 160, 191, 202, 211, 223, 243, 246,
    260, 265–81, 286–93, 296, 299, 304–
    9, 312, 324–30, 334, 361, 364–65, 369–

77, 388–90; tacit, 61, 239, 289–94, 305–
    8, 324
Knudsen, Thorbjørn, x, 67, 71, 81–82, 102,
    168, 277–79, 316–19, 321, 389
Kogut, Bruce, 324
Kollmeyer, Christopher, 358
Kornhauser, L., 114
Kraakman, Reinier, 78, 204, 230
Krall, Lisa, 201
kratophobia, 285
Kraus, Michael W., 369
Krebs, Dennis, 72, 241
Kripke, Saul, 28
Krippner, Greta, 143
Krueger, Anne O., 5
Krugman, Paul R., 5
Kuisel, Richard F., 303
Kuran, Timur, 304
Kurzban, Robert, 72
Kusch, Martin, 271
Kwon, Seok-Woo, 194

labor: bonded, 4, 121, 135, 185–86, 243, 247,
    249; disutility of, 273; division of, 91,
    113, 144, 176, 267–68, 274–75, 293–98,
    327, 365, 369; skilled, 5, 184, 223, 243–
    45, 267, 293, 322, 329–30, 334, 342, 344,
    357, 361, 364, 370–74, 377, 379, 390
labor theory of value, 6, 111, 166, 176, 184,
    190, 197, 275, 353–54
Laclau, Ernesto, 29
Lake, David A., 340
Lakoff, George, 265
Lamb, Robert, 363
Lamoreaux, Naomi R., 302
Landa, Janet, 84, 87, 107, 119, 125
Landauer, Carl A., 282
Lane, David, 37, 277
Lange, Oskar R., 283, 285, 288–90
Langlois, Richard N., x, 4, 212, 296
language, 58, 61, 82, 132, 151, 293; as an in-
    stitution, 45, 57–58, 64, 388, 392; origins
    of, 19, 53, 73
La Porta, Rafael, 83
Lascaux, Alexander, 116
La Torre, Massimo, 12
Latour, Bruno, 271
Lave, Jean, 37, 277–78
Lavoie, Donald, 288, 381
Lavoie, Marc, 164

law, ix, 2–21, 25, 40, 45, 52, 57–66, 72–126, 130–31, 136–41, 148, 151–57, 161–63, 168, 171, 182–83, 186–89, 196–99, 204–41, 245–48, 254–60, 266, 279, 285, 297–307, 313, 317–18, 322–24, 331–32, 340–42, 345, 352, 357, 365, 370, 373–77, 380, 385–89; authority and, 14, 65, 75, 86–87, 94, 99, 124, 147; autopoietic accounts of, 81; Chinese, 110, 259, 342; civil, 83–84, 93–94; common, 80, 83–84, 91–94, 162, 324; company, 94, 130, 205, 208, 213, 219, 223–31, 234, 304, 322, 368, 376–78, 383; constitutional, 81; constitutive role of, 2, 6, 8, 16–19, 66, 256, 309; custom and, 8–9, 15, 77–83, 92–94, 97–102, 106, 116–17, 125, 153, 299–300, 389; definition of, 389; economics and, 12, 15, 162–68, 205; employment, 233–41, 248–49, 258, 373–75, 386; enforcement of, 14, 85, 89–90, 93, 99–100, 105, 113–20, 125, 162–63; English, 83, 94, 171, 236, 238, 247–49, 322, 342; epiphenomenal view of, 9, 62–66, 94, 168; equality under the, 37, 123, 141, 188, 249, 324, 352–53, 380–82; evolution of, 78, 80, 83, 87, 91–92, 96–99, 299; firms and, 205–8, 211–28, 231, 258, 304, 322, 368, 377; historical specificity of, 15; international, 79; Islamic, 94–96, 225, 304, 322; Justinian, 83–84, 225; limits to, 116–20, 125, 240–41, 297, 389; Marxism and, 6, 8, 65–66, 74, 94, 102, 106, 109, 254, 260, 275, 300; money and, 150–54, 157–58, 161–64, 171–72, 221, 255, 258; morality and, 87, 106; Napoleonic, 303, 324; natural, 79, 86; origins of, 79; private, 77, 80, 87–89, 95–96, 152, 162; property and, 103–24, 137, 160, 188, 190, 196–97, 210, 222, 224, 273–74, 279, 285, 298, 304, 307, 363, 381–82, 388–90; punishment and, 90–91, 97; religion and, 92; Roman, 83–94, 101, 104, 183, 224–25, 246; rule of, 9, 13, 15, 87, 96, 110, 114, 117–19, 122, 125, 300, 333, 338–45; Scottish, 83–84; spontaneous evolution of, 13, 76–79, 83–88, 94–97, 100, 116, 152; the state and, 76–80, 85, 88–94, 97–100, 108, 110, 146, 158, 205, 313; superstructural view of, 8, 62, 74, 102
law of one price, 139

Lawrence, William H., 162, 171
Lawson, Tony, 5, 42, 167
Lazaric, Nathalie, 49
Lazonick, William, 288
Leathers, Charles G., 167
LeBlanc, Steven A., 95
Lee, Doowan, 276
Lee, John S., 135
Lee, Ruben, 144
Leeson, Peter T., 84
legal aid, 118
legal entities. *See* legal personality
legal fictions, 211, 218–20, 229–30
legal impermeability, 114–20, 125, 240–41, 389
legal incorporation, 7, 15, 18, 172, 204–13, 221, 224–33, 304, 314, 377
legal institutionalism, ix, 12–16
legal personality, 131, 172, 204–34, 304, 307, 376–77, 388
legal pluralism, 77, 96
legal positivism, 79, 86–87; Hayek's view of, 79
legal realism, 87, 99, 300
legitimation, 9–10, 70, 75, 77, 88, 98–100, 103–8, 111, 124, 170, 300, 305, 370, 390
Leijonhufvud, Axel, 265, 276
Lejot, Paul, 104, 342
Lenin, Vladimir Ilyich, 257–58, 300
Lerner, Abba P., 164, 283
Levine, Ross, 96, 194
Levins, Richard, 52
Levitt, Barbara, 49, 240
Levy, Frank, 329
Lewin, Shira B., 48
Lewontin, Richard C., 52, 265
Li, Minqi, 342–43
Lie, John, 144
Liebknecht, Wilhelm, 257–58
life expectancy, 36, 274
limited liability, 204, 221, 226–28, 232, 314, 323, 376–78
Lincoln, James R., 190, 324
Lindblom, Charles E., 305, 376
Lindenberg, Siegwart, 191
Lindert, Peter H., 38, 135, 246, 247
Lipsey, Richard E., x, 194, 276
List, Christian, 219
List, Friedrich, 360
literacy, rise of capitalism and, 16

Littler, Craig R., 258
Llewellyn, Karl N., 300
Lloyd, Dennis, 93
Loasby, Brian J., 4, 138
London, 122, 136, 160, 252, 282
London Stock Exchange, 136
Lopez-de-Silanes, Florencio, 83
Lorenz, Edward H., 278
Louis XIV of France, 302
Ludwig, Arnold M., 70
Lueck, Dean, 109
Luhmann, Niklas, 81, 117
Luo, Jianxi, 278

Macaulay, Stewart, 84, 114–15
MacCormick, D. Neil, 12, 98, 117
Macfarlane, Alan, 37
Machlup, Fritz, 231
MacKenzie, Donald, 4, 61
MacLeod, Christine, 120
MacLeod, Henry Dunning, 101, 103, 113,
    125, 162–63, 168, 186, 205
Madden, Edward H., 48
Maddison, Angus, 35, 36, 333–38
Magazzino, Cosimo, 288
Maghribi traders, 84, 119
Magill, Michael, 141, 243, 245
Mahutga, Matthew C., 358
Maine, Henry S., 80, 92, 99, 241
Maitland, Frederick William, 77
Makdisi, John A., 94, 322
Malaysia, 133
Malerba, Franco, 37
Malone, Michael S., 192
Malthus, Thomas Robert, ix, 17
Mandel, Ernest, 254
Mann, Michael, 161
Mantzavinos, Chris, 13, 45, 88, 100, 120
manufacturing, 17, 159, 223, 227, 330, 334,
    338
Maoism, 300
Maoz, Zeev, 349
Mao Zedong, 257, 376
March, James G., 49, 240
Margolis, Howard, 293
Marimon, Ramon E., 150
markets, ix, 1–8, 11, 17–21, 29, 35–41, 45, 61,
    81, 89, 102, 113, 119, 123, 126–47, 159,
    161, 167, 171–72, 180–88, 197–98, 201–
    22, 227, 232–37, 242–45, 249–60, 271–75,
279–321, 327–28, 332, 335, 344–45, 348–
    50, 357–66, 369, 376, 379–82, 385–92;
    abolition of, 272–74, 282–85, 363, 381;
    auction, 134, 142; capital, 143, 182, 257,
    360; complete, 141, 242; definition of,
    143–44, 389–90; degraded concepts of,
    3, 129–31, 136–40, 296; early, 19, 133–
    37; emerging, 133; fear of, 146; financial,
    136, 164, 167, 172, 183; historical speci-
    ficity of, 136–39, 144; for ideas, 130–31,
    140; inequality and, 358–61; as institu-
    tions, 45, 141–44; internal labor, 213; for
    labor futures, 4, 243–44, 256, 360–61,
    379, 382; missing, 4–5, 18, 141, 235, 242–
    45, 256, 360–61, 379, 382; political, 140;
    regulation of, 1, 7, 13–14, 95, 131, 142,
    172, 285–88, 297, 299, 303–5, 311
Marquand, Judith, 371
Married Women's Property Act, 121
Marris, Robin, 208
Marsden, David, 213
Marshall, Alfred, 4, 67, 167, 173, 181, 190–
    93, 196, 244–45, 266, 270, 276–78, 329,
    354–56, 362, 379, 387
Marshall, Gordon, 54
Martinez, Joel, 340–41
Martinez, Mark A., 288
Marx, Karl, ix, 5–10, 18, 20, 28, 33, 38–39,
    41, 51, 54–55, 62–66, 74, 106, 109, 111,
    127–28, 162–66, 177–79, 183–84, 190,
    192, 196–99, 223, 235–36, 241, 245–47,
    250–55, 259–60, 266, 269, 274–75, 282,
    293, 300, 323, 325, 329, 332, 345, 353,
    358, 361, 366–68, 375, 379, 385–86, 391
Marxism, 2–11, 29, 33, 41, 50, 65–67, 74–75,
    94, 102, 109, 140, 144–46, 165–66, 184,
    190, 237, 254, 257, 260, 273, 297, 300,
    308, 316, 325, 342–43, 354, 361, 368. See
    also Marx, Karl
Marzo, Francesca, 192
Masten, Scott E., 77, 78, 204, 222
Matthews, Peter Hans, 69
Mauro, Paolo, 15, 339
Maxfield, Robert, 37
Mayans, 60
Mayer, Lawrence S., 108
Mayfield, John E., 279
Maynard Smith, John, 181
Mayr, Ernst, 31
Mazzucato, Mariana, 288, 309

McAfee, Andrew, 142, 281, 370
McCloskey, Deirdre N., x, 5, 37, 101–2
McGrattan, Ellen, 150
McMillan, John, 84, 142, 144
McNeill, William H., 323
Meade, James E., 250, 360, 365
Means, Gardiner C., 258
Meckling, William H., 217–21, 228, 233
Mehmanpazir, Babak, 304
Mehrling, Perry G., x, 164
Meiji Restoration, 324
Meikle, Scott, 33, 148
Ménard, Claude, x, 42, 45, 143, 213–16
Menger, Carl, 78, 148–53, 270
Merrill, Michael, 260
Merry, Sally Engle, 96
Merton, Robert K., 131
Mesoudi, Alex, 90
metaphors, 3, 18, 62, 166–67, 180, 265–66, 270, 277–80, 309, 329
metaphysics. *See* ontology
Metcalfe, J. Stanley, 31, 276, 328
Methodenstreit, 148
Mexico, 338–39
Miceli, Thomas J., 109
Michie, Jonathan, 332
Micklethwait, John, 225–28, 322
Middle East, 94, 133–37, 156–57, 253
Milanovic, Branko, 36, 347, 359–60
Milgate, Murray, 131
Milgram, Stanley, 14, 70–72, 87, 90, 98, 241
Milgrom, Paul R., 77, 84, 87, 114
Milhaupt, Curtis J., 83, 94
Mill, John Stuart, 177, 266–71
Minard, Philippe, x, 303
Minkler, Lanse P., 119, 240
Minsky, Hyman P., 172
Mirowski, Philip, 2, 61, 144–45, 167, 197, 265–66, 270, 280, 308
missing markets, 4–5, 18, 141, 235, 242–45, 256, 360–61, 379, 382
Mitchell Innes, Alfred, 78, 162, 164, 173, 181–84, 197–98, 361
mixed economies, 41, 274, 283, 288, 297
Mnookin, R. H., 114
Mo, Pak Hung, x, 15, 339
Mokyr, Joel, 18
money, ix, 3–7, 18–20, 40, 57, 60, 73, 78, 101, 113, 124–34, 139, 146–203, 221, 244, 252–60, 265, 270, 301, 314, 332, 336, 343, 356–62, 366, 385, 388; abolition of, 284, 376; capital as, 173–79, 189, 197, 199, 256; commodity, 126–28, 386; credit, 166–67; credit theory of, 161–63, 186; evolution of, 151–56; functions of, 148; Marx's view of, 164–66, 184; medium of exchange, 148–49, 152–53; ontology of, 148, 168; origins of, 150–54; physicalist views of, 168; spontaneous evolution of, 148–54, 228; state theory of, 20, 148, 153–54, 164; store of value, 139, 148, 390; substance view of, 5–6, 164–66, 176; unit of account, 148, 152–55, 390
Moore, Barrington, 17
Moore, Basil J., 163–64
Moore, John H., 221–23
morality, 9, 14, 72–79, 86–88, 97, 106–9, 116–19, 239–40, 321, 368; evolution of, 72–73, 88; law and, 86–87, 93
moral motivation, 9, 14, 70–80, 87–88, 107–8, 116–19, 240
Moreno, Carola, 340
Morgan, E. Victor, 160
Morris, Gillian S., 233, 237
Morroni, Mario, 276
Morse, Adair, 217
Moshenskyi, Sergii, 157
Moss, Laurence S., 167
motivation, 9–14, 19, 53, 67–68, 73, 75, 106, 108, 116, 170, 180, 235, 239, 254, 268, 274, 372, 375
Mouffe, Chantal, 29
Mousseau, Michael, 349
Mouzelis, Nicos, 192
Muchlinski, Peter, 378
Mumford, Lewis, 323
Mundell, Robert A., 166
Munier, Francis, 304
Murnane, Richard J., 329
Murphy, Anne L., 160
Murphy, James Bernard, 82
Murphy, Kevin M., 191
Murray, James A. H., 181
Murrell, Peter, 288, 296
Muslims, 94, 157, 322. *See also* Islam
Myrdal, Gunnar, 16

Nagel, Thomas, 28
Nagelkerke, Ad, 15
Naidu, Surech, 121, 248

Napoléon Bonaparte, 303, 324
Nash, David, 239
nationalization, 356–58, 367, 380
natural capital, 11, 201
natural law, 79, 86
natural state model, 31–34, 50, 345, 390;
    Marx's adoption of, 33
Naughton, Barry, 259, 342
Neal, David T., 82, 160
Nee, Victor, 110
Nef, John U., 323
negentropy, 279–80, 327
Neild, Robert R., 18, 321, 343
Nelson, Julie A., 364
Nelson, Katherine, 278
Nelson, Richard R., x, 31, 46, 49, 191, 258,
    277–78, 288, 293, 306–9, 315, 322, 372
Netherlands, the, 10, 20, 35, 83–84, 159–61,
    225, 316, 324, 333, 339, 346–48
networks, 84, 138, 144, 161, 193–97, 200,
    202, 224, 232, 285, 302–5, 330–31, 342
Neurath, Otto, 284
new institutional economics, 15, 66–67,
    108, 142
Newman, Peter, 131
Newtonian science, 26, 165, 266
New York City, 328
New York Stock Exchange, 136
Nielsen, Klaus, x, 344
Nietzsche, Friedrich, 191
Nigeria, 337–39
Nik-Khah, Edward, 61
Nitzan, Jonathan, 50, 190
Nivette, Amy E., 95
Nolan, Peter, 342
Nonaka, Ikujiro, 278, 292, 306, 371
Nooteboom, Bart, x, 115, 278, 304
Nordhaus, William D., 166
North, Douglass C., 11–17, 42–45, 66, 77,
    84, 88, 96, 120, 123–24, 126, 130, 134,
    140, 145, 160–61, 194, 219, 302–3
North Korea, 257, 335
Norway, 95, 346–48
Nowak, Martin A., 241
Nozick, Robert, 4
Nussbaum, Martha C., 30, 364
Nyssens, Marthe, 378

O'Brien, Patrick K., 18, 171
O'Donnell, John M., 48

Ofria, Charles, 277, 327
Oi, Jean C., 110, 287
Oliver, Christine, 192
Olson, Mancur, 15, 120, 194, 288, 332
Oneal, John R., 349
O'Neill, John, 29, 201, 284, 381
Ong'ong'a, Okomboli, 69
ontogeny, 322
ontology, 12–13, 21, 28, 30, 41, 47–48, 53,
    56, 59, 62, 64, 111, 148, 164–70, 183, 190,
    266–81, 390; of money, 148, 168–70;
    physicalist, 168, 197, 266–71, 280–81; of
    production, 21, 266–81
open government, 333, 339–42
Opitz, John M., 322
Oppenheimer, Stephen, 19, 53
Opper, Sonja, 110
opportunism, 67, 240
organizations, 9, 42–45, 49–50, 57–58, 67,
    72, 123–24, 193, 205, 212, 215–21, 225,
    228, 233, 277–79, 291–92, 295, 297, 302–
    9, 317–23, 339, 376–78, 388, 391; defini-
    tion of, 43–45, 58
Orléan, André, 111, 145, 154, 197
Orlikowski, Wanda J., 271
Orsenigo, Luigi, 37, 277
Orts, Eric W., 78, 204
Ostrom, Elinor, 15, 45, 58, 119, 125, 168,
    193, 196, 273–74, 298, 363
Ottoman Empire, 159
Ouellette, Judith A., 82
Outhwaite, William, 55
overdetermination, 28–29
Owen, Robert, 282, 293
Oxenbridge, Sarah, 239

Padgett, John F., 276, 304
Pagano, Ugo, x, 204, 239, 320, 344
Paine, Thomas, 352, 362–65
Palley, Thomas I., 353
Palombarini, Stefano, 33
parental bent, 69
Pareto, Vilfredo, 167
Pareto efficiency, 14, 243
Parisi, Francesco, 83
Parra, Carlos M., 168
partnerships, 171, 175, 183, 205–8, 212,
    220–21, 225–29, 234, 322
Payne, P. L., 227
Peacock, Mark S., 155–56

Pearson, Harry W., 134
Pedersen, Willy, 192
Peele, James, 175
Peirce, Charles Sanders, 27
Pejovich, Svetozar, 66, 104, 108
Pelikan, Pavel, 42
Pellegrini, Lorenzo, 15, 339
Pendleton, Andrew, 244–45, 268, 378
Penner, James E., 103
Penrose, Edith T., 227
performativity, 4, 61
Persia, 156
Pettit, Philip, 219
Petty, William, 176, 187
Philippines, 336
Phillips, Michael J., 78, 204
philosophy, 7, 10, 19, 26–28, 31, 34, 47–48,
    60, 62, 86, 98, 219, 277, 284, 355
physics, 180, 271
Physiocrats, 176
Pickett, Kate, 352
Pigou, Arthur C., 182
Piketty, Thomas, 10, 190, 203, 361–62
Pincus, Steven C. A., 160
Piore, Michael J., 213
Pipes, Richard, 17, 103
Pirenne, Henri, 135, 228
Pistor, Katharina, x, 12, 83, 94
planning, 7, 21, 40, 143, 212, 257–58, 274,
    283–97, 304–5, 309–13, 380, 391–92;
    democratic, 287, 291–95
Plato, 31, 34
Plotkin, Henry C., 82, 277–79
Plotkin, Sidney, 273
Poland, 83–84, 225
Polanyi, Karl, 127, 134, 143, 146, 293, 386
Polanyi, Michael, 292
political markets, 140
Pollock, Frederick, 77
Pol Pot, 376
Poole, Michael, 244, 268, 378
Popper, Karl R., 26–27, 31, 48, 315
population thinking, 31–32, 41–42, 50, 390;
    essentialism and, 31–32, 50
Porpora, Douglas V., 55
Portugal, 121, 159, 333, 348
positivism, 48. See also legal positivism
Posner, Richard A., 106, 219, 244
possession, 8–9, 19, 94, 101–11, 120, 124,
    131, 136, 176, 183, 188, 196, 244, 255,

285, 297–99, 313, 390; different from
    property, 9, 102–11, 131, 196, 244, 255,
    285, 297–99, 313
Postan, Michael M., 246
postmodernism, 10–11
Potts, Jason, 137, 138, 168
Powell, Ellis T., 39, 160
Powell, Walter W., 240, 276, 278, 304
pragmatism, 27, 277
Pratt, Christine S., 340–41
preferences, 55, 67–68, 75, 83, 129, 182,
    219, 270
prestige-based imitation, 69
Price, Michael E., 69, 319
primates, 69–70, 200
private law, 80, 87, 98
private ordering, 8, 13, 15, 78, 88, 97, 110,
    205, 212, 234
private ownership, 2, 20, 38, 136, 250–59,
    273, 283, 296–301, 307, 356, 363, 375,
    380–81, 385
production, 3–4, 8, 18–21, 36–40, 62–66,
    111, 119, 126, 134, 136, 145, 161, 165,
    167, 171, 173, 177–85, 190–91, 197–99,
    203, 206–9, 213, 217, 231, 234–41, 244,
    249–50, 253–59, 265–89, 292, 294, 297–
    98, 301–2, 307–8, 311, 314, 328–29, 353–
    55, 358, 360, 366, 368, 371–82, 385; as
    exchange with nature, 112; factors of,
    5, 181–86, 194–95, 198–99, 202, 207–8,
    235, 276, 279, 353, 356–57, 361–62, 387;
    ontology of, 275–81; physicalist views
    of, 178–84, 194, 266–74
production functions, 186, 189, 194, 203,
    265, 276, 338
property: abolition of private, 21, 255, 272–
    74, 282–84, 300, 358, 363, 366, 376, 381,
    391; collateralizable, 2, 6, 20, 104–5,
    108, 124–26, 163, 169, 184, 186, 196, 199,
    203, 256, 259, 301, 314, 356–57, 361–62,
    376, 385, 387; different from posses-
    sion, 9, 102–11, 131, 196, 244, 255, 285,
    297–99, 313; incomes from, 258, 356–
    57, 362; intellectual, 306–7, 375; Marx-
    ism and, 109; redistribution of, 364–65
property rights, ix, 2–21, 35–39, 51, 56,
    62, 65–67, 75, 79–80, 88, 90, 94, 101–
    43, 146, 160, 168, 170, 180–90, 195–
    205, 210, 216, 221–24, 232, 241–45, 251–
    60, 265–66, 271–75, 278–79, 282–85,

property rights (*continued*)
292, 295–307, 310–13, 320, 326, 354–
57, 361–63, 366, 375, 379–90; economics of, 105–10, 221, 223; extension of,
121–23, 126, 243; feudal, 123; registration of, 104, 114, 124; relatively secure
in England before 1688, 122–26, 160,
255; security of, 120–26; spontaneous
evolution of, 87–88; types of, 104, 124–
25, 390
Protestantism, 16
Proudhon, Pierre-Joseph, 103, 109, 252,
379
Prüfer, Jens, 77
Pryor, Frederic L., 328, 330
psychology, 7
punishment, 9, 69–72, 78, 86, 89–90, 96–
97, 119
Puranam, Phanish, 278
Putnam, Hilary, 28
Putnam, Robert D., 191, 193
Putterman, Louis, 69, 239, 268, 363,
378–79

Quesnay, François, 266
Quine, Willem van Orman, 26–27, 48, 151
Quinzii, Martine, 141, 243, 245

Radcliffe-Brown, Arthur R., 91
Radin, Margaret Jane, 95, 201
Raff, Rudolf A., 322
Rafferty, Anne Marie, 323
Rahbari, Ebrahim, 336–39, 343
Raines, J. Patrick, 167
Rajan, Raghuram G., 223
Rasmussen, Douglas B., 27
Rau, Karl H., 113, 125
Rauch, James E., 304
Ravaisson, Félix, 82
Raveendran, Marlo, 278
realism, 27, 48; critical, 284. *See also* legal
realism
Reber, Arthur S., 292, 326
Redfield, Robert, 92–93
Reed, M. C., 172, 227
Reibel, R., 379
Reinert, Erik S., 66–67, 288
Reinhart, Carmen, 172
Reisman, David, 382

relational exchange, 137–39, 207, 214, 216
relations of production, 8, 74, 269
religion, 16, 40, 60, 62, 77, 80, 83–84, 87, 92,
94, 96, 99, 114, 119, 155, 157, 191, 225,
304, 322, 380
Renan, Ernst, 191
replicators, 318–19, 321, 322, 386, 389–91;
definition of, 391
Rescher, Nicholas, 191
Resler, Henrietta, 241
Resnick, Stephen A., 29
Ricardo, David, 6, 164–65, 252
Richardson, Gary, 122–23
Richardson, George B., 137, 214
Richerson, Peter J., 67, 69–70, 90, 242,
296, 320
Rifkin, Jeremy, 280, 308
Rigney, Daniel, 359
Riley, James C., 36
Rizvi, S. Abu Turab, 141–42
Robbins, Lionel, 140
Robé, Jean-Philippe, 78, 204–8, 213,
228–29
Robinson, Andrew M., 245, 268, 378
Robinson, James A., 17, 120–23, 324, 339
Robinson, Joan, 181, 183, 199
Robinson, Paul H., 72
Robinson, Richard, 27, 46
Rochon, Louis-Philippe, 164
Rodrigues, João, 310
Rodriguez-Sicken, Carlos, 69
Rodrik, Dani, 8, 317, 332, 338, 350, 360
Roemer, John E., 290
Rogers, Everett M., 322
Rogers, James Steven, 77
Rogoff, Kenneth S., 172, 278
Rome, 93–94, 134–35, 157, 174, 224
Roosevelt, Franklin D., 305
Rorty, Richard, 27–28
Roscher, Wilhelm, 178, 191
Rosenberg, Justin, 345
Rosenberg, Nathan, 322
Rosenthal, Jean-Laurent, 302
Roseveare, Henry G., 39, 160–61
Ross, Edward Alsworth, 191
Ross, Michael L., 340
Rostow, Walt W., 316
Roth, Alvin E., 144
Rothschild, Emma, 201

routines, 46–50, 67, 88, 115, 138, 142, 234,
    277–79, 296, 318–22, 323–24, 327, 345,
    386–89; definition of, 46–50
Rowthorn, Robert E., 69, 247, 288, 338
Roy, William G., 226
Rubery, Jill, 330
Rueschemeyer, Dietrich, 328
rules, 6–9, 12–14, 42–45, 49, 53, 56–73, 78–
    100, 104, 107, 110–11, 115–20, 125, 134,
    138–46, 151, 160, 167–70, 193, 211, 213,
    221–22, 229, 234, 240–41, 256, 266, 279,
    290, 293, 300, 304–7, 312, 319, 322–25,
    330, 339, 352, 365, 370, 386–89, 392;
    definition of, 391; habits and, 99; struc-
    ture of, 99, 391
Runciman, Walter Garry, 59, 90–91
Runde, Jochen, 271
Ruskin, John, 129, 283
Russia, 287, 296, 300, 321, 336–39, 342–43,
    346–47
Ruttan, Vernon W., 67
Ryan, Alan, 308

Saez, Emmanuel, 362
Sainte Croix, Geoffrey E. M. de, 134
Saint-Simon, Henri D., 379
Sala-i-Martin, Xavier, 334
Salaman, Graeme, 258
Salerno, Joseph T., 313
Samuels, Warren J., 12, 100
Samuelson, Paul A., 166–67, 188–89, 203,
    235, 365
Sandberg, Sveinung, 192
Sandel, Michael, 116, 201
Sargent, Thomas J., 150
Sarkar, Prabirjit, 83
Satz, Debra, 116, 201
Saudi Arabia, 337
Saunders, Peter T., 327
Saviotti, Pier Paolo, 276
Sayer, Andrew, 30
scarcity, 317
Schaffer, Mark E., 320
Schäffle, Albert E. F., 7, 167, 252, 286–
    88, 296
Schank, Jeffrey C., 326
Schmoller, Gustav, 7, 139
Schotter, Andrew R., 45, 85, 142, 151
Schuller, Tom, 194

Schultz, Theodore W., 186–89, 191, 198
Schultz, Walter J., 89
Schumpeter, Joseph A., ix, 5–6, 18, 20, 40–
    41, 62, 148, 162–64, 169–71, 182–84,
    197–99, 240, 251, 255, 259, 289, 325, 328,
    361, 366, 385–86
Schurter, Karl E., 102
Schuster, Peter, 277
Sciabarra, Chris Matthew, 292
science, 3, 8–13, 18, 26–28, 34–37, 48–52,
    62, 75, 99, 105, 112, 125, 165, 173, 186–
    87, 190, 198, 232, 265–66, 269, 291, 293,
    304, 307–8, 321, 328–29, 373, 376
scientific management, 271
Scotland, 83–84, 122, 161
Scott, Bruce R., 12, 17–18
Scott, Maurice Fitzgerald, 280
Scottish Enlightenment, 83–84
Screpanti, Ernesto, x, 257, 368
Scully, Gerald B., 288
Seabury, Samuel, 238
Seagle, William, 92, 94
Searle, John R., 12, 62, 111, 154, 168–70,
    197, 266
Second World War, 334
Seims, Mathias, 83
Sekine, Thomas T., 41
selection, 81, 319–22
self-employment, 209, 217, 233, 237, 245,
    249–50, 256, 314, 356, 367, 369, 373–
    74, 378
selfishness, 14, 109, 152
self-organization, 81, 84, 153, 316. See also
    spontaneous order
Sened, Itai, x, 13, 88, 100, 102, 120
Senge, Peter M., 371
Senior, Nassau W., 177–78
Sent, Esther-Mirjam, 308
Shachtman, Max, 257
Shannon, Claude E., 277, 388
Shanxi Province, 133
Shaw-Taylor, Leigh, 247
Sheleff, Leon Shaskolsky, 80, 93
Shennong, Emperor, 133
Shleifer, Andrei, 15, 83, 289, 339
Shoemaker, Floyd F., 322
Sicily, 94
Sik, Endre, 191, 304
Sills, David L., 131

Silver, Morris, 225
Simmel, Georg, 112
Simon, Herbert A., 15–6, 119, 236–37, 365
Simpson, S. Rowton, 104
Simpson's paradox, 360
Singapore, 335–37
Singer, Peter, 320
Singh, Ajit, 83
situated cognition, 37, 277
Six, Frédérique, 115
Skaggs, Neil T., 162–63
Skocpol, Theda, 325
slavery, 4, 39–40, 65, 116, 121–26, 134–35,
    141, 185–90, 195–99, 203, 238, 243, 246,
    249, 256, 356–57, 361, 368, 379, 382, 385,
    387; abolition of, 121; as capital, 185–
    90; voluntary, 4
Smith, Adam, 6, 9, 14, 20, 75, 83–84, 101,
    109, 129, 147, 151, 164–66, 170, 176–
    81, 184, 186, 189, 196, 198, 203, 266–67,
    327, 385
Smith, Henry E., 111
Smith, Michael E., 91
Smith, Peter B., 70
Smith, Vernon L., 14, 102, 142
Smithin, John, 78, 164
Smyth, Andrew, 102
Sobel, Joel, 196
Sober, Elliott, 31–32, 68, 71
social capital, 10–11, 173–74, 191–203
social constructivism, 30, 271
social democracy, 257, 283, 286, 309–12,
    346, 363, 392
socialism, 1, 8, 21, 59, 65, 101, 190, 250, 252,
    257, 261, 281–90, 294–310, 314, 346,
    363, 366, 379–81, 392; definition of, 257,
    391–92; democracy and, 287, 295; feasi-
    bility of, 21; origins of term, 282; prob-
    lem with incentives under, 286–87; via-
    bility of, 21, 281, 285–305, 392
social positions, 49–50, 55–59, 71, 386,
    390–92
social structures, 6, 19, 37, 44–45, 49–50, 53–
    67, 71, 74, 103, 105, 111, 130, 143, 168,
    177–78, 184, 193–96, 242, 245, 269, 271,
    313, 385–86, 390–92; definition of, 54–55
sociology, 7–11, 56, 67–68, 105, 112, 125,
    129–32, 140, 143–44, 157, 174, 184, 191–
    96, 213, 313, 356
Socrates, 34

Solow, Robert M., 194–97, 365
Somalia, 95
Sombart, Werner, 7, 62, 139, 174, 178, 183–
    84, 198–99, 256, 361
Somefun, Koye, 145, 280
Somek, Alexander, 79
Sonnenschein, Hugo F., 141, 142
Soskice, David, 33, 320, 344
South Africa, 336
South Korea, 133, 304, 334–37, 343, 346–47
South Sea Bubble, 226
Soviet Bloc, 334, 380
Soviet-type economies, 40, 251, 257–58,
    296, 334, 358, 380
Soviet Union, 257–58, 296, 334–35
Spain, 17, 121, 159, 333, 346–48, 378
Spanish Armada, 159
Spence, Thomas, 363
Spencer, Herbert, 167
spontaneous order, 8, 13, 20, 76–89, 92, 95,
    97, 100, 114, 116, 146, 149–53, 221, 224,
    228–29, 316, 392
Spulber, Daniel F., 78, 204
Squire, Richard, 78, 204, 230
Sraffa, Piero, 181, 183, 199
Stabile, Donald R., 245
Stadermann, Hans-Joachim, 104
Stake, Jeffrey Evans, 102
Stalin, Joseph, 257, 376
Stalinism, 300
Star, Susan Leigh, 271
state, the: law and, 76–80, 83, 85, 88–89, 94,
    99–100, 205; origins of, 91–96; role of,
    1–2, 6–21, 40, 51, 65–66, 78, 81, 88, 91–
    110, 124–25, 146–61, 164, 166, 170, 172,
    205–8, 213, 218, 221, 225, 228–29, 232–
    34, 245, 259, 274, 282, 285, 288, 291,
    297–305, 309–14, 320, 345, 362, 364,
    367, 376–77, 381–83
state capitalism, 251, 257–59
Steele, David Ramsay, 288, 310
Steiger, Otto, 103–4, 154, 163–64, 299
Stein, Peter, 81
Steinfeld, Robert J., x, 121, 247–48
Steinmo, Sven, 321
Stephenson, George, 204
Sterba, James P., 382
Stigler, George J., 130
Stiglitz, Joseph E., 110, 240, 268, 289, 320,
    332, 353, 358–59

Story, Joseph, 157
Stout, L. A., 208
Streeck, Wolfgang, x, 33, 344
Streissler, Erich W., 183
strong reciprocity, 70, 90
Sturn, Simon, 320, 344
Suchman, Lucy A., 271, 277–78
Sugden, Robert, 83, 85, 150
surplus value, 190, 353–54, 358, 368
Swedberg, Richard, 144
Sweden, 83–84, 157, 225–26, 346–48
Switzerland, 345–48
Synopwich, Christine, 300
Szulanski, Gabriel, 324

Tabellini, Guido, 77
tacit knowledge, 61, 115, 142, 239, 278,
    289–94, 305–8, 324, 329, 373, 389
Taiwan, 334–37, 343
Takeuchi, Hirotaka, 278, 292, 306, 371
Tamanaha, Brian Z., 96
Tandy, David W., 133
tariffs, 37, 350, 360
taxation, 17, 133, 141, 156, 159–60, 187, 249,
    310–12, 362–63, 367, 382–83; inheri-
    tance, 312, 383; money and, 156; redis-
    tributive, 312, 358, 363–64, 383
Taylor, Alan M., 271, 332
Taylor, Frederick M., 283
Taylor, Frederick Winslow, 271, 373
Tea Party, 60
technology, 7, 36–37, 49, 66–67, 95, 171,
    194, 202–3, 239, 249–50, 253, 260, 271–
    76, 281, 293, 296, 302, 307–8, 322–30,
    333–35, 343, 349, 351, 359, 370, 372,
    376, 386
Teece, David J., 324
Temin, Peter, 134, 135
Terry, Deborah I., 369
Tett, Gillian, 61
Teubner, Gunther, 81
Thackeray, William Makepeace, 252
Thelen, Kathleen, 33, 245, 320, 344
Thomas, W. A., 160
Thompson, Grahame F., 304, 332
Thompson, Noel, 282
Thompson, William R., 332
Tilly, Charles, 17–18
Tilman, Rick, 273
Tobin, James, 156, 365, 367

Tobin tax, 367
Todd, Peter M., 278
Tomasello, Michael, 53, 82
Tomer, John F., 191
Tomlinson, James, 29
Tooby, John, 69
Toporowski, Jan, 378
Torstensson, Johan, 110
Toullier, Charles, 109
trade unions, 17, 43, 58, 248–49, 301, 312
training of employees, 4, 5, 186, 235–36,
    244–45, 330, 356, 360, 379
transaction cost economics, 8, 206–13, 234
transaction costs, 4, 109, 112–19, 125, 213,
    217, 228, 245, 250, 307
Triantis, George G., 78, 204, 222
Trotsky, Leon, 257, 345
Trotskyism, 257, 300, 345
trust, 102, 115–19, 137, 145, 170, 192–97,
    200–202, 226, 239–40, 296, 317, 352, 372
Tullock, Gordon, 107
Turgot, Anne-Robert-Jacques, 176, 252
Turner, Bryan S., 54
Turner, Henry A., 305
Tylecote, Andrew, x, 16
Tyler, Tom R., 82, 99
Tymoigne, Éric, 350

Umbeck, John, 108
uncertainty, 3, 4, 7, 13, 137, 201, 235–39,
    290, 311, 360
unemployment, 301, 312, 348, 353, 355, 364,
    371, 373
United Kingdom, 35, 157, 172, 183, 203,
    210, 226–27, 230, 247, 249, 288, 304–5,
    339, 345–48, 362. See also Britain
United States of America, 21, 35, 117, 120–
    24, 162, 172, 190, 226–27, 238, 245, 248,
    288, 304–6, 317, 323–24, 332–39, 343–
    52, 358, 363, 365, 378; emancipation of
    slaves in, 124, 190
Uno, Kozo, 41
Usher, Abbott P., 159
usury, 174
utility maximization, 12, 14, 56, 67–68,
    147, 167

Valiente, Wilfredo Santiago, 182
Vanberg, Viktor J., 89, 143, 151, 168
van de Klundert, Theo C. M. J., 350

Van De Mieroop, Marc, 155
van der Woude, Ad, 159, 161–62
Vanek, Jaroslav, 250, 368, 379
Van Horn, Carl E., 245
Van Kleef, Gerben A., 369
Van Parijs, Philippe, 320, 364
van Staveren, Irene, 194
Varela, Charles R., 55
Vatiero, Massimiliano, 99
Vatn, Arild, 382
Vaughan Williams, Ralph, 181
Vaughn, Karen I., 288
Veblen, Thorstein B., 7, 15, 34, 48, 67, 69,
    74–75, 82, 99, 109, 167, 179–83, 186,
    199, 266, 270–77, 280
Veitch, John M., 122
Veljanovski, C. G., 191
Venice, 135, 158, 225, 322
Vernengo, Matias, 164
Verter, Bradford, 192
Vietnam, 335–36
Vignes, Annick, 144
Vikings, 95
Vining, Rutledge, 167
Vinogradoff, Paul, 225
violence, 91, 96, 114, 352; class, 300; state,
    98; state monopoly of, 76; ubiquitous
    before rise of states, 95
Vishny, Robert W., 15, 289, 339
Voelpel, Sven, 278
Vogel, Steven K., 288, 304, 305
von Baer, Karl Ernst, 326
von Böhm-Bawerk, Eugen, 173, 179, 182
von Krogh, Groeg, 278
von Mises, Ludwig, 105–6, 112, 136–37,
    285–89, 296–301, 309, 312–14; on prop-
    erty, 105–6
von Savigny, Friedrich C., 80
von Wieser, Friedrich, 354
Vroom, Victor H., 373

Wagner, R. Polk, 95
Wainwright, Hilary, 292, 381
Wallast, Len H., 279
Wallerstein, Immanuel, 342–43
Wallis, John J., 11–12, 15, 17, 44, 96, 123–
    24, 126, 219, 302–3
Walzer, Michael, 201
Wang, Ning, 110, 130, 259, 287
Wang, Xiaotong, 133

Ward, Benjamin, 250, 379
Warsh, David, 328
Watt, James, 204
wealth, distribution of, 4, 21, 35, 89, 109,
    134, 199, 203, 252, 257–58, 265–71, 274,
    346, 354, 359–60, 364, 381
wealth tax, 364
Weaver, Warren, 277, 388
Webb, Beatrice, 283, 294
Webb, Sidney J., 283, 294
Weber, Max, ix, 5, 7, 16–17, 60–62, 107–8,
    132–33, 178, 183–84, 198–99, 254, 256,
    323, 361
Webster, Charles, 1, 252, 323
Wedderburn, Kenneth W., 233, 237, 247
Wei, Shang-Jin, 259
Weil, Simone, 366
Weingast, Barry R., 11–12, 15, 17, 44, 77,
    84, 86–87, 96, 114, 120, 123–24, 126,
    160–61, 219, 302–3, 339
Weiss, Andrew, 240, 268
Weissman, David, 55
welfare state, 249, 312, 381–83
Wells, Alan F., 53
Wells, John R., 247, 338
Wenger, Etienne, 37, 277–78
Wennerlind, Carl, 39, 160
Werther, William B., 377
Westergaard, John, 241
Westgarth, William, 185–86, 189
Whelan, C. J., 191
White, Harrison C., 144, 304
White, Nicholas P., 27
Whitfield, Keith, 244, 268, 378
Whitley, Richard, 33, 344
Wicken, Jeffrey S., 277, 279
Wiessner, Polly, 69
Wilde, Oscar, 294
Wilkins, John S., 26–27
Wilkinson, Frank, 330
Wilkinson, Richard, 352
Williamson, Jeffrey G., 38, 135, 246–47, 332
Williamson, Oliver E., 8–9, 15–16, 67, 84,
    118, 129, 137–38, 194, 205, 211–13, 217
Wilson, Bart J., 102
Wilson, David Sloan, 68, 71
Wilson, Edward O., 71
Wilson, Nicholas, 244–45, 268, 378
Wimsatt, William C., 326
Winston, Clifford, 382

Winter, Sidney G., 46, 49, 276, 293, 315,
  320, 322, 324
Wittenhagen, Elke, 324
Wittgenstein, Ludwig, 29
Wolff, Richard D., 29, 368
Wood, Stephen, 330
Wood, Wendy, 82
Woodruff, Christopher, 84
Wooldridge, Adrian, 225–26, 228, 322
World Bank, 193, 195, 335
Wray, L. Randall, x, 78, 164, 350
Wright, Mike, 244–45, 268, 378
Wunsch, Cornelia, 155

Yamamura, Kozo, 33, 321, 344
Yanikkaya, Halit, 340
Yavas, Abdulla, 288

Yellen, Janet L., 240, 268
Yoffee, Norman, 91
Young, Allyn A., 327–28
Yuchtman, Noam, 121, 248

Zamagni, Stefano, 239, 379
Zamagni, Vera, 239, 379
Zander, Udo, 324
Zejan, Mario, 194
Zelizer, Viviana A., 129–30
Zhang, Hao, 245, 268, 378
Zhang, Jun, 259
Zhang, Xueqi, x, 133
Zhou, Kate Xiao, 110, 287
Zingales, Luigi, 217, 223
Zuboff, Shoshana, 281, 329, 371–72
Zucman, Gabriel, 362